*Leaders, Teachers, and Learners
in Academe*

LEADERS, TEACHERS, AND LEARNERS IN ACADEME:

PARTNERS IN THE EDUCATIONAL PROCESS

edited by

STANLEY LEHRER

President, Society for the Advancement of
Education; President and Publisher,
School and Society and School &
Society Books

APPLETON-CENTURY-CROFTS
EDUCATIONAL DIVISION
New York   MEREDITH CORPORATION

Copyright © 1970 by

MEREDITH CORPORATION

All rights reserved

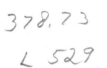

To
LAUREL,
who has tasted the fruits of higher learning,
and to
MERRILL and RANDEE,
who are reaching for these fruits

PREFACE

It was 1915. Across the Atlantic old empires were destroying cities, countries, traditions, and themselves. It was the year the Nobel Peace Prize had no recipient. It was the year Germany unleashed the scourge of the sea—the submarine—to encircle Great Britain. It was the year the *Lusitania* sailed into the sight of a German periscope and never reached port. It was the year the Panama-Pacific International Exposition was opened in San Francisco to celebrate the completion of the Panama Canal. It was the year of courage for Nurse Edith Cavell before a firing squad. It was the year *School and Society* was born.

This book is an offspring of *School and Society*. The educational journal has inspired the book's creation because of the goldmine of timely, learned thought found in its pages. To appreciate the quality of such scholarly wealth —much of which constitutes the value of this book—one should know more about its source, *School and Society*.

With the nation's interest absorbed by war headlines, 1915 was an unlikely year for the successful debut of an educational journal. Nevertheless, it was a time to give expression to the dynamic force wielded by education for the betterment of man. Nations that fed distorted facts into the minds of citizens during the war were converting the force of education into the energy of propaganda. *School and Society's* Volume I, Number 1 was published on January 2, 1915, with the vision and the vitality to foster an active, growing interest in U.S. and foreign educational problems, theories, and developments and to resist any complacency in educators generated by the war.

The first issue was inauspicious in appearance, but Editor James McKeen Cattell offered readers timely material such as G. Stanley Hall's "Teaching the War" and I. L. Kandel's "Education in England and the War." Also featured were an article, "Educational Evolution," by Charles W. Eliot, educational news events, a research paper on "Uniformity of Grading in Colleges and Universities," book reviews, and a report of a conference held by the Association of Urban Universities.

School and Society was not one of the fatalities of the war. It never missed an issue, and continued as a source of educational enlightenment throughout the postwar reconstruction of shattered societies and values.

   In 1939, German troops invaded Poland and the world once again tasted the bitterness of war. That same year, the New York World's Fair opened and had to share publicity in newspapers with war news. It was also the year *School and Society* was transformed from a commercial enterprise into a non-profit journal of the Society for the Advancement of Education. The Society was incorporated in September, 1939, especially to continue publication of the periodical as well as to "aid in the dissemination of news and the exchange of ideas and views among persons interested in education" and "foster other related enterprises designed to advance the interests of education." The Carnegie Corporation of New York provided funds for the Society to purchase the journal from Dr. Cattell, who was getting on in years and who wished to be unburdened. For more than half a century now, the publication has continued to serve education—and even to flourish—under the aegis of the Society for the Advancement of Education.

   Between two world wars and beyond, *School and Society* has mirrored the various trends in educational thinking, frequently sparking debates in print on many controversial issues. The questions of Federal aid to education, church-state-school relations, merit rating, segregation in education, and teacher education and certification, among others, caused years of furor on the part of educators, who sometimes declared editorial war on each other in defending their points of view in the journal's pages. Often the editors were criticized severely by educators for publishing articles whose theses were regarded as unpopular, factually incorrect, or theoretically unsound. Such was the case with the article, "On the Education and Certification of Teachers," by Arthur E. Bestor, Jr. (September 19, 1953), which is included in this book.* The editors were bombarded with letters complaining about Prof. Bestor's statements and expressing regret that the article had been published. However, the editors defended the right of Prof. Bestor—and all authors—to present views in *School and Society* that are genuinely sincere and of a scholarly nature. Several rebuttals to Bestor's article were given space in the journal as a matter of policy.

   Not all controversial subjects evoked criticism. "Federal Support, Not Federal Aid: The Murray-Metcalf Bill," by J. L. McCaskill (May 24, 1958), did not produce a torrent of correspondence, as happened with the Bestor article. Instead, and to the rare delight of the editors, the article was reprinted in the *Congressional Record* at the request of Senators Richard L. Neuberger and Hubert H. Humphrey. The latter stated that he "was very much pleased" to read this article.

   In addition to controversy, *School and Society* has left its door open for occasional pieces of refreshing, scholarly wit and satire, such as "Imaginary Advice to Students on Taking Examinations" (March 9, 1963), "The Great Revolt in Higher Education" (October 26, 1968)—both by Wm. Clark

_____
*This article was expanded in Prof. Bestor's book, *Educational Wastelands* (Urbana: University of Illinois Press, 1953).

Trow—and "Reasons Why My Mark Should Be Raised—by a Pre-Med," by Raymond M. Selle (May 15, 1954). These three items appear in this volume.

So varied are the articles in subject matter that *School and Society* defies a formal, specialized classification other than, perhaps, a "general educational journal." Take, for example, the bold indictments, in the tradition of Emile Zola's "J'Accuse," against politics mixed with public education in "Illinois, Illinois!" by George D. Stoddard (April 3, 1954) and "College Administration as Political Football," by T. Noel Stern (March 10, 1962). Both of these articles are reprinted in the book. Such statements are part of the panorama of educational history and, along with the journal's multiplicity of educational coverage, make *School and Society* a significant voice in—and on—education. Much of the magazine's contents have been reprinted and quoted in national magazines, newspapers, professional journals, and in books, thus attesting to the usefulness of the journal that, five decades ago, was launched with a dubious future.

Although this book is an anthology of *School and Society* and provides professional thought on several areas of higher education, it does not consist of unrelated readings. The purpose is to present selections that offer insight into problems, activities, responsibilities, and controversies concerning each of the academic partners—the administrators (Part II), faculty (Part III), and students (Part V). Part I, on the university and college, provides the backdrop for these principal players on the vast stage of higher education. Part IV, on the art of teaching, is included in the book to stress the importance of preserving the fragile partnership between professor and student by making it a stimulating experience. In this section we find analyses of techniques which can help to create a strong link between teacher and student.

Of necessity, the book is a comprehensive one because, unlike works that concentrate on a single subject, this volume brings together material on all the interdependent participants in the higher educational process. For historical value as well as added scope, the editor has selected eminent writers and significant essays appearing in *School and Society* over a period of many years; thus, he cannot be accused of favoring certain points of view expressed in papers solely of current vintage. In addition, the sweep of years reflects shifting trends in educational thought and action, new forms of crises and controversies, and evolving strengths and weaknesses in academe.

Many of the essays constitute a source of provocative concepts for the reader. The book is useful primarily in undergraduate and graduate courses in the general area of higher education. As a reference work, it is a storehouse of professional thought concerning administrators, faculty, and students in the realm of higher learning.

In the event that any author has changed his views since his article originally appeared in *School and Society*, it should be pointed out that such views remain relevant to the historical record of higher education because the article reflects the author's response to the times during which it was written.

I am indebted to William W. Brickman and the late I. L. Kandel, editors of *School and Society* with whom I have been associated since 1953, whose excellent choice of authors and articles for the journal has made the creation of this book inevitable. Dr. Brickman, professor of educational history and comparative education, Graduate School of Education, University of Pennsylvania, has been editor of *School and Society* for more than twice the number of years that Dr. Kandel served, and, consequently, most of the essays in the volume are representative of his keen professional selectivity. Of course, the selection and organization of all material in this book are completely my responsibility.

The assistance of Robert S. Rothenberg, Society for the Advancement of Education, was invaluable. He offered his help willingly and capably.

My wife's unique contribution to my work came in the form of encouragement that did bolster my spirit when it had sagged under the pressure of mounting problems associated with completing the book.

S. L.

New Hyde Park, N.Y.
August 25, 1969

CONTENTS

PART II

THE ADMINISTRATION

FROM LEADERSHIP TO COLLECTIVE PARTICIPATION

PART III
THE TEACHER, PROFESSOR, AND SCHOLAR
FROM PREPARATION TO RESPONSIBILITY

PART IV
THE ART OF TEACHING
FROM PERSONAL INVOLVEMENT TO COMPUTERS

PART V

THE STUDENT

FROM THE NEW YOUTH TO THE "FORGOTTEN MAN"

INTRODUCTION

Evolution has changed the structure and spirit of the American college and university—but not necessarily for the better. Within the past century, the institution of higher learning has been transformed from "a citadel of limited curricular offerings to a colossus of learning with expanding courses, expanding enrollments, and expanding research facilities and new buildings. Indeed, nostalgia is mixed with progress as the ivy-covered façades fade into the shadows of tomorrow's sprawling, sparkling structures."[1] The college of yesteryear could devote itself almost exclusively to the enrichment of the undergraduates' minds. Although the primary goal of the contemporary institution still is education of students, there is a tendency to overwhelm them by the gargantuan proportions of the school's multiple facilities and functions.

Students feel that their needs and interests are being dwarfed by the university's drive toward giantism. Time will tell how wise the concept of the multiversity is. The students believe they are not receiving enough personal attention and are treated as anonymous beings in their courses of study as a result of the intense dedication of the institution to research and community service. "The student seeking 'love and affection,'" explained Pres. Edward D. Eddy of Chatham College, "may have to stand in line with the Atomic Energy Commission, the poverty program, the Farm Bureau, and middle management."[2] There is the argument, of course, that a university exists to further the eternal search for truth, which is advanced through research, and not just to satisfy student needs and demands.

Student dissatisfaction first erupted in heated protests against the "system." Individual students felt lost among the teeming thousands on campus. It was difficult to receive personal attention from professors in crowded classrooms. The faculty was not always accessible for after-class

---

[1] Stanley Lehrer, "Preface," in William W. Brickman and Stanley Lehrer, eds., *A Century of Higher Education: Classical Citadel to Collegiate Colossus* (New York: Society for the Advancement of Education, 1962), p. 8.
[2] Edward D. Eddy, "The Student on the Boundary," *Liberal Education*, 53: 199, May, 1967.

consultation; many professors engaged in private research and writing encouraged by the university, and such pursuits often took them away from the campus.

The foundation of the academic establishment was shaken by the tremors of student discord. Some institutions hit by campus unrest have attempted to return to normal ("normal" being business as usual), while others have tried to fill the cracks of student discontent in their establishment with the mortar of improved cooperation and greater understanding between the schools and the students. Various institutions, such as New York University, have begun to take steps to implement student participation in policy-making, particularly when it concerns the behavior of students on campus. Perhaps a spirit of partnership will help to unite universities and students in their common cause: higher learning.

Problems in addition to that of student unrest are increasing for colleges and universities as enrollments, and plant and staff size, expand. New facilities, higher salary schedules, and scholarships are raising over-all operating expenses, thus putting pressure on the administration for more effective fund-raising to supplement student tuition and fees—and, in the case of public institutions, to supplement state and city financing. Endowments are one of the sources for large outlays of funds. There is reason to believe, however, that current institutions concur with the words of Oliver Wendell Holmes: "Learn to give money to colleges while you live." Foundation and corporation grants, as well as alumni support and some Federal aid, especially to government-instituted and university-operated scientific research projects, have helped to alleviate the perennial problem of fiscal hardship, but the search goes on for additional funds to fill the coffers of academe. Gerald P. Burns and Russell I. Thackrey offer some excellent thoughts on the financing of higher education (selections 15 and 16).

As enrollments continue to move upward, colleges and universities are confronted with the difficult task of screening the horde of collegiate candidates in order to select only those who are capable and worthy of occupying a limited number of classroom seats. College admission tests are useful in lieu of other, better means for selecting students, but they are woefully imperfect when they predict academic failure for certain students whose potentialities elude the built-in scrutiny of the examinations. Even more disturbing is that the absence of a creditable form of academic acknowledgment, acceptance, or encouragement might tend to keep such students' abilities untapped with benefit to neither these students nor to mankind. Lawrence H. Stewart and Charles F. Warnath decried any waste of student ability caused by the rigidity of test scores. "Frequently," they stated, "the university professor has observed a graduate student who can design and conduct a beautiful experiment but who has very low scores on tests of academic ability. With rigid cut-off scores on screening tests, this student never would have been admitted to college and later on to graduate study.

Yet if the college had refused to admit him, a grave injustice would have been done to both the individual and his future profession." [3] In case there is any seed of ability in a student, every means must be expended to assure the flowering of this ability. More effective methods must be found to sift the promising from the unpromising. Both W. Clarke Wescoe and Edward D. Eddy present their points of view on the best approach to college admissions (selections 19 and 20). William H. Angoff, executive associate for all board programs, Educational Testing Service, cautions us, however, that to "give up the use of academic criteria for academic selection because they fall short of some standard of forecasting efficiency is a counsel of perfection that does not seem likely to advance the cause of American education." [4]

What will the future bring for the academic establishment? In his satirical prognostications concerning "Locksley Hall: A College for the Future" (selection 31), Robert M. Hutchins sees a time when there are no academic ranks, no departments, no president, and "management is the function of the faculty and criticism the function of the Board [of Visitors]." The new-found power of faculty members saddles them with a strong sense of responsibility that normally had been the province of the president and trustees. One can only speculate whether the burden of management will prove to be professionally satisfying to the educational specialist of the future. Such managerial control of a college might seem, to the faculty, like holding a lion by the tail; the responsibility is so big and frightening that the professors cannot let go. Their teaching and research activities could suffer from inadequate attention as they grapple with the chores of management for which many lack skill and experience. The time might come when faculty members would wish they had not inherited the powers of the former hierarchy.

Contemporary chief executives perform the difficult, occasionally thankless job of supervising the over-all operations of colleges and universities. They are admired, maligned, honored, ridiculed, respected, resented, applauded—and even fired. They often are "accused of being out of touch with our campuses," said Pres. John W. Lederle of the University of Massachusetts. "Despite spending many years as a student and many more as a faculty member, once one of us joins the administration an academic iron curtain drops, and from then on we are accused of building public relations 'images,' of devoting too much of our attention to (of all things) raising money, forfeiting in the process any claim to respect as educational leaders." [5]

[3] Lawrence H. Stewart and Charles F. Warnath, *The Counselor and Society* (Boston: Houghton Mifflin, 1965), p. 153.
[4] William H. Angoff, "Written Test Scores and Prediction of Success in College: A Reply," *School and Society*, 96: 283, Summer, 1968.
[5] John W. Lederle, address on "Reflections on the Current Student Restlessness," annual winter dinner of Brandeis University, Statler Hilton Hotel, Boston, December 3, 1967.

The president of a college or university is many things to many people. Demerath, Stephens, and Taylor recognize five primary functions assumed by a president when he takes office: "Money Man, Academic Manager, Father Figure, Public-Relations Man, and Educator."[6] Each function "demands a varied repertory of skills and actions. In any one role the president may be expected to act as disciplinarian, planner, co-worker, public speaker, writer, analyst, persuader, expert, friend, and manipulator of power. Incompatibilities, conflicts, and frustrations are inevitable." [7]

At times, a president's self-confidence is shaken and his emotional strength painfully put to the test. "Trustees disgruntled over finances, faculty members opposing educational changes or embittered over promotions and salaries, alumni enraged at poor showings in intercollegiate sports events, editors and publishers seeking causes, students aroused by unpopular disciplinary measures, citizens scandalized by free-thinking professors—all direct their bolts at the president." [8]

Some criticism of the president reverberates for many years, one day exploding with such roars of denunciation that he is either forced to resign or is dismissed by the trustees. George D. Stoddard is a case in point. He resigned from the presidency of the University of Illinois in 1953 because of several "cumulative criticisms," such as "defending 'pink' professors (a running conflict with several legislators), refusal to honor a contract bill (a quarrel with a state senator), saying things 'hostile to religion' (a criticism of a minister on the board of regents), allowing the university radio to represent public questions unfairly (an intermittent argument with a downstate representative), and too many trips abroad with UNESCO (a conflict with the board chairman)." [9] Stoddard presents his historic case in "Illinois, Illinois!" (selection 38).

A president, in the performance of his duties, walks a tightrope at times between a cordial and a lukewarm relationship with the trustees. Tyrus Hillway indicates how this administrator is judged by the board (selection 37).

The power and responsibilities of the college presidency are derived directly from the board of trustees, which is the legal overseer of the collegiate structure. Some boards prefer not to pressure their presidents to pursue a particular educational policy, thereby expressing complete confidence in the judgment of their chief administrators to determine the academic plans and programs. Of course, the trustees who usually support the presidents' programs are not always so agreeable when certain innovations are proposed in their institutions. There is a tendency to resist any break in the

---

[6] Nicholas J. Demerath, Richard W. Stephens, and R. Robb Taylor, *Power, Presidents, and Professors* (New York: Basic Books, 1967), p. 218.
[7] *Ibid.*
[8] *Ibid.*, p. 219.
[9] *Ibid.*, pp. 219–220.

status quo. Many presidents have found themselves in the position of appealing to their boards till their throats went dry for endorsement of new programs, and the trustees generally approved. Other boards of trustees are not so acquiescent and exert an overbearing influence on educational policies and programs by insisting that their presidents implement those which are consistent with the trustees' wishes. On occasion, they even interfere with the faculty. They have been known, despite presidential protests, to oust professors who espoused beliefs that the trustees decided were unbecoming.

Robert M. Hutchins characterized the unfortunate, negative attitude of trustees of private institutions in the following manner: "The boards of trustees of private, endowed universities in the United States . . . have shown a tendency to behave like the directors of an American corporation, regarding the professors as employees and the students as a product to be turned out in accordance with the specifications of the directors. . . . The vitality of an intellectual community requires that it be free from such interference." [10]

Chairman William S. Paley of the Columbia Broadcasting System also has been critical of boards of trustees. Paley, who happens to be a trustee himself of Columbia University, looks with disfavor on a board which reaches decisions without representation of faculty and students even though the decisions might affect them directly or indirectly. "That a board of trustees should commit a university community to policies and actions without the components of that community participating in discussions leading to such commitments has become obsolete and unworkable," he said. [11]

It is regrettable, indeed, that faculty members actually are denied entrance to the inner sanctum of several governing boards. A sociologist reported that, in certain colleges and universities, professors still are not being asked to attend meetings of these supreme power units on which "few faculty members or students have ever served. . . . This concentration of authority has been a growing source of conflict." [12]

It is essential that faculty members, as well as trustees, presidents, and the entourage of vice-presidents, deans, directors, and departmental and committee chairmen, be given some voice in policy-making for their schools. The executive councils and academic senates, including various committees, tend to serve this purpose by involving faculty members or their representatives, as well as administrators, in such deliberations as curricular matters,

[10] Robert M. Hutchins, "The Learning Society," in Harry S. Ashmore, ed., *Britannica Perspectives* (Chicago: Encyclopaedia Britannica, Inc., 1968), Vol. II, p. 730.
[11] William S. Paley, commencement address, University of Pennsylvania, May 20, 1968, in *Current*, July, 1968, p. 58.
[12] Patricia Cayo Sexton, *The American School: A Sociological Analysis* (Englewood Cliffs, N.J.: Prentice-Hall, 1967), p. 16.

student discipline, and certain administrative appointments. In addition, any professor "should have the right to join, without fear of reprisal, any organization concerned with faculty representation. Local chapters of organizations such as the American Association of University Professors can be a constructive complement to the institutional academic senate." [13]

Progress, although slow, is being made in various institutions in the tapping of the faculty's mental resources for decision-making purposes. This constitutes an evolving and functional partnership between faculty and administrators. For example, Pres. James M. Hester of New York University stated in his commencement address in June, 1968, that "major steps were taken this year to give both faculty and students greatly increased responsibilities in the decision-making process in the university. Faculty membership in the University Senate has been increased and the powers of the senate have been significantly extended." [14]

Of course, many faculty members do not wish to have any of their energy diverted from teaching to the demands of administrative responsibilities, and, consequently, they do not seek such responsibilities or welcome the trend toward greater participation of the faculty in the governance of universities. Others on the faculty have innate leadership abilities or are masters of a particular specialization that is most appropriate for various forms of administrative activity. To these teachers the occasional or even frequent involvement in decision-making and in other administrative functions comes naturally. William A. Boram, director of Ohio University's Chillicothe Campus, believes that

the teaching faculties of most schools represent a wealth of administrative potential. For instance, the expertise of faculty members who are economists or communications authorities or mathematicians makes these people exceptionally able to perform certain administrative tasks.

The list of worthy administrative projects to which teachers might be assigned is bounded only by the range of creative thinking of administrators willing to delegate duties. It could include directing academic orientation sessions for students, planning various curricular innovations, representing the school at public or professional gatherings, directing conferences, assisting in formulation of budgets, or arranging for visiting speakers.[15]

John H. Callan endorses the partnership of faculty and administration (selection 44). He views the growing participation of professors in administrative affairs as a form of representative democracy.

[13] "Academic Senate Form of College Governance," *School and Society*, 96: 250, April 13, 1968.
[14] James M. Hester, commencement address, New York University, June 12, 1968, in *New York University Alumni News*, June, 1968, pp. 3, 5.
[15] William A. Boram, ". . . and Teachers Should Administrate," *Today's Education*, 57: 27, September, 1968.

Paradoxically, there has been a slight shifting of traditional roles. As faculty members assume managerial functions, in some instances unburdening the administration of certain responsibilities, some administrators have found time to teach a class or two.

The same enthusiasm that certain faculty members reveal in their willingness to share in the decision-making process of the administration also should be evident in their approach to teaching, but this is not always the case. Some of the faculty may find a greater challenge in administrative chores, or in the realm of research, than in serving regularly as transmitters of subject matter and stimulators of learning in the classroom. Others prefer to stick primarily to the task of teaching. There is a need for various types of teachers, of course, and we should not denigrate those who wish to contribute their specialties to the cause of education by serving in capacities other than as full-time teachers. In our society, many teachers are being called upon to help solve the problems of urban areas; of education in underdeveloped nations; of the clash between racial groups; of increasing resistance to law and order; of students using drugs for "trip-taking" and spiritual revelations; of the attraction of subculturists (beatniks, hippies, flower children) to young Americans; of automation and labor; of the decline in morality in the so-called age of affluence.

With ever-growing opportunities for faculty members to flee from teaching to meet society's requests for their services—and there is no doubt about the importance of such requests—what about the needs of the students? Why do many teachers find other areas of education more alluring and stimulating than teaching? These teachers, unlike the main character in James Hilton's novel, *Goodbye, Mr. Chips* (1934), may not know what it is to have a professional love affair with teaching. Very likely, their original preparation for a teaching career did not succeed in inculcating and nourishing in them a genuine affection for teaching. Perhaps the somber, pedantic nature of various teacher education programs tended to dull rather than inspire any dedicatory zeal for teaching. Or, it is possible that, regardless of the most effective teacher education programs, the particular personalities, abilities, and interests of these teachers prompted them to engage more and more in activities beyond the classroom (research, writing, travel, consulting, administration) in addition to, and often at the expense of, teaching. Allan O. Pfnister provides insight into the importance of teacher preparation (selection 46).

The subject of teacher education brings to mind a historical controversy of the 1950's involving the much-criticized Arthur E. Bestor, Jr., and some of the opponents to his views on the preparation and certification of teachers. The restudying of Prof. Bestor's original statement (selection 48) still can stimulate debate as well as provide an effective backdrop to controversies concerning contemporary theories on teacher education.

The policy of American colleges and universities usually is to emphasize the importance of their teaching staffs. Teaching ability and a definite interest in students are the desirable traits, for example, for which the University of Massachusetts looks when regularly screening the faculty. Treating students as individuals and not as IBM cards with numbers for names is the university's goal. [16] Yet, the function of teaching and professorial attention to students tend to decline in direct proportion to the frequency of faculty members' primary out-of-class activities—research and writing.

The dilemma of teaching versus research has plagued academe for years, and there appears to be no suitable solution in sight. Many professors believe that research enriches their specialties, thereby giving their students the advantages of courses of study that are re-evaluated from time to time, have new material added, and are updated and made relevant to the present. More and more students feel cheated, however, when professors are so involved in research that graduate assistants have to take over classes. They ask plaintively whether professors should be encouraged by administrators to pursue their own specialties at the expense of teaching.

A professor at Kalamazoo College has not joined the chorus of opposition to professorial research. In fact, he believes that research reinforces teaching. "Knowledge of a discipline is the prerequisite to adequate teaching," he declared, "no matter what the classroom style of the professor. If a man does not do research to maintain mastery of his discipline, if he does not keep up with the work that is being done in his field, his intellectual life is dying on the vine. What he teaches the student will be out of touch with the times. . . ." [17]

Another defender of the merits of scholarly research is a professor at American University. He sees long-term gains from research efforts that, despite some poor results, could have greater value than the influence of a classroom teacher. "In the sponsoring of research, just as in an investment in the work of businessmen or lawyers, risks are high and wastage inevitable," he pointed out. "In spite of all efforts to discourage frivolous or opportunistic work, we shall probably continue to have bad briefs, wasted business trips and useless scholarly articles. But returns may easily be proportional to risk. While a classroom teacher, with luck, will exert a useful influence upon several dozens of students in a year's time, one first-rate book will affect thousands directly, and will have incalculable effects through the other works that it stimulates." [18]

Obviously, research offers benefits to the teacher's craft and to courses of study. Nevertheless, students are unhappy because they do not have much access to many of their professors. Edward D. Eddy reported that the "reward

[16] Lederle, *loc. cit.*
[17] Richard L. Means, "Research Versus Teaching: Is There a Genuine Conflict?," *Liberal Education*, 44: 243–244, May, 1968.
[18] William R. Hutchison, "Yes, John, There Are Teachers on the Faculty," *The American Scholar*, 35: 435, Summer, 1966.

for good teaching today is less teaching. The professor who excels is given fewer contact hours with students. Particularly in the larger university the teaching function is often viewed as an exercise in popping in, popping off, and popping out." [19]

Eddy also exposed the danger in a professor's overdose of specialization. "Of greater moment to the student," he warned, "is the faculty member's inability to provide a 'wholeness' to learning. Wider knowledge leads to greater specialization. Specialization, in turn, seems to foster the self-perpetuation of the specialty. Some faculty members are more intent on reproducing their kind than on producing a wholly educated man." [20]

Robert M. Hutchins gave credence to a trend toward overspecialization when he pointed out that a professor's commitment "is not to his university or to education; it is to his subject." [21] Ironically, the specialist who does not feel this commitment to his university usually maintains a partnership with the institution for what it can give him. "The aim of the university," according to Hutchins, "is to tame the pretensions and excesses of experts and specialists by drawing them into the academic circle and subjecting them to the criticism of other disciplines. Everything in the university is to be seen in the light of everything else. This is not merely for the sake of society or to preserve the unity of the university. It is also for the sake of the specialists and experts who, without the light shed by others, may find their own studies going down blind alleys." [22]

While the specialists benefit from their association with universities, what kind of education do the students receive? A qualitative education is reflected in the typical smorgasbord of academic courses highlighted in the catalogues, which also feature a dazzling array of faculty names tagged with impressive credentials that invite student interest. But are the students being short-changed in their classroom instruction as various educators pursue, almost relentlessly at times, their own specialized interests? Clark Kerr seemed to think so. The former president of the University of California at Berkeley observed a decline in the quality of college teaching and gave the following reasons:

Teaching loads and student contact hours have been reduced. Faculty members are more frequently on leave or temporarily away from the campus; some are never more than temporarily on campus. More of the instruction falls to teachers who are not members of the regular faculty. The best graduate students prefer fellowships and research assistantships to teaching assistantships. Post-doctoral fellows who might fill the gap usually do not teach. . . .

[19] Eddy, *op. cit.,* pp. 199–200.
[20] *Ibid.,* p. 200.
[21] Robert M. Hutchins, "An Appraisal of American Higher Education," in William W. Brickman and Stanley Lehrer, eds., *A Century of Higher Education: Classical Citadel to Collegiate Colossus* (New York: Society for the Advancement of Education, 1962), p. 202.
[22] Hutchins, "The Learning Society," *op. cit.,* p. 724.

There seems to be a "point of no return" after which research, consulting, graduate instruction become so absorbing that faculty efforts can no longer be concentrated on undergraduate instruction as they once were. This process has been going on for a long time; federal research funds have intensified it. As a consequence, undergraduate education in the large university is more likely to be acceptable than outstanding. . . .[23]

The graduate assistants who make the effort to carry on with the teaching of undergraduates in the absence of the skilled master educators may be noble in attitude but deficient in practice. Victor A. Rapport and Bernard M. Goldman found the graduate assistant to be no ideal pinch-hitter for the missing professor. They concluded:

Whatever the virtues of the young teaching fellow, and they are many, he is not the experienced hand at teaching. His concepts of excellence, of standards, often show a rigidity that comes fresh from the crucible of theory rather than from the aging process of pedagogical experience. The often-expressed theory that the graduate fellow will be able to establish a close and sympathetic relationship with his beginning student because they are close in age and experience simply does not hold water. As any director of graduate assistants well knows, his junior partner in teaching is all too often austere and unrelenting in his application of the "rules" of behavior, of the concept of devoted pursuit of the intellectual ideal (for the freshman in beginning English composition!), and of the social distinction between the freshman plebe and the graduate school initiate. Unusual severity and snobbism can easily assume the guise of high standards. And the graduate assistant, like his senior colleague, has little spare time to devote to his students outside the classroom; he has the more important business of competing successfully in his own graduate classes so as to hold his assistantship against all comers. . . .[24]

Undergraduates are becoming disenchanted more and more with the universities to which they have gone with great expectations of gaining a meaningful education from learned professors. Instead of many, the students encounter few professors and several graduate assistants. The latter serve what is regarded as an intellectual feast consisting of slightly warmed-over subject matter that, because of a tasteless, inexperienced presentation, cools in the minds of the students. The assistants may fit into the academic shoes of the professors—and in some instances may do exceptional jobs in the classroom—but generally their limited teaching experience and relatively brief amount of time for in-depth mastery of their specialties do not help to titillate the intellect of undergraduates very much. "For solace," stated a

[23] Clark Kerr, "The Frantic Race to Remain Contemporary," in Kaoru Yamamoto, ed., *The College Student and His Culture: An Analysis* (Boston: Houghton Mifflin, 1968), pp. 26–27.
[24] Victor A. Rapport and Bernard M. Goldman, "The Lonely Student," in Esther Lloyd-Jones and Herman A. Estrin, eds., *The American Student and His College* (Boston: Houghton Mifflin, 1967), p. 124.

Cornell University professor, the students "can look forward to the day when they will be graduate students and thus entitled to come within conversational distance of a professor." [25] The big question is: How many students will look forward seriously to graduate work if their initial college experience is one of excessive second-hand teaching?

Luckily for the students who prefer the intellectual sparkle of professors in the classrooms, the academic gems of college and university faculties still include some dedicated teachers who have too much regard for students to abandon them as much as possible for the prominence and rewards of research and writing. The primary concern of these individuals is the careful filling of the cauldron of students' minds with the richness of learning. According to Irving Howe, professor of English, Hunter College,

There are thousands of men and women teaching in the American universities who care more about the quality of their work than the standard of their living. They are neither geniuses nor saints, their contributions to scholarship may prove to be modest, and many of them publish little or nothing. But they care about intellect, they nurture the minds of their students, and some of them are passionately caught up with the state of the world. On certain campuses they tend to be overshadowed by the small minority of research magnates and slightly larger minority of academic entrepreneurs; somehow, they do not sufficiently establish themselves as a force for standards in most universities; but they are serious men, much to be respected, who can transform the life and values of their students.[26]

It should be noted, however, that a professor's desire to devote most, if not all, of his time to teaching does not necessarily guarantee good teaching. Not every well-meaning professor is interested personally in an exciting interchange of knowledge and ideas in the classroom. His lecture might be based exclusively on a textbook that he probably had written. His recitation, following the textbook page by page, might be a dull, uninspiring chain of phrases. A Stanford University graduate student expressed this dim view: "In too many cases the classroom is not a place of sharing knowledge and wisdom. It is a place of mere esophageal expulsion by the professor. Truth, curiosity, challenge, even the chance to make mistakes and thus learn from them without being embarrassed, are all sacrificed. The student is required to parrot the gospel according to St. Bibliography!" [27]

Apparently, the inspirational teacher (whom Franklin R. Zeran describes in selection 80) is a rare breed, indeed. Few professors have the ability to inspire the intellectual curiosity of their students. "This lack of

[25] Andrew Hacker, "Who Wants to Teach Undergraduates?," *Saturday Review,* 49: 81, December 17, 1966.
[26] Irving Howe, "Beleaguered Professors," *The Atlantic Monthly,* 216: 118, November, 1965.
[27] David Doherty, "Spiritual Destruction in the Classroom," *Improving College and University Teaching,* 15: 29, Winter, 1967.

inspiration," wrote Robert Ulich, James Bryant Conant Professor of Education Emeritus, Harvard University, "is partly due to the academic teachers' early specialization, to their exposure in college to inefficient professors whom they unconsciously imitate, to lack of comparative and comprehensive knowledge, and to a training in which the critical and analytical attitude prevents the development of vision and the courage of interesting interpretation of human situations. . . . On the other hand, there are professors who know how to inspire through their oratory, who give their students a sense of logical structure and architecture of thought, and who fill their lectures with much more content and personality than is possible if students have constantly to listen to each other's half-baked wisdom. Also, there can be more real 'participation' in listening to one great man than in talking to many small ones." [28]

If a teacher succeeds in stimulating the thought processes of students, even arousing in them a hunger for independent study of a subject despite the termination of a course, then he has mastered the art of teaching. As for the *act* of teaching, what can replace the physical presence of the teacher? The interest of the students can be heightened especially through a challenging rapport with a knowledgeable master teacher, and often the lecture can be brightened by the warmth and wit of his personality. Images on a closed-circuit television screen, the mechanical wizardry of teaching machines, and computers that speed and feed information to students in certain classrooms may relieve the pressure on busy teachers and even teach students, but much more can be said for the electrical excitement of students actively engaged in discussion with a mentor who is present in class.

Looking beyond the attempted impersonalization of college teaching today, James E. Russell, former Secretary of the now defunct Educational Policies Commission, has predicted that the "successful college teacher of the future will be more concerned with how students integrate the curriculum than with how the scholars do it. He will look to each student, ask what has been the pattern of his intellectual activity, and plan the next steps accordingly. He will strive to help the student discover the relationship of new study to earlier knowledge; he will challenge him to bring to a problem many insights from many sources; and he will evaluate his success not only in terms of mastery of discipline, but also in terms of his progress in understanding relationships." [29]

Some of the mushrooming discontent among college students in the past few years is the direct result of "poor teaching," according to Pres. Lederle, University of Massachusetts. He believes students are reacting negatively toward "alleged institutional emphasis upon research rather than teaching,

[28] Robert Ulich, *Crisis and Hope in American Education* (New York: Atherton Press, 1966), pp. 177–178, 187.
[29] James E. Russell, *Change and Challenge in American Education* (Boston: Houghton Mifflin, 1965), pp. 91–92.

or on publishing or perishing." [30] More sincere and inspirational teachers in the classroom might help to encourage many students to return to their books and abandon their signs of protest.

Other students have borrowed the powerful device of labor unions—the strike—and will not attend classes unless their college offers a curriculum that is, in their opinion, relevant to contemporary life. These students are opposed to studies that are not applicable to the critical issues of our time. They also demand the right to participate with the faculty and administrators in the decision-making process concerning curricular changes and policies affecting the student body. In addition, they want the opportunity to rate the effectiveness of their instructors (as discussed in selection 113).

Unlike the 1950's, when students pounded on the doors of colleges and universities to gain admission, militant students in the 1960's have blocked the doorways to learning on several campuses, thus denying non-striking students free access to classrooms. Student unrest has galloped swiftly across many of the nation's campuses, trampling on the traditional process of higher education.

"Students would not raise the question of their rights so frequently if the process of their education were more meaningful to them and if they felt more respected," stated Joseph Katz and Nevitt Sanford. "We think that the most fundamental fact underlying the present situation is that student problems and student discontent have reached such proportions that nothing short of giving the situation major attention and moving towards major reforms will do. We must be prepared to accept discontent or even more destructive effects as long as the situation is given perfunctory attention and the arrangements of the college are allowed to remain as they have been in the past. That changes seem difficult or impossible does not matter. We must begin to make them." [31]

The student crusade for institutional changes is, in itself, a healthy response to outmoded programs and policies. However, those tactics that disrupt academic activities, and even bring an entire college to a standstill, are inexcusable. Student activists justify these tactics as a means to democratizing the campus, whereby they hope to have an influential "say" in policy-making.

CBS Chairman William S. Paley has reservations, however, about the need for a university to function democratically, as far as its students are concerned. "In many of the uprisings on the campuses," he said, "we have heard pleas for more democracy in university procedures. . . . Not all institutions that serve democratic societies must themselves be democratic in their procedures. Nor can they be. A hospital cannot be run by majority

[30] Lederle, loc. cit.
[31] Joseph Katz and Nevitt Sanford, "The New Student Power and Needed Reforms," in Kaoru Yamamoto, ed., The College Student and His Culture: An Analysis (Boston: Houghton Mifflin, 1968), p. 412.

vote of its patients, nor a research laboratory by that of its technicians, nor a newspaper by that of its reporters. . . ." [32]

It is ironic, indeed, that many students who demand greater democracy on campus have little or no faith or patience in using democratic methods, instead of disruption and destruction, to achieve their goals. Protesting by students is, of course, a democratic act, as long as it remains peaceful, but the militant groups believe that disrupting colleges is the most effective way to satisfy their demands quickly.

Those colleges and universities that have felt the thrust of student unrest and often requested the assistance of police or National Guard troops to restrain student rebellion have become resolute in their determination to resist further disruption of their institutions. In the wake of a revolutionary rampage involving dissident students at Columbia University in the spring of 1968, the faculty adopted rules that, in essence, permitted student protesting but attempted to thwart future campus disruptions by warning of disciplinary action. [33]

Recent studies indicate that student activists, in general, possess positive traits. Compared with nonactivists, they are "more intelligent, less prejudiced and psychologically more stable." [34] They also are "flexible, antidogmatic, democratic and relatively unimpressed with personal achievement," and they usually pursue courses concerned with the social sciences, avoiding subjects that provide training for a particular career. [35]

Pres. Lederle has sketched some negative characteristics of the campus activists:

Many of the present student activists impress me as completely cynical about government and about the democratic process as a decision-making vehicle. To them, government is the enemy. They talk of a credibility gap. Government starts wars, imposes selective service, buys napalm for killing innocent citizens in Vietnam, makes grants to universities for security-restricted research.

At my alma mater this past summer [1967] I participated in a sesquicentennial symposium on *The University and the Body Politic*. In session after session the present-day student activists (replete with beards, long hair, unusual clothing, and a few flowers) dominated the question period with lengthy lectures that revealed a total disbelief in our government. If there was any belief it was in anarchism, certainly not in the possibility of solving problems through the ballot box. And I hope I am not being too harsh when I say I detected an arrogance, a contempt for the fruitfulness of discussion. These activists appeared to know all the answers; they had no time for listening to opposing arguments, nor faith in the virtues of compromise and accommodation in achieving a viable society.[36]

[32] Paley, *op. cit.*, p. 59.
[33] *New York Times*, September 13, 1968, p. 34.
[34] *New York Times*, June 19, 1967, p. 29.
[35] *Ibid.*
[36] Lederle, *loc. cit.*

The GI's who filled every available college seat following World War II were "more constructive in attitude and more respectful of the role of the faculty" than are the student activists today, Pres. Lederle reminds us. The GI's "had come to the university to learn, not to run it. All that they asked was that the faculty shape up and get on with improving and updating university education." [37] Today, the dissident students believe *they* are the advocates of what is good and best for the campus. They feel it is their right to bring about the changes that will help their schools to relate to present-day problems.

New York University's Pres. Hester decried the popular belief of this minority of college youth that they are more in tune with the problems of the times than are the older generations. "No age group has a monopoly on sensitivity, moral awareness or idealism," he insisted.

The members of different generations can and do help one another in finding, sustaining and acting on ideals and principles. The intensity of youthful enthusiasm for ideal goals can and does reinforce aspirations of older colleagues. Those of greater experience can and do assist younger colleagues to achieve perspective that helps them persevere. Young people have the power to inspire new hope in older generations. They abuse this potential if they assume that they alone possess moral awareness and do not make contact with those who would help them. Teachers and administrators are equally insensitive and destructive if they belittle the earnest, if sometimes presumptuous, moral reactions of students. The purpose of the revision of university structure must be to make possible an enduring and mutually stimulating relationship between the generations.

But Hester warned,

For the university to achieve accord between the generations, far more is required than good will and patient deliberation. If the university is to be preserved and made more responsive to the urgent needs of today's world, we must instil in ourselves—all of us—a tough, clear-headed commitment to the rule of reason. We must be determined to prevent any irrational faction from abusing the freedoms we have won so that the university can be the forum in which reasoned discourse can take place. . . . Some argue that violent conflict in the university is essential to bring about major change. Obviously we must oppose such destructive negativism.[38]

Although student demonstrators have been capable of marshalling a large disruptive force on many campuses, they do not speak for all students. "There are other students who are looking for some standards, some guidelines, some laws," explained Pres. Lederle. "They don't like the permissive atmosphere, the chaos of the campus. They are looking to the administration

[37] *Ibid.*
[38] Hester, *op. cit.*, pp. 3, 5.

and the faculty for help in developing a philosophy of life. But they don't get many guidelines. They complain that professors defer too much. They even resent the minority of activists who dominate the spotlight. They complain that faculty and administration frequently don't have the strength of character to take a stand when canons of good taste are violated." [39] Perhaps these students are the vanguard of protest against the protesters!

As for the majority of students, a *Newsweek* survey revealed that they still are interested in "football, fraternities, dating, getting along in school, getting married, finding a job and securing a niche in society." [40] Even when students were granted the opportunity to select representatives to serve on committees that have an influential voice in college affairs, as was the case recently at Columbia University, only a small percentage of the undergraduates (15%) and the graduate students (4%) actually took the trouble to vote. The vast majority of Columbia's students were more concerned with their studies than with "student power." [41]

We should not conclude, however, that the yearning of the student minority for a share of policy-making is unimportant just because they are overshadowed by the traditional interests of the majority. There is much merit in giving students a slice of authority and responsibility in college administration—in a sense, some control over their own educational destiny. Herbert Stroup, professor of sociology, Brooklyn College, regards the participation of students on college committees as a step closer to a better understanding of the faculty and administrators.

Having students serve on committees may help to develop an awareness among students of the "realities" and perplexities of the total life of the institution. When impatient with certain aspects of the curriculum or the administration, students may then discover through their representatives, who have a chance to work closely with faculty members on these problems, that at least "there is more than one point of view." Under certain controls, it may be wise to permit student newspapers to "sit in" on some faculty and faculty-student committees in order that the genuine concern for the betterment of the college may filter through the newspaper to the students at large. It is obvious . . . that on many campuses antagonistic feelings create a real chasm between the students on one hand and the faculty and administration on the other. This chasm probably broadens and deepens unless there are unrelenting efforts to build bridges of understanding if not agreement between the young and their elders. Student membership on college committees provides one bridge of understanding. . . . Participation of students on faculty-student committees in specific areas and under carefully defined limitations seems to be not only permissible and advisable but even necessary and desirable. [42]

[39] Lederle, *loc. cit.*
[40] "Campus Rebels: Who, Why, What," *Newsweek,* 72: 63, September 30, 1968.
[41] Editorial, "Tyranny on the Campus," *New York Times,* December 6, 1968, p. 46.
[42] Herbert Stroup, *Toward a Philosophy of Organized Student Activities* (Minneapolis: University of Minnesota Press, 1964), pp. 158–159.

Various institutions across the nation have accepted the principle of student participation in certain areas of school affairs. At Teachers College, Columbia University, for example, two student representatives are serving for the first time on the Committee on Policy, Program, and Budget. Although the committee is advisory in function, it does render occasional policy decisions.[43] Active participation by students in committees dealing with the questions of student life, disciplinary action, and curricular improvements is a reality and not just a goal at New York University. On the agenda of student leadership is the eventual creation of a student senate for the entire university which is expected to give students a hand in determining university policy.[44] Following a sit-in at the University of Pennsylvania in early 1969, students joined with faculty members, trustees, and local community representatives to form a commission on which each group had equal voice concerning plans to develop the university area.[45]

The Association of American Colleges recommended, in 1968, that students take part in the policy-making of their institutions to help take the steam out of campus disruptions. The organization proposed that students and administrators decide jointly what forms of conduct should apply to all students. But not every administrator was happy about the trend toward this form of campus democratization. During the same year, Pres. James B. Donovan of Pratt Institute urged the then New York State Commissioner of Education James E. Allen, Jr., to hold a meeting at which administrators could discuss the problems caused by campus demonstrators. "The question now concerning us," he wrote to Allen, "is how far can we go in delegating the formulation of policy decisions to committees of students, faculty or independent advisers without violating the responsibilities vested in our board of trustees and our officers." [46]

In certain instances, one person—an ombudsman—might soothe student tempers and settle grievances more expeditiously and effectively than the changing of unpopular policies by faculty-student committees. His presence on campus would create the comfortable feeling that, when necessary, the students have a "friend" who is sincerely interested in helping them solve their problems. He could advise them of the right individuals to see in their attempts to gain faculty or even administration support for various requests. His sympathetic services could be most helpful in preserving a harmonious relationship between students and their faculty and administrators.

Samuel Gorovitz, associate professor of philosophy at Case Western Reserve University, offers these constructive views of the ombudsman:

[He should be] charged with the sole responsibility of championing the cause of

[43] *New York Times,* September 13, 1968, p. 34.
[44] Hester, *op. cit.,* p. 5.
[45] *New York Times,* February 24, 1969, p. 11.
[46] *New York Times,* July 16, 1968, p. 79.

student complaints and suggestions. He might be hired by a committee of the faculty senate, and should have no superior in the administration, nor any voice in the formation of rules or policies. But he should be thoroughly informed about the university's policies, precedents, vaguenesses, channels of communication, procedures for change, and loci of authority and responsibility—in short, he should know the workings of the university as few others do, and as students almost never can, and he should make available that knowledge for the championing of student interests.

An academic ombudsman could be of great help to students, especially to the student who lacks the confidence and aggressiveness to take up the cudgels on his own. The ombudsman would not be a buffer between student and administration, nor a liaison, but a non-judgmental pilot who would guide each student's efforts through the most effective channels. . . .[47]

For the college and university to prevail as functioning institutions in our society, the defects that trouble students must be eliminated. Students should be treated like the valued caretakers of our culture whom they will become. The best that higher education has to offer is not too good for them. They should be free to express their own ideas and learn all they can in addition to what they need to know as citizens of a free country. However, the needs and desires of students must be compatible with reason, lest chaos result on the campus. A good motto for all campuses should be, "Freedom to Learn Through Reason."

The most difficult time to apply reason is during campus demonstrations, when it is needed most. Raw tempers prompt students to malign professors and administrators for what they regard as unfair or ridiculous academic practices. This is unfortunate because the faculty and administrators have the heavy responsibility of upholding the standards of higher education, and they should be treated with respect. They do deserve to be criticized, of course, if they stubbornly refuse to correct imperfections in the curriculum and do not change those policies and practices that are out of touch with the needs of the students. The students should be guaranteed the opportunity to present grievances, and faculty and administration should act on all appropriate requests and not refuse to consider them. Instead of name-calling, students should try to work out their differences in as many meetings as necessary with faculty and administrators. And faculty and administrators should be willing to meet with students to discuss and consider problems. Neither side should lose patience with the other. However, when impatience dominates the mood of dissident students and they prefer disorder to discourse for dramatizing their demands, campus authorities should take steps to prevent disruptive acts. Mob hysterics and violence that deny the majority of students the democratic right of free access to classes are unlawful and should be stopped by any means at the command of college administrators.

[47] Samuel Gorovitz, ed., *Freedom and Order in the University* (Cleveland: The Press of Western Reserve University, 1967), p. 20.

Only demonstrations that are conducted in a peaceful fashion should be tolerated.

Discussions between protesters and college officials must be encouraged. With patience and the genuine desire to resolve problems together, the modern, sophisticated student demonstrators and the older, knowledgeable faculty and administrators should be able to find a way to relate to each other again. As partners in the educational enterprise, they all will reap maximum values from their interrelated activities—the search for knowledge, the dissemination of that knowledge, and, hopefully, the ultimate assimilation and intelligent use of that knowledge.

STANLEY LEHRER

PART **I**

The University and College

From the Contemporary Scene to the Future

1

The University in Contemporary Society

GRAYSON KIRK

President Emeritus, Columbia University. At the time his article originally appeared in *School and Society* (Feb. 5, 1966), he was President. The article is based on his commencement address, Columbia University, June 1, 1965.

There was a time, and not long ago, when in many countries higher education was by no means at the center of national life. It offered preparation for a few professions, principally the ministry, and a gloss of classical culture to a small elite of young men drawn largely from the more aristocratic segments of society. It was often derided even by those who had sampled its wares. Carlyle had his imaginary Prof. Teufelsdröckh speak of a university in which "the young vacant mind [was] furnished with much talk about Progress of the Species, Dark Ages, Prejudice and the like; so that all were quickly enough blown into a state of windy argumentativeness; whereby the better sort had soon to end in sick, impotent Scepticism; the worser sort explode in finished self-conceit, and to all spiritual interests become dead." Gibbon referred to his time at Magdalen College as "the most idle and unprofitable of my whole life." Max Beerbohm once wrote, "I was a modest, good-humoured boy. It is Oxford that has made me insufferable."

Today, higher education has a different place in the world. In this country we are familiar with the changes wrought by the land-grant college concept, which made university education more practical and more widely available. We are equally aware of the fact that our borrowings from the great German university system of the past century provided us for the first time with the concept of a true university based upon advanced teaching and research. From the British model of the residential college, the German university, and our own additions we have developed a vast and complex array of higher educational institutions with an aggregate annual expenditure for capital and operating costs of more than $9,000,000,000 and with a total enrollment of more than 4,000,000 young men and women.

In this tremendous development, the U.S. has been part of a world-wide trend that continues to accelerate as governments struggle to meet the needs of a growing population. It is a trend that places an ever-higher valuation upon higher education. Thus, in our day, the university has become one of society's most cherished institutions. It is everywhere regarded as the principal agency whereby a country may protect its future as well as its past. It has become the one indispensable source for trained leadership for almost every segment of a modern society. Access to higher education now is regarded as the right of all young people who have any claim to intellectual promise—and is demanded by many who have not. Throughout the world, in countries old and young, powerful and weak, authoritarian and democratic, new universities are rising to meet a seemingly inexhaustible demand for higher education. In short, for the first time in history the university finds itself at the very center and heart of society. The university of today is large, extremely diverse in its activities, very expensive, and very important.

This new eminence is gratifying, even exhilarating, but it has its hazards as well as its benefits. University leaders nowadays seldom are free from involvement in some public controversy. They must manage what is in reality a large business enterprise, but one that is dedicated to non-business purposes, and they must do so in a way that will be acceptable to four different publics: the students, the faculty, the alumni, and that portion of the general public which on occasion is more lavish with its criticism than with its support. Academic administration usually is disliked by the students, viewed with suspicion by the faculty, and castigated by the public for not exercising an omnipotence that, in fact, it does not, and should not, possess.

But this is merely a detail of a larger picture. Because the university today is the agency wherein virtually all our leaders are trained—or at least profoundly influenced in their attitudes—society has a mounting concern over what goes on in the university. Efforts to express that concern inevitably affect the life of the university—and possibly the longevity of university administrators.

Some individuals and groups, responding to this new feeling of concern, seek to dominate the atmosphere of the university so as to ensure that its prime function will be to defend and protect traditional and declared national beliefs, values, and attitudes, and to inculcate them in the youth of each generation. They are not concerned about research or scholarship. They view the university as a guardian, not as an innovator, an instrument to transmit to youth the heroic past of the nation, its special culture, and its ideals. When a university goes beyond this role, these groups are quick to rise up in condemnation and criticism. They feel that they have been betrayed.

Such a view finds fullest policy expression in any rigidly authoritarian state. There the university is merely an arm of the government, dutifully teaching an official ideology and carefully controlling student access to all contrary views or theories. Both *Lehrfreiheit* and *Lernfreiheit* are non-existent.

In other countries where universities are more free, but still are wholly financed by and under the official control of a ministry of education, academic authorities often find it prudent to be extremely cautious about curricular innovations that might evoke controversy or arouse official displeasure. Thus, for example, the teaching of political science, as we know it, is almost non-existent in Latin American universities.

In most free countries, other groups seek to gain dominance over the university, not to protect an ideological, political, or social status quo, but to destroy it, or at least to erode the foundations upon which it rests. These groups believe that the essential function of a university is to be the fountain-head of social, economic, and political reform, and they are determined to direct its official life to that end. This view of a university's role is widely prevalent in Latin American academic circles.

For all activists who seek drastic social change, the university is an obvious target and a potential instrument of the greatest value. It is filled with young people whose natural idealism is as yet untempered by the patience and tolerance of maturity. These students are at a time of life when a normal feeling of revulsion against all authority easily can be diverted into a violent antagonism toward existing political and economic institutions and policies. With the exuberant enthusiasm of youth, they are eager to find that Utopia that somehow all their elders have failed to discover. They may have studied history but they do not quite believe in it.

Moreover, the view that a university should be dedicated to social reform is not confined on campus to student leaders and their followers. Every university has many faculty members who by temperament and conviction are critics and reformists. They are not partisans for other ideologies or political systems, but some are restless under what they regard as the follies and the stupidities of their leaders. Nowhere else in society can such a group be as free to indulge in so much social criticism with complete immunity against any possible reprisal. This is as it should be; it is an invaluable asset to the university and to society, and it must be defended, even by a university president to whom complaints come from all those who believe that they have been the victims of the slings and arrows of outrageous faculty criticism. Nonetheless, and despite the fact that it is indispensable to the life of a university, the existence of this group on every campus does enhance the potential attractiveness of the university in the eyes of those outsiders who would like to use it as an instrument to help them achieve their doctrinaire ends.

Because of the university's contemporary importance and its assumed vulnerability, external groups seeking to provoke disorder or disunity are not likely to overlook such an opportunity. For example, it would be absurd and untrue to conclude that recent student protest movements and demonstrations across the nation all were externally inspired; it would be equally unwise to conclude that they were all wholly spontaneous, and that no element of professionalism lurked anywhere in the background.

Having said this, let me hasten parenthetically to point out what the press seldom has emphasized in its reporting, which is that only a very small minority of students is involved in these university disorders. The noisy clamoring of a handful of students may capture the headlines, but the vast majority of their fellows is either indifferent or even hostile to them. Some publicity, for example, was given recently to a demonstration on the Columbia University campus by a small number of agitated students and many non-students; the press did not feature the fact that within hours I had on my desk a petition, voluntarily circulated and signed by more than 1,200 students, demanding the expulsion of all the trouble-makers.

As we resist these efforts to make of the university either a bulwark of defense or an instrument of drastic change, we must never cease to proclaim to all concerned that the true and unchanging role of the institution is to be an open forum for *all* ideas and *all* opinions. The one eternal goal of a university is to foster the search for truth, however elusive it may be. We make progress toward that goal only as we encourage the fullest freedom of discussion on all matters which divide mankind into contending groups. If we fail to do this, we never will give to our students that quality of intellectual maturity that will enable them to become effective leaders and participants in an evolving democratic society. If we limit or constrain full freedom of discussion on any economic or political issue, we indicate thereby that we are unsure of the strength or validity of our own beliefs.

But, if the university is to maintain its independence and resist all assaults against its integrity, then it must keep its own house in order. Because it is so important to the health and vigor of contemporary society, the university of our time has a greater degree of public responsibility than in those days when it was content to inhabit a pleasant sanctuary of social unconcern.

This new responsibility runs throughout the institution. The modern university must seek consciously to hold and to deserve public confidence in the excellence of its work and the integrity of its purpose. Upon *all* members of the university community, therefore, there must be self-imposed *restraints* as well as asserted and recognized *rights*. These restraints cannot be imposed by any administration. But, unless they are recognized and observed, the university can ill defend itself against its critics or its would-be captors.

Let me illustrate briefly. Academic freedom for a professor means that his career may not be jeopardized by the expression of his views to his students or to the public. But however much a professor may assert his rights as a citizen to speak out on any topic, he ought to think twice before he makes a ringing public declaration of his views on a controversial subject, particularly if it is far removed from his own area of scholarly competence or expertise. He should hesitate before doing so simply because, no matter how loud or sincere his disclaimers, he can never entirely shed his scholar's gown. To his views the public tends to attach a special significance, no matter on what

subject, just because he is a professor in a great university. It may well be
that when he seeks to take off his academic gown he will have beneath it
only the Emperor's clothes, but he cannot escape a certain presumption of
intellectual authority—and he has responsibility not to abuse it. A scholar
has an implied professional commitment to approach all issues more in the
spirit of a judge than that of an advocate. He has an obligation, in Sir
Walter Moberly's words, to be "doubly watchful and critical of the un-
conscious operation on his mind of his own pet prejudices and sympathies . . .
an obligation more easily acknowledged than observed." When a scholar
fails to keep this admonition in mind, in the long run he puts in danger the
public acceptance of the essential integrity of the university.

The university student also has a primary responsibility, one that is a
part of his right to his intellectual freedom. This is the obligation to yield to
the views of others that respect he demands for his own. He may argue
heatedly with his comrades the long night through, but he may not in good
conscience attempt to interfere forcibly either with their free expression of
differing views or with the activities that derive therefrom. A student who is
unwilling to live by the simple rules of courtesy, decency, and good manners
that govern an academic community has no proper place in it, and he should
be invited to take himself elsewhere. The right to interfere with the rights
of others is no part of academic freedom.

A democratic society can exist in a state of health only if all citizens
observe a decent measure of courtesy and self-restraint in their dealings with
others. This does not mean that one should be supine in the face of something
that is believed to be dangerous or evil, but it does mean that one must attack
it through those devices and procedures developed by society for the peaceful
settlement of issues. Sir Walter Moberly also wrote that "An honest intention
to fight the Lord's battles is no guarantee against mistaken objectives or
illegitimate methods of warfare."

Moreover, we live in a world in which the communications gap between
expert and layman steadily widens. This is of little relative importance in
scientific or technical fields because the layman seldom undertakes to argue
with the expert; he is acutely aware of what he does not know, and he is
content to listen to those who do. But in the equally complex fields of public
policy, there is no such self-restraint and the layman frequently proclaims
that his opinion is just as valuable as that of a man who may have spent years
in the study of the problem in question, and who has at hand information
which may not be generally available to the private citizen.

This is a source of possible danger to a democratic society in a complex
world. Any layman has a citizen's right to disagree with policy decisions
reached by his public officials, but he ought to hesitate before he asserts that
his own view, which may be little more than a visceral emotional reaction,
is just as valid as that held by those who may have lived with the problem for
a long time, who have access to all sources of information, and who have the

responsibility for the consequences of the decision they have reached. Wisdom consists of knowing what one does not know quite as much as of knowing what one does know. Our graduates should have the sophistication of intellect to recognize the difference between the two.

2

The University in Our National Life

WALTER C. LANGSAM

President, University of Cincinnati. His article originally appeared in *School and Society* on Feb. 4, 1956, and was based on his inaugural address, Oct. 29, 1955.

The heart of any college or university in the United States is its faculty. Upon the members of this faculty lie three special responsibilities. First, there is the responsibility of good teaching. Although there apparently does not exist a really tangible definition of a good teacher, and although it probably would be difficult to prove legally that anyone is a poor teacher, there are certain generally recognized components of good teaching.

A good teacher knows his subject, is enthusiastic about it, and is eager to pass on his knowledge to the students in a way to arouse their interest. A good teacher is characterized by sincerity, and a great teacher also by humility. The classroom, filled with a captive audience of idealistic and trusting young men and women, is the last place in the world where one may justify cynicism, irrelevancies, unpatriotic utterances, or that cheap substitute for wit sometimes called smart-aleckiness. Finally, the good teacher has himself become so experienced and mature that he recognizes both the primacy and the integrating power of spiritual values. He never allows himself to become so overburdened with the urgent as to lose sight of the important.

The second responsibility of the university professor is research. This does not necessarily mean the prodigious production of learned books and articles; not every teacher can be a skilled writer. It does mean, however, a continuing thirst for further knowledge and a restless desire to take part in the everlasting search for truth, as this truth may be illuminated in a particular discipline or field of scholarly interest. And lastly, the effective faculty member provides patriotic leadership contributions to the life of his community.

The university faculty member is not an ordinary member of society. He is one of a select, respected, and honored group; as such, he owes special obligations to his American fellow-citizens, including that of leading a participating civic life worthy of emulation.

If the faculty be the heart of an institution of higher learning, then surely the students form its body. Created in the image of God, these students possess an innate dignity and worth that is sacred, and that, indeed, is protected by no less wonderful a document than the Constitution of the United States of America. I can think of no greater honor or responsibility than that of being entrusted with the guidance and development of the young men and women who someday will be the molders of America's destiny.

In a sense, our students are the unfinished product with which we work; but, as someone has well said, they are basic material with a soul. It is our task to fashion this material and to guide it not merely in the pursuit of happiness, but in the pursuit of the significant. It is our assignment not only to give the students a broad cultural background, specific formal knowledge, and technical skill, but to teach them how, eventually, to convert this knowledge and this technical skill into wisdom through the tempering influences of experience and ethics. We must be interested in the emotions as well as the reason of our students, for, whereas reason helps us decide on the means to reach a desired end, it is emotion, more often than not, that determines the end itself.

Perhaps the magnitude of our responsibility vis-à-vis the student, as well as of the honor involved, may become more apparent if we bear in mind that it takes only a year and some millions of dollars to build the world's tallest building, or its largest battleship, or its fastest airplane, but that it takes 21 years to develop one full-fledged citizen, who then is literally priceless.

It is in this spirit and with such understanding, incidentally, that we should contemplate a solution to the impending problem of multiplied applications for admission to college. Standards of academic excellence should not—and by the good institutions will not—be sacrificed to indiscriminate mass enrollment. But we must find a way, an American way, to give a chance to every worthy and reasonably well-qualified applicant who will be a better and more useful citizen because he went to college. No one, as far as I know, has yet found the answer to this problem; but I am sure that our institutions of higher learning, which thus far have solved every major problem that has beset them, also will find the correct and judicious answer in this matter.

In addition to its faculty and its students, every college and university has its administration. It has long been a source of regret to me that, in our way of academic life, many have come to look upon administration and faculty as if they were two separate groups, with varying interests, outlooks, and objects.

Actually, most American college administrators have had direct faculty experience. And I am not prepared to admit that these men and women automatically enter a new skin upon becoming administrators, nor that they lose overnight and completely the experience and outlooks which they acquired during their years as teachers.

It is, indeed, the aim of every good administrator to use this experience and his talents as a leader to make it as pleasant as possible for the faculty to work effectively with the students and to provide surroundings in which the students may develop their capacities to the fullest extent.

And now a few words regarding the type of institution that today may best be able to achieve all these goals. Our national system of higher education, with its parallel public and private institutions, was developed in order to meet our gradually evolving needs as a growing nation. And despite the fashion of breast-beating about all our educational errors, this educational system, on the whole, has been successful.

Today, moreover, there is discernible a further trend in our higher educational setup—a trend toward a combined public and private interest in one and the same institution. This trend, I am proud to say, has been fore-shadowed in the history of the University of Cincinnati—with its combination of public and private support, with its 50-year-old co-operative system wherein the university and American industry collaborate in educating the students in several of the colleges, and in the almost fierce pride of both alumni and non-alumni within the community in the progress of this institution. Whereas, in some areas, there still is misunderstanding and even dispute between the partisans of public and private higher education, the university and the City of Cincinnati have found a way to combine the best features of each in one enterprise.

Public support without political strings, returns from private endowment, corporate and private gifts, and income from tuition and fees together have financed an institution that has acquired an enviable international reputation. Surely we have found here a highly successful formula for town-and-gown co-operation—a formula that, with the passing of years, probably will be adopted and adapted throughout our great land.

With the continuing and expanding help of both our communities and our private firms and citizens, our American institutions of higher learning will be better than ever able to train more leaders—leaders who have learned how to think, how to search for the truth, how to use their knowledge and their skills wisely and for the good of society, how to rear future generations of sincere patriots, how to balance privileges and responsibilities, and how to leave their communities a little better off than they found them.

This is the paramount obligation of us all. Let us work hard together—community and university—to fulfill this obligation in a way to earn the gratitude of our country and the blessing of God.

3

The University Comes of Age

NATHAN M. PUSEY

President, Harvard University. His article originally appeared in *School and Society* on Oct. 17, 1964, and was based on an address at Vanderbilt University, Oct. 4, 1963.

A fully matured university is an educational institution which can set out on its own, deliberately and with confidence, to win important new knowledge. Any institution which makes such a bold attempt also has to have, of course, the ability to find, attract, and train individuals worthy of the task. It also is expected, under present circumstances, to send into our advanced technological society the many kinds of highly trained specialists the modern world demands. And though these exacting requirements are an essential part, even they do not comprise the full responsibility of a mature university.

World War II marked a turning point in the evolution of the university in America. At that moment in time, government, as the director of all aspects of the war effort, discovered it could not carry out its missions without the help of universities. Initially, it called on them only for personnel; then, also, for the training of specialists. But very quickly it came, in addition, to turn to them for most of the basic and much of the applied research on which the success of the whole complicated war undertaking depended. And so was inaugurated in the early 1940's a relationship new for government and new for universities which has worked a major transformation in our institutions of higher learning and which continues to be of tremendous, and growing, current importance to both parties.

In wartime, it was discovered that universities had a role to play in marshalling and training the military hosts, in devising and building the instruments of war, in acquainting military leaders with the languages, customs, and geography of unfamiliar parts of the globe. It was further seen that many kinds of knowledge and understanding indispensable for effective administration stemmed from the insights and ideas of professors.

31

So, during the war years, members of faculties from a wide range of disciplines were summoned to devote their knowledge and skills to government service. The result was that, all of a sudden, a professional group which had not hitherto held an especially elevated place in our society—indeed, had been often the butt of rather crude jokes among a people long inexcusably scornful of intellect—found its members called upon to provide essential assistance in one kind of program after another of crucial national importance and, in not a few such programs, actually to lead. This situation did not end with the war. Rather, it has continued and has gained strength, as professors increasingly have been drafted for important roles not only in the military and in government, but also in business and in many of the other manifold complicated specialized activities of contemporary society.

A single brief example will serve to illustrate the nature of this change in the role of universities and of professors. In 1936, just a few years before World War II, Harvard set up a Graduate School of Public Administration to help prepare young people for service in government. In order to guard its program against excessive academicism, to keep it related to the practical concerns of government, it was decided to associate with it a group of "consultants" to be chosen from individuals active in the work of government. They would come to the University from time to time to supplement the instruction of the professor and so give the program a feeling of relevance and immediacy. I need not labor the point that now most of this kind of consulting runs the other way. Professors are every week in Washington on a variety of missions, giving practical advice and sharing their knowledge and abilities with officials of government. And being involved in this kind of activity, they are in small need at home of help from outsiders from Washington to make their instruction seem vital and timely. The tables seem in fact to have made almost a complete turn.

This change in the activity of professors occurred so easily and naturally during the war that it almost escaped notice. As indicated, it derived from a change in what was expected of universities. And it has persisted because we are now in an age when almost everything we do depends upon highly trained professionals. It is the university alone which can find, recruit, and train the many kinds of well informed specialists needed to make our society work and, while doing this, develop the ideas and knowledge needed to enable the various professions to continue to advance. In the midst of such circumstance, it was inevitable that professors should move from their old haunts behind the backdrops and in the wings to positions near the center of our public stage. There for the moment, happily, they are performing quite well and presumably will continue to be needed in important supporting parts for a long time to come. Meanwhile, it is also clear that they enjoy these new roles and the increased prominence and give not the slightest indication of wishing to turn back from either to become once again merely observers and evaluators of the affairs of men.

The past 20 years have been exciting years for universities. First, immediately following the war, came the return of students in enormous numbers after frustrating years of dearth. All through the 1930's, colleges and universities had been plagued with too few students and too many teachers. Then, in the early 1940's, the stream of students almost completely had dried up as the young men, and many of the young women, were called aside for the pressing work of war. Suddenly, all that changed, and during the late 1940's, campuses literally swarmed with students as institutions sought eagerly to provide instruction for larger numbers than they had ever previously imagined they could cope with.

These happy years passed quickly, as one way or another their peculiar difficulties were surmounted in the enthusiasm of helping men returned from war. But after the veterans were graduated, more and more institutions discovered that the demand of applicants for admission did not fall off. What had been assumed to be a temporary condition did not vanish. Rather, it continued at even higher levels, with the result that more and more colleges found themselves freed from the old primordial necessity to compete fiercely to entice students—often even indifferent students—into their dormitories and classrooms. Now a large number of colleges have gained the opportunity to choose their entering classes from many more qualified students than they can admit. For the first time in our history, colleges and universities, instead of simply doing their best with the human material that presented itself at their doors, in recent years have been permitted actually to try to shape the composition of their student groups. It already is being discovered that this abundant supply of students is not necessarily an unmixed blessing; but as secondary preparation continues to improve, the population to increase, the number wanting to go to college steadily to advance, and the demand for college and university graduates to multiply, it would seem that the condition is here to stay and that it may be expected to spread at an accelerating rate. In such a time, the work of admission takes on a new and exciting dimension.

The reverse of the increased supply of students was inevitably an under-supply of teachers. All through the 1930's, teachers—even very good teachers—had been in oversupply, often tragically so. Now adequate numbers were nowhere to be found. Though in recent years this situation has been greatly improved, the problem has not yet been wholly corrected. And when we look at the increased enrollments still in prospect, it is clear that the relief thus far experienced may very well turn out to have been at best a temporary respite.

Another of the continuing baffling problems has been how to provide the new space demanded by a greatly enlarged educational enterprise. The physical facilities of the nation's colleges and universities, even under the relaxed conditions of those years, were only dubiously, if at all, adequate in the years before the war. The long years of depression and war had engendered neglect and found us in the postwar period quite unprepared in the matter of space for the magnification of activity that then came upon us. Ever since, we have had to struggle persistently, almost breathlessly, to try to catch up.

There was an immediate need in the late 1940's for living space for more students—especially for that new, unanticipated phenomenon, the married student—and, at the same time, need for more classrooms, for more libraries and laboratories, and not least of all, for more offices for necessarily enlarged faculties. But the greatest single need has been and continues to be the demand for more space for research. When the history of the American university in the postwar period is written, perhaps most prominent among all its themes will be an account of the enormous increase in research activity which occurred within it during this time, an increase which understandably has been accompanied by a very significant enlargement of graduate and postdoctoral study in all graduate and professional schools.

This great increase in research activity stems, of course, from the demands made upon universities during the war years. But other influences have since continued powerfully and increasingly to move the practices of universities in the same direction. Perhaps most important is a widespread conviction now held with irresistible determination that the answers to age-old problems can and must be found through increased research activity.

From their modern beginnings, research has been considered a distinguishing activity of universities. The basic dynamic for research in universities was and continues to be the desire for fundamental understanding. But research activity is now drawn increasingly into the service of urgent practical ends. The greatly enlarged contemporary effort was stimulated in the first instance by a pressing concern for national safety and for success in international rivalry. Since that time, a universal concern for health and a hoped-for achievement of improved control, if not extermination, of disease have contributed greatly to increased research activity in universities. Beyond this there is also a new realization of the importance, under continually intensifying competitive conditions, of research as the lifeblood of economic activity. But perhaps most influential of all forces has been the availability for the first time of something approaching adequate funds— chiefly government funds—to support research.

The Federal government will have spent more than three times as much on research and development in 1963 as it did during the whole five years of World War II—$13,000,000,000. Most of this, to be sure, will be spent in industry for development, chiefly weapons development. At best, one-10th of it, but still a sum of more than a billion dollars, will be spent in universities on their kinds of research. It is also important, in estimating the universities' involvement in, and importance for, the new greatly increased national research effort, to keep in mind that practically all the individuals who are working or will work on this great effort, in and out of the academic environment, will have had to be trained first for such responsibility in colleges and universities.

The account of forces making for change within the modern university does not stop here. The rapid advance of knowledge itself and the widened notion of the range of knowledge to be cultivated within the university have hastened the addition of new programs and the adaptation of old ones to meet the vastly altered conditions of our time. Before World War II, the social and humanistic concerns of the American university were largely limited to the Western world. Now our gaze has been lifted to embrace the whole globe. While natural scientists search further and further into the structure of matter or look outward, more perceptively than ever, into space, others among us in the university investigate languages hitherto denigrated as "exotic." Literatures are being examined which were formerly almost unknown and cultures explored which earlier were held to be of little intellectual worth. Today area studies pursued with increasingly complex interdisciplinary approaches are a part of every university's normal curricula. It is now true in fact, not merely a pretension, that the whole world at last has come to be of concern to cultivated men. And this in a time when there is an almost wholly new and very lively interest—again largely the result of technological advance—in the space within and around our world, both the infinitely small close at hand and the infinitely great far away.

The human mind may very well be bewildered by the scope of the modern university's concern. One has only to consider what has happened to the fields of chemistry or biology, or to a medical subject like anatomy, to shatter any comfortable illusion that one human mind can ever neatly comprise all knowledge. Today the startling array of new approaches and imaginative instrumentation dazzles the intellect. It has been said, for example, that in the field of medicine alone, more new knowledge has been achieved during the past generation than in all previous human history. Ethics, once a special topic in philosophy or theology, is now a subject of specific concern to students of law, business, medicine, or sociology. (And, one might add, is beginning also to be of interest to many lay people.) Mathematical considerations touch almost every field of university endeavor. And the living arts demand a place alongside the pursuits of scholarship.

In such a complex situation, it is not surprising that traditional departmental barriers are breaking down within universities. Furthermore, older patterns of instruction seem inadequate to present need. There is new recognition of the importance of independent work even at the undergraduate level; perhaps, I should say, especially at the undergraduate level. "Learning" in the old sense of getting by heart what others have thought and said seems much less important now than finding ways quickly to introduce young scholars into the experience and joy of investigation. And, at the other end, universities are increasingly involved in providing programs for more and more kinds of mature professionals who find repeated contacts with universities almost essential if they are to keep up with the onrush of knowledge and new opportunities in any field.

Perhaps enough has been said to indicate that today the American university is an extraordinarily dynamic, busy, relevant, and exciting place, and, to substantiate my point, that in responding to the increased range of expectation with which it is now confronted, it in fact has become an advanced and an almost wholly new kind of institution. And yet, happily, most of the perennial concerns of the old university live on within it.

With all the new demands made upon them, American universities remain the citadels of our culture, the strongholds of our humane learning. Set aside from field, factory, and market place, they are both apart from and part of the bustle of life and the responsibilities of government. Within them are many corners and yet, at the same time, quiet places where dedicated people work to keep our intellectual experience known, to evaluate it, to find present meaning in it, and, through it, give a new generation guidance, incentive, and direction. Universities have had, and always will have, a critical function to perform. Again and again throughout history, people, misled by mistaken ideas, have rushed on in self-deception to embrace irrational and illusory aims and, as a consequence, hideously have inflicted what might have been avoidable injury on themselves and others. The temptation to do this is always present. The cloak of civilization is easily rent; repeatedly, decency proves a thin veneer. This being so it always has been and remains a primary responsibility of universities to work to protect individuals and societies against mistaken ideas, to strive always to clarify knowledge and to increase understanding. It is not, finally, considerations of national safety, health development, or even exploration into space which call forth and define the essential nature of the university. It is, rather, this critical function and what the university can say to inform succeeding generations of the reach of human potential and what it can do and be to continue to arouse young people to devoted allegiance to humane responsibility.

It is comparatively easy to undermine sham and pretension and to drive the pietistic and the obsequious from the life of intellect. We all have had considerable practice at this sort of thing in recent generations and have scored repeated successes. It is also easy to swagger and to be merely assertive. But it is difficult—as it is now much more deeply needed to criticize and evaluate the human tradition—to find beauty beneath the cheapness seemingly so all-prevailing in everyday life and, in doing so, to engender a strength and a force within the human will that will lead to humane advance.

Is not this what we now most need from our universities? Is not this the most important and most challenging expectation which now confronts them? It seems to me it is. The two basic considerations for the life of a university are a sense of high standard in thought and conduct, and a widely shared faith in the importance of its mission. This standard and this faith are not fully contained in the search for new knowledge; they imply beyond this a clarification of moral values. And this perennial task of the old university happily lives on and is served in the new.

4

The Autonomy of the University

GEORGE I. SANCHEZ

Professor of Latin American Education and Director, Center for International Education, University of Texas. His article originally appeared in *School and Society* on March 19, 1966, and was a condensation of a lecture given at the University of Texas in 1965.

Years ago, someone asked the distinguished scholar, my esteemed friend Prof. Frederick Eby, "To whom does The University of Texas belong?' Unhesitatingly, he answered: "To the world of scholarship." Prof. Eby, then chairman of the Department of the History and Philosophy of Education and now professor emeritus, thus succinctly stated an overriding truth that often has been misunderstood, ignored, and sometimes consciously violated in the university in the United States and in the university abroad. The university belongs to the world of scholarship, to those who search for truth at the highest levels of intelligence, and who, then, promulgate truth to their younger colleagues, the students, who, too, are seeking truth.

This search for truth must operate in a climate of freedom, untrammeled by crass mundane restrictions or lay interference. Just as one cannot teach democracy in a concentration camp, so one cannot pursue truth fettered by handcuffs and leg irons. The university must be free. While the beautiful concept, "Ye shall know the truth and the truth shall make you free," is unchallengeable, it has to be predicated on the fact that, unless one is a mystic, only under freedom can he know the truth.

What is "freedom"? What is "truth"? In the university, it is what the world of scholarship says they are. The world of established and prospective scholars. Indeed, what is "scholarship"? Again, what the scholars say it is. Who are the established scholars? Their peers, and only their peers, shall judge them; and then only by their deeds in the world of scholarship.

The role of the university, and of the scholars who form it, is not social or political. It is an intellectual role, though their teachings may have profound effects on socio-political goals and processes.

The medieval university, of course, had variety in its structure. However, essentially it was an autonomous university. Its policies were set and it was administered by the "colleagues," professors and students. Admission, to the faculty or to the student body, was on demonstrated merit (*oposición*, as it is called in Spanish—that is, by a test before a competent jury, still practiced by many universities which follow the medieval tradition). The entire operation of the early university was what could be called "democratic" (quotation marks for obvious reasons).

This idyllic status of the embryonic university in the Western world soon encountered trouble. The universities needed more than special privileges and immunities; they needed economic support. This could come only from the city or principality, from the Church, or from both. Acceptance of such aid, however, soon involved the relinquishment by the university of some features of autonomy—the selection of the chancellor, the rules regarding the operation of the faculties, the degree of freedom to be enjoyed by faculty and students. A see-saw battle developed as now the university retrieved some losses, now the government (Church or State, or both) imposed more limitations. Throughout this struggle, the scholars (faculty and students) resisted lay interference, always striving to see to it that the university was a place where knowledge could be pursued in freedom; on the terms set by the scholars, the colleagues in scholarship.

The direct descendants of the medieval university inherited this struggle for the control of the university, a struggle in which the scholars sought state, or church, or church-state support without lay interference in the free pursuit of knowledge and in which the givers of financial and political support sought to direct the course of the university, to tell the university what it could or could not teach, who could teach, who could be a student and under what conditions; and the like. This struggle transferred to America when the first universities were founded, one in Mexico City and one in Lima, in the middle of the 16th century. Both of them were patterned after the University of Salamanca, founded in the 13th century. Increasingly, the crown and the Church made inroads into university autonomy in these institutions; and in those which followed them and were patterned after them. While Charles III restored some features of autonomy to the university in Spanish-America in the latter part of the 18th century, the revolutions for independence in the early years of the 19th century were responsible for the takeover of control of the university by the state.

The role of the university in Spanish America during the 19th and early 20th centuries was a sad one. Absolute government domination—over the protests of students sometimes, sometimes faculty, sometimes both—kept the university in constant turmoil. The economic poverty, the lack of administrative and governmental "know-how," and the lack of full-time faculties made higher education in all of Hispanic-America much of a shambles. Scholarship became individual, rather than institutional. Autonomy, the right of the university to pursue truth under freedom, went by the board. Institutions were suppressed and disbanded, reinstated, suppressed, and disbanded again; the quality of instruction became the child of haphazard luck. In most cases, except where clergymen such as the Jesuits were permitted to teach, the faculties were made up of men with no professional qualifications as teachers. A teacher taught a course or two at the university for prestige value or because of financial need. A doctor (M.D.) might teach a course in biology; a lawyer, a course in Latin, to say nothing of those who taught a course in the area of their specialization. In any case, they were "on campus" (and I use that term loosely), under the best of circumstances, for the brief hour of their respective lectures, and no more. The only persons who were more or less fulltime at a college (or *facultad*, as it is put in Spanish) were a handful of students who, at the beginning, were dedicated students. These students and their mentors soon became dissident, and began talking in generalities about university reform.

Reforma universitaria quickly became a catch-word, a slogan, a garbled creed; it became confused with university autonomy. And it became entangled with political issues and political parties. University reform is something more than irresponsible agitation. It takes "bricks and brains," money and scholarship. It takes responsibility in the pursuit of knowledge. It takes freedom to pursue that knowledge, by the economically poor student and rich alike; by dissident professors as well as by conformists and the faint of heart.

It is extremely unfortunate that the movement towards *reforma universitaria* occurred in Latin America simultaneously with the burgeoning of political democracy. The fountainhead was the University of Córdova in Argentina, where the fight for university reform and university autonomy became, sad to say, one and the same thing as political democracy, which was the theme of the day. That was early in this century. There, the idea that government should have no control over the university, but simply subsidize it, reached its zenith in the proposition that control of the university should be vested in councils in which alumni, students, and faculty had equal voice. Further, the idea of university autonomy was associated with exaggerated privileges for the students of the university and with rampant political partisanship in the affairs of government. While extremism in these matters is not uniform in Latin America, the pattern is much the same. The Latin-American university exhibits an undue preoccupation with national politics and with matters which have little or nothing to do with the pursuit of knowledge. This is true at the University of Chile in Santiago, at the University of San Marcos in Lima, Peru, at the Universidad Central in Caracas, Venezuela, as it is in many other schools. All are tainted in some degree with a confusion of the concepts "university reform," "university autonomy," and "political democracy."

In appeasing or in rewarding the students for their political actions, governments have been forced to grant extraordinary privileges to the university. The universities in Venezuela cannot be invaded by the police or the military, no matter what violence, what crime is taking place. They have the right of sanctuary. By law, property rights to land, buildings, and equipment in the Venezuelan university are vested in university councils, made up of professors, students, alumni.

When the students in Lima strike for some reason or lack of reason, the students in Caracas strike in sympathy. When the students do not like the dates for course examinations, they strike. The police catch some high school students at the headquarters of an extremist organization, where they are employed to make "Molotov cocktails." Their fellow students become incensed and threaten reprisals (strikes, riots, and so on) unless the culprits are released. It is shocking to witness the panic into which this throws the high government officials, from the president and cabinet on down. The culprits are released.

The students in most of Latin America use their power to prohibit scholastic probation or dismissal, no matter how many courses they fail. So, some agitators become "professional students," staying on and on. In Venezuela, by law, the professor can examine students only over the *materia vista*, the material covered when the students were present, but not that covered when they were on strike, or in mass absenteeism for whatever purpose.

This is a harsh portrayal of *autonomía universitaria,* Latin-American version. However, there are dedicated professors and dedicated students who seek, impart, and exchange knowledge calmly and seriously, who decry the antics of the extremists; and there are both public and private universities which do not suffer from the miscarriage of university autonomy.

Now, let us take a quick look at our own university, the composite of U.S. American universities. Here, too, we need to take a penetrating look at university autonomy, for the record, by far, is not one entirely of faultlessness, of perfection, and not one to justify smugness. Here, too, in varying degree, negative factors have entered into the concept that the university belongs to the world of scholarship. The established scholars and the incipient scholars need to examine the goals to which they are dedicated, the defensibility of those goals, and the extent to which the structure and policies of the university further those goals. I am just as unhappy at what I see here and there on our university scene as what I see in some universities in Latin America. The university of the U.S.A. cannot cast the first stone. Our university, too, belongs to the world of scholarship; and it, too, should be free to pursue truth—it should be autonomous; and, often, it is not.

The invasion of university autonomy takes violent forms in Latin America. The invasion is almost completely non-violent, or the reaction to it is non-violent, in the American university. The end result is the same: the pursuit of knowledge is hampered, is violated. I object to both forms of violation, for the university belongs to the world of scholarship—not to the politicians, not to the rabble, not to the extremists, not to the economic vested interests. Again, I am distressed and angered when a board of trustees is presumptuous enough to tell a faculty that it must not exercise, in the area of its competence, its inherent and perfectly ethical right to give advice and counsel to students, even on matters unrelated to the classroom.

In this field of university autonomy, and of the inherent right of the scholar to pursue truth freely, professorial heads have been bloodied many times; and they will be bloodied again. It is cheap at the price. I am angry because many self-anointed authorities have failed to see that the invasion of the autonomy of the university is not just a foreign manifestation. It is right here, and it is as dangerous here as elsewhere. It is up to us to stop it. Maybe a few more bloodied heads will do it. The university belongs to the world of scholarship, and scholars should be free to pursue truth freely.

5

What Is a College ?

EDGAR C. CUMINGS

Director of Community Services, Economic Opportunity Commission, San Jose, Calif. At the time his article originally appeared in *School and Society* (March 20, 1954), he was vice-president and dean of Hiram College.

Confusion exists concerning the real purposes, aims, and goals of a college. What are these? What should a college be?

Some believe that the chief function of even a liberal arts college is a vocational one. I feel that the vocational function of a college, while important, is nonetheless secondary. Others profess that the chief purpose of a college is to produce paragons of moral, mental, and spiritual stamina— Bernard MacFaddens with halos. If they mean that the college should inculcate students with the highest moral, ethical, and religious standards by precept and example, I am willing to accept the thesis.

I believe in attention to both social amenities and regulations, but I prefer to see our colleges get down to more basic moral and ethical considerations instead of standing *in loco parentis* for four years when the student is attempting, in his youthful and awkward ways, to grow up. It has been said that it is not our duty to prolong adolescence. We are singularly adept at it.

Some complain that a college is not extolling the merits of a given religious denomination. I am not decrying the benefits to be derived from a healthy church relationship for a college, for religion and education have a stake in one another. I am criticizing the tendency of many religious denominations, both Catholic and Protestant, to regard a college as a place where education takes second place to religion, and where the strings may be pulled by those who are confused about the chief tasks of an educational institution. I favor the general requirement that each student have a course in religion, but only on condition that this course leads to a questioning of and strengthening of the student's faith. It is of little concern to me whether or not a

43

student can recite the "begats" or the Bible chapters from Genesis to Revelations; an atheist can do that, too.

There are those who maintain that the chief purpose of a college is to
develop "responsible citizens." This is good if responsible citizenship is a
by-product of all the factors which go to make up a college education and
life itself. The difficulty arises from a confusion about the meaning of responsible citizenship. I know of one college which aims mainly to produce, in a
kind of academic assembly line, outstanding exponents of our system of free
enterprise. While really free enterprise has much to commend it, I hesitate to
commend to posterity students who live according to the gospel of John D.
Rockefeller or Engine Charlie Wilson. Likewise, I hesitate to praise the kind
of education which extols one kind of economic system to the exclusion of the
good portions of other kinds of economic systems. It seems to me, therefore,
that a college should represent a combination of all the above aims, and should
be something else besides—first and foremost an educational experience, the
center of which is the intellectual exchange between teachers and students.

When my father went to teach geology at a state university, it was only
a few years after the departure of one of the great university leaders of our
history—David Starr Jordan. The aura of Jordan still hung over the campus
and electrified it. Despite poor buildings, little equipment, and a small
student body and faculty, education was the magic watchword of that time
and there was hardly a student who had not fought his way there or who was
not motivated by a now forgotten fervor to gain knowledge and culture for
the sake of knowledge and culture. Not yet arrived was the time when going
to college was "the thing to do," or when the almost automatic receipt of a
diploma somehow opened the door to all enterprises. In those days, apparently, a college education still emphasized the gaining of knowledge the
hard way, the thesis that mental discipline is a necessity and not something
that modern psychologists and experts on education have discarded as
obsolete.

Along with the times, curricula have changed and multiplied as new
vistas of knowledge have been opened up. Along with genuine new intellectual avenues, however, we have indulged ourselves in some so-called intellectual activities and subjects which must have the ancients or the early leaders
of our higher education in stitches. I refer you to the catalogue of most of the
larger universities and many of the smaller colleges. It remains to be seen
whether a college is foresighted or merely foolish when it offers a course in
"Travel in Outer Space." I should advise students not to rush to make their
reservations for a trip to Mars or the moon; they still have time left and, in
any case, it is still problematical whether the boys with their hydrogen
bombs are going to leave us any space to fly around in.

Along with the change in times has, I fear, come a change in the attitudes of many students toward a college education. I have read entirely too
many statements such as this one on admissions application papers: "I want a

college education because I feel that this will help to support me and my family." I suspect that a job as a bricklayer would help this student to support himself and his family much better than a college education.

In his address, April, 1953, to the Ohio Association of College Presidents and Deans, Charles Allen Smart said,

When I see silly floats in student parades, and fraternity and sorority house decorations, I wonder whether our art departments aren't slipping. When I note the energy that goes into campaigning for 'prom-kings' and 'prom-queens,' while the students remain relatively indifferent to actual politics or, much worse, have learned that there is less and less room and safety for unorthodox opinions in this country, I begin to wonder what goes on in the classes in the various social sciences. When I see how vulgarly and publicly the students choose to make love, I wonder whether I myself, as a teacher of literature, expounding texts from Chaucer, Shakespeare and Browning, for example, in which love is felt and made most beautifully, have not failed to make these passages come alive in my students' minds in such a way as implicitly to expose and so lessen their own vulgarity. I happen to share Cardinal Newman's conviction, as I understand it, that if education does not strongly help to make ladies and gentlemen, there is something wrong with the education. He seems to say that liberal education can and should do nothing else, and if we accept his broad and deep definition of a gentleman, I am inclined to agree with him.

One of the best articles I have read in a popular magazine appeared in the spring of 1953 in the *Saturday Evening Post*. It dealt with Reed College (Portland, Ore.) and what made it a remarkable article was its emphasis that Reed is first of all an educational institution. Reed proves that students will flock to a college which is known to be difficult, which is known to place a premium on the acquisition of knowledge. It is also an example of a college which can flourish without the benefits thought to be derived from intercollegiate football on a grand scale.

A college should be an educational institution. This should not have to be said, but so many colleges and universities (and students) have become sidetracked concerning the matter that it needs to be restated, trite as it may sound. A college is a place where the teacher and the student are the two most important people; where young people should improve their thinking and deepen it, broaden it, refine it, and make it rational and objective. It is a place where they should, first and foremost, find the tools and the knowledge on which this thinking will be predicated.

6

The Dimensions of a College

SAMUEL B. GOULD

The author was president of Antioch College at the time his article originally appeared in *School and Society* (March 2, 1957). The article was based on an address at an Antioch College Assembly, Oct. 9, 1956. He resigned as president of the State University of New York effective Oct. 1, 1970.

According to what dimensions do we build a college?

Our first concern is the *intellectual* dimension of a college. It is a dimension projected along a never-ending line which marks the search for truth, a line reaching into the infinite because we know the whole truth is ever beyond our grasp, but at the same time a line upon which we can place our feet surely and take steps toward the light of understanding. The search for wisdom through knowledge is part of this dimension, for as Socrates said, "Surely, . . . knowledge is the food of the soul . . ." or as Shakespeare put it, "Knowledge is the wing wherein we fly to heaven. . . ." And such knowledge, if it is to lead to wisdom, should be sweeping in its outreach, set along many and varied roads for man to explore without limitation; it should cause him to read and reflect and, thus, to substitute judgment for opinion; it should be rooted in an unwavering integrity which spurns the twisting of it for base purposes.

A college in its intellectual dimension should be broad enough to take in all ideas, popular and unpopular. It should be strong enough and discerning enough to recognize and to withstand the pressures of those who would pervert the college for their own expediencies, or those who guilefully use its welcome and shelter to spread their own particular brand of propaganda, and all with pious protestations in the name of freedom of speech. It should be merciful enough to suffer eccentricities gladly, yet firm enough to banish sloth and superficiality from its midst. It should be humble enough to sense the infinitesimal character of the knowledge it transmits or the wisdom it engenders by comparison with what is still unknown; at the same time, it should be proud enough to sense the true worth of its calling.

A college in its intellectual dimension should have no part of the snobbery which occasionally and unhappily becomes scholarship's masquerade and protection against the world. C. T. Bissell says quite rightly that "scholarship is the fruit of dedication and loneliness."[1] Such dedication and loneliness, however, should have the effect of developing a certain magnanimity of character as well as a desire to disseminate with clarity and simplicity the conclusions drawn from one's study and meditation. There is no place in such an intellectual dimension for the poseur, whether teacher or student, who invites the kind of bantering attack which W. H. Auden makes in his decalogue prescribed for the literary intellectual:

Thou shalt not do as the dean pleases,
Thou shalt not write thy doctor's thesis
        On education,
Thou shalt not worship projects nor
Shalt thou or thine bow down before
        Administration.
Thou shalt not answer questionnaires
Or quizzes upon World Affairs,
        Nor with compliance
Take any test. Thou shalt not sit
With statisticians nor commit
        A social science.
Thou shalt not be on friendly terms
With guys in advertising firms,
        Nor speak with such
As read the Bible for its prose,
Nor, above all, make love to those
        Who wash too much.
Thou shalt not live within thy means
Nor on plain water and raw greens,
        If thou must choose
Between the choices, choose the odd;
Read the *New Yorker*; trust in God;
        And take short views.

The scholar, said Ralph Waldo Emerson, "is the world's eye. He is the world's heart." And so, besides being sharply investigative, he should be warm and responsive to all about him, even from his comparatively detached point of vantage. Out of his compassion and his urge to help, as well as out of his conviction that he must follow his inquiry wherever it leads, comes the quality of a college's intellectual dimension with room all along its sides for teachers and students alike.

[1] C. T. Bissell, University of Toronto *Varsity Graduate*, July, 1956, p. 127.

A college should be measured next by its dimension of *adventuresomeness*. It should base its program of study upon the premise that restlessness or dissatisfaction with the *status quo* is the sign of a healthy urge toward betterment. And such an adventuresome spirit, such a desire to probe into new methods, new theories, new practices, should evidence itself in positive creativity. Here is a dimension which takes the free inquiring mind of the intellectual and sets for it exciting tasks of exploration in which the only limits are those of man's imagination. It challenges the ability to devise new forms of intellectual enterprise or new avenues of moral or spiritual inquiry.

A college is a meeting place of ideas, jostling each other for recognition, stirring faculty and students to flights of imaginative yearning which either melt away or become hardened into practical possibility as they fall into the crucible of investigation. It is a place for daring and courage, not for complacency and acquiescence. By very definition its dimension of adventuresomeness reflects a willingness to risk or hazard, in spite of our awareness that all the trial balloons will not escape being punctured or deflated. Knowledge of the past is its resource but not its infallible guide for action.

Encouragement of the adventurous approach not only nurtures that most priceless asset of youth, creative imagination, but transmits that same asset to the faculty. In such an atmosphere mature people are constantly charged and recharged by the electrical excitement emanating from youthful restlessness and eagerness to explore. Working with young people keeps one young in heart, but only when the young people themselves are imbued with irresistible urges to meet the challenges of the time. And such an atmosphere spreads beyond a college into the community, helping to shape the latter into a more flexible pattern.

The dimension of adventuresomeness in the realm of ideas guarantees to a college that there is no tether or hitching post for the ideas of its constituency. It makes of the institution an exciting oasis of mental activity in the arid desert of conventional educational procedure. It opens both ends of the learning process and allows the fresh air of new ideas to blow through. "Art certainly cannot advance under compulsion to traditional forms," says Judge Augustus N. Hand, speaking of literary work, and we can add that neither can any other aesthetic or intellectual endeavor. "In the cultivation of creative power lies the greatest joy of the teacher, and the greatest hope for a better world."[2] To step boldly into the untried and unknown is the exhilarating possibility for a college with the dimension of adventuresomeness.

The third dimension of a college is the *spiritual*. Of all the dimensions, this is the most intangible, the most unmeasurable, the most difficult to fit into the college's structure. It is here that we move into a greatly debated

---

[2] D. Cowling and C. Davidson, *"Colleges for Freedom,"* p. 39.

and unresolved area. How does a college teach matters of the spirit? Is it actually something about which the college should be concerned? On one side stand men like Robert Hutchins, who maintains that education of the whole man is one of the most meaningless phrases in educational discussion and that "the task of education is to make rational animals more perfectly rational."[3] On the other side stand men like Theodore Greene, the philosopher, who says, "The final test of our efforts *must* be the deepest convictions, the actual behavior, the character and lives of our students after they leave our sheltered campuses. Have we really helped them to become more alive and sensitive, better husbands and wives and parents, better citizens, more humble and resolute and tolerant as human beings?"[4]

Both men want to achieve what amounts to the same thing but cannot agree on how to achieve it. Is it possible that all these facets of character mentioned by Greene can be acquired, as Hutchins suggests, merely by steeping oneself in the literature and accumulated wisdom of the past? Or must the college, as Greene implies, do something more to insure that its dimension of the spirit will be as great as its other dimensions? I believe it must, yet I can only grope for the ways by which it can be done. I believe the spiritual quality of a college must be its never-ending concern, regardless of how that quality is achieved. At Antioch we seem to think such a quality can be developed through the individual responsibility of the student, through his sharing responsibility with adults for finding solutions to his own problems of becoming and being mature, a sort of "learning while living" process. But we must admit that in this process we often find ourselves so involved with methods that the principles and purposes remain beyond the horizon. And when this happens, we have an intricate form with little spiritual substance.

I believe a college's dimension of the spirit is a totality formed of many parts. Each could be the object of careful scrutiny and the basis for educational effort if a college so desired; while each cannot be "taught" in the rigid sense of the word, each can be shown to be either present or lacking in every major or minor action within the college, whether by the individual or group.

The first of these parts of the spiritual dimension is the *stature of a man's vision*.[5] A man increases his stature as he recognizes the inadequacies of his present dreams and envisions higher ones. He increases it with the recognition of his unique potential and the use of that potential in helping to meet the world's need. We should not forget that a youth's vision is at least as much a predicator of his future as is his native endowment.

Vision, alone, however, is not enough. It must be accompanied by a

[3] R. M. Hutchins, "*Education for Freedom*," p. 37.
[4] T. M. Greene, "*The Surface and Substance of Education*," p. 22.
[5] The quotations and ideas in this and the next five paragraphs are largely drawn from E. M. Ligon, "*Dimensions of Character*," pp. 213-268.

dominating purpose, developed by the person and not forced upon him. Let us not confuse this with good intentions. I am speaking of the kind of purpose which dominates one's actions. It can be measured by observing how much of what a person does consists of aimless behavior contrasted with how much goes into achieving some definite objective. It takes both vision and dominating purpose to describe the forcefulness of a man's behavior. One can have vision and be a visionary, accomplishing little, or one can show much ado about very little. But one who gains in college a high vision of what he wishes to achieve and bends all his efforts to that end is profiting from the dimension of the spirit provided by that college in subtle or direct ways.

The second major part of the spiritual dimension is the *force of magnanimity*. The dictionary defines this as "loftiness of spirit enabling one to sustain danger and trouble with tranquillity and firmness, to disdain injustice, meanness and revenge, and to act and sacrifice for noble objects." The ability to rise above injustices and personal grievances is not easily obtained, but it is worth working toward. The mature individual in his daily life needs to practice both self-expression and self-renunciation many times. "He will need to learn," as one biologist put it, "that to satisfy his deepest desires he will often have to deny his most superficial desires." The urge for autonomy on the part of the individual and the urge toward magnanimity are linked together when he learns that "true freedom has to be earned and carries with it proportionate responsibilities. The dignity and importance of the individual is guaranteed only when he accepts his role in society with all its restrictions as well as its privileges."

A third component of the spiritual dimension is *faith*. I am not concerned here with defending the theological implications of faith but am content to interpret it merely as man's belief in a friendly, orderly universe. This implies a determination to search even in evil for the good it can reveal, for one believes that the good is present. Scientists, although some may not wish to admit it, also have faith. Theirs is a belief that the universe is governed by laws. It is this faith which makes them approach a problem over and over again in spite of repeated failures, never doubting that there is an answer. The great achievements of science during the last century testify to the power of such a faith.

Faith generates courage and optimism, both of which are necessary in the spiritual dimension of a college. Certain types of physical courage are comparatively easy to inspire. But the more difficult types involve years, not moments; indefatigable patience, not bursts of heroism; continual optimism in the fact of endless discouragement; the ability to face ridicule and misunderstanding, and similarly the ability to withstand the heady wine of popular acclaim.

Perhaps a college can best teach its students in these areas by making of *itself* a continuing example in all that it does, an example of vision, dominating purpose, and faith with its accompanying courage and optimism. Then, in its spiritual dimension, it may be broad enough to foster and enlarge the vision of its students and their determination to make the conflicts among men creative rather than destructive, broad enough to keep alive their faith in something which gives them strength for this work.

The fourth and completing dimension of a college is that of *community*. Here is a unifying dimension both within the college itself and beyond its campus. It is unifying because through a sense of community the college welds together the various elements of its campus population; furthermore, through the same sense it creates bonds between itself and the region where it is located. These are not the inevitable bonds of physical proximity which both region and college must accept willingly or reluctantly; they are, rather, the bonds which can be knit voluntarily between the two on the basis of a mutual desire to bring new cultural and intellectual enrichment to our area.

The dimension of community takes on increasing significance today as I see the mounting pressures and the impact of increasing numbers upon all levels of our educational system. Again and again I find myself reaffirming the essential goals of education, not so much because they need reaffirmation as they need to be remembered and re-emphasized. We are dedicated to an educational system based upon equality of opportunity for all, devoted to a conscious effort to develop a mature and dynamic citizenry, and concerned with seeking out and strengthening the potentialities of leadership and of professional skill. Most of all, we are dedicated to a system eager to inculcate in young and old a continuing desire to learn and, thus, to understand and enrich life generally. Such are the glorious concepts and yearnings of America.

These are our missions in education and their fulfillment will come about in many diversified ways. One of the important ways will be by the building of closer relationships between institutions of learning and the communities they are located in or near. Such relationships should and will make possible our leaping over the artificial barriers to learning set up by our formal educational curricula and other structural elements and giving to all our people opportunities for individual growth which spring from their sheer joy in expanding their mental and spiritual horizons. We need all skills and abilities in America, both greater and lesser, particularly in the areas of the mind.

It is my conviction that a college, in addition to its more readily accepted intellectual dimension which provides room for the highest kinds of scholarship and training, should have the dimension of community which offers a place for the general life enrichment of all who live nearby: young and old, artisan and farmer and member of a profession, and college graduate and the comparatively unschooled. Thus, many of the gaps or weaknesses which the new pressures of numbers are bound to create in formal education can be filled or strengthened as a college opens its doors and its resources to all in a friendly and informal fashion, without thought of credits or degrees or anything more than to assist the burgeoning of understanding in the individual as a member of a personal, physical, political, economic, artistic, and spiritual world. Out of this dimension can come a new strength for America. It can be born of a desire to make of each community a meeting place for ideas and fostered through the leadership of our educational institutions. It can create new and exciting uses for the great physical facilities and the intellectual or cultural resources which so many of our schools and colleges possess. Out of such a dimension can come a new unity of the people.

In the midst of day-to-day tasks, with their oppressive and wearying minutiae, it is good for us to pause and consider the dimensions of the college we are building together. And it is important for us to measure truthfully the depth and width of each dimension as it now stands so that we may continue to add to a structure that never will be completed. Each one of us individually, whether student or faculty member, adds to or detracts from the college's dimensions by what we are and what we do to show what we are. We add or detract also according to the degree of our willingness to work toward the extending of these dimensions both within ourselves and in this institution. Each student or faculty member is a microcosm of the college, even though the college itself should be more than the sum of its students and faculty. Its dimensions should and can reach new heights when it is peopled by those who work with power of intellect, with spiritual zeal, with eagerness for adventure, and with unflagging desire to serve others.

7

The Mission of the Liberal Arts College

LOUIS T. BENEZET

President, Claremont Graduate School and University Center. At the time his article originally appeared in *School and Society* (March 2, 1957), he was president of Colorado College. The article was based on the first Annual Report of the President to the Board of Trustees, Colorado College.

There is a good deal of vagueness as to what a liberal arts college today ought to be and do. In fact, the very vagueness of the term makes it harder to get together on plans. Liberal arts, apparently like politics, makes strange bedfellows. At the risk of rehashing old maxims, it may be important to look first at what kind of college a liberal arts college is and what it is not. If we can agree on a few specifics, then we shall be farther along at the start.

A college beginning life as a liberal arts college is under no divine law to keep that identity. Current pressures for change, in fact, are causing many a liberal arts college to ponder alternatives. It might become a small university, increasing master's degree programs in strong specialities and taking on others which do not present prohibitive costs. It might build a business school, a school of geological and petroleum engineering, a school of fine arts, and perhaps even schools of law and theology. This might require five years of planning, 10 years of execution, and several millions of dollars even for these graduate programs with limited technical needs. The future population of the Rocky Mountain States would justify this development; we are woefully short on universities. It would require a campus twice or three times our size; and it might entail an eventual student body of 5,000 with a faculty of 400. Because professional groups look for better avenues to their own profession, it might actually be easier to get money for this kind of development than for an undergraduate liberal arts college.

Another choice might be the building of a college of perhaps twice or more our present size of 1,000 students, merely by letting the enrollment drift upward and adding faculty without adding expensive new major fields. The increased enrollment would probably arise from the coming boom in college-age population, and this mainly from our own region. A natural development along with this would be increased programs of community service such as retail merchandising and household arts. Our growth, in other words, would be like the development of private but community-oriented institutions such as University of Kansas City. Along with this could come junior-college programs with various semiprofessional specialities. Such a development would undoubtedly lead us in the direction of outright municipal support; and it would provide the answer to what almost certainly will be a pressing local demand for a junior college within the next decade.

A third kind of college we might become is a so-called liberal arts college of limited size with a few major specialities geared to our region, such as geology, fine arts, and public administration—an odd kettle of fish to be sure, but no stranger than what appears here and there on the college scene. Such a college would not aim at being a graduate school but would sell itself as one of the best preparations in the country for a few selective careers.

It may appear that there is little difference among the three types of institutions just described. This is because all three types actually exist under the name of "liberal arts colleges" in different parts of the country. Each represents a highly worth-while educational operation, but none is a liberal arts college. During this year earnest suggestions have reached us for Colorado College to move in each of those directions—that is, a small university; a community-type college with more practical programs for better local consumption; and a selective undergraduate college emphasizing a few salable career fields.

A true liberal arts college is none of the above. A liberal arts college is primarily concerned with liberating the individual—liberating him from fear of himself, fear of others, from fear and ignorance of his world. It is concerned with breadth and depth of ideas and with a variety of interests. It is concerned with adjustment to a universe of ever-increasing complexity. A liberal arts college is concerned with achieving growth inside the mind and spirit of each student. It does not reject career selection or preparation; that is what the major is for. But it treats this aim as secondary to intellectual growth and breadth of understanding, believing these to be the straightest roads to success in any field. It is less concerned with the right answers in life than with the right questions.

Because of its attitude toward learning as personal development, the effective liberal arts college will produce more than its share of researchers, teachers, and creative business executives. In people like these it can accomplish the best working combination of broad understanding, keen intellectual tools, and dedicated purpose.

The preparation of enough new college teachers to take care of tomorrow's demands is just one task that could occupy liberal arts colleges exclusively for the next decade. Ten years from now we shall need 150,000–200,000 more college teachers than we have today—two professors for every one now. A prediction made by the Office of Education is, however, that there will be in that period less than 50,000 new Ph.D.'s—and at present only half the Ph.D.'s go into college teaching. Thus, the seedbed of college education itself will be dried up unless we find ways of turning more of our best minds into teaching the next generation at the college level. Similar shortages exist in the ministry, public health, high-level civil service, and, needless to say, scientific research.

The Knapp survey of the origins of American scholars, conducted at Wesleyan University six years ago, showed us that men and women of the professional leadership we need have come more frequently from independent liberal arts colleges than from any other type of college. Colorado College enjoyed a national ranking for the production of scientists during the first 40 years of the century. Yet, we need to re-think our mission in terms of greater and better production: production not so much in mass numbers—for this defeats our kind of college—but in the proportion of graduates whom we send on to careers of high calling. Basic to this, in my judgment, is a college program which educates for length, breadth, and depth.

For these reasons, it seems to me, our course should be to say "no" to the university, the community college, or the college of a few high-powered specialties, and to say a firm "yes" to an undergraduate liberal arts college which has breadth, clarity, and impact, and which, *because of its strength of program,* not just its scenery or climate, brings here as fine a selection of able and willing students as can be found anywhere. Ours can be one of those colleges where graduate and professional schools find their highest proportions of able recruits. It can be a place where education is considered important—important not only to the teachers or to the men who write the catalogues, but primarily to the students themselves. There are not many places like this in the country today.

8

A Liberal Arts College Is Not a Railroad

SOL M. LINOWITZ

Chairman, Special Committee on Campus Tensions, American Council on Education, Washington, D.C. At the time his article originally appeared in *School and Society* (Nov. 23, 1957), he was a partner in the law firm of Sutherland, Linowitz and Williams, and a member of the Board of Trustees, University of Rochester.

Businessmen and efficiency experts have recently been taking a hard look at our liberal arts colleges trying to find out what is wrong with their operations and why they are so far in the red. A number of them have now come up with the same conclusion: Measured by business standards and efficiency formulae, the liberal arts colleges are simply bad business operations. *Q.E.D.*: If the colleges want to make ends meet, they will just have to get on a sound, businesslike, efficient operating basis precisely as in the case of any other organization which is having financial problems.

The liberal arts colleges have long had this kind of thing coming. A lot of them have regarded "economy" as a nasty word and they have been reluctant either to tighten their budgets or to hitch up their braces. At the same time, our colleges and universities have been frankly and unabashedly making a pitch for funds at business and industry, arguing that our corporations have a real and basic stake in what happens to the private liberal arts college. And they have been succeeding admirably. Businessmen have responded by pouring in millions of corporate dollars. In doing so, however, they have been asking—as they have a right and a duty to ask—just how these dollars are being spent.

What they have learned has often appalled them: They have found out that, while the operating costs of colleges and universities have gone way up, faculty salaries are still way down; that there are large classroom buildings which are used only in part or only for a portion of the school year; that there are some college classes which have but a few students; that there are teachers who teach but a couple of hours each week; etc. This understandably has been disturbing to the businessman who looks for efficiency in his own business operations and knows that you can't (or at least couldn't) run a railroad on any such basis. With the best of intentions, therefore, the businessmen have been prescribing some answers which are based on business experience. And this, I think, has been causing a lot of misunderstanding and is apt to cause a lot more in the future.

As one who has been actively and directly involved in the business operations of corporate clients, I know how tempting it is to try to find solutions to these problems of higher education which will appeal to the businessman as efficient and sensible. And it is unquestionably true that there are many things which can be done at our colleges to help overcome some of their financial difficulties. But the heart of the matter is simply this: To a great extent, the very thing which is often referred to as the "inefficient" or "unbusinesslike" phase of a liberal arts college's operation is really but an accurate reflection of its true essential nature.

Perhaps it is worth re-emphasizing what a liberal arts college is all about: That it seeks to offer a long look into what has been said, thought, and written in the civilizations of the past and an opportunity to see the workings of different societies in perspective. A liberal education is supposed to give us a feeling for the depth of our roots and a sense of the stuff of which we are made. The right kind of a liberal education should create thoughtful and responsible citizens who will exercise their obligations with moderation and wisdom. Its essence is, as Plato put it, "learning to like the right things." Or, to use William James' phrase, it ought to lead to a "feeling for a good human job anywhere, the admiration of the really admirable, the disesteem of what is cheap and trashy and impermanent."

This kind of thing comes high. It cannot be achieved easily or by spending energies reshuffling curricula, faculty assignments, or classrooms. It means keeping an eye on what makes an education liberal.

One of the major steps frequently recommended by businessmen in order to get our liberal arts colleges on a sound financial basis is to try to cut down the number of faculty members on the assumption that this will make more money to be spread around among those who remain. Some would do this by reducing the number of hours which the student spends in class or under faculty supervision. Others would invoke a numerical ratio of so many students to one teacher as a guidepost for educational efficiency.

If a man is really convinced that it is harmful for the student to spend too much of his time in class or with faculty members, then (although he would have a hard time satisfying me on this score) I can understand his position. What I am bothered by, however, is the clear implication that the objective of increased efficiency might even override the desirability of having faculty members spend more time with the students in order to do their jobs right. In my own experience I have found that the common complaint on our campuses is not that there is too much faculty supervision and companionship, but that there is not enough. One of the things which it seems to me youngsters should and do look for in a college education is the chance to get to know faculty people of eminence and learning and to spend time with them in that close association which is blessedly unique at a college or university.

As to a numerical ratio of students per teacher, I am deeply disquieted —not because I am nurturing a romantic kind of Mark Hopkins hangover, but simply because I think this is the result of regarding a college as first a business operation and only secondarily as an educational institution trying to turn out the right kind of men and women.

A college may offer a course in Persian history, for example, which only five students will attend during a particular term. Should we abolish the course? Or should we hope that the few students who do learn something of Persian history will thereby become uniquely qualified to perform some important service for which this particular aspect of their education has especially fitted them? Or, if our students today seem to be drawn in ever larger numbers into the "bread-and-butter" courses, should we give up Greek and Latin and the other studies which I have always thought are the hard core of our liberal education?

In other words, would not a fixed numerical ratio really operate to change the character of a liberal arts college so that it would become something quite different from the kind of place it was always intended to be? Is there not a real danger that we may end up with an institution in which everything is off balance except the balance sheet?

What, then, is the answer? I think it is really quite simple and ought to be faced frankly and clearly: American business and industry will just have to continue to dig down deep. I think they will have to understand that much of liberal education which is urgently worth saving cannot be justified on a dollars-and-cents basis.

I think the time has come for American business and industry to say to our colleges and universities things like these, which badly need saying:

We need your help even more than you need ours. We are anxious to have young men and women who know how to assume responsibility and offer leadership. We ask you to give us young men and women of breadth and perception who can look beyond their desk or their workbench, who will understand where we have been and where we are going, who will know about the kind of world in which we live and the kind of future we are trying to achieve.

We want men and women who will be able to communicate with one another and with other people in other places, who will know how to transmit and stimulate ideas, who will know that things human and humane are even more important than the IBM machine, the test tube, or the slide rule.

We want people who will try to understand what goes on in a man's mind and heart, who can appreciate "know-why" as well as "know-how."

We want men and women who can see our problems as part of total human experience and who can understand something of what yesterday teaches us about tomorrow. We want and need young people who will be able to dream dreams and who will be unafraid to try to make them come true.

Because such men and women are basic to our very existence, we pledge you our full support so that you may properly do the job which in your interest as well as ours is required to be done.

If American business and industry were willing to place such a charge upon our liberal arts colleges and our universities, then our institutions of higher learning would be challenged as never before. They would be required—as they should be—to examine their own programs of study and to see if they are indeed ready to educate whole men. They would be able— they would be compelled—to concentrate their resources on the strengthening of human values. They would have the chance to prove that American liberal education can produce men and women of open mind and an understanding heart, with the wisdom, the maturity, and the humility to help us achieve our American destiny.

In such a way could American business and industry make the greatest contribution to American higher education to the greater profit and the lasting glory of both.

9

The Contributions of the Small College

ALLAN O. PFNISTER

Provost, Wittenburg University. At the time his article originally appeared in *School and Society* (Oct. 20, 1962), he was associate professor of higher education, Center for the Study of Higher Education, University of Michigan.

The small college, one with fewer than 1,000 students, has made and continues to make a more significant contribution than do the larger institutions in the U.S. Three rather broad studies provide some evidence for testing this statement. One deals with the production of American scientists, the second with the production of promising scholars, and the third with the production of college teachers. While these categories of contributions may be limited, there is probably general consensus that each constitutes a worth-while contribution.

The basic study of the contributions of colleges to the production of scientists is reported by Knapp and Goodrich.[1] Without going into the details on the way in which the authors determined the various indices of productivity, we can only note that the indices ultimately developed allowed them to set forth a list of the top 50 colleges in terms of the number of scientists "produced" per 1,000 graduates. Among the top 50 colleges, somewhat over half of them enrolled, according to 1958 enrollment statistics, less than 1,000 students—clearly "small" colleges.

Before we leap to any conclusion, however, we should recall that, in 1955, roughly 70% of all colleges in the U.S. enrolled less than 1,000 students. During 1924–34, the period covered by the study, an even larger proportion of colleges enrolled fewer than 1,000 students. On a proportional basis, therefore, one would expect not 50%, but over 70% of the first 50 to

---

[1] Robert H. Knapp and Herbert B. Goodrich, "Origins of American Scientists" (Chicago: University of Chicago Press, 1952).

have been small colleges. Knapp and Goodrich found that geographical location of the baccalaureate institution was probably the most significant factor related to the productivity index.

The second reference is a sequel to this study, "The Younger American Scholar: His Collegiate Origins." [2] Again, we can note that ultimately a list of the top 50 institutions was developed. Roughly 20 of these enrolled, according to 1958 figures, less than 1,000 students. The small colleges actually were not represented in proportion to their numbers in the sum total of institutions in the nation. Geographical location again appeared, according to the authors, to be one of the most important factors in the productivity index.

The most significant finding of these two studies was that selected small independent colleges were proportionally very productive, but that small colleges as a group were not particularly distinguished. The conclusion of the authors of the last report was that "the production of promising young scholars, in general, rests on a particularly narrow segment within the American system of higher education, with some three score institutions, at the most, showing significant and impressive rates of production, while among the remainder the dedicated young scholar is a rare exception among their graduates." [3]

A recent investigation begun by Frank Kille, then dean of Carleton College, and carried through to completion in the Center for the Study of Higher Education, University of Michigan, provides data on the baccalaureate origins of liberal arts and education college faculties. The study is based on a carefully selected 25% sample of American liberal arts colleges, teachers colleges, junior colleges, and/or education faculties of representative American institutions. Details on the statistical analyses undertaken can be found in the report itself. [4]

Assuming that it is desirable for an institution at least to perpetuate itself over the years, the baccalaureate origins study developed a ratio between the number of teachers in each class of institutions in the sample and the number of teachers produced by the corresponding class. Thus, among the "small" institutions in the sample, 6,640 faculty members were employed in 1955–56. However, over the years, the "small" institutions in the group of 836 produced only 4,770 teachers for the sample. These two figures give a ratio of 71.8. This may be compared to the ratios for the medium institutions (enrolling 1,200 to 5,999) of 86.1, medium-large institutions (6,000 to 11,999) of 332.3, and large institutions (12,000 and over) of 130.8. Certainly, such evidence is far from conclusive, but it hardly supports the

[2] Robert H. Knapp and Joseph J. Greenbaum, "The Younger American Scholar: His Collegiate Origins" (Chicago: University of Chicago Press, 1953).
[3] *Ibid.*, p. 93.
[4] Allan O. Pfnister, "A Report on the Baccalaureate Origins of College Faculties" (Washington, D.C.: Association of American Colleges, 1961).

contention that the small colleges are making the greatest contributions.

Using a per-capita index, *i.e.,* an index based upon the number of faculty produced for the institutions in the sample per 1,000 undergraduates, the small institutions came out in a much more favorable light: they produced 14.2 teachers for 1,000 undergraduates. On the other hand, the very large institutions (those over 12,000) produced 14.4 teachers for 1,000 undergraduates. This last figure is surprising, because the divisor obviously discriminates against complex universities; the divisor included all undergraduates, professional as well as arts and education people, while the dividend included only persons teaching in arts and education. Furthermore, a close analysis of the contributions of the small colleges revealed that the high score for this group was due to the spectacular contributions of a limited number of these "small" institutions rather than to a clear contribution across the board.

On the basis of such evidence as the above, it becomes rather clear that the contributions of small colleges as a group have not been particularly outstanding, but those of a limited number of small colleges have been quite significant. There are some very definite reasons why the small colleges as a group actually have made only a limited contribution to the world of scholarship. It also is obvious why some small colleges have made a rather spectacular contribution.

Let us consider some of the forces working against the small college. First of all, even at a relatively expensive (low) student-faculty ratio, the small college must depend largely upon one-man departments. In a day when knowledge is growing rapidly in all fields, the demands upon one person to offer a comprehensive major are next to impossible. If a standard major involves 24–28 hours, this means eight or nine different three-hour courses. Even alternating the courses requires a person to devote constant effort to keep up, to be creative, and to reflect and stimulate students to the best of their abilities. Teaching loads of 15–18 hours are not at all unusual in small colleges.

One also could mention the general sense of isolation that a faculty member in a small college may feel. At the same time, as the only member in a department, he may settle back into a well-established rut. He has no competition in his area. He can be as creative or as sloppy as he pleases, and he finds no one to call him to task. He does not have to produce, or write, or meet with other persons in his area of discipline. He can avoid quite successfully any new ideas. I am not arguing thereby for the "publish or perish" philosophy that obtains in many complex institutions, but I am simply indicating that, without some contact with his peers, the professor in a small college successfully can avoid creativity.

It is claimed that the professor of the small college can strike up an intimate acquaintance with his students, that he can carry on what is virtually tutorial work. As a matter of fact, he seldom does. In my interviews with students on small college campuses, I find many who sing the praises of the small college and speak of the opportunity for close acquaintance with their professors. When I ask them how many times they actually have sought out one of their professors, disappointingly few indicate that they even darken the door of his office.

Small colleges must perform the same general functions organizationally and administratively that large universities have to perform. Obviously, however, the administrative staff has to be smaller and the tasks have to be grouped under a smaller number of individuals. The faculty finds itself called upon to do more and more work in the form of committee activity. So we find in the small college 15 committees with every faculty member participating in a minimum of five. One of two things happens: either the work of the committee is not done—the committee meets once a year, if at all—or if some eager person wants his committee to work properly, he works 26 hours a day or lets his teaching slip. In short, the faculty member in the small college has some very potent forces working against him.

The small college also faces basic problems in the area of facilities. Think of the library, for example. When a faculty member wants to engage in some research, or even to broaden his knowledge of his own field, he finds the library of 15–20,000 volumes—and this at a time when library experts talk of a minimum undergraduate library of 100,000 volumes. Laboratories in the sciences tend to be limited in small colleges. Of course, one can be inventive. I have seen some interesting equipment in physics laboratories fabricated from all sorts of odds and ends, yet presumably well-equipped, and where the instructor is happy with his $65-per-year allotment for equipment—and this at a time of such rapid advancement in the sciences that $65 is hardly downpayment on a piece of equipment.

The students in a small college also face a number of problems. For the most part, students find a small college to be a friendly place; they get to know one another—because they cannot avoid seeing one another day after day. Because they tend to come from the same general background, however, they only have their prejudices well reinforced; the whole group becomes even more homogeneous than it was when it entered. I recall a visit to one campus where we tried to find a few rebels among the student body but, after a couple of days, could not even locate one. The atmosphere was one of glorious conformity.

Furthermore, upper-division courses are likely to contain only two or three students. Two or three majors in a field do not experience much competition, do not feel much of a challenge. Sometimes the professor is so glad to have someone taking his advanced course that he does everything possible to avoid frightening him away. The professor would rather teach eight or nine different courses and offer a major than to be deprived of his few senior students. The last year's work of a student in a small college may or may not be stimulating. The chances are that, if a student goes on to a respectable graduate school, he is shocked at his inability to engage in research, at his inability to state and defend his position, and at his lack of acquaintance with different points of view.

A small college also faces problems in developing its curriculum. For the most part, it tends to be proliferated. Small colleges tend to be imitative rather than imaginative. They face all sorts of pressures from the outside—pressures from professional agencies and from graduate schools. They are afraid to offer too much experimentation or innovation.

One could recount other interesting problems. But enough of the grimmer side of the picture. Let us turn rather to the potentialities. And there are potentialities, because the studies of the baccalaureate origins of scientists and scholars and teachers show significant contributions from a selected group of small colleges. Some small colleges are exceedingly productive; they stand at the top of the list in almost any study of productivity.

What are some of the ways in which the small college can become productive, can realize its potentialities? The following points might be mentioned:

The small college can resist the pressures of trying to be everything to everybody by seeking to be distinctive, offering a limited number of majors, and working at some depth in the limited number of majors which it is providing. Making use of the rather simplified channels of communication possible, it can keep the entire faculty and student body informed and stimulated. It does not face some of the problems that a larger institution faces because of the sheer magnitude and complexity of the latter's operation. The small college can counteract the threatening provincialism among its faculty by forcing them to take leaves, providing generous sabbatical allowances, and having faculty members attend conferences and meetings in their various disciplinary groups.

The small college can exploit the sense of community. It can work closely with the students if it wants to do so. It cannot assume because it is small that the proper relation between faculty and students will obtain, however.

The small college can dare to be different. With the simplified organization and with limited offerings it can engage in campus-wide planning and thinking more readily than can a large institution. It can be flexible enough to vary its program to meet the needs of the students with whom it is working.

Above all, the small college can avoid exalting smallness for its own sake. Small size only provides certain opportunities for doing things. It does not guarantee that these things will be done. The small college can keep alive the option for students to choose to attend small and independent enterprises of quality. The small college has many opportunities. Let us exploit these opportunities rather than assume that smallness *per se* is its supreme justification for existence.

10

Cooperative Relations Involving the Liberal Arts Colleges

WILLIAM E. CADBURY, JR.

Director, post-baccalaureate fellowship program, Haverford College. At the time his article originally appeared in *School and Society* (April 16, 1966), he was dean of the college.

When the British founded a new college, they usually placed it near an old one, and these clusters became great universities. Our forefathers in this country, true to the pioneer tradition which wanted breathing space, tended to place a new college in a handy wheat field near a village far from any educational competition. Or, if they did place it in an urban setting, they made sure that any neighboring colleges were so different as to offer little or no competition. The result has not been great universities—they developed otherwise—but many small, autonomous, widely scattered institutions of variable quality. These are now the independent liberal arts colleges about whose imminent death so many tears are being prematurely shed.

Each of these colleges glories in its independence, but of late we are beginning to wonder if this is not being bought at too high a price. Small segments of autonomy are being surrendered here and there in the interests of better education.

I have chosen nine markedly different cooperative arrangements as examples of what is being done: two groups of closely integrated near neighbors; four regional clusters of more widely spaced colleges, each with its own executive officer; and three groups less formally affiliated.

The nearest thing we have to the English pattern is perhaps the group at Claremont, Calif. Pomona College, the oldest of the group, was founded in 1887 and, by 1925, when the group plan was born, was a well-established coeducational college of high quality. It was Pomona's Pres. James A. Blaisdell who was the author of the group plan. His vision for the colleges was expressed in a letter which he wrote in 1923: "My own very deep hope is that instead of one great, undifferentiated university, we might have a group of institutions divided into small colleges somewhat on the Oxford type—around a library and other utilities which they would use in common; in this way I should hope to preserve the inestimable personal values of the small college while securing the facilities of the great university. Such a development would be a new and wonderful contribution to American education."

The first new unit was founded in 1925 as the coordinating institution and graduate school of the group; at first called Claremont College, it is now the Claremont Graduate School and University Center. Dr. Blaisdell served as its president for a decade, beginning in 1926.

Scripps College, a women's college which emphasizes the humanities and the arts, was the next to be founded, in 1926. Then came, in 1946, Claremont Men's College, concentrating on preparation for business, government, management, and law; in 1955, Harvey Mudd College was founded primarily for engineering and science, and, most recently, Pitzer College, for women, stressing the social and behavioral sciences. Although each of these institutions has a different emphasis, each, except for the Graduate School, is a self-contained and autonomous undergraduate college with a board of trustees and president.

Although each college has most of the facilities common to small colleges everywhere, some facilities are supported and used jointly. Most important, perhaps, is the Honnold Library, which, with more than 400,000 volumes in the regular collection and more than 3,000 periodicals and several special collections, is more like a university library than one for a small college. A joint science library serves five of the colleges. There is only a single Health Service and Infirmary, one Psychological Clinic and Counseling Center, and no duplication in such services as the business office, the heating plant, and the telephone switchboard. These, like the single Campus Security Force, serve all members of the group. For the faculties, there is a single faculty club.

The colleges publish a joint list of courses, almost all of which are open to students of all the colleges except where restrictions are placed by the home college. Needless to say, from the point of view of the student, the freedom to select courses elsewhere adds tremendously to the attractiveness of his college; and there is no extra cost to him.

Altogether, these institutions have more than 300 faculty members and more than 3,000 students—by all but our most recent standards, a fair-sized university.

The cooperation of Negro colleges in Atlanta began in an atmosphere of crisis. In the late 1920's, Atlanta University, Clark, Morehouse, Spelman, and Morris Brown Colleges were all small liberal arts colleges with financial problems, whose relationships were notable more for intense rivalry than for anything else. Morehouse and Spelman were colleges for men and for women, respectively; the others were coeducational. The General Education Board had recently increased its support for Morehouse, but had turned down an appeal from Atlanta University. The president of Atlanta had resigned and the trustees were hunting a successor. One constructive event occurred in the summer of 1928: Atlanta, Morehouse, and Spelman had gotten together to the point of conducting, for the first time, a joint summer session.

In June of 1928, John Hope, then president of Morehouse, received an honorary degree from the University of Toronto and, while there, was impressed by the strength of the university, which many years before had joined forces with several other Toronto colleges. He contrasted this with the unhappy scene in Atlanta, and so was receptive to the idea of some kind of cooperation. At this time, when there were many rumors flying about as to what was in store for the institutions in Atlanta, Hope received a letter from the General Education Board saying that the Board "might be willing to provide the funds necessary for the construction, equipment, and maintenance of a library for the Negro colleges of Atlanta."

This was the background against which a number of forward-looking men and women, including influential trustees of Atlanta University, conceived the idea of electing Hope president of Atlanta, to guide a re-organization which would limit Atlanta University to graduate work and affiliate it with Morehouse and Spelman; these colleges, in turn, would deny themselves the possibility of granting advanced degrees. On April 1, 1929, a Contract of Affiliation was signed and a reconstructed Board of Trustees elected Hope president of the new Atlanta University. Morehouse and Spelman successfully absorbed into their own student bodies the undergraduates of Atlanta University, and financial support came not only from the General Education Board but from the Julius Rosenwald Fund and from other sources. In the summer of 1931, the new library was opened, giving these institutions for the first time adequate library facilities. By 1936, Clark and Morris Brown also had become fully cooperating members of the group, which now is called the Atlanta University Center, consisting of Atlanta University (which has absorbed the Atlanta School of Social Work), the four undergraduate colleges, and a new combined Inter-denominational Theological Center.

In forming the Atlanta University Center, there was reallocation of physical plant, including moving Morris Brown and Clark Colleges from northeast and south Atlanta, respectively, to campuses adjacent to the others. The six board chairmen, the six presidents, and three individuals elected by the other 12, form a Trustee Committee on Cooperation. Combined library and laboratory facilities, extensive exchange of students, and consultation on faculty appointments are only a few of the ways in which cooperation functions.

Cooperation of quite a different kind is found in three mid-western college associations: the Associated Colleges of the Midwest (ACM), the Great Lakes Colleges Association (GLCA), and the Central States College Association (CSCA). Each association is guided by an executive officer, with the title of president, who is responsible to a board of trustees composed of the presidents of the member colleges. Each association has had only one president, the present incumbent. Since associations like these are something new in the educational world, these men have very little in the way of precedent to guide them. They, and their boards of trustees, busily are working out new ways for colleges to do things.

The Associated Colleges of the Midwest is the oldest of the three. Member colleges[1] are all strong liberal arts colleges located west or north-west of Chicago. Since most of them (Monmouth and Knox, Carleton and St. Olaf are exceptions) are too far apart for ready exchange of students, their cooperation takes a form quite different from that of many other kinds of groups.

Financial support for ACM activities comes largely from contributions of the member colleges and foundation and government grants. Although the association is only in its seventh year, its general budget, plus programs and projects, amounts to several hundreds of thousands of dollars annually, and its staff already has outgrown its original quarters. Large items in the budget are for a cooperative program with Cuttington College, in Liberia, and a program of Non-Western Studies, for which the association recently has received a grant of $450,000. Other projects include institutional research, joint activities in the insurance field, student conferences, circulating a borrowed telescope among member colleges, and several others, two of which I shall describe briefly.

A Program of Field Studies in Central America enables faculty members and students from ACM colleges to work in Central America jointly with colleagues from institutions which are members of the Confederation of Central American Universities. Insights from various disciplines such as biology, geology, geography, and social sciences are used in "interdisciplinary studies of the adaptation of man and other forms of life to different climatic environments." Students are granted academic credit for the work done. Some of them remain in Central America for a year, others for only six months. Obviously, their home campuses are enriched from their experiences when they return.

Since 1960, the ACM and the Argonne National Laboratory have cooperated in the "Argonne Semester" program. As in the Central American program, students and faculty leave the home campus—but to Argonne is not very far—and spend time in a different environment. At Argonne, they have the use of the superb facilities of a major institution and the stimulus

[1] Beloit, Carleton, Coe, Cornell, Grinnell, Knox, Lawrence, Monmouth, Ripon, St. Olaf.

of working alongside of outstanding research scientists. Most students stay only a semester; faculty members stay for as much as 15 months—two summers for research and an academic year of research combined with the direction of seminars and the other academic activities of the students. About 25 students and three or four teachers from ACM colleges are involved each year. Students and faculty members profit from the experience and, like those who have been in Central America, contribute to their fellows from their own experiences when they return.

The Great Lakes Colleges Association, consisting of 12 colleges[2] in Ohio, Michigan, and Indiana, is a little younger than the ACM, this being its fifth year of active existence.

Among the programs sponsored by the GLCA is a project on programmed instruction. More than 100 faculty members from GLCA colleges have received training and experience in the design and use of programmed materials, and more than a score of actual programs have been written and are being used, although cautiously, in as many fields in several of the member colleges.

Improvement of teaching also is being fostered by a plan for teaching interns in chemistry and biology. In 1965, 11 men at or beyond the Ph.D. level taught and studied how to teach at GLCA colleges. Each of them came from a research background. It is hoped that, by giving them a taste of teaching—half time—and an opportunity to learn how to improve their teaching, they can be persuaded, if they are successful, to remain in the teaching profession.

Perhaps the most important of GLCA programs are those which promote "the evolution of an intercultural environment for undergraduate education (with generous subsidization of relevant faculty development and with overseas study opportunities for highly motivated students)."

In 1964, the member colleges agreed to a division of labor to permit the offering of five new foreign languages and study of the related cultures. Antioch is responsible for Portuguese, Earlham for Japanese, Kenyon for Arabic, Wooster for Hindi, and Oberlin and Wabash for Chinese. Studies of these languages and cultures are available to all member colleges. A student can transfer, temporarily or permanently, to the college concentrating in the special area of his interest. Special summer opportunities, visiting professors, periods of study abroad, materials for self-instruction, and other devices still to be developed, are ways in which the use of these resources can be made available to all the member colleges.

The third and youngest of these three associations, the Central States College Association, is in its first year. The articles of incorporation were signed in April of 1965 and the first president (Dr. Pressley C. McCoy) took office a few months later.

[2] Albion, Antioch, Denison, DePauw, Earlham, Hope, Kalamazoo, Kenyon, Oberlin, Ohio Wesleyan, Wabash, Wooster.

Member colleges are 10 in number. They are all liberal arts colleges with strong church ties, located in six midwestern states.[3] An early joint effort was an amplified telephone conference. Plans are going ahead for a number of other projects. Undoubtedly this association will profit from the experience of others, especially the ACM and GLCA. There is, however, a difference in that all of the CSCA colleges are committed Protestant institutions, whereas most of the members of the other two associations are either independent of any church or have very tenuous church connections. A statement which has been prepared for use in the catalogues of member colleges includes a paragraph which suggests an approach different from that of others: "Through close collaboration among administrators, faculty, and students, CSCA hopes to strengthen the scope and quality of liberal education among all its members. This will include serious exploration of the theological, philosophical, and ethical dimensions of their church relationship and its relevance to the quality of education, to the intellectual life of the church, and to leadership in a democracy. As an expression of their commitment, the colleges are planning cooperative action to help prepare students for the range of problems and opportunities arising from urbanization, from varied scientific and technological developments, from treatment of minority and underprivileged groups, and from conflict within and among persons, groups, and nations. Special attention is being given to our joint responsibility in the realm of public affairs and to the development of an international perspective."

Still another type of interinstitutional cooperation is that of the University Center in Virginia, which was founded in 1946. It is the least homogeneous of any of the groups I am discussing. It originally had nine members; now it has 24, all of them located in Virginia. They include universities, such as the University of Virginia; coeducational colleges, men's colleges and women's colleges, such as Lynchburg, Washington and Lee, and Hollins; predominantly Negro colleges, such as Saint Paul's; a military college, Virginia Military Institute; and professional schools, such as the Medical College of Virginia.

Its founders were brief and suitably vague in stating its purposes: "to strengthen and enlarge the respective programs of the cooperating institutions."

One of the earliest of the center's activities and one of the most important, was a strengthening in research activity among the member institutions. Through the center procedures were established for procuring research funds. When the center was established, faculty research was almost entirely lacking at all but two of the institutions; now some research is being done on every one of the campuses.

[3] Millikin and Illinois Wesleyan Universities; Alma, Augustana, Carroll, Gustavus Adolphus, Luther, MacMurray, Manchester, and Simpson Colleges.

Another significant program of the center is one for visiting scholars. At first subsidized from outside sources, this program is now paid for by member colleges themselves, depending on the use made of the scholars, each of whom spends some time in Virginia, lecturing and conducting seminars at several of the member schools. Cooperative use is also made of teachers from the member schools themselves. A list of available people is published, together with topics on which they agree to lecture, and they go where they are invited. Being relatively local, these scholars may not have the glamour of some of the outsiders, but, like them, they enrich the offerings of the colleges which use them. Arrangements have also been made for cooperative professorships, as two or three institutions in the group share the services of a single professor.

The center is involved in so many activities that they all cannot be listed here; among the more interesting are library affairs, a program of Asian studies, a program of adult education, and cooperative programs in music and art.

The institutional groupings discussed so far have been more or less formal, but there are many other colleges which are sharing students and cooperating in other ways with less explicit organizational structure. For example, four institutions in St. Paul, Minnesota—one Methodist, Hamline, one independent, Macalester; and two Catholic, St. Thomas and St. Catherine—have been cooperating in a modest way since 1953. In that year, the Hill Foundation began to support area studies courses—the Far East, Russia, Africa, Latin America, and the Middle East. These courses—one area each year—are staffed by teachers from all four colleges and rotate among the four campuses. In 1957, St. Catherine (for women) and St. Thomas (for men) began exchanging students, and last year provision was made for student exchanges among all four in other courses.

The Connecticut Valley group—Mt. Holyoke, Smith, Amherst, and the University of Massachusetts—has been cooperating for several years. Distances, while not great—a dozen miles at most—are a problem, especially in the New England winters, but the colleges supply transportation by bus which runs among the colleges on a regular schedule. Once-a-week seminars obviously lend themselves better to this kind of cooperation than do three-hour-a-week classes.

The most dramatic aspect of the cooperative experience of these four institutions is their plan for establishing New College. One person from each of the four faculties served on a special committee to draw up the plan, which received wide publicity a few years ago. It has been suggested that small colleges should make the advantages of smallness available to more people by taking in more students. The Connecticut Valley plan seems sounder, namely, to establish a new small college, using some of the facilities of the older colleges, with special arrangements to promote less waste of resources. This idea is an interesting and potentially valuable consequence of small-college cooperation; but it may be significant that a state university was involved, too.

The last group which I will mention is the one I know best—the Philadelphia group, consisting of Bryn Mawr, Haverford, Swarthmore, and the University of Pennsylvania. Exchange of students among all four is permitted without extra cost to the student. Each year, a few undergraduates from each of the small colleges, and more than a few from the Bryn Mawr graduate school, take part of their work at the University of Pennsylvania, but Pennsylvania undergraduates seldom study on the other campuses; I suspect that very few of them know that they can.

Bryn Mawr, Haverford and Swarthmore have a good deal in common. The grouping is a natural one, but it is extraordinary how long it took for them to begin really to work together. Now, the three presidents meet monthly to consider joint problems. Each college keeps the others informed of impending faculty appointments, and efforts are made to avoid duplication of subspecialties. Library facilities are shared extensively. Certain programs have been carried out in common, including non-Western seminars for faculty members—a fertile field, apparently, for intercollege cooperation.

Student exchange is much more extensive between Bryn Mawr and Haverford (more than 100 students each way, each seminar) than between either of them and Swarthmore (about half a dozen or less). A simple matter of geography—a mile and a half from Bryn Mawr to Haverford, against 10 or more miles to Swarthmore—is one reason. Another is that Swarthmore has students of both sexes, and the others, one each. Thus, Swarthmore does not need the others as they need each other.

Bryn Mawr and Haverford have a joint drama club and a joint orchestra. The glee clubs often sing together; yet unlike the orchestra and the drama club, they have separate directors. The two colleges recently bought jointly a computer; the computer center is on the Haverford campus but is open to students and faculty of both colleges alike, and it is heavily used.

The most important aspects of cooperation are in the curriculum and in the day-to-day exchange of students. Some subjects are offered on one campus only—for example, astronomy at Haverford and geology at Bryn Mawr. A Haverford student who majors in geology takes all of the work in his major field on the Bryn Mawr campus, but receives the degree from Haverford. An introductory course in history of art is offered on each campus; beyond that course all of the work in that subject is given at Bryn Mawr. Similarly, the Russian language, both elementary and intermediate, is offered on both campuses; Russian literature and some other aspects of Russian studies are given at Bryn Mawr, while Haverford offers Russian history and work in Soviet economics and politics.

Several departments are moving closer together. The economics departments recently have "federated," a step which may well serve as a model for others. Federation means that, while each college's economics department has its own chairman, the courses are completely integrated; this year one faculty member is on joint appointment. Introductory economics is offered on each campus; beyond that, no course is duplicated, so that a student majoring in economics takes about half of the work at each college.

Cooperation is not necessarily easy. Calendar differences can be disastrous. The University of Pennsylvania's academic year is very different from that of the others, and in some years even Haverford and Bryn Mawr are out of step. It took many hours of committee work, plus faculty meetings, to get agreement on identical calendars for next year; but, since neither faculty is altogether satisfied, and students less so, the committee still has work to do.

I do not pretend to have described all of the significant cooperative arrangements now in effect, or even all aspects of any one cooperative group. The examples given show how a number of small colleges, in a variety of ways, use cooperation to enrich the intellectual lives of their students and faculties. Some of the things being done cost money; a good many others save it. Most of these groups are looking for still more ways to profit by helping each other. All of the signs indicate that the real use of such cooperation is only just beginning.

11

The Special Mission of the Church-Related College

EARL J. McGRATH

Director, Institute of Higher Education, Teachers College, Columbia University. His article originally appeared in *School and Society* on April 6, 1963.

The church-related liberal arts colleges occupy a much less prominent place on the stage of higher education than they once did. To a considerable extent, these shifts in attendance have resulted from economic and social factors in American society. In spite of its relatively declining position, social forces at work suggest that the liberal arts college is now in less danger of extinction than ever before. The sheer demand for education beyond the high school will guarantee an ever-increasing reservoir of students for all types of institutions. Any discussion of the survival of church-related colleges is, therefore, academic. But whether they can or should be preserved as institutions with a distinctive mission is a much-debated question.

Some members of the profession and laymen question whether its special mission does not prevent it from performing the essential functions of an institution of higher education. They believe that to the extent that a church-related college has a special religious mission, it ceases to be an institution of higher education. They affirm that, when such an institution affiliates itself with, and accepts the support of, a church body, it perforce surrenders the basic right and *sine qua non* of an institution of learning—that is, the unrestrained pursuit of truth. They also contend that a church relationship inevitably results in undesirable limitations on the selection of faculty members and students and, consequently, imposes a stifling parochialism on the intellectual and social life of the institution.

In regard to the relinquishment of the rights of academic independence, some central church authorities improperly have demanded a control of educational policies and practices in exchange for financial and other support. They have imposed policies and regulations on administrative officers and faculty members which stultify vigorous, imaginative minds and, in the long run, change the dominant purpose of the institution from the cultivation of the habit of free inquiry and the evaluation of new ideas to the indoctrination of youth in a closed system of thought. Perhaps a free society ought to tolerate even the latter type of institution, but intellectuals hardly will characterize it as an institution of higher learning.

A supporting church has the right to ask that the academic practices and the atmosphere of the institutions it supports advance its own interests. But such a body will do well to leave to administrative officers and the faculty the responsibility for determining how the purpose of the church shall be reflected in the educational program and in the student life. Pres. Edgar Carlson of Gustavus Adolphus College tersely has stated this idea in the following words:

> It must be recognized that education in general and colleges in particular have an independent basis of existence which is rooted in the mind's quest for truth and in the nature of the learning process. It cannot allow itself to be regarded as solely the instrument of some other "order," be it the family, the Church, or the State. It transmits the cultural heritage from one generation to another but in doing so it applies the critical apparatus of sound scholarship to that heritage. It interprets the present and explores the unknown with all the resources available to it and with a mind that is not predetermined by any obligation except faithfulness to truth. This is its particular and distinctive service.

A church-related college can remain a genuine institution of higher learning by not only tolerating, but by encouraging the unrestrained pursuit of truth, a critical presentation of conflicting philosophies, and a steady growth in independence of judgment in religious as well as earthly matters. An unexamined faith provides a weak foundation on which to build a stable, a meaningful, and a secure life.

Church organizations supporting denominational colleges should recognize the responsibility of academic bodies to establish policies and practices consistent with the principles of freedom of teaching and freedom of learning. Under these conditions, the church-related college can join secular institutions in the great enterprise of expanding the corpus of reliable knowledge and accustoming students to the habit and the satisfaction of intellectual inquiry.

The validity of the argument that a church relationship inevitably results in parochialism must be tested also in terms of individual institutional practices. If faculty members are drawn exclusively from a single denomination and discouraged from expounding the ever-emergent theories and facts of their respective disciplines regardless of the effect on established doctrine, the intellectual atmosphere of the institution will be provincial. If, however, a college chooses teachers for their demonstrated competence in their fields and assures them complete freedom in their teaching and research, and if a college admits students of different social and denominational background, such an institution can provide as cosmopolitan and stimulating a community of learning as its secular and government-supported counterparts.

Moveover, even within a single social group like a church denomination, provincialism today is not common. In this day of easy communication and travel, a casual observation refutes the assumption that Baptists, Lutherans, or the members of any other denomination constitute a group narrowly homogeneous in their intellectual, social, economic, political, or even their religious characteristics. The crucial elements in this situation are the selection of faculty members and students of genuine intellectual interests. In considering the stultifying influence of dogmatic teaching, one may fairly ask whether many teachers committed to a philosophy of positivism or scientism do not as effectively narrow the student's intellectual interests and close his mind to alternative views of the world and of man as teachers with particular religious convictions. Under proper circumstances, the church-related college can carry out its special mission and still maintain the essential conditions of a high-quality educational program.

Indeed, the most compelling argument for the preservation of the church-related college is its special purpose. It is, or should be, committed to a meaningful interpretation of human existence and to the exposition of a doctrinal system upon which students can build an ordered and stable life. One of the most striking and disturbing features of our culture is the lack of steadiness in our personal and social values. Many of our people lack any commitment to a system of reasoned values which gives direction to their personal lives and firmness to their decisions on social policy. The guiding principle in their lives seems to be expediency based on material self-interest and social advancement. If, as some studies show, youths today exhibit these qualities, the fault lies not so much with them as with their elders.

Many college students express a deep concern for the welfare of their fellow-men without regard to race, creed, color, or social status, and they earnestly seek a more satisfying set of life goals based on less materialistic values. Their higher education too often fails to assist these young people in formulating a consistent philosophy with which they can integrate their intellectual and emotional life. Indeed, teaching in all subjects has become so preoccupied with a detached analysis of reality and with the transmission of fragmented and so-called objective truth that it fails to consider whole areas of human experience of undeniable significance in any well integrated life. Charles E. Raven, a biologist and theologian and former vice-chancellor of Cambridge University, in analyzing the relation between religion and science, has this to say in criticism of our present limited conception of the purposes and the instruction in institutions of higher education:

> ... in any adventure after the interpretation of reality, we have got to use the whole of our available material and evidence; we have got to bring in the artists; we have

got to bring in the mystics; we have got to bring in the people with a wide human sympathy, a wide human knowledge; we have got to get away from the idea that intellect and intellect alone can express and interpret or can give us an adequate picture of the universe in which we live.[1]

Committed as they are to the objective and impersonal interpretation of all aspects of the world and of man, teachers characteristically neglect completely to discuss the matters which most acutely concern young people. As one teaching fellow at Harvard with strong religious convictions put it,

Not only religion is stifled. More fundamentally, it is possible—it is even common—for a student to go to class after class of sociology, economics, psychology, literature, philosophy, and the rest, and hardly become aware that he is dealing with issues of life and death, of love and solitude, of inner growth and pain. He may never fully grasp the fact that education is not so much information and technique as self-confrontation and change in his own conscious life. He may sit through lectures and write examinations—and the professors may *let* him do merely that—collecting verbal "answers," without really thinking through and deciding about any new aspect of his own life in any course.[2]

Yet, unless we wish to drift aimlessly with the ebb and flow of events, decisions must be made and actions taken in regard to personal and public matters of the most profound significance. The illustrious Mr. Justice Holmes put the idea with typical force when he said, "Life is action and passion. I think it is required of a man that he should share the action and passion of his time at peril of being judged not to have lived." But the great jurist would have been the first to admit, as his life so amply demonstrated, that action had to be directed by vision. He would have agreed with Socrates that, "If a man does not know to what port he is sailing, no wind is favorable."

The church-related college, free from the legal injunctions imposed on tax-supported institutions and the deliberate eclecticism of secular private institutions, can assist students in clarifying their philosophy and organizing their lives on the basis of a systematic body of religious doctrine—doctrine not authoritatively imposed and uncritically embraced, but rather voluntarily accepted in the critical light of relevant knowledge and informed opinion. The nurturing of such a faith, supported by reason, must be the dominant aim of church-related colleges. Like other institutions of higher education, they will have a wider range of goals, but without this purpose, it is doubtful that they have a special reason for existing.

Many questions must remain unanswered today when one considers how the special mission of the church-related college—the education of young

---

[1] Charles E. Raven, "Recent Changes in the Relation Between Religion and Science," *Journal of General Education,* 14: 190, October, 1962.
[2] Michael Novak, "God in the Colleges," *Harper's Magazine,* 223: 174, October, 1961.

people in the doctrinal framework of Christianity—is to be accomplished within the larger purposes of higher education. All colleges with a denominational affiliation presumably will have formal instruction in religion which not only expounds Christian doctrine and reviews the development of the church in western society, but also involves comparative analyses of other faiths. Likewise, all such institutions will provide some type of chapel or other community experiences for worship and spiritual rededication. Without completely excluding from the faculty those of other faiths, teachers generally will be sought whose personal convictions do not require a rejection of religion as an element in human life or who would find living in a church-related college community intellectually intolerable. What is needed are teachers thoroughly competent in their various disciplines and capable of dealing with the basic theories and findings of their subjects in terms of theological doctrines. Thousands of such teachers now find satisfaction in working in a church-related college; in fact, they reject offers of larger salaries and enhanced status elsewhere to do so.

The religious objectives of the college can be achieved, however, as effectively through the atmosphere of the institution, the informal relations between teachers who have religious convictions and students, and the extra curricular program of student activities, as well as through formal instruction. No church or college group pretends as yet to be able to project a plan by which the purposes of the church and of higher education can be fully realized in the church-related college. But the Commission on Higher Education of the National Council of Churches and the Council of Protestant Colleges and Universities have various commissions and committees at work on the related problems which in the early future should produce helpful reports. One, particularly, involving the joint efforts of theologians, philosophers of education, and practicing educators, is attempting to develop the philosophic basis and visualize the practical implications of a Christian philosophy of education stemming from Protestant themes, history, and experience. The work of this distinguished group of theologians and laymen should be of great help to trustees, administrative officers, and faculty members in reshaping the purposes and redesigning the programs of the church-related colleges so as to enhance both their spiritual and intellectual achievements.

If those interested in the church-related college wish to preserve its distinctive character and, indeed, its very being, they will have to be more generous in their financial support. Most church families can do this without serious financial burden. A study, in 1961, of the members of one prominent denomination showed that the estimated annual contributions of their synods varied from seven cents to $2.26 per confirmed member, the cost of a daily newspaper or a football ticket. Without substantially increased support from church members and organizations, these colleges will be struggling against insuperable odds to sustain themselves as institutions of quality.

The church-related liberal arts colleges have particular and worthy functions to perform in American society. Under proper circumstances they can be preserved as essential elements in our complex system of higher education with their own special mission. They unconsciously have imitated or deliberately competed with their secular, and usually more richly endowed, sister institutions. Even now, some are misled by the undiscriminating emphasis on an excellence defined solely in terms of intellectual achievement— achievement increasingly measured by the acquisition of knowledge. In the face of the present trends in education, it will be difficult for the church-related college to keep a clear vision of its special mission of providing a higher education within the context of the Christian faith.

Yet, among our people generally, there is an insistent yearning for an interpretation of life not inconsistent with modern learning but illuminated by a faith which even the most learned require to guide them in the important realms of living. Whatever their other aspirations and activities, the dominant purpose of the church-related colleges must be to provide a place in which this faith can be nurtured and strengthened. Without this purpose, they inevitably will lose their vitality and ultimately disappear. With it, they can occupy an enhanced position in American higher education and immensely enrich our common life.

12

Function and Evaluation in Higher Education

HAROLD H. PUNKE

Professor of Education, Auburn University. His article originally appeared in *School and Society* on Sept. 24, 1960.

Recent interest in evaluating and improving higher education is part of an evaluative surge in American culture. The surge appears in efforts to evaluate public education, industrial processes, personnel selection, and fiscal practices. Colleges and universities cannot avoid closer evaluation—if they are important in a dynamic culture.

One index of the importance of American higher education is the extent to which it has become big business: budgets, employees, student bodies, service projects, and plans for development. Another index concerns its role in the living standard with respect to vocational preparation, civic competence, and personal satisfaction. When higher education was a small enterprise, it did not seem important to insist on clear-cut statements of function or achievement.

Of the two historic university functions, instruction and research, the latter has moved extensively to industry and government. This is largely because of budgets, imagination in directing research, range of projects on which private groups want research done, and tax policies which encourage research by industry. Scrutiny of projects by unimaginative donors or legislators, who provide funds for university budgets, seems unlikely to stimulate university research. Broader co-operation among universities, industry, and government might improve the outlook—if all three have comparable status in setting up projects, participating in benefits, and preparing future research personnel.

Most individuals who pursue research careers complete substantial university study before embarking on those careers. Hence, universities hold a unique position regarding influence on the attitudes of young people, their choices among fields, and selection of persons for advanced study. Producing competent personnel is more important than the facilities produced by the competent personnel of a particular time.

Teaching responsibilities of universities apparently will increase, even though industry develops additional training programs. This is reflected in enrollment forecasts and in an increase in knowledge needed for effective civic and vocational participation. Expansion of personal interests and intellectual horizons also reflects teaching demand.

Americans think of universities as extensions beyond secondary schools. To most people this means transmitting more knowledge and perhaps developing certain physical and mental disciplines. People, as a rule, have hazy ideas about research. The development of clarity is largely a teaching job. Because of our social and political structure, people of the kind described greatly influence the resources available to universities and the ways those resources are used.

"Service station" programs of universities have been criticized. But in one sense, any institution which the people support is intended to serve them. This holds in any society. Thus, research and teaching are services. By somewhat imperceptible degrees, other services are added. Among early additions were "extension" services, to carry teaching beyond university campuses. Testing water, soils, minerals, and pathological specimens are parts of the picture, along with making surveys, furnishing consultative personnel, and undertaking community development projects in university towns.

Entertaining the public recently has become an important responsibility. Major activities often concern ball games, especially during football and basketball seasons. Large stadiums and sports arenas become essential university facilities, with comprehensive staffs—and regional agencies—to supervise operations. Minor activities include bands, glee clubs, debating teams, etc. Sometimes the demand that universities supply entertainment seems greater than the demand that they prepare teachers, technologists, or research personnel. As coaches and others know, evaluation of ball games is simple, immediate, and precise. The same does not hold for outcomes in research or in preparing technologists and teachers. As enrollments and alumni increase, there may be a larger percentage of enrollees whose net "take home" from the university is ball-team enthusiasm.

Three main reasons for entertainment and "service station" activities as important university responsibilities are noted. Universities often have more suitable space and personnel than exist elsewhere. Legal requirements may include "service station" functions, as in land-grant institutions, and university status may be enhanced through serving beyond the legal call. Moreover, dynamic promotion groups may grow up within institutions. But Americans now include the functions indicated as part of what "university" means. Through such activities, many people learn about the university—and develop willingness to support more than teaching and "service station" functions.

Research interests of universities might be fostered by extending the conception of research. The creative element in research is hypothesis formation. But creativeness is not confined to experimental, documentary, survey, and similar research. Hypotheses and creativeness are involved in the arts, philosophy, mechanical invention, government, city planning, business administration, etc. If universities increased their tempo in extending recognition to creativeness in such fields, along with concern for research in the conventional sciences, they could expand their potential as centers for growth of knowledge and cultural development.

This might gradually involve degree recognition beyond the Ph.D. in some fields and of more systematic recognition for high-level creativeness in others. As knowledge increases and higher levels of education are required before one can make a significant contribution to cultural development, the Ph.D. and similar levels of attainment increasingly signify apprenticeships rather than mature accomplishments. The United States, unlike some countries, has passed out of the era when the high-school diploma represented significant attainment. We gradually are passing out of the era when the doctor's degree represents superior attainment. A development such as indicated might help universities gain support for their less immediate teaching and "service station" functions. It also might be helpful if university instruction included a more co-ordinated effort to explain to students what the functions of a university ought to be—in an expanding democratic culture. More thought and agreement on this point, among educational leaders, would be an asset.

The attitudes, values, and economic productivity of the people determine what colleges and universities will do. Attitudes regarding birth control, mental illness, religious beliefs, and units of government have diverted research from these areas. We are more ignorant and guided by tradition in such fields than we probably would be if critical research had been directed earlier toward them. During the Middle Ages, social emphasis was on religion and cathedral building. In Classical Greece, it was on philosophy and art rather than on economic production, health, or housing.

After cultural trends gain momentum, it may be difficult to modify their force or direction. America now seems to be in a trend in which responsibility for research and some other avenues of developing knowledge is leaving the university. Greater responsibility for teaching, entertainment, and "service station" functions is flowing in. Whether this appears desirable depends on one's philosophy. Of course, any social trend can be changed—through insight and planning. But evaluation must relate to function. Universities cannot be evaluated as substantially research institutions if society increasingly forces them into a framework of entertainment and "service station" agencies.

13

Federal Aid and Higher Education

GUY E. SNAVELY

Executive director emeritus, Association of American Colleges. His article originally appeared in *School and Society* on Feb. 23, 1963.

The American four-year college of liberal arts and sciences is unique. In other countries there is generally less time between completion of secondary school studies and admission to university courses. Furthermore, their institutions are mostly state-supported and controlled.

The tendency toward the latter status in our country is frighteningly apparent. Our four-year college, independent of state domination, has been the continuing bulwark of free enterprise against a creeping socialism. The picture of the present situation is vividly portrayed in a recent article in the new journal, *The National Observer,* by Carroll V. Newson, former Associate Commissioner for Higher Education, New York State, and former president, New York University:

> It is inevitable, in the future, that public colleges and universities will become increasingly important in the field of higher education. In fact, the percent of students attending public institutions will grow year by year. By 1975, perhaps not more than four percent of the postsecondary students of the country will be attending private institutions.

The tendency toward complete state control of higher education can be and is being held in check by the strengthening of the independent college and university and a continuous reminder that our free enterprise system will fail if the college succumbs.

During my 17 years as executive director of the Association of American Colleges, whose membership is composed of the presidents of practically all the accredited colleges and universities in the U.S., I called attention in most of my annual reports to the danger of state control in the wake of increasing state support. I repeat that the governments, both state and

Federal, are adding almost unbearable burdens on the taxpayers by their continuing acceptance of responsibilities that can be handled otherwise.

In my book, "The Church and the Four Year College," I outlined how many church-related and a few other independent colleges had passed out of the picture in the earlier years because they had insufficient financial backing from the beginning. Many were started as part of a plan to boost real estate ventures in the steady movement to the West. However, in the past 50 years hardly an accredited four-year college has succumbed. Most of the colleges now supported by the Roman Catholic and the larger Protestant groups continue to grow stronger. They receive in many cases substantial annual contributions from their church constituencies; likewise, alumni and friends give sizable amounts each year.

Many foundations contribute sporadically to the support of these church-related and other independent colleges. Four decades ago, the world was electrified by the announcement that the General Education Board of the Rockefeller Foundation was giving to each accredited college in the country grants on a two-year basis for salary raises. More recently, the same pleasureable shock came to the presidents of the accredited colleges when the Ford Foundation made its first large gift to higher education and it was earmarked for the same purpose.

Conspicuous is the support given by the larger Protestant groups. Most noteworthy are the annual grants by the state conventions of the Southern Baptist Church. For example, in one state the Baptist college has been receiving $200,000 yearly for operating expenses. When it was found necessary to remove from a cramped campus, adorned with worn-out buildings, to a suburban community with several hundred acres available, the church constituency donated promptly several millions for purchase of land and the construction of appropriate buildings.

A nearby Methodist college was enabled at the same time to increase its endowment by over $4,000,000. To meet a challenge gift of $700,000 from the General Education Board, it had to raise $1,400,000. The controlling Methodist conference raised $1,000,000 in a few months, and the college planned to raise the balance of $400,000 in the local community.

Before this effort could be undertaken, the Ford Foundation grant of $450,000 for this college was announced. In 1962, the community responded fully to the appeal for $1,500,000 to meet another pledge of nearly half that amount by the churches in its supporting conferences.

In a neighboring state, a well-known Episcopal university has had similar experiences. The same can be said of several nearby Presbyterian colleges. In Pennsylvania, a small Lutheran college has been receiving for some 10 years nearly $100,000 annually from the churches in its supporting synods.

Until the founding of the University of North Carolina in 1789, all American colleges were established by some church group. The Congregational Church was conspicuous in this area. In due time, the church's interest and support seemed to lag and gradually the colleges it founded became completely independent. Through support of alumni, friends, and foundations, they have become financially strong. With income from endowment and annual gifts, the independent colleges and universities hold their own in competition with the state-supported schools. For some years past, more than $1,000,000 have been given annually to their respective colleges by the alumni of Dartmouth, Harvard, Princeton, and Yale.

There seems to be no real reason why the state must offer free tuition to any high school graduate who applies. It is logical that each state university maintain few or no fees for those within its borders competently prepared and really motivated for a higher education.

In my 1949 annual report to the Association of American Colleges, I included this paragraph:

On the other hand, if there are aspects of the predicted situation which you dislike, you may exercise your influence to try to change pertinent aspects of present circumstances that are their cause.

The proposal for Federal scholarships will be of interest to many colleges. Several objections to such a plan immediately suggest themselves. First, there is the question of how the government can meet the budgetary advances that will be necessary. In the second place, is it clear that all competent high school graduates have exhausted scholarship, loan and work facilities now available? Furthermore, is it wise for the national welfare to encourage students to go to college when they may not have an especial urge to do so and may not be able to find a satisfactory niche in life after they have gone to college?

An ambitious and needy student still can find ways and means to go to college, as many of us did a generation ago. There are available many scholarships, work opportunities, and large loan funds. Very recently, many banks have established loan funds for students up to $10,000 over the four-year college period. A bank in Washington announced a similar plan in early August, 1962.

With the increasing liberality in Federal scholarship subsidy, young people will get the notion that we must have a real "welfare state" where the government not only will guarantee a college education, but will furnish suitable and good paying positions thereafter.

Another reason for opposition to Federal aid is the inherent danger of Federal control through a central office in Washington. Common sense and a knowledge of human nature affirm the old dictum that he who pays the piper calls the tune. Regulations of schools and colleges has been concomitant with dictatorships.

In support of this last statement, one can adduce concrete examples where, in recent years, state officers have interfered blatantly and unfairly in the operation of their state universities. A few years ago, when the governor of Mississippi summarily dropped the presidents of four state colleges and universities, the accrediting association of the area forthwith cancelled their accreditation. This meant that their graduates no longer could be admitted without examination to nationally known postgraduate schools in such fields as law, medicine, theology, and teaching. Accreditation was restored only when a new governor was elected and protecting laws passed by the Mississippi legislature.

A little later, a distinguished president was eased out of the University of Illinois by the trustees, so no accrediting action seemed necessary. In Iowa and Louisiana, state officials have been known to put improper pressure on the administration and faculty.

Distinguished presidents of state universities have indicated from time to time the healthy rivalry involved in competition with the independent university. A late utterance on this point comes from Milton Eisenhower, formerly president of Pennsylvania State University:

It is the private institutions that set traditions, the standards of academic freedom in America. And because the private institutions do set and maintain these standards, we of the public institutions also enjoy the benefits of such freedom. If private institutions were ever to disappear, the politicians would take over the universities, and there would then be neither educational freedom nor any other kind.

For the welfare of the country and the continuing maintenance of free enterprise, the state-supported and the independent college and university must continue to complement and supplement each other.

14

Constructing a College on a Shoestring

M. K. WOODHOUSE

Professor of European history, Radford College. At the time his article originally appeared in *School and Society* (Jan. 4, 1958), he was a member of the faculty of Coastal Carolina Junior College.

There are very few of us who, as yet, have had actual experience in starting a college. But in the next 10 years there will be an enormous demand for experienced people to develop a dream into reality—people who know the hazards, the short cuts, the logical necessary steps. Since we started Coastal Carolina College in 1954 with three faculty members, two chairs, and a table, I know from personal experience the problems of inception and development. The first problem is money.

Money presents two major problems in education, one of which is usually obscured. Everyone can readily see that, before a college opens its doors, sufficient money must be in hand to guarantee the faculty salaries for a year. Operating expenses, other than salaries, can be held to the minimum, however. For instance, our college has been most fortunate to have the unqualified support of the public-school system. We are guests of the local high school. We have two rooms for offices, but otherwise we share all the facilities of the high school.

Our classes are held after high-school hours in the classrooms occupied all day by the high school. Thus, our operating expenses are held to the minimum, and this help from the public-school system makes it possible to start a college under the simplest conditions. The hazard here is that people may get the impression the arrangement is satisfactory enough to be permanent.

The second aspect of the financial problem is not readily seen. The accrediting agency, the regional association of secondary schools, colleges, and universities, has, as one of its standards, the rule that a college may not be self-supporting from fees. Extra money must be put into the college annually by outside sources. The money is ordinarily provided for by endowments.

If a college education is to be available for more than an infinitesimal minority, colleges must have outside financial support. This is a point that a person must recognize before he becomes a valuable trustee of a college. Once a businessman-trustee accepts that a college always will be in the red, he can be an enormous asset in keeping administrators from making the deficit unnecessarily high.

Trustee orientation is as important to a new college as student orientatation. Some new colleges make their first effort the briefing of trustees as to their role in the development of the college. As in any other activity, once the trustee knows what kind of activity is appropriate to him, he is able to function effectively on the school's behalf.

For a college to initiate operation effectively, yet on a small budget, it is best to be sponsored as a branch of an already accredited institution. Our college is an off-campus branch of the College of Charleston (S.C.), an institution which has maintained an enviable reputation for superior work, especially in the sciences. The administration at the College of Charleston, having the know-how as well as high standards, saved us from innumerable errors which might have been made in the process of becoming established. It also provides College of Charleston credits to our students with which no admissions officer of a senior college or university will argue, since he knows the standards of the parent institution. When a local community can get a substantial sum of money from leading citizens to underwrite the first few years of a college's life and then secure the support of a college nearby to provide the necessary guidance, which in the long run is more important than the accreditation, the possibilities of a college are at hand.

The current trend is towards junior or community colleges. Certainly, becoming a junior college is the first step and, unless millions of dollars are readily available, this is the obviously sensible way to start. At this point, the college meets its greatest hazard—the student.

The faculty of a new college must accept that the average high-school graduate who is going to college prefers the school with the football team and the dormitory. The scion of leading families in the community continues to go to the leading colleges. In your first few years you will not attract the student who is already predestined for another college: he goes on. That leaves two general types: the superior student who, for financial reasons, would never have gone to college, and the boy who thinks that, as long as it does not cost much, he might as well have the prestige of going to college. The latter group dominates. It must be understood that all of these people have the "paper credentials" to be admitted to accredited colleges.

The first type, the student who is intelligent and industrious, is a rather rare creature. The other type comprises the close to 50% of freshman classes which leave most colleges at the end of the first year. There just will be a bigger percentage of them in your school. He is the ill-prepared, he is indolent, and books could not interest him less. He probably has gotten through high school without the proverbial "cracking of a book" and is slow to realize that college is not an extension of high school in this respect. This realization decimates the sophomore class.

For the first few years you walk a tightrope. You become an expert in maintaining a minimal standard on one hand and in maintaining a continuing student body with the other, while keeping the community enthusiastic about your work. So far, in our case, this has worked. Each year a new college can anticipate that the entrance examinations of the students will show an increase in intellectual calibre of the students and, over a long stretch, the college will establish a reputation for good work which will attract more students who are really college material.

The student is not only a hazard in his classroom performance, but he becomes your best ambassador to bring in new students. Publicity can pour out of your office into the newspapers week after week, year after year, and yet people will not know you are in the community or know what you are doing. But when a student speaks, he is heard. From each incoming class you gather comments of how tolerantly ex-students regard you. The student who fails usually recommends the school as a hard place where one learns something.

No college can afford to postpone plans for a permanent plant with expensive equipment and buildings involving the expenditure of large sums. Perhaps the first illusion which people eager for educational advances are prone to drop into is that the wealthy businessmen of a community can be tipped over for several hundred thousand dollars simply by your dream. This is not true. The average corporation is not going to give large sums to formless enthusiasms, even when they need to save on their income tax. Also, junior colleges so far have had little success in cashing in on money being distributed by the large foundations.

Therefore, some concrete planning must be done on fund-raising. No end of small schemes for acquiring grass-roots support can be concocted to fit the individual locality. And such small contribution campaigns should not be overlooked, as anyone familiar with alumni-giving programs will testify.

One of the most expensive parts of a college development program is the building program. Conventional ideas of college campuses run to Georgian red brick or stone Gothic, and these ideas are expensive. Interesting new campuses are going up in wood construction and contemporary design. Almost any community can afford a small campus tailored to its true needs.

Curriculum tailored to real needs also will save money. The latest trend in education is away from cake decoration and back to Latin. To us who were educated in mathematics, Latin, and English, these are the very backbone of true education. Now they have the value of being revived and popular. Not only for the inherent value of being educated or the social prestige of "being in vogue" does the new college's curriculum need to adhere to the classical subjects, but it is cheaper. Fewer instructors can handle a normal student body if too many frills are not introduced.

I am not contending that a few faculty members should teach hundreds of students; our college restricts classes to 35 students each. But even in a simple situation, the frills are the deficit-builders.

A college on a shoestring is a possibility. It takes careful planning, wise use of resources, a sure tread, and a creative flair.

15

New Trends in Administering and Financing Higher Education

GERALD P. BURNS

President, Johns Hopkins Fund, Baltimore. At the time his article originally appeared in *School and Society* (Nov. 5, 1960), he was executive director, Independent College Funds of America.

The explosion of the frontiers of science occurring today is the direct result of the education that occurred yesterday. In order to continue solving the riddle of the universe and improving man's life on earth, we must expand the quantity and heighten the quality of this most basic force—education.

One way to increase educational productivity is for all of us to be aware of what has happened in the past, what is taking place at present, and what trends are developing for the future. Having made such observations, we can take appropriate action in line with those trends of greatest value and eliminate those with negative implications. Seven promising trends are presented.

1. The public interpretation of higher education has taken on new importance. Educators realize now more than ever that they and their institutions are not separate and apart from the community but, rather, are related to and provide services for this trend, this new emphasis on public relations.

Whether a college or university is publicly supported or privately supported, ultimately its support comes from the people. In the private institutions it comes chiefly from tuition and gifts. To insure a continuance of support, it is necessary to interpret adequately the services of the institution to the public. Obviously, the general public is composed of several segments with different relationships to the institution. There are the legislators, trustees, alumni, donors, prospects, and potential students. And, internally, there are the students and faculty to consider. Because of these different publics, and the variety of media and techniques used to contact them, the job of interpreting has become difficult and important, calling for skilled, professional workers. Then, too, since educational institutions are all interested in doing the best possible interpretive job, because many of the potential students and prospective donors are the same, some competition inevitably occurs.

The important point is that the American public has become genuinely interested in education. Action has been taken on the local, state, and national levels to improve and expand our educational programs. This kind of interest and action is highly desirable. We hope this trend will continue and we must answer, honestly and accurately, the questions the public is raising.

2. Greater support of higher education by the Federal government is a clearly defined trend. Most educators recognize that a certain amount of Federal financial assistance is essential especially for the maintenance of their physical plants. By the same token, many leaders in private education feel that there is great value in preserving the identity of private colleges and that such identity and even some independence might be lost by accepting heavy government subsidy.

There is little doubt that certain aspects of the difference between public and private institutions are becoming blurred. Publicly supported institutions, needing more money than their appropriations provide, have turned to their alumni, foundations, and corporations for gifts. Privately supported institutions, needing more money than tuitions, gifts, and endowments provide, have turned to the Federal agencies for certain kinds of financial assistance.

Some of this blending of support, relationships, and control is salutary; if carried to the extreme, however, adverse effects undoubtedly would accrue. It has been stated repeatedly and adequately proven that one of the great strengths of American higher education is its diversity—especially the balance and difference occurring between public and private institutions.

While one might hope for a continuation of this trend of the Federal government providing some special subsidies for higher education, a careful system of checks and balances should be established so that governmental aid does not replace that provided freely and voluntarily by corporations, foundations, and individuals.

3. Private support of higher education is increasing in a desirable fashion. While the presidents of most independent colleges would not agree that there is ever enough money to meet their pressing needs, it has been documented that despite last year's recession the number of donors giving and the amount of dollars given to educational institutions increased markedly.

Reports from many of our state associations of independent, liberal arts colleges indicated that this trend of increased support (especially to private institutions) will continue in 1960–61. Corporations, especially, have been in the forefront of this trend. From corporate giants such as U.S. Steel to the corner drugstore, business and industry is solidly behind the idea that the voluntary support of American higher education is both an opportunity and a responsibility.

The needs of higher education are great. For several years, our private colleges and universities have been subsidized, in part, by the low salaries paid to their faculty members. For an even longer time, these institutions have deferred essential plant maintenance and expansion. With corporations helping correct the former by providing a portion of the much needed operating funds and the government helping correct the latter by providing loans and grants for capital projects, the situation is beginning to brighten perceptibly. But the job is not finished. Americans must continue on a voluntary basis to support these private colleges generously.

We must preserve our position of leadership in this turbulent world. As both Herbert Hoover and Adm. Hyman Rickover have emphasized, the best way to accomplish this is to make certain our system of educating leaders and training scientists is second to none. This kind of first-class education and training can best be provided through our dual system of public and private institutions of higher education. Therefore, let us not complain about our taxes (heavy as they may be) going to public institutions. And, let us preserve our private institutions by raising the level of our gifts to them.

There are not enough desks, classrooms, or institutions to cope with the flood of college students that will engulf us next year. The American people have come to recognize that a college education is the birthright of their children. Certainly, they will not permit very many academically sound but financially impoverished colleges to close up. On the contrary, they will demand that these colleges be kept open by the local, state, or Federal government. Should this come about, then the amount of increase in our taxes would far exceed the modest voluntary contributions it takes to keep these private colleges operating.

4. Colleges and universities, both public and private, are doing their share to improve their situation by operating more economically. Although there was some complacency in the field of higher education between World Wars I and II, there is now a visible trend toward critical analysis designed to increase efficiency academically and administratively.

On the academic side, frequently aided by the philanthropic foundations, institutions have researched the needs of society generally and their communities particularly. They have studied their methods of meeting these needs and their progress in solving related problems. They have made, in many instances, constructive and creative changes in their operations. By so doing, they have begun operating with greater efficiency, effectiveness, and economy.

There is still room for improvement. In some institutions, a poor and wasteful job is being done. Admittedly, some of our colleges and universities are still glorified country clubs. Perhaps some should be closed up. But, in the main, the institutions of higher education are doing a vitally important job and doing it well.

One of the interesting facets of this trend toward internal improvement is that of experiments in co-operative endeavors. Educational institutions have one thing in common—no two are exactly alike. They have preserved and capitalized on their traditional differences. Because they are ruggedly individualistic, until recently anything resembling bona-fide co-operative effort was chiefly a pious presidential platitude. In the last few years, however, great strides have been made in various parts of the nation to co-operate in matters academic as well as administrative.

New Mexico and Oregon have led the nation in having all tax-supported colleges and universities co-ordinated by unified Boards of Higher Education. Other states have followed suit, and even New York City plans to employ a chancellor to increase the effectiveness of the four great city colleges.

5. A trend closely related to that of co-operative effort among colleges and closer to the administrative than academic side is that of collective fund-raising. About 10 years ago, under the leadership of Dr. Frank Sparks (then president of Wabash College), several small liberal arts colleges in Indiana decided to pool their efforts in promotion and development. They were eminently successful, as history has proven, moving from two donors and $15,000 to 8,647 donors and $8,791,972 in the brief span of one decade.

The basic principle of this collective fund-raising effort is similar to that of a community chest or united fund campaign. It enhances rather than impairs the fund-raising efforts of participating institutions by liberating funds from corporations which, for one reason or another, cannot or will not give to an individual institution but will give to the group.

Frequently referred to as the "state association way of giving," this collective effort has gained tremendous support throughout the nation. There are now 40 state or regional associations representing 488 private colleges in every part of the country. This is the largest group of independent colleges ever to federate for a specific purpose. By virtue of its size and representative nature, it offers business and industry the broadest possible base for giving to the greatest number of private institutions in the United States.

On Dec. 1, 1958, these 40 state associations federated nationally in the Independent College Funds of America, Inc., and opened an executive office in New York City. A constitution was adopted, a board of trustees formed, and a small national staff employed. The primary functions of this newly formed federation are to co-ordinate the solicitation of major corporations considered as joint national prospects, secure greater identification for the state association movement, and encourage greater co-operation among the 40 state associations.

6. The co-operative efforts on the academic side and this collective fund-raising on the administrative side have eased some of the most pressing problems even though they may affect the entire institution. As the executive head of the college or university, the president is ultimately responsible for the solution of all the operating (if not policy) problems facing the institution. Before we examine the trend of assistance, let us look at the problems.

Most of the problems are financial in origin or implication. They reside largely in inadequate endowments, underpaid faculty, plant deterioration, and insufficient scholarships. Of nearly equal importance are the serious questions raised by the burgeoning curriculum, extracurricular over-emphasis, enrollment fluctuations, and competition for new faculty members. Other related problems exist such as faculty-administration disharmony, alumni disinterest, and trustee disorientation.

Educational administrators, foundation officers, corporation executives, and even the general public have evinced a keen interest in these problems and their solution. All recognize that the college or university is the capstone of our educational system; that the institution and its president must operate in the best interests of the community, locally and nationally; that it and he must operate efficiently, effectively, and economically.

During the last few years, a great step forward has been made toward providing some training and orientation for presidents and trustees. In addition, many excellent studies and publications have appeared and graduate courses, special seminars, and national conferences have been held in various parts of the country to enhance and improve presidential and trustee performance. In fact, even presidents' wives and academic deans are now afforded "on-the-job training."

Part of the dilemma of the presidency will be solved when trustees find better ways of selecting presidents. Currently, they are influenced by faculty advisory committees toward electing distinguished scholars, by religious congregations toward electing men of the cloth, by chambers of commerce toward electing retired generals and admirals, and by business and industry toward electing corporation executives. Actually what the job calls for is the rare bird that has something of each of these fields in his make-up. He should have a good, broad undergraduate education, some graduate work in a subject field, some postgraduate courses in educational admini-strations and some experience in research, teaching, and communicating. If he has served as dean or vice-president of a college or university, this is a plus value. If, on top of that, he has had some war service, church, business, and financial experience, he is a valuable man. If, in the end, he has a pleasant personality, makes a good appearance, and wants the job—grab him!—he is the find of the century.

7. A final trend to be observed is that of providing orientation and training for college trustees. It is wishful thinking to expect that all college board members come to the job knowing what is expected and able to perform expertly. Much time is lost and effort wasted by institutions which select poor trustee material and do nothing about improving it. Care in the selection should be followed by appropriate "training" for the job.

It is a pleasure to note that although the selection process is still questionable in some quarters, presidents and other administrative officers are providing some splendid programs of orientation for their trustees. In addition, there now are publications available that offer valuable guidance to the trustee as well as the president. Courses, seminars, workshops, and conferences have been scheduled by foundations, associations, and collegiate institutions specifically for the training and orientation of trustees. For example, Reed College and the Oregon State Board of Higher Education helped accelerate this trend by sponsoring the first West Coast Conference on Trustee Orientation in December, 1958. And during the following summer, a special seminar for trustees and administrators was offered at Portland State College on the facet of their responsibility concerned with college promotion and development.

It is vitally important to everyone, lay and professional people alike, that a board of trustees function at maximum effectiveness. When it functions at these optimum levels, its contributions permeate the entire structure of the institution. When the board is apathetic or ineffective, it adversely affects the morale and the operating efficiency of the institution.

The trusteeship of a college or university is no mean responsibility. Service to educational institutions of any type at any level is one job that should be taken willingly and exercised at the individual's peak of efficiency. Few voluntary acts pay richer dividends in our society than that of helping the education of our youth and thus the future of our country.

The next step, after pondering the seven trends, is implementation or action that will strengthen trends judged worth while. Since education is too important to be left entirely to the professional in this field, we need and should welcome the advice and assistance of interested and informed board members, committeemen, and other lay leaders.

16

Thoughts on the Financing of Higher Education

RUSSELL I. THACKREY

Executive Director, National Association of State Universities and Land-Grant Colleges. His article originally appeared in *School and Society* on Oct. 12 1968.

Events of the past few months, and the prospects ahead, make it clear that the most pressing problem ahead for both public and private higher education, in our states and in the nation as a whole, is the financing of higher education. Who pays for education: the student and his family or society as a whole? How is higher education paid for, through institutional support making it possible for the vast majority of students to pay college charges without outside help; or through subsidizing students to pay college expenses? *When* is it paid for?

These are not "either-or" propositions. It is difficult to project a situation in which the student or his family will not pay a substantial portion of the cost of higher education, no matter how much public and voluntary support is increased. It is difficult to imagine the complete withdrawal of public and voluntary support from colleges and universities as institutions, no matter how successful the drive to have education financed either by or through students. No matter how much college charges to students could be reduced there will be many who need some form of grants or loans to make higher education possible. But the direction, the thrust, the major emphasis which financing of higher education takes in the future is at stake, is going to be decided for some time to come during the next few years, and the time of decision will be sooner, not later.

In focussing on the problem of finance as the major problem in higher education, I am not taking a materialistic view and have not succumbed to

The views and observations expressed in this paper are the writer's own, and are not necessarily shared by the association by which he is employed.

97

the philosophy of economic determinism. Quite the reverse. As John K. Galbraith said in April, 1967, at the University of California, Berkeley, "One of these days, without doubt, someone will urge that universities be put on a profit-making basis with all student accounts handled through the Diners Club. None of this is a proper subject of complaint. A university must accord liberty even to those who would destroy it or place its assets in the hands of the sheriff. But while we must accord freedom to damaging nonsense, we must never be passive about it. . . ."

Dr. Galbraith proved prophetic. Less than five months after he made these remarks, a press conference was held in Washington to unveil a proposal called an "Educational Opportunity Bank," under which the university would charge what the market will bear, the less-affluent student would borrow to meet the charge, and the Internal Revenue Service would be substituted for the Diners Club as the collection agency.

Today, there are serious and thoughtful people, some of them in high policy positions and concerned with priority allocations of national resources, who feel that higher education's financial needs should be solved by making the student pay increasingly more of the cost of education, on the theory that he is the primary beneficiary of higher education and should regard it as a sound investment in strictly economic terms. This view is held in spite of the fact, or perhaps in ignorance of the fact, that the student now, in real economic terms, pays three-fourths of the cost of higher education, in charges made and income foregone. My authority for this is a distinguished economist, Pres. Howard Bowen of the University of Iowa.

Some of this thinking is the result of chickens coming home to roost. As Charles Gelatt, a thoughtful trustee of the University of Wisconsin, said recently, "Whoever first said that a college education is worth $100,000 in lifetime earnings to an individual managed in one phrase to do more harm and good than most of us can accomplish in a lifetime." The good, Mr. Gelatt pointed out, was that many youngsters were motivated to go to college by the allurement of this pot of gold, and, as a result, are contributing to the civilizing process. The harm done was to create the impression that the primary purpose of going to college is to get a highly paid job, and—more seriously—"the idea that the individual reaps the major benefit from higher education has given society an excuse for its failure to support our institutions with any degree of adequacy."

Proposition number one in discussing and advancing the future of our society through higher education, Mr. Gelatt said, is that *"Society is the primary beneficiary of the education of its members."* This proposition long has been accepted by the vast majority of those in higher education, and we have assumed its general acceptance by society as a basis for its support of higher education through public tax support and tax-assisted voluntary giving. It would be a serious mistake to assume its continued acceptance, particularly in national legislative and administrative policy. It is being challenged increasingly by many individuals and some groups, for a wide variety of reasons. A few people in private higher education are challenging it out of sheer panic about their own financial problems. They feel, in essence, that the main hope of survival of private higher education is to make public institutions private, and the way to do this is to make them dependent on student charges for their financing. Allied with them are two groups: Federal and state officials caught in the squeeze between tax resources and needs for public financing; and those who always have been with us, who will support any argument to reduce taxes for any purpose except protection of their persons and property.

If one could assume, optimistically perhaps, that the philosophy that society should bear a substantial proportion of the cost of financing higher education will prevail, then the question of *how* the financing is provided is a major issue. To those in public institutions, the proposition that society should finance higher education through tax-support of institutions, as it does other public services and functions, seems clear and unassailable. Higher education thus is made available to all who can benefit from it, and equality of opportunity is provided. Those who benefit the most economically from higher education pay more in taxes. The virtues of this proposition are so apparent that those in public higher education repeatedly have expressed willingness to extend it—at the national level—to all higher education through the mechanism of formula operating support. While many in private higher education would welcome such an approach, some would not. Their desire to get substantial public support is equalled only by their desire to avoid either the appearance of getting it, or the responsibility of accounting for it. Hence, they favor what is described by some as indirect aid, and others are unwilling to call public aid at all public support tied to an income tax credit for tuition and related expenses, financed 100% through public funds, but transmuted miraculously into non-public support by taking it off the income-tax bill. Also sympathetic to this approach are those who want to reduce government to the least possible common denominator by letting individuals determine the expenditure of public tax funds. There is, of course, a long and valued tradition of public encouragement and subsidy of private giving for educational and charitable purposes. When it is advocated as a "way of life," it presents a somewhat different aspect. Its ultimate projection would be a society in which everybody is taxed, and everybody then is given a tax rebate to support the school of his choice, the fire department of his choice, the policemen of his choice, and the water system of his choice.

There is a considerably larger group who believe that society should finance education through *subsidizing students* so that they can afford to go to college. Again the proposition has considerable merit within limits, but serious and probably calamitous consequences if pushed to such extremes as to become the major method of financing higher education. Financing higher education primarily through the student, particularly if it is tied to paying the "required charges" of colleges and universities, whatever they may be, is, of course, an open invitation for colleges and universities to support themselves in the style to which they would like to become accustomed by simply raising fees. Indeed, they would have no alternative. And the inevitable result of this process would be strong pressures either to limit the right of colleges to set their own fees or limit the number of students to be financed.

Who selects who goes to college, and how, if college charges are so universally high that the vast majority of students must have a scholarship or be denied entrance to higher education?

And who calls the tune for our colleges and universities if all the money to pay the piper is channeled through the student—either through subsidies or borrowing? Are college curricula to be designed like television sets, automobiles, and women's skirts—with a view toward sales appeal, rapid model changes, and quick product obsolescence? Finally, if we do decide that public money calls for substantial financing of educational institutions, as such, how and by whom will Federal funds be channeled? Through the states? And if through the states, through the governor's office, or a master coordinating board? Through the legislatures directly to institutions? If not through the states, then nationally only on the basis of specifically identified national needs and programs? Many contend that this, coupled with rigid qualitative evaluation of individuals or institutions, is the only sound method of handling Federal funds. Again, it has much to commend it in some areas— as the basis of most of our present support in science and of the programs of some of our great foundations.

Yet, should this be the exclusive way of national financing of higher education? Since government is manned by fallible individuals rather than omniscient deities, cracks already are beginning to appear in the picture window. Many defenders of the "qualitative approach" say that many colleges should be allowed quietly to "die on the vine." Who decides which should die, and why? Is the determination of "national interest and purpose" in a program really and invariably the result of careful study by distinguished and representative panels of experts? Or did a busy group of men and women simply assemble for a half-day in Washington and give their blessing to a staff paper prepared by a young man with a burning desire to reform education on the basis of his unhappy experience at one out of over 2,000 colleges and universities?

Surely, past experience would indicate that, whatever the faults of our system of higher education—and there are many—they have shown considerable success in meeting the needs of American society in many diverse ways. Surely, it would indicate that, within every institution to which substantial numbers of parents are willing to entrust the education of their sons and daughters, there is a considerable awareness of things that need to be done, an interest in doing them well, and a capacity for improvement if given resources.

In this context, higher education is in something of a state of disarray and division. I do not refer to relationships among the major national organizations in higher education, but to the fact that there has been a great outburst of articles and statements in recent months about the fiscal plight of higher education—and particularly private higher education—with remarkably little consensus as to what needs to be done. Some—though by no means all—of this has taken the form of attributing most of the ills of private higher education to the existence of public higher education.

The remedies proposed vary widely. They include general state operating support, raising fees at all institutions combined with massive borrowing, general Federal operating support, tax credits. My point is that, unless the higher education community is able to arrive at some consensus on programs that will be mutually acceptable, and in the public interest, it is likely to find itself involved in increasingly destructive and divisive conflicts within the states and nationally, and to find that its legitimate needs will get low priority indeed. Some of the claimants for sharply increased public funding clearly have a priority of emphasis over higher education. There are others which should have substantially lower priority. But, unless higher education speaks with unity and emphasis, it is likely to have no priority at all.

The Federal government has provided many forms of support for purposes related to higher education: grants and loans to students, facilities support, research support, support for all sorts of special programs. Many of these programs, by requiring institutional matching or assumption of substantial administrative costs, actually detract from the capacity of the institution to carry on the major function of instructing students. Aside from limited instructional funds going to the land-grant institutions on a formula basis, and substantial support of the operating costs of graduate schools of public health, the Federal government has done virtually nothing to solve the most critical financial problem of our institutions of higher education, public and private.

My belief is that there is a clear case for the next new Federal program of higher education being one of operating support, on a formula basis, to all accredited institutions of higher education. At least it would help to solve the critical financial problems of both public and private institutions, and help curb the spiraling of student charges. The case for such support for private higher education is, in my opinion, much clearer at the national level—and distinctly preferable from the standpoint of the institutions involved—to proposals for state support of private higher education. One among many reasons is that, while all students have a claim to the "national interest" in their advanced education, state support inevitably must be linked to the specific and demonstrable advancement of the educational interests of residents of the state and subject to state restrictions on the use of public funds.

A national "operating support" program must be devised carefully to avoid diminishing other and non-Federal sources of support through voluntary gifts and tax funds. It would not, and should not, become the major source of operating support for higher education, but rather a supplementary and "gap-closing" means. Nor can it be expected, other than in very broad and general terms or categories, to give differential financing on the basis of "quality" programs—distinctions which everyone agrees may be desirable, but which almost every institution defines differently and in its terms. These can be left to non-Federal support, and to other types of Federal programs, and it is in the interest of diversity and variety in American higher education that this be so.

17

National Research Goals and University Policies

SAMUEL B. GOULD

The author was chancellor of the State University of New York at the time his article originally appeared in *School and Society* (Oct. 14, 1967). He resigned as president of the university effective Oct. 1, 1970.

As the Federal government's role in research, education, and training continues to enlarge, it increasingly becomes incumbent upon all in the government, as well as in colleges and universities, to establish certain fundamental directions, to define both long- and short-term national goals, and to communicate these determinations to one another. Goals should be determined for the level of investment in the development of natural resources and for the level of investment in the development and application of new knowledge. Also to be determined are forecasts of manpower and facilities required to attain these goals, and the level of investment in education and training for developing this manpower.

Only against this background can colleges, universities, foundations, and the Federal government itself plan and carry out the types of programs and missions increasingly needed to make our limited resources match our high aspirations. The total need must be identified, defined, and assessed. Once there is a greater degree of common agreement on national goals and methods of achieving them, many of the frictions that now mar the relations between the Federal government and the universities will be eased greatly. To a large extent, much of the current distrust, suspicion, and lack of understanding can be replaced by an atmosphere founded upon mutual agreement on objectives and on our respective roles in achieving these objectives.

But there is an even more elementary problem to be solved: We must focus upon finding better ways to make use of the vast amount of existing information on Federal programs, policies, and goals. There is a fundamental and immediate need for a better system of gathering and disseminating this information to the academic community, as well as to the Federal government itself.

Significantly, only in the fall of 1966 did our government publish a comprehensive report on *Federal Support for Academic Science and Other Related Activities in Colleges and Universities*. In the absence of such material, we at State University of New York did one of our own in April, 1966, comparing support to our own institution with that being given to others. Obviously, because of our limitation of resources, we were forced to center upon certain selected institutions, and our report was not so comprehensive as it should have been.

This shocking lack of information was revealed dramatically in a recent Library of Congress study, reported in the *Washington Post:**

"A Library of Congress study pictures a Federal science research establishment so vast and so ill-coordinated that it does not know how many research laboratories it has, where all of them are situated, precisely what kinds of people work in all of them, or exactly what work all of them are doing.

"Federal research is so fragmented, the report said, that research on environmental air pollution is handled by 192 different laboratories.

"The report was prepared by the Science Policy Research Division of the Library's Legislative Reference Service at the request of the House Research and Technical Programs Subcommittee.

"Subcommittee Chairman Henry S. Reuss (D.-Wis.), in releasing the report, said the Federal government spends about $16 billion a year on research and development. About $4 billion of the total is for work in Federal laboratories, he said. The rest is handled through contracts and grants to non-Federal groups.

"Reuss said there is no regular single, coordinated annual report on projects undertaken by the Federal laboratories, on how the different projects tie in with overall Federal goals, or what facilities and staff are available."

What better evidence is there to support the need for improved reporting on Federal programs related to our nation's educational and research needs? What better argument is there for an efficient central clearinghouse of information on Federal programs and policies? What better tool is there for colleges and universities to use both for long-range planning and day-to-day operations?

The State University of New York has begun experimenting with its own computer-based data bank of information on Federal programs. Clearly, the Federal government should be doing this, but we cannot wait.

Because of the urgency of this unfulfilled need, the setting of priorities for investment of our money and knowledge in basic and applied research and in the full development of our natural and human resources represents

* *Washington Post*, Nov. 15, 1966.

our most difficult planning task. Here again we require the closest cooperation between the Federal government and the academic community with its
huge reservoir of knowledge and talent.

As one looks at the complex problems facing our society in the latter
part of this century, it becomes clear that one very high priority must be
placed upon seeking solutions for the difficulties man has in relation to his
environment—the city, the suburbs, and the rural areas in the advanced
technological societies, and those problems of the less-developed societies in
Africa, Asia, and Latin America. Here we seek solutions to the problems of
education, health, poverty, housing, transportation, air and water pollution,
population control, and food and agriculture. If we are to deal adequately
with this priority, then we clearly must make a shift in the resources we
presently are allocating for research on defense, atomic energy, and space,
unless it can be shown that we can encompass *all* of these research needs
equally well and at the same time.

One illustration will suffice to cite just one of our unmet needs. The
vast amount of new knowledge being generated, and so swiftly, is a characteristic of our world. How is it to be gathered and organized and categorized?
And once so gathered and organized, how is it to be assimilated? Do we
know enough today about how people learn so that we can set forth ways
by which they can encompass this new knowledge and keep themselves
relevant to their times? To these must be added the new demands being
made upon higher education, demands caused by our expanding population
and by the increasing desire of more and more people for higher education.
The dimensions of the problems begin to emerge clearly. We see facing us
unprecedented demands upon faculties and facilities, demands that cannot
possibly be met by our traditional approaches to learning, whether organizational, psychological, or physical.

Nothing less than a revolution in teacher education is necessary if we
are to meet this issue squarely. The products of our teacher training departments or schools must emerge thoroughly aware of the new conditions they
face. Even more important, they must be capable of using new approaches and
techniques based upon a better understanding of how the human mind
learns. New devices for learning are coming steadily to the fore, but, in
spite of the testing some of them have undergone, they still are regarded with
suspicion. Such suspicion persists, at least partially, whether in regard to
devices or patterns, because not enough is known about the learning process.
And, unfortunately, not only has there been insufficient research up to now,
but a good deal of what has been done is open to question. The fact of the
matter is that not many of our teacher education institutions are research-
oriented, and even fewer conduct their research with the same rigor that is
characteristic of research in the sciences.

All this becomes an even more disconcerting set of circumstances when
we keep in mind today's outcry over the lack of attention being paid to

teaching as opposed to research in our universities. Part of student restiveness in our larger institutions is traced to the research emphasis, and the prestige of research seems to have more than its appropriate share of consideration when faculty promotions and granting of tenure are being weighed. More and more we hear the call for better teaching, for more attention to teaching methods, for more care in the selection of prospective teachers. What ought to be accompanying this call is a similar demand for more understanding of how teaching becomes most effective, a goal that cannot be reached without the most thorough knowledge of the learning process itself. Scattered bits of information filter down to us, based upon the experiences of more imaginative teachers or upon occasional research projects, but they give us only the outlines of the full picture we need. Teaching is both an art and a science; to practice it requires more than an instinct for communication, a sense of goodwill or even of evangelism toward youth, and a knowledge of subject matter. It requires the acquisition of a set of teaching principles, scientifically discovered and proven, all with the same depth of exploration characteristic of other disciplines. We are faced with a lack of innovative approaches to the teaching problems of today, with a paucity of teaching models to examine, and with a reluctance of teacher education institutions to break with traditional content or methods.

There has been a far too limited movement of the Federal government toward correcting this situation. Funds for educational research *have* been increased; educational research and development centers *are* being established, together with regional educational research laboratories. But the total resources devoted to these efforts are far below what is offered to other disciplines, even though the problem they must attack is fundamental to our future.

Three elements combine to militate against the growth of educational research and its support in a greatly increased fashion. The first is the lack of prestige such research thus far has been able to attain in the eyes of the academic world. Part of this, of course, grows out of academic snobbery from which schools and departments of education always have suffered, and reflects the general lack of interest colleges and universities always have had in the learning process as a whole and more specifically in the techniques of teaching. Part of it, however, stems from the very uneven quality of the research performed in teacher education institutions. The third element has been the development of a species of educationist jargon that has been overused to the point where strong reactions of antipathy have set in.

Obviously, the educational problem of our country is so vast and so vital that a tremendous effort must be made to change the status of educational research. It must be lifted out of its present reputation for mediocrity, it must be supported in a manner that matches its importance, and it must be pointed toward the most carefully constructed projects designed to grapple with our most fundamental necessities and to interpret the solutions cogently and clearly to the widest possible audience. Furthermore, there must be some sort of grand pattern or strategy in all of this to insure the comprehensiveness of the approach and the broadest scope for communicating results.

One foundation, with which I am familiar, is making a valiant effort in this direction, even with limited resources. In December, 1965, the Kettering Foundation created a separate organization, with its own staff as a nucleus, called the Institute for Development of Educational Activities (IDEA). The title is not fully descriptive of the purpose, since the Institute actually is broader in scope than the term "educational activities" might suggest. It is, in fact, making a most comprehensive attack on the total problem I have described, with major emphasis upon elementary and secondary education thus far, but with some effort in higher education as well, and with more of the latter to come. It is based upon the premise that, while education must be academically sound and quality-centered, it also must be innovative.

IDEA is organized in four major divisions. It has a basic research center linked to university research; a learning system center linked to laboratory and experimental schools; an innovation and implementation service linked to demonstration schools; an information service that makes certain that findings in research and innovation will reach educators and school systems all over the country. Judging by the kind of response IDEA has had to its first year of effort, it already is beginning to fulfill its objectives.

But now let us return to the broader role of Federal involvement in higher education. National goals must be defined to determine those necessary to the academic community and to the Federal government for intelligent planning and operational purposes. The question to be faced is how to go about it. It once seemed possible that the newly formed Interstate Compact for Education might be the vehicle, but the very nature and structure of that organization makes this impossible. The Compact was created to counteract the influence of the Federal government, rather than to channel it; furthermore, there is a preponderance of political and lay membership, together with heavy emphasis on other than higher education or research.

What seems to be necessary for our particular task is the creation of a forum or council or commission on higher education and national research goals. This could serve as a common meeting ground for leaders, those primarily responsible for making and carrying out the long-range plans of colleges, universities, and the various Federal agencies. It would address itself to the immediate problem of better communication among all concerned with national research goals and higher education. It would define problems and areas where studies should be undertaken. It would issue periodic reports on national goals and manpower needs in terms that are practical for academic and Federal administrators.

Such a forum or council should be financed jointly by the Federal government and the university community it would be designed to serve. As for membership, its academic members well might be nominated by the American Council on Education, the National Association of State Universities and Land-Grant Colleges, the Association of American Universities, the Association of American Colleges, the Association of State Colleges and Universities, and the American Association of Junior Colleges. On the Federal side, the membership should represent all the agencies with research, development, education, and training programs. Most of the work of such an organization, once agreed upon by the membership, could be done by contract with universities and other agencies.

We, as educators, are not expressing at present our views to the Federal government, even though it is our instrument. Our communication with its representatives is sporadic and incomplete, and our knowledge of what they are doing or why they do it is meager. The government should not be determining national education and research goals unilaterally. We are not merely handmaidens in the process of creating new institutions, defining goals, developing new types of basic and applied research, or in doing anything else that relates to education; we are full-fledged partners. Otherwise, something very basic to the future of universities and, indeed, to the democratic process itself, soon will become weak and eventually disappear. Together, however, each with full understanding of its respective role, the Federal government and universities can strengthen and give deeper meaning to research in America.

18

The New Federally Supported Ciceronianism

WILLIAM MARSHALL FRENCH

Chairman, Department of Education, Muhlenberg College. His article originally appeared in *School and Society* on Oct. 14, 1967.

Just as the undersigned was working on his 1966 income tax returns, there came to his office, unsolicited, a copy of *Phoneme-Grapheme Corres- pondence as Cues to Spelling Improvement,* a study "performed pursuant to a contract (No. 1991) with the Office of Education, U.S. Department of Health, Education, and Welfare, under the provisions of Public Law 83-531, the Cooperative Research Program."

This *1716-page* report indicates that other studies of phonemes and graphemes had been limited and unsatisfactory: The Hanna-Moore research had dealt with only 3,000 words, and these, it was thought, consti- tuted "insufficient samples of the American-English language to determine the amount of phonemic-graphemic relationships in the orthography." The contract investigators decided, therefore, "to go as far beyond the 3,000 most frequently used words as time and *project finances* would permit." (Italics are the present writer's.) How unfortunate that the project funds would permit only 1716 pages!

But no matter, for the contractors only scratch the surface, apparently. In the section on "Conclusions, Implications and Recommendations," one finds the suggestion that several more studies are needed. These are: Analysis of the algorithm to determine "to what extent it might be improved in the statement of individual rules, which rules produce the greatest degree of predictability, and why certain rules appear to fail," and to what extent "phonemes of doubtful distinctiveness (possibly allophones rather than phonemes) might be combined to obviate the possible adverse effect of minor dialect differences upon the efficacy of the phonological approach"; an extensive analysis of an error list to "identify all of the morphological factors that bear upon these mis-spellings"; words spelled correctly naturally also need an analysis "to assist the pupils to arrive inductively at the generalizations underlying the phonological structure of the orthography"; a study of the "effectiveness of the algorithm upon monosyllables alone"; a study of "words in the corpus on the basis of their frequency of usage in running text"; and a study of "relationship between the errors produced by the algorithm and the actual errors produced by children in their spelling efforts"; —and others.

I do not mean to ridicule the work of the contractors, though it does sound frightfully pedantic. I agree with Herbert Spencer that all knowledge may be of *some* value to *some* people, but our primary concern should be with knowledge of greater utility to more people.

Now, the question is this: How much Federal money are we squandering to elucidate the obvious, to penetrate the impenetrable, or to make much ado about nothing? To what extent are we researching promising fields and to what extent are we jumping on the Federal research gravy train? How many of the $60,000–$100,000 research contracts will modify our educational philosophy and procedures? Who reads the stuff? Where has it significantly altered school practice? Is it worth $163,105 to find out "Effects of Automated and Nonautomated Responsive Environments on the Intellectual and Social Competence of Educable Mentally Retarded Children" or $71,623 to research the "Cognitive Originality, Physiognomic Sensitivity and Defensiveness in Children"? When do we put on the brakes? Are we subsidizing the modern equivalent of gerund-grinding Ciceronianism?

Lest the writer be written off as a William McKinley-era reactionary, may I say that I have been sympathetic to the program of Federal aid to schools and to the Great Society; but if this is what it results in, I will have to research myself. This is my money they are squandering.

19

Open Door vs. Selective Admission

W. CLARKE WESCOE

Chancellor, University of Kansas. His article originally appeared in *School and Society* on March 23, 1963.

The college enrollment panic is familiar to all of us. A flame lit in the east, it has been swept westward by gusty winds of national publicity until today every parent is obsessed with the problem of getting his child admitted to college. Anywhere the parent looks he sees such articles as "The Race for College" or "Can Your Child Get Into College?"

Like all panics, this one is self-defeating. The major concern of prospective students becomes getting into a particular college instead of getting an education. Critics have said that such concern warps high school programs from college preparation into coaching for college entrance examinations. Another effect of the panic may be even more significant: selective admission tends to be equated with the quality of education.

Time magazine, in its influential, reprinted article, "The Race for College," stated flatly: "What is a quality college? One that selects quality students." The same magazine, in a later cover article about state universities, said: "As enrollment goes up, state universities now have the chance to grow up—not just to grow. All they have to do is grab the chance. Across the country, their entrance standards are rising. Only five states (Kansas, Montana, Ohio, Oklahoma, Wyoming) still require state universities to admit all high school graduates. Admittance tests are becoming fashionable."

In an article distributed to alumni magazines across the country, Frank Bowles, president, College Entrance Examination Board, divided institutions of higher education into "preferred," which are difficult to enter because of selective admissions policies; "standard," which may be purposefully lenient in their admissions and stiffer later in "weeding out" during the first year of college; and "easy," which are, by definition, non-selective.

The hidden assumption in all these articles is that difficulty in getting

111

into college automatically insures a quality education and that ease in admission leads automatically to the opposite. Another hidden assumption is that everyone is affected by the selective admissions policies of a small number of colleges. But *Time* admitted, after the 1961 Ivy League acceptances and rejections were mailed, "In a year when 900,000 freshmen will enter U.S. colleges, the news affected only a handful." That handful, even without the duplications of multiple applications, amounted to less than three percent of the total U.S. freshmen. A third hidden assumption is that there is a truly efficient method of selection—but even those institutions which select most rigorously admit that this is not true.

The overriding fact about selective admissions is that the institutions which practice it do so because they have no choice. This includes many "glamorous" private institutions which receive applications from many more high school graduates than they can accept. It also includes some public institutions which have achieved a similar kind of glamor or which may be located in areas of rapidly rising college-age populations or which may not be able to gain the kind of public support necessary to a larger effort. It does not include many good private institutions which "glamor" has passed by nor many public institutions in areas where the spirit of substantially free public education is strong and where the college-age population has not inundated the colleges. This last description fits the University of Kansas.

Predictions that college enrollments will double in the next 10–15 years have frightened educators as well as laymen. What they have forgotten is that such growth is a commonplace not only of U.S. higher education, but of all U.S. education. And the same voices that said we could not afford universal primary education or universal secondary education now have shifted their jeremiads to the college scene.

With the single exception of the abnormal period of the Depression and World War II, with its economic and sociological problems, college enrollments in Kansas have doubled every 15 years, as surely they have elsewhere. Today Kansas ranks with half a dozen other states in the nation in a percentage of college attendance near or past 50%.

In the past decade, indeed, Kansas already has gone through what others have dreaded: college enrollments have doubled from less than 29,000 in 1952 to more than 60,000 in the fall of 1962. Today, the University of Kansas is getting better students and doing a better job of educating them than it did 10 years ago.

The accomplishments of states like Kansas, in which four-fifths of the youth complete four years of high school and one-half enroll in an institution of higher education, was described as "majestic" by President Eisenhower's Commission on National Goals. The Commission did not call for selective admissions but asked that "within the next decade at least two-thirds of the youth in every state . . . complete 12 years of schooling and at least one-third enter college."

Despite the fact that 50% of the potential college students in Kansas are attending college and despite the Kansas law that every graduate of an accredited high school be admitted, the University of Kansas is not deluged by students who have little chance of earning a degree. More than 82% of our freshmen who were graduated from Kansas high schools ranked in the top half of their classes; over 50%, in the top fifth; over 30%, in the top 10th.

One out of every 18 entering freshmen in the fall of 1962 was the top student in his class; one out of every 12 ranked either first or second. This is self-selection, very much an American tradition.

Everyone agrees that those academically talented students who rank highest in their high school classes have the best chances of succeeding in college and that those who make the highest scores on various college entrance examinations may have better chances than those who score low. Selective-admissions schools which admit only those in the top five or 10% of their classes no doubt will have a lower drop-out rate than those who admit the top half or who do not select at all.

But the selection process is not infallible. Harvard, *Time* points out, graduates only 75–80% of its entering students.

In the middle ranges of academic ability, selection becomes most fallible—among the potential "B" and "C" students who may make a contribution to society as great or greater than the academically gifted— if they have the opportunity to prepare themselves properly.

Vice-Chancellor George B. Smith has demonstrated in studies of recent graduating classes at the University of Kansas that,

If restrictions for admission had eliminated [all K.U. freshmen] who scored below the fiftieth percentile on both the A.C.E. and the Speed of Reading Examinations, and provided, of course, that these students had not gone elsewhere to school, the loss to the state and to the nation would have been over 1,100 individuals in only five graduating classes, including 202 teachers, 176 engineers, 22 journalists, 31 lawyers, 25 medical doctors, 43 pharmacists, and 482 graduates of the College of Liberal Arts and Sciences and the School of Business who majored in areas where the supply of trained manpower is in equally short supply.

Similarly, hundreds of students who scored better than average on K.U.'s placement examinations dropped out of the university because they did not have the motivation to work hard enough to succeed.

Educational measuring sticks simply are not good enough to predict whether any individual will fail or succeed in college, and sometimes even the measuring sticks contradict each other. Students who ranked in the top 10% of their high school classes have scored in the bottom 10% of our placement examinations, and students who ranked in the bottom 10% of their high school classes have scored in the top 10% of our placement examinations. Top-ranking students have flunked out, just as students ranking near the bottom in high school or in examinations have earned degrees and won honors.

We have no tests to measure determination, motivation, and desire, and in getting a college education these qualities are not merely important, they are all-important. The best predictor of success in college still is the first year in college.

In times when this nation needs not fewer educated men and women but more, a selection process should promise more accuracy than any now available. This is particularly important when the varied preparatory backgrounds of Americans are considered. Academic selection processes automatically discriminate against the child whose parents are not fond of reading, against the child from a large family, against the child from a small high school, against the farmer's child and the laborer's child, and the child born into an underprivileged minority.

Higher education—particularly publicly supported higher education—owes these children a chance to prove themselves, not only for their sake but for our own. Education is the key to the social and economic mobility which is this country's most prized possession—and the key as well to the future.

Even those institutions which select most carefully are beginning to back away from the results of their own methods. Harvard's former Dean of Admissions Wilbur J. Bender has warned that strictly academic standards, neglecting "passion, fire, warmth, goodness, feeling, color, humanity, eccentric individuality," may well produce "bloodless" Harvard students.

Henry S. Coleman, director of admissions at Columbia College, has said that his "enchantment with statistics has faded considerably." He called test scores imperfect yardsticks of students' "staying power" and desire to learn.

John E. Sawyer, president of Williams College, expresses the concern of many educators when he charges that too many high school students are learning how to answer test questions rather than how to study and think independently. Williams recently got a Ford grant for a 10-year experiment of harboring academic risks.

Amherst's Pres. Calvin Plimpton wants "a good mixture of city boys and country boys, rich boys, and poor boys, bright boys and average boys, athletes and physically handicapped boys, Americans and foreigners, boys of all races, of all faiths and even of no faith." Except for the absence of girls—to which I, for one, never could become reconciled—that is a remarkably accurate description of K.U.'s enrollment.

It is better, however, for the student to select himself for the college than for the college to select the student, and the results may be superior in many ways.

One major reason offered by those who are urging selective admissions is economy; but not only is selection not perfect, it is not cheap, and if junior colleges and technical institutes are provided for those not admitted to universities, the cost to the nation may not be less but more. I do not urge the selective institutions to abandon their traditional methods; since they cannot or will not expand, they have no choice but to select. Their problems of selection are their own. They become ours, however, when the institutions or other critics urge these methods on the rest of us.

Perhaps these advocates of selective admissions are in the position of the unhappily married man or woman; they would like to see their unmarried friends share the same problems. There also may be economic motives: as the gap between the tuition costs of private and publicly supported institutions continues to grow—in spite of increases at publicly supported institutions that averaged 64% from 1950–59 and have gone up more since then—the private institutions feel under considerable pressure not to raise tuition precipitously.

Spokesmen for some private institutions have urged publicly supported institutions to solve their financial problems by raising fees. By whatever means needy students are aided, however, high fees represent another kind of selection.

The more insidious influence operating to further more selection is prestige. A number of liberal arts colleges and universities frankly admit that they require certain test scores for admission because of prestige factors, because they—or others—believe that "a quality college is one that selects quality students." But the proof of the pudding still is in the eating.

The University of Kansas, operating with only the self-selection provided by its reputation, stands with the best in the nation in the achievements of its students. Three examples: in three of the past five years, K.U. students have received one of the 32 Rhodes Scholarships awarded in the U.S.; the 37 Woodrow Wilson Fellowships received by K.U. students in the past two years place the university among the top 10 recipient institutions in the nation; and the five Danforth Fellowships received by K.U. students in the past two years, only one less than the total possible number, is unequaled by any U.S. college or university.

The quality of the instruction at K.U. and the quality of its student body are not dependent upon selective admissions. Far from being handicapped by the lack of such an admissions policy, K.U. finds it completely in accordance with its philosophy of American public higher education.

20

Pretense and Honesty in College Admissions

EDWARD D. EDDY

President, Chatham College. His article originally appeared in *School and Society* on Nov. 11, 1967, and was based on an address to the Association of College Admissions Counselors, Potomac and Chesapeake Chapter, at the University of Delaware, May 11, 1967.

I propose to throw the usual presidential cautions to the wind—and try to be completely honest even if it may not be possible for a college president, after years of pious preachment, to speak the whole truth. I am tired of, unhappy with, and confused by what the present system of admission to college is doing to colleges and universities, high schools, parents, and, most of all, to the students themselves.

It is time we stopped the nonsense, cut out the ridiculous claims, and began to act as if we were human beings who care more about people than we do about institutions, statistics, or percentages. There is too much pretense and far too little honesty in college admissions and college education.

Now it would not be fair for me to make all these sweeping condemnations without including my own institution and myself. Furthermore, others would have every right to sneer and ask, "What have you done to help turn chaos into sufferable confusion?" My first honest answer would be to say that Chatham College is only one small institution—so do not expect too much. Like most colleges and universities, it is a fragile institution, capable of suffering irreparable damage in the academic market place if it gets too far out of line. But I can point with some pride to one or two small steps.

First, we resolved, at least several years ago, not to grab every phone call, every postcard, every tentative inquiry as a statistic to be used in counting how many young ladies apply as compared with the number we accept. Furthermore, we resolved to discourage the clearly unadmissable student from completing an application and plunking down the fee. This tactic has not worked with everybody—there still are those who want to take a long, admittedly futile chance. But we have tried to prevent a few disappointments and certainly a lot of work for guidance counselors and for us by being honest about admissions chances when it is clear that we can be honest.

These two moves in themselves have kept Chatham College off some of those lists which describe the "terribly selective" and "frightfully selective." Such false measures of the value of a college are based in part on how many were admitted or enrolled compared to how many applications an institution was willing to accept or to promote. Unfortunately, honesty is not always the best policy for either an admissions officer or a guidance counselor whose effectiveness is measured by comparative statistics.

We have done something else. Last year, our director of admissions made a special plea for a "viewbook" to supplement the catalogue which, like most college catalogues, principally serves as an intellectual seduction machine for the prospective student. We resolved to attempt a publication which would be as honest as we dared to be and as enthusiastic as we actually are. The result is called "Letter to a Student." It is written "from the President of Chatham College."

"Letter to a Student" breaks a few well-established rules governing what is acceptable to say about a college and about higher education. It says to a prospective student: not all students ought to go to college, and not all women students ought to go to a women's college; perhaps the biggest mistake of high school students is to over-idealize college experience and the particular college or university in which they enroll; there is no magic whatever in the size of a class, but rather in the teacher and the student.

"Letter to a Student" is not the breakthrough which we need so badly in college publications, but, hopefully, it is the beginning step in honesty for at least one college. I mention all this to establish that possibly I am not just a complainer—but I still want the chance to register some of those complaints. Let us take a few of higher education's pretensions or assumptions and see what they are and what validity they have.

Number one is the pretension that colleges and universities actually are capable of educating a student. If we are honest, we would confess that few, if any, of us could ever be that sure of the process of education in order to make such a wild claim.

Education, as we know it in American colleges, is an irrational mixture of hopes, misty dreams, personal and social needs, and giving time to a generation to grow up. It is training the mind of youth to think reasonably; providing background and skills with which to earn a living; opening windows so that sensitivity may have fresh air and flourish. It is Grecian in method, Gothic in architecture, and ghastly in the insistent perpetuation of established ways. It is the near-automatic conferral of social status and community respectability.

For the woman, it is a husband with a better chance of "success." For the parent, it is gratification—whether the parent had no college education and always dreamed of one, or had one but at the wrong place, or had one at the right place and never recovered. For the principal, counselor, and school board, it is a sigh of relief and a welcome statistic to quote to an angry parent. For a confused youngster, it is a place to spend four basically pleasant years before one has to stop rebelling and start proving.

We know where the process of higher education probably occurs; we have a few clues on how it occurs; but we patently are dishonest if we claim that it *does* occur. To my knowledge, no one has found an effective way to undertake a longitudinal study comparing those who go to college in terms of personal development with those who do not go. Until that study is undertaken, I shall continue to wonder how much happens to a youngster merely because he or she is passing through some interesting developmental years between 17 and 22, regardless of what else is taking place.

In all honesty, some of our most prestigious colleges and universities apparently are successful because they "capture" the right students at the right time. I call this "the dry ice theory of education"—keep the good student well-preserved for four years, thaw him out in time for commencement, and claim all the credit. It does not happen quite that easily, but we should never make the mistake of equating normal process of personal development with intellectual growth.

What, then, can be our claim for education? Colleges and universities are part of our society for the very simple reason that some people know more than other people. This does not presume a process, then, so much as a relationship—the effective relationship of those who do not know to those who do know. An institution of higher learning exists to provide an organized framework and a place where students may study under and work closely with those who know more than the students do.

Let us move on to pretension number two: That colleges and universities can and should be all things to all people and, further, that those institutions which are must be better for the student than those which are not. This is verbal nonsense. All people do not need and never would be capable of using all things. The all-to-all is not the important factor. But it is important that, within whatever institutional framework is chosen, there must be something of value for each who comes to it.

The simple undergraduate, for example, could not possibly enroll in 200 courses in a history department manned by 65 professors of history. The usual academic schedule will permit the usual student to take three or four history courses, unless the student is a history major. Then the number goes to 10 or 12, but not 200.

So I return to the conclusion—the possibility rather than the pretense— that undergraduate years should be regarded as an *experience,* not as a sum total of earned credits in a necessarily sumptuous setting. It is better to have the specialty of the house than to have a four-page menu of short-order items.

Let me say just a word about the gravediggers with spades in hand who merely are awaiting the arrival of the coffins carrying separate men's and women's colleges. These same gravediggers, a few years ago, were waiting through the night for the end of the liberal arts college. Jacques Barzun was reciting the last rites. But the grave has not been filled. It is not the small, private liberal arts college—whether for men or for women—which has died, in effect, but the large city-centered, private university, such as Pittsburgh, Akron, Temple, and Buffalo.

The college or university which stakes out a claim to certain areas of human knowledge and limits itself to those areas, despite all the other pressures upon it, will do the better job of teaching and of providing a particular kind of educational experience.

There are some students who ought to go to college in an isolated, rural area, and some who ought to go to college in a teeming city. There are students who ought to jump into highly specialized disciplines and some who ought to be free to roam for awhile before settling down. Why do we have to assume that we must pretend to be everything to everybody?

Pretension number three is an extension of number two. It is concerned with the false notion that there is *one* college or *one* university which is the absolutely perfect one for any one individual. I just cannot believe that collegiate marriages—between the student and the institution—are made in heaven. For any one student, there are at least 100 institutions of higher learning in which that student could be equally happy.

This is why I would like to wage total war on The Myth of the First Choice. Somehow, and in great error, we have allowed our students to think that there is a relationship between potential happiness and college preferences. Pure joy and unending satisfaction come automatically if one is accepted into his first choice college; partial happiness and incomplete satisfaction, from admission to the second college on the list; deep questions of self-value and brooding despair, from the third choice admission.

Let us establish first that there is not a single institution in the country which is admitting *only* those students who had that institution in mind as first choice. I talked with one student last year who completed seven applications and listed each one respectively as his first choice because he was sure each one only took those who gave the institution such a rating.

Many of us are in the happy circumstance of having a majority of our students content with what happened. But every college or university has a minority who allow the fate of the admissions draw to twist their college careers into disgruntled disasters.

Can't we at least begin to talk about the top three choices without encouraging students to pick and choose among them? I am not as concerned about the effect on colleges, which have a habit of surviving, as I am about the effect on individual students—the student who has his heart set on admission to East Siwash as the only fountain of knowledge worth a splash, and then receives an admission only to West Siwash.

We are worse than students in our tendency to over-glamorize institutions of higher learning and to allow prospective students to concentrate their romantic idealism on a particular heaven. It is not good for colleges and universities, and it certainly is not healthy for students who are unwilling to make the most of a splendid, but third choice, opportunity. Thus, disillusionment and frustration are built into the picture before it even is unveiled.

Finally, pretension number four. This is the mad scramble among all colleges and universities, but particularly those in the East, to appear "terribly exclusive" and "mobbed beyond belief" by "incredibly good" candidates for admission.

Why can't we just admit that we all go through the same agony as students and their parents? The one valid reason we are "mobbed beyond belief" is because we have tolerated so many ghost applications in recent years. We are haunted by that "tidal wave" of students which was supposed to engulf us several years ago. It came, we survived, and the wave receded to manageable proportions. But I guess nobody bothered to tell high school students.

The admissions crisis, the college entrance hysteria, or whatever you want to term it, is a condition of our own making. The fault lies squarely with the colleges and high schools. If one chooses wisely and well, it is not necessary to apply to more than three colleges. And if one happens to miss, there are hundreds of good colleges also missing.

The Episcopal minister, Malcolm Boyd, has written several books of prayers which have special appeal to college students. I think he may have been thinking of college presidents, admissions officers, and a few high school guidance counselors when he wrote this line:

"Lord, show him how to be very cool and quiet, and let him start being honest with himself."

Amen.

21

University Branches: Solution for College Crush

N. A. SICURO

Director of Program Planning and Development, Academic Centers and Continuing Education, Kent State University. His article originally appeared in *School and Society* on Dec. 10, 1966.

Emerging rapidly as a potential solution to burgeoning college enrollments is a system of university branches enrolling many of the country's 5,570,271 students. Among the states adopting this concept are Ohio, Pennsylvania, Wisconsin, Indiana, and Kentucky, led by Ohio's 34 branches of its seven state universities. The university branches are fully accredited, usually two-year undergraduate centers, strategically located in communities away from the parent campus. The branches serve the functions of assisting in servicing an overflowing number of students, affording an avenue for more mature persons with ability to take college course work close to their homes, providing means for men and women with home and occupational responsibilities to pursue a regular college credit program, and assisting students in determining their potential for degree aspirations.

Some educational leaders hold that the primary objective of a university branch is to provide a college education for those who cannot afford to go away from home. Others espouse the principle of universal education as the chief reason for establishing these centers. Nevertheless, over 2,000 institutions of higher learning in the U.S. are bulging at the seams, with the public institutions being taxed most. The projected college enrollment of over 10,000,000 for 1980 has resulted in prompt, speedy action by many officials of higher education to make it possible to accommodate this rising tide of college-seeking youth. Some states have utilized the community college as the instrument of solution, but this concept is not universally accepted.

Ohio's recently formed Board of Regents has supported the university branch concept, in existence even before the Regents became a reality. Already in operation are 34 branches operated by Bowling Green, Central State, Kent State, Miami, Ohio, and Ohio State Universities. Kent State leads the group with 10 branches, enrolling nearly 7,000 students in the autumn of 1965. Permanent campus buildings for Kent State branches are being built in four communities at a cost of over $10,000,000. Others are projected. Ohio State has branches in five cities, Ohio University in six, Miami University in five, Bowling Green in four, Cleveland State in three, and Central State in one. These 34 branches enrolled 23,894 students in the fall of 1965, representing a 500% increase in 10 years.

Indiana's regional campuses are operated by both Purdue and Indiana Universities. Purdue's four campuses, located in Calumet, Fort Wayne, Indianapolis, and Michigan City, enroll 10,261, while Indiana University's eight campuses enroll 15,141. Pennsylvania State University, a pioneer in the branch campus movement, has a system of 20 commonwealth campuses enrolling 7,376 and stretching from Erie to Philadelphia. Wisconsin's freshman-sophomore center system enrolls 4,697 in nine centers, located at Green Bay, Kenosha, Marinette, Manitowoc, Marshfield, Menasha, Racine, Sheboygan, and Wausau. The University of Kentucky's branches, once known as centers, are now called the community colleges of the University of Kentucky and are located in Ashland, Elizabethtown, Fort Knox, Hopkinsville, Henderson, Covington, Prestonburg, Somerset, and Cumberland. They enroll 4,723 students.

Those who accused the branches of restricting their offerings to transfer programs overlooked Penn State's long history of providing technical education in engineering technologies leading to the associate degree. Critics further are being silenced upon learning that Purdue's four regional campuses now enroll nearly 3,000 associate degree students. Kent State has accepted the challenge by establishing Ohio's most comprehensive associate degree program in history, slated to begin in the autumn of 1966. Spurred by local as well as national needs for technicians in engineering, business, and health fields, officials of branch operations have broadened their programs to reach nearly every segment of society.

These recent developments have resulted in many soul-searching moments for philosophers of higher education. Selective admissions policies are under constant pressure by those supporting the emerging concepts of total service to communities. Unquestionably, a revolution has taken place in American higher education. Healthy aspects are most prevalent. The awareness that education holds the hopes of the world's future has resulted in unparalleled action by local, state, and Federal governments to insure opening the doors to a college education to anyone who seeks it. The university branch concept undoubtedly will gain stature as the crescendo of college students progresses to the once unimaginable number of 10,000,000, expected by 1980.

22

Semester System vs. Quarter System: The Missouri Compromise

D. W. TIESZEN

The author is deceased. At the time his article originally appeared in *School and Society* (Feb. 24, 1962), he was Dean of Instruction, Central Missouri State College.

American colleges and universities traditionally have been organized either according to the semester plan or the quarter plan. As countless transfer students, college registrars, and others concerned with interpretation of credits will testify, there frequently is confusion resultant from the operation of the two systems. The increasing popularity of the trimester plan provides opportunities for increasing this confusion. Yet, no one pattern of organization is sacrosanct, and in the years ahead we will have to study these systems with open minds.

College faculties are not particularly agreed upon the arrangement they prefer. Possibly the majority prefer the semester system to the quarter system. Yet, with the demands in higher education for more effective use of facilities, it may be the semester plan which will become obsolete first. College and university programs increasingly will be in operation for 12 months per year. The school year more and more will be divided into three or four parts. How many parts are immaterial as long as they are interchangeable parts. The highly mobile American college population makes desirable as much uniformity as possible in "counting credits."

The "semester hour" has the value of a long history and popular understanding. It may continue in use after the semester, as we now know it, has disappeared.

In Missouri there is an interesting adaptation of the semester plan. Some Missouri state colleges operate under a program which, in effect, is a "Missouri Compromise" of the semester-hours-vs.-quarter-hours question.

The author of the system is unknown, but he was an educational Henry Clay. The state colleges, which were formerly normal schools, operated on the quarter basis. This was quite necessary in a rural society. Some of the graduates hoped to transfer to the state university, which operated on the semester basis. So the normal schools, in order to expedite transfer of their work, computed their credits as semester hours, although organized on the quarter plan. This procedure dates back to 1914.

This has been accomplished by having classes meet more frequently each week. Ordinarily, in colleges, a three semester-hour class in a semester of 17 weeks meets three times a week, or a total of 51 class hours. Under the Missouri plan, the same class will meet five times per week during an 11-week quarter, or a total of 55 class hours. This plan, or a minor modification of it, is now in use in three of Missouri's state colleges.

The advantages and disadvantages of the plan appear to be as follows:

ADVANTAGES

1. The quarter system, with its greater flexibility and smaller tuition payments at one time, is retained.

2. Hours earned are in semester hours, a commonly understood form of educational coinage.

3. Faculty members and students alike are engaged in fewer preparations at any one given time than under either the semester or quarter plan. For example, assume a 15 semester-hour load for a student in any institution which is under the semester plan. If he is taking all three-hour courses, this means he is enrolled in five different classes and possibly with five different professors. Under the "Missouri Compromise," the same student, in class for 15 hours a week, may be enrolled in only three different courses and with possibly three different professors. This same advantage also accrues to the teacher—fewer different preparations at any given time. This may well be the most important advantage of the system.

4. Since two semester-hour classes meet three days per week, the usual complaint against two semester-hour classes that there is not enough continuity between class sessions is minimized.

5. Since most classes are three semester-hour classes and are in session five days per week, this is excellent utilization of the physical plant.

DISADVANTAGES

1. Faculty members who have lectured on Monday find their next lecture comes not on Wednesday, but the very next day. Somehow the process does

not appear as leisurely. Reading must be accelerated. Laboratory periods come closer together.

2. The additional registration and short 11- or 12-week periods are retained in this plan.

There is much of sentiment and tradition and little actual factual basis which governs the calendars for institutions of higher learning. Actually, we do not know that a learning experience which lasts for 17 or 18 weeks is a better learning experience than one which lasts 11 or 12 weeks. In the years ahead there may be much more flexibility in college calendars than there has been. Some day we may attain such sophistication that we may eliminate quantitative credit measurements for qualitative educational experiences. Until then, however, there will be advantages for our mobile society in providing easily understood credit measurements, as best we know how to measure such things. The semester hour has much to recommend it for the purpose. And the principle involved in the "Missouri Compromise" may enable us to attain increased flexibility in the college calendar in the years ahead, while not surrendering an easily understood unit of academic measurement.

23

The University and Anti-Communist Pressure

HENRY KING STANFORD

President, University of Miami. His article originally appeared in *School and Society* on March 5, 1966, and was based on "A Report from the President," 1964–65.

Last year I presented, as part of my annual report, the text of a talk I had made on "Universities and Political Invaders." It seemed appropriate, in that talk to the National Association of Broadcasters, to emphasize once again how the university is a trustee of the legacy of civilization; how the university cannot administer this trust effectively unless it is free to roam where honest, rational, and critical inquiry takes it. I emphasize further that the true university can never be the pliable servant of political authority or any special group.

Now, a year later, it seems appropriate again to examine the nature of the university in view of the interest and activities of "special groups" who, in their fervor to expose communistic forces in our society, see in the integrity of a university a possible threat to the security of the United States. The University of Miami itself was subjected to criticism and innuendo by a local "fringe" group for seeking to maintain its campus as a forum for free inquiry and discussion during the year 1964–65. It was insinuated, in a novel means of character assassination, that the University had let itself become, wittingly or unwittingly, a tool of the international communist conspiracy.

These are anxious times for both the Town and the Gown. Anxiety, of course, is not rooted exclusively in the uncertainties of international politics. The theological existentialist tells us that man, being able to perceive that he exists, and also that he may cease to exist at any moment, is foredoomed to an anxious state by his capacity for this duality of contemplation. There is no question, however, that whatever state of anxiety is peculiar to man's nature, the growing tension in international affairs has multiplied his apprehensive moments.

I confess myself a gnawing uneasiness ever since the Soviets launched the Cold War following World War II. I became even more concerned after the Soviet development of nuclear power and missile technology. Now that the Chinese communists are becoming a nuclear power, my alarm is compounded.

One manifestation of this age of anxiety is the tendency to see the enemy at every turn. The Western sheriff would hardly have survived had he interpreted every sound as the presence of the outlaw and fired straightaway. But, today, we do have trigger-happy, self-appointed vigilantes, who startle at the slightest rustle of an idea with which they disagree. The Cold War, turning hot once again in Vietnam, has unnerved them. Professing to see communists behind every sound of free discussion, they fire at random at university campuses.

In fighting the Cold War, we are confronted with a phenomenon which we did not know in the earlier history of our country. To be sure, we have known different kinds of wars. There have been different wars for different generations of Americans. Our forefathers fought the chivalrous Civil War. Men fought adventurously in the war with Spain, which John Hay called "a splendid little war." The doughboys marched off idealistically to the first World War, the "war to end war." The GI's fought the second World War with grim and realistic determination to get a tough job over with as quickly as possible.

The Cold War of the 1960's, however, is an altogether different kind of warfare. It is much more than a war of potential nuclear destruction. The Soviets, it appears, prefer to fight on the battlefront of ideas or native insurgents rather than risk the radioactive ashes of mutual death and destruction. The big weapons are evidently going to be kept hooded. There will be comparatively little opportunity for citizens to participate directly in military engagement, except those who will have to bear arms in wars of containment. But all of us are drawn inexorably to the battleground of ideas.

The university worthy of the name cannot afford to shield the minds of its students from the mind of the enemy. How else are students to learn the fundamentals of dialectic materialism and thus discover its weakness if they are not exposed to it? How can students learn to recognize and cope with communist propaganda if they never see or hear samples of it? Young minds must be toughened by exposure, by testing, by exploring all the ideas of man, free to question, argue, reject, and accept. They must be free to read about, to discuss and analyze all the communist systems. Totalitarian education, whether Nazi or communist, can brook no expression of opinion contrary to the party line. What stultification of the vitality which the university student has the right to expect in the humanities and the social studies! We in America can build more inquiring, and therefore stronger, minds on the foundation of free discussion.

During the spring, I was questioned about the appearance on our

campus of a periodical allegedly published by communists to take advantage of the struggle for civil rights in the U.S. My answer to the question
was in effect: "So what?" I am not afraid to subject the minds of our
students to any publication which the communists can muster. And what is
one isolated publication in comparison with the thousands of communist
publications we house in the Otto G. Richter Library? The University has
prided itself on its agreement with the Library of Congress, by which our
librarian, Archie L. McNeal, is given the opportunity to select duplicates of
all Soviet publications received by the Library of Congress. Today, our
collection of Soviet documents, ranging from 1948 down to the present,
numbers more than 100,000 items. We are enthusiastic about the possibilities
for study and research into the Soviet state, ideology, economy, culturo,
and a hundred aspects of Soviet life which this great storehouse of documents
provides. Similarly, our librarian is eagerly and successfully building up
one of the country's greatest collections of documents published by the
Castro regime in Cuba. We want to provide students and researchers with
all possible materials that shed light on the particular brand of communism
that has sprung up in Cuba. The beginning of the defense against the spread
of communism is to know accurately the species and the environmental
conditions which nurture its growth in a particular locality.

An attack upon this library collection is certainly possible by those
anxious individuals who regard censorship as the surest weapon against
free discussion of ideas. Their brand of superpatriotism expresses their fear
and anxiety that freedom is itself suspect. It is a refuge of those who have
lost faith in the United States, its democratic governance, its educational
system, and its ability to defeat the Soviet challenge. It is a virulent form
of disunity. As Henry Steele Commager said recently:

Those who cultivate and spread the gospel of hatred throughout our society bear
a heavy responsibility. They do not really weaken communism; they weaken
democracy and liberty. By their conduct and philosophy they lower the moral
standards of the society they pretend to defend. Eager to put down imagined sub-
version, they are themselves the most subversive of all the elements in our society,
for they subvert that "harmony and affection" without which a society cannot be a
commonwealth.

My plea must not be interpreted as an appeal to eliminate such criticism
from our society. Progress results from exposure of weakness at either end
of the ideological spectrum, and its correction through remedial change.
Exposure means evaluation of shortcomings. There is much to criticize.
Higher education itself, faced with the unprecedented task of coping with
swollen enrollments and exploding fields of knowledge, should not be
immune from criticism from layman and professional educator alike. What
this essay does inveigh against is the frenzied attack upon free expression;

the vicious denunciation, as subversive or communist, of the individual who disagrees.

With the support of faculty and trustees, I will continue to keep this campus a forum of free inquiry and discussion. I am proud of the consensus we have reached in the support of this principle. The tradition for freedom of investigation by research, discussion, or lecture has long been present on our campus. During 1964–65, the Faculty Senate wished to have a policy, in writing, supporting the right of faculty and student groups to invite to the campus outside speakers who they believed would "enhance the intellectual development of the audience." The proposal from the Senate had my endorsement and gained the unanimous approval of the Board of Trustees.

The task of the university in the Cold War is clear. It must commit itself and its students to the most rigorous scholarship within its means. Mediocre standards cannot meet the communist challenge. Any institution doing less than its best to strengthen the minds of Americans weakens the nation in a perilous hour. The university must ever seek to graduate students who will enter into the responsibilities of citizenship with zeal, not apathy. The responsible alumnus-citizen will guard the liberties of vote and free discussion and oppose encroachment masked as superpatriotism, the easy solution of terming everyone who disagrees with us "communist" or "pink." The responsible alumnus-citizen should be inspired by the standards of his alma mater to work wisely and insistently for improvements in our system of government and in our society. Thus inspired, the responsible alumnus-citizen should be influential in bringing to the underdeveloped peoples of our own nation not only hope but progress in the democratic way of life.

The world is not sanforized; it keeps shrinking. Our neighbors press upon us. Barring nuclear war, there will be 6,000,000,000 people on this planet by the turn of the century. We cannot plan our lives to exist apart from these peoples and their aspirations. The communist powers hope to encircle us—in Latin America, Africa, Asia, Indo-China—with a vast mass of people who believe their best chance of progress lies with the totalitarian, communist directed way of life. The U.S. must offer them another choice, no matter how difficult it is or how long it takes to bring it about. The university lies squarely in the middle of this struggle: to produce students today and citizens tomorrow, whose commitment in this battle of ideas is total, unflinching, deadly serious, and based on sound, informed convictions.

24

The Invitation of Speakers to the College Campus

HAROLD W. STOKE

The author was president of Queens College of the City University of New York at the time his article originally appeared in *School and Society* (March 10, 1962). He resigned his post in 1964.

Colleges exist to conserve the values of accumulated knowledge through teaching and to add to knowledge through research. The notion that colleges are forums from which everyone has a "right" to advance his ideas is, in my judgment, questionable on both practical and intellectual grounds. The fact that society at large permits activities to be carried on freely or ideas to be circulated freely does not obligate colleges to give them hospitality under the guise of academic freedom or of constitutional rights. Prize fights, burlesque shows, and propagandizing are not proper college activities, no matter how acceptable they may be elsewhere.

Colleges are constantly making judgments, guided by good taste, educational values, or even by law, as to what books they should put into their libraries, what courses into the curricula, what faculty members they should hire, and what visitors should be invited to their campuses. To have such judgments forced upon them is repugnant to the whole idea of academic freedom. Academic freedom grows out of the conditions which colleges— *with themselves as the principal judges*—require for their work; it is not the creation of the First Amendment.

That freedom is indispensible to the work of colleges needs no elaborate justification. Colleges need it in the research they do, the courses they teach, the faculties they select, and the visitors they invite to their campuses. Their freedom to investigate and discuss should extend not only to observable facts, but to areas of opinion and to the emotionally exciting subjects of social concern—war, peace, ethics, religion, sex, politics. We have found no better technique than that of freedom for the discovery of truth. For a college to be

130

cut off from the investigation and discussion of the heats and passions of its day is to kill its usefulness.

In the exercise of its freedom, however—the selection of its faculty, the construction of its curriculum, the organizations and activities it permits, the visitors it invites—a college must meet a single generic test: does the exercise of its freedom serve the purposes for which the college itself exists? Nor is it enough to justify the exercise of its freedom on purposes for which it merely can be said, "There is no law against them," or that "They will do no harm." This is too aimless to be compatible with the importance of colleges and with the conservation of the time, energy, and resources required for their work. Colleges have little justification for engaging in anything for which there is not a presumption of positive educational value. Academic freedom is quite capable of deterioration into academic self-indulgence and triviality; it is the obligation of the academic community to see that it does not. Certainly, if a college is to preserve its integrity, it must not be used to serve purposes incompatible with its own.

Such a broad principle of guidance, however sound, leaves much room —as it should—for choice, and, in application, it leaves broad grounds for controversy. People may agree on the work of colleges in general, but they will not agree in all details. Today the problem of controversy is how the colleges should handle the discussion of communism on the campuses; tomorrow it will be something else.

It would be a serious mistake to forbid the discussion of communism— even by visiting communists—on college campuses. The discussion of communism is difficult and confusing. The difficulty and confusion come from the fact that communism is not only a complex social philosophy about which we must be informed, but it is also a political conspiracy. The question is how can communism be studied as a system of thought without fostering it as a conspiracy? Our society is in the position of the physicist who must study atomic energy while avoiding lethal radiation.

Policies which will meet the increasing involvements of colleges in our society today call for more thought and more discriminating judgment than they have called for in the past. The concern of a college for freedom must extend not only to freedom for itself, but for that of the society in which it lives. One thing is certain: no college ever enjoyed academic freedom in a society which, as a whole, did not enjoy a corresponding degree of freedom. A college which is concerned only about freedom for itself will lose it when freedom in the society of which it is a part is lost.

This is why a college must exercise the utmost care if it insists on providing a forum for those within its own society who are dedicated to the destruction both of academic freedom and of freedom in general. To justify such insistence, the case for a truly academic need must be all but overwhelming. A college must provide an understanding of communism; it is equally obligated to lend no aid to its conspiracy. This is why invitations to communists to speak on a campus must be discriminating. Thus, an invitation to the Soviet Educational Advisor, obviously a communist, to visit a college to describe the system of Soviet education is one thing; an invitation to the National Secretary of the Communist Party of the United States is another. One invitation serves a legitimate educational purpose which the college needs to fulfill; the other, in effect, invites the Communist Party to make use of the college.

The claim that the actual physical presence of a member of the Communist Party of the United States is necessary (which I question) for students to be adequately informed about communism must be set off against the contribution which his presence makes to the political advancement of the Communist Party. (The vehement insistence of the students that they would be unaffected by such appearances must be, I should think, very discouraging to prospective communist speakers, but it also makes one wonder why they ever should be invited!) Even so, I doubt that the educational sacrifice students may make in foregoing the privilege is very great in comparison with the contribution which the college makes to the communist cause in lending itself as a forum.

The college should be permitted to make these kinds of judgments for itself. No one else is in a position to do so. It is not feasible for legislatures, city councils, or even boards of trustees to exercise such judgment for the college any more than such groups can select its library books or its faculty members or determine the content of a course in quantitative chemistry.

If a college claims and is given freedom to decide who is to visit its campus, it will be held responsible for the choices it makes. If it can defend its choices as sound, all the better; if it cannot, those who make the choices will be relieved ultimately of their responsibility.

Who, then, within the college should make such decisions? The students themselves, for reasons which I believe are educationally sound, exercise great freedom of choice. But I cannot believe that it would be wise to place upon them the full responsibility or that they morally or educationally can claim an exclusive and unreviewable right to decide such matters for the college. Too many, besides themselves, have an interest in such decisions. But neither should the faculty and administration make such decisions without regard to the wishes and interests of the students. The problem for the college is essentially to devise a procedure whereby a consensus, if at all possible, can be reached. In the vast majority of instances, no problems will arise. There will continue to be differences of opinion in a few instances as to the wisdom of decisions, but if those decisions are reached by a procedure understood and agreed upon, and if they serve the purposes of the college while protecting it against exploitation, the usefulness and integrity of academic freedom will be maintained.

25

The University and the High School

LAWRENCE A. KIMPTON

The author was chancellor of the University of Chicago at the time his article originally appeared in *School and Society* (March 1, 1958). The article was based on an address to the Conference on the American High School, Oct. 28, 1957. Dr. Kimpton is now retired.

The number of people at the conference on the high school, including interested members of our Chicago citizenry, indicates the importance the public attaches to the education currently being provided by the American high school. And the trouble is that it really is important and no mere passing fad of public concern.

Everyone, or almost everyone, is aware of the fact that the future of our free way of life depends upon an educated citizenry; and over the last half century, as the percentage of young people attending the public high school has jumped from roughly 10% to well over 90%, our public interest began to center in secondary school education. There has been an enormous amount of criticism of the high school in recent years, and, while some of it has been uninformed and irresponsible, some also has been informed and telling. I should like to try to make a fresh start upon the problem from the only vantage point that I possess—namely, that of a philosopher by training turned administrator by profession.

Whenever we talk about education, we base our statements, consciously or unconsciously, upon certain very fundamental philosophical ideas. Philosophy has been said to be the science of bewildering oneself methodically, and there is something in this definition. Philosophy really is bewildering and this is the reason so few people are able and willing to reveal the fundamental philosophical presuppositions that direct their educational judgments. What knowledge is and how one acquires it are the problems of epistemology; and epistemology, in turn, is based upon certain even more fundamental ideas about the nature of man, the universe, and man's relation to the universe, collected under the name of metaphysics.

The metaphysician and epistemologist who has played the greatest role in the determination of the methods and objectives of contemporary elementary and secondary education is John Dewey, who was a professor of philosophy at the University of Chicago from 1894 to 1904 and one of the founders of our Laboratory School. Dewey had the misfortune of being widely misunderstood and so unwittingly has served as the great philosophical instigator and prophet for what has come to be called "progressive education." It seems clear that he had little realization of what he had wrought until his later years when he made several efforts to correct the misunderstanding that had occurred.

Dewey was a pretty good philosopher and what he really had to say, if correctly understood, has relevance to the educational enterprise. He was concerned with the problem of how we think, and this was the title of one of his earliest and best books. To express his conclusions in the jargon of the philosophers, all thinking originates in a problematic situation and is brought to a conclusion within a context which shapes the thinking and determines the relevance and, indeed, the truth of the conclusion. For example, Robinson Crusoe finds himself upon an island which he believes to be deserted. One day while walking on the beach he sees a footprint, and this datum, as Dewey calls it, constitutes the problematic situation. Who made the footprint? Is he friendly or unfriendly? And if I assume the latter, what ought I to do about it? We all know the rest of the story. He decided that the footprint was made by a cannibal and took steps to defend himself; and he did, in fact, successfully defend himself later against an attack. This is what Dewey is saying in essence, and there is nothing very earth-shaking about it. We think when we have a problem to think about. The way we think is determined by a complex context involving certain partial information and certain desired conclusions (for example, in the case of Robinson Crusoe, saving his own life). It is understandable, therefore, that Dewey emerged with a somewhat new definition of knowledge and of truth. Knowledge is what we seek in trying to solve a problem, and truth is the answer that satisfactorily solves the problem.

There is one other fundamental idea about Dewey's philosophy developed in his later work—namely, the concept of value or the end of human life. The object of living, according to Dewey, is growth, and all he really means by this is that you must go right on having problems if you are to realize the full richness of life. We all know from our own experience what he is talking about. Too many minds become frozen at a certain point: they possess all the answers. Thinking ceases, according to Dewey, when all one's values become fixed and there are no live, interesting, and new things to think about. The essential principles, then, of Dewey's philosophy are that the learning process occurs within a context of concern and challenge, and life takes on values as long as this continues as an active process.

What happened when certain persuasive teachers of teachers began to explain what Dewey meant? Thinking begins, says Dewey, with an interest or a concern. Therefore, said the educator, our problem is to interest students; and this interpretation passed over easily into the distortion of amusing and entertaining them. Dewey certainly did not mean anything like this. It is true that one way of interesting the child in mathematics is to play games that involve the use of arithmetic, but another way of getting him interested is to require him to learn enough mathematics so that he becomes aware of problems that had not previously existed for him. It is a valuable thing, of course, to interest a child in learning to read, but this does not mean keeping the child amused and entertained whether or not he learns to read.

Still another kind of unfortunate misunderstanding occurred as to Dewey's theory of truth. For Dewey, truth is the solution, the particular set of facts and hypotheses that actually work to solve a problem. This became translated into some kind of inverted "adjustment to the environment," a phrase which Dewey himself often uses. Dewey is really saying that thinking begins in maladjustment to the environment and continues as an active, tough, and difficult process, whereby we solve the problems that occur within our experience. This was misunderstood by certain professional educators, whose influence exceeded their wisdom, to mean that the end of the educational process is the adjustment of our youngsters to their environment with no particular concern or activity on their part. For example, grades were eliminated so that the young person might not suffer the frustration of feeling inferior to others. Students were promoted in both the elementary and the secondary schools whether they deserved it or not in order that they might have no sense of maladjustment. This enormous sensitivity and tenderness for the sense of security and adaptation of the child is a frightful travesty upon Dewey's thinking. His was really a rigorous mind, believing that the adjustments we make to the problems arising in our experience occur only through hard and active thinking, and, if the adjustments are made for us, nothing of any educational significance occurs.

And a final grievous error is made in the interpretation of Dewey's theory of value. He did say that value was growth, meaning that the good life is being endlessly challenged and endlessly dissatisfied with the limitations of the present. This is how we grow and stay alive, said Dewey, but this principle was translated by certain thoughtless Progressives into a complete lack of discipline for youth. Let them express themselves, it was said, and give them complete and unrestrained freedom of action and speech, of manners and lack of manners; only then will they grow. This is a curious kind of confusion of the philosopher, John Dewey, with the woolly-headed Frenchman, Jean-Jacques Rousseau. Rousseau really did believe in the noble savage, as he expressed it, and he honestly felt that, if all human minds could only completely and fully express themselves, the millennium would come. But Dewey entertained no such stupid idea. Growth, for him, was a thoroughly disciplined kind of concept, in terms of which the human mind was constantly beaten back and forth between brute fact and the flights of human hope and aspiration. John Dewey was one of the most significant philosophers of our time, and the serious misunderstanding of him—unlike most philosophical misunderstandings—has affected millions of lives.

I am greatly troubled when I turn, as a university administrator, to consider this serious philosophical and educational misunderstanding. I believe that universities, in large part, have been responsible for it by separating themselves from high-school education and the training of high-school teachers. I fear that this separation has resulted not only in a distortion of the philosophy upon which much of our secondary education rests, but also in a watering down of the subject matter taught in many of the classrooms. Let me try to state some of the origins and causes of this separation and make some suggestions about the need of directing the attention of the entire university toward the problems of the American high school.

For reasons that I do not altogether understand, the field of education spelled with a capital "E" came into disrepute at the universities. The professional educator was looked down upon by his colleagues within the university community until a professor hesitated to admit that he was a member of the school of education. It has been the habit of oppressed minorities through the centuries to band themselves closely together for common defense and, even though separated from the main part of the community, to play a powerful role in its life. And this is precisely what happened in the schools of education at the great American universities. Sneered at by their colleagues as second-class citizens, the educators withdrew from the general life of the university, but proceeded through active and strong lobbies in the state legislatures to set up requirements for the licensing of teachers that involved taking their courses and their degrees. Always apart from the universities were the normal schools, established to train the teachers of the communities, and most of these became teachers colleges. The schools of education of the universities began then to train these teachers of teachers for the teachers colleges, thus cutting off the high school even further from the mainstream of the universities. As the schools of education, independent of the universities, became stronger, they developed their own courses, not in psychology but in educational psychology, not in physics but in how to teach physics, and not in history but in the techniques of presenting history to the student. With the combination of state licensing laws, schools of education, and teachers colleges, the circle became complete. The American high school was cut off from the main body of the American university.

What is the solution to this problem? It is simple enough to state, though not easy to realize. The universities must stop grousing about the education of our high-school students and get back into the business of training teachers. The schools of education must become a real part of the universities and the universities must begin to relate themselves properly and effectively to the work of the schools of education. The philosophy of education must be taught by a member of the department of philosophy. The department of physics must stop regarding the master's degree as being of no importance. The high-school teacher of mathematics or the teacher of teachers of mathematics in the school of education must receive his training in subject matter at the hands of a competent mathematician. This does not mean that the school of education ceases to have a part to play in this educational program. It has been conspicuously successful over a number of years in the development of useful and valuable educational techniques. Because of the schools of education, a great deal is known about curriculum development, tests and testing, the techniques of counseling and vocational guidance, and school administration. These things are important and necessary to the teacher and to the school administrator. And if Dewey is right that knowledge begins with interest and challenge, there are techniques of stimulating these among students. The school of education, moreover, is and will remain the real link between the university and the high school, translating the theory and new discovery of the universities to the high-school classrooms. We are all too acutely aware of the enormous time lag that now occurs between new development in any field of knowledge and the high-school classroom. Mathematics, for example, has made enormous progress within the last half century, and yet the program of high-school mathematics has remained substantially unchanged over this same period. And if it is the role of the school of education to stand between new knowledge and its applications, this bridge should support traffic going in two directions. It is of considerable importance that the universities know more than most of them now do about the real activities and problems of the classroom teacher. So much of the research in education seems sterile and irrelevant to the teacher because the research worker is unacquainted with what actually happens in the classroom.

We have long prided ourselves in America on our ability as administrators. We are an efficient people and our universities reflect this; upon the whole, they successfully accomplish the ends to which they are directed. But somehow we have failed with the high school, and we are paying a high price. We have allowed a part of the university to drift out of its proper relationship with other parts and to take over the entire problem of the secondary education of our youth. The school of education must be reestablished as one of the important focal points within the university where the content fields converge. The school of education must give this content appropriate configurations for the high-school program and add the necessary techniques of presentation. The minds of our youth are the future of America, not to be entrusted to a single part of our educational enterprise. It is our responsibility as citizens, as teachers and administrators in high schools and universities, to insist that these minds receive the best that all of American education can provide.

26

The University's Stake in Problems of School Administrators

WILLIAM H. CARTWRIGHT

Professor of education and chairman, Department of Education, Duke University. His article originally appeared in *School and Society* on Oct. 30, 1954, and was based on an address to the Conference on School Law, Duke University, June 15, 1954.

The university's stake in problems of school administrators grows from many causes. First, the university is eager that its students should have sound preparation for college. Second, the university trains teachers for the schools. Third, the university prepares school administrators themselves. Fourth, the schools and the universities are parts of the same educational system.

The university must broaden and deepen the understanding of its students and improve them in mind and spirit so as to make them more effective members of our free society. Further, it must provide most of them with specialized knowledge, understanding, and skill so as to enable them to enter one of the professions. The university can carry out this assignment well only if it has a firm foundation upon which to build. The broader the knowledge, the deeper the understanding, the greater the intellectual skill of those who come to institutions of higher learning, the more rapidly and efficiently can the college further the development of well-rounded personalities and enlightened, useful citizens.

Our secondary schools were founded as college-preparatory institutions. And, during most of the history of education, college preparation has been the principal purpose of secondary schools. This situation has changed greatly in America during the past two generations. The secondary school has become a part of the American common school. We now assume that all normal children have a right to graduate from high school if they apply themselves. The primary function of the secondary school is now preparation for citizenship. And a host of lesser, but nevertheless important, functions have asserted themselves. As a result of these changes the natural bonds between the schools and the universities have been weakened. There has been a loss of sympathetic understanding between the two.

In part, this deterioration in understanding results from the fact that many college professors seem not to realize that the high schools have many functions to perform and can no longer devote all their attention to the task of college preparation. Frequently this is reflected merely in lack of enthusiastic support of the schools. Sometimes it results in bitter hostility.

But not all of the blame for the lost contact between school and college is to be laid at the doorstep of the college. It does not take very deep reading of the literature of professional education, or very earnest listening to some of the speakers at education conventions, or very detailed study of the proposals of some would-be curriculum-makers to discover this. Too many professional educators have given more consideration to the fact that preparation for college is not as important a function of the secondary school as it once was than they have given to the fact that college preparation is still a very important business of the secondary school. As a matter of fact, nearly half as many persons are enrolled in our institutions of higher learning as are enrolled in our high schools. The majority of the graduates of many high schools are planning to go to college. In this situation we might expect the curriculum-makers to devote proportionately less of their time to life-adjustment education and the "emerging" curriculum than they do in order that other aspects of high-school work might also be improved.

The schools have a right to expect the universities to be sympathetic and understanding. More than this, the schools have a right to expect the universities to give active support to curriculum improvement for the schools of everybody's children. This improvement will require experimental education in which the university must co-operate. At the same time, the universities have a right to expect that school administrators will not give up the business of preparing students for college. The universities, and society, have a right to expect that educational experimentation will be carefully conducted and that it will be conducted only on a small scale. They have a right to expect that new practices will be extended over large areas only when they have been proved more effective than those now followed.

The second concern of the university in the problems of school administrators is that of obtaining the best possible teachers for our schools. Here the two have a common cause. The administrator is eager to secure superior teachers, for without them the school system for which he is responsible cannot carry out its duty to society. The university is eager to prepare superior teachers for the good of society, for the sake of its own reputation, and in order to obtain well-qualified candidates for its student body.

America has evidenced serious interest in the quality of its school teachers in many ways. Teacher-training institutions seek promising candidates for the profession and try to provide them with the best education for their purposes. The state establishes requirements for teaching certificates which are designed to insure that candidates have attained a minimum educational status and have had courses necessary for their work. Employing officials try to screen otherwise qualified candidates carefully so as to secure the best available talent for their communities. And the profession itself has been active in recent years trying to set up reasonable standards. Law enters the picture at several points. The state charters or approves teacher-training institutions; it establishes certification requirements; and it governs the contractual relationship between the teacher and the administrative unit.

Teachers will never attain the professional status to which they all aspire until the profession itself establishes and maintains professional standards of preparation. That happy situation is not likely to exist for many years to come. It is no derogation of the great teachers' organizations to say that their principal concern has not been along this line. It is quite understandable that these organizations have been principally concerned with attracting members and with improving the economic security of those members. Meanwhile, the only effective guarantees of adequate teaching staff are the integrity and ability of teacher-training institutions and of employing officials. This is not to belittle the importance of certification regulations. They have been a very important factor in raising the level of instruction. In fact, without them we would not have been able to achieve the present high standard of education in this country. But there is a limit to what can be achieved or should be attempted through legal certification. Certification cannot determine personality, character, or ability. And these are the most vital characteristics of a teacher. In fact, these qualities can make up for lack of all that certification can guarantee. All that certification can do is to guarantee that the candidate has spent a minimum period of time in college and has passed certain courses. This it should do.

But the matter of specifying courses required for a teaching certificate has been carried beyond reason in some places in recent years. And it has become a matter of serious import both to colleges trying to give the best possible education and to school administrators seeking the best possible teachers. When a superintendent cannot employ without penalty a teacher who has demonstrated her superior teaching ability under a standard certificate issued in another state, or when a teacher-training institution cannot possibly pack into a degree program the courses required for an appropriate certificate in all of the several states in which a candidate may have to live, the situation is little short of ridiculous.

The time has come when school administrators and universities might make common cause in petitioning that the details of certification requirements be kept at a minimum. This is not a recommendation for lowering standards. We should maintain the college degree as a requirement for a teaching certificate. We should require prospective teachers to have a sound general education, additional work in the subjects of their specialization, and professional training in the art and science of teaching. But teacher-training institutions have educational leaders on their staffs who may be as competent as those in government service to define these requirements. And school administrators are usually competent to select the best-qualified applicants. In a time of critical and growing teacher shortage, the university and the school administrator should do all in their power to attract into the teaching profession persons of superior personality, character, and ability. After the state has established a high, general standard of education for certification, it can make its greatest contribution by paying teachers well and by making good teachers secure in their positions.

The third concern of the university in problems of school administration is the training of those administrators themselves. In this connection it is important that we share our thinking in order to work out the best possible training program. A great deal has been accomplished along this line in recent years. We should pay tribute to the Cooperative Project in Educational Administration. It has achieved more in three years than anyone would have thought possible. Among its important contributions has been bringing together, at many times and places and for many purposes, university personnel and school administrators. Already important changes in the program of educational administration in many universities have resulted from CPEA activity. Never did so many superintendents and professors of education work so closely together for so long.

But have we brought the other departments of the university into the program as much as we should? They have entered here and there, but have they been exploited to the utmost? In the perilous times ahead, our school administrators must be educational statesmen of the highest caliber. Can we not call on the social scientists to give substantial help in preparing them? It is of great importance that we have lawyers with us here giving generously of their time and understanding. May there be many other conferences on school law to follow this one, and may we always have the counsel of the legal profession. But can we not extend the practice to make more use of the historians, the political scientists, the economists, and the sociologists? Can we not use these experts in social science in the formal education of school administrators more than we have as well as consulting them on specific problems?

It was stated that we really have one great educational system in this country. This is not true in a legal sense, but, from the point of view of social purpose, it is very true. And it is true in the view of the man on the street. The past few years have been years of sharp and continued attack on education. Sometimes the charge is that the universities or secondary schools are subversive. Sometimes it is that the secondary or elementary schools are anti-intellectual.

Whatever the charge, at whatever level, if it is true, the situation weakens education at all levels. If the charge is false, it damages the reputation and increases the danger at all levels. If the schools do not give effective instruction, the effectiveness of the universities is lessened. If the colleges do not give a sound education, the efficiency of teaching in the schools is lowered. If academic freedom is curtailed in the colleges, teachers trained by college professors and textbooks written by college professors are less serviceable in the education of an enlightened citizenry. If freedom to learn is restricted in the schools, the students who come to college are unable to bring their critical faculties to bear fully on the issues which are raised in their deliberations.

This interdependence between school and university should make college and school personnel eager to understand and help each other. It may be amusing to find some of those who are most critical of experimentation in the school curriculum in the vanguard of those carrying out nearly identical experiments in the colleges. But it is very unfortunate that some college professors are leading attacks on the schools rather than trying to co-operate with the harassed school administrators in seeking solutions to their mutual problems. The needed co-operation will be facilitated if schoolmen will make it known that they welcome the interest and help of the college faculty.

27

Ideas and the State University

ELI M. OBOLER

University librarian, Idaho State University. His article originally appeared in *School and Society* on Feb. 4, 1967.

Matthew Arnold once described Oxford as the "home of lost causes, and forsaken beliefs, and unpopular names, and impossible loyalties." This description could well be used for every responsible and worthwhile university in the U.S. today. If a university is not the "home of lost causes, and forsaken beliefs, and unpopular names, and impossible loyalties," what is it?

The university, particularly the state university, today all too often is the home of the causes that have already been won, of beliefs that are held by everyone else, of faculty and administration who strive only to be popular, and of those who have perfectly ordinary and conformist loyalties. Indeed, for many state universities, the question of the relationship of ideas and the university hardly comes up. The state university today is much too busy with taking care of the workaday problems that it must face, what with inadequate space, too few faculty, too few library books, and an ever-growing student body, to have any time to think of such *outré* things as "ideas."

Most of our state universities have some kind of slogan which indicates that they are trying their best to be "the servant of the state" or, as some universities have put it, "the state is our campus." If this slogan is carried through to its logical potentialities, it means the destruction, rather than the regeneration, of the university.

That university which strives to put as its primary function that of being a service agency to a government, whether local or state or Federal, is, by that very action, abnegating its most important role, which is to be the creator and disseminator of new and updated ideas. Very rarely, indeed, do political entities countenance new ideas. Their function is to maintain the status quo and to protect that which is, rather than to look into that which may be, and even, possibly, to try their best to circumvent the possibility that what now is may develop into some kind of ineluctable necessity of what must be.

Sacrifices to political or other non-university-related exigencies affect, to a greater or lesser extent, just about every university in the country. Even without going into panic about the possibility of "socialism" in the ever-increasing role of the Federal government in almost every phase of American civilization, it is still possible to be concerned, if one cares about the facilitation of free inquiry, with the dire potentialities of the current trend toward centralization of control of research and even teaching. For example, in the tremendous library at Moscow University, which numerically is perhaps the largest in the world, certain books are denied to students. Some other books may be given out only with the approval of the powers that be. Every piece of reading material that is charged out must be signed for, and this record is maintained for each student or faculty member, to show what he has read throughout his years at the institution. This is not quite the way in which the records of libraries in American state university libraries are kept.

Getting down to specifics on the campus community's responsibility toward freedom of inquiry, the faculty of a university has a very heavy responsibility, which transcends meeting classes, advising students, or even that most vital of all duties, participation in faculty committee meetings. The basic responsibility of the faculty of a university is to encourage and to disseminate ideas of past time, our time, and of time to come. Nowhere else in our society can this obligation be placed. Nowhere else is there such a comparatively free group of individuals, with the sound educational background, and with the time and opportunity to do the job that needs to be done.

But what is happening to the faculty's basic job? Just as one example, according to a *New York Times* article of Aug. 1, 1965, written by the education editor, Fred M. Hechinger, "The nation's universities are entering a new phase as they respond to a growing demand that higher education become the agent of urban service and renewal." There is still one more job for the university and its faculty. There are voices to the contrary, however. The president of the American Council on Education, Logan Wilson, has urged educators to remember that "our primary obligation to students in residence implies a top priority for the teaching function."

This gets into rather a complex question, namely, one of priority. What good is having ideas and communicating just to students in residence? On this basis, it would take a long, long time for the fermentation of ideas of universities to reach the general public. Even today, just five and a half million of our population are attending academic institutions at any one time. The obligation to get ideas out from the cloistered, ivy-covered walls is as important as the one of having the ideas in the first place.

These ideas must be, by their very nature, destructive, iconoclastic, new ideas. The majority of the population is always against destroying the old, and must always be reassured that whatever suggestions there are about the new will not be of a revolutionary character. All ideas, to some, are dangerous—but to suppress ideas is much more likely to be dangerous.

There is a new phrase which has come to signify the so-called new trend in our universities, that of "community involvement." It is only a new phrase, not really a new idea, however. The University of Wisconsin has said repeatedly that "the boundaries of the campus are the boundaries of the state." It becomes more and more apparent that the university of the future must have as its boundaries the world. This sounds very idealistic. But when have new ideas coming from a campus not sounded idealistic?

We are all too closely tied together under that sword of Damocles of which the late Pres. Kennedy warned us—the constant threat of nuclear destruction—to have any delusions about being able to be as parochial as the state-as-boundary motto would make us. Perhaps it is a necessary motto, for the sake of getting backing from provincially minded legislators, to help in getting basic budgets. Perhaps, in order to get nationally based grants, this may, at this time, have to stop at being some such slogan as "the boundaries of the campus are the boundaries of the United States." The importation of ferment-stirring new students into practically every institution of any consequence in the country, the exportation of professors by such means as Fulbright grants, and the new idea (at least new for most of the many institutions which now have it) of sending students away for intervals of from one to several years into institutions of learning throughout the world, are examples that tie in with the notion that ideas are universal, rather than parochial.

What is the place of the student body in this idea of the relationship between ideas and the university? Our generation of students is quite different from the so-called "quiet generation," of which some of us complained, back in the 1950's. In the 1960's, it is being a conformist to be a protester, to be an activist, to cry out against silence, apathy, privatism, and to be actively involved in national problems. The student "explosion" at Berkeley has been only the outward sign of feelings that are present in almost every institution of higher learning these days. It is not only proper to picket and march these days; it is almost *de rigueur*.

The average college student today is faced with quite a dilemma. He normally comes to an academic institution for the purpose of learning. He does not see himself in the role of a crusader or a picketer or as the leader of a revolt. He is simply going to spend four years in learning those things which he needs to learn in order to fit into our society. This is a fair description of the wants of the majority of students at a majority of American universities. But, of course, there is a very active minority which sees the university as a place to do as well as to learn.

What should be the role of ideas in a university, both for students and for faculty—and, perhaps most importantly of all, for the administration? Ideas should be central in the university, for all three groups mentioned. The sacred fact is but a tool, and the sacred idol of an established opinion or a generally accepted idea is, except to the confirmed believer in the sacredness of that which is, again but an instrument.

Nobody wants irresponsibility in the university. It is not a gathering place for the crackpots of the world. It should be a place where those who have something to think about, who are able to express their thoughts clearly and understandably, who have responsible and measured facts and opinions underpinning their beliefs, may express those beliefs, whether or not it pleases a legislature, or a pressure group, or even the president of a university.

The university, ideally speaking, must treasure the individual who brings new ideas as its true leader. That individual, whether instructor or full professor, whether a freshman or a graduate student, whether a white Anglo-Saxon Protestant or a brown Buddhist or a member of the Jewish faith, may have something to add to the ideas which are the only justification for the university's existence.

It is true that there are very clear indications, if public opinion polls are to be believed, that the general public is not necessarily in agreement with what has been offered hereinbefore as the ideal. According to what pollster Louis Harris found out from what he calls "a carefully drawn cross-section of the adult public," the American public is not very tolerant of non-conformity. To quote him, "the man who stands apart from the crowd—because he does not believe in God, because he pickets against the war in Vietnam, because he demonstrates for civil rights—is regarded as harmful to the American way of life by two out of three of his fellow citizens."

Here is the way the question was asked: "America has many different types of people in it but we'd like to know whether you think each of these different types of people is more helpful or more harmful to American life, or don't they help or harm things much in one way or the other?" When asked about college professors active in unpopular causes, 58% of this cross-section of the American public considered this kind of behavior more harmful than helpful to American life. Only six percent considered it helpful, and 36% said it did not matter. It is rather disturbing to find that college professors active in unpopular causes were ranked as more harmful to American life than members of the John Birch Society, who received a vote as follows: 48% said they considered them more harmful than helpful, four percent more helpful than harmful, and 48% said they did not matter to American life as far as helping or harming is concerned. This may all be irrelevant, because universities can hardly be run on the basis of public opinion polls. What is more significant than what people think of the thinking individual is what happens to his thought, which ultimately is the more important in deciding what action takes place.

The ideas which truly matter are those which change the world. The ideas which keep the world as it is are of some importance, but only until the newer ideas come along which will make the older idea obsolete. Out of the university, the American university in particular, have come many, if not most, of the ideas which have created the civilization we have today. If this civilization is to be improved—and certainly in every aspect of life a need for improvement is evident—most of the ideas for the improvement, perhaps even for the preservation of the very structure of that civilization, will come out of the university.

So long as the university is willing to hire and keep the men who have the unconventional ideas, to keep in school the students who question the conventional wisdom, and to make public proudly and freely those ideas which do come from the university, rather than to pretend that somehow these controversial ideas have nothing to do with the university as such, the American university may be proud of itself. Once it begins to go down the road of denying in any way the opportunity for ideas, the university, as such, is dead.

28

Academe's Cult of Innovation

WILLIS N. POTTER

Professor of education, University of the Pacific. His article originally appeared
in *School and Society* on Feb. 4, 1967.

A large segment of American higher education seems to be in the grip of an
innovative fever. This current condition manifests itself in what is happening
on campuses ranging all the way from obscure, back-country colleges to the
eminent universities; in fact, innovationism plays no favorites and the educational phenomena which it creates are everywhere. It is a preoccupation with
great power, and with undoubted significance for the future of our colleges
and universities. In an American academic world avid for sensational change,
I would like to enter a plea for the other side of the case.

To form a conception of a new idea first, to translate it into action first,
to profit first from its appeal and its publicity—this purpose is causing
sleepless nights and turbulent days for the dynamic administrator. He is
hard-pressed by the urgent expectations of some of his trustees, his fellow
administrators, and a part of his faculty. How can he sleep? Or, even, how
can he find much time by day to attend to the proven, on-going aspects of
his job? He must strain for the different, the unique, something to produce
the eye-catching item of educational news.

Thus, there come into existence scores of new-type curricula, new forms
of university organization, new programs for "instant" training, and spectacular methods of attacking old problems. At best, some of these innovations
may develop into permanent and valuable elements of education, contributing to stimulating and scholarly experiences for students; at worst, the
results may be ephemeral, time-wasting, and damaging.

There is no intention of underestimating the worth, in higher education,
of self-evaluation, self-criticism, and experimentation. As a social institution,
the college cannot meet its responsibilities by standing still. But what many
colleges and universities need is some clear understanding of what their

purposes really are, and, in particular, what limitations must be set for their duties and activities. Obviously, the statements of objectives appearing in college catalogues provide little basis for such understanding, aside from the fact that they notoriously are as unread as anything in all literature.

If purposes were well-defined, and if, from year to year and from decade to decade in the life of the institution, a reasonable and discernible pattern for progress has been laid out, then there exists a valid basis for experimentation and innovation. Such a pattern need not prevent the conception of new ideas on campus; on the contrary, it can give them meaning and often facilitate, in a salutary way, their transference into fact and substance.

What are the compulsions producing a more-than-usual struggle for innovation beyond the limits of well-considered planning? One of these forces is all too evident. Forty years ago, Thomas Beer said that "governors of universities fall into their natural place behind the golden calf, bearing shovels."[1] This surely is an unkind way of describing the dilemma of the academic directorate—a dilemma basically unchanged in nature since then, but now accentuated seriously.

The need for gifts and grants to bridge the gap between tuition and endowment income and operational costs increases year by year. And newness or uniqueness of proposals in order to secure such funds, especially of the government and foundation types, demands more and more of the college staff's energies. The colleges find themselves caught in a whole series of races against time. Deadlines must be met for the hundred and one exigencies of expansion and change.

Under such conditions, the valued independence of the college or university hardly can be maintained. It might appear that the administrators and faculty can do what they wish. But such is not the case, for the "image" of the institution must be considered. That overused term, perfectly good in original concept, has done much harm when applied, or misapplied, to higher education. Many of the undesirable connotations of cheap advertising and publicity are there. The "image" must not suggest that the college is doing any less than plunging forward, taking advantage of all possibilities for self-aggrandizement, and meeting in every aspect the requirements of an up-and-coming commercial house.

An attitude of this kind, in the long run, will not succeed even from the standpoint of promotion and public concept, for the picture it presents is not one of a community of scholars engaged in a sound educational enterprise. It suggests, rather, an association of opportunistic individuals interested in exploiting the knowledge industry.

Another influence tending to produce the rage for innovation lies in the changing interests and concerns of a good many college teachers. Can we

---

[1] Thomas Beer, *The Mauve Decade* (Garden City, N.Y.: Garden City Publishing Co., 1926), p. 207.

assume that the faculty member is employed to teach? He well may conduct research and he may publish (whether he be perishable or not); but his primary reason for coming to the campus is to teach. By virtue of the competence of his teaching, along with that of his colleagues, the college can be good, or even great.

I would like to assume as a corollary that this faculty member has not been employed to serve on the traffic-and-parking committee, nor to tinker endlessly with the curriculum, nor to stand on his head in the downtown square. Others can accomplish these things more effectively and more gracefully. It is true that the college teacher, as a member of the society on campus, may have some academic chores to do. Above all, however, his obligation is to be a strong representative, both as scholar and teacher, of whatever discipline his is.

But something strange has been happening to an increasing number of college teachers. It must be a result of an element in the spirit of the times pervading the campus atmosphere. For, just as not a few students no longer feel a first interest in studying, so some of the faculty seem to have lost their drive for teaching. They have come to the belief that there is a multitude of more vital things to do.

Ferment is the word of the day. The classes are met, the lectures given, the seminars conducted, and the students counseled, but all these are rather dull anachronisms now. There must be ferment, lest the campus become an enclave of quietude. Thus, the innovation, no matter how questionable, catches the eye and, indeed, the mind and heart. The faculty member then may become a willing instrument for ill-considered academic schemes and devices which can detract from his value as an able teaching scholar.

What remedies can be proposed to moderate this hyperactivity in pursuit of the new and the unique? It seems to me that there is a single remedy—not easy, not simple, but essential to the future good health of many colleges and universities. The total faculty and administration of the institution must come to some positive and substantial understanding of its goals as an educational agency. Then, without by any means rejecting new ideas and proposals, the college should establish a compelling connection between innovations and objectives. The whole community of the campus should be eager to identify, develop, and put into action all proposals which give promise of significant, long-range values for the students. On the other hand, quick improvisation should be avoided. The academic adventure should be approached with more than a little caution. And the college must learn to recognize the factitious glamor of the academic gimmick, no matter by whom proposed, no matter how well-financed.

About 10 years ago, J. B. Priestley, commenting on the distinguished merit of certain universities, said, "It lies in their successful creation (not quite what it used to be, perhaps) of an atmosphere of disinterested scholarship, an environment in which thought itself is triumphant. . . . In such places knowledge is in the very air. Not the formal courses of instruction but the atmosphere and the surroundings enrich the student."[2] Here, indeed, is the uniqueness most to be desired and not cheaply earned. It is expensive, not so much in money as in faculty dedication and high learning, and in unusual administrative skills. I believe that such an atmosphere, wherever it can be created, is innovative and unique in a manner all its own, and that for our colleges and universities there is no better way.

[2] J. B. Priestley, *Thoughts in the Wilderness* (New York: Harper, 1957), p. 51.

29

The Comprehensive American College: A Forecast

STEPHEN E. EPLER

President, Ohlone College. At the time his article originally appeared in *School and Society* (July 9, 1955), he was Director of Day Programs, Portland State Extension Center, Oregon State System of Higher Education.

The next major development in free public education may be the comprehensive American college. This college, with a variety of programs for serving the diversified needs and abilities of students, would serve the majority of the 18–21 year olds as the high school now serves the 14–17-year-old group.

Education for all is a democratic tradition in the United States. Over 100 years ago, Alexis de Tocqueville stated, "It cannot be doubted that in the United States the instruction of the people powerfully contributes to the support of the democratic republic."[1] Since 1900, the high school has become an accepted part of the nation's education program for its youth, and college enrollments have increased tenfold. Before 1999, it is probable the majority of all American youth will finish four years of college.

Our rising level of civilization will require and support a mass educational program longer than our present 12 years. This will challenge American public education to develop post-high-school programs which will assist the individual to be a better citizen and to be better equipped for his life work.

The comprehensive American college should provide the variety needed to serve all American youth, not just the 50% recommended by the President's Commission on Higher Education (1947). This college of 1999 would include the best of our present post-high-school programs. For example, technical institute type of work will be available in many more areas for those who want to combine college work and on-the-job experience.

[1] "Democracy in America," Vol. I, p. 329 (Vintage edition, 1954).

New developments in science and other areas will bring curriculum changes. A higher civilization with more generous support of education will improve instruction.

Most of the youth of the future will live at home while attending college as they did when attending grade school and high school. Transportation developments and strategic locations will permit the comprehensive American college to have an enrollment of sufficient size to provide the diversity of faculty, curriculum, and facilities the students need. The enrollment considered a desirable minimum may prove to be 500, 1,000, or even 2,000.

How will the development of the comprehensive American college affect the existing types of post-high-school education? The bulk of the students in the comprehensive American college probably will come from the group corresponding to the 75% of college-age youth not now enrolled in higher education. More professional fields will follow the lead of medicine and theology and begin professional training on the post-college level. The church-related colleges will continue to serve their particular clienteles as will other private colleges with their unique missions which led to their establishment and continued support.

All existing phases of American higher education can be expected to contribute some elements to the development of the comprehensive American college of the future, but the public junior college and the urban university will probably exert more influence. Both serve local students and are sensitive to community needs.

In the past 50 years, the average amount of formal schooling has increased from less than eight to nearly 12. It does not seem unreasonable to expect a continued development of American civilization and a corresponding expansion of our educational system which would provide the average citizens with as much as 16 years of schooling.

30

The Future of the Private University

JOHN T. RETTALIATA

President, Illinois Institute of Technology. His article originally appeared in *School and Society* on Oct. 29, 1966.

In an age which calls for the utmost development of our educational resources, we must take a fresh look at all aspects of American education—including our traditional reliance upon the leadership of the private university. Friends of the private institutions quite rightly uphold them as standard-bearers of excellence and bulwarks against government domination. Our faith in the ability of such institutions to serve these purposes in times of enormous problems and pressures must be based upon a clear understanding of their sources of internal strength and vitality.

It is facile to say that the mass job of higher education today belongs to the publicly-supported institution and the selective job to the private institution. While public institutions, offering tax-assisted tuition rates, are most crucially affected by the problem of numbers, private colleges and universities are sharing also in the responsibility for serving more students.

The real strength and unique capability of the private university in our modern society lies in the way it is structured and financed, and in the effect of the following factors:

1. The governing bodies of major private universities constitute a remarkable cross section of the nation's business and professional leadership. Voluntary trusteeship brings this leadership into an absolutely unique relationship to higher education. No other system of citizen responsibility presents as strong a challenge to dedicated participation.

2. Gift support programs, necessary for the maintenance and development of a private university, link the institution with a constituency ranging from alumni to heads of national corporations and philanthropic foundations and from parents of students to interested people in the community with a concern for education. Every donor shares an investor's interest in what the institution is doing.

3. The private university, in turn, is subject to the moral and legal requirements of good stewardship which such investor relationships demand.

4. Sound fiscal management and continual evaluation of results achieved are encouraged by these relationships and requirements.

5. Additionally, the private university is subject to the external evaluation placed upon it by faculty and students in the "educational market place." Its very survival depends on earned recognition.

6. Finally, the responsibilities which build the sinews of the private university are matched by an unusual degree of freedom in the shaping of its purposes and goals. It is vital for a university to be sensitive to the needs of its constituencies and of society at large. But to be worthy of its role, it must act as well as react; it must lead as well as respond. In its freedom to decide what it shall be, the private university has an opportunity to provide directions for higher education which are greatly needed in an age when sheer proliferation tends to obscure the very meaning of the university concept.

The question frequently is raised as to whether gift support can be maintained on a sufficiently high level to perpetuate truly independent institutions of university scope. Part of the answer lies in clearly defining the areas in which the institution proposes to justify its existence. Institutions that can do this have been conspicuously successful in attracting support from private sources in amounts which even a decade ago might have seemed unrealistic. On the other hand, it seems unlikely that there is enough money, either public or private, to sustain a university that wishes to be all things to all men.

In regard to securing financial support, it is both hopeful and challenging to note the increasing sophistication of business leadership concerning education. The extent to which it is necessary to build a case in support of a request for a corporate grant imposes a new burden on university administration, but one which we should welcome. The private university must stake its future upon the proposition that an informed constituency will put its money on the independent decision-making process which this kind of university is designed to cultivate in its students and faculty and to exemplify in its programs and practices.

31

Locksley Hall: A College for the Future

ROBERT M. HUTCHINS

Chairman of the Board, Fund for the Republic. His article originally appeared in *School and Society* on Sept. 12, 1959, and was based on an address to the Conference on the Shape of a College for the Future, Miami University, April 18, 1959.

I have thought that instead of presenting an article of my own, I might offer here the annual report of the Chairman of the Faculty of Locksley Hall for the year 1988-89.

The report begins:

To the Board of Visitors of Locksley Hall:

As the elected representative of the faculty, I have the honor to submit its report for the year 1988-89. At this time, which marks the expiration of my five-year term and the end of the first 25 years of the College, it seems appropriate to review the history of the College since its foundation. This will necessarily involve some account of the origins and progress of the state of Rancho del Rey.

As is well known, the state of Rancho del Rey originated in the gift to the public by the owners of the King Ranch in Texas of 100,000 square miles. The reason for the gift was that the owners of the ranch had become convinced that the development of people was more important than that of animals. They therefore determined to provide a refuge for those who could not face the prospect of having their children go through the American educational system, but who did not wish to secede from the Union. Two conditions were attached to the gift. First, the land was to be organized into a state in accordance with the provisions of the treaty between the Republic of Texas and the United States. Second, American women of child-bearing age who had children under 12 were to have priority in gaining entrance to and owning land in the new state. Those who were married were permitted to bring their husbands with them if they wished.

The financial resources of the donors were such that they easily persuaded the legislature of Texas to see the merits of their plan, and since both houses of Congress had for many years been controlled by residents of Texas, no difficulty was experienced in Washington. President Stevenson signed the measure on Christmas Day, 1964, and Rancho del Rey was admitted to the Union on January 1, 1965. Immigration began at dawn the next day, and our state, which was formerly occupied by a few cowboys and a couple of million cattle, is now the most densely populated in the Union, having passed Rhode Island in 1975. As loyal Americans we hope that the depopulation that has taken place in other states will prove to be only temporary.

It cannot be too often emphasized that Locksley Hall is only one unit in the educational system of Rancho del Rey and that its dependence on the other units in the system is complete. For example, the average student at Locksley Hall finishes his formal liberal education at the age of 18. This would not be possible in the three years ordinarily spent here if it were not for the organization of the six-year elementary schools and three-year high schools of this state. On the other hand, 50% of our graduates go on to the University, and this would not be possible if it were not for the recognition by the University that liberal education is the best preparation for professional study and research. If I may be pardoned a personal word, I may say that one of the most moving experiences of my life was that day in 1967 on which the Cosmological Faculty of the University, at the insistence of the sub-faculty in medicine, voted down special requirements in mathematics and science for entrance to medical work and decided to admit applicants on the basis of their fulfillment of the requirements of Locksley Hall in liberal education.

First, then, Locksley Hall has flourished because of the excellence of the educational system of which it is a part. A second reason for its success is that there never has been any doubt about its own role in the system. It is devoted solely to liberal education, the education that every citizen ought to have. In the schools and colleges of Rancho del Rey vocational training is unknown. The constant acceleration of technology since the '50's and the steady reduction in the working week to the present 20 hours have made direct preparation for earning a living in the educational system an obvious absurdity. In this state young people are trained for jobs on the job. The object of the educational system is to teach them what they cannot learn on the job—how to be citizens and human beings. As the Commanding Officer of the United Nations Police Force, Chief John Eisenhower, has nobly said, "The one certain calling is citizenship; the one certain destiny is manhood."

Locksley Hall has no departments. All members of the faculty are expected to be able to give instruction in all the subjects studied in the College. It has, however, three divisions. In addition to the division devoted to the instruction of youth, it has a division for the preparation of teachers and one for the education of adults.

Among the many blessings conferred upon us by the Founding Fathers of Rancho del Rey, the constitutional prohibition against academic degrees must come high on the list. The statutory prohibition of schools of education has proved equally valuable. The two together have meant that in this state it has been possible to educate teachers. In the early days there were fears of a teacher shortage; but they did not materialize. Every intelligent man and woman teaching in the United States started for Rancho del Rey as soon as the state was opened up to settlement. In the effort to establish their priority, many of these teachers adopted children under 12, and I regret to say that one distinguished male scholar from Columbia was detected at the border disguised as a pregnant woman. Candor compels me to add that teachers' salaries in Rancho del Rey have always been somewhat higher than elsewhere. This is because of the constitutional provision known as the General Motors Index, which stipulates that the compensation of teachers must always be equal to that of junior executives in that great corporation.

A powerful inducement to teachers to join the faculty of Locksley Hall is the complete independence and freedom that we enjoy. Locksley Hall has no president and no board of trustees. The Board of Visitors has no power; the faculty of the College has the legal as well as the moral responsibility for its management. The faculty is aware, however, that all bodies of privileged persons inevitably tend to deteriorate and therefore welcomes the public and private criticism that the Board has lavished upon it in the last 25 years. The faculty knows that its rejection of many of the recommendations of the Board would have provoked, in lesser men, some feelings of resentment. The principle that management is the function of the faculty and criticism the function of the Board is now established, and all parties are agreed that it must remain forever inviolate.

It must be added that the freedom we enjoy is accompanied by a responsibility we did not expect. It is very convenient to have somebody else to blame. Here at Locksley Hall we of the faculty can blame nobody but ourselves. We cannot evade the consequences of our weakness and self-seeking by relying on the President or the Trustees to save us from them, and we are denied the consolation of attributing whatever anybody in or out of the College does not like about it to the arrogance of the administration and the stupidity of the Board. In the early years of the College some of my older brethren, who had been brought up under a different system, felt so un-comfortable when called upon to cast votes for which they would be held responsible that they echoed the cry of the ancient Israelites, "Give us a King to rule over us." Fortunately, wiser counsels prevailed. We have been much assisted by the fact that we have no departments and no academic ranks. These fruitful sources of group bickering and individual animosity being absent, we have been able to think for an increasing part of the time when we are together about what is good for the College and for the community. But it is no use denying that the path has been a hard one. We record again our gratitude to the Board of Visitors for helping us to be better than we otherwise would have been.

The number of teachers required in Rancho del Rey was small in proportion to the population because the number of subjects taught was somewhat less than a third of the number taught in other states. My great predecessor, the first Chairman of the Faculty, had emblazoned on the walls of the senior common room as a constant reminder to us all the words of Sir Richard Livingstone: "The good schoolmaster is known by the number of valuable subjects he declines to teach." The excellence of the elementary and secondary schools and the fact that students do not come to us until they have passed the examinations in these schools mean that Locksley Hall never has had to offer remedial work in Greek or Latin, to say nothing of mathematics or English. The students arrive at our gates prepared to go on with these subjects and to add to them the exploration of the world of ideas, which is, of course, their main business with us. These limitations on the number of subjects taught have made possible the level of teachers' salaries that the General Motors Index requires.

Of course, a good deal of re-training was necessary to permit our educational system to absorb the teaching immigrants to whom I have referred. Most of them never had had any liberal education. By the use of films, television (open and closed circuit), and the teaching machines invented by B. F. Skinner, we were able to expedite this process.

Today prospective teachers at Locksley Hall get a liberal education. They then go on to the University to study one or more of the three fields to which the University confines itself—theology, cosmology, and law. Thereafter, they work here as apprentice teachers with the more experienced members of the staff. Every seminar and discussion group at Locksley Hall has two teachers—a senior and a junior member of the faculty. The teachers learn to teach by teaching.

The constitutional prohibition of academic degrees has had one incidental benefit: commencement exercises are unknown in Rancho del Rey. At no time, therefore, is a citizen of this state given the impression that he has completed his education. The state is a community learning together, and the citizen is expected to keep on learning throughout his life. This is why the curriculum of Locksley Hall could remain simple and clear: the College has been under no pressure to teach every young student everything that he might need to know at later stages of his career. The aim of the College is to teach the student what he needs to know in order to keep on learning, to awaken his interest in continued learning, and to train him in the habits that will help him to learn whatever he wants to learn.

Locksley Hall is the realization of the ambition that Woodrow Wilson expressed just 80 years ago. He said, "Here is the key to the whole matter: the object of the college . . . is not scholarship . . . but the intellectual and spiritual life. Its life and discipline are meant to be a process of preparation, not a process of information. By the intellectual and spiritual life I mean the life which enables the mind to comprehend and make proper use of the modern world and all its opportunities. The object of a liberal training is not learning, but discipline and the enlightenment of the mind. . . . What we should seek to impart in our colleges, therefore, is not so much learning as the spirit of learning. You can impart that to young men; and you can impart it to them in the three or four years at your disposal." Having acquired this spirit, the 50% of our graduates who do not go on to the University are expected, like the other citizens of this state, to enroll in discussion groups in which their intellectual interests and capacities may develop. The faculty of Locksley Hall organizes such groups for adults of this community who wish to continue their liberal education.

In the educational system of Rancho del Rey, time-serving and the accumulation of credits are unknown. Goals are set up for the students to reach. The examinations determine whether or not he has reached them. The student may present himself for the examinations whenever he is ready to do so. If he fails, he may take them again. The chronological age of students and what used to be called their "adjustment to the group" are matters of supreme indifference to everybody, including the student himself and his contemporaries. I have said that in Rancho del Rey the elementary school takes six years and the high school and the college three years each. But these are statements of averages. The goals having been set by the teaching staff, it was found that in the ordinary case six years of instruction prepared the pupil for the examinations of the elementary schools, three years for the high schools, and three years more for the college. As far as Locksley Hall is concerned, 10% of our students graduate in less than three years, and 10% in more. Eighty percent take the average time.

The goal that was set for the students of Locksley Hall was the acquisition of that education which in the opinion of the faculty was necessary for a free man in a free society. It cannot be too strongly insisted that the educational program of Locksley Hall was designed for everybody and that experience has shown that it can be mastered by everybody, though at different rates of speed. If there is one thing that the history of Locksley Hall demonstrates, it is that the ancient American doctrine that the course of study must be trivial and the life of the student frivolous because most young people cannot be interested in anything important is as fallacious as it was popular. The Latin motto of the Students' Association of Locksley Hall is *sero sed serio*—we may be young, but we are in earnest.

All citizens of Rancho del Rey are expected to achieve the education that is offered by Locksley Hall. Although the intellectual attainments of the people of this state are clearly higher than those of any other, there is no evidence that their native capacities exceed those of persons born elsewhere. Since the founding of this country, experience everywhere has shown that the young American will respond to the best that can be offered him. The reason he has been offered in some places less than the best is that his elders do not want to take the trouble to find out what the best is or to find out how it may be effectively offered. We have known, moreover, since the time of Plato that what is honored in a country will be cultivated there. The state of Rancho del Rey was established in honor of the human mind. It was to be a community learning together. The culture of this state, therefore, supports at every point the serious intellectual purpose of the educational system of this state.

To descend to a more practical level, consider, if you will, the effect upon the interests and, hence, upon the development of the young of a system in which everybody has studied or is studying the same things and has a common language and a common stock of ideas. At Locksley Hall, for example, the faculty and all the students have followed or are following the same prescribed curriculum and are discussing the issues it raises throughout their waking hours. The multiplication of the power of the individual through the support of the academic community is added to the multiplication of this power that comes from the support of the larger community outside. We are perfectly prepared to believe that students who have succeeded with us would have failed elsewhere. We suggest, as Edward Gibbon did long ago, that like conditions produce like effects.

The conditions obtaining in Rancho del Rey have made it, as everybody knows, the cultural center of the world. The head of the Chinese delegation to the United Nations remarked last year that Peking even today had not achieved the beauty, serenity, and vitality of our capital, and the President of Greece has applied to our state the words in which Pericles described his native city. The principal newspapers, publishing houses, magazines, dramatic groups, film studios, and television networks now have their headquarters here. The leading artists, writers, musicians, scientists, and scholars of the world now reside among us.

But it would be selfish of us to be concerned only with the happiness of our own state. In every walk of life the citizens of Rancho del Rey and the graduates of Locksley Hall—the oldest of whom are now about 40—are making a world-wide contribution. It often has been remarked that it is fortunate the graduates of Locksley Hall are not much interested in making money, because their equipment is such that if they wanted to, they would make all the money there was. In the professions, in politics, and in business they have distinguished themselves, earning the affection of their alma mater and the admiration of their fellow citizens.

The period through which we lived in the '40's, '50's, and early '60's of this century is now commonly called the Age of Illusion. It was a period in which things were not what they seemed, or at least not what we said they were. At this epoch Americans were in the habit of saying one thing and believing another and thinking one thing and doing another. Numerous efforts were made to repeal the Law of Contradiction. The fact was that our situation had changed too fast for our ideas. The result was that we could offer no rational explanation for much that we did. For example, we had an economic theory built on the mindless mechanism of the market and a political theory based on the conception of the night watchman state. When these theories appeared inapplicable and unworkable in an advanced industrial society, we had no guide to intelligent action. The educational system of those days was suitable to the production of consumers, jobholders, objects of propaganda, and statistical units. The universities were not centers of independent thought. They appeared designed for vocational certification and highly specialized research. In their never-ending quest for money, they felt compelled to sell themselves to the highest bidder. Instead of enlightening the society, particularly about its own shortcomings, they flattered it. Hence, they flattered and perpetuated its illusions.

The era that now seems to be dawning will be called, we hope, the Age of Reason. The change began with the end of the Cold War and the transfer of all weapons to the United Nations 15 years ago. That made it possible for us to begin to think what we were doing and to reflect at last in a rational way about how we might use our resources for the benefit of our fellow citizens in America and throughout the world. The change has been accelerated by the example of the State of Rancho del Rey and by the work of its people. In this change, Locksley Hall is proud to have played a modest part.

PART II

The Administration

From Leadership to Collective Participation

32

Leadership in Higher Education

EDGAR C. CUMINGS

Director of Community Services, Economic Opportunity Commission, San Jose, Calif. At the time his article originally appeared in *School and Society* (Sept. 28, 1957), he was Director of Education, American Social Hygiene Association.

The decline in leadership in higher education may be attributed, in part, to the methods employed by boards of trustees in selecting their new leaders and to the changes in the kinds of people chosen. The primary cause of these changes has been the growing emphasis placed on the fund-raising ability of the potential president. Trustees seem to assume more and more that only a person with a business or industrial background can possibly extract money from corporations. How wrong they are can be seen from the example of Harvard University, which has achieved a degree of success in keeping the larder full but has not yet resorted to the practice of choosing a tycoon or a retired admiral as president.

It is my belief that the business-type or military-type executive has been an unsuccessful president, all things considered. It is not sufficient to cite facts and figures which point to the amount of money raised by such leaders. A college can be fully solvent financially and still deteriorate educationally if trustees and others regard it as a business venture instead of what it actually is—an educational institution with business elements attached to it.

Another tendency of college and university trustees is to appoint an outstanding secondary-school principal or superintendent of schools as president. This has not occurred often, but it has happened too frequently to give one a comfortable feeling. It has happened recently, for example, in at least two of our largest universities.

While a schoolman or professional educationist occasionally will grasp the meaning of higher education and become a good leader, too often such a person enters upon his position without the respect of his faculty members and is never successful in gaining this respect, which is necessary for ultimate success. The typical faculty member, rightly or wrongly, has a healthy disdain for the professional educationist, a disdain which frequently is matched by that of the professional for the "content" people on our faculties. A pathetic example of the outcome in terms of low institutional morale can be seen at present in one of our state universities. Here, according to published reports, the chief executive is a professional educationist with an autocratic bent of mind who is unable to comprehend the fact that any university belies its name if it is not a center of intellectual controversy and a haven for intellectual freedom. And yet, this same university is regarded by many as having made great progress because of additional financial support, more buildings, and similar material developments.

There is, too, the continuing custom of appointing ministers to presidential chairs. Doubtless, at one time in the history of higher education, there was considerable justification for this practice. That this custom should be continued for the sake of tradition, and little else, appears somewhat indefensible. Presumably, ministers are still becoming college presidents because of the belief of faculty members and trustees that the presence of a minister in the highest campus office will assure the cultivation of a Christian education and will preserve the institution for the supporting (?) church constituency. The fact is that some of the colleges which long ago gave up their ministerial presidents and their church affiliations have stronger and more thoroughgoing religious programs on their campuses than many institutions which are still religiously affiliated.

There is little basis for the supposition that an ex-minister will make a good college president. He may make a good speaker, in the popular sense, and he may make a good promoter and fund-raiser, but he is unlikely to have too much awareness of what a higher education entails. Some ministers, in fact, look upon a college as though it were still a quasi-seminary, or as if its chief reason for existence were religious training rather than the inculcation of knowledge. In addition, most ministers have had no experience with congregations which could be remotely compared with the unique (and frequently uncanny) legislative methods of the average college faculty.

Faculty members are a different breed. They have been taught to think, to question, and to discuss freely and openly. They have traded the opportunity for great financial rewards for a degree of security, a relatively pleasant way of life, and the world of the intellect. They are not easy to handle, even for one who has grown up in their own ranks and who has become a dean or president. He may understand them and their ways, but it is the gifted administrator who can overlook their personal and curricular foibles and give them the kind of leadership they want and deserve.

It is difficult, therefore, for an executive from an unrelated field to enter an educational institution and come to any very satisfactory relationship with his faculty. If he does not regard faculty members as "queer ducks" or as cantankerous individualists, he is likely to suffer the pangs of unbearable impatience over what he considers to be the circumlocutory methods employed by faculties in arriving at decisions.

In many instances, such executives enter upon their jobs with the feeling that the faculty members are the employees of the college or university and its board of trustees. Some of these presidents never learn until it is too late that the faculty and students *are* the university, that a university is a community of scholars—and rather individualistic scholars, at that.

Those trustees who let their eyes wander from the central educational task of a college in choosing an executive make a grievous blunder. All the endowment in the world and the most beautiful buildings are unlikely to obscure the fact that an institution is no better than its educational leadership and the faculty and students which this leadership has been able to assemble.

Another factor which has affected our educational leadership is confusion over the dictum of "equality of opportunity." Originally this phrase was created as a demonstration of the necessity for educational democracy in a democratic society. Since we were all created "free and equal" under God, we should all have equal opportunity. I subscribe to this theory, but I also submit that it has suffered in the hands of those who have distorted it to mean something quite different.

There are, for instance, college and university presidents—particularly those who head public institutions—who maintain that everyone can feel free to apply for admission to their institutions. I do not argue with this doctrine, either, although it contains some obvious weaknesses. To mention only one, it is debatable whether it is wise and charitable for a state university to admit any high-school graduate, including those with a clear lack of ability to cope with a higher education, when the chances for success are remote. While a few students of this type may graduate, many more will suffer failure and will recognize that their post-high-school education should have been of a different sort. In addition, many of our state universities are now so cluttered with mediocre students that the time of the dean's office is taken up primarily with them instead of with students who could profit from special handling of a different kind.

Confusion in this area exists because it is not clearly stated that there shall be equality of opportunity for those who can qualify for a higher education. This statement in no way nullifies democratic procedures, nor does it establish the cult of the elite. No university should accept a student who obviously does not have the qualifications for a higher education.

One result of the acceptance of anybody and everybody has been a deterioration in the standards of some institutions. If most high-school graduates are ultimately going on to college—and the percentage is rising every year—then the standards of our higher educational system are bound to suffer, just as the standards of our secondary schools have suffered because of their legal necessity to attempt to educate the masses.

The public institutions, in particular, have tried to solve this dilemma by offering such a wide variety of curricula that even the intellectually mediocre student is able to obtain some kind of a degree. It is difficult to reconcile the practice of permitting hordes of students to major in, say, physical education or horticulture with the exacting education other students are required to obtain in some of our better institutions. And yet, both kinds of students obtain degrees which have virtually the same market value. The chief difference, unlikely to be generally recognized in our present-day society, is that one kind of student has obtained a genuine higher education, while the other kind has what must be called a watered-down degree.

The ultimate question is, of course, what constitutes a higher education in this country. In the face of almost constant criticism, in several fields, of the great lack of education in many of our college graduates, we continue to dilute our offerings, too often with the pious feeling that more educational opportunity for everybody equals a better educational system. Perhaps we should take stock of our boast that our educational system is the best in the world, merely because more and more young people are getting "educated." If this country now suffers from a lack of real leadership, as we are told by many thoughtful critics, it is conceivable that the dilution of our educational system must bear a share of the blame. And the leaders of this educational system must be held responsible both for the dilution and for failing to give to our society the kind of far-sighted leadership needed to sustain and improve our people and our land.

33

Presidential Leadership in Academe

ARCHIE R. DYKES

American Council on Education Fellow, University of Illinois. His article originally appeared in *School and Society* on April 1, 1967.

It frequently is observed that there is a notable absence of strong, directive leadership from the presidential offices in the contemporary world of higher learning. Some say that, because of the absence of such leadership, higher education is adrift, muddling along without any clear sense of direction. Only peripheral influence is assigned that legendary repository of power—the office of the president. Many lament that today's presidential office-holders do not compare with the great presidents of the past—the Eliots, Harpers, Gilmans, and Whites—who not only molded in an intimate way their own institutions, but left an indelible mark on American higher education generally.

Such an assessment of presidential leadership results from an inadequate understanding of the world in which today's presidents must labor. The circumstances which today affect executive leadership in higher learning bear little resemblance to those of the past and dictate radically different behavior from those who occupy presidential offices. It is clear that the circumstances which enabled strong, forceful, and quite autocratic presidential leadership to flourish, which made it possible for earlier leaders to shape unilaterally higher learning with bold, imaginative strokes, are no more. Those who occupy academic presidencies today work in a profoundly different milieu; one that has as its dominant characteristics effective constraint on unilateral action from *any source* and a delicately balanced system of countervailing power. The stereotype of the college or university president as a man of great power, exercising large, independent, and unchallenged authority in managing the institution over which he presides, now belongs to history.

Many developments have contributed to the changed nature of presidential leadership in higher learning. We will discuss three of the more important of these. Perhaps the exposition will contribute in some measure to an improved understanding of and appreciation for the character of academic leadership today.

When colleges and universities were small, when internal complexity was non-existent, and when teaching and research were carried on under relatively simple conditions, a strong personality in the presidential office could be and usually was the dominant force on the campus. The lines of influence between the president and the workaday world of the institution were direct and strong. Countervailing forces or effective restraints on presidential power were, by today's standards, almost non-existent. Moreover, the social and cultural temper of the times lent legitimacy to strong, directive leadership, generously sprinkled with authoritarianism. When the president spoke, he was listened to; when he decided, his decision largely went unquestioned. Thus, when Pres. Charles W. Eliot of Harvard was asked by a faculty member why the faculty had to accommodate itself to so many changes, he could answer simply, "There is a new president."[1]

By contrast, consider the presidential officeholder today. The colleges and universities have changed dramatically; not only are they larger and more complex, they also encompass competing sources of power and influence, all tightly tensed with an intricate system of checks and balances. They are, as Rudolph noted, characterized by a "delicate balance of interests, a polite tug of war."[2] No one source of power can act effectively without approval or compliance from others, and the necessary approval or compliance can be secured effectively only through persuasion, never by coercion. As now ex-Pres. Clark Kerr of the University of California aptly commented, "there are more elements to conciliate, fewer in a position to be led."[3]

Presidential authority in the contemporary world of higher education is dispersed and tempered by countervailing forces. The president who will make his influence felt must do so through persuasion, consultation, and suggestion. Instead of the charismatic, autocratic leadership qualities of an Eliot, the conditions surrounding the academic presidency today require men with talent for getting things done collectively—men who can secure consensus through consultation and mediation. But this does not mean that leadership cannot be exercised. The relentless pursuing of important goals and objectives through the processes of consultation, persuasion, and mediation can mold the shape of a college or a university just as effectively, if not as dramatically, as the autocratic leadership of another day. Given the present conditions in higher learning, it is in this muted, more modest, and administratively more demanding style of leadership that the hope lies for maintaining the viability of higher education in these times of rapid change.

[1] Frederick Rudolph, *The American College and University* (New York: Knopf, 1962), p. 291.
[2] *Ibid.*, p. 423.
[3] Clark Kerr, *The Uses of the University* (Cambridge: Harvard University Press, 1963), p. 34.

There are two kinds of authority which may be exercised in an organization: collegial and hierarchical. In the days of the "great presidents," hierarchical authority was supreme. (Lord Bryce spoke of the almost monarchical position which the college president occupied towards the professors and the students in the early years of the present century.4) Authority derived from position, and the top position was the office of president. In such a setting, the incumbents of presidential offices could and did rule in a high-handed fashion. Eliot's reply to the questioning faculty member has been cited. His successor, Pres. A. Lawrence Lowell, thought the president should conceive a plan for the university and, while suggestions from the faculty should be welcomed, the basic elements of the plan should not be subject to interference.5 A professional contemporary of Eliot and Lowell remarked on the seemingly free rein of the president to alter the fundamental character of Harvard: "To such an extent is the university the plaything of its president."6 The image of the president as a molder and maker of institutions hardly could be clearer.

But high-handed administration based on hierarchical authority already was under attack. "The argument for giving a free hand to the president is that this is the way to get things done," complained Prof. Cattell of Columbia. "It should be remembered, however," he warned, "that it is quite as important—and this holds especially true in the university—not to do the wrong thing as it is to do the right thing." He went on to say that "in a democracy leaders are the men we follow, not the men who drive us. . . . The trouble in the case of the university president is that he is not a leader, but a boss."7

As hierarchical authority increasingly became inapplicable in academe, collegial authority became more relevant. Concurrent with the growing fractionation and subsequent specialization of the scholarly disciplines, authority became more a matter of expertise and competence than of position. Inevitably, the professoriate more strenuously questioned the prevailing arrangements for academic administration, resting as they did on the principle of hierarchical authority, and claimed for itself a larger role in administration and governance. "The faculties, each for itself, should control appointments of professors and instructors; should determine all matters concerning curricula; should decide questions as to expansion or contraction of work; should have the final word respecting internal arrangements of

4 James Bryce, *The American Commonwealth,* new edition, vol. II (New York: Macmillan, 1913), p. 718.
5 A. Lawrence Lowell, *What A University President Has Learned* (New York: Macmillan, 1938), pp. 3, 12.
6 "J. McKeen Cattell on Reforming University Control, 1913," in Richard Hofstadter and Wilson Smith, eds., *American Higher Education; A Documentary History,* vol. II (Chicago: University of Chicago Press, 1961), p. 801.
7 *Ibid.,* p. 788.

buildings—in short should be the supreme authority in all matters directly affecting the educational work."[8]

Today, the role of the faculty in governance is an influential one in almost all colleges and universities worthy of the name. Riding a wave of increasing respect for expertise and reinforced by the professionalization of the academic disciplines, the professoriate increasingly has become independent. Pre-eminently expert and with special knowledge its stock in trade, autonomy is the hallmark of today's faculty. The things most valued in the cosmopolitan world of academe are status in one's discipline and respect from one's peers. These no administration can give or take away; they stand independent of the official institutional authority structure.

Thus, responsiveness to administrative or hierarchical authority is reduced and collegial authority is controlling increasingly. Given such a condition, the ability of a president unilaterally to assume leadership and make of his institution what he will is constrained greatly. And, as Riesman has pointed out, "no great revolutionary figure is likely to appear."[9]

Students of administration and organization long have maintained that clearly understood and agreed-upon goals are essential if any enterprise is to be administered effectively. Without goals which can be related meaningfully to the individual task of those who have membership in an organization, it is difficult to bring the disparate parts together for the common good. The result is a loss of singleness of purpose, imbalance within the enterprise, and a tendency to drift aimlessly, thus seriously reducing the ability of the enterprise to serve the purposes for which it exists.

In an earlier day, when institutions of higher education were smaller and less complex, when their functions were less diverse and better defined, and when the demands placed upon them were far more limited, the question of goals and purposes did not pose a serious problem. The members of the faculty knew what the goals of the institution were; a common interest in teaching bound personal and institutional goals together. A single animating purpose gave direction and coherence to the efforts of the faculty, individually and collectively.

But circumstances have changed in the day of the multiversity. Teaching is less central to the interests of the faculty and the institution; research has become more important. The scholarly disciplines have been fractionalized and professionalized. The professor has become a specialist. Professorial orientation is less to the *place* where the professor works and more to the far-flung disciplinary group. Instead of common goals, there are many diverse goals, some in contradiction to others, but all laying claim to professorial loyalties. Unlike its predecessor of an earlier era, rarely does the large, multipurpose college or university manifest a clear, generally understood

[8] "An Academic Scientist's Plea for More Efficient University Control, 1902," in *ibid.*, p. 769.
[9] David Riesman, *Constraint and Variety in American Education* (Lincoln: University of Nebraska Press, 1956), p. 22.

set of goals or purposes. As Corson has noted, "The American college or university exists to serve not a single purpose, but several. It exists to instruct students, . . . to carry on research, . . . to provide a variety of student services, . . . and . . . to provide a wide range of community services. . . . The task of gaining consensus on what an institution shall be and how it should carry on its work is made difficult by this broad range of activities, by the various interests of many specialists, by the relative independence of many of the activities that are carried on. . . ."[10]

Such is the character of the institutions which college and university presidents must now administer. This welter of diversity and complexity adds to the difficulty of presidential leadership. In such a milieu, shared concerns and common interests are difficult to come by; loyalty and commitment to common goals even more so. "It has become a commonplace to observe," lamented one student of academic government, "that most of our large university organizations are held together by little more than a name, a lay board of trustees, an academically remote figure called a president, and a common concern for the power plant."[11] Clearly, a unifying mission is not a pervasive characteristic of the contemporary college or university. And this fact adds immeasurably to the burden of presidential leadership.

Central to this discussion has been the contention that conditions peculiar to the contemporary world of higher learning require a style of presidential leadership radically different from that of an earlier day, and, moreover, that the widespread inclination to denigrate the leadership of today's presidential office-holders is unjust. In order to understand or assess presidential leadership in the present era, we first must know something of the conditions under which the president labors.

The great presidents of the past were great because their leadership styles were consonant with the age in which they lived and with the character of the colleges and universities which they headed. Today, their autocratic tendencies would be resisted fiercely.

But, if the charismatic, autocratic style of leadership is unsuited for the present, this does not mean that leadership is at an end. Rather, it means it must be exercised in keeping with the characteristics and the cultural expectations of the present; it must be manifested in less dramatic, less romantic, and more muted form. But, if the president has a strong will to lead and is willing to commit himself and his energies to that objective, he indeed can be an educational leader, indeed can play a decisive role in formulating the goals and objectives of his institution and in steering the institution towards them. But it probably will not be said of his college or university, "here is the lengthened shadow of a great man."

[10] John J. Corson, *Governance of Colleges and Universities* (New York: McGraw-Hill, 1960), pp. 19-20.
[11] Edward H. Litchfield, "The University: A Congeries or an Organic Whole?" *AAUP Bulletin*, 45:375, September, 1959.

The College Presidency

WILLIAM W. BRICKMAN

Professor of educational history and comparative education, Graduate School of Education, University of Pennsylvania, and editor of *School and Society*. His article originally appeared in *School and Society* on Nov. 18, 1961.

Resignations and involuntary retirements of college and university presidents seem to have become more frequent in recent years. For some executives, the position, with its multifarious duties, many of them having little direct connection with the basic mission of higher education, has become excessively onerous, spirit-crushing, and body-weakening. Others have lamented the lack of time to devote to educational problems, to research, or even to read at will. In short, what appears to be a position of glamor and influence turns out in many cases to be a bore and a man-killer.

The refusal of outstanding individuals to continue as presidents should give anyone concerned with higher education sufficient reason to reflect upon the entire system of college and university administration. Perhaps a fundamental revision should be considered.

The system of selecting university presidents is undoubtedly rooted in historical, ideological, economic, and other factors. Since it is evident that the presidency has become more of a social, diplomatic, financial, and administrative post than one of scholarly and educational leadership, it is justifiable to inquire if a change is in order at this time. If education is to be worthy of the adjective "higher," then it seems that its destiny ought to be handed over to those who really exemplify the ideals for which it stands. If the university aims at a combination of teaching, scholarship, and public service, it would seem that its scholars should direct its functions and activities.

This is hardly a radical suggestion. The rector of European universities has been drawn traditionally from among the professors. The position generally rotated each year and the incumbent was *primus inter pares*. A permanent staff of experienced administrators and financial officers took care of the various day-by-day details of running the institutions. The universities remained first and foremost an educational organization—to the students, professors, and the public.

In all probability, there will be no frantic rush to reform the administrative setup in American higher education. Many of those associated with or interested in colleges and universities will doubtless devise reasons for not adopting a practice which apparently has been satisfactory a long time in Europe. What should not be forgotten, however, is that a system whereby a president is elected by the faculty represents actual democracy in education, a procedure which has persisted more in publications than in practice. Further, a chief executive does not give up his scholarly and intellectual interests, but for a year or two at the most becomes relatively unproductive. This is a rather small price for the freedom of keeping the university perpetually under the direction of the persons who make it what it is.

There are other possibilities of making the presidency a more palatable professional position, assuming that the European tradition is not adopted. Let the presidents be scholar-teachers and let them be given by the boards of trustees sufficient encouragement, time, and recompense to continue their intellectual labors. Such executives will appreciate the fundamental problems of the university and will have enough insight to be able to work together with a faculty of peers. Presidential assistants and associates should be appointed to take over many of the variegated and time-consuming duties of the president.

A faculty, deans, and a president dedicated to the fundamental objectives of a university would bring about an elevation of intellectual standards, a rise in the esteem in which the institution should be held, and an expansion of its influence. Under the present system, extraneous values and considerations rule all to often. It is obvious that the time is ripe for reform.

The university is a community of individuals devoted to scholarship, teaching, and intellectual service. It should be directed by one who has an intimate knowledge of these functions.

35

Leaves from a President's Notebook

LLOYD MOREY

President emeritus, University of Illinois. His article originally appeared in *School and Society* on Dec. 24, 1955, and was based on an address to the National Federation of College and University Business Officers Associations, Estes Park, Colo., June 27, 1955.

I have had the rare good fortune to serve in several professional groups: teaching, governmental and institutional accounting, music, and educational administration. Educational business administration has occupied the greatest part of my time, energy, and interest.

There is one name that will always stand higher in the contribution to educational finance than any other. To the late Dr. Trevor Arnett we all owe a debt of unrepayable gratitude for the part he played in the improvement of college and university financial administration.

What evidences are there of progress toward better business administration?

The business officers have finally gotten together on a national basis. I congratulate this Federation and hope it will fulfill its expectations and opportunities.

There has been a very important restatement of principles of accounting and reporting in Volume I of "College and University Business Administration," as well as of various business operations in the recently issued Volume II.

While I continue to have strong doubt over most so-called "Federal aid," there has been good progress in contractual matters. Most agencies now recognize the basic principle for which business officers so valiantly strove: adequate reimbursement to institutions for all indirect as well as direct costs.

One practice which crept into programmatic classified defense contracts and has caused internal difficulty is the "bonus" plan of compensation for staff transferred to such contracts. Such a provision has little to justify and much against it. A recent report, "Faculty Compensation—Policies and Practices," by a Committee of the Association of American Universities, analyzes it and questions its propriety. I hope and believe it is on the way out.

A new danger has now asserted itself in the gradual increase of continuous fiscal controls over operations of state-supported institutions. The states have in large numbers gone far in the direction of autonomy for higher education. But, even in the face of this widespread recognition, the exceptions are numerous.

It is time to turn back this trend and put authority where responsibility lies and where the public intended it should be—in the hands of the boards duly constituted by law to manage these institutions. Responsibility requires methods of control *within* the organization as an integral part of management. When these are adequately set up with proper means of financial reporting and independent audit, continuous external controls are not only unnecessary but are undesirable both in the public interest and from the standpoint of the institution. Illinois is one of the states which have gone far in following this principle.

This subject has had the active attention of the Association of Governing Boards of State and Allied Institutions, the Association of Land-Grant Colleges and Universities, and the National Association of State Universities. They have set up a joint committee to take active steps to reverse the present trend and endeavor to bring practicality and sanity back into these relationships. Each of these has devoted time to it in recent conventions.[*]

There is increased attention to comparative costs as among comparable institutions. The results of a comparative summary of a group of moderate-sized private institutions under auspices of the Business Officers' Federation will be watched with interest. The most significant comparative cost study is the joint one of University of California and the "Big Ten" Mid-west group. Major problems in securing reliable bases of comparison are involved here, and if they can be overcome the results should be of much value.

How does the business office look from across the hall?

The business office is just as important as I thought it was in the administration of a university. It is one of the many essential mechanisms needed to help administrators and faculty get the real work of the institution accomplished, to keep the affairs of the university in good legal and procedural channels, to present essential financial facts convincingly, and to maintain

[*] *See* L. Morey, *College and University Business,* June, 1955.

records that are beyond challenge. A business office serves best if, instead of saying decisively and quickly that the thing wanted by a department or professor cannot be done, it seeks to find a way that the objective can be accomplished within the limitations in which the institution must work. Even though it is but a service division, the better the business office, the better the institution.

Many problems presented to the president are similar to those presented to the business officer, because nearly every problem in a university has its financial aspect; unless that aspect can be satisfied, the proposal stops or must wait, whatever its merit otherwise. It is just as important for the president to show a sympathetic and helpful attitude toward every proposal as the business officer, and more often than not help of the latter is needed.

The president does not want from his business office frequent voluminous reports or a mass of financial detail. He does not have time to read them and should not have to concern himself about most of them. The top question that he wants a ready answer to is: How much free balance is there in general current funds out of which he can make assignments or recommend such to the board of trustees? Details of departmental situations he wants to leave to the department and the business office.

This does not mean that complete reporting at the proper time and place is undesirable or unimportant. It is a fundamental of good practice and of good public relations. Even for the public, however, condensed, pin-pointed reports, attractively illustrated, are better than lengthy accounting schedules. By all means, have the latter, but keep them in reserve and use them sparingly.

The president expects the business officer and other executives to solve their own problems in every instance possible; and, if they must be brought to him, to give him a recommendation for a solution. In other words, he wants not merely reports of difficulties or plans, but he wants to know chiefly what he can and must do if necessary to resolve difficulties or make plans work.

Although the University of Illinois business organization has always differed from that of most other comparable universities, I have found no reason to change it. The basic difference is the separation of the *comptroller* functions from those of *business management* and keeping them attached directly to the president and the board. I have been strengthened in my belief in these principles at least for large institutions such as Illinois. Such an institution should have an officer of high level, not concerned with management of activities on a wide scale himself, who can review and report independently on every institutional operation. To do this he should have direct responsibility to the president and the board. Responsibility for management of general business enterprises should be assigned to another officer.

What are the basic principles of educational executive management?

After over 40 years in the business office and two in the president's office, one should have a complete formula for educational executive management. Save for the following important principles, there is none:

1. Set up channels of communication and means of discussion, and respect and use them.
2. Listen first, decide afterwards. Do not be too quick or too positive with your answers; allow time for consideration, for discussion with others, even for the possibility of changing your judgment after further consideration.
3. Discuss with those affected and with advisers any proposed changes before they are initiated. Try to get others to agree with you as fully as possible in advance.
4. Be honest, fair, and consistent in your dealings and your decisions.
5. Delegate responsibility as fully, wisely, and freely as possible, but give authority with it; then hold your delegates responsible for results and for errors as well.
6. Praise freely, publicly as much as possible; criticize only privately.
7. Give yourself as much as you can to your staff and your public.
8. Do not develop or hold grudges, even though you are certain the other party is wrong and is treating you unjustly.

What are the fundamentals of good relations in educational administration?

The most important function and feature for successful management is the art of getting along with people. Best results are secured by working *with* people rather than *over* them, making them feel that they "belong" and that they are in a partnership rather than merely being hired. Workers of all kinds, whether they be ordinary laborers or internationally known scientists (and a university has the whole gamut of services in its personnel), produce effectively only when they are personally happy. Happiness depends on many circumstances—home, employment or business, church and social contacts, and world affairs. Primarily, however, it is conduced by freedom from anxiety, fear, and uncertainty; in an organization these are relieved by a sense of confidence in the methods and attitudes of the administration, by reasonable security of employment, and by good conditions in which to work and produce. When this element is good, production is good, whether it be scientific or manual; without it, the maximum usefulness of every individual is reduced.

Such an attitude can be encouraged by providing adequate means of discussion and conference on all matters, by opening adequate channels of communication, by giving evidence of fair and objective consideration of every proposal, and by giving the staff a feeling of certainty and confidence in methods of administration. These I have endeavored to carry out, and the results have been highly gratifying and rewarding.

But internal organization and relations are not enough. The external or public relations of an educational institution of any size, especially a public one, are of at least equal importance. In a large institution they are legion, and they are demanding. They tax the time and ingenuity and often the patience of the president and many others. But they are not insurmountable, and, as in the case of the staff, the right approach from within will usually win and hold a friendly attitude from without.

With the great help of many others, I have found it possible, within a relatively short space of time, to convert a general and widespread attitude of dissatisfaction and often hostility toward the University of Illinois to one of friendly interest and approval. It is impossible to tabulate just how that has been or can be done. A few points may be worthy of mention:

1. There must be a receptive and friendly attitude toward every individual or group to which the institution is related or which has or expresses an interest in it. The way should be open to anyone to present suggestions or complaints, and every one of these should receive attention and reply with reasonable promptness. If the situation warrants, and it is practicable, personal consultation is better than correspondence. No one should be neglected.

2. A spirit of integrity and fair dealing among all must be continually practiced, as this is the only way to build up confidence among all concerned.

3. All interested groups and, in a public institution, the general public as far as possible should be informed as fully as feasible about the plans, policies, and programs of the institution with clear but concise explanations of the reasons for them.

4. The president, to the fullest extent of his time and strength, and other principal officers as well, should lend themselves to other groups and organizations by appearances at their meetings when requested and by friendly interest and helpfulness.

5. Co-operation should be given the press and friendly attitude and fairness maintained toward its representatives—and strict impartiality.

6. I, at least, attribute our success at Illinois considerably to the encouragement of a high moral tone in the institution, the interest in religion, and an emphasis on high ideals of family life, citizenship, and clean living. These are dear to the hearts of most citizens who are glad to see them upheld by their educational leaders.

Pres. Herman B. Wells of Indiana University, in a magnificent address in October, 1950, before the Newcomen Society, said:

Look about you. Not, of course, within the confines of this room, but at the broad expanse that is modern Higher Education. Consider it well, for in it you see the marvel of the world and, I firmly believe, the hope of the world. What you observe is a testimony and a result.

Modern higher education is the direct descendant of a long tradition and stands on the shoulders of its ancestors. The college and university have been for many centuries the stronghold of learning. Their task today is more challenging and more significant than at any previous time. When a staggering proportion of the peoples of the world are being deliberately misled, deceived, and misinformed, there is greater need than ever before for the staunch bastion which is the university. "Give me a place to stand, Sire," said Archimedes, "and I will move the world." The modern system of higher education is such a place.

36

What Professors Want in a President

TYRUS HILLWAY

Professor of education, Colorado State College. His article originally appeared in *School and Society* on June 20, 1959.

A college without a leader is like a ship without a rudder. It will drift aimlessly. But the leader must be thoroughly competent and absolutely honest, with a true sense of the direction in which the vessel should be steered. That statement of a president's place in the academic scheme of things represents the consensus of some 400 American college and university professors who recently were asked to identify the characteristics of good and bad college presidents.

Previous attempts to learn what qualities make for success in the presidency have consisted largely of collecting the opinions of the presidents themselves or of consulting the trustees, who hire presidents. The author believes, despite several objections that might be voiced against his assumption, that valuable judgments regarding the desirable and undesirable traits of college executives may be secured from professors, who daily observe and work with presidents.

During the past year, the writer sent a questionnaire to 500 full professors in 93 accredited American colleges and universities. The names of these professors were taken from the current catalogues of these institutions, which included both public and private colleges geographically distributed among 24 states in different sections of the country. While the names actually were chosen at random from the faculty listings in the catalogues, considerable pains were taken to make certain that all the principal academic departments had representation in approximate proportion to their size.

Each professor was invited to indicate what, in his judgment and on the basis of his experience, he considered the characteristics most highly desirable in a college or university president and to rank them in what he felt to be their order of importance. In addition, he was requested to enumerate those traits which he regarded as least desirable in a president and to give these items their rank order. To encourage frankness, respondents were promised anonymity. Of the 411 questionnaires returned to the investigator, 403 proved usable in the study. Eight were blanks or had generalized comments only.

An unexpected amount of agreement was found among the lists and, to a slighter degree, in the rankings. On the lists of traits considered most highly desirable, the most popular by all odds was *integrity*. Twenty-four percent (97) of the respondents put this quality in first place, and it ranked high on almost every list. Next in importance, in the judgment of the professors responding, was *intellectual ability*, which 22% (89) listed in first place. Closely following these two essential traits was a third, *the ability to organize and lead*, which over 20% (81) of the respondents thought extremely important or even indispensable.

Only 10 characteristics in all proved popular enough with the professors to capture more than a handful of first-place votes. All 10 of these, however, appeared upon the vast majority of the lists. The 10 traits, representing what professors appear to consider most desirable in a college president, are listed in the order of their popularity (Table 1).

Table 1

DESIRABLE CHARACTERISTICS OF COLLEGE PRESIDENTS

CHARACTERISTICS	NUMBER OF FIRST-PLACE VOTES	PERCENTAGE OF FIRST-PLACE VOTES
1. Integrity in personal and professional relations	97	24%
2. Intellectual ability and scholarship	89	22%
3. Ability to organize and lead	81	20%
4. Democratic attitude and methods	44	11%
5. Warmth of personality		
6. High moral and intellectual ideals	24 / 21	6% / 5%
7. Objectivity and fairness	20	5%
8. Interest in education (an educational philosophy)	8	2%
9. Culture and good breeding	5	1%
10. Self-confidence and firmness	4	1%

Although many additional suggestions were offered, these recommended presidential characteristics contain all that most respondents indicated to be essential in a successful president.

The professors had very definite ideas regarding the traits which they identified as clearly undesirable in the head of a college or university. Of all the undesirable characteristics, there was almost overwhelming agreement upon a *dictatorial* or *undemocratic attitude*. Twenty-four percent of the group (98) thought this the worst possible fault in a president. Other undesirable traits identified by the professors are shown in Table 2.

Table 2

UNDESIRABLE CHARACTERISTICS OF COLLEGE PRESIDENTS

CHARACTERISTICS	NUMBER OF FIRST-PLACE VOTES	PERCENTAGE OF FIRST-PLACE VOTES
1. Dictatorial, undemocratic attitude	98	24%
2. Dishonesty and insincerity	61	15%
3. Weakness as educator and scholar	60	15%
4. Vacillation in organizing and leading	60	15%
5. Poor personality	36	9%
6. Bias or favoritism	24	6%

While a number of other undesirable traits were mentioned, the above list includes all those which the majority of respondents thought to be of outstanding importance.

Combining the two lists, one might say that the ideal college president, as far as the professors are concerned, is a person of unquestioned personal and professional integrity and of superior intellectual ability and scholarly attainment; an exponent of the democratic method in management who also has the strength of character to organize and lead; a warm and friendly person with high intellectual and moral ideals and a positive educational philosophy; one who is objective and fair in his dealings with other people and who represents a superior degree of culture and good breeding; and one who displays firmness and self-confidence rather than vacillation in his leadership. However, the professors have not placed anywhere on their list of desirable attributes that quality which trustees are likely to consider of the utmost importance—the ability to raise and handle money.

Since most of the traits mentioned by the professors may be called personal rather than professional, one might conclude that professors are somewhat less concerned with the training which a prospective president may have than with his attitudes and personality. True, a number of those who answered the questionnaire expressed the opinion that every president should have the doctor's degree, but these were in the minority. A few specified requirements like the following: "Should be college-trained" or "Should not be a professor of education" or "Should have the Ph.D. degree rather than the Ed.D." Perhaps most of those replying assumed that any candidate for a college presidency would have to be a person with college or university training and some prominence in the field of education. A few particularly stated that he should be an educator instead of a business man or military figure. Nevertheless, neither in the lists nor in the numerous voluntary comments written on the questionnaire forms did professional status appear to rank as high in the estimation of the professors as did factors of character and personality.

In choosing a college or university president, then, it seems clear that the professors would wish, first of all, to have *the right kind of man*—above all, a man of integrity. That he should be worthy of the faculty's respect for his academic attainments remains a secondary, though still very important, consideration. Some dissatisfaction with both methods and results of presidential selection by trustees was readily apparent from the large number of comments upon that subject written on the questionnaires by various respondents. On the other hand, several professors warmly praised the presidents they had known and worked with. To such professors, who are able to speak with a genuine glow of pride about the joys of serving on a campus presided over by a capable, honest, and inspiring leader, the ideal college president is not merely a possibility but a happy reality.

37

How Trustees Judge a College President

TYRUS HILLWAY

Professor of education, Colorado State College. His article originally appeared in *School and Society* on Feb. 11, 1961.

How and upon what grounds do trustees in our colleges and universities evaluate the work of college presidents? How do they determine whether a president is effective in carrying out his responsibilities or whether he ought to be replaced? These are questions upon which only the faintest light has been shed by recent educational research. A vast amount of heat admittedly has been generated in debates regarding the characteristics and functions of the people who sit on boards of trustees,[1] and numerous comments have been forthcoming regarding the proper selection of college presidents.[2] For information about the actual (and extremely important) relations maintained between presidents and boards, however, the sources are chiefly a handful of interesting memoirs by retired presidents and a few sensational case histories rather gruesomely displayed in the newspapers.

In the American institution of higher learning, over-all control ordinarily resides in a body of laymen trustees, among whose principal duties is the selection of a president or chancellor. The arrangement very closely resembles that of an American business or industrial corporation. The president, as general manager, administers the affairs of the institution under broad policies approved not by the faculty, but by his board.[3] In Europe, on the

---

[1] For some recent examples, see, among others, K. F. Burgess, *Association of American Colleges Bulletin*, 44: 399–407, October, 1958, and H. L. Donovan, *Peabody Journal of Education*, 36: 259–263, March, 1959.
[2] *Cf.*, R. M. Hughes, "A Manual for Trustees of Colleges and Universities" (Ames, Iowa: Iowa State College Press, 1945), pp. 34–43; M. A. Rauh, "College and University Trusteeship" (Yellow Springs, Ohio: Antioch Press, 1959), pp. 23–33; and H. W. Stoke, "The American College President" (New York: Harper, 1959), pp. 71–88.
[3] Evidence need not be adduced here to show that, in many American institutions, members of the faculty are looked upon by the trustees merely as contractual employee-specialists rather than as intellectually independent professional men.

other hand, the policies of universities are determined for the most part by
the professional men who comprise the faculties, though these are subject in
some degree to general control by governmental ministries of education.
Which plan operates the more effectively remains a matter of controversy.[4]

Since the typical American board of trustees manages its institution
through the agency of the president, some form of supervision by the trustees
and periodic evaluations of the president's achievements and failures may
logically be assumed. Only a dull-witted or a lazy board, one may safely
assert, would so cavalierly shirk its duties as to select a president and then
allow him completely free rein to run the institution in any manner pleasing
to himself. Boards customarily weigh the president's educational policies,
pass upon his proposed annual budget, serve sometimes as courts of appeal
against his decisions, and perform a number of other functions of a clearly
supervisory nature. If a president should prove incompetent, untrustworthy,
or in any other way unsuitable, for the welfare of the college they may—and
should—put him out of office.

To seek further light on the various methods by which the trustees
measure success or failure among our college presidents, the writer made
an attempt early in 1960 to secure information on the subject from a representative group of board members. After eight preliminary interviews at
which board of trustees' methods of evaluation were discussed in detail
with individual trustees of higher institutions in the New England and Rocky
Mountain regions, it was possible to compile a list of 25 likely factors for
trustees to consider in deciding upon the worth of a president, a list of the
four main competencies (i.e., institutional management, educational leadership, public relations, and money raising) in which a president might be
expected to demonstrate his abilities, and a list of 16 methods that the
trustees might employ as the means of learning what a president has actually
accomplished. From these lists a questionnaire was prepared and mailed to
355 trustees of colleges and universities in the 48 continental states, both
private and public institutions being included and only one trustee being
selected from each.

Respondents were asked, first, to identify those factors on List 1 which
to them appear most important in evaluating the effectiveness of a college
president; second, to specify which of the four presidential competencies
mentioned they regard as most vital to the welfare of a college or university;
and, third, to mark on List 3 those methods which they most often use in
determining whether the president is functioning to the satisfaction of the
board. A total of 148 (or about 42%) of the 355 questionnaires were returned
in usable form.

With respect to those factors which are considered by trustees in judging

[4] Ruml and Morrison urge a greater exercise of authority by the trustees. See B. Ruml and
D. H. Morrison, "Memo to a College Trustee" (New York: McGraw-Hill, 1959).

the work of the president, the respondents agreed overwhelmingly on 10. These appear in Table 1 in the order of preference.

Table 1

FACTORS CONSIDERED BY TRUSTEES IN JUDGING PRESIDENTS

FACTORS	NUMBER OF VOTES	PERCENTAGE OF VOTES
1. Leadership in maintaining high academic standards	133	90%
2. Good judgment in selecting faculty and staff	131	88%
3. Ability to maintain high morale among faculty and staff	128	86%
4. Facility in making friends for the institution	127	85%
5. General intellectual leadership in college and community	125	84%
6. Fairness and honesty in treatment of faculty and staff	119	80%
7. Good judgment in promoting faculty and staff	119	80%
8. Ability to maintain a balanced budget	116	78%
9. Respect accorded him by other educators	114	77%
10. Influence of his moral character on students and faculty	113	76%

In relation to the second list, which names areas of presidential competency, it should be noted that, although each respondent was requested to vote for only one of the four named (the one rated as most vital to the welfare of his institution), many respondents voted for two or more. Perhaps it is permissible to conclude from this multiple type of response that the trustees believe their presidents ought to be versatile men, skilled in more than one aspect of their work. Whether specifying only a single competency as most vital or indicating some combination of two or more, the trustees gave their preference to presidents who are competent primarily as educational leaders—that is, concerned more with academic than with business matters. They expressed the least preference for the president who is a good money raiser and business man.[5] The votes cast for each competency and the percentage of the total vote represented in each case are shown in Table 2.

[5] This expression of high regard for the educational leader and comparatively low regard for the money raiser may surprise members of college faculties. See T. Hillway, *School and Society*, 87: 306–308, Summer, 1959.

Table 2

MOST VITAL COMPETENCIES OF A PRESIDENT

COMPETENCY	NUMBER OF VOTES	PERCENTAGE OF VOTES
1. Educational leader	78	52%
2. Management executive	67	45%
3. Public relations expert	41	27%
4. Money raiser and business man	24	16%

This leaves the question of what methods trustees actually employ to judge the president. Out of a list of 16 possible methods, only five seem to be used with any regularity. These are listed in the order of their frequency in Table 3.

Table 3

METHODS USED IN JUDGING PRESIDENTS

METHOD	NUMBER OF VOTES	PERCENTAGE OF VOTES
1. Discussions with other trustees	114	77%
2. Examination of president's report	105	71%
3. Over-all impression from many sources	103	70%
4. Discussions with alumni and the public	101	68%
5. Discussions with the faculty	84	56%

Such likely methods of evaluation as periodic visits to the campus, visits to other colleges for purposes of comparison, discussions with students, attendance at social and athletic events, and classroom visitations appear to be used only rarely. Three institutions among those included in the study have gone to the trouble of preparing systematic standards for judging the president's performance.[6]

That college and university trustees are quite satisfied with their present methods of judging presidents may be inferred from the comments volunteered on many of the questionnaires. A few respondents objected to the questionnaire itself on the grounds that a trustee "simply knows" when the president is doing a good job. No suggestions of acceptable methods other than the 16 listed were offered. While one may well wonder about the reliability of such methods of evaluation as an "over-all impression from many sources," at least it seems clear that the trustees know what kind of

---

[6] Davis has provided an interesting score card by which the achievements of a president can be rated. See P. H. Davis, *Liberal Education,* 46: 395–404, October, 1959.

performance they expect. If their responses on the questionnaire are to be believed, what they value most highly in a president is leadership in maintaining academic standards and skill and honesty in dealing with other people. Effectiveness as a business manager would appear less important. While trustees and professors probably arrive at their judgment of a president by different routes, they nevertheless agree in general upon what they desire in a president and upon, at least, *the basis* for judging his effectiveness.

38

Illinois, Illinois!

GEORGE D. STODDARD

Vice-Chancellor for Academic Affairs, Long Island University. At the time his article originally appeared in *School and Society* (April, 3 1954), he was the former president of the University of Illinois, having resigned the previous year.

> *The weight of this sad time we must obey,*
> *Speak what we feel, not what we ought to say.*
>
> KING LEAR

For the regularly scheduled meeting of the Board of Trustees of the University of Illinois in Urbana on July 25, 1953, all appeared to be in order. The members of the board had received from the office of the president of the university the usual notice of business to be transacted. Only one item was thought to be controversial—moving the university health center to another location in order to improve its facilities and services. The big business, overriding all other matters, was to be the final approval of the internal operating budget for the year 1953–54.

This *one-year* operating budget, based upon the total income of the university, showed in detail how the sum of $52,000,000 was to be spent. It was one of the largest sums ever received by an institution of higher education. (There was also a *two-year* appropriation of $7,500,000 for new buildings.) Although most of the members of the board were familiar with the budget, several hours were well spent in a further analysis of the proposals, with special reference to reductions and increases over the previous year. The review of the budget, together with some attention to 24 other items on the agenda, took up the time of the board from the 6:30 dinner hour until 11:30. This was on Friday, July 24, the board sitting as a committee of the whole.

Only two items revealed any lack of rapport between the president of the university and some members of the board. Since there was resistance to moving the health center, the matter was deferred. On the other hand, while not accepting my recommendation that the office of the vice-president in charge of the Chicago Professional Colleges (Medicine, Dentistry, Pharmacy, and Nursing) be abolished in favor of a return to the plan of having the dean of the College of Medicine act as a general executive dean, the board at this meeting decided not to continue Dr. Andrew C. Ivy as vice-president beyond the expiration of his term on August 31, 1953. It retained the post but not the man. (I had also recommended that Dr. Ivy be continued as distinguished professor and head of the department of clinical science, and this was done.)

The long session, while fatiguing to all in view of the complex budget, progressed smoothly. In a corner of my mind I began to think pleasantly of my flight to London and Edinburgh which was scheduled for the following Sunday, permitting me to board the battleship *Iowa* for a portion of its fleet maneuvers. But this was not to be.

Mr. Harold E. Grange, the newest member of the board, called for a private session to be held at once. Accordingly the members of the staff of the university left the meeting but stayed in a corridor "on call." This group included the president of the university, the provost, the comptroller, the legal counsel, and the secretary of the board who was also assistant to the president of the university. Later, word was sent out that only the president and the provost need stand by.

Shortly after midnight I was called in. As I came through the door Mr. Wirt Herrick said in an undertone, "Prepare yourself for a shock!" I took my place at the table in the quiet room as Mr. Park Livingston, president of the board, announced abruptly that the members present had taken a vote of confidence in my administration and that the vote was "no confidence." Since the president of the University of Illinois serves "at the pleasure of the Board of Trustees," I submitted my resignation immediately and started to write it on a slip of paper. At this point Mr. Wayne Johnston asked me to correct the text from "In view of the vote of the Board of Trustees" to "In view of the vote of the majority of the Board." The only discussion was in reference to the effective date of the resignation. It was quickly decided that it should be at the end of the first semester of the coming academic year in order, as Mr. Grange said, "not to inconvenience me." I then left the room and Provost Coleman R. Griffith was called in. I learned later that he, too, was given a vote of "no confidence."

At nine o'clock the next morning, just before the meeting of the board, Mr. Livingston telephoned to say that what the majority of the board really wanted was my resignation at once, even though my salary would be extended for five months. On reaching the Illini Union at 9:30, I corrected the slip of paper to read "as of August 31, 1953." Mr. Griffith resigned as provost at the same time. There was no discussion of these actions during the board meeting—only an announcement to the press after adjournment.

Now, to back up a bit. The midnight session of the board sitting as a committee of the whole as indicated had no items on the agenda; no members of the staff, press or public, were present. In fact, only the members of the board who voted against Stoddard and Griffith knew that the meeting was to be held; the three members present and voting in favor of the administration, Mr. Wirt Herrick, Mr. Wayne A. Johnston, and Mr. Herbert B. Megran, had not been informed. Mr. Robert Z. Hickman, who was absent on a vacation trip, stated subsequently that he would have voted with the minority. This procedure was followed by a board of trustees that had long taken pride in the open and forthright character of its meetings. As far as I know, there was no precedent in the history of the University of Illinois.

The faculty (largely absent from the campus during the summer session), the press, and friends of the university throughout the state soon demanded an explanation. The 22 department heads in the College of Liberal Arts and Sciences, headed by Dean Henning Larsen, released a strongly worded resolution referring to my forced resignation as "contrary to all accepted standards of academic procedure; technically legal, it is morally unjust." Later, the University Senate (the faculty governing body) in a formal resolution expressed deep concern, stating that "there is a strong feeling among the faculty that the drastic procedure followed was unfair and has resulted in serious danger to the university's reputation and prestige."

In the meantime almost all the former members of the board of trustees put themselves on public record as follows:

We, the undersigned citizens of this State, all of whom were formerly members of the Board of Trustees of the University of Illinois, wish to record our protest against the unprecedented action of the present Board of Trustees in forcing Dr. George D. Stoddard to resign as President of the University. Dr. Stoddard has long been considered one of the outstanding educators in the United States. Common decency required an orderly procedure and a fair hearing for him. Instead, those who initiated the midnight action against Dr. Stoddard did not even inform him or their fellow-trustees that any such subject was to be brought up for consideration.

We commend Trustees Herrick, Megran, Hickman and Johnston for opposing these Star Chamber proceedings. They were faithful to their trust and to American standards of fair play.

For many years, the University of Illinois was kept out of politics. Recently, attempts to use the University of Illinois for political ends have become all too common and now have culminated in action which cannot fail to do great harm. It is an interesting coincidence that two of the trustees who participated in these disgraceful proceedings were substituted for candidates whom the University of Illinois Alumni Association had recommended.

The University of Illinois is not the property of its faculty or its alumni or of any group of politicians. It belongs to the people of this State. We feel confident that when our fellow citizens understand what has happened they will express their indignation in ways that will be understood.

Of the two trustees mentioned above as not backed by the Alumni Association, Mr. Grange was one.

It will be asked: If there were no formal complaints, no charges, no information, what *was* the basis for the action taken? Mr. Grange said that certain legislators in Springfield kept asking him "when were they going to fire Stoddard," but he did not name them. On July 26, Mr. Livingston, through an exclusive interview in the *Chicago Sunday Tribune,* listed 14 controversies that he claimed led to dissatisfaction among the trustees. Also, by stressing the absolute need for tranquility, six of the trustees have confirmed Mr. Livingston's selection of the big issue as *controversy.*

Hence, it may be well to mention a few of the growing pains in my seven-year term at the University of Illinois. Some of them strike me as inevitable, but others, in my opinion, were intensified by the failure of the president of the board of trustees to place the welfare of the university above politics. That these struggles did not materially affect the progress of the university may be gathered from my "Notes for a Seven-Year Report of the President of the University of Illinois" (*School and Society,* Nov. 28, 1953). Throughout, faculty and student body worked with zeal and imagination to move the University of Illinois forward on all fronts—to wake up what President James L. Morrill of the University of Minnesota once called the "sleeping giant."

On August 3, the *Chicago Tribune* published in full my reactions to the 14 controversies described by Mr. Livingston on July 26. Only four of the items are reproduced here and one of them is abridged with respect to my part of it.

I

Livingston: In November, 1946, soon after taking office, Stoddard began the first of a series of trips abroad, mostly on business of the United Nations educational, social, and cultural organization. He helped organize the global group, which has produced many controversial proposals, and he became head of the United States delegation to it under the Truman administration.

Altho Stoddard used his vacations for some of these trips and gave up part of his salary to make others, the frequency of them kept him away from his desk while squabbles arose at the school. The board of trustees told him in effect—in July, 1951, after raising his salary from $22,000 yearly to $23,500—that seven foreign trips on outside business were enough. He was to stay home, the trustees explained, and run the university instead of UNESCO.

Stoddard: First a slight correction: I have not been head of U.S. Delegation to UNESCO, although I have been Deputy Chairman and I was for three years Chairman of the U.S. National Commission for UNESCO.

The Board of Trustees understood that practically all my time away on UNESCO was vacation time. Also one "squabble" (in the College of Commerce) arose after I had been steadily in Urbana for eight months—and within a few days of my departure for Italy.

In any case, I felt that whatever contribution I could make to UNESCO was in the public service and consistent with the purposes and ideals of a great university.

II

Livingston: In June, 1949, Rep. Cutler [R., Lewistown] assailed Stoddard for allowing an allegedly "pink" professor to remain on the faculty. Cutler suggested an investigation to "comb Russia lovers" out of the school. Stoddard said he was against Communists as teachers but added socialists were all right if they advocated the replacement of capitalism with socialism by legal means. The statement came a month after he had fenced with legislators about medical school personnel.

Stoddard: The professor concerned was no "pink"; he was a conservative Kiwanian. As to medical personnel, the less politics, the better.

III

Livingston: That summer, Rep. Dillavou [R., Urbana] charged there were "50 reds, pinks, and socialists" on the university staff and that the university was "being used to indoctrinate youth with radical political philosophies." Stoddard demanded that he send a list of the suspects' names.

Stoddard: The explanation for this one was due, and still is, from Representative Ora Dillavou. He could not find 50 reds, pinks and socialists; he could not find one!

The charge was made on the occasion of the political maneuver in Peoria by which Mr. Harold Grange was substituted for Mr. Chester Davis on the Republican slate of candidates for the Board of Trustees of the University. Mr. Davis had been approved in traditional fashion by an alumni committee of the University; Mr. Grange had not.

The fact is that while the Broyleses, Cutlers, Dillavous, Horsleys, Libonatis and Marzullos shout themselves hoarse about Communism in the University, those of us in charge have worked quietly, through our own security officers, the Federal Bureau of Investigation, the State Department and the military establishment, to make sure that no Communists are on the staff. This is important for we have a number of classified and secret research projects at the University. All staff members of the University of Illinois have signed a standard loyalty oath, and the Security Officer has announced publicly that there is not, to his knowledge, a single Communist in the University of Illinois.

IV

Livingston: About that time, Stoddard began a feud with Sen. Miller [R., Chicago] over a $617,000 bill which Roy Warner, Chicago contractor and friend of Miller, charged was owed him by the school for building a women's dormitory. Warner later was paid.

Stoddard: As Mayor LaGuardia of New York used to say, "This is a beaut!" . . . Mr. Warner had obtained a contract for the construction of the Lincoln Avenue Residence (a dormitory for 500 women) on a *cost-plus* basis at a final maximum of $2,012,000 and, concurrently, a contract for the Utilities Distribution System at a *final fixed* price of $807,000.

The Warner Construction Company proved to be inefficient and negligent and not above an attempt fraudulently to transfer personnel and materials items from the fixed price utilities contract to the cost-plus contract. It took constant vigilance on the part of University staff and attorneys to prevent this. The "controversy" paid handsome dividends to the University and the taxpayers in that the net claims waived by the contractor (after his affairs had been taken over by the First National Bank of Chicago) were *$328,000 less than his original bill.* This is the extra sum the University would have paid if it had not endured this unpleasant, long-continued struggle.

In these negotiations Mr. Livingston was of no help. In fact, he was so eager to settle this dispute favorably to the Warner Construction Company and against the interests of the University that on several occasions he by-passed the officers of the University in attempting a settlement.

As I said at the time: "Through the efforts of countless persons over the decades, the University has become great and strong—truly an enduring monument to the intelligence of the people of Illinois. It is far too fine a heritage to be turned over in silence to persons whose loyalty is mixed. I am confident that the faculty and the new administration will defend the ancient tradition of scholarship and academic freedom."

The faculty, individually and collectively, has indeed been heard from, and large sections of the public, following the lead of such newspapers as the *St. Louis Post-Dispatch* and the *Chicago Sun-Times,* have been alerted to a sense of danger in this new merger of politics and public education. In education, at least, it is important to resist both the inherent badness of power-hungry politicians and the suffocating goodness of men without ideas.

39

College Administration as Political Football

T. NOEL STERN

Chairman, Department of Political Science, Southeastern Massachusetts Technological Institute. At the time his article originally appeared in *School and Society* (March 10, 1962), he was a research associate in government at Indiana University.

I was dismissed in 1961 as president of West Chester State College in Pennsylvania. The Board of Trustees acted within its legal power and stripped me of authority and salary within 48 hours. No specific charges were filed. No hearing was granted by the Board or by state authorities in Harrisburg. However, the State Superintendent of Public Instruction, who is a member of the board, announced that my work with state educational officials was satisfactory.

The publicity hurt my family. Leaks from the Board of Trustees set the press after me before I had any knowledge of official action. I made my own charges, afterward, to present the issue to the taxpaying public. The trustees replied with silence and clamped a censorship of fear on the faculty.

The sharp spasm of administrative pain at West Chester is part of the national growing pain. We are injecting more analytical thought into college teaching. We are moving away from the anti-intellectualism which still holds a number of campuses.

In the South, the movement toward intellectualism is tied with integration. In the church-supported schools, many boards of trustees are split between old-fashioned "un-think" religion and modern intellectualized religion. In the state-owned colleges—including teachers' colleges—progress frequently is slowed by politics, patronage, and sports. The problem for Pennsylvania's state colleges is to provide a good education at low cost for able students from low-income families—without interference from politically minded coaches and patronage-minded politicians. Should students at

Pennsylvania's state institutions be short-changed intellectually or should they receive the full benefit of public financial support?

Education is presented as a central issue by Gov. David L. Lawrence. Recently, the Governor's advisory commission on education completed a study at a cost of $300,000. The report foresees a tripling in enrollments at the state colleges and recommends that teacher training programs consist of a solid course in subject matter or liberal arts offerings.

Thus, the written proposals endorsed by Gov. Lawrence will be judged in a measure by the public in terms of the actual practices at the state-owned institutions of higher learning. The last session of the General Assembly failed to pass $28,000,000 in new taxes to finance the Lawrence educational program in the state colleges and in the public schools throughout the state. The willingness of future legislative sessions to back new taxes to finance education will be affected by the type of trustee appointed by Gov. Lawrence to the boards of the 14 state colleges, by the policies which the trustees follow, and by their educational standards. In other words, the theoretical proposals of the Governor are judged by actual practice in the 14 institutions where the Commonwealth has direct control.

There are 1,300 professors and 22,000 undergraduates at the state colleges. Their educational programs are knit together by statute, by state budget control, and by policies of the State Department of Public Instruction and the Board of State College Presidents.

West Chester State College is in the public eye since it is close to the state's largest center of population. The 3,000 student enrollment at West Chester is the second largest among Pennsylvania's state colleges. Thus, the influence of football and political football pressures on academic standards at West Chester is a concern for the 13 sister institutions.

No college president ever had an ideal board of trustees. The West Chester board is remarkable only in its distance from the ideal. The tradition of politics is more thoroughly engrained at West Chester than at most of the other state institutions. Divisiveness in the nine-person board at West Chester comes from its assorted membership: two are professors; three have no college education; and more than half of the trustees are active politicians.

The board can offer no facts in reply to my charges. It ducks the issue and speaks in generalities. I am simply told that the board "lacks confidence" in my administrative performance and that it is disturbed by a "series of little things."

Unofficially, I understand that the problem centers on:

1. *Football Line Coach*—I was reluctant to hire a football line coach who was recommended for a position as assistant professor. One trustee accused me of "prejudice" against the candidate because he used bad English. The candidate thought that Machiavelli's "Prince" was a "novel."

2. *Athletic Admissions*—The Athletic Department pushed to admit 80

students who were below West Chester's admission standards. I worked to reduce such admissions. I wanted to eliminate the double standard: classes at junior high-school level for a minority of our students who were admitted for athletic skill, and college-level instruction for the mass of students. This divergence in standards had been criticized by the Middle States Association's evaluation team in 1959.

3. *Athletic Finances and Loans*—The athletic group on campus seeks independent control of the $65,000 in athletic money under the budget of the Student Activities Association. This money comes from student fees and from gate receipts at athletic contests. The accounts of the athletic office are muddled. All records of gate receipts from football and other sports are regularly destroyed before audit. The accounts of the student loan funds also are muddled. The report by Henry Sanville and Company, certified public accountants, states, "Of the fifty-six loans granted during the year ended May 31, 1961, we observed only fifteen loans supported by signed promissory notes. This is a departure from procedure in the past." Thus, nobody can say where the money went or when it will be returned to the fund.

Criticism is levelled against West Chester by officials of other Pennsylvania state colleges. They ask whether unauthorized subsidy is paid to football players at West Chesler State. Is this the reason why West Chester always wins the state college championship?

4. *Jobs for Trustees*—One West Chester trustee applied for two professional jobs at the college—director of public relations and director of administration. Her nephew-in-law applied for director of administration. He later was appointed by the Governor to the Board of Trustees. Neither candidate has adequate educational background. Thus, I politely refused their applications with the help of other board members.

5. *Patronage*—Like many other schools, West Chester is plagued with political patronage. We have 160 patronage jobs on our maintenance force. All contribute cash to whichever party is in power.

The board includes a woman who is vice-chairman of the State Democratic Committee and who is the strongest figure in Chester County politics. The board also includes another lady who is on the State Democratic Committee.

Local politicians were excited when I fired a painter who was partially blind, a tractor driver without fingers, a rapist working in the girls' dormitory, and a fireman who was subject to fits and who had a long record of assault and stabbing. One of the women board members pleaded at a board meeting for reinstatement of this employee.

6. *Factionalism*—Factionalism in the Democratic Party arose from the old issues of religion and of workingmen versus middle-class intellectuals. The split in the party broke out on the West Chester board. It was intensified by the precarious position of the Democratic Chairman in Chester County

and by the electoral race for judgeships. It was further agitated by a difference within the trustees as to whether the Miss Pennsylvania Beauty Contest should be brought back on campus or whether it should be permanently banned as non-educational.

7. *Gossip*—West Chester is like other campus communities. It fights its vendettas with gossip. At West Chester each faction has enough voltage in its gossip to destroy its rivals but not enough power to dominate. After I was dismissed, I learned some of the foolish gossip about myself. My daughter was supposed to have married a Negro. This was not true. It also was rumored that I had joined the Society of Friends to escape the draft. This, too, was inaccurate, since I had been interested in Quakerism and in pacifism since childhood.

8. *Conservatism*—Community conservatism affected some board members and faculty. Some felt that the traditions of the college were violated by increased emphasis on subject-matter courses, intellectual content, research, and graduate study. Concern was expressed that the new emphasis would shift interest away from athletics and from extracurricular activity. Some of the coaches found that I asked "Socratic questions." Others were concerned that my inaugural address dwelt on the philosophy of Albert Camus and avoided the standard stereotypes about the mission of education in America.

Past history at West Chester resembles that of other teachers' colleges which now are converting to a broader frame. The college was founded in 1812 as an academy at the secondary level, in a center of culture and of Quakerism 25 miles southwest of Philadelphia. West Chester grew into a normal school, then to a teachers college. Recently, the 14 Pennsylvania state colleges dropped the word "teachers" from their titles, reflecting the national trend. Although the Pennsylvania state colleges still grant degrees only in teacher training, a new law permits them to add other programs. Thus, many supporters see West Chester as a future university center for southeastern Pennsylvania, with undergraduate schools in teacher training, liberal arts, music, and physical education and graduate work toward the master's degree.

During my year in office at West Chester, I worked toward the goal of raising academic standards and improving the physical plant. The experience was exciting and challenging. Despite its abrupt ending, it was the best year in my career—thus far.

The college administration made improvements which had been desired by the Board of Trustees and by the majority of the faculty for many years. We raised admission standards, including standards for athletic candidates. Faculty recruiting procedure was democratized, and 32 new faculty of high calibre were appointed. The business structure of the college was modernized and a new dean of administrative affairs was appointed without regard to past political affiliation. The appointment had the approval of the Governor.

But local and state patronage dispensers objected that the new dean was a "carpetbagger" from New York City and a former Republican.

A new campus plan and a 10-year building program were drafted. This spring the college will break ground for $4,000,000 in new structures.

There also has been a negative side to the ledger over the years. My dismissal is the product of past history. It results from factionalism which existed long before I came on campus and which exists now. It surrounds the present acting president and will affect whatever new man is inaugurated as "permanent" president.

A number of administrators and professors have been caught in the pincers. The college was black-listed by the American Association of University Professors for more than a score of years and was removed from the list of censured administrations just a short time before I took office.

Some of the past troubles involved the Student Activities Fund. The largest part of the fund goes to athletics, and most of this for spectator sports. Although West Chester has been blessed with winning teams, it has long been plagued with politics—under both Republicans and Democrats. This stems in part from the cynical attitude which many Pennsylvanians still maintain toward a state patronage system which is reputed to be the largest in the nation. The political tradition at West Chester also stems from provisions in the state law. State college trustees at each of the 14 institutions are appointed by the Governor and confirmed in office by the State Senate. The president of the college and the chief business officer must be approved by the Governor. There is no civil service for non-instructional employees. Professors and instructors are granted rank and salary in accordance with arbitrary provisions in the law. Yet, professors have no legal tenure beyond the will of the local board of trustees and their annual contracts.

This helps explain the general fear and conformism which pervades the faculty at West Chester. Several faculty members spoke to me of fear for their own safety after I was dismissed. They offered this as reason for their silence.

Past presidents at West Chester have had trouble. A generation ago, West Chester's most famous president was called in by his board for hearings. He refused to testify, but he kept his job since he was long established in the community. The next president of the college was forced to retire under a cloud. He was accused of pocketing student funds, but he made restitution. At the same period, another college official was sent to prison.

In 1959, a president died in office after serving a quarter of a century. For four years prior to his death, he engaged in a running dispute with the trustees. The issues included politics, athletics, educational standards, and a lack of democracy in faculty-administration relations. During the 1959–60 academic year, a board member served as acting president while the board sifted through 40 applications for the presidency. The acting president antagonized community leaders by opposing the Miss Pennsylvania Contest and many faculty members by seeking to shake up the academic program. Thus, he was dropped from the board by the county political machine shortly after he left the position of acting president.

Although I am a professor myself, I do not feel that all professors make ideal board members. Some are not seasoned in business, and many are beguiled by gossip. There is a tendency for some professors to carry their anti-authoritarian theory to an extreme. While it is good to believe in democracy, one need not don a French revolutionary bonnet every time that he sees a college president.

Professors on the West Chester board were caught in community and political vendettas. They feared the anti-intellectual group in the party—with reason. Thus, the professors on the board wound up by attacking their own image. They were afraid to stand up for the president whom they had selected after extensive search. They yielded to athletic pressures which sought to make the college into a big-time football school.

The case at West Chester has had national publicity. I have received letters of support from all over Pennsylvania. A dean at the University of California remarked that I was one more man caught in the West Chester "nut-cracker."

If local groups in West Chester can combine with national organizations to clean up the situation at the college, the sting of publicity will have been worth while. The Commission on Tenure and Professional Rights of the National Education Association recently made a two-day preliminary investigation on campus. Another group which entered the case is the Commission on Higher Education of the Middle States Association of Colleges and Secondary Schools. It sent a representative to the campus and two representatives to Harrisburg to confer with the Superintendent of Public Instruction. The commission has been concerned for some time with the controls exerted by Harrisburg upon the state colleges. Other groups which are studying the West Chester situation are the American Association of University Professors and the National Student Association. The American Civil Liberties Union is studying the need to amend Pennsylvania law in respect to the tenure of state college administrators.

My recommendations for a reorganization of West Chester include action at the regional and state level:

1. *Accreditation*—The Middle States Association should withdraw accreditation of West Chester until courses for physical education students are raised from sub-high school level to college level. These include science courses for physical education majors and the course in baseball where the final examination asked in one of its five questions, "How many positions are there in a baseball game?"

2. *Trustees*—The boards of trustees of the 14 state colleges should be abolished. In their place should be appointed a single statewide board of trustees for all 14 colleges, following the pattern which exists in Maryland

for its teachers' colleges. Members of the new central board of trustees in Pennsylvania should be chosen without regard to political party. They should confine their work solely to questions of policy and should not intermeddle in administrative work. The new central board should give each of the 14 state colleges freedom to develop its individual program and institutional personality.

3. *Civil Service*—All employees of the state colleges and Department of Public Instruction should be placed under civil service. The Governor of Pennsylvania can take immediate action by placing educational personnel under "executive civil service" in anticipation of later legislative enactment by the General Assembly.

4. *Academic Freedom and Tenure*—Faculty tenure under civil service is needed to guarantee academic freedom. Thus, faculty should be guaranteed both tenure and freedom of expression under law. I emphasize the point, since the American Civil Liberties Union found serious cases of faculty insecurity at some of the Pennsylvania state colleges.

5. *Contract for Presidents*—After careful screening and selection, the new president of a state college should be given a three-year contract. This would give him time to "get his feet wet" and to put his academic program into effect.

6. *Dismissal*—Administrative personnel should be granted a hearing when faced with dismissal. Charges should be in writing. A period of leave should be granted after dismissal in order that the administrator may have full opportunity to find new employment.

7. *Macing*—No college employee should be "maced"—forced to make a political contribution in order to hold his job.

8. *Admissions*—Admissions should be based solely on the high school academic records of students and on their professional potential as evaluated by admissions officers. No student should be admitted merely on athletic ability.

9. *Physical Education*—The physical education program at West Chester should meet the needs of all students. All should have a chance to participate in intra-mural sports and in individual physical recreation. Spectator sports should not monopolize the program.

10. *Financial Controls*—Careful financial controls should be imposed on the spending of student funds. Large purchases of athletic supplies should be bought on competitive bid. There must be more careful audit of athletic expenditures and student loans.

West Chester supplies a large portion of the teachers south of Philadelphia and many in the city itself. Graduates in music and in physical education go to jobs all over the state. The quality of teacher produced by West Chester affects the future of Pennsylvania schools for the next generation. Thus, it is hoped that the latest explosion at West Chester will have a positive result and will produce reforms needed by the college and by the Commonwealth as a whole.

40

When Is a College President Successful?

EDGAR C. CUMINGS

Director of Community Services, Economic Opportunity Commission, San Jose, Calif. At the time his article originally appeared in *School and Society* (March 5, 1955), he was vice-president and dean of Hiram College.

Although there are probably no official figures concerning the tenure of college presidents, rumor has it that the national average is something like three and a half years. In any case, a president who lasts 10 years or more is regarded as something of a latter-day miracle.

The brief interludes enjoyed by a good many presidents cause one to ponder the criteria for success in this hazardous field. One's ability to achieve longevity does not appear to be a chief measure of success. In fact, some authorities believe that the most energetic presidents are probably the ones who fail to last. Let us explore the reasons for this curious situation.

Every president has a certain number of specified hurdles to surmount. Foremost among these is doubtless his own board of trustees, with whom he must spend a honeymoon fraught with difficulties and of indefinite duration. All of the trustees will assure the lucky candidate that they want him to be a "strong president" and provide "outstanding leadership" to the faculty and the board. In addition to the very necessary requisite of a strong constitution, the new president must be strong academically, spiritually, socially, emotionally, and morally. He must have a "strong" wife and family, and he must be a "strong" money-raiser. If he comes from an Army or Navy background, so much the better.

The chief difficulty surrounding his honeymoon with his trustees is the dubious fact that it is never over. Where his wife has learned through trial and error that he is possessed of certain human vagaries and is understanding enough to put up with these qualities indefinitely, his trustees are unlikely to be quite as long-suffering.

Another hazard is the faculty, who also want a strong president, or think they do. They want the institution to progress, particularly with regard to good tenure conditions and salaries, but they typically do not want to have the internal applecart upset too much in the process. The new president is quite likely to feel that one way to make progress is to raise academic and instructional standards and to believe that one of the best methods of achieving both ends is by a long enough tenure, he can outlive many faculty members who are just going through the motions, but the danger is that they will both outlive and outmaneuver him.

The boast that many a faculty member has made to the effect that he has outlived "old so-and-so" and will outlive "you" is no idle one. Any president will do well to remember that Machiavelli himself could have taken lessons from a good many faculty members. The writer knows of one situation where a genuinely outstanding president ran afoul of the American Association of University Professors within a short period of time and subsequently lost his job over a professor who, as almost everyone admitted, richly deserved whatever radical treatment he received.

A third major hazard is the alumni of any given institution, particularly one with good athletic teams. As Hutchins has said, most alumni want to remember their alma mater as it was, or as they fondly believe it was, when they were in school. A president who does not remember the importance of "tradition" is walking on eggs. One example will suffice to describe this tenuous situation. At one college the trustees and the president decided that the original building on the campus had better be scrapped before it fell down and hurt somebody. As soon as work commenced and the alumni got wind of it, irate letters began to inundate the president like the waters of the Nile. While he did not lose his job over this incident, it did begin a movement of calculated distrust which eventually made him decide that a public relations position would offer more peace of mind.

If our president surmounts the first three hurdles, he may find himself facing another one in the form of financial matters. Unless he is one of the few who have entered upon such a position with a written understanding that no money-raising is entailed, he may find that his success is measured, especially by his board, by his ability to locate and mine the root of all evil. On the other hand, if he happens to be a good fund-raiser, he will find that this quality may save him from the attacks of the other groups mentioned above. It is a sinister indictment of higher education that the president who turns up dollars in sufficient quantities hardly has to bother about raising standards or increasing the academic reputation of his school. A balanced budget "answers" many embarrassing questions.

One or two case histories, embellished a bit to make them unrecognizable, may cast some further light on this question of success.

The first case is that of a man who is now one of the better-known public figures of this country. Some 20 years ago he was enthusiastically called to the helm of a medium-sized college of excellent, if static, reputation. This man was in his early 40's, physically and intellectually vigorous, dynamic, aggressive, decisive. He was a brilliant speaker and a better-than-average money-raiser. He was also a Christian gentleman in the unhackneyed sense of this phrase. In short, if his trustees had prayed for the ideal president, he was their man.

What happened? He obtained a good academic dean to run the institution internally (his first mistake, of course) and proceeded to busy himself with matters of important policy, with spreading the gospel of his college across the land, with raising money and making friends. The result after a few years was a college whose very atmosphere was electric. The students grew to adore him, and the alumni and faculty grew to detest him. He made "mistakes" on the campus, when he was there—which couldn't be very often because his main task was to increase the outside reputation of his college. The basic mistake he made was to insist that his college be made a place where things happened, where the air was alive with intellectual ferment, where curricular changes did not have to wait an eon for the slowly grinding gyrations of the average faculty to occur. To his students he was a god; to his faculty, a dictator with the soul of the Grand Inquisitor. He lasted six years, during which the country came to know of his institution for the first time (and perhaps the last). He was replaced by a morale-builder.

The second case involved the 30-year span of a kindly old gentleman who has long since gone to his reward. Everyone liked him, even his trustees. He was kind; he was saintly; he was a genuine "democrat" with his faculty; he beguiled all and sundry with his trite, gracious little speeches which all sounded the same. He was a "character" when he was appointed president, and he became a legend.

Everybody was happy, in a way. The professors performed their mediocre instructional tasks in genteel poverty. His alumni praised the school's fine basketball teams. His trustees loved him dearly because he never once challenged them. And his students came to his charming teas in droves, left them talking about how delightful Old Chips and his wife were, and continued to study the minimum amount. One day Old Chips died a natural death and was buried on the campus. Someday a novel will be written about him. But was he successful?

Let us not belabor the point. Someone has said that every college or university needs a certain kind of presidential cycle. Every 20 years or so, following the regime of some sweet old soul, every college needs a regular human dynamo to sweep out the dry rot, retire a certain number of faculty members, tell off the alumni, make all the trustees hopping mad, and do away with football. Things get shaken up, complacent people become ruffled, buildings get built, and curricula become changed for the better. Then a morale-builder assumes the presidency again.

Is there a solution? No, not as long as graduates become alumni, trustees are appointed for their prestige and wealth, and faculty members worship tenure. Perhaps the cycle is the solution after all.

41

The Administrator in Higher Education as an Educational Leader

JOSHUA A. FISHMAN

Distinguished University Research Professor of Social Sciences, Yeshiva University. At the time his article originally appeared in *School and Society* (Oct. 19, 1963), he was dean of the Graduate School of Education, Yeshiva University. The article was based on an annual talk to the faculty.

I was neither born with an administrative spoon in my mouth nor bred for educational administration. In American higher education, most administrators are drawn from the ranks of teachers and researchers rather than from the ranks of administrative trainees. Although this is as it should be—for the greater good of higher education—the result is that many administrators practice their newly found "black art" with a great deal of ambivalence. In my own case, the strains and stresses were particularly great, especially because I determined to continue directing a large and demanding research project at the very same time that I undertook administrative responsibility. I quickly discovered that these two areas of endeavor—creative research and creative administration—were very uncongenial companions.

Occasionally, there is some conflict between them in terms of the cognitive styles and the personality attributes which they require. Administration is all too likely to be concerned with immediate solutions, with individual cases, with practical and tactical decisions and compromises. Research is all too likely to be at least one step removed from the world of immediate application, to be oriented toward abstract and theoretical considerations, to seek out integrative concepts rather than particularistic phenomena. Nevertheless, much more serious than these seeming differences in cognitive orientations (which I do not believe should be taken too seriously) is the fact that both research and administration are alike in one very basic sense: they both require an 18-hour working day. In both pursuits, there is simply no end to what needs to be done or what can be done. In both domains, constant and complete dedication is called for, and the successful protagonist tends to create more, rather than less, work for himself and for others. Just as the testing of one fruitful hypothesis leads to the generation of 10 others, so the creative administrator constantly tends toward newer and more demanding functions.

Although the struggle between research and administration has been a difficult one, I can, nevertheless, recommend it to others. As a researcher, I became a more academically oriented administrator. As an administrator, I became a more organized researcher. However, at some crucial juncture, one or another of these two aspects of my life had to receive undivided attention.

Since 1960, I have had a truly unusual opportunity to observe the administration of higher education, to engage in it, to read it, and to think about it. Why should any academician in his right mind leave his classroom, his laboratory, and the intellectual and interpersonal companionship which great universities provide and seek a home in the world of administration? Even if, as in my case, it is not necessary to give up completely one's citizenship in one world in order to take up residence in the other, why should one bother?

A common academic view of educational administration is that it is a necessary evil at best and an unpardonable, if not unspeakable, evil at worst. Certainly, it is viewed as something to which no really decent spirit and no truly vigorous mind could possibly be devoted. Indeed, not merely does one school of academic thought hold administration and administrators in low esteem because of their moral and intellectual deficiencies, but it even prescribes such individuals because only they are suited to administration. In this view, educational administration is no more and should be no more than the filing of records, the preparation of catalogues, the scheduling of classes, and sundry other duties like the raising of money. Anything more directive and creative is considered an affront to intellectual and moral giants by intellectual and moral pygmies.

Strangely, there is a very similar view of administration within certain administrative circles themselves. Just as all social relationships tend toward our view of social reality, so some administrators, like members of "disadvantaged minority groups," tend to take on the characteristics attributed to them by others. This self-view of administration claims that its major function is to avoid trouble, to balance budgets, to save money, to guard against scandals, to smooth ruffled feathers, to keep things running efficiently, and to engage in similar manifestations of academic Babbitry and spigotry.

Oddly, the individuals who hold such views are the same who decry such behavior on the part of administrators in the elementary and secondary schools. Indeed, good training programs in educational administration are explicitly concerned with the preparation of educational leaders who will be research-oriented, sophisticated in organizational, social, and psychological theory, and concerned with fostering academic excellence in their staff and in their student bodies alike.If this is what we are really after with respect to administrators for elementary and secondary education, why should we settle for anything else, or be astounded by anything else, in the administration of higher education?

The administration of higher education—at its best—is the exercise of leadership toward rigorous, conceptually integrated, and socially challenging intellectual goals. It requires an allegiance to more than the usual trinity of bromides (early spring, mother, and honesty—which, in academese, become translated into "quality," "standards," and "democracy"). It requires a university-wide and school-wide perspective, but, even more, a philosophy which relates intellect to society in a particular way. Ultimately, it requires not a budgetary goal or an operational efficiency goal, but a socio-educational philosophy and the capacity to dedicate one's self toward the realization of that philosophy; to inspire others toward that same goal; and to lead and assist them toward it. Thus, a consistent socio-educational philosophy will guide the administrator with respect to budgetary allocations, programmatic priorities, personnel policies (promotions, sabbaticals), recruitment, public relations, etc., much differently than would be the case if he were guided primarily by blame-avoidance. If this is what administration is, then it requires and only will attract able stewards.

Almost every faculty member is involved in administrative efforts of some kind—when he assigns grades and must choose between the gratitude of his students and the respect of colleagues and students alike; when he serves on dissertation or oral-examination committees and is in a position to hold out for an extra ounce of candidate effort or not to bother; when he is on a faculty committee and either can direct the formulation of policy and the implementation of policy so as to advance conceptually the field of higher education or simply so as to make things nicer for himself and his colleagues. Faculty members frequently accept the responsibility of rising above expertise in separate fields, and of rising above self-interest camouflaged as faculty "rights," to consider the role of their particular university in its particular environment, the purposes of academic excellence, the justifiable claims of society upon them and the university, and how they can contribute to the needs of the university that gives them sustenance and freedom. A faculty concerned with broader socio-educational goals and means is concerned with administration at its best. A faculty that is not genuinely concerned with such matters—and at the same time decries administrative leadership in these areas—is both intellectually and organizationally immature.

If there is anything unique about the deanship, it is not a concern with issues such as these, since these are issues which must be of concern to everyone, from the president and the board of trustees to the graduate students themselves. The real uniqueness of the dean lies in his role as a middleman, representing his school and his faculty to upper administrative authorities at the same time that he represents the upper administration on the local scene. This is an inherently difficult position to be in and one deserving of a study to be entitled "The Deanship: A Portrait of Academic Split Personality." To those on the outside, it may seem simple to resolve the dean's "middle management" problems by suggesting identification with one or another of the major bodies with which the dean must work. However, such a solution quickly would render the dean's office inoperative as the meeting ground where university affairs receive intensive and impartial study, although such a solution is probably sought frequently by one dean or another in avoiding ulcers or premature old age. However, while an effective bridge must be anchored securely on both sides rather than merely on one, in human affairs marginality is frequently the price of being an objective intermediary.

There already has been a recent study entitled "The Dean as a Marginal Man," which claims that deans are sentenced to the status of perpetual wanderers, constantly plagued by approach-avoidance conflicts in conjunction with each of their two possible reference groups. This may be true, but the solution to the problem of the bridge which has only one secure anchor hardly can be found by building bridges with no secure anchors at all. Rather than be a marginal man, the dean should be a truly bicultural man, fully at home in two neighboring cultures, fully accepted by both, committed to both, and, therefore, able to interpret the one to the other and able to be the instrument of social change between them to the end that they operate as one rather than as two cultures. Unfortunately, biculturism is not a very stable state—particularly in a bi-polar world—and is likely to degenerate either into the marginality of the *mestizo* on the one hand, or into complete assimilation on the other.

The dean must be a truly bicultural individual and his leadership must be bicultural. To function in this way he must gain and maintain the trust and co-operation of his faculty and of higher administration alike. Either one or the other can frustrate him by too narrow or too self-centered a view of their goals and their priorities, by too limited support of his mediating leadership role, and by constant demands that he either must be 100% with them or against them. When this occurs, successful "deaning" becomes impossible; administration degenerates into either clerkship or dictatorship; and the best minds and spirits leave the field.

42

The Dean as Humanist?

FREDERIC W. NESS

President, Association of American Colleges. At the time his article originally appeared in *School and Society* (Summer, 1960), he was academic vice-president and dean of Dickinson College. The article was based on an address at Dickinson College on the occasion of the installation of the first W. W. Edel Professor of Humanities, November, 1959.

Academic deans are instinctively on the defensive. Most of them start out as teachers, burning for lives of scholarship and service. Then, by some grotesque switch of fate, they discover themselves immured in a nine-to-five cell, suffering the guilt of betrayal and noting for the first time the Dantesque inscription over the doorpost: *Lasciate ogni speranza, voi ch'entrate.*

The dean, however, who wakes up one morning in the swivel seat, where he spends so many penitent daylight hours, to discover himself installed in an endowed chair of humanities experiences a sense of remorse so exquisite that he is the object of pity even from fellow deans—men who, by definition, have long since abjured such tender emotions. In fact, one of my deanish friends whispered to me recently, "Does this mean you have been kicked upstairs?" He could conceive of no straightforward reason why a dean should be honored with a chair of humanities. Nor, for that matter, can I.

There is a solemn convention about chairing ceremonies, dating back over the centuries, which requires the incumbent to speak learnedly about his discipline and then close with a highly charged *apologia pro vita sua* explaining why everyone else in the field is wrong and he is right. Since deans, if anything, are conventionalists, I am bound to this format.

Before beginning, however, I must quote a brief excerpt from Ten Hoor's recent article in *Liberal Education*:

The general public assumes that because a man is made president or dean, this is an indication that he is a "deep thinker" on educational problems. Sometimes the president or dean agrees with this assumption; it is more or less natural to do so. . . .

Now I do not mean to assert that a president or a dean may not actually be a "deep thinker" on the subject of education as such. But this is not necessarily so. Even when it is so, the faculty is certain to be reluctant to acknowledge it, for they are inclined to look upon it as against nature.

Because I am inclined to agree with these sentiments, I have chosen to deal with the subject of "The Dean as Humanist?" Note the question mark. There is indeed a very real doubt as to whether the two terms, dean and humanist, are at all compatible.

Most of us, when we think about the humanities, are clearer about what they are not than what they are. Specifically, they are not the social sciences and they are not the physical sciences. They comprise, in the usual liberal curriculum, the third slice of the academic pie. If, however, anyone thinks that the professor of humanities is *ipso facto* conversant with everything that is not a physical or social science, he is in for some academic disenchantment. Moreover, if anyone thinks that the study of humanities produces humanitarians, he should consult with any undergraduate now on academic probation. As for breadth of vision or liberalization of thought, the specialist in the humanities pursuing like Browning's Grammarian "the doctrine of the enclitic *De*" is moving in no larger an intellectual circumference than the zoologist clocking the wiggles of a newt.

In short, the humanities, academically speaking, are simply one phase of the total curriculum. Despite the many false claims made in their behalf, they cannot provide an answer to the total man anymore than can the physical sciences or the social sciences. But since these claims are more often made in the name of "humanism" than "humanities," the time probably has come to offer a new term. Humanism is defined as the study of the humanities or, more often, as "polite learning." For the most part, though, it has remained man-centered. Thus, when the neo-classicist Alexander Pope in the 18th century wrote, "The proper study of mankind is man," he was uttering an essentially humanistic doctrine.

One of the difficulties with humanism—with the study of the humanities, in general—is that it tends to get off the track. It was born in a spirit of reaction. In its several resurgences over the centuries, it always has retained this characteristic of reaction. Irving Babbitt, founder of the school of neo-humanism with which I came in contact in the early '30's under Louis T. More, the brother of Paul Elmer More, and the tutelage of his sophisticated disciple Robert Shaffer, wrote in 1908, "The humanities need to be defended today against the encroachments of physical science as they once needed to be against the encroachments of theology."

The trouble with all such defenses is that they lead to extremes. Thus, the study of the humanities tends to become esoteric. For example, Henry S. Dyer of the Educational Testing Service provides a kind of institutional definition when he characterizes measurable knowledge of the humanities as "Familiarity with basic terms in literature, music, and art, sensitivity to form and technique, and comprehension of complex meanings and inter-relationships in specific works of literature." Where, one might ask, is the proper study of mankind in all this?

Even when the emphasis of humanism is upon man rather than upon man's art for art's sake, it has a natural inclination toward exclusiveness. It is not so much interested in *l'homme naturel* of a Rousseau as in *Il Cortegiano* of a Baldassare Castiglione. In other words, the proponents of the humanities have tended either to withdraw into ivory towers of esoteric formalism or to parade on peacock walks gracefully flicking specks of dust from their fine lace cuffs.

There is, however, a new humanism now beginning to materialize in the intellectual circles of America—in fact, throughout the Western world—a humanism which is seeking to protect itself not so much against the physical sciences or the social sciences as against the built-in obsolescence of humanism itself. I offer three bits of evidence of this rebirth.

In his provocative essay entitled "The Misbehavioral Sciences," Jacques Barzun sets realistic limits upon the humanistic context: "The humanities will not rout the world of evils and were never meant to cure individual troubles. . . . Nor are the humanities a substitute for medicine or psychiatry; they will not heal diseased minds or broken hearts, anymore than they will foster political democracy or settle any national disputes."

Howard Mumford Jones' recent "American Humanism" stated: "Humanism implies an assumption about man. It implies that every human being by the mere fact of his existence has dignity, that this dignity begins at birth, that the possession of this dignity, even if dimly realized by the possessor, is, or ought to be, the continuum of his life, and that to strip him of this dignity is to degrade him in so outrageous a way that we call the degradation inhumane. . . . Modes of expressing the dignity of man constitute the substance of humanism."

And third, from the reports of the fifth annual assembly of the International Council for Philosophy and Humanistic Studies (1959), there is evidence that the humanist is now seeking ways of peaceful coexistence with the physical and social scientist toward the successful amalgamation of man's rapidly unfolding knowledge of man. Thus, Gustave Reece, the musicologist, admonished his fellow humanists at the Michigan meeting that they should feel no alarm at living in a world in which science is in the foreground. After all, they have been living for years in the world of industry. "It should be at least as easy," he said "to coexist with scientists as with tired business men."

Let me return, finally, to the administrator, the former teacher of freshman English and Shakespeare, the erstwhile explicator of literary criticism, now transmuted into a college dean. Robert Graves might well have had his ilk in mind in the little poem which appeared in the October,

1959, *Atlantic* under the title, "Established Lovers." Note this third stanza:

> Observe him well, the scarlet robed academician
> Stalled with his peers, an Order on his breast,
> And (who could doubt it?) free
> Of such despairs and voices as attended
> His visits to that grotto below sea
> Where once he served a glare-eyed Demoness
> And swore her his unswerving verity.

For the humanist teacher-turned-dean makes certain choices which are generally irreversible and irrevocable. He may like to think of himself as a teacher, but this is a form of pleasant self-deception. Nor is it any less a deception if he teaches a course now and again. However he wishes to conceive of himself, his certain choices inevitably make him different. Some of them are conscious choices and obvious ones; others are as subtle as sea-change, so gradual that he may be unaware of their implications for months, perhaps years. I shall review only a few of them.

First, the humanist turned-dean becomes a generalist, reversing the natural bent of the college teacher towards specialization. The life of scholarship becomes an illusive Holy Grail which, if ever clutched again, will probably be by the feeble fingers of retirement. As a generalist, he must transcend the boundaries of his own subject field and develop a sympathy for, if not an understanding of, the objectives and aspirations of the total academic curriculum. So elasticized, it is questionable that he can ever return to his original dimension.

Second, he necessarily becomes a compromiser. Although the successful administrator never will yield his few basic principles, a substantial portion of his working day is spent in an effort to balance antithetical forces. He finds, for example, when he is invited out to dinner that his chair is usually placed at the table leg because he is the only guest exercised in straddling issues. The teacher and scholar enjoy the luxury of pursuing truth to its logical conclusion. The administrator daily suffers the agonies of inching along tortuous pathways through relativistic jungles.

Third, he tends to lose his identity and to become instead a kind of symbol of an institution. A blurred symbol at that, for an academic institution is a complex of many meanings, a compound of many simples. Thus, the casual observer never can be sure which mask the dean is wearing at any one time.

However much he may deplore it, the dean inevitably becomes more of a conformist than his colleague in the classroom. He follows tradition until he becomes one. He is a public figure, often at untold sacrifice to his private life. If I were to sentimentalize, I could point out that he is the lonely man ever in the midst of a crowd. Although sometimes described as the "official visionary" of the institution he serves, he is in fact usually too hobbled by details ever to put his feet on the desk and raise his eyes to the stars. Finally, as the "big stick," the campus "hatchet man," the enforcer of rules, he may well find that he has mislaid his essential humanity.

To adapt an observation once made by John Erskine, "A college dean is like a small boy walking a high picket fence—thrilled, but in constant danger of being impaled." Thus, the question mark in my title, "The Dean as Humanist?" Can he in truth, even if he has been thoroughly schooled in the humanities, reconcile these concomitants of office with the essential goals of humanism?

This, of course, is the typical leading question to which we expect an answer in the affirmative. To the contrary, my answer must be a qualified no.

The dean as humanist is at best a vicarious humanist. At the same time, if he is to be a moderately successful dean, he must perforce be a vicarious scientist and a vicarious social scientist. His only salvation from a schizophrenic dissolution is to adhere to a unifying belief in the power and perfectability of the human intellect.

This must be his faith, his single creed. In the confusion of his multivalent universe, this must be his sun, his source of light, the well-spring of his strength, his personal "Hymn to Intellectual Beauty."

But intelligence is not an attribute of the animal; nor is it, essentially, an attribute of God. It is the singular characteristic of man. It is also the focus of the highest form of humanism. Therefore, to the extent that the academic administrator identifies himself with this unifying principle, to that limited extent he perhaps may lay claim—an uneasy claim—to a chair of humanities.

In his poem, "Kittyhawk," Robert Frost offers a superb definition of humanism and at the same time a potent nostrum for the humanist-turned-dean:

> But while meditating
> What we can't or can
> Let's keep starring man
> In the royal role.

43

The Solution to College Administration Problems

ALVIN B. QUALL

Director of Graduate Studies, Whitworth College. His article originally appeared in *School and Society*, October, 1969.

Academic freedom is a term which warms the hearts of faculty members while it is raising the hackles of many college presidents. The turbulent reactions of these two groups as they struggle to define academic freedom results from the different philosophical positions which each group holds. Violent disagreement on such matters as curriculum change, selection of personnel, and faculty tenure grow out of the basic beliefs of men and women who are charged with administrative responsibility.

How can college and university presidents avoid campus riots and, at the same time, keep up with the mainstream of higher education unless they possess an adequate philosophy of school administration? What must an administrator believe and how can belief be put into action?

Of course the easiest way is to follow practices of the past. The traditional approach, however, obviously has failed. In a day full of new problems, new procedures are demanded.

The university had its earliest beginnings in Greece. University life at Athens, in the fourth century, was spirited, but hardly moderate, in a period noted for its lawlessness. Universities were organized in the 12th century in France and Italy. The administrative organization was very simple. It consisted mainly of students and instructors who met in a quiet place free from the cold and the rain. The teacher, or master, was so close to the student in the beginnings of the university that teacher and pupil banded together and exacted certain privileges from the communities in which they lived. Among their privileges were freedom from taxation, from military service, and from compulsory contributions to the locality. One of the greatest privileges was that of self-government. The right of the self-governing of a college or university is endangered today because campus students demand exemption from many of our civil laws. If modern students continue to abuse established civil laws, they may lose much of the freedom they now have in their academic and social life.

In the period from 1900 to the present, colleges and universities have became large and complex, and careful organization has been necessary—someone has had to direct the show. This resulted in the appointment of college presidents, deans, and registrars.

From the time when higher education became organized, up to the present, administrators became entrenched in their positions. Many presidents and deans held their posts for long periods of time. Inevitably, such men began to think and act as if they were the only ones who knew how to run an institution of higher education. Between 1900 and 1965, students and laymen accepted administrative autocracy, and thus was born the authoritarian administrator. This person's word was law and most people obeyed his mandates, even though they resented his directness.

In the 1960's, doubts began to arise about the infallibility of long-term presidents and deans. As people became better-informed, they began to question directives which were illogical, even though the edict came from venerable presidents and deans.

No doubt, some of the questioning began when colleges became so large and unwieldy that one person found it impossible to know all of the answers. This situation, along with changed attitudes toward morality and freedom, has spelled the death knell for authoritarian administration.

When faced with a major campus problem, the traditionalist administrator attempts to follow the pattern he knows is expected and whose precedents he can find out about. He quotes records of committee minutes and official school publications. The carefully worded records provide a life jacket for an administrator floundering in the present stormy sea of confusion and violence. A favorite practice in college administration is to clutch a straw—write to several institutions and find out what they do in regard to teaching loads and dormitory regulations. Such a study reveals an average of what other schools are doing, but it does not prove that what they are doing is correct. One difficulty in relying on past practices is that they may have been ineffective or downright wrong. It is hard to tell whether a practice is good or bad after much time has elapsed because the necessary information may not be available currently. A practice that may have succeeded in previous times might not be what is needed to solve today's problems.

Being bound by the past is illustrated by the registrar in a midwestern college who proposed to enroll students in the gymnasium where there was plenty of room rather than in the library where space was limited. The business manager of long standing in this institution said, "We can't use the gym because we have always used the library and we don't know how our registration procedures will work in a new place."

Established administrative organization is bogged down in routine and inertia. Secure in its old momentum, it continues at a set pace. Of course it is easier to let conditions remain as they are because it takes a real effort to emerge from a rut.

The administrator who slavishly follows the past does so through lack of experience. He has no knowledge or beliefs on which to base his actions. Management consulting firms easily detect unproductive practices in an organization because the persons engaged in them frequently lack a clear purpose for what they are doing. For example, one large educational institution planned to spend over $1,000,000 on its radio facilities without ever having put on paper the specific objectives they wanted from the radio station.

The prudential administrator attempts to live "a day at a time." If a problem occurs for which there is no precedent, he proceeds to do whatever is necessary to solve that problem. He often changes course because he finds himself on the wrong tack. At Columbia University, the administration decided that the militant students were correct in stating that Columbia should not engage in classified research, seeming to imply, "We don't want more student unrest and rioting, so we surrender." This kind of action solves a problem temporarily, but it is not good sense because an objective set up for the welfare of many will have to stand against the opposition of a few.

A high percentage of college presidents and deans have taken the position that college students may be compared to buyers of merchandise and that the "customer is always right even when he is wrong." Educational leaders who take this position obviously act on the principle that what a student wants is what he needs; and, furthermore, young people today are so much more intelligent than students used to be that college administrators really can learn what is most valid by listening to the teenagers and youth in their early twenties. College administrators not only listen to students, but often they give in to what the young people want. A popular practice today is for college officials to ask students for their opinions on almost any phase of the school program, ranging from what they want to eat (which seems reasonable) to what they think they should study (which may be impracticable).

A careful look at the student-centered approach reveals that the administration frequently has responded to unreasoned pressure tactics. The administration which responds too quickly and too completely to student demands may find that it has sacrificed long-range stability for a quick answer to a current problem.

The mutual means, or "mod-vue" approach, is the only one which holds an answer to current administration problems. This united approach draws its resources from students, parents, faculty members, and board of trustee members. It derives from each group the knowledge and insight which each holds in the light of that group's strategic place in today's society. There are many things to be learned from college students. For one thing, they know what they like and this desire can be used to motivate them. Students also have ideas on how to vary classroom procedures. They are good at detecting flaws in teaching and in administration. Their criticisms should be heard and checked for validity.

However, educators obviously should not draw all of their objectives from students because, though they may be intelligent, they clearly have not lived long enough yet to cope with all situations. Also, it would be expecting too much for youth to prescribe remedies for all current problems when they lack the background to know whether some procedure is an experiment, an expedient, or a tested solution.

The parents of college students are the most illogically and thoroughly disfranchised of all groups involved in this "state of confusion." There are the soundest of reasons why parents should have a voice in what goes on at a college or university. One, they generally pay for their son's or daughter's schooling. Then, of course, they are determined that their children must succeed in learning so they will be prepared for life and future employment.

Most parents have specific ideas of what they want their children to learn. Intelligent, caring parents want their offspring to be responsible, to exercise sound judgment, and to have a broad and solidly based sense of values; however, they do not have any way to make parental desires known where it really counts. Administrators should ask and listen to parents and incorporate their ideas into the various programs of higher education. Parents also should have a voice, because the knowledge they have learned from experience often will solve unprecedented problems facing educators today. The good and bad aspects of permissiveness in the home well might be shared with college authorities as the degree of freedom a student possesses seems to be one of the "hang-ups" on the modern campus.

Faculty members, along with students, occupy the center of the stage in higher education. Faculty members should help with the matters which are related most closely to their own disciplines and their everyday responsibilities. This means that teachers of all ranks should assume major responsibility in curriculum planning, research, and improvement of classroom instruction. Frequently a teacher is asked to help in an area of his "non-competency." This occurred when a college president asked the members of his faculty how they might raise money for their institution, to which a department chairman responded, "If I knew the answer to that question, I wouldn't be a teacher. I'd be an administrator." If the average faculty member is asked to help with administration beyond that closely related to his own field, he probably will contribute out of his ignorance rather than out of experience or knowledge.

The members of the boards of colleges or universities generally are professional or business men and women. This background provides them with business acumen and ability to establish sound financial policies. If a college needs to borrow money for a major building or decide upon a suitable campus plan, board members can be of inestimable help. Whenever a board member starts to remake the curriculum or decide how a class should be taught, there is grave doubt that his efforts are in the best interests of the institution. He probably will be sincere in his attempts; but, unless he has had some experience as an educator, he will be unable to function in the most effective manner.

A "mod-vue" of college administration suggests that five major groups of people should make significant contributions to colleges and universities as they strive to establish "acceptable academic freedom" and maintain forward motion in the pursuit of "the good life." If students, faculty members, parents, board of trustee members, and college presidents can communicate and are allowed to contribute the wisdom of their own education and experience, this mutual-means approach to present-day college administration possesses real promise of success.

44

Faculty Participation in College Administration

JOHN H. CALLAN

Dean, School of Education, Seton Hall University. His article originally appeared in *School and Society* on Feb. 18, 1967.

Today, perhaps more than ever before, higher educational institutions need the great wealth of knowledge and skill that, for the most part, has yet to be explored in their faculties. The problems besetting colleges and universities indeed are too many and too complex to overlook this important source of available competence to help solve them.

Campuses throughout the country are in a state of change. The once revered, placid halls of ivy have been replaced or overshadowed by modern brick and steel structures. Expanding parking facilities only have begun to meet the needs of a society on wheels. The docile, insecure, quiet, contented scholar of yesterday is no more. In his place is the involved, controversial, knowledgeable, and effective faculty member who not only wants, but demands that his voice be heard. These are indications of change and vitality that are welcomed by anyone who takes pride in seeing his profession come of age.

With these changes, it becomes apparent that authoritarian administration, with its paternalistic regard for faculty and students, also must change. For the most part, the college administrator accepts and welcomes the changing role of the educational leader. He recognizes that there is both a need for and value in faculty participation in college administration. He is willing and eager to explore avenues for effecting cooperation among the members of the academic community. He is aware of the fact that effective college operation is the result of the involvement of the total academic community: students, faculty, and administrators. He also is aware that an administrator can delegate authority, but never final responsibility—that the ultimate responsibility rests with one person. He also knows that he cannot avoid his responsibility by delegating authority—it is his, traditionally, legally, and morally.

Democratic administration should be based on the principle of representative or indirect democracy, rather than pure or direct democracy. Prof. Bartky of Stanford University emphasized this point very clearly when he wrote, "Those who emphasize only freedom and equality will resent leadership of any kind. . . . On the other hand, those who think decisions should be made directly by the majority would have use only for a leader of opinion, a man who could formulate a policy and argue its merits. There is little need for an administrative leader in a pure democracy, where all decisions are made and carried out by the masses. It is only in a representative democracy that a leader can find full employment for all his talents."*

Democratic administration needs the involvement of mature, responsible, and intelligent faculty members. The degree or extent of involvement will depend on the unique purposes of the institution, the human resources available, the legal implications, and the willingness of the faculty to participate. Faculty involvement will be effective only if there is basic good will on the part of both faculty and administration. There must be a relationship based on mutual respect of the parties involved—a relationship that is characterized by a willingness to work cooperatively toward a common good. It is one thing to demand to be heard; it is quite another to be willing to listen.

Another important consideration is that both administration and faculty must recognize the limits of their individual competence. No man can be competent equally in all areas.

In order for representative democracy to function effectively, the appropriate representative must be responsive to the attitudes and interests of his constituency. There always is a very real danger of the abuse of position and power, and appropriate safeguards must be provided to obviate this possibility.

In summary, the nature of faculty participation in administration must be guided by the principles of representative democracy, must be responsible, must be based on mutual respect and good will, and must be creative and productive.

*John A. Bartky, *Administration as Educational Leadership* (Stanford, Calif.: Stanford University Press, 1956).

45

Interdependence of Administration and Faculty

RICHARD F. HUMPHREYS

President, The Cooper Union. His article originally appeared in *School and Society* on Feb. 8, 1964, and was adapted from the President's Report, 1961-62.

Unlike a business or government enterprise, an institution of learning operates under a dual system of responsibility. To the administration it looks for details of management, housekeeping, financing, broad policy, and, hopefully, leadership. To the faculty it looks for educational programs, ability to convey knowledge, contributions to its students and to society, prestige, and, hopefully, leadership. Actually, this is not a balanced partnership, for the true purpose of a college's existence is acquitted by its faculty, not its administration. Though instructors, unsupported by funds, cannot build a college's future, no amount of money put into laboratories, studios, research equipment, or the rest of the material of education can produce an institution of quality without a faculty of quality.

The qualifications demanded of a teacher—as of all people who contribute significantly to society—are so many they are almost overwhelming. He must be a scholar in his own field, but sensitive to other scholarship. He must be a capable instructor willing to exercise great patience with the student, but must find time to make his own contributions to his profession. He must not allow himself to be burdened by academic trivia, but he must assume responsibility for the system of education of which he is a part. He owes allegiance to his profession, but equally to his institution. He devotes his life to the teaching of others, but he himself never must stop learning. Above all, he shares in a remarkable phenomenon: as an individual he is part of an academic community whose stimulating and reinforcing influence produces a whole that is greater than the sum of its parts. It is the joint responsibility of faculty and administration to make this non-Euclidean process possible.

Just where do these responsibilities, taken separately, lie? Since it is easy to be wise about what others should do, let me first touch on the role of the faculty. A major component of this role is the willingness to accept participation in the making of the college—in the acknowledgment that a school is good or not good partly because of faculty choices and decisions. Effective participation must be accompanied by readiness for responsibility. This in turn demands the breadth of mind to think of interests beyond one's own professional specialty. It means an almost continuous re-study of the methods and content of the educational program—not only minor adjustments for next year, but major ones to match the progress of knowledge. It means the recognition of weaknesses, including those of other members of the faculty. Realistic evaluation of academic brothers in terms of their contribution to education is a responsibility almost no faculty member likes—and yet who is more qualified to exercise it?

Certainly the faculty shares a large responsibility in helping to answer the question: What is the proper role of a professional school in the educational community? In the liberal arts college it is possible to escape into rhetoric—to declare, for example, that the college should "educate for life." Such evasion is less easy in professional schools. We enroll students who have made a career choice and, therefore, we owe them a program meticulously tailored to that career. What will the young architect, the chemical engineer, or the graphic designer be doing in our society five or 10 years from now? We must forecast his role now, to determine how best to prepare him.

Another faculty responsibility that must be more actively assumed is that of giving academic and professional guidance and help to the individual student. Small classes, of which we are so proud, are no guarantee of success in this area. Nor have we cause for self-congratulations on a relatively low percentage of academic failures; with a selective policy we should be concerned about even one failure. We should consider how we could have prevented that failure rather than how small a fraction of a class might fail. In a college of professional schools, we assume a responsibility for directing our students into successful careers. Therefore, their individual problems demand individual attention.

Perhaps the responsibility a college teacher most easily can compromise, either inadvertently or knowingly, is that which he owes himself as a scholar. Yet, here his value to his students, to his institution, and to his profession is at stake. The field of knowledge, most especially technical knowledge, changes rapidly, and only by keeping pace with it can the educator sense the future demands of his profession. The difficulty that leads to compromise on this responsibility is not the lack of scholarly ability, but rather the lack of encouragement, support, and recognition.

Any faculty member and any administrator can add to this list of responsibilities. If we agree that these are some of the obligations of faculty, then it is time to look at those obligations that administration must assume.

A distinguished faculty is fashioned of promising individuals set in an environment that fosters both individual and collective development. The creation of that environment is a joint enterprise, with administration carrying the brunt of the effort. Its essential elements are not hard to describe, but to achieve them requires intelligence, good will, patience, and, usually, money.

A key asset any school must have to attract and hold a distinguished faculty is a superior student body, one that is a challenge, a provocation, a delight. Again, administration bears the brunt of the responsibility for attracting a good student body, although the soundest means of attracting good students is the assembling of a superior faculty. Selection of superior students on the basis of their own qualifications is manifestly more nearly possible for a private college than for a state university, but in either case the successful recruitment of good students should depend largely on the administration's other obligation to encourage excellence in faculty and curricula.

The pursuit of scholarship requires time, whether for self-study, painting, writing, research, or simply maintaining liaison with other scholars. Administration should make sure that teaching schedules are not so demanding that other scholarly pursuits are thereby discouraged and it should be able to encourage extensive individual work in some cases. We should be in a position, when we identify the exceptional writer, painter, or researcher, to give him the time to do what he does so well. To encourage faculty creativity is a special responsibility of a professional school, for everyone gains—the profession, the professor, the student, and the school.

There can be little doubt that one of the most salutary experiences a scholar can have is a year away from his customary surroundings, spent in a new and refreshing atmosphere of scholarship and research. Administration should be in a position to encourage such experiences. Ideally, for the good of the college, sabbatical leaves should be almost mandatory rather than the rare exception.

In a similar category rests our responsibility to encourage younger members of our staff to complete their formal graduate work. Encouragement, in material terms, means granting them time for such work without reduction in salary and even helping to underwrite their academic expenses—practices increasingly prevalent in industry these days. Whatever false values may be assigned to the Ph.D. (the teacher's "union card"), it nevertheless represents several years of intense study in the forefront of technology.

I do not think that creative output should be the prime criterion of a faculty member's stature. I do think that creative work is a lively correlative to good teaching and that it must receive the institution's support and encouragement. The enthusiasm of the researcher permeates his being and adds confidence and excitement to his teaching. In the evaluation of our faculty by educational standards, creative effort neither should be overlooked nor overemphasized.

In this brief recital of some of the responsibilities of administration, financial responsibility has been implied rather than stated. But this responsibility underlies all others. We must try to be financially prepared to recognize that the teaching profession should receive pay commensurate with its preparation and its contribution to society; that physical facilities should be adequate for the comfort and stimulation of students and faculty; that an environment conducive to excellence in both faculty and students must include some of the fringe benefits as well as the basic necessities of academic life. Finally, in the face of an abundance of problems, administration finds this generalization inescapable: only the best possible faculty, functioning under favorable conditions, can win us the best solutions.

PART III

The Teacher, Professor, and Scholar

From Preparation to Responsibility

46

The Preparation of College Teachers

ALLAN O. PFNISTER

Provost, Wittenberg University. At the time his article originally appeared in *School and Society* (Oct. 8, 1960), he was associate professor of higher education, Center for the Study of Higher Education, University of Michigan.

Many of our current debates about the suitability of various programs for the preparation of college teachers arise out of a failure to define with any clarity the role of the teacher. By initially confusing "faculty member" with "teacher," we erect almost insurmountable barriers to fruitful discussion of the issues. At the undergraduate level, it may be psychologically difficult to distinguish between "faculty member" and "teacher"; admittedly, it is much easier to do so at the graduate level. Psychologically possible or not, however, the only way to begin a logical discussion of the preparation of the college teacher that will lead anywhere is to abstract that portion—greater or less, depending upon circumstances—of the faculty member's role that is called teaching.

If we examine the teaching situation, we find that by reducing it to the most simple elements we have: one who is called a *teacher;* one person, or more, designated *student(s) or learner(s);* and *subject matter* with which teacher and student(s) are concerned. (I am not ignoring all that recent literature has said about objectives involving attitudes and skills and values. We must speak of attitudes with respect to something or someone, skills with respect to something, values with respect to something.) And with teacher-student subject matter we must have the means by which the teacher *communicates* subject matter or something about subject matter. The above does not exhaust the complexity of the teaching situation, but I believe that other elements may be subsumed under these basic categories.

Let us consider first the teacher *vis-à-vis* subject matter. Subject matter in the teaching situation is something personal. As Newman suggests, knowledge or subject matter is "a state or condition of mind."[1] It is more than a collection of discrete items; it is the individual creation of the mind. Or, as Philip Leon suggested in his inaugural address at University College, Leicester, a professor (and I would insert the word "teacher") is one who "manufactures a subject . . . he makes English literature as a Professor of English and French literature as a Professor of French; as a historian he makes history and determines which part of it shall be ancient, which medieval, which modern, and which the end of history."[2] The teacher is not a phonograph, playing back bits of information which he has gathered hither, thither, and yon. Rather, he is personally responsible for having encountered the world of knowledge and for having fashioned out of this encounter something called subject matter.

Although the teacher cannot be considered apart from subject matter, the possessor of subject matter may not be a teacher. For the teaching situation demands the student and the communication between teacher and student. Here we must emphasize that in relation to the subject matter of the teacher, the student is relatively ignorant—for the subject matter is a personal creation of the teacher. The student stands in need of the teacher because he stands in need of the subject matter which is the teacher's.

The relation of teacher to student is dynamic. The teacher, who has confronted the world of knowledge, forms his subject matter and communicates with the student. Communication implies give and take. It is not passive receptivity or absorption.

When the teacher is involved in communication, he faces the whole question of methodology. As is true of the creation of subject matter, communication is personal and alive. Methodology varies with the personality of the teacher, and it also varies with the subject matter. Communication in the physical sciences or in mathematics may be different from communication in a second language or in music. But essentially, methodology involves the best possible conversation between the teacher and the student. The conversation is not haphazard; it is initiated, carried forward to an end, and it has purpose and direction.

In effect, we have sketched above the outline of a theory of teaching. Let us see if this theory helps in our consideration of the preparation of college teachers. Some of the propositions developing out of this theory are:

(1) The preparation of teachers is a lifetime task. This is trite—but in its triteness it is ignored too often. No level of formal education is wholly responsible for preparing college teachers, nor is any one level wholly to be blamed if teachers are not better teachers.[3] The undergraduate school shares

---

[1] J. H. Cardinal Newman, "The Scope and Nature of University Education" (New York: Dutton, 1958), p. 93.
[2] P. Leon, "The Professors: An Inaugural Lecture" (Leicester, England: University College, 1955), p. 5.
[3] *Cf.*, J. S. Diekhoff, "The Domain of the Faculty" (New York: Harper, 1956), pp. 50ff.

in the preparation. The undergraduate school introduces the student to the subject matter of a discipline, and, if it does the job well, begins to make him realize that the subject matter is more than a collection of sense impressions, isolated facts; it assists him in gaining the "philosophy" of knowledge, as Newman would term it—the ability to view things in relation to one another—and it assists him in making a start at formulating his own approach to the world of knowledge.

The graduate school takes the process further. And the graduate school does not finish the process, for it only can assist the student to gain more tools, more insight.

In terms of time spent in any institution, the employing college may have the greatest responsibility. It must provide the opportunity for the teacher to continue to grow and to create. If, for various reasons or conditions, the employing college is not able to provide circumstances for growth, then it cannot wholly blame the schools that preceded it. The preparation cannot be completed at some arbitrary point such as the Ph.D.

(2) What I have just stated *vis-à-vis* subject matter applies equally to communication. Recent studies suggest that relatively few students look back to a particular undergraduate college faculty member as the source of inspiration to enter college teaching. Less than one-third (29%) of the college teachers in one study[4] reported that the desire to enter college teaching came in undergraduate college. On the other hand, in a study in which I am involved, it is found that a few colleges produce an inordinately large number of future college teachers. In the medieval university, the masters constituted a guild, and completion of the academic program led to induction into the guild. Perhaps in this latter day we need more of a sense of "guild" in the undergraduate college. Perhaps those colleges sending large numbers of persons into college teaching have a high sense of "guild." Perhaps teachers therein are more successful in communicating a view of knowledge rather than isolated bits of information.

The graduate school clearly has a responsibility in the area of communication. By the time of reception of the highest degree, 75% of the future faculty members have decided upon college teaching as a career.[5] By conducting inquiries into the nature of communication in a specific discipline, the graduate school can assist the future teacher in developing skill in communicating.

But 25% of those who enter teaching decide upon a college teaching career after completing graduate study. Moreover, one study shows that only 45% of new teachers enter directly from graduate school into college

[4] J. E. Stecklein and R. E. Eckert, "An Exploratory Study of Factors Influencing the Choice of College Teaching as a Career" (Minneapolis: University of Minnesota Press, 1958).
[5] *Ibid.,* p. 7.

teaching.[6] Thus, the employing institution also has a responsibility to assist the teacher in gaining skill in communication.

Skill in communication develops over a period of time. Perhaps the most meaningful discussions of methodology occur in the teaching situation rather than in courses generalizing about methodology. But reflection on communication cannot be left to chance. Some systematic investigation and discussion are necessary. As the orator gains skill through practice—guided and systematic practice—so the college teacher gains skill through practice—guided and systematic practice. Rarely does one become an effective orator who does not reflect systematically upon what he is doing. Similarly, I fail to see how the college teacher can be effective without reflecting systematically upon what he is doing.

(3) Not only is the preparation of a college teacher a lifelong process, but the theory of teaching outlined above requires that we think always of the three-dimensional teaching situation. We cannot argue the relative importance of subject matter and communication. By definition, a teacher must be both a master of his subject and a skillful communicator. By definition, he is not a teacher if he cannot communicate. By definition, he is not a teacher if he does not have something to communicate. By definition, he is not a teacher if he does not have students with whom to communicate.

(4) If our theory of teaching is valid, we cannot equate publishing with good teaching. I do not depreciate publication as an important part of the role of the faculty member; however, publication may vary in importance with the type and complexity of the institution in which the faculty member is located. Publication implies addressing one's peers, requiring their evaluation.[7] Teaching vis-à-vis the indispensable student implies communication with one who is less than equal.

(5) Need the teacher engage in research? If research implies publication, the teacher as such need not engage in research. If research is likened unto continuous inquiry into the discipline, the making of subject matter, the teacher fails to do research at his peril. He stops growing. He always must be mastering his subject matter; he always must be looking for the relations of one discipline to another.

(6) Is the Ph.D. degree the right degree, or is the Ph.D. program the best program? Assuming that the Ph.D. program is to assist the student in gaining skill in creating subject matter through investigation, it presumably is good preparation for college teaching. If the dissertation represents an honest investigation into a portion of subject matter, it may be an excellent experience in the methods of inquiry. If it is simply training in the skill of developing a publishable piece, it contributes much less to the depth and skills required by the teacher.

[6] "Teacher Supply and Demand in Universities, Colleges, and Junior Colleges, 1957–58 and 1958–59" (Washington, D.C.: National Education Association, 1959), p. 17.
[7] G. K. Plochmann, *Journal of General Education*, 12: 170–175, July, 1959.

Ironically, "Ph.D." includes the term "philosophy." To have a "philosophy" implies to have an overview, a command of the science of the subject matter, to know how to deal with it and to see it in relation to other subjects. If the Ph.D. program leads to a philosophy, then it is good preparation for teaching, If it does not, then it contributes less to teaching, and perhaps it contributes less to mastery of the subject matter than we are willing to admit.

47

The Preparation of Teachers in a Liberal Arts College

THOMAS M. CARTER

Professor emeritus of education, Albion College. His article originally appeared in *School and Society* on April 17, 1965.

There is, at present, a growing interest in the education of teachers in liberal arts colleges. However, a good liberal arts college must not be taken for granted. It is good only if it meets certain standards. Such a college has a clear vision of what it is trying to accomplish and reveals its vision in its stated aims. The end result of all college experiences should be thought of in terms of human abilities, habits, attitudes, appreciations, skills, powers of judgment, and other similar characteristics. A clear understanding of what these are and a general agreement as to what department of the college should be held responsible for them is necessary.

The general aims of the college should be clearly stated and accepted by all who teach in it:

1. A vivid, stirring picture of *what has been*. Someone has said that "to be ignorant of what has happened before one was born is to be always a child." This statement was never truer and never carried more weight than at the present time. The past is "the dead past" only to those who do not understand it.

2. The ability to see and understand *what is*. Much of what is, is in terms of present possibilities which, as yet, have not been discovered, implemented, and made use of. The power to go around the world many times within a few hours has been here all the time. We did not create it; we only implemented it. Some of what is, is in our universe of things, while others are in our universe of humanity.

3. Sufficiently cultivated, creative imagination to project oneself into what is, as yet, unreal. An important function of liberal education is to enable man to see *what could be*. A liberal arts college is a place where, if anywhere, a young person should formulate a utopia for himself and a utopia for others in the world about him. He should be helped to see how his life could be different and how society could be different.

4. A clear, broad, and enlightened vision of *what should be* and a warm espousal of it. That old fatalistic notion that "whatever is to be will be" must give way to whatever should be must be. If there is a hierarchy of values among the aims of a liberal arts college, this one possibly would take first rank. Men must be led to live and, if necessary, die for what should be.

5. An orientation toward a career. There is no more sacred obligation than that of determining what one should do with his life. What a person can do and do well contributes greatly to his own happiness and to his usefulness to society. The college student should be increasingly career-minded, and the sooner he begins the better, even though he changes his career perspective several times while in college. With a career perspective, one more effectively can appropriate for himself the many phases of general education which are not related specifically to any career but which are related to his life in a career.

Each department needs to articulate a series of specific objectives for guiding thought and judgment through the endless and intricate maze of materials and activities available to it. For illustrative purposes, we will set forth appropriate aims of two departments in a liberal arts college.

THE MATHEMATICS DEPARTMENT

The highly divergent mathematical needs of various vocations must not be allowed to dictate the content of a general education course which has no particular reference to the vocation into which one goes. On the other hand, the general training in the field of mathematics must not serve as a limitation upon the mathematics prescribed for career purposes. Mathematics often is thought of as a tool subject. It is that, since quantitative thinking is called for in the study of other subjects. For this reason, there should be a close relation between the mathematics department and other departments of the college. However, mathematics has a place of its own in the pattern of general or liberal education. Four objectives of mathematics may indicate the two categories of functions of mathematics:

1. Ability to supply the needed quantitative aspect of thought involved in each of many activities in which one, at one time or another, engages.

2. The ability to read and interpret statistical and graphical material, to organize and express facts statistically and graphically, and to do one's thinking along many lines in statistical and graphical terms.

3. A proportional intellectual comprehension of the subtle abstract world of number and quantity with the necessary accompanying awakened interest and appreciations.

4. A proportional intellectual comprehension of the world of form and space relations with the necessary accompanying awakened interest and appreciations.

Of the four aims stated above, the first two are career-oriented and the last two are liberal education-oriented. They also are stated in terms of human adaptations, attitudes, and abilities rather than in terms of subject-matter mastery only.

THE DEPARTMENT OF EDUCATION

The teacher needs a clear understanding of the origin, function, and present nature of the school and its relation to its cultural setting. He also must possess the ability to process the elements of culture and make them comprehensible to the learner. The aims of the department of education may be stated as the cultivation of appropriate personality characteristics, liberal education, professional knowledge, and professional skills.

Desirable characteristics of teachers are physical and mental vigor, freedom of neurotic tendencies, open-mindedness, judiciousness, resource-fulness, decisiveness, cheerfulness, sympathy, tolerance, tact, kindness, teachability, loyalty, high ideals, modesty, courageousness, sincerity, patience, consistency, altruism, refinement, and self-control. It is unreasonable to expect to find all these qualities to a high degree in all teachers. Moreover, it is still an open question as to whether selection or training can be most relied upon to provide schools with teachers who have good personality qualities. Students in a liberal arts college are likely to be a selected group. Another selection is made from among them for admission to the teacher education program. However, personality traits undoubtedly can be affected by training.

Liberal education can be assigned, in large measure, to departments of the college other than the department of education, but not all of it. No department of a liberal arts college can be more vital to its mission than the department of education. Most great philosophers, from Plato to John Dewey, have spent some of their most fruitful years considering education. This is natural, since education affects and, in turn, is affected by all other aspects of life.

Professional knowledge obtained in such courses as principles of education, history of education, comparative education, and educational psychology can contribute to liberal education as well as to professional knowledge. Some educationists do not favor giving much attention to these courses because they think of them as too theoretical. People who think this way would do well to consider John Dewey's statement that "theory is the most practical of all things." It is so because it has wide implications and long-range applications.

The need for professional skills is so obvious that superficial thinking has led some educationists to favor confining teacher preparation to skills gained in the classroom as an apprentice teacher and in closely related situations. This is unwise, because a teacher who is short on theory is likely to be short on growth. Some liberal arts teachers discredit teacher education because some time must be given to gaining professional skills. This seems strange when they readily admit the educational respectability of skill training in graphic art, music, science, and linguistics.

Not only do teachers need a liberal arts setting in which to prepare for their careers, but also the liberal arts college needs to include in its program the kind of training needed for the education of teachers. Liberal education is the means of interpreting and transferring civilization to oncoming generations. The five great agencies of civilization are the home, the church, the school, the state, and the vocation. Why should one of these great agencies—the school—be neglected by a liberal education agency?

48

On the Education and Certification of Teachers

ARTHUR E. BESTOR, JR.

Professor of history, University of Washington. At the time his article appeared in *School and Society* (Sept. 19, 1953), he was professor of history, University of Illinois. His article was excerpted from an address at the University of Wyoming, July 29, 1953. The article was expanded for inclusion in Prof. Bestor's book, *Educational Wastelands* (Urbana: University of Illinois Press, 1953). This artiolo and tho book oauood oonoidorablo oontrovoroy.

The division between elementary and secondary education on the one hand and higher education on the other is an administrative fact, natural and probably inescapable. In recent years in the United States, however, it has been converted into a momentous intellectual schism, threatening the soundness of our public educational system and even the intellectual welfare of the nation. The schism has spread to the universities, where the education of teachers has come almost completely under the control of departments or colleges of education, so-called, which are affected little, if at all, by the educational thinking of the rest of the university faculties.

This process has been facilitated by a misuse and misapplication of the word *education*. The Department of Education actually concerns itself with "the art, practice or profession of teaching; especially, systematized learning or instruction concerning principles and methods of teaching." The quoted words are the dictionary definition, not of *education*, but of *pedagogy*. What calls itself a Department or College of Education is, properly speaking, only a Department of Pedagogy.

This is not a mere matter of words. The faulty terminology at present used has warped, in subtle but dangerous ways, the thinking of almost everyone in America concerning public educational policy. The fact—obvious, undeniable, and yet forgotten— is that the university *as a whole* is concerned with education. Every department in it is a department of education in the legitimate sense of that word. My own department is actually a Department of Education in Historical Thinking. The term Department of History is merely a convenient abbreviation of this concept. The division that calls itself a Department of Education is in reality a Department of Education in Pedagogical Methods. It has no right whatever to abbreviate its name to Department of Education and thereby to imply that it has a greater concern with education than some other department.

The abuses to which this faulty terminology has led are numerous and obvious. Taking advantage of the unfortunate laxness of academic terminology, professors of education represent themselves to the general public as the only members of university faculties who need to be consulted with respect to the ultimate aims and purposes of education. And they have contrived to put across the completely unfounded notion that the proper way to prepare for a career in teaching is to take course work in education, so-called, that is to say, in pedagogy.

Let me not be misunderstood. Pedagogy itself—that is to say, the careful investigation of the processes of teaching and learning—is a legitimate field of research. Important work has been done, and it must continue to be done, in investigating the psychology of learning, in developing effective textbooks and teaching aids, in experimenting with classroom procedures, in adapting instruction to students of differing intellectual capacity. As a teacher of history, I am directly interested in every improvement that increases the effectiveness with which history is being taught. But the effective teacher of history requires many qualities of mind and personality, many varieties of knowledge, and many intellectual skills, among which pedagogy is only one.

Obviously every teacher must have some knowledge and skill in pedagogy just as a doctor must have some adeptness at what we call "bedside manner." It is far from certain that the best way to acquire these skills is by listening to lectures about them. But granting that it is, such courses are not the central thing in the preparation for either profession. What counts in a doctor is his knowledge of medicine, and what counts in a teacher is his knowledge of the subject he is teaching. To expect to produce a good teacher by training him mainly in pedagogy is as foolish as to expect to produce a good doctor by loading him down with courses in bedside manner. And yet at one midwestern university there is a course entitled "Science in the Elementary School," the catalogue description of which says frankly, "no science background is assumed and no attempt is made to cover content." If medical schools were run as colleges of education are, we would all be done to death by cheery and plausible doctors who would know all about *how* to practice medicine but who would not be quite sure whether human beings have gizzards or not.

The preparation of teachers for the public schools is one of the most important functions of the American university. It is a function of the university as a whole. It will never be satisfactorily performed until it is performed by the university as a whole. The fact that it has largely been delegated to the department or school or college of education is a principal cause of the alarming anti-intellectualism of so much public education today.

University faculties of liberal arts and sciences must bear much of the blame for permitting this situation to develop. They should have exercised constant vigilance over developments in secondary education. They should have studied the actual educational needs of prospective and experienced teachers. They should have devised programs especially adapted to the needs of teachers, yet soundly based upon the fundamental intellectual disciplines instead of upon long-drawn-out training in the mere tricks of the pedagogical trade. They failed to do so, and the educationists rushed in to fill the vacuum.

Faculties of liberal arts and sciences must retrieve their past mistakes. They must take seriously the problem of devising sound and appropriate curricula for the education of teachers. They must show themselves ready and willing to assume again, sincerely and with a sense of highest obligation, the responsibility for teacher training which they permitted (with culpable negligence) to pass out of their hands.

At the undergraduate level the education of the future teacher should be an education in the liberal arts and sciences. This ought to be self-evident The ideal of liberal education is to produce men and women with disciplined minds, cultivated interests, and a wide range of fundamental knowledge. Who in our society needs these qualities more than the teacher? We increasingly recognize that the doctor, the lawyer, and the engineer, if they are to achieve true professional eminence, must receive balanced training in many intellectual disciplines which are not directly related to their professions. How much more does a teacher need such an education? For him the fundamental intellectual disciplines are not supplements to, but the very essence of, his professional stock in trade. The teacher never knows when he may be called upon to give instruction in any or all of them. The students whose work he directs have a right to expect of him a genuine and sympathetic understanding of their various intellectual interests and ambitions. The last profession in which narrow vocational considerations should be allowed to interfere with thorough and well-balanced under-graduate preparation in the liberal arts and sciences is the teaching profession. Opportunity to satisfy minimum pedagogical requirements should be provided through electives that are a normal complement of a college program of liberal education, but under no circumstances should the depart-ment of pedagogy be permitted to exercise any sort of control over the undergraduate programs of prospective teachers.

Continued training in the fundamental intellectual disciplines is the recognized and proper purpose of graduate work. American universities, it seems to me, have failed, and failed most miserably, to apply even rudimentary common sense to the problem of devising a sound and useful graduate program for public-school teachers. We force the teacher to choose between a research program that is thorough and scholarly but too highly specialized for his needs, and a pedagogical program that is superficial and blatantly anti-intellectual and that solemnly and tediously reinstructs him in vocational skills he already possesses. The university ought not to compel the teacher to choose between such unacceptable alternatives. It should offer him a program that satisfies the highest academic standards and at the same time faces realistically the actual facts of secondary and elementary school teaching.

A little imagination should enable the university to devise a program that will be of a truly advanced scholarly character and that will possess genuine relevance to the intellectual tasks which a public-school teacher is called upon to perform.

We must begin by considering the actual situation of the public-school teacher. He is usually called upon to teach two or more distinct disciplines. Even in a single course he ought to be bringing to bear upon the subject in hand appropriate information from other fields. A wide range of accurate knowledge is his most useful asset, rather than an intensive knowledge of a limited though rapidly advancing segment of learning within which he may hope to make original contributions of his own. In simplest terms, the graduate work of a school teacher ought to be a prolongation and deepening of the liberal education which he received (or should have received) as an undergraduate. The university ought to provide him an opportunity to continue that liberal education for as long as he is willing to pursue it, and it ought to reward him with a suitable degree for conscientious and thoughtful work when rationally directed to that end.

Let me illustrate by a specific example. A student, let us assume, has received a four-year liberal education, in the course of which he has met the pedagogical requirements for teaching. He has majored, perhaps, in history, and has done a considerable amount of work in English. He has taken introductory courses in the sciences, economics, and political science, and acquired a reading knowledge of one foreign language. His first teaching assignment is to a course in the social studies, to a course in English, and to one in algebra. He is to return for several summers to the university for advanced work. What should the university encourage him to do?

The university should permit him, first of all, to take courses that will really round out his knowledge of the various fields of history. For this purpose many undergraduate courses may be more appropriate than the graduate courses offered to research students, and he should be permitted to elect these. When he has completed a sound program in history, he should be permitted to go back to the point at which he dropped mathematics in college, and work that field up systematically in the way in which undergraduate majors in mathematics would do. So it should be with each of the fields in which he has done previous work, or in which he is required to teach, or in which, perhaps, he develops an interest for the first time.

The results of such study should be an exceptionally well-prepared teacher. More than that, the results would be a liberally educated man or woman, with a far deeper and wider range of knowledge than a four-year undergraduate program could give him. Study directed in such a way and to such ends is advanced study, no matter what parts of it may have been pursued in nominally undergraduate courses. It is the kind of education which a university should be proud to offer, and which it has a legitimate right to reward with an advanced degree. A student who pursues such a well-thought-out program for a full academic year beyond college graduation and who brings his command of two subjects up to certain pre-established standards should receive a Master's degree. A student who pursues it with distinction for three years beyond college graduation and who brings his command of five subjects up to the standards set should be entitled to a doctorate.

Much careful thought must go into the establishment of these standards in each subject. In order to receive a degree, a student should be required to demonstrate, in each proffered subject, a comprehension at least equal to that which an able undergraduate might be expected to obtain through a strong major program in the discipline. Course credits might aggregate about 30 semester hours, including undergraduate work. But the number of courses should not be the principal criterion. A comprehensive written examination in each of the subjects offered for the degree would be indispensable. In addition, an oral examination for the doctorate should cover all the five fields presented. A careful reading of certain basic works—the classics of the discipline—should be specifically required and tested. No thesis would be submitted for either degree, but a student should have been required to write at least one substantial original essay in each of his fields during the course of his studies, and these should be part of the record upon which his degree is awarded.

The traditional research program of the university, and the teaching program that I have just described, should be considered parallel but distinct. Both should be under the administration of the graduate school of the university, but the degrees ought to be different. Corresponding to the traditional degrees of M.A. and Ph.D. which would continue to be awarded in the research program, the university might make use of the degrees of Master and Doctor of Education (M.Ed. and Ed.D.) for the teaching program. These degrees, of course, already exist. The present proposal, however, would put them under the jurisdiction of the university as a whole, not the department of education or pedagogy, and would permit a student to earn them by work in any regular department of liberal arts or science in the university.

To administer its re-established responsibilities in this wide realm, the university might well set up a distinct Faculty of Teacher Training, with its own committees and administrative officers. To this newly created faculty would belong all the members of all the academic departments offering work leading to the M.Ed. and the Ed.D. In many universities a professor already belongs to two or more faculties—to the Faculty of Liberal Arts and the Graduate Faculty, for example—hence, such an arrangement has ample precedent. Most of the administrative and public-relations functions of the old college or department of education would be transferred to the committees of the new Faculty of Teacher Training. These would not only approve curricula, but would also supervise teacher placement. Co-operation of the university in school surveys and in educational commissions of various sorts would be handled through the new faculty.

This new all-university faculty would also assume direct authority over the curriculum in the demonstration and laboratory schools which the university maintains. To the general public a university school signifies an institution of elementary or secondary education devoted to the ideals of science and scholarship for which the university stands. It must be made precisely that. Its program should be determined by scholars, scientists, and educationists together, and it should concentrate its experimental work upon the problem of effectively teaching the basic intellectual disciplines, organized as they are in the real world of science and learning.

Advanced research in educational problems will be conducted, as it ought to be, by the university as a whole and on an interdisciplinary basis. In other words, psychologists, sociologists, and statisticians will be asked to collaborate in investigating various problems of teaching and learning. Historians, political scientists, and economists will co-operate in studying various aspects of educational administration. The university will serve public education, not by delegating its responsibilities to a department of pedagogy, but by itself providing the opportunity, the facilities, and the funds to bring specialists from various disciplines together for co-operative research without detaching them permanently from the departments to which they belong.

One great barrier stands in the way of a rational program of teacher training—the certification requirements which are imposed by the state. These requirements are, in reality, special-interest legislation—a kind of protective tariff—enacted for the most part at the behest of professional educationists. As the very first step toward educational reform, citizens, scientists, scholars, professional men, and classroom teachers must unite in demanding that the legislatures of the 48 states review, carefully and realistically, the statutes governing the certification of teachers. The present laws must be replaced by ones which will protect the schools against incompetent teachers rather than the professors of pedagogy against losses in enrollment.

Looked at from the point of view of logic or common sense, the present arrangements for certifying teachers are completely topsy-turvy. Local school authorities, who can interview teachers individually as well as examine their credentials, are in a far better position to judge a candidate's probable skill and competence as a teacher than can a bureaucrat who works solely from records of courses taken. Conversely, an agency of the state is far better equipped than a local school board to determine a student's competence in his chosen subject, for it can compare his academic record with hundreds of others, it can administer standardized examinations, and it can call upon specialists in all fields of knowledge for advice and assistance. Under the existing system, however, the responsibilities are completely reversed. The matters that local authorities are competent to determine for themselves are precisely the ones that the state educational bureaucracy insists on controlling from above; and the kinds of minimum requirements which the state is in the best position to enforce are precisely the ones that are left largely to local discretion, or to quasi-official accrediting agencies.

The first step to reform is to clear the statute books of those provisions which specify a fixed number of hours in education (that is, in pedagogy) as a requirement for certification. This means simply dethroning these requirements from their peculiarly privileged position. Then a new system must be worked out which will give assurance that a certified teacher is both proficient in teaching and well-prepared in the subjects he or she is to teach.

Different certificates should deal with these different matters. One certificate should testify to the teacher's proficiency in teaching. There ought to be several ways of earning this certificate. An experienced teacher ought to be granted it simply upon presentation of satisfactory evidence of a successful teaching career of a specified length of time. For a candidate without previous experience, successful completion of a period of practice teaching should be the principal requirement. The institution that supervises practice teaching usually specifies certain pedagogical courses as prerequisites, hence the state has no need to lay down pedagogical course requirements of its own in granting certificates of teaching proficiency. Provision should be made for students without either experience or practice teaching to obtain a temporary certificate enabling them to offer instruction in specially designated schools, which would guarantee to give on-the-job training and special guidance and supervision to those without experience. Such programs might well be financed by the state to aid in the recruitment of teachers, or they might be conducted by the extension departments of universities. After completing a specified period of teaching under such conditions, an instructor should be entitled to a permanent certificate of teaching proficiency. An arrangement of this kind would enable the schools to draw upon a large and brilliant group of liberal arts graduates who are at present excluded from public-school employment by unjustifiably arbitrary pedagogical requirements. After the basic certificate in teaching proficiency has been earned, further course work in pedagogy should be entirely optional with the individual teacher.

Another certificate should be provided for each of the fundamental disciplines of public-school instruction. Ideally these certificates should be granted on the basis of state-administered comprehensive examinations in the subject, periodically offered to all persons who believe themselves qualified. There should be at least two levels of such examinations, one leading to limited, the second to advanced certification in the subject or discipline. Pending the development of such examinations, limited certification might be granted on the basis of 15 or 20 semester hours of college work in the subject, advanced certification for 30 or 40 hours. The certification should be in specific subjects rather than general ideas. In other words, there should be certificates in history, in political science, and in economics: a teacher of social studies would be expected to possess at least limited certification in two or three of these subjects.

A prospective teacher would be encouraged to meet certification requirements in as many subjects as possible during his undergraduate years. The teacher already in service who returned to the university for advanced work during summer sessions and regular terms would have a definite purpose in view: to bring his certification in the subjects he had been teaching from the limited to the advanced classification, or to secure certification in additional subjects. The recognition or accrediting standards applied to schools themselves could easily be geared to this system of certification. The ideal school would be one in which every course was being conducted by a teacher possessing advanced certification in the subject or subjects covered by the course. Every deviation from this would lessen the standing of the school.

Salary increments could likewise be effectively tied to this scheme. The term "professional growth" frequently appears among the criteria for the promotion and the advancement in salary of teachers. At present this is a vague phrase. It could easily be endowed with a definite meaning. Under the proposed system, a teacher would be giving tangible evidence of professional growth every time he raised his certification from limited to advanced in a given subject and every time he acquired a limited certificate in a new field. Each such step might well entitle him to an increment in salary.

Besides the certificate of teaching proficiency and the certificates in the various subjects, provision would have to be made for various types of special certificates. Elementary school teaching, for example, presents special problems. A certificate in Educational Psychology for Elementary School Teachers, in addition to the general certificate in teaching proficiency, might well be established. Care should be taken to make its requirements clear and specific. This certificate should not be granted for a mere potpourri of pedagogical courses, but only for a carefully designed program comprising extensive work in the regular academic department of psychology. Another certificate in Educational Administration should also be offered, to be obtained by specified work primarily in the departments of political science (or public administration), economics, and law, with only such work in the department of pedagogy as seemed clearly justifiable. Other special certificates—and several will doubtless be needed—should be set up on analogous principles.

A reorganization of teacher training and certification requirements along the lines here outlined would correct some of the gravest abuses in the present situation. It would bring to an end the aimless accumulation by experienced teachers of credits in pedagogical courses. It would restore to teacher training a realism and a clear sense of purpose that it has lost. It would, in fact, make teacher training "functional" once more.

A new curriculum for the education of teachers, based wholly upon the liberal arts and sciences rather than upon the mere vocational skills of pedagogy, will do more to restore the repute of the public schools than any other step that can be taken. Not only will teachers be adequately trained in the disciplines they undertake to teach, but they will also be imbued with respect for those disciplines and will be prepared to resist the anti-intellectualism that currently threatens the schools. And when the tide begins to turn, young men and women of genuine intellectual interest and capacity will be attracted in increasing numbers into the profession of public-school teaching. They will not be repelled at the outset by being asked to lay aside their intellectual interests and fritter away their time in the courses of the pedagogues. Under a well-ordered plan, the gateway to teaching will be the gateway of learning itself.

49

The Intellectual and the Schools

FRANCIS KEPPEL

President and chairman of the board, General Learning Corporation, and former U.S. Commissioner of Education. At the time his article originally appeared in *School and Society* (Feb. 6, 1954), he was dean of the Graduate School of Education, Harvard University.

The following comments are concerned with Arthur E. Bestor, Jr.'s "On the Education and Certification of Teachers" (*School and Society*, September 19, 1953) and his expanded views in "Educational Wastelands" (University of Illinois Press).

There should be no question about Dr. Bestor's right to study the policies and procedures of the schools and to publish his conclusions. The controversy between certain professors of liberal arts and certain professors of education has been costly in energy and wasteful of talents desperately needed in the development of the schools. It can lead to useful results only if there is full freedom of speech, and only if there reigns also a sense of scholarly integrity and rigor. The reader must judge whether Dr. Bestor's article, and this comment on it, live up to these requirements.

It has been suggested that Dr. Bestor is unfriendly toward the basic political purpose of public education and the right of the children of each generation to educational opportunity. A careful reading of his book will show that this is incorrect and unfair. Unfortunately, others may quote him for purposes with which he might not agree. Bestor, however, is concerned about one important aspect of the work of the schools and his motives should not be impugned if he criticizes weaknesses which have been of equal concern to many "professional educators."

Dr. Bestor, however, is not without responsibility for creating a querulous atmosphere. Some of his comments about professors of education are far from courteous and the very title, "Educational Wastelands," is open to question. Both the general public—ultimately responsible for our educational system, which continues to produce honest and intelligent citizens and distinguished scholars—and those sincere individuals who are accused of laying waste the land have a right to protest.

It is not that two parts of the academic world—the liberal arts and the "professional educators"—are hopelessly separated in their aims or procedures. There is common ground. Bestor's recommendations for a sound liberal education for all teachers are obviously sensible and should be directed to those planning liberal arts programs as well as to those who serve on faculties of education. Everyone who has studied the schools will agree that far too many of the nation's million teachers are inadequately or badly prepared in the subjects they teach. Many of the proposals he makes on pp. 83-84 of his article are good. But the fact that they are set forth as though they are new ideas demonstrates again the shocking failure of communication or the lack of adequate investigation which bedevils the daily task of those who prepare teachers. For more than a decade, some of these ideas have formed the basis of the Master of Arts in Teaching program at Harvard, and more recently of similar programs at Yale and other institutions. Certain teachers colleges were among the leaders in establishing programs of general education. Current misunderstandings are the result of more than a simple confusion about the meaning of words used by educators to describe their activities: there is ignorance of what is now being done and what has been done in some teachers colleges and schools of education. A full exchange of information is needed.

A basic policy proposed by Dr. Bestor is that the schools' "particular job . . . is to provide intellectual training in every field of activity where systematic thinking is an important component of success" (p.16 of his book), particularly in the separate and fundamental disciplines of history, chemistry, mathematics, philosophy, and the like. These ways of thinking, when combined, form a liberal education, the purpose of which is the deliberate cultivation of the power to think. Dr. Bestor believes that the nation desires intellectual guidance from the scholarly world in defining these areas ever more accurately and in devising school policies and programs to accomplish this end.

To many a hard-pressed teacher or principal, this definition of purpose must bring a wistful smile. Life in the schools would be much simpler if the local communities agreed with Bestor. But the fact is that in most parts of this country such a statement of purpose does not accurately or completely describe the public's instructions to the schools. The teacher is expected to develop "good moral standards" as well as "train the mind," to help children to get along with each other in a reasonable and democratic manner as well as to study history and science. These instructions are not usually clearly stated, and one set of instructions is often in conflict with another. But it is clear that the public does not accept "intellectual training" as the "particular job" or the only purpose of the schools.

No doubt the "professional educators" have played a part in influencing public thinking in this regard over the past half century, as Bestor points out. But has he explored far enough in this area, or weighed his evidence sufficiently? Others believe that school programs designed for other purposes than "intellectual training" are not primarily the result of the plotting of professors of education. They reflect rather public opinion, which is, in effect, saying two things at the same time: that learning decent behavior, honesty, how to live by democratic values, etc., is important and should take place in the schools as well as the home; and that the public (to which belong parents of highly gifted as well as highly ungifted children) is of two or more minds about disciplines of thought, intellectual training, "scholarly standards," and the like. Scholars are necessary and should be supported, but it is the American way to laugh at their impracticalities and illusions. Outside their specialty they have been known to lose scholarly objectivity. There are a good many Americans who would have grave doubts about a university scholar's wisdom in planning for Johnny's school life. There is a certain ambivalence in the attitudes of American families toward the intellectual, an ambivalence which has deep roots in American history.

In the area of public policy formulation, then, one may ask whether Dr. Bestor's position does not assume too much for the intellectual's role. When it comes to his definition of the study of education, which he would prefer to describe as "pedagogy," the opposite question is appropriate: Is his position intellectual enough?

The reader's answer will depend on the faith he has in the contemporary social sciences as a means of understanding human behavior. How far can he trust theories developed in anthropology, psychology, sociology, economics, and political science to guide him in determining educational policy? A body of research over the past half century has resulted in theories which emphasize the essential role of emotion and of social forces in the learning process. The definition of the nature of the mind itself has been radically changed. Many educational policies during the same period of time have been based on these theories, though all too often with inadequate evidence or with too hasty a leaping at generalizations. Dr. Bestor is probably correct in wishing to discard certain careless practices, but he has not clearly decided whether to discard careful theories as well. He seems to welcome in the teaching of education only the results of investigations in one rather narrow aspect of the psychology of education, though his book bristles with problems which should be handled by historians and philosophers, political scientists and sociologists, as well as psychologists and experienced educators. For example, his proposal to concentrate the work of the schools on developing the pupil's "power to think" in apparent isolation from other aspects of emotional and social growth would seem to neglect contemporary learning theory and studies in human development. To what extent should those who study public education isolate themselves in the future from these broader aspects of science and scholarship? My colleagues and I have faith that the social sciences have already advanced the understanding of human behavior, and will continue to do so in the future. "If it is a sign of anti-intellectualism to understand a human being in his rational, moral, and emotional totality, and not *only* as an intellectual being, then we must courageously bear the blame of anti-intellectualism," one of my colleagues has said.

Bestor proposes that the preparation of teachers become a function and a concern of all professors in the college or university. This is obviously a desirable goal. But is it likely that his proposed pattern of organization will focus enough of the attention of these professors on the problems of the schools to accomplish his aim?

Specialization is a mark of the academic world, and the difficulties of interdisciplinary programs are by now a familiar story. At Harvard, our approach to the problem of how to define and to study the range of problems raised in the educational process has been to appoint, to full-time membership in the Faculty of Education, scholars in the arts and sciences, with heavy emphasis on philosophy and social science, as well as scholars in the professional fields.* We believe that the development of close personal and scholarly relations between faculty members of diverse intellectual training and experience will be mutually beneficial. I emphasize the importance of full-time membership because, with regret, I must report my impression that Bestor underestimates the difficulties facing his colleagues whose primary interests are in college teaching and research when they try to focus their attention on the problems of the schools. The past record of professors of the liberal arts, as Dr. Bestor has himself pointed out, is not good in this regard. What are the grounds for expecting a change in the near future? The present system of academic rewards and prestige does not favor his plan of organization. A special academic group of high quality and high morale, devoting a major part of its intellectual life to the study of this aspect of our society, and serving as a stimulating force to the entire academic community, seems to me still to be necessary.

The acid test comes, of course, when a teacher faces a classroom of pupils somewhere in the United States. He has to deal with the children as they are, with their wide range of ability to learn and their apparent lack of interest in the intellectual disciplines. He has to face the grave implications of imposing his cultural standards, and his view of what is important and unimportant, on a captive audience. As Dr. Bestor correctly points out, there is little dependable evidence to guide us in preparing teachers for this task. Imaginative experiments are needed. For this reason we welcome the present trend of certifying officers toward approving over-all, institutional

* I speak here only of the study of education itself: future teachers of any subject should obtain their basic preparation under scholars whose major task is the advancement of their specialized fields. A faculty of education should not be a duplication of a faculty of arts and sciences.

programs for the preparation of teachers rather than the counting of so many hours of this or that. One concern with Dr. Bestor's proposals on certification of teachers is, therefore, that his plan might turn out to be more rigid and complicated than our present arrangements. An ironic observer might even suggest that the result of his proposal would be to change the guard, not to free the prisoner.

My colleagues and I believe that much can be done to improve the elementary and secondary schools. The task is difficult, far more difficult than it seems on the surface, and likely to become more difficult as year follows year. We do not much care about organizational patterns or titular responsibility. We wish simply to help in this improvement of the quality of the public schools, and to make sure that by our actions the academic civil war does not interfere with carrying out our responsibilities as educators.

50

Bestor's Bad History

H. G. GOOD

The author was dean of the College of Education and Home Economics, Ohio State University, at the time his article originally appeared in *School and Society* (Feb. 6, 1954). Dr. Good is now retired.

Nothing less than a straight denial will be the proper response to the opening statement in Professor Bestor's article in *School and Society* (Sept. 19, 1953). It is not true that "the division between elementary and secondary education on the one hand and higher education on the other is an administrative fact, natural and probably inescapable." The old division was, and for several centuries continued to be, between elementary, on the one hand, and secondary-higher education, on the other. That division was based upon the separation of the social classes. Before and especially after the Reformation, the elementary school was for the lower classes, while the secondary school prepared upper-class boys for the university. The "administrative fact," at that time, was contrary to the "fact" stated by Mr. Bestor; and, except in a figurative sense, it was not "natural and inescapable." It was the result of historical conditions.

Moreover, it is a major achievement of the American nation to have linked the three schools—the elementary, secondary, and higher—to form a single system. The present "administrative fact" is that state universities are subject to all the winds that blow in the social climate. So, also, the professors. They are teachers, not always more intelligent than their students. The American people working through elected legislatures and boards and through school administrators and professors of "pedagogy" are creating an educational highway. The idea has commended itself to other peoples. For a number of years, but especially since World War II, through the Butler Act and the Langevin Plan, respectively, England and France have been trying to create similar systems. They are trying to end educational segregation based upon social class.

Those who write about education should take some account of its history, if they know that history. Professional historians are notorious for their neglect of the history of the institutions which provide them the opportunity to earn a living. Any who belong to a "Department of Education in Historical Thinking" have a special obligation to get the facts and to use them. And if historians considered that *history* has at least two meanings they might not be so greatly disturbed by the two senses of *education*.

The program in the article is so unrealistic that it need not occupy us very long. One or two points can be briefly made. The "university as a whole" does direct the work of the College of Education just as it directs the work of the College of Arts and Sciences with its renamed "Department of Education in Historical Thinking." The highly specialized courses, each buttressed by a series of prerequisites, which are offered in some liberal arts departments are often very inappropriate for the teacher who wants to acquire usable knowledge and understanding of his teaching fields. I suppose this is "anti-intellectual." But, in some universities, some departments have seen that there is a difference between the needs of a high-school teacher and those of a specialist in a highly developed field. Other departments should be, at least in part, controlled by the College of Education. I wonder how long it would take a teacher to complete all the work described by Professor Bestor. I wonder, also, how much additional work would be required if the arts departments were in undisturbed control. I wonder, finally, how long it will take to change the certification laws of the 48 states.

51

Errors in Dr. Bestor's Thinking

WILLIAM I. PAINTER

Consultant to the State Department of Education, Columbus, Ohio. At the time his article originally appeared in *School and Society* (Feb. 6, 1954), he was an associate professor of education, University of Akron.

It seems regettable that Dr. Bestor has allowed himself to make errors in reflective thinking with reference to professional education that he would lament if applied to his own field. He reasons from partial data, inaccurate data, and false associations.

Had he checked the professional education requirements of the 48 states, he would have found that so-called pedagogy is no major portion of the required pre-service education of public-school teachers. Secondary school teachers in particular are seldom required to take as much as one sixth of their work in a College of Education. Furthermore, his proposals relative to the amounts of training to be required in academic areas have largely been met in most states for years. Colleges of Education have raised few objections to this system of academic majors and minors.

When he refers to a catalogue description of a course entitled "Science in the Elementary School" as stating that "no science background is assumed and no attempt is made to cover content," is he so gullible as to think that an attempt is made to teach science methods in abstraction? Such description is solely for the purpose of citing that the course is not to be used as credit toward a major or minor in the academic field. Elementary teachers cannot complete even minors in every academic field which they must teach. The reasons such courses are taught in Colleges of Education are the failure of academic departments to keep in touch with the interests, needs, and psychological maturity of boys and girls in the elementary school and the lack of interest on the part of academic faculties in developing such courses.

Dr. Bestor urges that the graduate student with a major in history should take more courses in the field of history to round out the program, and he implies that Colleges of Education do not permit the student to do so. First, Education faculties have urged secondary school teachers to do this for years, but in only a few instances have academic departments reciprocated by accepting Education as a graduate minor. Second, if academic departments, such as history, would offer broad survey courses in the initial stages of the training period, teachers with even minors in a field would not be faced with the problem of trying to teach that in which they have no academic background. The evil lies in the continuous bifurcation of courses in the academic area with such emphasis on advanced material that the individual with a Master's degree in a subject field is often acquainted with little more of what he must teach than is the college freshman.

The author's insistence on the participation of the whole of a college in the planning of teacher education comes a little late, since professional groups have been working for some time to bring about such a liaison. (The American Association of Colleges for Teacher Education has even introduced this item as an evaluative criterion.) Unfortunately, our efforts often have not been met in true co-operative spirit.

Dr. Bestor grants that careful investigations into the processes of teaching and learning are legitimate functions of professional educators; yet he wishes to take all opportunities for effecting the results into educational practice away from them. If he wishes to be consistent in his thinking, he will grant those students of the current needs of youth and of teachers as much respect for their judgment in such matters as he would grant the scholar of history for his judgment in that liberal-art field.

State certification requirements, which Dr. Bestor criticizes, are no more a protection of the interest of professional educators than of the subject specialists against their own competitive departments. The chief purpose is to protect the prospective teacher from influences which often would permit and encourage him to complete four years of college without sufficient breadth of training to find any public-school position for which he could qualify. Neither the university nor the state can tailor-make a job for each candidate for teaching. Local school district factors largely determine the patterns to which the training program must conform.

Effective teaching is not mere scholasticism; it is that which improves the thinking and behavior of youth now. Such application of learning to thought and action is the highest level of intellectualism.

52

Better Teacher Training

BARRY T. JENSEN

Director, Behavioral Sciences Division, General Systems Industries, Inc., Torrance, Calif. At the time his article originally appeared in *School and Society* (Dec. 21, 1957), he was Human Factors Scientist, System Development Corp., Santa Monica, Calif.

Many of the student complaints about teaching in the schools of education reflect thinking in terms of theory-practice dichotomy with a request for more "practical" ideas and less "theory." We face not an either-or situation, but a question of defining interrelationships of theory and practice. Coladarci has contributed greatly to thinking in this matter.[1] He indicates that educational psychology is a body of knowledge which could serve the educational worker in making hypotheses regarding specific situations.

When a teacher faces a class, he brings with him his goals, he assesses the present situation, and makes hypotheses about his most effective procedures. A good teacher continually checks the situation for changes and makes new predictions as his pupils progress. His predictions and hypotheses are based upon *his* theory, even though it may be unsystematic and non-rigorous. In short, there is no such thing as practice without theory. The foundation fields of philosophy, sociology, anthropology, and psychology all contribute to development of this educational theory of learning and to the acquisition of skills. The procedure described below requires the acceptance of this principle that the fields are inseparable.

In the last three decades, considerable experimental data have cast doubt upon the universal efficacy of lectures or even lecture-discussions.[2]

The opinions expressed here are those of the writer and not necessarily those of The System Development Corporation or of any other employee.
[1] A. P. Coladarci, *Educational Leadership*, 8: 489-492, 1956.
[2] B. T. Jensen, *Journal of Educational Research*, 45: 175-181, 1954; R. Birney and W. McKeachie, *Psychological Bulletin*, 52: 51-68, 1955.

On the other hand, much is said for close integration of laboratory experience and other instructional methods. Therefore, I propose changes in organization of the teacher-training program and begin by recommending the elimination of the basic course in educational psychology. One cannot abolish the need for educational psychology, however. The educational psychologist would participate as a member of the teacher-training staff—not as a lecturer, but as a discussion leader and guide in the series of seminars described below.

During their first term in Education, students observe classes in a public school. As part of their observation program, they would participate in seminars with a staff including representatives of the foundation fields. In the seminars the students would consider what the teacher is trying to do (his goals), why he does what he does (his theory), and examine the conditions facilitating or preventing the attainment of these goals.

In a subsequent term, the students would participate in seminars devoted to the development of an educational theory of learning. Here the educational psychologist would meet with small groups of students to examine such questions as "What are the relationships between 'theory' and 'practice'? " and "Is there any difference between 'practice' and 'drill'? " The aim of this activity would be to help each person develop his own theory so that it is meaningful to him and thereby useful.

During a third term, the students would participate in a laboratory in human behavior. One of the hoped-for outcomes would be greater self-understanding and an increased ability to "manipulate" others. Any number of approaches might provide the means of inquiring into motives and developing an ability to recognize defense mechanisms and positive attempts to gain self-enhancement.

The fourth major contribution of the educational psychologist could be made in an area in which observations indicate very little transfer from a formal course—practice teaching. He would observe student teachers at practice and then meet with them in seminars and conferences outside of their classes. Here in little cultural islands, the psychologist, the philosopher, the sociologist, the methods instructor (if there is one), and the student would inquire into the nature of the situations facing that student. They would help him to clarify his goals and the goals of his pupils, assess the situation, and hypothesize by describing appropriate procedures and determining if operations were carried out as specified.

In summary, instead of acting in separate instructor-subject-time blocks, the several foundation people should work together to provide for the student a series of seminars correlated with other experiences throughout his entire teacher-training program.

53

The Place of the Humanities in Teacher Education

ALVIN C. EURICH

President, Academy for Educational Development, New York City. At the time his article originally appeared in *School and Society* (July 21, 1956), he was vice-president and director, Fund for the Advancement of Education. The article was based on an address to a joint meeting of the American Association of School Administrators and the NEA Department of Classroom Teachers, Atlantic City, N.J., Feb. 20, 1956.

No thinking person would regard the humanities as unimportant in teacher education. The questions are primarily how much, how, and by whom?

How simple and satisfying it would be if we could approach these questions in absolutes. On the question of how much, we could say, for example, that all prospective teachers should have the following humanities courses in their basic preparation: The humanities, American literature, English literature, philosophy, music, art, and two years of German, French, Spanish or Latin.

Although this list may be longer than usual, it typifies liberal-arts college requirements in the humanities. Teachers' colleges, by and large, would require a much shorter list. From a surface observation, then, one could say that teachers' colleges think the humanities less important in the education of teachers than liberal-arts colleges.

We might all agree that with automation, toward which we seem predestined in an age of fissionable elements, far greater emphasis should be placed on the humanities. We might argue at length, as faculties do, about the relative merits of adding another course possibly in World Literature. Or we might argue for extending some of the courses from one semester or five credit hours to two semesters.

Without meaning to be cynical, I have come to regard such an approach to the problem as sterile. All we need to do is to compare the requirements in college catalogues to realize the absurd situation into which this approach has led us. The juggling of courses, credits, and hours within academic circles is a political expedient: the strong political forces within a faculty usually come out on top with their fields of specialization well represented in the requirements. Seldom, if ever, does such juggling add up to a balanced education. The requirements so arrived at never really express what is expected of the student as an end result of the process.

It would be presumptuous indeed for me even to suggest an answer on the question of how much humanities should be included in a program of teacher education. All we can do is to explore some approaches that promise to yield a greater return for time and energy spent than those we are now using. In doing so, I assume that all of us are eager for prospective teachers to have a well-balanced education.

The first major issue on which many flares—or shall I say flashes—of heat have been generated in recent years without in the least pulling us out of the quagmire of intense emotional confusion is on the proper balance between professional education and liberal or general education. In planning our programs of professional education we have assumed that a prospective teacher knows nothing about education until he takes a course in it. Thus, we have failed to recognize teaching and education as unique in comparison with every other profession. Unlike every other field, the person who enters teaching has lived with his profession day after day for 12 to 16 or more years.

Suppose, in the interest of making the point more concrete, a person had spent five days a week for 12 to 16 years in a hospital. We would regard as utterly absurd an assumption that at the end of that period he knew nothing about hospital practice. We would assume on the contrary that he has had a very extensive chance to observe good and poor practice and, given average intelligence, that he has learned a great deal. With 16 years in a law office, the same would be true in law, or in any other field.

But, fortunately, we need not stop with an assumption. We have evidence that students learn much about education without taking courses in the field. At Cornell University, for example, a group of liberal-arts college graduates, no one of whom had been exposed to a single course in professional education, were given the National Teachers Examination. Their average score was higher than the average for teachers' college graduates.

Furthermore, the deficiencies of our present balance are also becoming apparent through other evidence. The Carnegie Corporation, in its January, 1956, Quarterly Report, pointed out that fewer and fewer students are taking mathematics in high school and that even those with high scholastic aptitude are mathematically incompetent. As a partial explanation, the report indicates that

although all states require education courses for secondary mathematics teachers, a third of the states require no mathematics for certification of math teachers. At the elementary level the situation is even worse. In the majority of instances a prospective elementary school teacher can enter a teachers' college without any credits in secondary school math. In most states, a teacher can be certified to teach elementary school math without any work in math at the college level.

Such results suggest that another approach is needed. If we were first to determine what in the field of professional education is desirable for a teacher to be effective, we might then set out to ascertain the extent to which the desirable has been acquired by living with the profession over a period of years. The task of professional education would then be to fill in the gap between the desirable and that already acquired. This procedure would be essentially the same as that long advocated by professional educators in urging prospective teachers to take into consideration the development levels of pupils in their classes. If this process were generally applied we might have an opportunity to achieve a better balance between the professional and the general education of the prospective teacher. We might, then, provide greater emphasis for the humanities and at the same time develop a higher degree of competence in mathematics.

The second issue relates to the way in which we assemble a program of liberal or general education and the number of parts or pieces of the humanities that we include. There is a constant need for curriculum reorganization. Instead of juggling courses and credits, however, could we not achieve a real balance by determining the basic or major ideas that have evolved with our ever-emerging civilization which we believe a prospective teacher should thoroughly understand? Such ideas as freedom, law, democracy, love, beauty, custom or convention, honor, desire, and eternity are all basic in the lives of every human being. They are ideas that are so important, so significant, so all-pervasive, they cut across various fields of discipline. If, in our preparation of teachers, we emphasized an understanding of these ideas and, in the process, drew upon many fields of knowledge, we could be more sure than we are today with our fragmented courses that we would achieve a balanced curriculum with the humanities receiving greater emphasis.

In developing an understanding of freedom, for example, we would draw upon the Bible and other great pieces of literature by such authors as Milton, Tolstoy, Locke, Bacon, Shakespeare; we would draw upon political science with such documents as the Declaration of Independence, the Constitution, the Bill of Rights; we would draw upon science and the arts and any other fields that contribute to an understanding of freedom. Furthermore, in the process we could deal with successive levels of maturity in thinking about freedom. We would not be caught, as we are so frequently now, duplicating elementary levels by treating the same idea in several different fields.

Of course, beyond the basic ideas we would have to include in our preparation of teachers the various skills as in communication.

Such a fresh approach might possibly lift our teacher preparation—or college education generally—to new levels of understanding and make it possible to save much instructor and student time.

A third basic issue relates to procedures. If the humanities are to be important in teacher education, they must be taught by superior and inspiring teachers. Even though we were to achieve a proper balance between professional and general education, and economize through curriculum reorganization with an emphasis on understanding major ideas, how can we, in the face of the critical teacher shortage, provide our prospective teachers with superior instruction? If we insist upon maintaining our present ratio of one teacher to every 13 college students, we will need in the next 15 years two and one-half times the number of college teachers we now have. High quality with such numbers is obviously impossible. Our only alternative is to utilize every possible means at hand to make available our most competent and inspiring teachers to the largest number of students. This means, in addition to curriculum reorganization, full use of motion pictures, visual and auditory aids, and television, both open and closed circuits. We have at hand the means for making a great teacher in the humanities, such as Mark Van Doren, for example, available to many students. This does not mean that any aspect important to optimum conditions for learning need be eliminated; it means merely utilizing *all* resources for learning as we have learned to use books.

Exciting and thrilling opportunities for a better balance in the education of teachers and for further emphasis on the humanities lie ahead of us. I have merely sketched some new approaches: that we base professional education upon the understanding acquired through observations; that we concentrate in liberal education and especially in the humanities upon developing maturity in thinking about the great ideas that have contributed to the evolution of our civilization; and that we make our most gifted and inspiring teachers available to the largest number of students through the use of every possible means now at hand.

There is a chance that through these approaches the education of teachers might acquire new dimensions and be lifted above entrenched practices that perpetuate mediocrity.

54

Standards in Teacher Education and the New Image Makers

BERNARD MEHL

Professor of history of education, Ohio State University. His article originally appeared in *School and Society* on Feb. 6, 1965.

There exists today a very laudable, yet highly questionable, urge within the administrative ranks of professional educators. After being bombarded by criticism against teacher education, professionals have joined the ranks of "image worriers" and now work to try to shore up the image of teacher training programs. Acting in this manner through such bodies as NCATE and TEPS, deans and professors of education at last have acknowledged that the critics are correct in pointing out that the public does not grant great esteem to teacher education. What the educator has admitted is not the specific charges levelled against the teacher training program (the educational journals are filled with rebuttals to the Rickovers, Bestors, Liebermans and Kirks), but that the critics serve as indicators of an anti-education bias on the part of the public.

Schoolmen always have been disturbed at any form of criticism, seeking to act in such a way as to escape severe scrutiny of their internal program. The reasons for this are understandable. Since the schools and agencies serving them are fair game for dissident groups of the left, right, and center, anonymity, therefore, has been an effective shield. The schools have paid the price of anonymity, the lack of critical self-inquiry. Yet, the gain gathered from the use of this technique cannot be overlooked.

The "image worrier" among professional teacher educators is concerned with this anti-education bias. He does not want to yield to the specific arguments taken up by his critics, yet he knows that he depends upon "public opinion" for support for funds to meet the teacher shortage and for power recognition to effect political decisions affecting public school financing policy and programming. To deny the importance of the image as a power

creator would be an act of sheer folly. Given the practical political situation
of today, we realize that Federal aid to education is no closer to realization
than it was a decade ago. We view with alarm the austerity programs at the
state and local levels in regard to school tax levies. We can feel with educators
and thus not take the easy way out by scoffing at their concern with their
image. Then let us admit that the "image" is important. What we need to do
is to explore what steps to take to improve that image, knowing full well that
each step taken carries with it consequences which go beyond an immediate
image projection. That is to say, in order to put oneself in a somewhat more
favorable light *vis-à-vis* a certain segment of the public, one may tarnish his
picture with another segment. If we hold to an advertising analogy, we can
say that the campaign will get only a certain group to buy the product in
large quantities. If that group already is buying the product, then the
advertising campaign will be different than if one addresses oneself to a
group that is not buying the product. The issue here is to examine the tack
taken by the professional educators who are concerned with image-building
and then argue that they are not even following those who have made a life's
career out of this enterprise. Let us then accede to the importance of image-
building and try to ascertain if educators at least are following the "book."

With this in mind, we can state the business at hand.

Educators read the public bias concerning teacher training in the
following way: Teacher training colleges are inferior because they are
overrun with inferior students who fail in other schools maintaining higher
standards. George Bernard Shaw's famous statement to the effect that those
who can, do, and those who cannot, teach, is now admitted to be part of the
public's stereotyped image about teachers in general and teachers in training
in particular. Because of this bias, professors of education are held in low
repute by their colleagues in the arts, sciences, and engineering faculties and
are tarred with the same brush as their students. The argument goes like this:
By making himself a party to avowed student mediocrity, the professor of
education, too, must be mediocre.

One remedy proposed by NCATE and TEPS is to raise grade-point
standards, and it is this remedy that bears investigation (NCATE and TEPS
have not stopped at this and have realized fully that more is involved, but
many institutions looking for fast results have made higher grade points the
all-important image repairer). With one simple act, the major barrier to
recognition for college students, professors, and deans of education would be
wiped away. Besides, these same groups could point with long-awaited
glee to an arts faculty, which retained lower grade-point standards, having
to accept those very mediocre people turned away from colleges and schools
of education. All these hopes have the earmarks of a stirring melodrama
wherein the evil witch is punished by having to take back her ugly toad and
return Snow White to her rightful parents. We need not remind these educators that this fiction is quite unreal. But more is at stake than revenge in

two reels. The reason may be that a "C" gained in an arts faculty cannot be viewed in the same light as a "C+" or even a "B" in the higher standard-conscious education college. The case may well be that raising admission standards to colleges of education will not appreciably affect their "image."* It could work to its detriment if it is discovered (and who can hide such matters) that, in spite of new packaging techniques, the product still is deemed mediocre. At least it might be wise to set up a limited number of standard-conscious programs generally unpublicized and check out the results with care. If the results are positive, we must begin the promotional campaign; if not, then we must discard the idea. I will insist that quality is basic to imagery and will affirm that the teacher-training image still will be bad in the not-too-long run if the only difference is limited to a higher entering grade-point standard. If we are to measure the gains of the new image by the amount of political leverage allotted to professional educators in their quest for improved educational facilities so needed in this era of domestic and world crisis, then the necessity of broadening our analysis beyond the stereotype stage becomes more and more evident.

---

* Agricultural colleges, home economic departments, and physical education departments have long used the sliding grade point as the lever to obtain higher status with little or no success. Whatever image has come to these "lower order" colleges and departments has been the result of bringing in prestige programs, e.g., agricultural economics, physiological research, chemistry, etc. That is, when the body of subject matter was made challenging.

55

Teacher Education for the Next Decade

FRANCIS S. CHASE

Professor of education, Graduate School of Education, University of Chicago. At the time his article originally appeared in *School and Society* (March 21, 1964), he was dean of the Graduate School of Education. The article was based on an address at Idaho State University, Oct. 1, 1963, and on an address to the Conference of Academic Deans, Boston, in January, 1960.

The provisions for the education of teachers during the next decade will condition the quality of American education for the remainder of the century. If we are serious about increasing the effectiveness of education, we must think deeply about how we can improve the selection of prospective teachers and the measures through which they are prepared for and inducted into the practice of teaching.

A good program of teacher education represents an extension of, and not a replacement for, liberal education. By liberal education, I mean studies that, in the words of Everett Dean Martin, will serve "to free the mind from servitude and herd opinion, to train habits of judgment and of appreciation of value, to carry on the struggle for human excellence in our day and generation, to temper passion with wisdom, to dispel prejudice by better knowledge of self, [and] to enlist all men, in the measure that they have capacity for it, in the achievement of civilization."

Teacher education should be built on elements which form the basis for understanding our own and other cultures; it should extend acquaintance with the best thinking of our own and previous ages; it should deepen the meaning of knowledge through application to a variety of teaching-learning situations; and it should develop a spirit of speculative inquiry. Such an education will be calculated to produce teachers who will motivate the learning process through a rich variety of approaches rather than depending on some rule-of-thumb method or slavish imitation of observed procedures.

The young people in our schools are more likely to become students when their teachers exemplify a spirit of continuing scholarly inquiry. A scholar is driven by passion to enlarge his own knowledge and to project his thinking into uncharted areas. The good teacher couples this passion to know with an urge to enlist others in the joys that come from the discovery of new ideas. His enthusiasm for his subject impels him to unfold its marvels to others. This leads him to search for ways of arousing in young minds a hunger for knowledge and for ways of feeding the whetted appetites with the best that his field can offer.

If our schools are to be staffed by any considerable number of individuals who can qualify as teacher-scholars, four conditions must prevail:

First, *intellectual curiosity on the part of those who choose careers in teaching.* Criteria for the selection of candidates for teacher preparation should include possession of the abilities and interests essential to sound scholarship in the chosen discipline.

Second, *assimilation by teachers of a substantial body of organized knowledge, together with methods of inquiry through which knowledge can be extended.* To fulfill this condition is part of the task of teacher education.

Third, *a certain amount of leisure and freedom from demands that swallow the day without allowing pause for reading or reflection.* To create this condition is a task of educational administration, but one often not well performed.

Fourth, *the cherishing of scholarship and its fruits by the teaching profession, the local community, and the larger society.* In the face of the anti-intellectualism that pervades much of American life, this condition will not be easy to achieve; but the teaching profession cannot be absolved from exerting itself toward this end.

Is it too much to ask that the ablest and most dedicated scholars in our universities and colleges allot some of their time for the education of those who will play a large part in determining the caliber of college entrants and the future of civilization?

How can we expect to produce good teachers of science unless their own education includes contact with genuinely creative scientists and provides the excitement of participating in discovery of new knowledge? How can we expect to produce gifted teachers of history unless they are taught by historians of the first rank and inducted into the study and criticism of the sources of historical knowledge and the arts and sciences of historical interpretation? How can we expect teachers to introduce our children and youth to great literary achievements unless they themselves are taught by scholars who understand the uses and abuses of the art of criticism and who retain a fresh and spontaneous enthusiasm for great ideas aptly expressed? How can we expect a teacher to develop in the young a mastery of a foreign language unless he himself is taught by those thoroughly at home with the language and the culture of which it is a part? And how can teachers be expected to acquire the art of exciting the desire for learning in their pupils unless their own instructors stir in them a hunger for knowledge?

It will not do simply to vary the prescription as to the number of parts of content to be purveyed by one department and the number of parts of method to be mixed in by another group; teacher preparation thus compounded contributes to our educational ills rather than to their cure. Under this devitalizing division of labor, content tends to become a body of ideas to be acquired and to remain inert and unused; and method is reduced to a set of vessels emptied of meaning. Only through a blending of content and method can we restore vitality to teacher education. This is not to deny that there are different kinds of scholars who play different parts in the education of a teacher; but it is to say that the scientist or historian participating in teacher education is communicating both content and method and is using method consciously or unconsciously as a carrier of content. The pity is that he often uses it so badly. His own teaching may become more effective with all students by reflection on what the prospective teacher is learning from him about how students may be led to share the excitement of discovery and the satisfaction of achieved understanding. To be sure, there are understandings about teaching mathematics, or other subjects, at the earlier stages of development that are not likely to be acquired from the teacher of the higher branches. For this reason the prospective teacher, while extending his scholarship in his special field of study, should maintain a steady contact with learners of the age groups he expects later to instruct.

There are many ways in which the preparation of teachers may be shaped, but all of them should have in common such features as a broad general education to provide understanding of the major contributions to Western thought and an insight into at least one non-Western culture; advanced study in the field of specialization, including methods of inquiry through which new knowledge is discovered and tested; opportunity for early identification with the teaching profession and for continuing observation in schools and participation in guiding the learning of others; induction into the art of teaching by gifted and sympathetic teachers, followed by an internship in which full responsibility is accepted for directing a group of learners; and analytical study of the teaching-learning process and penetrating evaluation of one's own and others' teaching procedures, under the guidance of instructors who have a deep understanding of child development and needs, the nature of learning, and the role of the teacher in a modern democratic society.

Teachers for early childhood ideally should have at least as much general education as is commonly represented by a bachelor's degree from a good college. The important thing is not the possession of a degree or the number of years spent in college, but the possession of a truly alert, cultivated, and inquiring mind. It is as important for teachers of young children as for teachers at later stages of growth to exhibit the characteristics of an educated person.

Beyond this, the need is more for specialists in child development than for specialists in the subjects to be taught. There is a respectable body of professional knowledge which is an important attribute of the teacher of young children: an understanding of the needs of the young child; the psychology of learning; the role of the school in the American culture; and the problems encountered by the child in developing an adequate self image, adapting to his environment, and acquiring the ability to read, use numbers, speak and write the native language. In all these, there is content as well as method.

While scholarship in a specialized field is not essential for all teachers of young children, there should be some teachers who have unusual artistic ability and skill in nourishing the creative impulses of children, some who excel in music and the teaching of music, some who have special skill in diagnosing reading difficulties, and some with other types of specialized knowledge and ability. Specialization in particular aspects of knowledge may be increased somewhat for teachers of later childhood and early adolescence. Even though the major part of the young child's day may be spent with one teacher, there is no valid reason for not giving even very young children the opportunity to be introduced to music, art, mathematics, and science by teachers who have special enthusiasm for, and knowledge of, the particular subject.

Although a five-year program is preferable, excellent teachers for elementary schools can be produced in a four-year college program, provided the high school preparation is adequate. For a high school teacher the task is not readily manageable because of the desirability of considerable specialization in the teaching field. In cases where it is deemed necessary to qualify for high school teaching in as little as four years of college, the emphasis should be on a program of liberal studies, including specialized and professional studies so pursued as to reveal the relatedness of special and general studies.

The specialized aspects of the preparation of high school teachers should be the responsibility of an active faculty group, including scholars in the specialized area of knowledge, one or more first-rate specialists in education, as a field of study, and one or more persons with extensive experience with high school teaching in the particular subject. This faculty group or committee should assume responsibility for choosing the content, organizing the program, and conducting a seminar through which all that the students are learning may be focused on the teaching roles for which they are preparing.

Wherever possible, the preparation of high school teachers should include graduate study in the teaching field. There should be provision also for graduate studies of genuine significance in the field of education; but the amount of time required for such studies may be reduced as education receives its appropriate treatment in courses in history, psychology, sociology, and other fields. In institutions with graduate schools or departments, the committees for the preparation of teachers should include strong representatives from the graduate departments.

The faculties of graduate schools and undergraduate faculties of arts and sciences again have an opportunity to assume major responsibility for the education of teachers. If they give serious attention to the task and exhibit a willingness to work with those who have special knowledge of educational institutions and processes, they will mend the broken links between higher education and the lower schools and give a lift to learning everywhere. On the other hand, if they fail to give their best thought to the education of teachers, they will have turned aside from an opportunity to reinvigorate the whole stream of American education.

The liberal arts colleges have a major obligation to develop in those headed for teaching a spirit of speculative inquiry and understanding of methodologies appropriate to different kinds of inquiry. They also have an obligation to offer in their own instruction diverse models of good teaching. All these things constitute a part of the obligation for preprofessional training. The specialized professional preparation should be left to those institutions which have well-qualified specialists in the psychology of learning, curriculum theory, and other aspects of education, as well as competent faculties in the arts and sciences. No institution of whatever size and reputation should undertake the preparation of teachers except for those subjects in which creative scholars are ready to give time and thought to the education of teachers.

Teachers in our schools should exemplify in high degree the qualities of educated persons. No major aspect of human knowledge and no human culture should be wholly closed to them. They should be able to learn from and to use symbols of many kinds—linguistic, mathematical, and/or musical. They should be able also to learn from direct observation of objects and living organisms and to express ideas clearly through speech and writing in their native language and with some facility in at least one other language and/or through a universal medium such as mathematical symbolism, music, or painting.

They should know how to estimate probabilities by selecting and analyzing relevant evidence; but they should recognize the limits of what they can know objectively and the vast extent of the unknown to be dealt with through the insights provided by religion, philosophy, and great literature of many kinds when illuminated by one's own reflection and imagination.

They should have a just perception of themselves and a just appreciation of the rights, needs, and potentialities of others. They should understand how the health of society is conditioned by freedom of judgment and expression for the individuals who compose it; and they should value, and be willing to sacrifice for, institutions which buttress these and other human freedoms. They should be guided more often by reason than by unconsidered emotion or prejudice, and should prize those things that contribute to the well-being and elevation of mankind above those that provide only temporary pleasure.

They should continue to learn by re-examining their values and assumptions, broadening their knowledge, extending their understanding, deepening their appreciation of life in its many manifestations, and putting their faculties increasingly in the service of their aspirations.

When we have more teachers who exhibit these traits, our prospects of extending these characteristics among our population generally will be materially enhanced. To this end, the institutions of higher education should bend their efforts.

56

Teacher Education and Preparation for the 21st Century

RICHARD I. MILLER

Vice-President for Academic Affairs and Dean of the College, Baldwin-Wallace College. His article, based on an address given at the inauguration and dedication of the Education Building, State University of New York at Albany, Nov. 8, 1967, originally appeared in the Summer, 1970, issue of *School and Society.*

The aspects of teacher education that are significant for the future are related to three generalizations: teacher preparation is an integral aspect of the total education program; many creative and promising innovations are being undertaken, but on a piecemeal basis and often without adequate conceptualization, planning, and evaluation; and teacher education is now the best ever, but woefully inadequate to move ahead with the future.

Teacher education programs[1] need to consider seriously the use of system analysis and quality controls, including cost-benefit analysis. The simple system approach used in this essay includes three parts: objectives, program, and evaluation.

What objectives might prepare teachers better for the future? Certainly, a clear and concise statement of objectives should precede program considerations. Objectives should be defined carefully so that evaluation measures can be applied to them. These student-oriented goals are suggested: a broadly literate person—one who has a broad and liberal education; a scientific person—one who understands mathematics and computer programming; a compassionate person—one who understands human frailty and is slow to censor; a technically competent person—one who is fully modern in the skills of a chosen content area; a pedagogically competent

---

[1] For a useful summary of research and studies in teacher education, see George W. Denemark and James B. McDonald, "Pre-service and In-service Education of Teachers," *Review of Educational Research,* 37: 233-247, June, 1967.

person—one who is knowledgeable and relatively experienced in techniques of teaching and ways of learning; an organizational person—one who understands the institutional bureaucracy known as the school and who knows about processes and strategies for bringing about improvements; an inquiring person—one who is able to analyze problems and make appropriate adjustments, and one who constantly is evaluating his contribution as a teacher; a communicating person—one who has learned how to talk and work with colleagues and with students; and a dedicated person—one who believes education is very important.

What programs are needed to attain carefully defined objectives? Most of the following 16 suggestions are in operation in the nation, but nowhere can one find a comprehensive model featuring more than a few of them.

1. Two years of broad, non-professional education should constitute the freshman and sophomore years. An alive and enriched person is an essential prerequisite for successful teaching. Toward this end, the first two years of undergraduate college work should be exclusively liberal and fine arts and natural and physical sciences—with the exception of one education course. This emphasis exists in some teacher education programs, and the trend is in this direction.

2. The first exposure to the challenge, frustration, and excitement of teaching and learning should be a stimulating one, provided in a one-semester course during the second year. Utilizing television, slides, filmstrips, tapes, and explanations by classroom teachers, as well as by psychologists and educators, this course needs to be stimulating and provocative. A dynamic, multi-media approach has been in operation in a few places—for example, at the Harkness Center, a Board of Cooperative Educational Services operation in Erie County, New York.

3. A summer or semester abroad should be a part of undergraduate study. The effective preservice program in the future will include an authentic immersion in another culture. Those who raise technicalities as major obstacles may be rationalizing their inability to understand the importance of this experience. Summer-abroad programs have not been organized by many universities, yet such programs have distinct advantages over the regular semester. In any case, every education student should live abroad for at least one summer in an area that coincides with his linguistic fluency.

4. Preservice programs should have a strong inquiry bias. Almost all educators and administrators pay allegiance to the importance of developing methods and procedures for inquiry to foster lifelong adaptability in education, but no serious effort to this end is evident in teacher education programs. Certainly, lifelong technical skills cannot be developed since these change rapidly, but an attitude toward inquiry and flexibility can be developed. One way to accomplish this is exemplified by North Buckinghamshire College of Education, a small, new college just outside of London, where an inquiry approach is used. Starting with practical problems, students are

expected—with guidance from the professor—to find solutions using theoretical bases and substantiated points of view.

Another approach might be a year-long course during the junior or senior year which focuses on inquiry training. The course should be taught on a team basis, combining the intellectual skills of a philosopher, psychologist, educator, and classroom teacher. This team approach needs careful planning and coordination and, in addition to lectures, small-group discussions, independent study, and personal consultation, should include a field project requiring original research by all students.

5. Competence in research methodology and design should be expected of all students at both undergraduate and graduate levels. A single well-designed, three-hour undergraduate course in research methodology and design should be mastered, or some similar standard should be required for students, regardless of the grade level or subject area. Every student, furthermore, should undertake and complete some piece of original theoretical or action research as part of this course. Teachers must be knowledgeable about research if the teaching profession is to acquire a greater scientific base. In addition, competence in research methodology and design should be required of all graduate students.

6. Preservice programs should include study of new innovations and the process of change. Considerable literature on change processes is available in anthropology, social and industrial psychology, and rural sociology, and less extensive, but important, contributions are available in education. Rarely do students come into contact with this important body of knowledge, and even more rarely do they study systematically how change takes place. As innovations become more complex, as institutions and teachers become more specialized, and as the tempo of change increases, special attention to the process of change becomes more compelling.

7. Teacher education programs should have some features of continuous pupil progress and of team teaching. Former U.S. Commissioner of Education Harold Howe observed: "At a time when the public schools are realizing the importance of individual differences and are adopting individualized instruction, independent study, flexible scheduling, team teaching, nongraded classes, and similar practices, most colleges and universities still subscribe to a uniform four-year, 125-unit system." If nongradedness, team teaching, and other such innovations are good for elementary and secondary education, they may have some applicability to teacher education.

Team teaching is a natural way of bringing academicians into education. For example, educational psychology would benefit from a well-coordinated team approach consisting of an experimental psychologist, a social psychologist, and an educational psychologist.

8. Independent study should be an important dimension. Every professor assigns independent study—or does he?—is it not individualized library retrieval rather than independent study? As used here, independent

study means pursuit of individual interests, singly or by small groups. The topic for research and study should be chosen by the student with guidance from his assigned faculty member, who would meet with the student from time-to-time to check on progress and make suggestions on the research. At least one three-hour credit course of independent study should be part of every preservice program.

9. Student-planned courses should be included. College students are old enough to fight in Vietnam, to marry, to hold responsible positions, but not to decide what kinds of educational preparation they need. At least this is the implication one draws from the absence of student-planned courses. Students in their junior or senior year could be divided into groups of, say, 25, and asked to develop three-credit hour courses around their areas of interest. Faculty members could help recruit professors around the campus as well as city officials and "open doors" in general.

10. The professional semester should extend for two semesters, alternately during the fourth and fifth years. The professional semester requires a five-year teacher program for most students, although individualized accelerated programs should be available. An extra year for most students is just around the corner, for the traditional four years no longer can provide experiences necessary for effective teaching, especially if student teaching is given a more important role.

Patterned after the successful five-year teacher intern program at Central Michigan University, the approach suggested here is designed to satisfy two assumptions: teacher preparation can be improved by providing extensive realistic experiences through paid intern positions, and a university can involve good school systems in active and responsible ways in the preparation of teachers. Thus, a student spends his final two years in alternate semesters on campus and as a full-time, paid employee of a school system. During the first intern semester, the student might receive half of a beginning teacher's salary, and more during the second experience.

Extended professional teaching experiences produce a close working relationship between the university and the public schools; more extensive, realistic, and careful supervision; and a five-year preservice program.

11. Supervisors of secondary level student teachers should be subject matter specialists, mainly. Most university supervisors for student teachers are practitioners rather than scholars, so we have student teachers receiving pedagogical advice from both the classroom teachers and the university supervisor. But who provides a critique of the subject matter being taught? —everyone and no one. Both the teacher and supervisor provide and offer suggestions in subject matter, but neither has the credentials essential for advising student teachers on content.

12. Volunteer community teaching by preservice students should be encouraged and facilitated. All preservice students should be urged to serve in community agencies, working with poor children and adults. This experience

could come during the junior year, and carry with it three hours of credit or some other device necessary for satisfying certification requirements. These late afternoon, evening, weekend, and/or summer assignments could provide invaluable teaching experiences, as well as genuine help for youngsters who need it most.

13. Organizational charts of colleges of education should reflect a functional, rather than a structural, bias. The antiquated and political nature of many university bureaucracies is revealed by even a cursory examination of organizational charts.

Colleges of education often have been organized more on the bases of campus and state politics and availability of outside monies than on the basis of a conceptual design that ties theory to best practice. As a result, some programs are given undue weight and influence. Their importance has contributed to the anti-intellectual bias toward education on the part of other faculties.

In the future, colleges of education should have departments of communication, educational change, educational technology, and research development. (In the area of educational change, there are not more than six programs presently in operation.)

14. The college of education should have close working relationships with the state department of education and with local school systems. The University of Iowa has joint appointments with the State Department of Education, and the New York State Department of Education has taken a leadership role in encouraging colleges and universities to join with public schools in relating academic study to professional practice. Indeed, these types of relationships should be encouraged.

Some colleges of education have been providing services to communities effectively, but the majority are only going through the motions. An example of good university-community relationships is the Cornell-Ithaca Teacher Associate Program. Prompted by an address given by James B. Conant, local educators were aroused to explore more effective university-public school approaches to teacher education. The continuous progress education (nongradedness) and the teacher associate are direct products of this increased collaboration.

15. Some graduate education programs should be devoted solely to developing specialists in research, evaluation, and processes of change. A study by Clark and Hopkins indicated that only about 1,500–2,000 professionals could be classified as "hard-core" research and development personnel, spending more than one-half their time on research and development and producing for several years. Another 2–5,000 might be called "occasional researchers," with their major professional focus outside research and development activities, but doing occasional research reports. Clark and Hopkins predict that, outside of government and foundation programs, education will require a "hard-core" research and development personnel

pool of 130,000 by fiscal year 1972. In terms of full-time workers, the figure is approximately 65,000.[2] The need is critical, yet graduate schools of education have not made strong commitments to develop the scientific personnel, including specialists in computer technology and programming. Without these competencies in abundance, education will not move ahead dramatically.

16. Teacher education should be an all-university function. Many universities and colleges subscribe to this concept, but few earnestly and persistently have worked out programs to provide it with meaning. In judging whether or not the all-university concept is feasible, these questions might be raised: Have the president and his staff taken initial leadership, with sustaining thrusts whenever necessary? (Without vigorous leadership at this level, the all-university concept has little chance of real success.) Does the university have appropriate organizational structure to facilitate multidisciplinary programs? Do university reward systems provide realistic bases for involvement of academic professors in education?

Colleges of education need to ask themselves three questions in respect to their role in the total university community: What activities and programs are uniquely the responsibility of a college of education? What activities and programs should be shared by other faculties? What activities and programs should be turned over to other faculties? Perhaps, colleges of education should be renamed "colleges of pedagogy." All faculties within the university are involved in education, but few are involved in the art, practice, and science of teaching and learning.

The next six points pertain to evaluation—one of the most under-developed areas in education. The "calibrated eyeball" approach, authority of a father figure, tradition, opinion, and non-replicated evidence have constituted the major bases for inadequate evaluation. Herein, evaluation is viewed as a decision-making, as well as a judgmental, process. Evaluation is an integral part of system analysis, serving as feedback and guide. More or less continuous monitoring procedures need be set up to determine whether programs are fulfilling stated objectives.

1. Colleges of education should maintain contact with every graduate. Those who spend four to seven years in an institution usually develop a lifelong interest in it. Furthermore, they are an invaluable source of data for improving the college's program, and also can provide opportunities for field research. A full-time research specialist should maintain contact and undertake studies to provide valuable feedback and guidance for the college of education. Such an individual is not known to be employed anywhere in the nation.

---

[2] D. L. Clark and J. E. Hopkins, "Preliminary Estimates of Research, Development and Diffusion Personnel Required in Education." Special U.S. Office of Education project memorandum, Sept. 1, 1966, pp. 15-16.

2. Professorial evaluation should be individualized. This evaluation should be partly in terms of his own objectives, in the context of those developed for the total college. Each professor should be expected to state his objectives generally and specifically, and these would be agreed upon by the chairman and the professor. His performance, then, would be judged by how well he attains his objectives. Student appraisal of faculty performance is valuable in many cases, but irrelevant in others, depending on the kind of objectives established. Colleague appraisal, outside appraisal, and self-appraisal should be utilized also.

3. New methods and procedures for evaluating student performance are needed. Actually the problem is twofold: applying and testing what research and evidence is now available, and developing more precise approaches to evaluate student performance. Micro-teaching is one successful innovation that also has brought about more careful study of student performance.

4. Cost-benefit approaches should be applied to colleges of education. From these and other types of evaluation, a college of education should be able to develop a cost-benefit profile that will not impinge upon academic freedom or upon "pondering time" necessary for some kinds of creative endeavor. Heretofore, many have assumed that cost-benefit studies would not be applicable to education. Sufficient evidence is now available to indicate that education is indeed an important area for such measures.

5. A monitoring committee could provide the dean and president with periodical feedback. Established from the university as a whole, with perhaps one-half the members from the college of education, a monitoring committee would provide thoughtful and constructive evaluation. Many colleges of education have advisory committees, but these usually neither have university-wide membership nor include evaluation as their major focus.

6. Periodic visitation by outside teams should be scheduled. Perhaps every other year, a five-member team of outside educators and/or a consultant firm should spend three days intensively examining the college's objectives, programs, and methods of evaluation. Such appraisals should help provide independent input and fresh points of view.

Colleges of education need to be one step ahead of the future, for education is too important to be left to antiquated colleges of education. If we do not take upon ourselves the urgently needed reforms, other power structures likely will force them. These forces are becoming increasingly restive and impatient with the second-rate programs across the nation, perhaps in the spirit of Dr. Charles Mayo, who said: "In the practice of surgery, second rate is not only unsatisfactory, it is apt to be dangerous, and therefore is intolerable."

We are now entering into a third phase of the more-or-less continuous ferment that has characterized education since World War II. We have gone through the *Why Johnny Can't Read* groundswell in the early 1950's, followed by an unprecedented interest in content revision. We have moved into individualization and organizational flexibility in the early 1960's, and recently into massive Federal assistance. The latter thrust may serve as an effective catalyst in moving teacher education toward major innovation and change.

Many Elementary and Secondary Education Act projects under Title III are forcing colleges of education to reexamine the kinds of teachers they are developing—teachers that do not fit into "swinging" Projects to Advance Creativity in Education (PACE) programs. Also, expanded provisions under Title XI of the National Defense Education Act, as well as the potentially important Education Professions Development Act, offer challenging opportunities for colleges of education.

Our attitude toward change needs further emphasis. Unless a college of education really wants to be different, and unless its members are willing to work as a team, improvements will be hit-or-miss and in small increments. We do not need more tinkering in teacher education. We need full-blown, courageous models of something new—new in the sense that the many parts are molded together, a whole that differs from the sum of its parts. Who will be first?

57

The College Professor as Teacher

GEORGE B. CUTTEN

President emeritus, Colgate University. His article originally appeared in *School and Society* on Oct. 25, 1958.

A large number of persons on the faculties of our colleges and universities lack teaching ability and have no interest in the teaching function. Indeed, with the possible exception of the Sunday school, probably the poorest contemporary teaching is that to be found in our colleges.

William Lyon Phelps tells us in his "Autobiography" that, when he entered Yale in 1883, he found that "a curse hung over the Faculty, a blight on the art of teaching." He would have probably found a similar condition in other universities and colleges, a blight which his brilliant efforts did not remove. In the three-quarters of a century which have passed since then, it is probable that the art of teaching has suffered more blight than he observed, and that the curse has become so common that it no longer surprises us.

Twenty years after "Billy" Phelps entered Yale as a freshman, Prof. William James published an article, "The Ph.D. Octopus," which shocked the educational world. Of course, anything James wrote was and is worth reading, and it seemed that what he said at that time would deflate the Ph.D. and detract from its assumed value, but, as we know, such has not been the case. Among other things, he had this to say regarding teaching:

Is not our growing tendency to appoint no instructors who are not doctors a pure sham? Will anyone pretend for a moment that the doctor's degree is a guarantee that its possessor will be successful as a teacher? Notoriously his moral, social, and personal characteristics may utterly disqualify him for success in the classroom, and of these characteristics his doctor's examination is unable to take any account whatever.

The truth is that the Doctor-Monopoly in teaching, which is becoming so rooted an American custom, can show no serious grounds whatsoever for itself in reason. As it actually prevails and grows in vogue among us, it is due to childish motives

278

exclusively. In reality it is but a sham, a bauble, a dodge, whereby to decorate the catalogue of schools and colleges.

When Phelps entered Yale, James was a professor at Harvard, and, during the early years of the 20th century, one could hardly select any other two persons in the educational world whose opinions would be more popular and whose conclusions would be in little danger of being brushed aside. But their criticisms might well be transferred to the present time; committees are still being appointed to examine and report on the value of the Ph.D. and its effect on teaching, though the reports so far have had few beneficial effects.

To require a certificate for effective teaching before one could become eligible for an academic appointment would be about equal to questioning his moral character. To call persons who occupy professors' chairs "teachers" is a splendid example of the law of compensation when applied to nomenclature and can well be classed with calling the young people sitting in front of the professors "students." In each case the designation is a distinction rather than a definition. In fact, the title "teacher" is almost taboo in colleges and universities. "Teachers" are found in the elementary and secondary schools; colleges and universities are inhabited by "professors." We thus can see that, if you happen to inquire whether a professor is a good teacher, it really would mean nothing, for the word "teacher" has lost its specific meaning when applied to a college professor. Research and teaching are different poles of intellectual attainment, and one does not naturally lead to the other.

There is no doubt that the Ph.D. degree and training have been of value, but it is seldom that we find a professor failing in his work in the college of arts and sciences because he does not know enough concerning his subject to teach it. The criticism of the Ph.D. as a preparation for teaching in colleges is that it implies if a person knows a subject, he can teach it—a false and dangerous assumption. If a professor is a poor teacher, is the remedy to add to his stock of knowledge of his subject? The false assumption which the Ph.D. has impressed on us is "the more knowledge, the better the teaching." This is about equal to saying, "If you want a particularly beautiful and cleverly wrought piece of furniture, apply to a lumberman; he has an abundance of wood."

So the Ph.D. fallacy continues: the more research a professor has done, the more books and articles he has written, the better teacher he is supposed to be. But the opposite is more likely to be the case. The fault for this lies not only in the applicant and his choice of qualifications, but, also, even to a larger extent in the demands made by the college trustees, the college president, and the heads of departments.

When seeking a professor to fill a vacancy, what questions do they ask concerning the applicant? They want to know about his age, his family, his college, his university, his degrees, his books, articles, and lectures, and also what books he has in the making. Anything about his success as a teacher? Only occasionally, for there are some college presidents and heads of departments who cannot escape from the tradition that young people come to college to learn, to examine, and to think, and the most efficient means of accomplishing this is by the use of capable teachers. In general, however, an applicant who has a good research record is supposed therewith to be a good teacher, regardless of naturol ability or of training to make him one.

The choice of "productive scholarship" as the most appropriate preparation for the career of teaching seems to be well established and is usually demanded in preference to any other training program. The following may be considered proof of such a preference for productive scholarship.

At one time I was seeking a professor to fill a vacancy in the faculty and heard of a man in one of our larger and most famous universities who might be available. I discovered that he was one of a group of a dozen or more faculty members which formed a separate department in the university. All the members in this department taught the same subject to the pupils in the freshman class. On inquiry I heard much favorable comment concerning this man, and among the most flattering statements frequently made by colleagues and others was that he was the best teacher in the department. "Why, then," I asked, "is he being permitted to go?" The answer was this: All the faculty members in that department were appointed for a period of four years with the same official titles and with the understanding that, at the end of the period, they must have had published some research book or article of a creditable quality. Without this proof of their "productive scholarship," they no longer could consider themselves as members of the faculty. This man had taught most successfully and acceptably but had done no research and, consequently, was discharged.

The lack of efficient teachers is nothing new. How many first-class teachers did you have in college or in the university? Did the number add up to one, or were you fortunate enough to have two? Had this one good teacher written the most books or magazine articles, or was he just a teacher?

My college experience began 66 years ago, and I never can forget the first class I attended. With boundless expectations concerning the superiority of a college professor, and assembled with 35 other freshmen for a lesson in geometry, I awaited the great man's entrance into the room. He appeared just in time to occupy the chair behind the desk before the bell sounded. His first gesture when seated was to reach into his pocket for a black skull cap which he fitted on his head. He then mentioned the name of a member of the class who immediately went to the blackboard, drew a geometrical figure, and was about to recite. The professor, by this time, had adjusted himself comfortably in the chair and, closing his eyes, said, "Is A at the apex?" These words and the name of another student to continue the recitation were all that we heard. His eyes remained closed. That was college teaching as I was introduced to it in 1892.

Six or seven years later, I attended a professional school in a university where only college graduates were admitted to the class. The professor was one of the greatest authorities in his subject in America. He had written copiously and published many books on the subject, one of which was designated as a textbook for the course. This class was in the second year and had not met this professor before. We found it was his custom, as soon as the roll was called, to open his copy of the textbook at the prescribed lesson and read aloud for the remainder of the hour. After about a month of this experience, the class assembled, responded to the roll call, and, with the exception of three or four, left the room, one by one, disgusted by the waste of time.

In the university, each senior was required to choose one course out of three presented by the department in which I was most interested. These three courses were taught by the three highest trained professors in the department; they were all poorly taught but contained some variation.

One of the professors had a unique method of presentation. After each pupil was seated and the professor was behind his desk with notebook before him, and with his right forefinger ready to indicate the progress of the dictation, he would give the room a sweeping glance and say, "All ready." He would then start to dictate from his own notes, and every pupil was supposed to write down the notes which the professor dictated for the next 49 minutes. If the professor should suddenly look up from his notebook and detect anyone apparently not writing, the pupil would be ordered to leave the room.

Each pupil was required to present his notebook to the professor at some particular date each semester, which, after being presumedly examined by the professor, was returned for further use. The pupils who profited most from this method were those who were trying to pay their own way through college. They would procure a half-dozen blank notebooks, of different kinds and appearances, and copy the notes into these with as much individualism as possible and sell or rent them to other students who had more bank notes than class notes. There was little risk involved if the notes copied were from the dictation given a few years earlier.

Looking over the 12 years spent as a pupil in college or in the university, I am sure I had only one superior teacher and three or four capable ones. In the university where I studied eight years, the best teacher I had was an instructor in Hebrew, and the next in order of teaching ability was a professor of anatomy in the medical school. The poorest teachers were the ones who had written the most books and magazine articles. I did not have a teacher of even average ability in the subject or department in which I received my Ph.D., except in one laboratory course.

Almost every institution of learning in this country, of 100 years of age or over, claims a former member of the faculty, now long since deceased, who is supposed to have been, and is always referred to as, "A Great Teacher." He was usually almost canonized, rarely had any competitor, and, strangely enough, never had been imitated.

It may be that in future universities the faculty will be divided, one-half choosing to follow the chase of research to produce and provide the material for the other half to teach. The faculty may then represent two different crafts, according to the ability and choice of the individual. As a matter of fact, there seem to be lines of demarcation within the Ph.D. itself. Not all Ph.D.'s go into teaching, and those who are not teachers are not confined to productive scholarship of an academic nature. Some of the Ph.D.'s become businessmen and direct their fondness for research to business interests and business and manufacturing problems. If this tripartite division could be determined and developed early in the process, each chosen applicant might be directed into a distinctive task and the process might end in greater rewards—greater teachers, more prolific scholars, and more successful directors of business and super-industry.

In addition to teachers, research professors, and business consultants, the Ph.D. training serves as a preparation for a number of other occupations with less numerous demands, such as scientists, government experts, and foreign service. Not long ago, Dean Benjamin Fine reported that during 1957 only 24% of all new college teachers, serving full time, held the Ph.D. degree, compared to 31% in 1954, and this notwithstanding the fact that the production of Ph.D.'s is four times greater than it was 10 years ago. But even at that, we cannot be sure that the 24% were all good teachers. The most laudable claim that we can make for them is that they could not escape some knowledge of the field in which they were employed to teach.

What has become of the Ph.D.'s who did not continue to work in the academic fields? Probably business and industry and government have captured them; but why, after an academic training and environment for the seven to 10 years preceding, should they choose a business life? The answer usually given is this: "On account of the comparatively large salaries which business offers." It is true that business displays a beckoning finger, but there is something more than that. They refuse the teaching task because they do not know how to teach. They are also ignorant of the fact that teaching is an art which can be learned, or at least improved.

If there is any connection between the knowledge gathered in the Ph.D. course and the art of teaching, which is somewhat doubtful, the outlook for the teacher who is helped this way is rapidly deteriorating; more teachers than ever before with no degree higher than their B.A. to encourage and prepare them are employed by the colleges, and this is especially true of science teachers. One out of three new Ph.D.'s does not teach. Four years ago 18% of college faculty members did not have even an A.M.; now it is 23%.

What is to be the end of all this? In the last few years, the colleges, reduced to starvation, have developed cannibalistic tendencies and are raiding the high schools and robbing them of their best teachers.

Last year, President Eisenhower, in an address made in Oklahoma City, suggested four things *we should have*. The first two were the testing and stimulating of high-school students to procure prospective scientists; and the third and fourth, the stimulating of good quality teaching of the sciences and the provision for laboratories and fellowships to help train the students chosen. But in this and in practically all other suggestions, the emphasis is placed on the subject matter to be taught, rather than on the skill of the teacher employed to present it.

In most universities, when a faculty member is promoted to the rank of professor, he has tenure. There can be little doubt concerning the benefit of such a scheme and as little doubt concerning the objectional features. Tenure often restrains the adventurous spirit and may curb the ambition. Fewer new courses are probably presented, and there is less and less revision of the older ones. Tenure is the most disastrous for the lecturer and is the first step toward retirement for him. After tenure has become a fact, lectures are composed, delivered, and carefully laid to one side for next year. There may be an occasional addition of an idea out of a new book, but these become less frequent, and last year's lectures, tests, and examinations are annually repeated with less enthusiasm and increasing dullness.

When the freshman returns home after first entering college, he is filled to overflowing with the extraordinary events of the first few weeks which he tells with great enthusiasm to the other members of the family at the dinner table. Among other things, he relates the story Prof. Thomas Thompson told yesterday to his class. All the family seem to enjoy it except the father, and when the laughter has subsided, the father dryly remarks, "Is old Tommy still telling that story to the freshmen? It is 30 years since he first told it to our class."

Lecturing is not teaching. The best that can be said for it is that it could well save the pupil from reading a book or a magazine article, or it might be inserted among the sources of information to supply a deficiency in the textbook. For this purpose it could be used once or twice during the semester. Its advantage is that it is best used for large classes, and, with the development of television, the size of the audience is unlimited. There is a drawback which professors may not have considered; the TV technicians demand hours and sometimes days of the lecturer's time to prepare him for an appearance, and they also require many repeat performances before they are ready for a showing. Would professors consider all this technical training worth while?

But not ever graduate student is a professional lecturer. A lecturer should be a master of his craft, a magnetic personality, and an enthusiast concerning his subject. He should have a good voice and an excellent command of the English language. This is not the program we have for the pupils. The lecturer appears before a class of small or medium size and does not know the pupils' needs or understand their problems. The pupil may feel no need of the subject, and it may soon become irksome to him, and so he becomes unco-operative. The pupil has only one contact with the subject, and and one word lost may be fatal. Besides these inconveniences and difficulties, he frequently thinks of it as a waste of time. Was it not Prof. Thorndike who reckoned that 90 hours of listening to lectures covered about the same ground as nine hours of reading the same from a textbook? The textbook, moreover, was always on hand for further consultation.

If lecturing is not teaching, neither is lesson hearing, for they are both off the same piece, except that the information given is contributed from another source, although not from as reliable a source perhaps in the lesson hearing; one pupil, at least, has the advantage of reiterating the answer. Lesson hearing may save the pupil from taking a written examination, if that is worth while, and professors who use this method suffer less deterioration from tenure than the lecturers, for they receive some guidance and inspiration for their work from the recitations of the new classes, year by year. Nevertheless, there is deterioration, especially if the same textbook is used.

It is doubtful if tenure affects the real teacher very much. He has his craftsmanship which constantly inspires him, and his habitual method is not easily shaken off. The pupil is more of an inspiration to him than to either the lecturer or the lesson hearer.

58

The Professor as a Leader

LOUIS WILLIAM NORRIS

President, Albion College. At the time his article originally appeared in *School and Society* (Feb. 15, 1958), he was president of MacMurray College.

Through whatever gate the professor enters teaching, to succeed he must be a leader. A teacher will not succeed in arousing the student to think about the subject unless he thinks about it himself. Teaching is a situation in which a man or woman thinking sets a student thinking to the point where he is intrigued into doing it on his own. Imitation remains, by far, the most basic transaction in the learning process. When students come to college, they have their family, public school, and church written all over them by the osmosis of imitation.

Gilbert Highet, professor of Latin at Columbia, says this in substance: "The most obvious qualities which the liberal educator ought to acquire are those which he wants his pupils to possess. . . . The young . . . will tend to imitate any good qualities he himself manifests." Hilda M. Neatby states in her notable volume, "So Little For the Mind," "When educators set the example of bad writing, vague thinking, and slavish imitation, how can they possibly convey to others, as they profess to do, 'the art of communication,' 'creative writing,' 'critical thinking,' and 'a sense of moral values.' " The bad teacher may well be a bad writer, vague thinker, slavish imitator, or all three.

The successful teacher must be a leader in the field of his choice. He leads students by conveying to them the excitement of finding out things of great importance *at the time students are with him*. This discovery of important things must go on in the professor's life contemporaneously with the student's search. Otherwise, learning is clearly detected by the student to be something you do only during school terms, for that was when the professor learned, or else it is merely to get a grade, which the professor is paid to see that he earns.

William E. Hocking shows brilliantly in his "Experiment in Education" (p. 10) that "Leadership which does not at the same time educate fails to lead. . . . To educate, it is not enough to be able to formulate principles ideally laudable, which are incompletely related to the habits of [one's] nation or of oneself." Teaching is leadership in the enterprise the professor wishes the student to undertake. Learning to teach successfully is learning to lead toward "the stimulus of distant futures," as Richard Cabot put it many years ago.

Teaching as leadership requires the professor to manifest several basic gestures or attitudes. First, the good professor as a leader is a man digging. The highest privilege of the teacher is that he gets paid for going on with learning for life. If he does not claim this incomparable opportunity for himself, his students will not follow. They will know instinctively that learning is only make-believe. Old textbooks (even if they are better!), old lecture notes, no publications—all give the professor away. They advertise that the professor either has lost the zest for learning or else he never has had it.

Perhaps the chief need of the teacher after graduate school is competent criticism of his intellectual life. Publications, public performance, competitive exhibitions, and other criteria are tests for the man digging. No excuses will do for avoiding these tests. Let the professor never be guilty of saying it does not pay, the publications are too crowded, or there is no time! The successful professor does not teach for pay. He knows there is always room for good work and time for doing it if he wants to. Let him come up on term paper day with one of his own just published in his favorite journal. When he asks his students for one of theirs, let him give them one of his. They will know without his telling them that learning is for keeps.

Second, the good professor is a man running. He seeks an end, or series of them, in his own learning. Some planned objective must stand before him and be known to his students. What is the professor's five-year study plan, his summer or vacation plan, or indeed his lifetime plan? He must have such plans he diligently seeks in order to be sure he is busy about the right things. The will-to-scholarship must be the most evident trait of a professor in a student's judgment. It will perfect in the teacher the habits of looking-it-up, writing-it-down, and sticking-to-it.

Academic life requires the professor to learn to work in short stretches. Little jobs get done regardless of how busy one gets. The big ones can usually be done in small units. A sense of immediacy may pervade the professor's life, so he moves steadily toward his master plan. He will have to keep comfort at a minimum, for, if he has the will-to-scholarship, the delights of the mind will mean so much more than those of the body. Conservation of accomplishments can be learned by keeping an eye on the record of publications and on other such performances. Life is always too short for the good professor. He rejoices as a strong man running a race that has new goals each time one is reached.

Third, the good professor is a man catching. It is the catcher who runs the team. He motions the fielders in place for each batter, but, most important of all, he expects the right pitch from the man on the mound. He talks to the pitcher, signals for just the right ball, and pounds his glove in masterful glee when a called strike is delivered. He keeps the pitcher on his toes, steadies him in a crisis, and praises him when he does well. No pitcher can win unless the right thing is expected of him. A good professor expects great things of his students. Let him never write off a class as hopeless because the students are "flunkers," "probationers," "general educationists" majoring in another department, or "riders" in a required course. No student can honorably be allowed just to sit, to memorize merely, or to doodle. Nothing dignifies learning more to a student than the expectation by a good scholar that his students will become good scholars, too.

Fourth, the good professor is a man with his hat off. Humility before the learning of the masters in his own field becomes the professor who is a leader. Courteous regard for those whose attainments lie over the fence in neighboring fields belongs to him, too. A smug presumption—that all scholars who have gone before have ignored the greatest insights—always sounds hollow. A professor who refuses to take off his hat to any other scholar only makes himself small in trying to be big in the student's eyes.

A truly educated man respects learning in all fields of knowledge. He seeks illustrations, applications, influences, and origins of his own subject in other fields. The complex interrelation of ideas corresponds to the complex interrelations of factors which make up a mature personality. Any scholar who confines his studies to his own field alone hinders his progress in the field of his choice and becomes remote from his students. A professor needs often to take off his hat to other professors and, perhaps, on occasion to an enterprising student. He never will catch cold for doing it.

Fifth, he must be man with a baton in his hand. Teaching is fundamentally an art, not a science. The professor transforms his subject into an art work peculiar to his particular medium. What he wishes to lead his student to learn is put before the learner half-concealed and half-revealed, awaiting completion of the art transaction. Notes on a page remain to be created by the player. Notes in the atmosphere, after being put there by the violin player, await the interpretation by the listener. This completion by the listener is the seat of his enjoyment. The student finds joy in learning as he participates with the professor in completing his meaning.

The professor's task is to put his subject in such form as to make the student unable to let it alone. Like the concert-goer, who returns home humming the tune of the symphony, the student should leave the classroom pondering what the old prof said, unable to put it down. The day after Toscanini died, *The Chicago Sun-Times* carried a cartoon showing a group of angels in one part of heaven getting ready to play a harp concert. Before them stood the director with baton poised, ready to begin. To the players the director said, "Everybody on their toes! Toscanini just arrived." The good professor should find the angels as ready to be on their toes for him, for he must be an equally good artist.

59

The Functions of the University Professor of Education

FRED N. KERLINGER

Professor of educational psychology and head of the Division of Behavioral Sciences, New York University. At the time his article originally appeared in *School and Society* (Feb. 2, 1957), he was associate professor of education.

Schools of education are plagued with value conflicts. In the early days, the educational value structure and hierarchy were clear; there was little real fundamental value conflict. Most professors of education were committed more or less to the teachings of Dewey and Progressive education—and learning was by doing. Now, however, it is being discovered that the problem is not nearly so simple. Dewey's teaching, it is realized, has been misinterpreted. Many education professors now believe, for example, that we do not learn just by doing; we learn by doing and by thinking about and reflecting upon what we are doing, have done, and will do. And educators generally are wary about the use of the word "Progressive." There are also some difficult and disturbing newer developments: "group learning," "group dynamics of the classroom," the "needs of the individual in a social context," "authoritarianism in the classroom," and so on. One of the most difficult of these problems is an outgrowth of earlier educational thinking, especially Dewey's thinking on the use of community resources in teaching. In the university this germ of a good idea has grown vigorously, in some cases to enormous size. The basic idea is that the community should be used by the university as an educational resource—for teaching, research, student teaching, and for getting professors out of the ivory tower.

The growing idea seems to be that part of the university campus is the community. Students should be taken into the community to make their academic learnings real. Professors should work actively on community projects, helping the community solve its problems and growing themselves in the process. The student who spends all or most of his time in the classroom is not being educated. He is learning only words, verbal abstractions, and these verbal abstractions will not help him solve future teaching problems. Rather, he must get out of the classroom and get immersed in real-life situations. Only then will he really learn. The professor, too, runs the danger of becoming immured in the ivory tower, of becoming "academic" in his approach and thinking to educational problems. He, too, must get out of the classroom and the laboratory and into the community. He must steep himself in the ongoing, meaningful, difficult, and, above all, realistic situation of the community. The community can mean rather precisely the schools in the community or it can be vaguely defined as "out there." [1] However defined, the fundamental idea is the same: the student and the professor should get out of the university, the classroom, and the ivory tower into the community. And this "getting into the community" extends to almost all phases of the university school of education program, but especially to teaching and research. [2]

What are the implications for a university school of education program? Above all, what are the functions of a professor at a university school of education, and how does the whole off-campus idea square with these functions?

A university has two main and interrelated functions: to advance knowledge on all fronts and to impart this knowledge. The first function means research and creative, critical thinking. This pursuit and advancement of knowledge must be untrammeled, must not be dictated to by the university administration, industry, the military, schools, communities, or by anything or anyone but the individual researcher himself and his precious curiosity. The university must be a meeting-ground for curious and active minds exploring intellectual matters. The two functions of research and teaching go together; one would dry up without the other. In a true university, both functions must be alive and active. And for them to remain alive and active, the ivory tower is clearly essential for most professors. What I am suggesting for professors of education, in brief, is more ivory tower.

The education professor is said to be different from other professors because he has to deal mainly with practical teachers who want practical answers to practical questions about practical problems in practical school situations involving practical children who have practical parents who want practical results, and so on. This is, of course, partly true. But it is even more true that the professor—of education, engineering, liberal arts, or any other kind—should be precisely the person to fight *against* practicality and the

---

[1] Recently, at a national educational conference, a well-known educator was speaking about the program at his institution, and he pointed out the window and said something like, "We don't teach sociology in the classroom; our classroom is out there."

[2] The research end of it is now being categorized as "action research." *See* Stephen M. Corey, "Action Research to Improve School Practices" (New York: Teachers College, Columbia University, 1953).

consequent narrow ends and narrow means enforced by practical view-points and problems. The so-called practical answer to a question of any complexity is usually oversimplified, sometimes downright false. An example may make this clear. Teachers want to be democratic. The question boils down to, "What shall I do to be a democratic teacher?" If the professor is a "practical" person, he may say, among other things, "Break your classes down into groups, have the children decide on topics, and let them go to work. The basic principle of democracy is participation. Therefore, this method is democratic." [3] This is a practical answer to a practical question. But, unfortunately—or perhaps fortunately—it does not solve the problem. The question has been raised by some thinkers as to whether this method may not also contain the germs of autocracy. [4] A further question has been raised as to whether any method, *per se,* is democratic, autocratic, or anything else. Strictly speaking, there is no such thing as a practical answer to a practical question. All questions, especially educational questions, have "impractical," ivory-tower connotations. All questions have behind them theoretical foundations, without the exploration of which the questions are impossible to answer. There are no short, direct answers to the questions, "What shall I do to be democratic?" and "What is the best way to teach reading in the third grade?" Each of these questions, and hosts of others like them, are enormously complex requiring time, study, and much effort even to understand the ramifications of the problems they raise.

Now, for the education professor to understand these questions and to find out the answers he must spend a good deal of his time in the ivory tower. And he must often slam the door of the tower and keep the community out if he wants to preserve his professional objectivity and integrity. If he does not do this, if he continually listens to the hundreds of practical questions that the community throws at him, and if he continually tries to answer these questions directly and practically, then eventually and willy-nilly he will sacrifice the most precious thing the university professor has—the sharp, insistent voice of the professorial superego which keeps telling him to get at the root of problems. And getting at the root of problems means curiosity, thinking, speculation, and scientific research. Naturally, our professor has to come down from his tower. How often he does so is partly an individual matter. But he does so only to sharpen his curiosity, to try out his answers, and to get fresh leads and new problems *along lines of his own interests.* When he forgets this and rarely or never goes into the ivory tower—indeed, he may even claim that he is *not* an ivory-tower man—then he may lose the intellectual leadership that is so characteristic a function of the university professor. In fact, he may even become a huckster selling the wares of the university to community and student cash customers.

[3] *Cf.,* E. C. Kelley, "The Workshop Way of Learning" (New York: Harper, 1951).
[4] *E.g.,* D. Riesman, "The Lonely Crowd" (New York: Doubleday, 1953), and F. N. Kerlinger, *Progressive Education,* 31, 1954, 169-173.

On the presumed difference between the education professor and the traditional academic professor, it has been argued that the education professor's function is not so much research and the pursuit of knowledge as it is teaching and working in and with the community. To some extent this is true. However, to the extent that any professor does not serve the two basic functions outlined above, he is not a university professor. The answer to this dilemma is that any professor, before he takes on any community commitment, with or without compensation, ask: Will my doing this work help make a contribution to knowledge? and Will doing this work give me leads on how to teach better? If the answer to both these questions is "No," then the work should probably not be undertaken. In short, community work would be better left to other agencies or to the community itself if involvement in the work distracts the professor too much from his basic purposes of advancing knowledge and teaching. It may be objected that the professor *is* teaching in his community work. True, but further questions might be asked: "Could I convey my ideas and knowledge better on the campus? Am I not limiting my ideas and knowledge to too narrow a field— and wasting my time and energy in the bargain?" [5]

The same arguments apply to consultations. More and more professors are being called upon by schools, communities (community councils and the like), and industry to help solve "outside" problems. This can be, of course, a function of the university. Yet, if it occupies too large a portion of any professor's time, then it is not serving the university's functions. If it actually becomes university policy—and this seems to be happening—then the university becomes either a social work agency, a consultation and lecture bureau, or, generally speaking, a "do-good" center.[6] This does not mean that education professors should not go to schools and work with teachers. It is a question of how much and what for. The professors and the university, if they are to preserve their basic functions, must be ruthless. Each request for assistance must be critically examined.

To sum up, the university professor belongs in the ivory tower. He only leaves the tower to try out his ideas and to get new ideas. This is a rather severe and extreme statement, but it is a necessary one because the trends toward practicality, money-making, foundation grant-grabbing, doing good, and what not are alarming. If they continue, then the education

[5] A good example of some of the waste of time and the dissipation of professorial energy is some extension teaching. Much of this teaching is justified. But probably just as much of it could be done, and done much better, right on the campus. This is an important university value question which apparently has not even been examined. On the contrary, it seems to have been accepted as a wonderful thing by some elements of the university and as a necessary and inescapable evil by many professors.
[6] This is illustrated by the growth of "human relations," "group dynamics," and "community" centers in universities. If the functions of these centers are those of research and teaching, then their existence may be justified. But too often they do little or no research, or poor research, and actually deteriorate into "do-good" agencies.

professor will find himself without the essential leadership that is his pride and right—the leadership in intellectual matters, the leadership in ideas, the leadership in criticism of the community, and, finally, the leadership of the whole field of education.

No amount of rationalization can change the fundamental issues. One of the assumptions behind such community commitment is that we learn by doing, so what better place to learn than in the community itself where we must "do," where we must be realistic and practical. This argument is misleading on two counts. One is that, as indicated above, we do not learn just by doing. The second is that so-called learning in the community can be, and most often is, disorganized, emotional, and distracting. On the additional point often made that universities must show communities *how* to solve their problems, must communicate know-how, the university is *basically* not the place to teach know-how, techniques, methods. It is a place where methods may be an outgrowth of the pursuit of knowledge, the study of the relationships among phenomena, be they methods, techniques, or community and personality dynamics. It is a place where theories are conceived, systematized, and tested. This is, or should be, as true of education as of any other discipline. The university professor needs detachment, he needs to be away from the community with its endless and multifarious demands which can distract him from thinking about, say, community problems. And it is impossible for him to keep this detachment if he insists upon "getting into the community," if he insists that his research is "action research" to bring about community change. Only by sedulously guarding his right and duty to work in the ivory tower, and only working at least a good bit of his time in the ivory tower, can he fulfill the important and indispensable functions of the university professor.

60

Faculty Load in a School of Education

ALFRED ELLISON

Professor of education and head of the Division of Early Childhood and Elementary Education, New York University. At the time his article originally appeared in *School and Society* (Feb. 15, 1958), he was associate professor of education. The article is from "A Partial Study of Faculty Load," a report by the Sub-Committee on Faculty Load, School of Education, New York University.

What is a professor's load? One of our faculty members, in his response to our request, put it this way: "The principal problem of load is the amount of time and its pattern for establishing one's right to be one of a community of scholars."

Certainly a basic responsibility of a professor in a school of education is his contact with students, both in and out of class. Consequently, it seems reasonable to establish teaching time and counseling time as two main professional tasks. In relation to his teaching, a professor will devote much time to the preparation of his class work, reading of students' papers and projects. A professor is certainly concerned with students, and various professors devote various amounts of their time in the personal and professional counseling of students—some in terms of the professional development of students and others in terms of the students' personal growth. Often the two are inseparable. Curriculum advisement of a freshman, or orienting a transfer student, through to the doctoral advisement on a research project can be involved.

A professor, however, has many other responsibilities. He must continually be alert to and master of the latest developments in his own and related fields of competence. He may be one of those pushing forward the frontiers of knowledge in his special area. He may be involved in research which itself contributes to the advancement of knowledge.

He needs to devote some of his time, energy, and ability toward the development of his profession as a profession. Thus, he devotes some of his efforts to the profession itself, possibly through the various professional organizations to which he belongs. He may discharge this responsibility by his research, by sharing his insights, by speaking at various professional organizations, or through his writing.

A school of education, with its roots in actual practices in schools for children and youth, has specific responsibilities to those schools. Consequently, various professors may devote time and energy toward the upgrading and continual development of those schools. A professor thereby also renews his own first-hand contact with practical school problems and resolves a key problem of all professors: the gap in time elapsed since their own first-hand contact with children, young people, and their schools.

In his own institution, a professor has responsibilities both to the institution and to his colleagues beyond his responsibilities to students. Some of his time is devoted to the faculty organization and the committee structure in the institution. The task of a professional school cannot be discharged without a certain amount of bothersome and sometimes irksome administrative and routine detail. Professors must share in the discharge of those duties, although in varying amounts.

Some of our professors make significant contributions to the community at large and, in their effort to help community growth, spend much time working with various levels of community leadership. In involving students in the processes of understanding the community, professors range all the way from the immediate local community or neighborhood to the ends of the world through overseas workshops.

If his field is one of the specifically creative ones, the professor has a real necessity to renew himself through his own personal act of expression, his own creative act. Above all, a professor needs time to think, to cogitate, to mull over, to chew, to taste, to test, to work out, to battle through the conflict of ideas. And he needs to be a human being, alert, aware, warm, responsive, and responsible, and tremendously concerned about the world of man. He needs time to live fully and the wherewithal to do so decently, with dignity and integrity.

Feelings about faculty load assignments are part of that generalization, "faculty morale." Assessment of faculty load assignments as fair and reasonable can very positively influence the morale of faculty members. Similarly, high general morale of a faculty operates to define as satisfactory that faculty load which exists, and low morale due to other causes can be revealed through a feeling that any amount of load is oppressive. Consequently, it is extremely difficult to separate those facets of a professor's professional life which may stem directly from load factors.

One professor commented, in his reaction to our questionnaire, "A load is not a load even when equated with students, hours, course credit. A small load is a big load if you are not interested in what you are doing, feel underpaid or frustrated in doing what you want most to do." Similarly, a big load does not necessarily feel oppressive if other factors are correct. Such factors as office facilities can make a very real difference in feelings about load. Another professor stated that his hidden load is considerably increased by lack of privacy, lack of adequate office space, and lack of adequate secretarial help. "The telephone rings incessantly. Students and faculty members come into the room. . . . These interruptions put a great burden on the continuity of our effort. I have an idea that I would feel my present load less intensively if I could have an ordinarily decent arrangement which is associated with this type of work." These factors not directly related to work load or teaching or counseling assignments can increase the feeling of oppression which correspondingly increases the feeling of heavy load, regardless of whether the load is actually heavy.

An important factor of morale which influences one's feeling about work load is the general attitude of a professor about his treatment by the administration of the institution, particularly with reference to promotion and salary increment. A professor who feels that his work has not been adequately recognized and who never has been given any reason to think otherwise may very well assume that the hard efforts which he has been applying are unwarranted, that they are unappreciated and unrecognized by the powers that be. "What's the use?" may permeate his general feeling tone. Under a merit system of salary increments, a professor who receives no increment could possibly interpret this to mean "no merit," and he often wonders why no one has told him in what way his merit is lacking.

The problem of equalization of load is probably intended both to protect the professor who inherently finds it difficult to protect himself from accepting more and more assignments or requests for his services and to protect the institution and this type of professor from those few on the staff who may tend to shirk their fair share of duties and, if they have their way, may tend to do as little as they can "get away with." An administration must accept its share of responsibility, particularly if there are many of this latter group present. Consequently, factors related directly to administration such as supervisory procedures, departmental chairman procedures in relation to individual staff members, promotion policies, and salary increments all have a direct relationship to and influence on feelings about work load.

61

Professor vs. Student

ARTHUR E. LEAN

Professor of education, Southern Illinois University. His article originally appeared in *School and Society* on Feb. 15, 1958.

> We could get something done around here if it weren't for these blankety-blank students!—*Anonymous Professor*

This pitiful plaint, oft quoted in academic circles, points up a curious anomaly which has impressed more than one observer of the American educational scene. Although it seems fairly obvious to most educators that the teacher's role should be, above all else, a *helping* one, many good teachers are traumatized repeatedly by displays of pedagogical disdain and superciliousness on the part of their colleagues toward those very individuals who are, after all, the *raison d'être* of the entire educational enterprise.

This lamentable state of affairs may be found most commonly (though by no means exclusively) at the college and university level. Here the range of professional attitudes toward the objects of their endeavors runs the gamut from outright contempt and derision through amused tolerance to genuine respect. But there is sufficient faculty representation at the former end of the scale to furnish a disquieting spectacle.

Such ignoble feelings are, to some extent, a reaction to the modern trend toward excessive sentimentality which—in the opinion of many, at any rate—has accompanied an over-emphasis upon "child-centeredness" in education. One of the more reactionary of this group was the late (and possibly unlamented) Latin professor who regarded with a jaundiced eye the current tendency to emphasize the importance of knowing the "whole student," including his personality traits, family background, extracurricular interests, etc. This particular professor each semester would fix incoming classes with a baleful glare and sternly admonish them, "I don't know who you are, and I don't want to know. I'm not in the least interested in your private lives or your doings outside of this classroom. Just be here at the appointed time, recite when you're called upon, and you'll get your 'C' at the end of the course." Could it be that this misanthropic attitude on the part of a genuine scholar has had something to do with the steady decline in the study of the classical languages?

The "sink or swim" treatment is not at all uncommon in universities. Some professors make it a point to maintain a forbidding reserve toward students. Speculating upon the motivations behind this practice, one might identify a basic feeling of inadequacy beneath an expressed disinclination to be bothered by a lot of silly questions and apple-polishing. Availability of professors for conferences with students is often limited to one or two hours a week, and even these schedules are sometimes disregarded in the most casual fashion by faculty members.

In certain institutions, amazingly enough, there is a well-recognized and overtly expressed "weed 'em out" policy which manifests itself in a deliberate attempt to banish large numbers of students after they have been admitted. This practice probably occurs most often in state universities required by law to admit all graduates of accredited high schools in the state. It also is found in certain types of specialized and professional programs, such as first year of medical school. The military ruthlessness and callous indifference of such policies contrast strangely with the current national emphasis upon the conservation and best utilization of human resources.

Although this "kick the students around" attitude is certainly not confined to institutions of higher education, it is probably much less common in the lower schools. One high-school teacher, after visiting university classes being attended by some of his former students, was visibly shaken by the experience and later commented to a professor friend, "If we taught them in high school as you do here, we'd lose our jobs in a hurry—and rightfully so."

This entire generalized attitude of teacher vis-à-vis student is easily rationalized by equating it with maintenance of academic standards. College professors and administrators are typically almost pathologically sensitive about academic respectability. And here we are presented with a situation which reminds us of the smear techniques of recently notorious politicians. Whenever a new educational proposal is made, be it in curriculum, evaluation, admissions policies, or any other area, opponents often can effectively quash it by claiming that its adoption would "lower standards." Usually no real proof is required; the charge alone suffices; the proposal becomes a "dead duck."

There is much loose talk about "standards," and often the most voluble users of the term would be hard pressed to define it save in terms of superimposed requirements and of relatively meaningless phrases, such as "solid, substantial work." Now, no educator in his right mind would deny the value and importance of achievement. At the same time, however, much has been accomplished in the study of the learning process and the optimum conditions under which learning takes place. Unfortunately, some of our most learned teachers either are ignorant of all this or they deliberately disregard or violate it.

Many a toiler in the educational vineyard has remarked upon the spectacle of professors who seem to assume that the institution which they serve exists primarily for them and their convenience and only incidentally for the students, who are treated as "the lowest form of college life." But, obviously, the faculty members are at once the employees and, in a sense, the *servants* of those students. There is no room in the teaching profession for practitioners who believe that students are a necessary evil and a back- ward, inferior lot; that respect and concern for students is somehow a sign of weakness; that pomposity and superciliousness toward students is, after all, no more than they deserve. Unfortunately, there are a few teachers who seem convinced that anything more than a mere mechanical, routine effort on their part is "soft pedagogy"; that deliberate obscurantism, trickery, cheating, and all sorts of unethical practices by the teacher are actually laudable and perfectly legitimate aspects of the educative process; and that the best way to maintain academic respectability and high scholastic standards is to make it as difficult as possible for students to learn anything.

62

The College Teacher as Counselor

HERBERT STROUP

Dean of Students, Brooklyn College. His article originally appeared in *School and Society* on April 13, 1957.

In current discussions of the college instructor, a myopic stress is often placed upon the single function of classroom teaching. Such a valuable study as Gilbert Highet's "The Art of Teaching" suffers basically from an overly narrow conception of the task of the teacher. In outlining the teacher's methods, Highet recognizes "lecturing," "tutoring," and "recitation," but he fails to include such functions as counseling, campus activities, and off-campus responsibilities.

The observer of college teaching can never quite be sure that the college instructor fully enjoys non-classroom functions. Perhaps the claim by some instructors that they are engaged in scholarship is not only indicative of their primary interest, but a left-handed way of showing disdain for other than classroom activities.

The rise of the man of knowledge as a social type in the 17th century and beyond is a theme entirely pertinent to the academic scene today. The man of intellectualization in the past was also a man of responsibility— primarily of social responsibility. Is it not significant that the "Columbia Encyclopedia" lists Francis Bacon as an "English philosopher and statesman," and then proceeds to give about equal space to each of these attributions? Is it not significant that George Berkeley spent three years in the Bermudas seeking to found a school which was to convert the Indians and that for the last 40 years of his life was so active in the execution of his churchly responsibilities that he failed to write a single book? Was not the aim of Hume, in part, an effort by the use of reason to discredit that type of intellectualism (as exemplified by Locke) which grossly exalted "pure reason" as the rule of the whole of life? Is it not significant that Edmund Burke's finest speeches were uttered at the impeachment trial of Warren Hastings—speeches which pointed out the responsibility of the country to its empire and the heretofore unappreciated injustices of India? The list could be multiplied, with some clear exceptions, of the man of intellectual skill and concern who saw his teaching function pre-eminently in the maintenance of active social responsibility. Probably there is no one term today which approximates the meaning granted to such intellectual leaders of the past; certainly "professor" hardly fills the bill.

But with the rise of popular education, with the increasing differentiation of economic function, and with the growing impact of other related technological and ideological innovations, the social function of the college teacher radically changed. Chiefly the changes brought about a situation where the intellectual was not a person of general knowledge, but of a specialized knowledge. The college instructor became the technician in a knowledge area so ramified and so changeable that it took most of his time and his best efforts to survive as an academician. As a member of a well-defined class, the instructor regularly held no special responsibility in society. He became what Prof. Albert Salomon wisely calls the "coffee-house intellectual," who, in bohemian-like fashion, knew all of the answers to vexing problems but held none of the responsibility for their solutions. Thus, the possible link between "high" scholarship, the cult of so-called academic and social liberalism, and bohemianism—lack of direct social responsibility—is more causal than casual.[1]

The college instructor who worships at the leaden calf of scholarship divorced from social responsibility can hardly be expected to understand fully his role as counselor of students in groups (classrooms and student activities) and of individuals. Yet there has existed and still remains the task of counseling students.

The development of the student personnel movement in American higher education is the result of many complex historical factors. But surely one of the bases for its growth lies in the fact that college instructors oftentimes, and especially in recent times, have so shunted off their responsibilities as able guides of the young in non-scholarly problems that the vacuum quite naturally was filled by those who cared enough to secure specialized training for the job. In a sense, moreover, the resulting change has been cumulative and interrelated; that is, as college instructors no longer took counseling as their responsibility, they encouraged the growth of specialists, and as specialists became available they tended to discourage the instructors from maintaining their responsibility.[2]

Fortunately, a small but growing group of educators is increasingly showing concern and some understanding for the counseling responsibility

[1] Read the provocative analysis by Russell Kirk, "The American Intellectual: A Conservative View," *Pacific Spectator*, Autumn, 1955.
[2] The intellectual's failure of the ethical nerve (here termed "social responsibility") is dramatically discussed by Julien Benda in "La Trahison des Clercs" (Paris, 1927).

of college instructors. Part of this interest is a result of a variety of efforts recently to define the nature of higher education in a period of mass demand. The Harvard Committee's "General Education in a Free Society" (1945) and the Report of the President's Commission on Higher Education (1947) are prime examples of the effort at redefinition.

Unfortunately, however, the growth of interest in the responsibility of college instructors for counseling is an indirect result of these and similar studies rather than an integral part of them, for they do not—nor do a number of other important redefinitional documents (e.g., Huston Smith's "The Purposes of Higher Education")—make systematic room for a re-examination of the function of counseling in higher education. Yet, because these studies have been directed toward asking the question, "What should college education be like?" they have encouraged a re-examination of the broad setting in which education takes place within American colleges. Undoubtedly there have been other institutional influences, such as the high cost of specialized counseling, the occasional sharp rift between faculty and professional counselors (in some institutions replacing the traditional antagonism between faculty and administration), and the distrust of some students of professional counselors.

Teaching and counseling at many points are very close to each other. One example of the similarity was expressed recently in the statement of goals by the Department of Personnel Service, Brooklyn College:

1. Develop appropriate educational and vocational interests so that the student may choose a program of studies wisely, may succeed in it, and after graduation succeed in his chosen field.
2. Become a responsible, effective, and contributing member of one or more student organizations, thereby developing skills in human relations and a sense of at-homeness in his environment.
3. Understand and accept himself and the people around him, learn acceptable ways of expressing emotion, learn to trust his own feelings and judgments.
4. Develop a philosophy of life which will enable him to take his place effectively and responsibly in our democratic society.
5. Develop interests and attitudes which will enable him to grow in wisdom and understanding throughout his life.

In actual practice, the department co-operates with the faculty in the organization and maintenance of a variety of student service programs.

The number and variety of so-called in-service programs in student personnel services for faculty members who possess an interest and a responsibility are encouraging. Several dozen colleges and universities are presently operating such programs. Some of these appear to be efforts simply by professional counselors to make quasi-professionals in short order out of faculty members, while other programs seem to be based upon sentimental ideas of improving faculty awareness and skill without a genuine reliance upon the store of professional support and guidance. Whatever the results in specific programs, no amount of professionalism can replace the fundamental and clear responsibility of every faculty member for the counseling of students. On the other hand, there surely will continue to be a need for the expert counselor to whom the instructor may refer those students whose problems are obviously beyond his competence to solve.

It is in the spirit of the pilgrim that many instructors and their students seek that guidance by which they may affirm "the new creation," the creative, security-granting possibility by which the "new age" may be marked.[3] As pilgrims they are able to realize the fundamental possibilities of counseling—in the classroom, in student activities, and with individual students. They may not have the perfect skills, they may be acking in professional knowledge, they may feel more inadequate than their students, they may distrust the manners and contributions of professional counselors, yet, despite all, they have begun the long and sincere trek of the pilgrim. If this spirit increases in college faculties, the observer will concomitantly see the further development of counseling as a well-acknowledged element in the role of the college teacher.

[3] This language mirrors that employed by Paul Tillich in "The Courage to Be" (New Haven: Yale University Press, 1952).

63

The Scholar as Teacher

LEWIS LEARY

Professor of English and chairman of the Department of English and Comparative Literature, Columbia University. At the time his article originally appeared in *School and Society* (Sept. 26, 1959), he was professor of English at Columbia.

For more than 50 years, people who talk about teaching in American colleges have been beguiled by William James' essay attacking "The Ph.D. Octopus." Much that he said needed saying half a century ago. And much that George B. Cutten has said of "The College Professor as Teacher" (SCHOOL AND SOCIETY, Oct. 25, 1958) needs saying today. But Pres. Cutten's article is so filled with half-truths that it requires reply, not in argument, but to complete the record. [See selection 57.]

The popular image of the scholar as pedant immersed in library or laboratory and with no skill in teaching has about the same validity as the popular image of Mr. Chips, Miss Dove, or Mark Hopkins and his log. It derives from a conception of scholarship which is medieval in origin, ubiquitous in survival, but with little relation to the contemporary situation. Any of us in retrospective moments can recall, as Pres. Cutten has, examples of strangely disorientated men who taught strangely. My favorite is the professor of Renaissance studies who, when called against his will to teach literature of the United States, devoted the first term to Longfellow's translation of Dante and the second to Bayard Taylor's translation of *Faust*. And the longer I remember him, the less convinced I am that he was really strange. He taught what he knew rather than give lip-service to something of which he was unfamiliar.

The fact is that our best teachers are almost without exception our best scholars. The professor whose notes yellow with years is ineffective precisely because he has not remained alive in his subject. The trouble with most Americans, one educator is supposed to have said, is that they die at 30 and are not buried until they are 70. If this has anything to do with the

Ph.D. and teaching, it suggests that the degree sins in omission rather than commission.

Scholarship is not at a different pole from teaching. It is a continuing investigation of the validity of what is taught. It is a search back through the tangle of premises and suppositions on which knowledge is erected. Whether done in laboratory, study, or classroom, its function is the testing and accumulation of knowledge. Scholarship has been called honest intelligence at work and our only defense against every version of vulgarity which tempts us to tranquility. In the largest sense, it is state of mind, incessantly inquiring, testing, correcting. The teacher who is not scholar moves backwards through standing still, and the college moves backwards with him.

There are many things wrong with college teaching, but we are ungrateful to the thousands of dedicated and inspiring men and women who teach well under conditions not of their own making when we underline popular misconceptions of the teacher's function or accomplishment. There are teachers who teach badly, even when they know their subject. But how much less are they to be feared than the teacher who teaches well without knowing what he is talking about.

That is why we must examine so carefully Pres. Cutten's pronouncement that "criticism of the Ph.D. for teaching in colleges is that it implies that if a person knows a subject, he can teach it—a false and dangerous assumption." And that is why we must turn it to its reverse side to examine its implied parallel, equally false and infinitely more dangerous, that knowledge of subject is not necessary. We have learned enough of techniques of persuasion to discover that when cleverly presented almost anything can be sold. We have lived through times which have seen attractively packaged falsehoods taught as truth. The college teacher, for all his quaint ways, is a very powerful person. The untaught teacher is subversive of values on which sanity and civilization depend.

To insist on the necessity for continuing scholarship by the teacher is not of itself a plea for emphasis on academic degrees. Among things wrong with college teaching is the insistence of a Ph.D. for every teacher—when it is insisted on. But the teacher has not made this requirement, nor have the graduate schools. Another is the withholding of promotion or tenure until books or articles are published, and this is a stumbling block which, when erected, is put in the teacher's way by college officials. The teacher works on amazingly well, I think, in spite of administrative policies which tempt him to evade his first responsibility, which is to informed communication. Professors learn to speak softly to academic executives, but my quiet advice to Pres. Cutten is that he hold his fire long enough to discover the proper target, so that his shots can be effective.

Nor is this to deny shortcomings among college teachers. Much needs doing to make them better and allow them to be more effective. The Ph.D. is certainly not sacrosanct. Many of my best friends among fine teachers are unembarrassed without it. But the Ph.D. has been whipping boy, I think, long enough. Surely, we have not so little confidence in ourselves that we imagine that, if we had really been tormented half a century by so iniquitous a device, we should not have done something about it. Or, having been tormented, have not done something.

However tattered, the Ph.D. is worn today, if as nothing else, as reminder that the aim of education is knowledge and of teaching the communication of knowledge. A wiser generation than ours may discover it unnecessary, but when it does, something very much like it will be substituted in its place.

64

Scholarship, Research, and Teaching

I. L. KANDEL

The late I. L. Kandel was professor emeritus of education, Teachers College, Columbia University, and editor of *School and Society* at the time his article originally appeared in the journal (June 13, 1953).

The pressure to publish is one of the burdens borne by college and university teachers. The reason for this pressure seems to be primarily to enable academic administrators to impress the world with the weight of research produced by their faculties. Pressure of this kind too often leads to publication for the sake of publication and not infrequently to premature presentation of research results.

The Carnegie Foundation for the Advancement of Teaching with financial support from the Carnegie Corporation of New York undertook in 1946 an experiment to demonstrate another and more important value of continued study and research by college teachers. The report of this experiment, concluded in 1952, has been prepared by Howard Lowry and William Taeusch, president and dean respectively, College of Wooster, and issued by the foundation under the title "Research—Creative Activity and Teaching." Grants were made to a number of institutions, grouped together regionally, to enable them to assist faculty members who wished to engage in study in their own field of competence either by reducing their teaching loads or by leaves of absence. The end looked for was not in the results of study or research but in the improvement of teaching on the principle that "research and good teaching are vitally connected," and that

No teacher or scholar should be judged or promoted by the sheer weight of his annual bibliography. Very often, at its best, scholarship does not consist merely in what are usually called "discoveries," but rather in the fresh and creative synthesis of facts already at hand.

A line of demarcation should be drawn between scholarship and research. The latter term has been carried over from the sciences in which research is expected to result in discoveries. Such research tends, on the whole, to be narrowly directed to a specific end, whether anticipated or not. The paraphernalia of scholarship cannot be limited in this way, for the essence of scholarship is breadth which is accompanied by imagination and vision and is constantly expanding as new relationships and directions are recognized.

Were such a line of demarcation accepted, it would lead to a radical reform in the requirements that are usually prescribed for the Ph.D. This degree should attest to the completion of a period of apprenticeship to a master of scholarship, the acquisition of the canons of scholarship, and training in the methods of intellectual activity, all of which are more essential as bases of good teaching than the production of an "original" work or "the advancement of knowledge" often by less than one quotable sentence.

It does not detract from the importance of the experiment to say that the most exciting description of the scholar teacher is that given in the following statement in the report (p. 16):

One of the greatest teachers we have ever known was a man who published almost nothing. In the technical sense, he discovered nothing. But daily he read deeply and widely, thought in fresh ways about what he knew and was coming to know— learning, relating, comparing. His fifty-five years on the campus where he taught were years of increasing mastery of what he knew, and to his students his life and daily habits were a perpetual invitation to learning.

The whole passage from which this is cited is worth profound study. For ordinary mortals, however, a successful direction has been opened up by the experiment, initiated by the Carnegie Foundation, "to improve instruction is to stimulate creative activity among faculty members."

65

Teaching, Research, and Academic Freedom

JOHN D. GARWOOD

Dean of the Faculty, Fort Hays Kansas State College. His article originally appeared in *School and Society* on Nov. 11, 1967.

One of the most hallowed and time-honored of all academic practices of college and university administrators is the meeting where the priests of the academic world with their cup bearers gather to listen to the mystic incantations of those who preside in the inner temple. The presiding high priests, in majestic splendor, raise their hands and bless those who have come to participate in the sacred rites.

No ritual is more sacred in the ceremony than that which deals with the act of teaching. Hands and voices are raised in commending those who perform this holy act, while sack cloth and ashes are donned in demonstration of grief for those who have desecrated this most holy sanctuary of human endeavor. They pontificate the great and eternal truths. But, alas, although the ritual symbolizes the creed of the great and the near-great in the academic hierarchy, although the sacrificial lambs are slain and placed on the wood, the fire never is ignited, the sacrifice never really fulfilled. Although they invoke the "peace which passeth all understanding," there is no peace and little understanding.

The quality of collegiate instruction is being probed by legislators, trustees, recipients of foundation grants, and others. No longer an economic or social pariah, the professor is being worked over by the "pros."

In Boeotian legend, the virgin huntress, Atalanta, was famed for her beauty and swiftness of foot. So great was her love for her father, King Schoenus, that she vowed to wed only the man who could outdistance her in a footrace, the loser to drink the poison cup. She was vanquished by Hipponemes, who cast three golden apples on the ground during the race. As she ran, she retrieved the apples and placed them in the bosom of her tunic. The apples grew heavier. Hipponemes finished the race in front. Those who teach also have their golden apples.

Research and consultant roles are an anathema to good teaching. For every academician bringing the fruits of his off-campus experiences back to the classroom, there is the loss of teachers for extended periods of time. Off-campus commitments beget more of the same and a penchant for the accolades of government and business. This choice is forced on the professor by the rules of the game.

From the university's point of view, research and publication are vehicles for the expansion of knowledge, an academic aegis to be donned by presidents when interrogated by Boards of Regents. Ubiquitous by nature, research represents a mosaic in many colors, and is handy to have around when the sacrosanct idea of teaching is discussed with the Regents.

Every self-respecting institution of higher learning conceives of itself as a chosen vessel of history. Research becomes a teleological mission of university life. Innovations which bear the university's name are status builders, as projects bring money, students, faculty, and recognition. Among alumni, such activity is second only to football.

The professor is motivated by similar kingdom-building forces. Good teaching does not pay off. As an operational sphere, it is the most difficult of all academic phenomena to measure.

Research grants bring an independence not associated with the classroom, which has a refined type of time-clock punching. Research and consultation have attendant with them an amalgam of time for vicarious reflection, Braniff bourbons, the mystery of the filled attaché case, State Department briefings, the romance and pervasiveness of change, and the seductive idea of becoming known on a national basis.

Publications may be seen, felt, weighed, evaluated, and distributed. A man who has his name emblazoned in gold on the back of a book may ride aboard that book in majesty, glory, and grandeur for years. Most men in academics do not bring forth a new idea which revolutionizes thinking. Most efforts result in a rearrangement and shuffling. Academic homage is paid for these efforts, which bring promotions, higher salaries, status, recognition, and a camaraderie with others who are following a comparable course of action.

Research, foundation grants, and consultative roles off campus breed more of the same, which, in turn, bring less interest in teaching. Once the ground rules are laid out, a neophyte in the field plays accordingly. Presidents, deans, and department chairmen piously call for better teaching and then reward most highly those who teach the least. The most talented, the most vigorous, teach in a perfunctory fashion. To those who attain this exalted station in life flows the power, honor, glory, and larger pay checks.

The most inviolate of all areas in academia is the classroom. Administrators are not permitted by tradition, academic mores, or the American

Association of University Professors to observe the instructor teach. A student may be glued to his chair by the magnetism of the professor's remarks, or he may stir restlessly, his eyes taking on the glazed look of a soul venturing in distant places. Editor John Fischer put the matter most succinctly: "Typically the president is a sort of Merovingian king, presiding nervously over the savage and powerful barons who run their separate schools, departments, laboratories, and institutes like so many feudal fiefs. He has only very partial command over the university's budget; because of the tenure rule, he cannot fire a lazy or incompetent professor; and his control over what happens in the classroom is marginal."*

A salesman is judged by the amount of his sales, a lawyer by his success in court, an architect by the aesthetic and functional qualities of his buildings. It is possible for a young Ph.D. to isolate himself and move through the years on the academic momentum generated while in graduate school. His Ph.D. does not mean he is able or willing to teach.

Obviously, all teachers do not operate in such a fashion. College and university teaching lends itself to "dogging" it. As in other areas of human endeavor, there are the slothful, the incompetent, and those given to off-campus peccadilloes. The professor is not worried about building up a consumers' preference for his product.

The third golden apple which weighs heavily in the tunic of those on the lecture platform is the freedom from responsibility. As Sen. Gale McGee (D.-Wyo.) stated to the student body at Oregon State University, July 6, 1966, Prof. McGee has more solutions to the problems of the world than does Sen. McGee.

As a wholesaler and retailer in ideas, the professor need not stand back of his product, need not affix his seal of approval, provide a money-back guarantee. He may toss his ideas in the air, bounce them off the blackboard, and proceed on the easy assurance that it is up to the student to decide. He has the right to blow where he listeth without ever sailing

The decision as to what is Truth is placed in the hands of the student. The incisive factor of responsibility for decision-making is not regarded by the academician as a responsibility of his. The fact that the professor is not held responsible for the results of his efforts dulls the edge of his motivation, removes the incentive for a follow-through. His professorial success is not laid on the line as in other professions. He can pass the puck back and forth and never need bother to attempt to score.

The competitiveness of the market for staff members is evidenced in continually lighter teaching loads, greater salaries, more fringe benefits, and a minimum of direction on the part of administrators. Do some take advantage of this situation? Ask the students.

---

*John Fischer, "Is There A Teacher On The Faculty?" *Harper's,* February, 1965, p. 18.

If teaching is as important as men in high places say that it is, then it must be treated as such in the college hierarchy of values. Our traditional concepts of academic freedom are permissive in the extreme, however, they do not bring with them responsibility.

The theoretical concept of academic freedom is premised on the grounds that the academician is a scholar, a seeker, and a purveyor of Truth, and, in the pageant of progress, he lives to communicate Truth in the classroom. A learned diagnostician and theoretician in his discipline, one assumes that he unceasingly toils to bring his thoughts to his students and is himself above anything but an optimum effort. His life on earth is regarded as a trying preamble to life eternal as made manifest in his students.

He is the disturbing yeast in the leaven of society, his words the butterfly inside the chrysalis, they illuminate the entire landscape. His *modus operandi* is associated inextricably with freedom from restraint, which is the shibboleth of creativity. Ideas are the raw stuff of his idyllic existence and his allegiance of intellect to ascertaining the Truth is as certain as a proposition from Euclid.

This pearl of great price is canonized and trotted out in brocaded prose with razorlike edges whenever the efforts of God-fearing men in the classroom are brought to question. When questioned, men wring their hands, wrack their brains, and call upon the spirit of Tom Paine, Thomas Jefferson, and John Dewey to sustain them.

This concept does not recognize that all teachers are not scholars who yearn for the Truth. The "goof-offs" are there. Some are there "to make a living." They are the ones who have discovered, quite correctly, that college teaching provides an avenue for a comfortable living, a fair amount of status coupled with a minimum amount of responsibility for one's own activity. Although not predatory by nature, yet, in terms of shaping the master images of a culture, they represent the cat among the pigeons. They only shuffle back and forth and hope they do something. In a word, academic freedom posits an ideal classroom situation, which exists in relatively few instances.

Students have been aware of this for a long time. Battle-scarred though they may be, academicians have a passion for their own structures. Too long have administrators and teachers stuttered in the margins as year after year, in apostolic succession, they follow the cliché of yesterday in erecting the scaffolds of presumed adequacy in the classroom. It remains for those on campus to cast aside the golden apples of Atalanta and teach as the academic myth suggests they do.

66

Schizophrenia on the Campus

EDMOND L. VOLPE

Professor of English, College of the City of New York. At the time his article originally appeared in *School and Society* (Nov. 26, 1955), he was an instructor in English.

The successful American college professor is a healthy schizophrenic. His body houses two incompatible personalities. He is a teacher and a scholar.

The effective teacher is a social being, sensitive and responsive to the emotional and intellectual needs of students. He is a ham actor, a mezzo-voce orator, an amateur psychologist, a part-time sociologist, a spiritual leader. The scholar need be none of these things. He is, in fact, necessarily anti-social, capable of spending hours, even whole weekends, alone in a library or at his typewriter. He is often shy and uncomfortable in the presence of others; he is a writer rather than a speaker. The scholar is a solitary; the teacher, a social being.

The human character, it is true, is capable of surprising contradictions. But men like Lord Byron or Albert Schweitzer, who function successfully with opposing personalities, are rare. The average college professor is no such extraordinary being; yet every day at the sound of the bell he must come out of his isolated corner—a teacher.

The schizoid academic is a modern phenomenon. Earlier faculty members were primarily scholars; they were required to teach but not to be teachers—a significant difference. Today, however, the American college is breaking new ground, and the professor, straddling the fissure, has been split in two. And all his complaining and all his planning will not put the professor together again. He must be both a scholar and a teacher.

If the professor has to alter his ego on demand, he needs assistance, particularly from those who are, to some extent, responsible for his dual existence—his students, future students, and their parents. Before they can aid him, however, these groups must know the cause of the professor's schizophrenia and recognize the part they played in its development.

313

The task of the expanding American college is to erect an institution with a Gothic foundation and a modern façade. It must, in other words, retain its medieval traditions and at the same time fulfill its responsibilities to the national community. Traditionally, the college is a congregation of scholars, and the campus is a center of study and research. Though, at present, the university graduate schools have become the major centers of research, colleges cannot abandon their tradition of fostering scholarship. Few scholars begin their teaching careers in graduate schools, and the quality and quantity of American learning is still mainly dependent upon undergraduate faculties. Whatever adaptations colleges make to changing social conditions, they must continue to promote research in all fields, science and the humanities.

In the past, scholarship as the sole requirement for an appointment to the college faculty caused no difficulty. The scholars formed a living library. Young people, desiring knowledge, came to the campus and listened to the professors. It was wonderful, of course, if the scholar was also an excellent teacher. But his teaching ability was a minor consideration. He had something important to say and the students wanted to hear him. The scholar did not have to metamorphose into a teacher in the classroom. Students considered a college education a privilege, not a right.

Today, however, the professor cannot successfully fulfill his duties in the classroom without changing from scholar to teacher. The modern college is no longer merely a center for study. It has become an industry turning out a required commodity—the educated specialist.

Our complex industrial society requires men and women with broader educational backgrounds than are provided in secondary schools to man its administrative and technical posts. It needs technically proficient young people with the proper mental discipline to grasp the broad view of any situation. Such discipline is achieved only by a deliberate process of extending the boundaries of thought. An introduction to many subjects, as diversified as geology and world literature, has proved to be an effective process for awakening young minds. The number of college graduates in the better-paying jobs has been constantly increasing.

Parents, eager in the American fashion to push their child into a higher economic and social bracket, conceive of a college education as an investment that will pay off huge financial and social dividends. They direct the child towards a profession or towards occupying a front office in the factory where the father has labored in obscurity. The youth's goal is set before his June graduation from high school. He eagerly awaits the new life September will bring him, but his eyes are not focused on the campus: he sees only the bright distant star of a good paying job or an office door with a professional title under his name.

At college, the freshman suddenly discovers that he will be expected to learn how to write coherent compositions, read Milton and Chaucer, know something about history and philosophy, even know how to swim. What, he demands to know after his initial awe of the large institution has passed, do these courses have to do with the goal he has set for himself? Will history, ethics, English make him a better engineer, guarantee him a better salary?

The American college student has changed. He reflects the need of industry, but not its thinking. He does not realize that educated men, not just technicians, are in demand. Many of these new students, in an earlier period, would never have gone to college. They would not have measured up to the entrance requirements. Colleges then were considered something more than preparatory schools for industry and the professions. And the greatest problem of educators today is to resist public pressure and keep their colleges educational institutions with programs that will awaken and expand the intellect.

Such institutions require real teachers who can pry open young minds sealed by a monomania—financial success. Today, instructors must create interest in courses that have no apparent relevancy to a professional program of study. They must, in other words, sell their subjects. Some students react to a subject; most react to the personality of the teacher. To turn out educated graduates, therefore, colleges need professors who can overcome the lethargy and hostility of the modern American student.

Many college administrators and professors resent the new type of student and deplore the lowering of entrance and course standards. They struggle against the broadening curriculum and demand limited registration. They denounce the increased emphasis upon technological subjects and the debasement of the humanities. And they are right in feeling as they do.

Colleges should remain havens for scholarship; they should preserve their function—turning out educated graduates; they should not follow the trend of many modern parents and become abject slaves of the young. Colleges should be fountains at which the adolescent comes to drink, not snack bars which provide whatever is demanded.

But these educators representing the traditional view are also wrong. Their arguments for limiting registration are weak echoes from the past. The American college has accepted the challenge of the middle-aged 20th century. It has expanded and admitted large numbers of people who, in an earlier period, could not have entered the academic gates. These new students belong on the modern campus. They may not, as a group, achieve the distinction of previous students because they do not initially bring as much intelligence or interest with them. But no one goes through four years of college without reaping many benefits. And certainly there can be no question of the value of extended higher education to the democratic community.

The belief that colleges should be reserved for the few, that the advancement of learning and human knowledge is to be achieved by educating the best minds only, is anachronistic. The finest students very rarely receive no extra attention from their professors. Most colleges offer honors programs for the best students, and future scholars and scientists go to graduate schools for specialized training. The broader the base of well-educated people in a society, the higher can the pyramid of knowledge be built. No poet, scientist, or philosopher was ever hampered by a large sympathetic public.

It is no easy task, however, to produce that base of cultured graduates out of a Cyclops student body, an unwieldy giant with vision limited to financial success. The job requires a schizoid faculty—scholars who are also effective teachers.

Within the last decade or so, the American college professor has become increasingly aware of his duties as a teacher. But the failure of students and the general public to understand the aims and functions of both the professor and the college has made teaching more of a battle than it need be. Two orientation programs—one for the student and one for the instructor before either reaches college—would improve the professor's chances of producing something more than college-trained technicians.

A series of talks given by professors and extending over the full period of secondary education should be a part of the high-school student's training. The program would acquaint the prospective student long before he enters college with the aims of advanced education. The high-school pupil and his parents should know that college is more than a preparatory school, that, though it can lead to better jobs, its primary purpose is to educate. He should be taught to respect the college as a center of research and scholarship and be made to realize that his future teachers are also scholars who are eager to make available to him their wide backgrounds of specialized and general knowledge. At present, most college students catch a glimpse of the great world of ideas, but only towards the end of their four years of study. Even then, too few try to venture into that exciting realm. They have struggled too long against believing in its existence, choosing to see reality only in practical technical training. With proper orientation, perhaps, they could live in that kingdom of ideas for four years and leave college better prepared for a career and for life.

The prospective college instructor also requires orientation. In graduate school he is trained to be a scholar, nothing else. Very little in a Ph.D. candidate's course of studies prepares him to be a teacher. When he meets his first class he usually knows as little about teaching as do his students. Education courses, no matter how many, will probably not make anyone a college teacher. But a special course or two added to his regular program— perhaps educational psychology or a methods course—could make the future scholar conscious of himself in the role of teacher and could better enable him to assume his dual role on the modern college campus.

Such orientation programs would not cure the professor's schizophrenia, but they certainly would aid him in his struggle to turn out educated college graduates.

67

The Professor: Educator, Scholar, or Both?

THOMAS O. BRANDT

Professor of German, University of New Hampshire. At the time his article
originally appeared in *School and Society* (Nov. 12, 1966), he was professor of
German, Colorado College.

There is a tendency, perhaps even an obsession, at American universities to
deduce the qualifications of a professor from the number and circumference
of his publications, chiefly books. The reason for this desire is twofold. To
be effective, he must be a scholar and a gentleman. His character is revealed
by his general behavior; his decisions and actions can be judged by his
colleagues, his students, and administration officials. Since his aptitude as a
scholar can be verified best by colleagues in his field, he should publish
significant and comprehensive studies which then would be easily accessible
to experts in his field, in this country and abroad. When the fruits of his
endeavor are committed to print, objective appraisals can be made in the
form of reviews and discussions. This, of course, is entirely legitimate in the
case of a man who wishes to publish the results of his studies, and scholars
will be much indebted to him if his treatise or book proves to be essential.
However, a scholar, defined as "a learned or erudite person," is not necessarily
one who produces a treatise or a book, as being an author in a given realm
of science does not make him automatically a scholar.

The insistence of university administrators, deans, and executive
officers on the production of learned studies seems to stem from a desire to
see the value of their faculty members recognized and verified. Therefore,
persuasion is exerted to have them pursue research projects with their sights
set on the printing presses. Since advancement in rank and salary, as well as
tenure, often depends on whether manuscripts are accepted for publication,
every conceivable effort is made by the harassed profession to fill the prescription. This laborious activity not infrequently resembles either a game of
chess or an immaculate procedure which may prove a point of little interest

and no significance whatsoever. An unimpeachable method, needless to say, is a *conditio sine qua non* for any scientific endeavor, but as a means, not as an end in itself. Perhaps this frequent confusion is the reason for the insignificance of so many learned dissertations which the awed layman is inclined to consider profound. This is particularly true in the realm of the humanities and the social sciences. In one way or another, all of us are laymen in relation to fields not our own.

Thus, the accumulation of manuscripts is extraordinarily great. Lately, the enormous pressure upon commercial publishers has been somewhat eased, particularly since the end of World War II, by our ever-increasing university presses, by partly subsidized presses abroad, and by vanity presses.

The publication of a book is accepted as the ultimate proof of one's ability, subject to reviews, which frequently are small articles in themselves displaying erudite knowledge, rather than critiques. Books are the agents for promotion, for offers from other institutions, and for prestige. They may even prove that the scholar is a scholar.

Doing research in a narrow and specialized field will help the professor little in his educational task, unless he limits himself to highly specialized courses. Research in a broad and varied manner, if it is to be valid, is rare and requires the genius of a comprehensive mind. He who knows too much in one particular field is in danger of losing educational perspective and of making his students into research assistants, to the detriment of a well-balanced education.

There are admirable educators who are excellent scholars without having published a line. They succeed in kindling judicious enthusiasm among their students, in opening eyes and minds, in revealing knowledge with perspective and circumspection. If they do, why not commit their wisdom to print? If they should, we are prepared to answer, they often would not offer new findings and, moreover, their verbal presentation may not be equalled in significance by their writing. It is the "How" that counts with them decisively, in addition to the "What." Their disadvantage is their relatively small audience. This does not help their peers and academic superiors in arriving at a judgment about their ability as scholars when the printed word as a measure for evaluation is so much more convenient.

For this reason, the faculty member at a university—less often at a college—feels haunted and compelled to produce, literally at any cost. Striving to be original, he may contrive topics and rely on speculation without offering a hypothesis. The positivist will arm himself with the requisites of Sherlock Holmes and triumphantly offer proof that a certain piece of literature was actually written on one specific date instead of another date, as previously assumed. The psychologically-minded will indulge in symbolism and gladly run the risk of making a phenomenon more complicated than it is. Most will prove things for the sake of proof and employ a host of footnotes which are as much to serve their claim to accuracy as their desire to display private erudition. Others, rendered breathless by their labor, will be content to edit with little change works that have been edited capably before, or will rearrange books by others to provide them with a new look. Whose look?

Where, then, is the equation between educator and author? When hard pressed, the educator, in many instances, will have his teaching load substantially reduced to cope with the publishing race. Administrations will often gladly agree to this—indeed urge him to do so—for his crowned efforts will be reflected in the university's dearly cherished "university image." The educator then will rely more upon assistants to do his teaching, so that he may do research leading to publication. The assistants, as a rule, are graduate students who hardly can be expected to match the skill and experience of a good educator. The scholar-educator naturally will avail himself also of frequent leaves of absence—sabbaticals, fellowships, special arrangements with his administration, etc. Again, the gain in published research must be regarded as a loss in teaching.

A few well-endowed universities can demand that their faculties engage in research leading to publication, since they are in a position to grant and to provide for leaves without hampering the teaching process. This is particularly true where the tutorial system is prevalent, with its interplay of teaching and research, and where the relation between teacher and student is a very personal one. Where this is not the case, administrations would do well to show reasonable consideration to those who are real scholars, and not only "knowledge technicians," by reducing their teaching loads, while being content with excellence in teaching in the case of those who are in no position to offer important new findings.

Even in the case of the prominent young scholar who earned his Ph.D. at 25 and has been employed as an instructor at a university for two to three years, it does not seem fair to hang the sword of Damocles over his head by telling him that he can be kept and promoted only if his research assumes printed form. Some rare and outstanding young scholars undoubtedly will succeed in meeting this rigorous expectation. Others will need more time to have their thoughts and insights mature and deepen, and may lose their bearing altogether when confronted with demands resembling an ultimatum, let alone the opportunity of reappraising and refining the results of their research. If an instructor has begun his career at a prestige university—that obviously appointed him in good faith and as a promising scholar—and if he then is sent into academic Siberia for not having made the promotion grade, the blow may well prove to be destructive as far as his future scholarly ambitions are concerned. Libraries in Siberia generally are inadequate for real scholarship.

The criteria for judging an educator as a scholar—as practiced today—are largely invalid. Moreover, whether a certain piece of investigation is accepted by a periodical for publication depends so much on an array of external circumstances that the rejection of a manuscript, particularly of a relatively unknown author, cannot necessarily be equated with a value judgment. Conversely, its acceptance does not mean unqualified recognition *per se*. It depends upon the frequency of previously published articles in the author's particular field of research, upon the judgment of readers, upon available space, backlog of manuscripts, etc.

Perhaps there is no way out of this dilemma. On the one hand, one realizes that "he who rests, rusts," that competition is the father of all achievement, that a scholar, in addition to sharing his knowledge, should enrich it by investigation, and that the results ought to be made known to the largest possible number of interested scholars. On the other hand, one cannot deny that a full teaching schedule, with its many demands on the faculty, rarely allows a man to indulge in thorough research to be displayed in learned treatises and books. True, there are rare scholars who are both excellent teachers *and* authors. But many educators, even very able ones, do not have the ability to cast their findings in writing or to do research. These then will prefer to do the house chores of research or pseudo-research, compile lists of one kind or another, indulge in statistics, busy themselves and others with questionnaires, or belabor the obvious. They will endeavor to make up lack of quality in depth and breadth by pieces of writing that serve no particular purpose in the realm of scholarship.

The fact that such writing may be recognized as valid by reviewers still does not necessarily prove its value or that its author is a scholar. Even if it is proved beyond any doubt to be a work of scholarship, it has indicated nothing yet as far as the aptitude of its author as an educator is concerned. If the excellence of a study or book alone were a testimony to the ability of its author as an educator, the latter could well stay at home and leave the matter of study and exploration to his students in our excellent libraries.

Instead of making promotion and tenure dependent almost exclusively upon publication records of sometimes dubious value, would it not be more reasonable to grant substantial recognition to scholars who dedicate themselves to truly educating students? The gain for the developing mind of students and future scholars would be immeasurable. Instead of classes of several hundred—which might well be administered by tape recordings—there could be smaller groups, some extensively and intensively on a seminar, colloquium, or symposium basis, even at the undergraduate level.

An insistence on what has been called "Publish or Perish" reveals that lack of reasonable judgment and that lack of genuine scholarship which it hopes and pretends to be able to cure by it.

68

Renaissance of Teaching

WARREN L. HICKMAN

Associate director, Social Studies Curriculum Center, Maxwell Graduate School
of Citizenship and Public Affairs, Syracuse University. His article originally
appeared in the Summer, 1966, issue of *School and Society.*

The United Steelworkers and the International Longshoremen's Association,
among others, have been slipping quietly from their role as social revolu-
tionaries into the position of entrenched conservatives. Industrial pioneers
and financial innovators of the American 1930's and 1940's had carved
comfortable niches by the mid-1950's. Professional military minds comfortably snuggled down beside impressive piles of mothballed aircraft,
tanks, and ships.

Despite nostalgia for the straining controls of a wounded aircraft in the
firm hands of a pilot officer, the military mind has had to face the cold,
impersonal atmosphere of shining control rooms with whirring computers
and fantastic memory banks directing the course of missiles. Unions are
stirring restlessly under their more comfortable leaders, shying from the
scent of automation like a horse at the smell of blood. More than one union
leader will lose his saddle before calm is restored. Industry has been gal-
vanized into meeting competition of automated mills in Europe and Japan.
Banks are installing computers to match the speed of the new generation.

With the exception of a few alert universities, American higher
education has continued to provide more and more wall space for the niche-
carvers of the postwar era. Like a slumbering giant, American higher
education is just beginning to shift in uneasy sleep prior to full awakening.
Automation is about to revolutionize industry, finance, labor, and the
military. Higher education cannot expect to be spared, nor should it be.
We can expect the loss of fine traditions, but we may find compensation if
this new revolution also brings about a renaissance of teaching. Already
there are numerous indications that the computer may push research and

writing off the undergraduate campus and turn the emphasis once more to students, teachers, and classrooms.

For 15 years, academic deans have met at annual conferences to moan over the demise of the teacher and the rise of the disinterested "research" faculty on undergraduate campuses. These are the same deans who previously deplored the short supply of Ph.D.'s and the lack of research which left so many marginal college faculty unable to present the latest developments of their discipline to their classes. We have witnessed the swing from one extreme to the other. Today's complaint is not directed against research. It is aimed at the specific type of research which is not creative, which develops no new ideas or theories, and which contributes little or nothing to the discipline.

The new breed of "researcher" is being criticized by eminent scholars for being afraid to "go out on a limb." Fear of professional criticism has led to a practice of qualifying almost every new statement. A body of critics exists who sift through articles and books seeking an unqualified statement they can challenge as the basis of an entire article of rebuttal. So research for the not too brave has deteriorated to a point of cataloguing and collecting. The mechanical task of reading volumes to sift out a series of related material is not too different from a law clerk's patent search, an attorney's preparation of a brief leaning heavily on a century of court precedent, or an auditor developing a financial analysis of a corporation's last 20 years of operation. An aura of mystery and rare ability has been woven around a routine task. This job cannot be accomplished by an I.Q. of 100, but it is little more than a clerical job for a professor with eight to 10 years of college and university study and several years of teaching and research behind him. We are speaking, of course, of uninspired cataloguing of documentation, not of scholarly interpretation and experimentation which add new insight to the field.

There is little relationship between teaching ability and ability to perform as a research technician. This high-level clerical technique contributes nothing to the classroom, but does draw the professor away from his students. Automation now promises to shake the institution of research to its roots, resulting in a much higher grade of *creative* research and a renaissance of teaching.

General Electric and *Time-Life* jointly have financed Silver, Burdette & Co. Xerox has purchased the *Weekly Reader* publications. IBM is deep in educational research. RCA has been negotiating with publishers. Further progress in the development of computers soon will make the computer an indispensable adjunct to any first-rate college or university library. Complete cross-reference of disciplinary and inter-disciplinary materials may require years, but even in the beginning the computer will be able to store and return far more information than a small team of researchers could in an entire lifetime.

We can expect to see machines sort, evaluate, and present in printed form all available evidence on subject X within a decade. Major universities are now searching the country for historians, economists, chemists, and professors of literature who have background in storing and retrieving data. This is no new idea. Graduate faculties already are being offered a choice of faculty seminars on the use of computers on the larger campuses. In some cases, computer "language" may be substituted for the foreign language requirement for doctoral degrees.

Eventually, small- and medium-sized colleges and universities will be able to purchase memory bank tapes from the large research libraries. There temporarily will be a heavy demand for the routine "read and compile" researcher who learns to store data. The 1970's will bring the machine to the small college library, which will enable a student or a professor to push a series of buttons and in return receive a chronologically, chorologically, or topically ordered presentation of any desired subject. This may be a brief survey or a thorough study, depending on the buttons pushed. Within minutes, a college junior will be able to obtain materials sorted from 500 or 1,000 books related to his term paper on an obscure historical event, whereas a professor reading the same 500 books would be unable to complete the same research in 10 years.

A book may be prepared by employing the services of one or more technician editors to rewrite or otherwise edit the ordered, evaluated, and related documentation pouring in printed form from memory banks. What then will happen to the "researcher" who spends 50%–75% of his time in research and 25%–50% in teaching? What becomes of the professor who says "I only remain in teaching because I'm committed to research"?

Perhaps more pertinent is the question of what will become of the life of the graduate student. If a graduate student can obtain more information on a given subject by pressing a button than he possibly could obtain in five years in the library or the laboratory, will there be a five-year graduate program? Under such circumstances there is every reason to believe the emphasis on graduate research will need to be altered. Graduate students will have more time to practice teaching. The entire Ph.D. program will require restudy and re-evaluation. In addition to 60 hours of post-master's courses required for a doctor's degree, a graduate student now spends half to three-quarters of his time in research. What will be substituted for this "research" by 1975? What advantage will there be in teaching present methods of research to potential faculty, except for those who plan to work in a level of research above and beyond the abilities of computers programmed by the world's leading scholars?

Professional articles which are so much a part of our "publish-or-perish" system are often chapters from projected books, rewritten excerpts from dissertations, or papers previously read before conventions. A re-evaluation of the "publish-or-perish" philosophy is inevitable when any undergraduate can press a button and obtain a term paper or seminar report of far more depth than the *average* non-computerized article written by a professor.

Even a good article may come to represent a reinterpretation of material drawn from the machine, and may not represent ability to research, but an ability in composition. Our faculty and administration are not prepared for this. We can insist that computer presentation of related material does not have the value of reading entire books in the process of searching for pertinent material, but no one can imagine it possible to prevent the easy way out once the button is there to push.

Research, to be real research, will need to be creative. Statistics, reviews of tested reactions, and comparative theories can be drawn from the past by the machine. Real research will involve new theories, new ideas, projections, predictions, and interpretation. It again may be dominated by and distinguished by creativity. Researchers will feel the need to "go out on those limbs" and to expose themselves to criticisms for their speculations in order to stand out above the production of the button pushers. Objectivity no longer will be a word which any technician can use to shield his semi-clerical compilations from the criticism of lack of imagination.

When this fate befalls tens of thousands of college and university researchers, teaching ability again may become a means of judging performance on *all* undergraduate campuses rather than on the present handful of elite holdouts. Students on some campuses are already in rebellion at the lack of faculty-student contact. They soon may witness automation at its best, when it replaces outmoded and overly expensive operations. The cost of education has risen to accommodate research and reduced teaching loads. Administrators have emphasized research and writing until it is supposed to be a goal in itself. What can be more natural than to produce the "end product," research and basic reporting of compiled research, by a more "efficient and economical" means? We already are pricing non-creative research out of the reach of employers of human labor.

Thousands of undergraduate faculty may be faced with a half-time job unless they move to data-storing centers or convert to full-time teaching. A solution to the "teacher-shortage" may come more quickly than anticipated. Most important, the performance in the classroom will not be hidden beneath a façade of non-teaching projects. At that point, the struggle for rank and salary may well introduce a renaissance in teaching.

69

Suggested Intermediate Graduate Degree

HOWARD PUTNAM

Professor of sociology and head of the Department of Social Sciences, East Texas State University. His article originally appeared in *School and Society* on March 18, 1967.

Varied suggestions have been made for a new university degree, at a level between the master's and doctor's degrees. For example, Yale University recently adopted a program for the master of philosophy degree,[1] requiring one year of work beyond the regular master's. Also at that level is the proposed doctor of arts degree.[2]

These programs are in answer to teacher scarcity in junior colleges, four-year colleges, and universities.[3] Many of today's college teachers complete all but the last year of a doctoral program. A new predoctoral graduate degree would give a completed status at the level most often attained. The program of academic degrees thus would reflect the situation more accurately.

Numerous institutions have an established program of study for the degree or certificate of Education Specialist, often abbreviated as the Ed.S. Usually, this is given for the completion of 60 semester hours beyond the bachelor's degree, with a master's degree required as part of that preparation.[4] The Ed.S., designed for specialists in education, is granted at a point between the master of education and doctor of education degrees. The degree may serve as a terminal one or may be a base for doctoral study.

Ideas and customs developed in the Ed.S. program may be applied in

[1] J. P. Miller, "Master of Philosophy: A New Degree is Born," *Journal of Higher Education*, 37:377-381, October, 1966.
[2] F. Bowers, "Doctor of Arts: A New Graduate Degree," *College English*, 27:123-128, November, 1965.
[3] D. G. Brown and J. L. Tontz, "Present Shortage of College Teachers," *Phi Delta Kappan*, 47:435-436, April, 1966.
[4] This is the rule, for instance, at the University of Arkansas, Louisiana State University, and the University of Tennessee.

creating a broader plan. Just as we have the master of arts and master of science, we might create the Specialist in Arts and Specialist in Science degrees. These could be abbreviated as Sp.A. and Sp.S. Each would carry the connotation that a "Specialist" degree is at a level of its own. Confusion attendant upon ambiguous use of the term "master" or "doctor" would be avoided. There would be three distinct levels of graduate degrees: the master's, specialist's, and doctor's degrees.

Following tradition in such matters, most institutions might require a knowledge of a foreign language as one of the hurdles for the degree of specialist in arts. For the degree of specialist in science, a substitute task of the same difficulty would insure equal status for the two degrees. For this purpose, the student might be given a thorough examination on the research procedures of his academic discipline.

A thesis, similar to that for the master's degree, might be required. In the Ed.S. program, some universities [5] require a thesis, and others [6] do not.

Demands that all college teachers must seek the doctorate keep administration and faculty alike under tension.[7] The Ph.D. shortage causing this may continue far into the future. The specialist's degree for all disciplines may be a realistic answer. The college teacher who does not pretend to be a research worker would be qualified formally for lower-division college teaching. Most college teaching is at this level. And deans or department heads would be under less pressure to find teachers with the doctorate. Accrediting agencies, too, might find the intermediate degree a useful compromise.

[5] For example, Arizona State University, Ball State University, and the University of Tennessee.
[6] For example the University of Arkansas, the University of Florida, and the University of Missouri.
[7] J. F. Rogers, "Staffing Our Colleges in the Present Decade," *Teachers College Record*, 67: 134-139, November, 1965.

70

The Ph.D. Fetish

JOHN W. DYKSTRA

Associate professor of sociology, Jersey City State College. At the time his article originally appeared in *School and Society* (May 24, 1958), he was instructor of sociology, Utica College of Syracuse University.

In American higher education there is probably no other single achievement that affects the educator's status more than the acquisition of the Ph.D. As a perusal of any learned society's listing of "positions available" will indicate, a high percentage are open only to those who have their terminal degree. Those with lesser degrees who do secure employment as instructors frequently find that mobility upward is absolutely barred until the Ph.D. is acquired, regardless of other achievements. The close relationship between employment opportunities at the college level and the Ph.D. has led understandably to the widespread reference to the degree as the "union card."

The vital importance to the young scholar of getting the Ph.D. is further indicated by the fact that many alternative opportunities for attaining recognition in the academic world are available only to those who have this degree. Scholarship and fellowship opportunities may be so limited; numerous research grants are restricted to Ph.D.'s. Although the evidence is not so clear, it is also probable that opportunities for publication are affected, in some measure, by the possession of the degree.

Despite this domination of the Ph.D., there exists among those conversant with the realities of American higher education a widespread recognition that the acquisition of the degree provides little assurance that one can competently fulfill the role expected of the American college faculty member. Successful completion of the Ph.D. program may be assumed to be evidence of a significant degree of subject-matter mastery, as well as an ability to carry out an acceptable research project. There is no measurement at all of the extent to which the candidate possesses the ability to convey knowledge of and enthusiasm for his subject to young men and women with little or no background in the field, an aptitude which is vital to the successful performance of the usual professorial role. Nor is there any provision in the program for appraising the future faculty member's ability to work harmoniously and productively on the committee work that occupies so much of the time of college professors. Skills in counseling students, guiding student organizations, and furthering college-community relationships are neither nurtured nor tested in the Ph.D. program. The Ph.D. program has about as much relation to classroom competence as a course in bullfighting has to proficiency in agriculture, to modify a well-known observation of Thorstein Veblen.

In the preoccupation with research qualifications that has dominated hiring and advancement in American higher education, there seems to be little recognition of the fact that good teaching plays a major role in attracting the next generation of researchers to a field. The Knapp-Goodrich study, "Origins of American Scientists," provides ample evidence that the most productive institutions are frequently those with extremely low percentages of faculty members with Ph.D.'s. To do a competent job of teaching, one must have research ability: unfortunately, the converse is not assured.

Why, then, does the steadfast devotion to the Ph.D. requirement persist in these days of increasing shortages of staff? The continued insistence seems, in part, explainable through an analysis of the unintended services which are thus rendered to many strategically placed groups in the academic world.

Sociologists have noted that the ostensible reasons for perpetuating practices in a society often are quite different from the real ones. From a college administrator's point of view, the existence of a Ph.D. emphasis has always simplified the task of selecting personnel to fill faculty vacancies. Meaningful evidence of an applicant's ability to perform with competence the duties expected of him is seldom available. Insistence upon persons with a Ph.D. for the job has served to narrow down the field to manageable proportions before the more amorphous, real considerations must be reckoned with. In a like way it eliminates would-be aspirants for higher rank without the necessity of surveying the significant qualifications that are such a challenge to objective appraisal.

The certainty of a requirement such as the Ph.D. becomes especially welcome if the job requirement is supposed to be concerned to a considerable degree with teaching ability. The sort of evidence that decisions are usually based on would be discarded by any court that made the slightest pretense of maintaining judicial respectability. Recommendations concerning teaching skill are frequently written by persons who never have seen the aspirant conduct a class. Surmises about an individual's teaching ability may be ventured on the basis of known personality traits. Other conclusions may be reached as a consequence of random comments made by students. In the latter case, the unsoundness of the student sample involved would cause any normally conscientious scientist to throw the evidence in the wastebasket without delay.

Vested interests that would suffer from a modification of the status quo have been widely recognized as a chief source of resistance to social change. Those who feel that their security and upward mobility might be adversely affected by a major change in attitude toward the Ph.D. can hardly be expected to be particularly receptive to proposals for a reappraisal. They are naturally cognizant that present practices now rule out of the competition persons who might have comparable or superior talents but who lack the essential badge of respectability. And, of course, those in a position to determine policy on such matters are disproportionately those who have long since acquired the coveted Ph.D.'s.

The support of Ph.D.'s for the retention of the doctoral qualification may stem from a frank awareness of the personal advantages involved or, more probably, from a rationalization that provides a more socially palatable reason for the real one. For some the Ph.D. was acquired only by dint of great sacrifices of time, money, and effort, so that the perquisites of the label are not likely to be readily abandoned in the interest of progress. Others, who have seen comrades fall by the wayside during the Ph.D. quest, may have become convinced that some sort of defensible, natural selection occurs.

The graduate schools that are busy turning out Ph.D.'s are another vested interest that can be counted on to support the ubiquitous Ph.D. requirements. These institutions will hardly concede their inadequacy in the field of vocational preparation in a day when vocational proficiency is so eagerly sought in education at all levels. Considerations of prestige and finance dictate that the flow of Ph.D. aspirants continue unabated. Administrators realize that many young scholars would prefer to probe into the unknowns of their field free from the confining restraints of the Ph.D. program, and submit to the latter only because it is the necessary passport to academic recognition.

In the determination of ratings among American institutions of higher learning, the percentage of Ph.D.'s on a staff has long been a definite criterion which the appraisers have welcomed. Accrediting agencies automatically assume an inferiority in the quality of the work done in institutions where Ph.D.'s are rare. Those colleges that have corralled, at some additional expense, a staff of Ph.D.'s will hardly wish to forfeit one of their claims to distinction, nor will they wish to concede that their past recognition has rested upon a somewhat dubious basis.

The dysfunctional aspects of the present uncritical insistence upon faculty members who have their doctorates are substantial. In a period when there is an urgent need for personnel for our colleges who can perform their roles with exceptional ability, the present system eliminates many gifted scholars. Since the pool of available Ph.D.'s often gives the college administrator little opportunity for being selective, it is little wonder that mediocrity is distressingly commonplace in American college faculties.

Perhaps the greatest impetus for a reappraisal of the Ph.D. prerequisite will come in the days immediately ahead, when the demand for a new staff is destined to far exceed the output of the graduate schools. There should be less of an inclination for professors to seek security behind the Ph.D. barrier. Positions worthy of the talents of brilliant educators lacking the Ph.D. may be opened to them for the first time as long overdue modifications of past policies are made. There may come belated recognition that new policies need not represent a lowering of standards but, rather, the adoption of much more realistic ones.

If the acquisition of the Ph.D. is to continue to be the key to academic acceptability for college faculty, the requirements for the degree should be made to bear a more meaningful relationship to the work expected of such professionals. Obsolete requirements, that rule out men of demonstrated talents from being considered for responsible posts, should be abandoned. With higher education the gigantic and responsible business that it is, the retention of the prevalent, ill-designed personnel standards is a source of incalculable loss to the nation.

71

The Folly of Faculty Rank

KENNETH D. YOUNG

Professor of education and head of the Department of Education, College of the
School of the Ozarks. At the time his article originally appeared in *School and
Society* (Nov. 7, 1959), he was dean of Oklahoma College for Women.

The faculty ranking system now employed by most colleges and universities
is causing many well-qualified teachers either to leave the profession or
seek positions in institutions in which a promotion is assured by reason of
the move. When salary and rank are tied together, it is often necessary to
establish a policy that will allow only a specified number of faculty members
for each rank. Does it make any sense for a dean or a president to say,
"Frank, you're a good teacher and an asset to both the college and the
profession, but we can't offer you a promotion to full professor until somebody resigns, retires, or dies"? Or, "Frank, we have an opening in the rank
of full professor, but our budget next year will not allow us to have another
full professor"?

Many promising young college teachers are employed with the rank of
instructor and do an excellent job for two or three years only to be informed
that there are few, if any, opportunities for promotion to the higher ranks.
That is not only unfair to the college teacher who would like to remain in the
profession, but it places a burden on college administrators for which there is
only one solution—change the present system.

The writer would like to submit the following plan for consideration
with the firm conviction that any change would be an improvement:

1. Eliminate the ranks of assistant and associate professors and refer only
to professors.

2. Employ new personnel either as instructors or professors, depending
upon the qualifications required by the employing institution.

3. If a faculty member is employed as an instructor, set up criteria
stating how long he must remain in that rank or just what performance is

required of him before he can be promoted to professor. A three-year probationary period is suggested.

4. Dissociate salary from rank.

5. Set up the best possible salary arrangement that the financial condition of the college will permit, basing it strictly on performance and not on length of service.

6. Discontinue the practice of offering blanket salary raises, except on a cost-of-living basis.

The implementation of this plan would not involve any reductions in present salaries; but, as the present group of full professors dwindle in number through retirement and death, adjustments could be made in accordance with whichever salary plan the college decided to adopt. This plan also would permit colleges and universities to continue, if desired, the policy of creating special professorial chairs designed to honor a learned and scholarly individual for unusually meritorious achievement.

The plan would permit more flexibility in salary arrangements, would eliminate a ranking system which has no good reason for existence among professional people, and very likely would encourage a great many young instructors to remain in the profession—a situation which must prevail if colleges are to meet the challenge of ever-increasing enrollment in the years immediately ahead.

Colleges and universities are seeking more money because more is needed, but prospective donors and economy-minded legislators have every right to question this ancient practice of ranking which, when used as a basis for determining the salary, actually denies well-qualified personnel the privilege of normal advancement within their own profession.

72

The Great Art of Public Relations

WILLIAM H. FISHER

Associate professor of education, University of Montana. At the time his article originally appeared in *School and Society* (Feb. 8, 1964), he was associate professor of education, Texas Western College.

A colleague and I were perusing a colorful brochure from the college of education of a prominent university. We were amused to note in the section, "doings of staff members," that the faculty was scattered across the land and to the ends of the earth. The professional activities were recounted in a manner obviously designed to evoke pride in alumni.

Does learning take place when professors are gone from their campus or is education best achieved by their steady, diligent work in the classroom? As president of the University of Chicago, Robert M. Hutchins showed leadership when he raised questions related to this issue. As he became impatient with the bandwagon tendency of his staff toward involvement in conferences, Hutchins once expressed public doubts concerning professors who competed among themselves over who could most frequently occupy hotel rooms at conventions.

The activities depicted in the public relations communiqué to which I have alluded no doubt should be a part of the work of an alert faculty. Research and publishing also have a place in our universities. The problem is one of establishing balance.

Evidence is accumulating that we have come to think that of greater importance than the day-to-day routine is what the public and alumni think of the job we are doing. Although among the strongest critics of the methods of Madison Avenue, college teachers are prone to observe: "It's the public image that counts!"

Quality in teaching remains as probably the major factor whereby most institutions of higher learning will be weighed in the balance. It does not seem unreasonable, therefore, to raise the issue as to how much is gained by faculty who are engaged in a myriad of off-campus endeavors. Especially is such a question related to the educational contributions which a staff member makes to his own college or university.

Work away from the campus may be rationalized on the ground that graduate assistants are capable of meeting the obligations of their superiors. Although assuming the duties of a professor is helpful to his assistant, embarrassment may arise with respect to the function of tuition fees. Parents as well as students are prone to believe that, when they are paying for the services of someone high on the academic echelon, they are entitled to such services.

It is, of course, expecting too much that our universities suddenly will close their public relations offices. But it seems relevant to suggest that the efforts of our institutions henceforth be evaluated in the crucible of solid educational achievement. This is, after all, of more enduring significance than a "public image."

If evaluation follows this line rather than the one of chimerical impressions, there exists a possibility that not a few summer sessions virtually will disappear. Irrespective of the enrollment explosion, directors of college summer sessions are bent upon the quest for ever greater numbers of students. This problem is, again, one of perspective, since summer terms do indeed have a place in American education. It seems nonetheless ridiculous that the kind of climate, for instance, enjoyed in the locale of a given institution looms as of greater importance than whether a summer program represents curricular offerings in depth.

Graduate degrees, including the great number which are awarded by certain universities, are known to have drawing power. Sustained effort and production on the part of students is considered as of less value than a quantitative listing of the degrees. It is plain though that the "degree factory" plan is by no means a universal one.

It is likely that staff members in our institutions of higher learning will assist in finding solutions to the various crises which confront mankind if they will show a greater willingness to meet their primary obligations. This, in the main, means performing their duties at home, on the campus, as they consciously allow the headlines to pass them by.

73

The Constructive Use of Faculty Mobility

ROBERT H. FARBER

Dean of the University, DePauw University. His article originally appeared in *School and Society* on March 18, 1967.

Although the title of this article is "The Constructive Use of Faculty Mobility," other titles might be used, such as "The Case of the Missing Professor." The fact is that teachers are on the move, upward and outward, horizontally and vertically. The accelerated trend in this direction is becoming more evident each year, and there is general agreement that this accelerated mobility is affecting the educational program of liberal arts colleges, with a number of positive and negative consequences.

In preparation for this article, I wrote to each one of the deans in the Great Lakes Colleges Association (Albion, Antioch, Denison, DePauw, Earlham, Hope, Kalamazoo, Kenyon, Oberlin, Ohio Wesleyan, Wabash, and Wooster) and asked them to comment on three aspects of faculty mobility: the current status of faculty mobility, the educational implications of faculty mobility, and constructive suggestions. This paper will be based largely upon the responses of the cooperative deans, and I want to record here my deep appreciation to them.

I received answers from all 12 GLCA deans, and it is apparent from their replies that there is a great deal of faculty mobility in our institutions. The deans estimated that, altogether, we had about 56 faculty members on sabbatical leaves and 45 on special leaves, for a total of 101 faculty members who have been away from our campuses for part of the current school year. The deans estimated that this number represented a range of from five percent to 12% and in most cases from six percent to eight percent of the faculty of the institutions represented. In these days of serious faculty shortages, the figure of 101 professors (who probably are among the better teachers) represents a significant number. In addition, several deans replied in a most definite manner that faculty mobility of this type had shown a marked increase in recent years and it was their impression that this trend would continue. When one considers the central importance of excellent teaching, it is apparent that faculty mobility of this type represents a significant aspect of the academic program.

On the educational implications of faculty mobility, the deans were most cooperative and explicit. On the one hand, there was almost complete agreement that faculty mobility represents a fine opportunity for the individual faculty members and for the institution. Such phrases as "new dimensions in education," "intellectual and academic stimulation," and "helping professors remain alive and vibrant" were listed many times. All of us have been affected in a most constructive manner by the Non-Western GLCA project, and we all can testify concerning the significant contribution made to the intellectual life of our various campuses by professors who have returned from these projects. The experience of involvement abroad with such program as AID, the Fulbright Lectureships, research grants, the National Science Foundation assignments are obvious to all. It was mentioned more than once that first-rate liberal arts colleges must remain competitive with large universities in terms of intellectual opportunities for faculty members. It therefore follows that cooperative programs of this type are essential for the attraction and retention of first-class faculty members. The unmistakable conclusion here is that faculty mobility of this type represents unique advantages for all of us, and we must continue in the future as we have in the past to encourage activity of this type.

Unfortunately, there also are several problems, and they are serious ones as they relate to the quality of college programs. The first one was expressed in several forms, but related to the lack of continuity in the departmental program, as well as the quality of instruction. Student expectation in terms of quality education is at an all-time high and it is difficult to cancel courses in any significant number over an entire year's period. The caliber of temporary replacements represents an almost impossible problem, not to mention the time and money involved by the appropriate officers of the institution in the search for replacements.

Constructive suggestions from the deans largely centered around the problem of suitable and available replacements. A number of persons suggested that the Great Lakes Colleges Association might serve a most needed area in developing a pool of possible replacements for one semester or for one year. One of the most obvious sources is represented by the faculty members who recently have retired from member colleges. Another source which has been used from time to time by the GLCA is represented by foreign scholars. Perhaps other resources can be discovered which will help us in our search for temporary replacements.

In addition, we need new guidelines concerning several aspects of sabbatical and special leaves. For example, what is the purpose of the leave?

How many special leaves should be granted to any one individual (in view of the continuity problem)? What are the requirements for return? In the past, we have made an important distinction (on the obligation to return), based on whether the salary was paid by the home institution or another agency. The responsibility of the professor as a member of the academic community really is not affected by this distinction, since the essence of the problem is continuity and consistency in the program. It seems reasonable, therefore, to require, in a substantive manner, that persons on either special or sabbatical leaves return to the institution for at least a minimum period of time.

It is apparent that faculty mobility in terms of enriched opportunities will be a part of any first-class program representing, as it does, new horizons and new dimensions. It also is apparent that we must be clearer on guidelines, purposes, and responsibilities if we are to be fair to the students and to the maintenance of a first-class program at home. As one dean put it, we need to emphasize freedom, but freedom with responsibility. We can do this with an awareness of the scope of the problem, as well as a recognition of our obligations to the faculty members and students involved.

74

Education and the Challenge of the Future

ARTHUR W. MUNK

Professor of philosophy, Albion College. His article originally appeared in *School and Society* on March 18, 1967.

Never before has America found herself in a more paradoxical position. While it is the richest and most powerful nation in all history, it finds itself increasingly more insecure. Not only do we find ourselves involved in a war that is so inhuman and so absurd that it has been repudiated by most intellectuals, and not only do we face a domestic situation that verges on chaos, but, worst of all, we are drifting toward a very uncertain future. The great danger is the destruction of democracy, followed by Armageddon: that is, through the emergence of an American brand of fascism resulting from a coalition of southern racialists and northern reactionaries.

While education certainly is not wholly responsible for this predicament, it at least is partly responsible. For, although our problems largely are the result of factors present in the total interaction of forces on the world scene, as well as on the American scene as a whole, education cannot be held entirely blameless. Moreover, as a potent molder of culture and of the public opinion of the future by virtue of its influence on the young, education has a vast responsibility both for the future of America and the future of mankind. This brings us to the question which has been raised so often that is has become trite, but which must be raised again and again if we are to avert unparalleled disaster: What is wrong with education?

As a philosopher, I venture to say that, fundamentally, American education suffers from two maladies. The first is the lack of a significant basic purpose. With its many strange antics, today's education suggests the knight who jumped on horseback and rode in every direction. The second is the fact that our education is dominated too much by contemporary American culture—a culture which has lost its vision. [1] Our culture may be characterized

---

[1] This is the charge that Arnold J. Toynbee makes in his stimulating little book, *America and the World Revolution* (New York: Oxford University Press, 1962). Every American teacher should read this little book.

as affluent, narrowly nationalistic and pragmatic, and—in terms of its preoccupation with the immense, the novel, the bizarre—as immature and sensationalistic.

Thus, educationally as well as militarily,[2] we are frittering away our resources and our energies. While educational administrators vie with each other in rearing their lofty towers (building ventures which are often ill-planned, wasteful, and too luxurious), deans and faculties glory in their craze for the novel and the bizarre. In the words of a young academician: "It's new, it's novel, it's exciting! We must have it."

The results of our educational process, in terms of the average American student, are far from flattering. Although there is a creative minority on whom the hope of the future depends, most students seem to have lost all sense of direction. Dominated by an easygoing relativism and a naive, irrational existentialism, youth probably never has been more immature, undisciplined, and confused. What else can one expect of a generation that feeds on *Playboy*, the more bizarre aspects of Sartre, and the jazz that excites the nerves but fails to arouse the creativity of the mind?

Coupled with all this, there are definite signs of efforts at escapism. Appalled by the dangers of the Nuclear Age, and in revolt against such evils as racism, poverty, and war (evils which we have tolerated too long), large sections of our youth seek avenues of escape through sexual adventures, alcohol, LSD, and even through outright violence. Often, even when youth does make a real effort at social protest against evils such as war, the protest is so bizarre and is executed so badly that it hurts rather than helps the good cause involved. There is no greater contradiction than the spectacle of the blatant libertine trying to register a protest against some social evil.

The beatnik certainly constitutes a strange figure. While at times he succeeds in registering a sincere and well-directed social protest shaming the rest of us for our cowardice, his irrationalism coupled with his queer ways seem to imply both a preoccupation with fads and an effort to return to the simplicities of barbarism. In his beard we also detect something of a profession of a maturity which he does not possess.

Alarmed by something that had happened elsewhere, I addressed my introductory philosophy class as follows: "First of all I want to apologize that my generation has done such a poor job. It has created this nightmare world into which you have been thrown. Nevertheless, I am also critical of your generation—chiefly because it has not made more creative responses. Unless your generation awakens to an astounding creativity, it may do even worse than mine. By its irrationalism and its anarchistic tendencies, it may provoke the totalitarianism that will set the world on fire."

What then can we, as educators, do to insure a better future, both for

[2] The Conference on National Priorities Problems, which met at Columbia University, Sept. 30-Oct. 1, 1966, stressed the danger to democracy inherent in our vast military system.

Americans in particular and for all mankind in general? While I have no panacea, I will risk a few suggestions.

First of all, as teachers, we must obtain a sense of direction. To obtain a sense of direction that promises creativity, we must get a clear idea of the significant basic aim or goal of education. Elsewhere, I have called this the humanization of man; [3] but for our present purposes this vital matter can be stated best in terms of its two most important and most relevant aspects.

The first consists of that discipline of the mind which always has been called academic excellence. Guided by the best that every field of knowledge affords, the student must be taught to wrestle with the tough problems involved. Here term papers and essay questions, together with lectures and Socratic dialogue (in which the teacher shows evidence of having done his homework well), are more helpful than myriads of objective tests which plague contemporary education. There is no substitute for this wrestling with momentous issues and problems that comes with carefully prepared lectures well garnished with opportunities for questions and Socratic dialogue, on the one hand, and the writing of essays and monographs, on the other. [4] Without academic excellence, creativity is impossible.

Yet, standing alone, the first aspect makes the scholar pedantic and leads to the curse of ivory-tower detachment. This brings us to the second aspect: creative living in the Nuclear Age. Education at its best and in the full sense of the word means creative living, as well as creative thinking: and, since both include creativity, as well as constituting vital elements of the total self, they supplement one another. If this is not forgotten, both the curse of ivory-tower detachment, which was so characteristic of pre-Nazi Germany, and that romantic irrationalism of reformers such as Rousseau, can be avoided.

Since these ideals cannot be imposed upon the student by fiat, the teacher also must supply a certain amount of motivation. Moreover, here he can call three basic motives to his aid—the first pragmatic and elemental and the others idealistic.

The pragmatic is based upon man's will to live—to which the alert teacher will appeal. Thus, upon occasion, the teacher will give his students a glimpse of hells—not the fictitious hells of theological fancy, but rather the outer hell of nuclear peril and the inner psychological hell, both of which man himself, by attempting to play the role of the old blood-and-thunder conception of God, actually has created. In this task, books by nuclear scientists will prove helpful. [5]

[3] In *A Synoptic Philosophy of Education* (New York: Abingdon Press, 1965).
[4] In science this also would, of course, include work in the laboratory—but the larger implications of scientific findings, problems, and questions also must be given due consideration.
[5] See especially, Ralph E. Lapp's *Kill and Overkill* (New York: Basic Books, 1962). Students are more likely to listen seriously to scientists than to clergymen or philosophers. In spite of doubts, scientists virtually have attained the role of high priests in our culture—fascinated as we are by technology.

The student, however, must not be left with this vision of hells. To avoid attempts at a futile escapism and to challenge his creativity, the two positive idealistic factors must be brought into the picture: the creative possibilities of this age of danger and the power of example. Spurred on by a greater danger than ever before and possessing—as we do—the total wisdom of the ages, such tides of creative power may rise that we actually may realize the ancient dream of a warless world. Moreover, we must incite our students to creativity by our own example.

After all, the wisest men of all times have made it clear that there is nothing more challenging than the power of example—this visible manifestation of creativity. Thus it was said of Kant that he did the "best things in the worst times." Similarly, Hegel put the finishing touches to one of his masterpieces while the thunder of Napoleon's guns was rattling the windows in his study. This also reminds us of the ancient proverb: "It is better to light a candle than to curse the darkness."

75

The Professor and Collective Negotiations

JAMES F. DAY and WILLIAM H. FISHER

The authors are, respectively, professor of education, University of Texas at El Paso, and associate professor of education, University of Montana. At the time their article originally appeared in *School and Society* (April 1, 1967), Dr. Fisher was associate professor of education, University of Texas at El Paso.

Today, we find increasing teacher unrest in our society manifested through collective negotiations, strikes, and other forms of group action. Teacher militancy has been chiefly in the public schools rather than in the colleges. It has been accompanied by the growth of the American Federation of Teachers (AFT), and of this organization's serious competition with the National Education Association (NEA). The AFT, through its challenge, has forced the NEA to represent the rights of teachers before their superintendents and school boards. Both organizations are concerned with collective negotiations. It is because they are in competition that different terms are used by each association—the AFT speaks of "collective bargaining" while the NEA uses "professional negotiations." In this article, the term "collective negotiations" is used as it has been coined by Lieberman and Moskow. It is a preferred term for the college professor in order to encompass both the AFT and NEA definitions.[1]

Public school teachers rapidly are moving toward organizing themselves, using collective negotiations as a method. Government professional workers are being unionized. Jerry Wurf, president, American Federation of State, County, and Municipal Employees, speaks of a revolution in employer-employee relations in public service. He says that the various states are passing laws that are helping government workers so that they can sit down and bargain as equals with the governments that employ them. Government professional workers (architects, engineers, nurses, personnel workers, social

---

[1] *Cf.*, Myron Lieberman and Michael H. Moskow, *Collective Negotiations for Teachers: An Approach to School Administration* (Chicago: Rand McNally, 1966).

workers, biologists, chemists, etc.) in increasing numbers are joining and forming local chapters of the American Federation of State, County, and Municipal Employees.

While other professional people are organizing in a manner enabling them to be co-equals at the bargaining table, the college professor, relatively speaking, is sitting still. The college teachers have the American Association of University Professors (AAUP). This organization has achieved much, especially in the area of academic freedom and tenure. The AAUP, in the past, has had modest success in the use of sanctions involving investigation, public exposure, and censure. Censure is the strongest tactic of the AAUP, and consists of the publication of a report and the listing of the offending institution's name in the *AAUP Bulletin,* until the college has removed the conditions which gave rise to the censure. The main (if not only) reason for an AAUP censure has been the dismissal of a professor who has tenure. In these cases, censure rarely produces real help for the dismissed professor. By the time censure is made, the professor usually has become a forgotten casualty. The AAUP does not use censure in connection with the vital conditions of college policy, denial of promotion, salaries, dismissal of non-tenure teachers, pensions, and fringe benefits. Because the AAUP has shown no convincing signs that it intends to move militantly, many college teachers are looking toward the AFT. There are local AFT chapters among the state colleges of California. The graduate assistants at the University of California (Berkeley) have chosen the AFT as their organization. Some 10,000 college teachers have joined the AFT.[2]

What should be done? There are a number of possibilities. These possibilities will be discussed following the presentation of a few facts that have a bearing on the professor's situation.

The college teacher has problems in regard to identity and loyalty. He is paid his salary in an institution of higher learning, and is a specialist and scholar in some discipline. College teachers could be classified in terms of their orientation to a field of specialized knowledge (*e.g.,* chemistry) on the one hand, and their loyalty to the college at which they work on the other. The chief personal identity for a professional comes with his field of specialized knowledge, while his rewards (salary, position, working conditions) come from the college by which he is employed. The point is that all the profession does is to pass judgment on the individual's initial qualifications. From then on, the judgment of his competence rests with the college in which he works. This requires that the college teacher expose himself to evaluation of his worth and ability in his own professional field by those outside his discipline—the college administration. We have the college

[2] Israel Kulger, "The A.A.U.P. at the Crossroads," *Changing Education,* 1:34-43, Spring, 1966. *Changing Education,* a new AFT publication, is an effective answer to those who have claimed that AFT publications lack real intellectual content.

teacher's authority which rests on specialized knowledge clashing with the authority represented by his superiors in the institution, and which mainly rests upon bureaucratic position and status. In this situation, the college teacher is not an equal, but, rather, is at the ultimate mercy of the president. His rights, his working conditions, and achievement in his discipline can be neglected and ignored. This undoubtedly contributes to many college teachers being chronically frustrated, dissatisfied, and neurotic. Unless something is done to make the college teacher a co-equal at the bargaining table, this situation only can get worse.

The college president inevitably is not only from a different discipline from most of the college teachers, but he also operates within a very different frame of reference. His frame is the one of power and prestige. He often dominates faculty committees by placing the "right" men on them, which results in a situation in which most of the college faculty are confronted by a small group of administrators supported by their henchmen from the faculty. College policies thus are shaped from the administrator's viewpoint, no matter what the situation may appear to be. It is not the college faculty to which the average administration listens. Rather, it is influenced by individuals and groups outside the college woo can exercise strong social pressures. The president will listen mainly to leading citizens of the community, such as members of boards of directors of banks and the like, editors of newspapers, etc. College teachers are working at the business of organizing so that they can bring their power to the conference table at a level approximately equal to that possessed by the administrator. Otherwise, college teachers could become second-rate technicians instead of genuine professionals.

College students are protesting and showing much discontent. We are witnessing student rebellions which reflect their dissatisfaction with American society. It is an educated guess that there would be far less student discontent if the faculty could have an important role in forming college policy. The college teacher certainly understands students, and can think and operate from their frame of reference better than the average administrator.

The enrollment in our colleges has increased greatly in recent years. In 1950, 2,214,000 were enrolled; by 1963, the total had risen to 4,207,000; and by 1970, it is predicted that there will be over 7,000,000.[3] Today, some 45 universities have 40% of all college students and about half of all faculty members. Lazarsfeld and Thielens have shown that the bigger the college, the more anxiety among faculty members and the more tension between administration and faculty, thus indicating that, as universities grow, there will be greater need for faculties to organize so as to cope better with college administrations.[4]

[3] Robert P. Wolff, "The Race to College," *The Atlantic,* 216: 145-148, November, 1965.
[4] *Cf.,* Paul F. Lazarsfeld and Wagner Thielens, *The Academic Mind* (Glencoe, Ill.: Free Press, 1958).

There is a shortage of college teachers, especially of professors with Ph.D.'s. One of the explanations for this shortage is the declining attractiveness of academic work as a result of increased administrative inroads on the professor's independence, freedom, and citizenship rights. An example would be situations where men recommended for tenure by their professional colleagues have had the judgment of their peers set aside by administrators who base their criteria upon factors other than competence in one's own discipline. Such administrative policy is reducing the professor to something considerably beneath that of a professional worker. If it continues, he will come to resemble a hired hand more than a professional man.

It is known in American labor that an economically good market position is enjoyed by those who are members of a large union. There is, in the final analysis, no substitute for collective bargaining. An increasingly larger segment of college teachers is coming to recognize this fact.

The college president ordinarily is selected by a board of directors, trustees, or regents. Most faculties have nothing to do with this selective process. Faculties resent the great authority exercised by the administrative hierarchy, and the resentment frequently is founded upon the method of selection of a president. Especially in the state-supported institutions where board appointment is controlled by political considerations, faculty members are well aware that some presidents are chosen by political "deals" rather than on the basis of merit.

Administrative policies in many colleges have caused teachers to neglect teaching in favor of other activities. Research, publication, and loyalty to the administration become more important than teaching. The students suffer, and probably research and publishing also suffer, because these are achieved more adequately when coming from the heart of the professor, rather than as the result of administrative pressure. Should an administration be allowed—without the consent of the faculty—to institute a policy of publication as the route to academic advancement?

Many of the professions are now on the way to establishing strong organizations that can represent them at the bargaining table as co-equals with their employers. But the college teacher, for the most part, is sitting still. He is at the mercy of the college administration, which may function in an arbitrary manner. College students' protesting and rebelling constitute part of this milieu. Faculty salaries are low, there is a shortage of professors, and an increasing trend toward the neglect of the college student and classroom teaching. A corrective for these conditions, among other professional groups, has been for employees to form large and powerful organizations that have the right to represent them.

Now what may the college teacher do? Here are some possibilities: The college professor can continue as he has in the past. This means that he will let the administration determine what his salary, his rights, and other working conditions shall be. In some states, he will be able to join an

organization of college teachers which operates on the state level, *e.g.*, the
independent Texas Association of College Teachers. These organizations
attempt to influence state legislatures in support of legislation designed to
help college faculties. However, such organizations only make recommendations; they do not operate as co-equals at the bargaining table. In such a
situation, the professor relatively is helpless. He can do little more than think
of the "good-old-days," such as those in the early universities of western
Europe when the authority of the university was vested in the faculty itself.
In those times, there were no administrators—the power was in the faculty
or its elected representatives.

Sitting still means that the professor can continue to dream of the
"good-old-days" and hope that administration, at the least, will leave him
alone. His working conditions, rights, and salary probably will lag behind
those of other professional workers outside the colleges. The professor will
become more and more a dependent within the administration's growing
bureaucratic domain. He certainly will not be a professional worker, if the
bureaucractic trend continues, he will become a kind of hired hand. As a
result, not only will the professor suffer, but students and the society of which
they are a part also will feel the results.

Another possibility is for the professor to turn to the AAUP as the
organization to represent his professional needs. There is a growing group
in the AAUP that is demanding that the organization be concerned not only
with academic freedom and tenure, but also with the many other facets of
the professor's working conditions. This group believes that AAUP (or some
organization) should protect the faculty from the power, authority, and
capricious decisions of authoritarian college administrators. If the AAUP is
to become the adequate representative for the college teacher, it will be
necessary for the members to undertake rather drastic changes in the
AAUP's policies, structure, and organization. Today, the national office of
AAUP tends to oppose local chapters' taking any real initiative in policy-
making—the authority rests with the Washington office.[5]

The AAUP has taken no significant action against the present situation
of allowing the various regional accrediting associations to police and regulate
the profession of college teaching. These accrediting associations are, in the
main, dominated by administrators. In short, in the present circumstance,
the AAUP has done too little. It must change, or many college teachers will
be turning elsewhere for help.

It is likely that the kinds of "splits" which have come to characterize

[5] "Report of Committee A, 1965-66, the University of Arizona," *AAUP Bulletin,* 52:125, June,
1966. In this well-known case, Committee A on Academic Freedom, acting under the aegis
of the central office of AAUP, reversed the decision of the University of Arizona chapter
which, by formal vote, had requested that the censure status of the Arizona administration be
continued. This clearly was evidence that groups in local situations no longer can depend upon
their national office for support.

the annual meetings of the AAUP will continue. Evidence is growing that members will demand more militant action, including possible merger with the AFT. Many AAUP members are beginning to recognize the importance of belonging to an organization that believes in collective negotiations. We have seen the signing of a collective bargaining contract with an AFT local chapter in a college in Yakima, Wash. In the 1965–66 school year, the AAUP was shaken by the AFT challenge at St. John's University, in Brooklyn. At the start of the 1966–67 school year, a strike delayed the opening of the largest community college in the state of Michigan, when some 150 members of the faculty at Henry Ford Community College (Flint) refused to report for duty. This apparently is the first college teachers' strike under collective bargaining, the teachers demanding salary rises of up to $1,000 per year.[6]

Another possibility is for college teachers to turn to the National Education Association (NEA). Though professors outside the ranks of teacher education may not like to admit it, the NEA has had many years' experience in grappling with some of the major problems which confront the colleges today. Through the Association for Higher Education, the American Association of Colleges for Teacher Education (both formed as the result of NEA impetus), and similar groups, the NEA has demonstrated that it is no neophyte in confronting a myriad of problems in higher education. The NEA recently has been prodded by the AFT into changing its policies. It now is sponsoring professional negotiations and sanctions. Soon it may have to recognize that, under certain situations, strikes are a proper and necessary method. William G. Carr, NEA executive secretary, now is asking the following questions: "Under what conditions, if any, could a strike be considered necessary? Under what conditions is a strike specifically unprofessional and unethical?"[7] It is time for the NEA to ask these questions, because teachers belonging to various NEA-connected organizations have been striking. For example, during the spring of 1966 there were four teacher strikes in Michigan which were led by NEA—Michigan Education Association affiliates.[8] It would be an educated guess that, before long, the NEA will accept strikes as a method of social-economic action. If this occurs, at last there will be no essential difference in policy between the AFT and the NEA.

College teachers would have problems in affiliating with the NEA, because it mainly is a public school organization. However, if we should have an NEA-AFT merger, there possibly would be less opposition by the college professor. Could there be even a larger merger, that is, NEA-AFT-AAUP? Perhaps this is the answer. A merger of these major organizations would come to have many of the characteristics of the AFT, if the teachers

[6] *U.S. News and World Report*, 61:90, Sept. 19, 1966.
[7] "NEA to Prepare Position Paper on Resolution of PN Impasses," *Urban Reporter* (National Education Association), 5:1, August, 1966.
[8] "Nine Strikes, One Mass Firing Attempt Hit Michigan," *ibid.*, pp. 2-3.

of America (college professors included) are to move forward. This is likely if the AFT can pressure the AAUP toward its image, as it recently has pressured the NEA. The AAUP may come to realize that merging with the AFT represents its ultimate salvation if it is to avoid eventual demise.

What does the future hold? It is, of course, too early to forecast precisely. All that may be said with certainty is that higher education inevitably will change, and it surely will change in the direction of greater power and influence on the part of the faculties. Certainly, the professor will not remain quiescent. Changing cultural values and increasing concern for the rights of employees will not permit this. The authors present the following points as educated guesses with respect to the future: The college teacher will organize into a tighter organization that more aptly will represent his rights. This development possibly may represent some kind of amalgamation of the NEA-AFT-AAUP, or portions thereof. Irrespective of its precise nature, in the new setup, teachers will find real strength. American labor has proved many times that a good market position is presented by those who belong to large, powerful unions or organizations.

The core of power representing the college teacher will be the method of collective negotiations. Only by such means can true professional status be obtained. This method will make the professors potentially equal to the administration in regard to vital questions of salaries, promotions, retirement, tenure, academic freedom, and other conditions. Kugler portrays graphically the importance of collective negotiations (collective bargaining) to the college professor when he says: "There is no other way. If the profession of teaching in our colleges and universities is to meet its responsibilities to the students and the teaching staffs, then it will organize itself in democratic fashion, on a national basis consonant with local autonomy, and equipped with the only known effective device for negotiating differences and establishing policy—collective bargaining."[9]

Collective negotiation is a process which goes beyond merely giving the professors the opportunity to be heard, or to be consulted. It will prevent college administrators from making unilateral decisions with respect to the conditions under which college teachers carry out their various and important functions.

In the future, the college teacher will realize that teachers' strikes may be justified in some situations. As a means of limiting the number of strikes, and, thus, protecting the public interest, colleges will create peaceful ways for the settlement of disputes. This doubtless will be achieved, however, without specific legislative ban upon strikes. It may consist of the forming of fact-finding boards (or committees) which will operate when collective negotiations between professors' groups and college administrators break down. It would be expected that both parties (teachers and administrators)

[9]Kugler, *op. cit.*, p. 43.

would follow the findings of fact-finding boards. It the administration and/or trustees failed to pay attention to impartial, disinterested fact-finding decisions, it naturally would follow that the college teachers then would have the right to strike. The professors' future course of action relative to collective negotiations inevitably will affect all of society, as well as higher education.

76

Faculty Responsibility and the Executive Conquest of Academe

DURWARD LONG

Vice-chancellor, University Center System, University of Wisconsin. At the time his article originally appeared in *School and Society* (Feb. 19, 1966), he was assistant dean of the Graduate School, University of Georgia.

The attention presently given to higher education by the quality newspapers, magazines, and popular publications is encouraging. Several recent, excellent articles clearly have pointed out some of the vital issues in higher education today, particularly editor John Fischer's "Is There a Teacher on the Faculty?" *(Harper's,* February, 1965), political scientist Robert Presthus' "University Bosses: The Executive Conquest of Academe" *(New Republic,* Feb. 20, 1965), and editor Donald Robinson's "How Sinister is the Education Establishment?" *(Saturday Review,* Jan. 16, 1965).

These analyses deserve serious attention. Fischer feels that "nearly all of our colleges and universities are capable right now of providing far better instruction than they actually put out" and the reason performance doesn't measure up to capability is "because our whole academic system is now rigged against good teaching." Presthus charges that one reason for the condition of our institutions of higher learning is the aggrandizement of university administration and the conquest of Academe by the "executive syndrome" existing in administration. The administrators, according to Presthus, are allied with a group of conservative faculty (academicians *qua* administrators) who share "administrative values of power and prestige." Together they rule and ruin our institutions, shortchanging parents and students, emphasizing non-academic trivia, and perverting intellectual values.

Certainly, there is a degree of accuracy and applicability to these charges. Many would applaud these views, but it does seem that a modified perspective also deserves consideration. Presthus' villain is the "executive conquest of Academe," Fischer's culprit is the "rigged academic system."

Neither places these two conditions within our cultural context or attempts to tell us "why."

One difficulty in higher education is the great expectations of so many groups. American institutions of higher learning are expected, even required, to do far more for the student, his parents, the surrounding community, industry and government, the faculty, and even the world, than was ever before imagined. Despite the fact that extremely valuable contributions are being made in all these areas, Academe is forever flayed for not performing them better. On the one hand, there is the accusation that colleges and universities do little which makes positive contributions to students. On the other hand, there is the charge that the institutions of higher learning are changing students, but into less-than-responsible citizens. The criticism is valuable but only when viewed in proper perspective.

Student protests and riots, subjects of a torrent of analyses recently, are alternately blamed on detached administrators and administrative systems or professors "who don't care about students any more." Few have been willing to connect the "riots" with the mass beach-party phenomena each spring or with the changes taking place in American high school youth, the "Beatle craze," the long years of permissiveness from birth to college, or American social developments in general. Nor has anyone emphasized the possible contribution of leading students to convictions stronger than the fear of majority condemnation.

Actually, there are many factors more profound than that administrators are responsible for the current situation in higher education. The continually expanding functions of colleges and universities, the increasing numbers of students, the changing characteristics of students with changing needs, the greater involvement of institutions in the life of the community and nation (and, therefore, in public policy), the changing college professor, the greater competition for and yet greater need for additional financial support have all operated to create an institution quite unlike that of the medieval institutions, present-day European universities, or 19th-century American universities. Many of the characteristics described by the critics were brought about by social changes in America rather than by administrators or academicians *qua* administrators.

One would agree that many of the problems described by Presthus do exist. There is considerable disagreement, however, whether the problems were created by "administrative aggrandizement," and whether the problems described exist in the same degree in all large universities in all sections of the country. One could point out many illustrations where administrative policy has encouraged and made research (which Presthus rightly evaluated as a main function of institutions of higher education) and teaching easier rather than more difficult; and where administrative decisions concerning tenure and position have actually relieved a professor's colleagues of "unpleasant and distasteful" discipline. The theory that professors will discipline their profession internally is at best a theory. One might maintain that professors have, in the main, shirked leadership and many of their responsibilities, thereby inviting "administrative inroads" and some aspects of the state of affairs described by Prof. Presthus. The tragic fact about the "executive conquest of Academe" is that the faculty sometimes has been affected at least as much as the administrators by the "executive complex." Perhaps Daniel Hollowell, in "What's Wrong With Our Students?" *(New Republic,* Feb. 20, 1965), should have added "Faculty" when he said, "administrators think and talk like G.M. executives."

It is easy for a faculty member to sit on the sidelines and condemn many of the entertainment and service aspects of the modern American university as "extraneous" and contradictory to the purposes of the institution. Also, it is easy for the faculty member to assume that the general American public appreciates institutions of higher learning as places where knowledge may be pursued for knowledge's sake. Yet, experience tells us that the American public judges knowledge and the organized pursuit of knowledge for what it can do in *practical* terms, and for the service (and entertainment) it can provide for the community. Cognizant of this fact, there are many faculty members who refuse to become administrators because they do not wish to become involved in this complex function of securing funds for their colleagues. Nor do they wish to become so involved with so many people of different types; mediating, persuading, leading as they know administrators must. Some do, and become subjects for Presthus' epithet, academicians *qua* administrators.

Along with the sound criticism, there are several "myths" in the current criticism of administrators. One myth is that the administrators are universally powerful and capable of making "inroads" into the intellectual values of the universities all the way from deans to graduate assistants. Perhaps the truth of this matter is that universities resemble to a great degree a collection of feudal "fiefdoms," to use John Fischer's term. There the analogy ends, for there are few high-level administrators whose power compares with feudal barons. Most of the time more change takes place by persuasion than by power.

Still another myth which ought to be explored, if we dare, is the idea that the great majority of college faculty are dominated by a love of seeking truth and of imparting knowledge to their inquiring students. This view says that the professor is a dedicated professional who is little concerned with material reward (though "professors must eat") and/or prestige and status. Practical experience plus a perusal of literature on the subject present a somewhat different picture. This questionable concept of the faculty member goes on to describe him as one who is close to the students while there exists a chasm between administrators and students that "no man can breach."

If a more accurate picture of the "new professor" is given, might it reveal that he is a mere human being subject to dedication about as often as other human beings and in the main very interested in material reward and prestige? Might it include the suggestion that in reality the "new professor" is much concerned with projects, theory, books, papers and other inanimate objects and not as closely nor deeply devoted to his students as persons? Would this view suggest that he is interested in research and, at least since the Johns Hopkins Idea, has emphasized it professionally more than teaching, and that administrators have simply taken their cue for evaluation from the faculty's professional emphases of the past rather than imposing it? It seems right to emphasize reseach, but in an over-emphasis, students and teaching are at least second on the professor's list of priorities.

This priority system is perpetuated through the assistantship system of teaching. The graduate student observes the low value that the professor places on excellent teaching, and the high value placed on other activities (research and writing) and therefore adopts a similar value system for his career. It is the faculty member's concern with consultantships, outside grants, and "practical" research as well as the administrator's permissive attitude toward them that has contributed to the present situation.

The faculty turnover of some universities might well be a product of the increasing marketability of the faculty members rather than administrative sins, though the latter do exist. Presthus' statement that "talented men will be unlikely to trust their careers to a system" where fair qualitative distinctions and rewards are not made by administrators implies that the other fields to which Ph.D.'s now are turning are not subject to this failure. Additionally, he also implies that Ph.D.'s always have had this choice.

One thing is certain: the effect of over-emphasis of research on small liberal arts colleges. There was a time when the small liberal arts college, nestled in some quiet rural community, was viewed as offering fulfillment to the academician who prized teaching and contact with students above all else. Perhaps that, too, has been a bit of academic mythology. Today, however, the fact is that the teaching-oriented graduate student is influenced so strongly towards research that he is no longer really interested in teaching after he is vested with the doctorate. If he is employed in a small college, he becomes dissatisfied with the emphasis upon teaching and student-contact and strives to move to a large university. There, he tells himself, he will not have to be "an intellectual wet nurse to undergraduates." If he is successful in making the flight, he is also unhappy in the university when he is assigned the large sections of freshmen and sophomores. He wants to do research and to turn out others like himself. This process widens the cleavage between university and college, threatens the performance of the small college, weakens the undergraduate's preparation, and does a disservice to a graduate student and scholar whose forte may not be basic research.

The academicians who are non-administrators exaggerate the views presented by Dr. Presthus. In fact, standards for promotions, tenure, graduate faculty rank, teaching load, and many prerequisites for the professor are set by the faculty in most universities, though they may be applied *pro forma* by administrators (department heads, deans, etc.) who were once faculty and who still hold faculty rank. In many cases the faculty rank of professor was necessary to receive the administrative appointment in the first place. Logan Wilson, quoted by Dr. Presthus, has also said, "The faculty *itself* regards relief from teaching as its chief reward for accomplishment or as the highest status symbol." The faculty member finds himself devoted to a never-ending cycle, research for publication, publication for reward, reward in time off from teaching for research, and back to research for publication in quantity. A recent study by the Brookings Institution revealed that a great majority of professors in the larger institutions preferred research to teaching and look down on faculty who teach mostly under-graduates.

Clark Kerr points out in *The Uses of the University* that American faculties rarely have been concerned with the over-all educational policy of their institutions, contenting themselves with control of certain internal matters and, one might add, issues that affect them personally and economically. This situation, in addition to other factors, causes the multiplication of administrative duties and functions, many of which are staffed by "non-academic" persons for which "we academicians" should be glad. As many have observed, the faculty is collectively an extremely conservative group regarding changes within The System and, as Fischer has pointed out, applies a given technological innovation about 28 years later than industry.

If we agree that the dismal picture painted by the critics is accurate, to what additional conclusion are we led? Is it supposed that faculty do not realize the sad state of affairs, that they do and exploit it, or that they had rather "switch than fight"? Once the situation is clear to faculty, what are the remedies? The tendency to "look to Europe" as an example and to visualize the early and present American colleges in terms of the European institution is at best less than promising in understanding the historical and future development of American universities. Kerr evaluates the American university as "a remarkably effective institution . . . which is as British as possible for the sake of its undergraduates; as German as possible for the sake of the graduates and the research personnel; as American as possible for the sake of the public at large; and as confused as possible for the sake of the preservation of the whole uneasy balance." Indeed, it is many things to many people, for it is an outgrowth of a pluralistic society undergoing rapid, momentous change.

It seems that there is a great number of faculty in American universities who are still devoted to teaching as well as research and who are sympathetic to certain administrative needs without necessarily qualifying for Dr. Presthus' term, academicians *qua* administrators. This group is interested in a parallel development of increase in material and prestige reward and professional contribution in teaching and research. Why should they not be? Also, it seems that there must be a great number of administrators *qua* academicians, approaching gigantic problems with courage, imagination and academic interest. It seems that it is an advantage to have each segment of the college community understanding the problems of other groups.

In conclusion, many changes have come to the American university. That most of the undesirable characteristics are the results of "university bosses," we cannot agree, unless the faculty are included among the "bosses." The faculty and administrator do bear responsibility for the state of affairs, but so does the public.

One must seek ways of remedying the situation rather than seeking to place blame. Each segment of American public life shares the responsibility. The solution will not be as simple as recommended by some who advise protests by parents and donors. These are persons who act also as legislators, businessmen, and promoters with motives different from "reforming higher education." Nor will the Federal government's largesse in itself correct the trend. Most likely, it will accelerate it. Imitating European universities offers little hope, too. Until we can convince the general American public that teaching is of equal value to any other profession's activity in society and that it contributes inestimable enrichment to lives of persons without necessarily "manufacturing" any concrete measurable product, our gimmicks will be ineffective. Perhaps the truth of the matter is that, despite the fact that the college teacher is centrally involved in American society today, he does not feel secure and properly evaluated for teaching. So he tries to make his contribution in research a concrete measure, however inadequate, in a pragmatic, utilitarian society.

PART IV

The Art of Teaching

From Personal Involvement to Computers

77

The Professor and the Art of Teaching

GEORGE B. CUTTEN

President emeritus, Colgate University. His article originally appeared in *School and Society* on Jan. 31, 1959.

If the colleges and universities are now lacking efficient teachers, as has been charged, what can we do about it? There have been occasional gestures in the direction of encouraging superior teaching in certain institutions, such as the Sterling Professors at Yale, the James B. Duke Professors at Duke, and the Kenan Professors at the University of North Carolina, but if there has been any accurate report concerning the success of these efforts, it has not become a matter of general knowledge. Are these special, highly paid professors superior teachers, or are they more active and prolific scholars? If they are the best teachers, what gives them superiority? If these specially appointed and specially paid professors are really superior, have we not a basis for training all college and university professors?

The only superior teachers which some people recognize are the born teachers. This means the same for lawyers, engineers, or artists and signifies that the native traits of character are such that they more easily accommodate themselves to the art espoused. But the peculiar personality should be so adapted to the art by study, practice, and experience that the product will be a master workman.

So there is one thing we can do, and one thing we must do: we must teach the teachers to teach. Teaching is an art or craft and can be taught and learned the same as any art or craft. What is an art? Let us see what the dictionary says: "Skill, dexterity, or power of performing certain actions, acquired by experience, study or observation." How does this fit into that to which the pupils in college are exposed? Have those who are employed to teach acquired by experience, study, or observation the skill, dexterity, or power of teaching? Or have they entirely eliminated that and learned to lecture instead? Or, perhaps, the teachers prefer to listen to recitations. If so, who will do the teaching?

The characteristic of an art or craft of any kind is its passing on from one generation to another the skills which have been learned by a craftsman from the journeyman to whom he has been apprenticed. These skills are taught to the apprentice, with exactitude and perseverance, so that they become second nature, and thereby the trainee is not only able to produce more results, but—more important—results of a superior quality. A spectator, watching the craftsman at work, may think that the workman holds his tools awkwardly and unworkmanlike but later notices that all journeymen of that craft use their tools in a similar way, for this is one of the skills taught by the journeyman and characteristic of all similarly trained workmen. Thus, many who have been trained in the same craft have identical tools and use them according to the skills which the craft demands. This is usually true whether we are speaking of carpentry, blacksmithing, or pipefitting; of surgery, dentistry, or radiotherapy; of painting, sculpture, or architecture. Why, then, should we expect that the art of teaching, with its delicate skills, should be bestowed upon us without our asking for it, to say nothing about our not working for it?

Perhaps teaching may best be recognized as a mutually complementary function: no one teaches unless someone thereby learns something. One reason why teaching is often avoided is that it is always hard work, no matter how attractive it may be. But, like many varieties of hard work, it returns great rewards. As has often been said, the demand today, as for many years past, is for "productive scholarship," but what is the graduate school supposed to produce? Is it to produce dissertations, or should it aim to produce teachers who are so much needed.

Let us come down to details and try to analyze the situation. There are certain universities, such as the University of London, for instance, which will act simply as examining agencies, examinations being provided under careful supervision, and, when these are passed successfully, a degree is granted. The pupil finds his material where he can. We have other universities where a variety of sources of material is recognized as valid— perhaps we might call it the textbook method. Textbooks are designated, lectures are given to classes, auxiliary material may be suggested, phonograph records are heard, and television is used to present the subject matter in various ways. Then, occasionally, there are other universities where the pupils are privileged to have teachers. Any new methods of presenting college courses are mostly enlargements of the textbook or lecturing methods and will probably be encouraged in these days of overflowing numbers of prospective pupils.

Much is expected from television, but it is simply an illustrated variation of the lecture method so common in many college classes. The experiments being tried, financed by benevolent funds, may be the best we can do under present circumstances, but perhaps the professors, being relieved from lecturing by these mechanical means, might be trained as teachers. In the few institutions where apprentice teaching is being attempted, so little time is devoted to it, compared to the time expended by masters and apprentices of such arts as carpentry and watchmaking, as to render it insignificant. Generally speaking, teacher training is most in evidence in the kindergarten and elementary departments, but gradually and decisively it loses its emphasis, and by the end of the high school it is usually lacking. What is needed is a revival of the art of teaching in colleges, for it is a fallacy to expect that the ability to teach in a college is a miraculous gift automatically bestowed as a bonus with the Ph.D. degree and which is, by some magical process, at the demand of every college appointee, without effort on the part of the recipient.

Real teaching is an arduous and difficult occupation. Much time must be spent daily planning an appropriate presentation of the subject so that the whole class will get it and the individual student cannot miss it. Lessons must be considered in the light of different personalities in the class and must be fitted to the pupils' previous training and experience. Pertinent questions must be planned, for these will excite the mental action which a simple statement does not do, and such questions should be clearly stated and be definite and answerable. They should also be suggestive and lead the pupils' minds beyond the simple answers expected.

While teaching is a demanding vocation, it is also a technical task, and to rise to the top level of the profession requires the help of a master who is familiar with the skills. In his daily preparation, a teacher has a real difficulty in keeping abreast of the new discoveries in the natural sciences; and the social and economic sciences, which did not bother the college teacher of the 18th century, now demand continual renewing and retouching. To expect a teacher to carry on research, and at the same time to read professional journals and the new books in the field of his subject, and also to prepare the lessons he must teach daily is asking more than one person can accomplish. Nevertheless, the colleges and universities demand that research shall have the preference, which necessitates that lesson preparation shall be neglected and probably omitted.

Of course, the professor's method of conducting his class is important. In a well conducted college class, there is no need of students' smoking, reading the daily paper, conversing with neighboring students, writing letters, or performing other tasks to entertain themselves. If the professor cannot entertain the "students" with the lesson, he is no teacher.

It is often said that the best university and college teaching is to be found in England, at Oxford and Cambridge Universities, where the tutorial method, at its best, has been developed. A limited number of students is assigned to a tutor, and these meet informally and occasionally with him, usually individually but perhaps in pairs, when the assignment is discussed and the problems which arise are thoroughly examined. A new assignment, consisting of collateral reading and related themes, as well as the central theme, is the lesson for the next meeting. Over the centuries this has proved to be good teaching, but the expense is prohibitive for our universities with the tens of thousands seeking admission.

There is a suspicion that the quality of the tutorial system in these English universities has deteriorated since the beginning of World War I, owing to the exceedingly high mortality among the carefully selected young tutors in these institutions. Conscription at that time was seeking the physically fit wherever found. If this is true, there may be a compensating consideration. The two great universities were so much in the limelight that their reputations attracted the most brilliant young men from all countries as students and helped to balance the poorer grade of tutors. The whole rumor, however, may be an attempt to lower Oxford and Cambridge to the level of the universities of other lands, as far as reputations are concerned.

Perhaps a modification of the tutorial method may retain many of its values and at the same time minister to the whole class. After the class has assembled, the teacher designates a certain pupil to answer the question which he is about to ask. The answer draws more questions from the teacher, and other members of the class may ask questions. The pupil first questioned is relieved, and others, perhaps those who have interrupted to ask questions, continue discussing the subject. The discussion and the questions are passed from one to another, but there is always some pupil definitely selected to discuss the subject with the teacher, who is never found off the course of the discussion which he has planned and whose skill is shown by the direction and quality of the answers. During the full hour the teacher is busy directing the discussion, correcting or criticizing the answers, and keeping all the members of the class participating and interested.

Knowledge cannot be transferred from one person to another; it has to be reborn in the recipient's mind. To accomplish this, certain mental activities must be aroused. Mere telling will not do it. Teaching is not completed until what the teacher wishes to impart becomes a part of the learner's mentality. The decisive element in the teacher's art is stimulating the appropriate activity in the pupil's mind, and this cannot be done without the proper excitement of mental energy awakened in the proper way.

If the art of teaching is studied by prospective teachers, we must not expect the result to be a group of teachers perfectly trained and capable of perfect teaching and faultless artistry. They would vary as have others who have experienced identical training. As with all kinds of training, their success will depend upon their personality, mentality, ambition, industry, and other factors of life, and upon how such training can be appropriated by each. Even with the best of training, there will be some comparative failures. One thing can be said of them, however: they have tried to improve and apply their native ability so as to get the best results of which their natural gifts are capable. They all will not teach exactly alike, but each will find it easier and more successful to develop one of the teaching talents with which he is endowed, and others will emphasize their special gifts.

Probably the best teachers in the American colleges are the athletic coaches. It might seem to be undignified to employ teachers as we do coaches: "Win the games or seek another position." But it works. Even our colleges should realize that it is as important to teach a boy his mathematics as his football.

It is very unlikely that there is a group of teachers in America of higher quality than those teaching in the New England college preparatory schools for boys. It is true that they are not employed exactly as are the athletic coaches, but if some boys from any one of these schools should fail to pass the entrance examination in English, for instance, and thus be debarred from entering Yale, Harvard, or Princeton, there would be a new English teacher in that school next year.

There are certain subjects which from their contents, organizations, and functions seem to demand superior teaching—and get it. Such a subject is medicine. Here teacher and student work along together for four years in intimate relations, similar to the master craftsman and his apprentice. They handle material together, perform experiments together, continually discuss available literature, etc. Besides this, there are medical board examinations (which the medical students have to pass successfully before they can practice) at which poor teaching as well as poor studying would be detected, and failures would reflect discredit upon professors. This close relationship is also somewhat true concerning engineering, and all laboratory courses have an advantage of this kind.

The best teachers in ordinary courses in college are likely to be the assistant and associate professors who are seeking promotion. They cannot escape the idea that good teaching may assist them in their upward climb.

The practice in large universities of assigning the class work of freshmen and sophomores to graduate students as teachers may be a financial necessity, but it surely is not a pedagogical success. Of course, if we had a system of training teachers, similar to the apprentice system of other crafts, not only would the graduate student be there with the class, but the master craftsman also would be there continually to superintend the teaching.

Why the teaching in colleges and universities should be considered unimportant is difficult to say, unless it seems that the college students are more able to protect themselves than the children in the kindergarten. But are they? In adopting the lecture method of teaching in the colleges, we have placed the emphasis upon the teacher instead of upon the pupil, as has been the general rule in former days, and it is the teacher, not the pupil, who is expected to do the hard work. The principal examples of this method which reach the general public are the Sunday sermons and the political speeches. How would you like to try an examination on the sermon you heard last month? Or, perhaps, on the one you did not hear?

Many of the conditions required for good teaching are more easily and naturally fulfilled in small colleges than in large universities: smaller classes, more intimate and friendly relations between the faculty members and the students, fewer and smaller demands on the faculty for "productive scholarship," and less likelihood of substituting lecturing for teaching. On the other hand, the faculties of small colleges may have heavier teaching loads and not have the financial resources to provide the most favorable conditions.

The nearest approach to a return to teaching is the seminar. It is, however, a poor substitute and does not fulfill the place or function of the professor as teacher. It is usually available only to seniors and graduate students, but real teaching is most valuable to underclassmen. The seminar offers too much opportunity to the garrulous student who wishes to impress others by his excessive speaking. It also puts all present on a common level. The real teacher never surrenders the command of the class.

Of all the breaches of educational etiquette, perhaps none would be considered more despicable than for a professor to visit the classroom of one of his colleagues during the teaching hour without an invitation or permission. It seems that this is a defense attitude and an acknowledgment of the failure of any professor to be able to teach acceptably. Knowing human nature as we do, when the time comes for us to insist upon having trained and effective teaching, we are sure that the professor will welcome any person to his display of teaching ability as freely as he now passes around copies of his latest piece of research. When teacher training is accepted as the most important part of the prospective teacher's preparation, the master teacher's classroom no longer will be his castle which no one dares to invade, but he will be honored to be selected by the director of teachers or by the teachers in training because these young people can learn their art from him.

Teaching is the pinnacle of the educational pyramid. While we do all we can to develop teachers, we also should claim and use teachers wherever we find them, whether in "productive scholarship" or among the janitors. Teaching ability without anything to teach would be far from solving our problem, but what about detailed knowledge to teach and no teacher to teach it? The master teacher should be rewarded by a salary at least equal to that of the "productive researcher," for his is not only a more important task but a more difficult one.

No honor which comes to man can be greater than to be spoken of as a great or good teacher. Mary Ellen Chase wrote: "Teaching, at its best, is not only the highest of arts, but the most exhilarating of occupations." Then she added, "I have never known a dull moment in nearly fifty years of it." To appoint a trained teacher to a deanship is a demotion, regardless of what the salary may indicate and it is a waste of precious material which is irreplaceable. It is slaughtering the ewe lamb. Jesus evidently accepted as appropriate and factual the statement, "We know that thou art a teacher come from God." This description of Him and His mission, coming from a man of Nicodemus' reputation and standing in the land, is substantiated by every historical fact of which we know. The events of His life, as portrayed by the Gospels' authors, show Him to have been a teacher rather than a preacher, a tutor rather than a lecturer, an instructor rather than an oratorical speaker.

Nothing we have said should be interpreted to favor the curtailing of real scholarship. We must expect every teacher to be a scholar, but we must draw a distinction between this and "productive research." The distinction might be expressed by saying, "No scholarship only for the sake of scholarship." The teacher's scholarship must be for one purpose—that of enriching his teaching.

Perhaps we may reach the final solution to our problem of "Scholarship and Teaching" by a bit of reorganization of the university. Let us try.

1. Separate the undergraduate departments entirely from the Graduate School, except as hereafter suggested. The professors in the undergraduate departments will be employed as teachers and will be paid as teachers. They will not be responsible for any program of research for themselves or for others, and they will receive promotions on the basis of successful teaching. The minimum training for these teachers will be a creditable B.A. degree, a stiff M.A. degree in the subject of their specialty, and one extra year's study and training in teaching as an art, leading to an appropriate degree, under the guidance of the director of teaching.

2. The Graduate School will employ its staff as research professors who will plan, participate in, and produce research on the part of their students, who are working toward the degree of Ph.D. The class obligations of these professors will consist of two duties. Once a week each one will hold a seminar of two hours, which all graduate students will attend and report on the various assignments previously given. The professors in the under-graduate departments, teaching similar subjects, also will be privileged or required to attend these seminars to keep in touch with the latest develop-ments in their subjects. In addition, once a week the professor will meet each student in his department, individually, to receive reports of the assigned work and to give advice and direction.

3. There shall be appointed, in addition to the various deans, two vice-presidents of the university, a director of teaching, and a director of research. In a few institutions a new office, dean of instruction, has been established. What are the duties and what are the results of the efforts of such an indivi-dual? As far as I can ascertain, the office seems to be mostly an honorary one, and the word "instruction" in the title refers to the subject matter to be taught, rather than to the method or necessity of teaching. The director of teaching, as suggested in this article, has a 24-hour-a-day task.

While there has been little advancement in teacher training during the past century, lately there seems to have been a revival of this important function. Yale, with its great resources and its combination with Smith and Vassar, is an important present example. This is most encouraging, but there is still a tremendous task to be accomplished.

78

The Nature of Good Teaching

HOLLIS L. CASWELL

President emeritus, Teachers College, Columbia University. At the time his article originally appeared in *School and Society* (Dec. 3, 1960), he was president of Teachers College. The article was based on an address at Buffalo State Teachers College, May 6, 1960.

What is good teaching? Are there carefully evolved standards for the work of the teacher? Can one readily distinguish between what is good and poor teaching and know the reasons why? Carefully developed answers to these questions will go a long way in helping clarify positions on educational issues and in aiding one to determine what educational changes he considers desirable. I shall indicate a few of the most important characteristics possessed by good teaching. Each characteristic of necessity carries implications for learning, because desirable learning is the goal of teaching and teaching can be tested only in terms of the quality of learning to which it leads.

1. *Good teaching is concerned with helping the pupil develop meaning and understanding.* There is a great tendency to equate education and command of facts. As a result, teaching often emphasizes memorization of prescribed bodies of knowledge. But modern research has shown that the ability to recite facts is a very different thing from understanding the meaning of those facts and having the ability to apply them to the solution of problems. The "walking encyclopedia" is not a fit ideal for modern education. We could produce a generation of quiz kids and fail completely to meet the real needs of our people for education.

Education that is worthy of the name helps people understand why things are as they are; it enables them to sense the meanings in situations. Reading is not calling off a list of words; it is getting the meaning lying back of the words. Mathematics is not primarily being able to manipulate numbers; it is understanding numerical and spatial relationships and being able to apply mathematical processes to make a situation meaningful and manageable.

366

Teaching that is concerned with meaning and understanding must be close to the pupil; it must build upon his own experiences; it must relate to the things he knows and understands. The only way to take a person from the known to the unknown is *to start where he is,* and good teaching is largely a process of guiding a student from the known to the unknown.

Firsthand experience is particularly important in providing an education which develops meaning and understanding. A young child can read with *meaning* a story about his own experiences in coming to school; a story unrelated to his experiences becomes largely word-calling. It has been said that one picture is worth a thousand words; it may appropriately be added that one firsthand experience is worth a thousand pictures.

2. *Good teaching is concerned with influencing the behavior of pupils.* A century ago, John Ruskin wrote:

Education does not mean teaching people what they do not know. It means teaching them to behave as they do not behave. It is not teaching youth the shapes of letters and the tricks of numbers and then leaving them to turn their arithmetic to roguery and their literature to lust. It means, on the contrary, training them into the perfect exercise and kingly continence of their bodies and souls.

More recently, one of England's and America's greatest philosophers, Alfred North Whitehead, stated much the same idea: "There is only one subject-matter for education, and that is Life in all its manifestations."

A great deal of teaching has overlooked this standard. There are many teachers of literature who become so engrossed with seeing that pupils gain certain knowledge about literary selections that they minimize or ignore the effects of their teaching on pupil behavior. The real test of the teaching of literature is to be found in the reading habits students form and continue after the course is over. It is better not to teach literature at all than it is to teach pupils to hate good literature.

Similarly in other fields, teaching should be directed at changing behavior. In citizenship instruction the central purpose is to get pupils to behave as good citizens. Much knowledge and many skills are essential to achieving this end. But when the mastery of knowledge and skills becomes an end in itself and behavior is forgotten, the real reason for the support of popular education in our country is subverted.

3. *Good teaching is concerned with the student as a person and with his general development.* Good teaching is a very personal matter. Review your own experience and recall the teachers who stood out, who made an important contribution to your development. Are they not the ones who took a personal interest in you, who saw your potentialities, who encouraged you to higher aspirations than you alone would have held?

With rare exceptions, the answer to this question will be in the affirmative. Occasionally, one may gain inspiration from the distant star, but for the day-by-day struggle of life it is the warmth of the intimate fireside that sustains one. The authority, the man or woman of great renown, may stimulate the ambition and serve as a source of useful knowledge to the student far removed; but if there is not the teacher near at hand with a warmth of personal interest, firsthand knowledge of the pupil's capacities, and continuing concern for his development, aspirations created by the stars with but few exceptions wither and die.

4. *Good teaching recognizes individual differences among pupils and adjusts instruction to them.* One of the striking facts in a system which provides elementary and secondary education for all the children of all the people and higher education for a substantial proportion is the great diversity of ability which must be considered. The range of potentialities and interests is as wide as the population, and as a consequence the variability of achievement in any field is tremendous. In a school system which provides for all, there is simply no way to eliminate or to reduce substantially these differences. They must be accepted and adjustments must be made to them.

Some adjustments can be made in general curriculum plans and some in school organization. But the major ones must be made by individual teachers in the classroom. It is here that the capacities and difficulties of the student must be understood; it is here that the varying rates of learning among pupils must be recognized; it is here that instruction which helps each pupil achieve at his optimum rate must be designed and given.

To make these adjustments is one of the most important elements of good teaching in American schools, for only in this way can equality of opportunity be provided for all our children and youth. This is a standard which we as yet are far from meeting satisfactorily. All too often slow pupils still have to struggle to maintain a pace appropriate to the average, and the gifted are not challenged because they, too, are led to set their sights on average performance.

But significant progress has been made and one thing is perfectly clear. It is in those situations, where good teachers can work with groups of pupils of such size that they can study each one individually and provide much small-group and individual instruction, that outstanding teaching is being done. Whenever the individual pupil is lost in a mass, this essential quality of good teaching disappears.

The White House Conference on Education stated, "Schools are now asked to help each child to become as good and as capable in every way as native endowment permits. . . . The talent of each child is to be sought out and developed to the fullest. Each weakness is to be studied and, so far as possible, corrected." If this great conception is to be realized, there must be inspired teaching in American classrooms.

5. *In good teaching a teacher must be competent in both content and method.* One of the most unfortunate aspects of the historical development of American education has been the tendency to separate content and method, often

throwing them in opposition to each other. I have observed teaching which was very poor because the teacher did not possess mastery of the subject matter he was trying to teach; I have observed teaching which was equally poor because the teacher did not have command of appropriate methods. Either situation is to be deplored.

The plain fact is that both content and method are essential ingredients of the equipment of a good teacher. It is high time that the two were not thrown in opposition to each other. In fact, it would be as sensible to argue which is the more important for the preservation of life, air or water, as it is to argue whether content or method is more important in the competence of a teacher. A good teacher must achieve competence in both.

6. *No single method will insure good teaching.* There often has been a tendency in American education to tie good teaching to a particular method. At one time the project method was thought to be the answer, the case method has had wide use in certain professional fields, the lecture method frequently has been damned, and the discussion method has been widely emphasized.

All of these methods, under certain circumstances, will result in good teaching, and, under other circumstances, will result in poor teaching. Method *per se* is no guarantee of the quality of instruction. The nature of the subject, the abilities of the teacher, the status of the pupils, and the availability of instructional materials all determine what method gets the best results. Some lectures are inspiring and highly informative; others put the class to sleep. Some class discussions are an obvious waste of time; others stimulating and useful. There are some teachers for whom it would be tragic if they could not rely largely on the lecture method and others for whom it was equally tragic if they did.

Good teaching adapts methods to purpose, content, pupil status, and teacher ability. It permits and encourages the use of a variety of methods. It finds no panacea in any single one.

What is good teaching? This is a basic question. It strikes at the heart of the whole educational process. Answer it clearly, thoughtfully, and soundly and you will have one good guide through the uncertainties of the future. Ignore it or answer it with catch phrases and clichés and you are certain to be in for confusion.

Many beliefs undergird the work of an outstanding teacher. Perhaps the most important is conviction in the potentialities of students. Teachers who love their work are motivated most of all by the belief that they can help their students become better, more effective men and women. This is the central dedication required of a teacher.

79

Creative Teaching for Excellence in Education

LINDLEY J. STILES

Dean, School of Education, University of Wisconsin. His article originally appeared in *School and Society* on Sept. 26, 1959, and was based on an address to the DuPage County Teachers Institute, Wheaton and Elmhurst, Ill., March 16, 1959.

Teaching, at any level, is an art. As such, it relies on scientific principles to promote learning, but the quality of teaching, itself, is determined by the creativeness, knowledge of content, ingenuity, depth of understanding, initiative, and insights of the individual teacher. The effects of teaching, like those of other arts, are frequently subtle and difficult to appraise; yet, at the same time, they may be long enduring. The way a teacher teaches not only determines whether students will master necessary skills and become familiar with areas of significant knowledge; it influences, also, attitudes, appreciations, values, behavior—the total outlook of the student toward learning and life.

The creative teacher must be, first of all, an educated person. He must be curious about many things, their interrelationships and meanings. A broadly and soundly educated scholar, he also must be adept at bringing knowledge to bear upon situations he faces. From a background of sound liberal preparation he will search continuously for broad generalizations which help interpret life in relation to given environmental forces.

Secondly, the creative teacher must be a specialist in his field of teaching. Unless he is thoroughly familiar with the content to be taught, its relationships to life problems and other fields of knowledge, he will be a slave to the textbook, an uncritical dispenser of facts and dogma, a recitation referee and possibly an uninspiring bore and a drudge. Only the teacher who keeps his own scholarship abreast of new knowledge, who joins enthusiastically in the search for truth and distillation of wisdom, can achieve the heights of creativity in teaching.

370

   Finally, the creative teacher must possess reliable knowledge of how students learn, how they react under a variety of stimuli, and how learning becomes permanent and useful to the individual. He must feel empathically with his students, understand what happens when one learns and another fails to learn, and know how to adapt his teaching procedures to change the latter to the former. The creative teacher will approach the teaching of each student as a new and unique assignment which demands the utmost of his knowledge and skill; at his command will be a wide variety of teaching procedures and aids to be used as required by individual situations. When one approach fails, he will be able to devise additional ways of transmitting the content to be taught, sharpening the skill to be mastered, or encouraging the attitude or appreciation to be developed.

   It is ironic that, at a time when teaching needs most to be strengthened, a nation-wide campaign is being conducted to support the premise that scholarship in a subject field alone is sufficient to successful teaching. These efforts are tending to convince the American people that skill in teaching is inherited rather than developed, that professional preparation for teaching is, therefore, unnecessary. As a consequence, when excellence in teaching is most needed, many have been led to believe that teaching ability is a matter of happy accident rather than a product of systematic study and practice.

   Sober reflection will remind everyone of brilliant scholars they have known, who knew their subjects but who were pedantic, uninspiring, ineffective teachers. Individuals who believe that ability to teach is innate are unlikely to feel they can improve on nature. Their chances of becoming creative teachers are small.

   To advocate that to know one's subject is sufficient to teach is comparable to arguing that knowledge of anatomy is all that is needed to perform surgery. Just as the surgeon must spend years in practice, under supervision, to learn how to translate his knowledge of medicine into a skillful operation, the creative teacher must learn through controlled and examined practice to guide the learning of his students with maximum efficiency and permanence. A slip of the surgeon's knife may be fatal to the patient, no matter how great is his knowledge; likewise, an erroneous approach by the teacher to a given child may inhibit learning in ways that damage future development beyond repair.

   The teacher without an adequate professional preparation for his mission subconsciously leads an existence of fear that knowledge may exist of learning and teaching about which he is ignorant. Those who maintain a cynical aloofness to the importance of improving their practice defend their own weaknesses by proclaiming that ignorance is a virtue. They attack all who dare to search for laws, knowledge, and empirical evidence that might challenge their resistance to learning how to teach.

   The creative teacher rejects the artificial separation of knowledge of the subject taught and professional skill in teaching. He knows full well that without both—comprehensive scholarship in his subject field and a highly developed skill in the art of teaching—he will be doomed to mediocrity as a teacher. Socrates gave us the wisdom that "the unexamined life is not worth living." Applied to teaching, this thought might be paraphrased to suggest that the teacher who does not examine his pedagogy, as well as his scholarship, is unworthy of the name.

Creative teaching is characterized by such terms as variety, inspiration, enthusiasm, imagination, insightfulness, empathy. It aims at helping students develop initiative, independent effort essential to self-direction and self-discipline, capacity to view the broad sweep of events, facts, and principles, as well as the organized use of intelligence to solve problems. The major motivational forces of the creative teacher are curiosity, desire, ambition, pride, and the satisfaction that comes from a job well done. Such teachers have the ability to maintain high standards as their goals of instruction while helping students of different abilities to make progress toward them, often by a variety of routes.

The creative teacher possesses characteristics and habits that are common to all creative endeavors: high sensitivity to impressions; ability to associate rapidly ideas and visual impressions; imagination—the capacity to perceive new relationships or something that does not exist; emotional responsiveness; capacity to absorb and retain knowledge; wisdom—the faculty of reasoning —ability to see patterns in events and facts and to sense relationships; empathy—power to feel experiences of others, both real and vicarious; artistry—habit of permitting the organization of knowledge and perceptions to flow from within in fresh and unique patterns of expressions.

The creative teacher must be a master of his subject, but sensitive and sympathetic to the stages through which mastery is eventually achieved. He must hate ignorance, but love students; seek to stamp out error, without extinguishing the spark of curiosity that ignites all learning; censor slovenly work, but let his praise for progress keep interest and effort high; encourage the slow and goad the bright, without creating contentment in the one or rebellion in the other; and he must stimulate independence in learning while subtly guiding the direction, rate, and quality of attainment. Above all, the creative teacher must give first priority to teaching, to his responsibility to his students; he must seek to know each learner as an individual as well as to understand the group forces that operate when a particular class comes together for instruction; yet, he must remain the scholar who shows by his example the excitement and satisfaction that comes only from seeking to know. Finally, the creative teacher must believe in his own capacity to teach, yet be humble about the need to continue to study the art of teaching throughout his career.

80

The Inspirational Teacher

FRANKLIN R. ZERAN

Dean, School of Education, Oregon State University. His article originally appeared in *School and Society* on Nov. 8, 1958.

Gibran, in "The Prophet," has Almustafa answer the teacher as follows, when the teacher asks him to speak to the group about teaching:

No man can reveal to you aught but that which already lies half asleep in the dawning of your knowledge.

The teacher who walks in the shadow of the temple, among his followers, gives not of his wisdom but rather of his faith and his lovingness.

If he is indeed wise he does not bid you enter the house of his wisdom, but leads you to the threshold of your own. . . .

And he who is versed in the science of numbers can tell of the regions of weight and measure, but he cannot conduct you thither.

For the vision of one man lends not its wings to another man. . . .

The inspirational teacher—the individual who knows his subject field, the laws of learning, and then applies them in the teaching process, and who can motivate the student to accept the goal as his own—that is the kind of teacher under whom we all want to study.

Since there is no hierarchy in teaching, we should expect to find this type of teacher at all levels—elementary, secondary, and collegiate. The faculty member at the college level who works with students in the classroom —in English, mathematics, chemistry, political science, history, or zoology— is a teacher just the same as a first-grade teacher or a high-school teacher of mathematics. They all need to know their subject matter very well—or no teaching can take place. They all teach subject matter—to individuals. The learning process is the same; and, furthermore, learning is likely to be a painful process for some. They all need to recognize that unless the "student" accepts the goal as his own—whether it be to spell correctly or to learn the structure and physiology of cells—little learning actually will take place. This is where the teacher "leads you to the threshold of your own mind." This is motivation.

The time has come to stop talking about "elementary teachers teach children and secondary and college teachers teach subject matter." The truth of the matter is that we all teach *individuals*, and if we "teach" we must teach "something." This "something" is subject matter. If the teacher does not know his subject matter, he simply cannot teach. The teacher, furthermore, must know how learning takes place if he is to teach the student. Many times, the failure of a student to "pass" a course is the result of the teacher failing to do a job of teaching through lack of knowing how learning takes place and his part in the process.

The inspirational teacher knows that to develop into the individual one potentially is, calls for identification of the potentials, the setting of goals, and the willingness to pay the price through self-discipline. He knows that he promotes this growth in the individual when he maintains standards. He also knows that this specific job as a teacher is to assist the student in obtaining and furthering a command of the fundamental process; that if he performs this task well, then citizenship, worthy use of leisure, ethical character, and vocational efficiency will emerge as concomitant values.

However, even when one identifies his potentials, sets goals, and imposes self-discipline, man cannot utilize his potential by existing in a state of vacuum. To function he must reside in a social environment. The society in which he finds himself will determine in large measure the opportunity he has to develop and utilize democratic procedures in his classroom, stressing, among other things, the aspects of responsibility for actions taken and the necessity on the part of the student to know the processes involved in arriving at a decision. The teacher is not to supply the answers but to direct the student in his search. He not only permits the student to disagree with his statements, but urges and stimulates the student to think for himself. By permitting the student to state his point of view and then defend it, the teacher knows that the student is learning. The student, at the same time, learns to assume the responsibility of being open-minded enough to permit others their right to be heard.

The inspirational teacher has no "pat" approach nor does he teach each group in the same manner. To teach he needs to learn what each one in the group already knows about the subject—at the start of the course— and begin at that stage with something new. Furthermore, he does not use his own textbook, with his own duplicated syllabus, and then confine his lectures to the same book. Also, his "depth of preparation" in his subject field has not been so narrow as to preclude "area." For example, the history teacher needs adequate preparation in sociology, economics, and political science to relate the historical events to the environment in which they took place.

Teachers at all levels are confronted with the same problem—individuals unable to do the work satisfactorily. The law says these individuals must attend elementary and secondary schools until graduation or until reaching a specified age. In most states the law says that if an individual graduates from a high school in that state, he is to be admitted to a state college. Teaching is difficult under this situation. However, instead of pointing fingers and raising our voices against the teachers in the sending schools—instead of fixing the blame—perhaps more good will be accomplished if we utilize our time and efforts trying to fix the mistakes. If "Johnny is silent," the teacher has an obligation to do something about making him vocal. That is what the inspirational teacher does. Should we accept less?

81

From Logs to Logistics

JOSEPH SEIDLIN

Teaching consultant, Agricultural and Technical College at Alfred, State University of New York. His article originally appeared in *School and Society* on Nov. 11, 1967, and was based on a talk to the faculty, State University College at Buffalo, Dec. 9, 1965.

A descriptive subtitle for this article could be: "Professor, All is Forgiven; Come Back to the Classroom." Real teachers are happiest "in the classroom." The better ones, the good ones, recognize early in their careers that to be happiest in the classroom, one must engage in activities outside the classroom. A homely illustration, an analogy, really, is enjoying one's fireplace on a cool evening. The enjoyment is enhanced by proper preparation, *viz.*, if the fuel for the fireplace is wood, clearly one must provide the wood, and, since wood burns up, one must keep replenishing the wood. Furthermore, the draw—the chimney draft—must be functional, *i.e.*, no eye-smarting, vision-obstructing, lung-annoying, lingering smoke in the room. *Mutatis mutandis*, this is applicable to preparation for teaching, both daily and long-range. However, returning to the analogy, one becomes so enamored of and enmeshed in the preliminaries, *viz.*, the most economical and automated ways of producing fireplace wood, or the most efficient way of laying brick so as to insure the most effective draw in the chimney, and then ignores completely the use of the fireplace. In the name of coherence, I turn from fireplace logs to the log so prominent in educational history— the log used as a classroom by Mark Hopkins and James Garfield.

Most of us have mixed feelings about the one-to-one, faculty-student ratio, even if it were practicable. For that matter, Socrates, however much he may have involved one person in his famous dialogues, appreciated the bystander presence of a group. Not many of us would accept a log as either a comfortable or otherwise desirable classroom. What about the auditorium, the armory, the amphitheater, the stadium? None of them is really a classroom. With appropriate gadgets—loud-speakers, microphones, etc.—the larger the room, the more students can hear the professor, and, usually, the fewer listen. If part of a professor's lecture is exposition, as generally it must be, the mere presence of a large number of students weakens the quality and effectiveness of the lecture. Actually, the poorer the teacher, the less important the size of the class. Not only programmed instruction, with or without teaching machines, but even the lowly textbook, can and does replace the poor teacher satisfactorily. None of these can replace or has replaced the human interaction between superior, or good, or live professors, and students thus recalled to life.

"What are professors for?" is a likely alternate title for this paper, except that Philip Abelson pre-empted it as the title of an editorial in *Science,* June 18, 1965. "The time has come," writes Abelson, "to ask, 'what are professors for?' The professor's primary activities should be teaching and research, with the priority in that order, but with research a close second." And, a bit further, "The professor's most important role is to provide various forms of guidance for the students. . . . We know that motivation and taste can be fostered by 'close association of professors with students.' " I am reasonably certain that, by "close association," Dr. Abelson does not mean "the two ends of a log." A real live teacher closely is associated with his students, even when there are 30 or 40 in a class.

But many of our "teachers" are not really teachers. They are mathematicians, physicists, historians, linguists, etc.—not teachers. Many of them are men—and women—of great stature; major contributors to science, technology, and the arts—but they are not teachers. On some scales of worth to humanity, they outweigh the teachers—but they are not teachers. They even might be indispensable to institutions of higher learning – but they are not teachers. To them, students are a means; to teachers, students are the end products, all else is a means.

A small pamphlet, *You and Your Students,* published some 15 years ago by the Massachusetts Institute of Technology, stated: "In the Massachusetts Institute of Technology there are many excellent teachers. For the most part, these men have gained their ability as teachers by hard and individual work, by a deep interest in their students' progress and welfare, and usually over a long road of individual experimentation and development. Good teachers are made, not born. Yet how few of us regularly spend even one percent of our annual professional time deliberately studying the mechanism of teaching—with a view to self-criticism and self-development. In the long run, such time is well spent, and it repays itself many-fold in improved teaching efficiency and in actual time saved."

Today, there is a strong trend in our universities, best expressed by the position that the worth and dignity—status—of a university professor are directly proportional to his teaching load; that, in fact, he reaches the most coveted position on the faculty when his teaching load is reduced to zero. In colleges, primarily teaching institutions, me-too-ism—aping the universities —is so strong as to make teaching the college professor's second choice.

One of the negative characteristics of a democracy is its allergy to resolving problems as they arise; one of the positive characteristics of a democracy is to solve what appear to be unsolvable problems. *Viz.*, deforestation was not arrested until it became a national threat. In like manner, we are faced with air pollution, water pollution, with car graveyards, etc., and with neglect of teaching. In 1965 and in 1966, vocal leaders—educators, editors of magazines and newspapers, statesmen, and others in growing numbers—eloquently and vehemently protested the anomalous dichotomy between teachers and teaching.

How did it all begin? There must have been some basis for minimizing the importance of a teacher's job in the classroom. When the teaching machine burst upon us in full flower, the popular question became, "Will the teaching machine replace the teacher?" My answer to that question was: "Since part of the teacher's job is mechanical, a machine can replace that part, and probably do it more effectively; since some teachers are 99.44% mechanical, machines can replace those teachers, with perhaps some gain for the learner." For that matter, a like situation must have arisen when the textbook first came into being. Then, too, the answer to the question as to whether the textbook was going to replace the teacher might well have been, "Since part of a teacher's job is to gather and organize material, a textbook could replace that part. Some teachers are little more than 'textbooks wired for sound.' Textbooks can replace those teachers, and 'they would never be missed.' " And so it may be that "no teacher" is better than a poor teacher.

Much of the present excitement in curricular revision in many fields, perhaps most spectacular in mathematics, also has its origin in a subconscious reaction to inexcusable, unbelievable, poor teaching. Thus, we hear the evangelistic exponents of "modern mathematics" tell us that "no longer will algebra be taught as a bag of tricks." No good teacher of algebra ever taught it as a "bag of tricks." I dislike to disillusion so many of my colleagues by warning them that, in the hands of an ingeniously poor teacher, the most modern of modern mathematics can be and will be taught as a bag of tricks, albeit less obvious tricks.

It would be unrealistic to minimize the importance of improved curricula, improved methodologies in all guises, and improved physical facilities. However, although the effective teacher may use any or all of the above improvements, he, as a person, is indispensable to the total process and structure of our educational system. Hence, when he shirks his opportunities and responsibilities in the classroom, he renounces his allegiance to the teaching profession.

We need not be overly concerned whether teaching is a science or an art. In principle, it is a science; in practice—like anything else in practice, even ditch-digging by hand—it is an art. It may be that most of the nonsense about teaching has run its course. However, nonsense, like old soldiers, never dies. I suppose that, even 25 years from now, there will be replicas of John Dooley's at one extreme, and "great lovers of children" at the other. But 25 years from now, teaching, like medicine, will be a strong enough profession to parry whatever thrusts come its way. In the meantime, we must elevate the status of a college professor as teacher. One way of doing it is to postulate that a competent teacher must be a scholar, and may be a researcher. Clearly, teaching, scholarship, and research, are not mutually exclusive. If the scholar-teacher is prized—and priced—as highly as the researcher, or even the administrator, the classroom once again will be able to attract and hold the potentially competent teacher.

Why or how have we become conditioned to use a qualifier alongside of "teacher," and nothing but a halo alongside of "researcher"? Thus, the college professor whose dominant activity is research, is a researcher; but his colleague, whose principal activity is teaching, is a competent teacher, or an effective teacher, or a poor teacher. Rarely, if ever, is he just a teacher. The quality of teaching and teachers has been accepted verbally as inseparable from the act or actor. Yet no other component of education can claim as many abortive "studies" nor as much unmitigated nonsense in the thousands of *ex-cathedra* pronouncements. At one extreme, teaching competency or effectiveness is equated with "love for children"; at the opposite extreme, it is equated with knowledge of subject matter.

It is not easy to analyze, perhaps even to identify, the variety of motives or reasons behind so general opposition to the evaluation of teaching. In part, it may be cowardice; in part, ignorance. A very few courageous and competent educators put into practice many known principles underlying the identification of effective teaching and teachers. There is no real iron or bamboo curtain which shuts off competent observers from "a look at" teachers at work; not that we have not made many, often successful, attempts at surrounding the teacher's castle—the classroom—with impregnable walls and abutments.

Then there is the formidable never-never land of "the total learnings of the whole person." Like Edgar Guest's "it takes a heap of living to make a house a home," it takes an infinite variety of influences to educate a student. How can we evaluate a process whose "results" are many years removed? And so, in the total scheme of schooling, the quality of teaching, or teachers, has become entangled with mystery, legend, and oozing mush. Most of these, I say hopefully, are part of the passing scene; some still plague us.

Is a teacher's job so intangible as to defy critical analysis? Is it really impossible to differentiate between inspired teaching and deadly dull teaching, between uniquely human teaching and machine teaching; between effective teaching and tainted teaching?

Those who resist teacher evaluation tell us: the number of factors that determine quality of teaching is beyond our ability to count, and we have no exact measuring instruments to enable us to evaluate these factors objectively.

Many years ago, an analogous situation existed in the field of physics. As we all know, the force affecting a body is the resultant of a great number of forces too many to count. Physicists tackled the "insoluble" problem by what has come to be known as isolating the system. That meant that a small number of the more dominant forces is assumed to comprise the total number of forces, and the resultant of these is computed. "Isolating the system" served as a great impetus in the development of the science of physics, both in theory and application. As for exact measurements, there are none, even in physics. As measuring devices become more delicately refined, approximations become finer and significant figures grow in number. But the physicist or the chemist who refuses to use available measuring devices, because they do not yield exact measurements, if he exists at all, probably is in an insane asylum. No applied science or technology or art marks time until all that is ever to be known is known; until mythical exact measurements become available. As rational human beings, we must put into practice whatever knowledge, whatever measuring instruments are available at any given time.

As an illustration, think of the history of progress in medicine. So many theories and practices of even 10 years ago have been replaced by more effective theories and practices. This is not to say that the older theories and practices have not, in their day, saved lives and combatted disease. Nor would any mature reasoning physician claim that the present theories and practices in medicine are the last word.

Let us "isolate the system," and concentrate on three dominant components of quality, or effective, teaching: knowledge of subject matter, of the vehicle of instruction, since one can not teach what one does not know, provided, of course, that it is knowable; ability, innate or acquired, to communicate knowledge to, or share it effectively with, learners; and an awareness not only of the unique importance, but also the organic relationship, of the teacher's job to the total structure of higher education.

Are these three components measurable?

Knowledge of subject matter.—While courses and degrees are not synonymous with knowledge, they are a fairly reliable first approximation, and certainly a significant symptom, not unlike body temperature and blood pressure in the diagnosis of disease. Since all knowledge is growing, a knowledgeable person also must keep on "growing." A teacher in a rut loses his effectiveness, since the difference between a rut and a grave merely is that of dimensions. Is knowledge of subject matter intangible, and therefore incapable of appraisal?

Ability and desire to communicate knowledge to or share it effectively with learners.—No other determiner of the teaching process is as uniquely characteristic of teaching as this one. This is perhaps the only unique characteristic of a teacher. Any of the other characteristics apply with equal force to other professions.

An awareness not only of the unique importance, but also the organic relationship of the teacher's job to the total structure of higher education.—However much of a star or a prima donna a teacher may be, he must be sensitive to and cognizant of the fact that he is a member of an organization. Generally, administrators can and do "measure" this complex quality of a teacher. They are perplexed somewhat, however, as to its relative position in the hierarchy of determiners of quality teaching.

For over 30 years, I have annoyed my colleagues at meetings, seminars, workshops, etc. by pressing upon them the following query: What essential determinants of the quality of teaching can be obtained from actual observations of teachers at work in their classrooms? I have accumulated, through actual observation of 200 teachers of college mathematics, a long list of such determinants. But dominant among them are the following 10: *exposition* (are the "explanations" clear, specific, pointed; involved, indirect, long, tedious?); *organization* (is there any discernible plan, or order, or sequence, or arrangement of both the content and the conduct of the recitation?); *presentation* (is the teacher dramatic and vital; informal and relaxed; laborious and sullen; dismal and dull?); *motivation* (aside from "required" work and examinations, what incentives, or genuine inducements, or real considerations are adduced to actuate "learning"?); *enthusiasm* (is there any contagious "force" or "energy" emanating from the teacher?); *richness of application* (what are the variety, extent, and sources of applications and illustrations?); *resourcefulness* (what is the teacher's reaction to an unexpected question, an unusual comment, or a strange turn of events?); *questions* (what kind of questions are asked by the teacher? do they serve the purpose of orienting and developing; or awakening interest; or regaining attention; or providing an oral quiz? are the questions asked by the students intended to gain information; to earn a grade; to test the teacher?); *use of textbook* (is the teacher guided by the textbook merely in plan and sequence? does he ignore it? is he enslaved by it?); *tests and examinations* (are the tests and examinations an integral part of the teaching-learning process? are they a "necessary evil" imposed upon the teacher by "authorities"? are they dreaded by the students as an instrument of torture?).

According to Dale Wolfle, "If great teaching is to be rewarded, the great teachers must be identified. . . . Any realistic effort to identify the outstanding teachers must depend upon the judgment of qualified observers. . . . The teacher who wishes for enhanced status must, therefore, make a choice. He can co-operate in efforts to see if the ablest teachers can be identified reliably. If that turns out to be the case, then rewards, privileges and other means of enhancing prestige can follow. Or, he can insist that good teaching is essentially a private and unmeasurable affair. But he cannot hold this view and plead that the ablest teachers be given special recognition, *and also honor consistency*."*

The quality of teaching is a spectrum ranging from the unbelievably dull to the dazzlingly brilliant. Before long, some group, agency, or organization, some sudden impulse of ineffectual administrators may impose upon college professors criteria for evaluating teaching and teachers. I am convinced that for the good of teachers and teaching, learners and learning —all of education, in fact—the most appropriate group to develop and employ criteria for evaluating teachers should be composed predominantly of educators: professors, deans, and even presidents. Evaluation of teachers is inevitable. Whether the consequences will prove to be educationally sound and desirable largely is up to college teachers and college administrators.

* Editorial, *Science,* Dec. 11, 1964.

82

Stuart P. Sherman—Master Teacher

MARK VAN DOREN

Professor emeritus of English, Columbia University. At the time his article originally appeared in *School and Society* (June 7, 1958), he was professor of English. The article was based on an address at the University of Illinois, Jan. 26, 1958.

To measure a school by its teachers is not to measure it by the only item that matters. Doubtless the item that matters most is the subjects that are taught—the things the students will be asked to learn. But the student meets the subject in the teacher, and the teacher for that simple reason never ceases to be crucial in the drama of learning. Just as the content of a mind cannot be known until a voice delivers it, so it may be said that a subject does not exist until the student hears it in the words of his teacher. And if these are good words, the subject, too, seems good. It seems better yet when style distinguishes the words. The proof of any statement is finally in its style, by which I mean its precision, its beauty, and its personal force. Teachers, then, are the voices of the university; and its best teachers may be thought of as those who deliver its content, its meaning, and its truth in such a way that they themselves become its style.

I had many good teachers (at the University of Illinois), and I could name them all, but it is better for my purpose that I should name just one. He was Stuart P. Sherman (1881–1926), professor of English. The fact that Stuart Sherman has been much praised does not discourage me from praising him again; nor is the fact that he helped in large measure to create the reputation of the university anything but highly relevant to what I have been saying about the teacher in his ultimate capacity as artist, as deliverer, as master of the style which content seeks. I can testify, as many have done before me, that Sherman was the finest teacher I ever had anywhere. But I should like to go on from there and say, to the extent that I can, why this was so. All of my reasons, I suspect, will be one reason in the end: the man was the subject, the subject was the man. Whatever he taught—Shakespeare, Matthew Arnold, Emerson, Carlyle—seemed to be of the deepest personal interest to him, an interest so natural in its depth, so convincing in its force, that I could think it only a sort of accident that he was teaching me what he knew. He knew it anyway. It was his pleasure to do so; indeed it was his very life, which I had the good luck to be living with him. The whole nature of the man stated itself in every sentence he spoke; he could not have concealed himself had he tried, and he was not trying. Not that it was himself he labored to deliver; it was of course his subject; but somehow his subject always arrived by way of him; the truth of it had to be the truth for this man who stood before us and showed in his face as well as by his words what it is like to be *spoken through*—the original meaning, some will have it, of that great word *person*: "sounded through." Sherman's face, always sympathetic with what he was saying, so that it seemed an actor's face though he himself was never in any obvious sense of the term histrionic, showed us sometimes that it was fun to be a medium, and sometimes that it was terrible. His humor was not left at home, and neither on other days was his tragic sense; but I mean more than that. I mean that we could see ideas being born in the person who spoke; he thought, in other words, while he talked—a rare spectacle, for it is easier to talk than to think, and it is hardest of all to do both simultaneously. The few teachers who do it are never forgotten.

Irving Dilliard, who in the St. Louis *Post-Dispatch* writes for one of the best editorial pages that can now be read, told me that he came to the university in 1923 because Sherman was here; he had heard about him from his high-school teachers and was determined not to miss so remarkable a man. Informed upon his arrival that Sherman taught no courses for freshmen, he sought him out in his office and begged permission at least to sit and listen. This was irregular, but he persisted until he got the permission; the result was that he heard every word Sherman spoke as a teacher in this last year he was to be at Illinois. And Irving Dilliard says he remembers those words because he remembers the way Sherman looked when he said them. The man was the subject, the subject was the man.

To be this sort of teacher is to be conscientious in the way great artists are conscientious: they do their best all the time, and they understand what they do; they feel their way through uncertainty to certainty. But Sherman was conscientious on another occasion that I remember, an occasion that had nothing to do with public speech. The master's essay I had written for him at the end of my fifth year at the university was in his hands, and I waited to hear what he thought of it. He let me know, by appointment, one day in his office. He went over it with me, almost word by word, while I sat in shame, listening to him say that here or there—and his finger was always on the place—I had not known what I was talking about; I had not understood the terms I used; I exaggerated; I pretended; I showed off. Only then did he astonish me by remarking that the thesis might be good enough to publish—

after, of course, I had cleaned it up. Publication did occur; but what I shall never forget is the lesson in writing I was given that day. It was given by a busy man who had immense concerns, and who could have let those concerns excuse him from attention to such details as a shallow phrase in one of his student's papers. Nothing, however, seemed more important to him at the moment than that I should understand my own mind and express it as capably as I could. And to Sherman, I think, nothing *was* more important than this. The great artist will not despise detail. He is doing at any time what needs to be done, and doing it so that it will stay done.

83

Sincerity in Teaching

REV. CHARLES F. DONOVAN, S.J.

Academic vice-president, Boston College. At the time his article originally appeared in *School and Society* (Feb. 15, 1958), he was dean of the School of Education.

A cynic has remarked that disputes between schools of thought are more apt to yield an exchange of fruit than a fruitful exchange. To be productive, a debate should have two opponents who see that there are two sides.

The now historic debate between Progressives and traditionalists is no exception. Combination, the addition of the opponent's strength to one's own (which is not the same as compromise), has not been energetically sought. Progressives, of course, began by reacting against an overconcentration on the material of education, knowledge or subject matter, as opposed to the process of education. Mortimer Adler has made the distinction between the order of knowledge in itself and the order of learning—that is, the way in which the human mind passes from ignorance to mastery of knowledge. It is tragic to consider this an either-or distinction, and still it must be admitted that, as a class, traditionalists have clung to the order of knowledge and neglected the order of learning, while Progressives have worked on the order of learning, with less regard for the order of knowledge. And still the word "learning" is both a noun and a participle; and, unless the integral meaning of the word in both senses is respected and acted upon, education will be either stunted or psychologically cross-grained, deficient in substance or inefficient in method.

With their scholarly devotion to learning in the objective sense and their conviction of the intrinsic worth and desirability of knowledge, traditionalists take an uncompromising attitude towards the student. It is up to the student, they say, to assimilate knowledge because of its intrinsic desirability, regardless of his personal feelings in the matter. Progressives, on the other hand, arguing that you may lead a person to intellectual wellsprings but cannot force him to drink, stress desire rather than desirability. They make the student's thirst the key factor in education rather than the quenching potential of knowledge. Traditionalists contend further that knowledge is not only desirable but necessary and that the knowledge they present is precisely what young people need for enlightenment, culture, utility, etc. Progressives counter that the dynamic of education is not a need felt by a professor or some other person but a need felt by the learner himself in his own experience. This is the doctrine, sometimes the dogma, of felt needs.

When we indicate the possible combination, the joining of the positive values of the two positions, do we not happily illuminate the role of the teacher? May it not be said that the central task of the teacher (not of the scholar) is to communicate to others the desire, the felt need, for the knowledge which to him is so desirable? The teacher, of course, communicates knowledge (and attitudes and ideals and skills) as well as desire. But no worthy teacher is satisfied to have students accept his instruction passively or reluctantly. He wishes to share not just his "subject" as an inert and detached mass, but also his enthusiasm, his feelings, his own desire for the subject as well, especially because once his students catch his spirit they, too, will be teachers, partners with himself, teachers of themselves and of each other. Traditionalists might well imitate Progressives in giving more attention to the student's appetite, his felt need, for learning.

Progressives are right in underscoring the self-active nature of learning. St. Thomas, before them, even raised the question as to the possibility of teaching, so impressed was he with the necessity of activity on the learner's part. But Progressives are wrong in implying that the thirst for learning has to come from within. The feeling of a need for learning is not always and only a spontaneous impulse within the learner. Desire can be aroused from without; felt need can be communicated. This is the central function of the teacher.

The teacher's role, then, is not to force upon students subject matter that is objectively desirable even though subjectively unpalatable. Nor, on the other hand, is it to play kite-tail to student whims and interests. Rather, it is to bring students to share the teacher's appreciation of the desirability of an area of knowledge. Then the student's own free will takes over and, with continued instructional guidance, normally leads to learning. I say normally, because realism suggests we admit that both Progressive and traditionalist teachers will meet ineducable people—people who are defective not mentally but spiritually, who can be driven to perform academic assignments but whose souls cannot be quickened to intellectual desire. The student is a free being, with his own emotions and his own will, and these can be set against the teacher. If the first step in successful teaching is the communication of a desire for learning, every teacher is doomed to some failure. But the obligation remains in every case for the teacher to do what he can, by appealing to the mind, heart, and will of the student.

If this is a fair analysis of the teacher's role, does it not suggest qualities basic to successful teaching? The scholar, as scholar, is rightly devoted to the mastery and extension of a field of knowledge. We take it for granted that a teacher is first a scholar of sorts; he must have academic competence. What turns a scholar into a teacher?

Great teachers are those who have enthusiasm, who can inspire. What is inspiration but the communication of a desire? And how can desire be communicated if it is not founded on the teacher's sincerity, on his respect for his own knowledge, for his own vocation, and for the student he would teach? This seems central and essential in teaching. Other characteristics that we list when we anatomize the teaching process—sense of humor, friendliness, voice quality, fairness of tests, etc.—are secondary or accidental. We all have known inspiring teachers who were deficient in one or perhaps many of these desirable but nonessential qualities. But it can be doubted if there ever has been a great teacher who lacked any of the sincerities enumerated here. The absence of any of them results in a shallowness, fraudulence, or superciliousness that is plain to the most naive and stands as a block to learning. Learning still may take place, but it will take place in spite of, not because of, the alleged teacher.

Sincerity is a moral quality. If sincerity is the cornerstone of teaching success, is teaching primarily a moral rather than an intellectual activity, as it is usually regarded? Again, sincerity is a quality of the person. Are we, then, to accept the old canard that teachers are born, not made? If sincerity is the cornerstone of teaching success, does this mean that techniques and pedagogical devices are really as vain as has been charged so often? Fortunately we need not give either-or answers to these questions. Education is intellectual, but not exclusively so, as perhaps traditionalists have been inclined to believe. Education is an art, with its proper skills, but besides the skills certain moral attributes are required of the artist.

Before learning there must come the desire for learning. Desire is in the realm of the will, the moral realm. It should not surprise us that an activity which deals so intimately with the "inner man" of other men, as does teaching, has an essential moral dimension. However, the sincerities described here are prerequisites to successful teaching, not guarantees of success. The sincere teacher will be an abler artist if he knows the nature of the learner, his normal levels of interest, the desires that may conflict with the desire for learning, and ways in which the quenching of intellectual desire may be facilitated. Hence, he will need all the skills and pedagogical lore of his profession. Indeed, his very sincerity about his task will lead the true teacher to equip himself as best he can for the performance of his art—the art of communicating desire for learning, the art of building two-way bridges, through human wills to human minds, for the delivery and for the pursuit of knowledge.

84

Teaching Through Stagesetting

GEORGE E. CARROTHERS

Professor emeritus of education, University of Michigan. His article originally appeared in *School and Society* on April 3, 1965.

Why are pupils' actions so unpredictable, even from day to day or hour to hour? Why do they act so well in certain classes or situations and so despicably in others?

The answer to these provocative questions has come to me in clarion clearness on many an occasion while observing teaching in hundreds of schools and classes, from rural elementary schools to graduate courses in universities. We, as teachers, must face the fact that pupils' actions are determined largely by what the teacher does and the spirit of interest, or lack of interest, in which he does his work. Teachers engender pupil responses. It is the teacher, not the pupil, who consciously or unconsciously determines the spirit, the performance, the quality, and quantity of learning.

A friendly, interested, prepared teacher in the classroom, in the laboratory, or on the playing field radiates his interest and enthusiasm. It was no accident that Fielding H. Yost of the University of Michigan was so successful with his football teams or that he was given the nickname of Hurry-Up Yost. He played football from whistle start to whistle stop; others were inspired to do likewise. With the prepared, concerned teacher, work starts on time, whether it be a football game, a lecture, a recitation-discussion, laboratory period, or other activity. The learning situation continues to the end of the period without any calls for order such as are heard frequently in classes taught by firmly entrenched, unionized teachers. The alert, prepared teacher, surrounded by his carefully selected teaching materials, is ready to see that every moment is occupied profitably by every student. Prepared teachers are as desperately needed as prepared medical men. Doctors, teachers, and efficient workmen are not produced by union or other pressure groups.

The pertinent question is, Why do parents permit their children to be taught by the mediocre when better teachers could be secured? Learning, unlike body operations, may be of the worst sort, yet the layman does not detect the difference. This makes it many times more important for school administrators to have the courage to select, promote, and encourage those persons who want to become great teachers. Boards of education ought to support administrators who can and do recognize merit and who are willing to pay salaries up to $25,000 a year.

Schools always will need large numbers of average teachers. They ought to be retained at fair salaries. There is *greater* need for a number of superior teachers to act as leaven for the whole group. Why short-change our children by driving superior teachers out of the classroom in order that they may obtain deserved salaries? Why force teachers into administrative positions for which they frequently are not fitted and for which they often have no desire? A few well paid thoroughbreds in the medical profession are an inspiration to all doctors on the staff. Likewise, teachers are inspired when they find opportunity to associate with teachers who can handle, with success, youngsters who for the time being are missing the way or who can teach effectively several times as many pupils as the average teacher. The most interesting and most helpful course I took during three years of graduate study was taught by a master teacher who nearly always had several hundred students in his classes. Dr. William H. Kilpatrick was a master at setting the stage properly. He knew how to keep all of his students interested and busy from beginning to the end of the semester. A few teachers of high order *can* be discovered and given opportunity to grow. The Kilpatricks, however, are not obtained through time-served promotions or union pressure.

During my freshman year at Indiana University, I took zoology with Prof. Carl Eigemann. He taught as if zoology were the most important subject in the university. He was a student and a collector. His classrooms and laboratories were filled with many kinds of teaching and learning materials. He seemed anxious to have every student become acquainted with the zoological world and to have them "love" it as he did. There never was a dull moment in any of his classes, whether he was lecturing, leading a discussion, or merely walking around the room observing his students at their laboratory tables. No student ever missed a class if he possibly could be present. Dr. Eigemann was a master at teaching through stagesetting.

I recall a similarly effective teaching atmosphere in another teaching field, one in which the teacher was equally competent at securing appropriate responses from all pupils. Mrs. Fred Jeffers, Painsdale, Mich., was teaching a large algebra class one afternoon. She had about 75 pupils in her class, even though she was aware that some so-called teachers insist on the upper limit of 30-40 pupils for high school classes. That was a challenge. The teacher was prepared, even for the varying abilities. At one point, a large boy at the blackboard seemed to have finished the assignment. Mrs. Jeffers stepped quietly up beside him. On ascertaining that he had finished the assignment satisfactorily, she suggested that he go to the other side of the room and see what he could do to help a fellow pupil. The student seemed proud to be asked to serve as an assistant to the teacher. Just then, another pupil had finished the assignment. Mrs. Jeffers asked him whether he would like to try some of the more difficult algebra problems printed in a teacher's journal to challenge teachers. With an alert step, the boy went to a table, picked up the journal, and started to work immediately. The teacher was prepared for any situation. Little wonder that Mrs. Jeffers was retained in that school for 50 years and paid a salary above the average. Schools everywhere are desperately in need of such concerned, skillful teachers.

For my first high school position, I was employed to teach in a Posey County, Ind., school. On reaching the town, I learned that I was to be the entire high school faculty for the rather large high school of three years. It was too late to change, even though I also was to be the township superintendent. The collecting of books and other teaching materials began in earnest at once. That year I taught freshman English, sophomore English, American literature; physical geography, American history, world history; freshman Latin, second-year Latin, third-year Latin (Cicero); beginning algebra, plane geometry, and a third year of advanced algebra and solid geometry— 12 preparations and 12 recitations each day, five days a week. A careful organization was arranged, and pupils were taught how to study and how to be helpful in collecting and using learning materials. At the end of the year, the county superintendent gave state-wide examinations. Every pupil passed. Successful teaching is possible even with large numbers when a person has a liberal arts background, a satisfactory salary, genuine interest in boys and girls, a willingness to make concerned preparation, and loyal community support.

Again and again, we need to ask ourselves seriously why pupils perform as they do. And we need to remember that much of the time they are reacting to the actions of school and community adults. In the auditorium at Rollins College, Winter Park, Fla., I could see from my vantage point on the platform that many students were whispering and showing a lack of respect for the speaker. The man was a nationally known writer, a friend of Pres. Hamilton Holt. Suddenly, the speaker stopped, apologized to the audience, confessed that he was not prepared, and said that if ever asked to return, he would be prepared. He was asked. The next time the speaker was fully prepared. Everyone gave rapt attention. The half-hour passed quickly with not the slightest indication of boredom.

The overwhelming need of schools today is a larger number of great teachers. Society has a fair number of great medical men, great scientists, and great business leaders, each of whom has had opportunity to develop individually without stifling bureaucratic control. These great leaders are showing the way and inspiring others to discover, develop, and live up to their innate possibilities. Schools are desperately in need of larger numbers of inspiring leaders, persons who are interested in becoming effective teachers, persons who are thinking and dreaming of continued study and preparation such as will enable them to inspire their students to stretch themselves mentally to their fullest individual possibilities. The greatest blessing school authorities can confer on the younger generation is to select, encourage, reward, and protect interested teachers. Time-served promotions are suicidal in the extreme.

85

The Teacher in the University

ROBERT F. GOHEEN

President, Princeton University. His article originally appeared in *School and Society* on April 2, 1966, and was based on a speech at the presentation of the E. Harris Harbison Award to eight distinguished college teachers by The Danforth Foundation, Princeton, N.J., Jan. 12, 1966.

The late Prof. E. Harris Harbison probably would be both gratified and embarrassed to find an award for distinguished teaching bearing his name and modestly would disclaim the tributes paid to him. But he would be proud that his Alma Mater was the scene of these ceremonies, for he was a loyal son of Princeton, with a deep appreciation of the tradition of vigorous teaching which goes back to its beginnings. "They proceed not so much . . . by prolix discourses . . . by burdening the memory," one early account of Nassau Hall states, "as in the Socratic way of free dialogue between the teacher and the pupil or between the students themselves. . . . In this manner the attention is engaged, the mind entertained and the scholar animated in the pursuit of knowledge." From those early days under John Witherspoon, through the 19th century with the great impact of Joseph Henry and other worthies, to the legendary "preceptor guys" recruited by Woodrow Wilson, and on down to our time—Princeton has respected great teachers, and benefited greatly from them.

As we honor Jinks Harbison, former Henry Charles Lea Professor of History, together with these eight so worthy recipients of the Harbison Awards for 1966–67, we are giving recognition to how precious a thing in our civilization is good teaching, and we appropriately may ask what it entails. In the educational journals, its definition seems always to elude those who chase to capture and pin it to the dissecting table. This is not surprising. There are many kinds of good teaching for many kinds of teaching situations at many different levels. Attempts to reduce it to a formula are doomed to failure, because there always will be a teacher who will break all the rules and yet be profoundly successful. In other words, it is the good teacher, not teaching in the abstract, that counts.

This is not to say that the art of teaching cannot be studied or its skills conveyed. It is to say that good teaching can never be successfully dealt with in a mechanical way. "Objective criteria" and "scientific evaluations" are attractive slogans to some in the world of education who are uneasy with anything that is not measurable. But such approaches to so complex and personal a thing as good teaching will always fall short.

What is important is the recognition of it. And here we should reject emphatically the proposition that "heresay" is somehow not admissible or legitimate in judging teaching. How, really, do we know that Prof. Harbison was a great teacher? Because of the testimony of hundreds of students and colleagues. I do not doubt that, similarly, the evidence on which the awards are based is partly hearsay; diligently sought, carefully sifted and examined, and yet—hearsay. Much of what we know of the teaching genius, apart from the scholarly work, of other great teachers—Joseph Henry lecturing on electrical magnetism at Princeton, Mark Hopkins on the legendary log, Louis Agassiz in his zoological laboratory at Harvard, or Socrates in the market place—is based on hearsay.

Is this not perhaps another way of saying that the successful teacher is known by the mark he leaves on his students? If so, it is *not* the mark of indoctrination. (Someone recently described the indoctrinal sort of teaching as pouring from a big pitcher into many little pitchers, then via the final examination back into the big pitcher, so that all you have left is a lot of dirty little pitchers—and I am not referring to visual aids.) No, the kind of teaching which is significant at the college or university level—the kind involved in these Harbison Awards—is not indoctrination.

When Louis Agassiz was asked his greatest achievement, he replied that he had taught men to observe. Socrates taught men to question. Each great teacher has his unique way. Yet, more often than not, two particular attributes will be found in the successful teacher. One is an ability to awaken and stimulate delight in the use of the mind. The second is attention to the effort to do so, together with a belief in its value to the student *in his own right*. Certainly, those teachers I have admired most in Princeton (and Prof. Harbison was one) seem to have engendered in their students a pleasure, a joy, a raised awareness, in intellectual activity. Perhaps their students were not always the keenest of observers, or the most skillful interlocutors—but they had discovered the pleasure in following ideas, the satisfaction in discovering where they lead, the lift in the journey that carries beyond the misty flats of one's own experience.

I do not mean that this always comes easily either to student or to teacher. Undertaking to deal seriously with ideas is often a messy, difficult job for the young (even under the best tutelage); and undertaking to deal seriously with ideas is always a demanding, often a lonely, necessity of the teacher (even with the best of students). But vital connections do occur. Somehow the maturity of the teacher gets translated to the students so that they go beyond their years. This was one of the qualities of Dr. Harbison: his *maturity* was manifest, and he conveyed it in everything he wrote and said.

There is another role that the good teacher plays. He is interpreter in the house of learning. Now, the word interpret has several connotations: to explain—to translate—to construe. All involve the making of a connection. This is what the teacher does. He puts the student *in connection* with the problem at hand and leads him to seek and press an engagement with it.

Finally, in the great teacher, no matter how unobtrusively, there will be found strength of conviction. Faulkner, in his Nobel Prize speech, said of the writer: he must "leave no room in his workshop for anything but old verities and truths. . . . Until he does so . . . he writes not of the heart but of the glands." We might say the same of the teacher. In his role of interpreter, his own heart and convictions will come through—subtly and quietly, perhaps, but they will come through.

We are hearing much these days about the bleakness of the impersonal university, the neglect of teaching, and the pressures of research and publication. There is ground for concern, as well as much exaggeration, in these charges. It is the more heartening, therefore, that The Danforth Foundation has taken leadership in recognizing the crucial role of teaching—*i.e.*, the presence and work of good teachers—in higher education. And it is most fitting that the Harbison Awards of The Danforth Foundation should give emphasis to the teacher's concern with the personal dimension in education and the relevance of religious faith to the problems of our age.

Let me mention briefly just three of the many reasons why better teaching must be nourished and sustained on our campuses. One is obvious enough: the rapidly growing number of college and university students. A report of the U.S. Office of Education, Dec. 27, 1965, indicates that enrollments rose 12% over last year's level to a total of nearly 6,000,000, more than double that of a decade ago. The new freshman crop is 18% larger than that of 1964. Every state and territory showed an increase. Place alongside this the fact that the number of college and university teachers being produced (with or without doctorates) is falling far behind these burgeoning figures. The inference is clear. There are going to be proportionately fewer competent teachers to the number of students to be taught. Accordingly, the role of those teachers who can by leadership and contagion encourage and assist others is ever more crucial.

A second compelling argument for doing everything we can to strengthen and enrich the teaching on our campuses grows out of the exploding diversity of knowledge. The house of intellect, once so relatively tidy, has swollen and burst into fragments. As the late Prof. Charles Osgood observed, he who tries to act as if this had not happened is like the man who gave up reading the encyclopedia because he could not follow the story.

Not only in the sciences and the social sciences, but also in the humanities, marked changes are discernible in the materials being studied and the approach to these materials. On the whole, the movement is a healthy one towards basic principles and fundamental analysis, away from mere memory work and dependence upon fixed segments of subject matter; but it does call for more, talented teachers. Rote learning never was much good. Today it is worth even less. The citizen of tomorrow must master the ways of analysis, must search deeply, if he is to cope with the uncertainties and changes of the decades ahead. But this kind of education cannot be offered by second- and third-rate minds using second- and third-hand methods of instruction.

A third reason for stressing the importance of teaching in higher education today is the emphasis and glamor now so widely and strongly attached to research. Please do not mistake me. The quest for new knowledge in the university and the college, too, is vital. On campuses all over the country, the stepped-up range and tempo of research have strengthened and enlivened instruction far more widely than they have deadened or disabled it. In the college or university, research and teaching are two poles of the same magnet; neither has much force without the other. That is what the ideal of the teacher-scholar is all about. But at a time when there are not enough good teachers to go around, and when the supply is falling still farther behind the demand, it is of national importance that such good teachers as we have not be lured or cudgeled away from teaching.

I am concerned here particularly with the drift toward sharply reduced teaching loads in many universities. It seems to me to have gone dangerously far. There is good reason for reducing the teaching duties of men and women with unusual capacities for research or great gifts as lecturers or writers. It enables such people to bring their talents to bear in the best way. All college or university-level faculty members should, as I suggested earlier, have the time for search and inquiry, for scholarship, in their chosen fields of study. What I am dubious about is that by-product of today's intense competition for faculty, wherein part of the lure is a weekly teaching assignment of no more than a few hours—and sometimes none at all. Whether they mean to or not, institutions which go in heavily for this kind of enticement are making the avoidance of teaching a reward and a mark of status in a way which cannot but be harmful to higher education.

I am making no defense of the overly heavy teaching load, which is still too often the rule in some types of institutions. It, too, is at odds with good teaching and brings low returns in students' learning. But, in many of the leading institutions today, the pendulum is toward the other extreme. So much so—that the day may not be far off when legislators or trustees will be inquiring into the budgeting of substantial salaries for college and university faculty members on ridiculously low teaching schedules where there is not the exceptional promise or achievement to justify it. Some embarrassing questions may be asked.

Let this not be taken as a wail of despair. The link between good scholarship and good teaching is strong and will remain so. I also believe that the common sense of America's academic folk will prevail so that good teaching will have its proper place of honor among them. Meanwhile, it falls to all of us to help to keep the balance and preserve the dignity of the teacher-scholar as teacher, not solely as scholar. This cannot be the concern of deans and presidents only, but of departments and individual faculty members. It is precisely there that the battle for effective teaching must be fought and won.

The nation cannot afford to have its best minds apart and aloof from the students thronging our college and university halls. There must be a meaningful connection between them. Woodrow Wilson once said: "America will be great among the nations only in proportion as she finds an adequate voice. . . . Her wealth will not interpret her, or her physical power, or the breadth of her uncounted acres, or anything she has builded; but only such revealing speech as will hold the ear and command the heed of other nations and of her own people. Our thinkers must assist her to know herself." In this same sense, America needs more than ever the men and women at all levels of education—school, college, and university—who will be interpreters to the coming generations, and leave their mark on them: the mark of maturity, of the use of the mind, of thoughtful conviction.

In recognizing this need, and establishing these awards in the name of a great teacher, The Danforth Foundation carries on its tradition of service to the nation and mankind. The eight Harbison Award winners afford us a high and striking example of all that I have been trying to say; and like the Chinese picture, each speaks in himself far more tellingly than all the words one can muster.

86

Thoughts on the Improvement of Instruction

EUGENE STANLEY

Specialist for higher education programs, Advisory Council of Higher Education, Baltimore. At the time his article originally appeared in *School and Society* (Oct. 13, 1956), he was assistant professor of education and acting chairman of the Department of Education, Morgan State College.

Any instructional practices worthy of the name must consider the uniqueness of the individual and necessity of the student having an active role in the teaching-learning processes. This does not mean, however, that the instructor is insignificant. Effective modern education lifts the instructor to a new level of operation, and, in the use of subject matter, to increased proficiency.

The most effective learning occurs when the individual is active in teaching-learning processes. Instead of being manipulated, he should partake in the manipulation of subject matter; instead of being merely "exposed" to an experience, he has an experience. Rather than having an incompleteness filled, he moves to action motivated by a sense of his own incompleteness. Though some would act upon him through patterns of isolated stimulation, he reacts to and with the totality of his environment. The true learning process is experiencing, doing, and reacting. Since he is a goal-seeking, purposeful being attempting to satisfy his needs, activity on his part is an indispensable condition for the fulfillment of those needs. The net result of this activity is an enlarged self, a phenomenon created in the very process of striving to achieve and maintain balance in the midst of fluctuating influences in his environment.

The acceptance of the foregoing statements compels one to take a fresh look at some of the current educational practices. Those instructional processes oriented toward securing the "right" answers, particularly in the realm of the social sciences, are educationally suspect. The authoritative approach to knowledge, whether exemplified in the person of the teacher or the textbook, renders the student a mere pawn in the largest possible game of chess. Such procedures can be reduced to mere routine. When that happens in the classroom, students are exposed to a state of educational debilitation.

The authoritative approach stands to be condemned on a variety of points: the functional value of facts is overlooked; the learner's nature is misconceived; a faulty conception of mind is supported; the development of the inquiring mind is discouraged; the nature of the learning process is misconstrued; concomitant learnings are disregarded; and the potential animation of the teaching-learning processes is destroyed. The challenge, therefore, is to see the potential for true instruction in "wrong" answers submitted by students. Though a response may be incorrect, it is potentially better than no response at all. The student must be encouraged to participate. His contributions are highly revealing, for they permit the instructor to assess the nature and quality of the student's prior experiences. Opportunities are granted for a look into the unique patterns of understandings, conceptions, and insights which serve to distinguish one student from another. Real teaching, therefore, becomes an immediate possibility as one gets *inside* the experience of the learner.

When the instructor gets *inside* the learner's experience, dynamic teaching can begin if certain preliminary considerations are met. The first is that of creating a classroom atmosphere which removes some of the traditional halo of authority from the teacher. Since it is a co-operative enterprise, the teacher's first task is probably that of convincing the students that he is an eager scholar in his field still looking for many of the answers. An essential companion-piece to this point of view is that of assuring the students that the quest for knowledge is a joint responsibility in which all must play a part. The stage is properly set when the student is made to feel that he is a valued member of the group and believes he is capable of making a worth-while contribution to the class projects.

When the teacher knows that he has achieved such a classroom atmosphere, he should then convince the students that he will accept their ideas as working hypotheses to be resolved through the efforts of the class, unless, of course, the ideas are contrary to basic fact.

The teacher who is sufficiently sensitive to the value of these procedures will also recognize the importance of attempting to meet other basic student needs. The need for a sense of belonging, for example, is gratified to a considerable degree by the steps just offered. It certainly could not be met in the classroom if the teacher's practices accented the student's academic infirmities.

Also to be recognized in effective teaching procedures is the need for security and integrity of person. Some indications must be given the student that the subject matter is not more important than his general well-being. Right or wrong in his answer, the sacredness of the personality of the student cannot be violated in successful instruction.

The student shares with his instructor the need for a sense of achievement or mastery. The teacher's deft handling of the student's response can contribute to his feeling some measure of progress, some growth in understanding. As is well known, a bit of carefully dispensed encouragement may prove its own reward in enhanced student achievement.

What can be done with some of these "wrong" answers which we receive so often from students? Much promise may be found in the following suggestions: attempt to secure a precise understanding of the response; examine and verify the plausibility of the response; ascertain the nature of the experiences upon which the response rests; test the logic supporting the response; estimate the conceptual routes essential for modification of the response; encourage wider student participation in the discussion; and guide the discussion toward some consensus of opinion which is as adequate and harmonious as possible.

Understanding the Student's Response

Since communication is truly difficult, the teacher should be sure that the student's response is understood at the outset. Frequently other students can be helpful in this "play-back" procedure. When the responding student agrees that he has been correctly interpreted, then additional progress can be achieved. Note that this inquiry can aid in adding to a student's sense of personal dignity, for when rightly performed he is not put on the defensive and his contribution is accorded status.

Examining and Verifying the Response's Plausibility

The sincere student's response makes "some kind of sense." When the student is offered the opportunity to explain why he gave the answer he submitted, the intelligence of the response is sometimes quite enlightening. It is precisely at this point that one gets a preliminary insight into the nature of the student's organization of his experiences.

Ascertaining the Nature of the Experience Upon Which the Response Rests

Further questions asked of the student may reveal the information desired at this point. A teacher's familiarity with experiences which are normal—and often quite the vogue—for students of a given age group, community, and socio-economic status may also prove beneficial. Once this broader base of cultural participation is grasped, the teacher finds himself nestled confidently inside the student's experience, and the real teaching potential of the situation emerges.

Testing the Logic Supporting the Response

This is an important procedure, for it will reveal the cause-effect sequences the student has established. This step is also of high value, for on occasion the pattern of reflection which supports an answer may prove more significant than the response itself. If the student is enabled to detect an error in his logic in the exchange, there is growth in perception on his part.

Estimating the Conceptual Routes Essential for Response Modification

The instructor now attempts to define again the relationship, if any, of the student's answer to one more appropriate. If, by chance, the student has been led to question his own contribution, skillful teaching can point him in a better direction. The alteration of the student's misconceptions may depend, in part, upon the sequential development of new ideas. However, this is not always true, for a new integration and synthesis may occur inside the learner without the need of external aids.

Encouraging Wider Student Participation

Students can often communicate more effectively with one another than they can with the teacher; they can be mutually helpful to one another. This technique also prevents the teacher from cutting short the dynamics of the interaction. It may add interest to the classroom activity and create an enlarged atmosphere of freedom essential to good instruction.

Guiding the Discussion Toward a More Adequate and Harmonious Consensus

The teacher must make certain that the discussion is getting somewhere. Agreement must be sought and those considerations to which they pertain must be brought to light. It is desirable that all contributions made in the discussion be given the respect and status due them, and conclusions drawn should reflect fully and harmoniously all of the intelligence generated.

Any one of these steps may produce good results. All experienced teachers know of the vast amount of unpredictability which characterizes an atmosphere of free inquiry on numerous occasions. To the dedicated teacher there are few developments which bring more excitement than demonstrable evidence of the growth in perceptions and understanding on the part of students under his leadership. As suggested here, teaching is a labored series of processes, but it is also a labor of love. The classrooms in our schools presided over by animated teachers who obviously enjoy their work hold the key to a safe and secure future for our country and for those ideals which we cherish. Good instruction keeps alive the spirit of inquiry, the zest for freedom which provides the best guarantee we know to combat totalitarian doctrines. The leaders of the next century should be well armed for their responsibilities if they can be taught the value of the free market-place of ideas. Much of this potential can be realized through those teachers who are able to see the instructional potential of "wrong" answers.

87

The Case Method of Teaching

FRANK P. FITZSIMONS

The author was professor of education, Brooklyn College, at the time his article originally appeared in *School and Society* (Oct. 3, 1953). Prof. Fitzsimons is now retired.

The method of teaching in the upper classes of high schools and colleges ought to be thoroughly re-examined and the more realistic approach of the case method of teaching should be considered for its presentation and for its value in analyzing subject matter. The case method of teaching has its basis in a situation or a series of situations to the end of formulating a principle for action.

This well-tempered, objective, mature, and inductive method was introduced in the law school of Harvard University in 1869–70 by Christopher C. Langdell. It was called the "case method." This "new method" of instruction was ridiculed in the early days and contemptuously referred to as "Kit's freshman" or "Langdell's chickens." The older members of the bar insisted that such method would make "case lawyers" unable to argue a legal question unless it was "on all fours" with the case as studied.

Nothing is further from the truth. The case method is bilateral. It displaced the old unilateral lecture and textbook system of instruction, and the student acquired a general view of the law through the pointed analyses of a classroom discussion.

It may be assumed that the case method of instruction in the field of education will be thought to develop "case classroom teachers." Perhaps it is more likely that the case method for the field of education may bring about the secret of effective teaching in teaching teachers how to teach so that the rule of good teaching will be known:

> People must be taught as if you taught them not
> And things proposed as things forgot.

Whether it is law, medicine, theology, or teaching, the persistent rule of procedure in the overt act of skillful teaching can be summarized in the following verse by an anonymous author:

A student of knowledge with tact
Absorbed many answers he lacked;
But acquiring a job
He said with a sob,
"How does one fit answer to fact?"

This, then, is the problem in a situation known as a case and in this method also there may be an answer to the fact, or a summary answer to a number of facts. However, there is a severe discipline of mental acuity in finding the answer to the facts in the problem of a case.

In this method, too, the mind of both teacher and student will become flexible and versatile seeking the "fitting" of the answer to the fact, even though it may be a "case answer." Such procedure also may be beneficial mentally if the case inference solution is hammered out from the facts at hand.

No clearer presentation of the case method of teaching can be found than in the legal education analysis of the American Bar Association in 1894 and reprinted in 28 Am. L. Rev. 709:

1. That law, like other applied sciences, should be studied in its application, if one is to acquire a working knowledge thereof. 2. That this is entirely feasible for the reason that while the adjudged cases are numerous the principles controlling them are comparatively few. 3. That it is by the study of cases that one is to acquire the power of legal reasoning, discrimination and judgment, qualities indispensable to the practising lawyer. 4. That the study of cases best develops the power to analyze and to state clearly and concisely a complicated state of facts, a power which, in no small degree, distinguished the good from the poor and indifferent lawyer. 5. That the system because of the study of fundamental principles, avoids the danger of producing a mere case lawyer, while it furnishes, because the principles are studied in their application to facts, an effective preventive of any tendency to mere academic learning. 6. That the student, by the study of the cases, not only follows the law in its growth and development but thereby acquires the habit of legal thought, which can be acquired only by the study of cases, and which must be acquired by him either as a student, or after he has become a practitioner, if he is to attain any success as a lawyer. 7. That it is the best adapted to exciting and holding the interest of the student, and is, therefore, best adapted to making a lasting impression upon his mind. 8. That it is a method distinctly productive for individuality in teaching and of a scientific spirit of investigation, independence, and self-reliance on the part of the student.

If the word "teacher" is substituted for lawyer, the value of the previous quotation for the field of education is evident. It will be noted that the case method of instruction rejects the idea that the instructor anticipates the course of the discussion in the classroom and seeks to devise ways of guiding or leading students around to what a teacher or some other authority has decided are the most important aspects of the case.

Usually, the guidance of a class discussion sets the wrong attitude or tone at the outset and takes from the student responsibility, because the student must learn to think for himself and to bear the responsibility for his conclusion. Besides, many classes seem now to be a series of bilateral interchanges between the instructor and the individual student, and will not the case method of teaching give a most fitting design of class instruction for a continuance of this pattern of student and teacher behavior?

The case method of teaching should not be a mechanical routine or procedural trick. Indeed, anyone can imitate a trick of class procedure to produce a desired result. There is no technique of teaching which does not reflect one's true self and any kind of synthetic word overlay without varied integral relation between the student and teacher is usually uncomfortable, ineffective, and ridiculous.

It takes time and struggle to reach a stage of thinking to be "case method"-minded and to attain faith and conviction in this sort of approach to teaching. Surely, man must combat and persuade himself before he can combat and persuade others to take up this case method of teaching. It is not a sure-fire way of teaching, but it has the merit of confrontation of a problematic situation seeking a solution that is not trivial, bizarre, but mature in proportion as it is reasonable.

In the case method of teaching procedure, it will be helpful to say: (1) Read the case. (2) Do you see the problem? (3) What is it? (This is the situation "diagnosis.") (4) Who will start or open up the case? (5) What have you said? (6) Did you say what you meant to say? (Critical thinking here.) (7) Summarize your point of view. (8) Any comment from the class? (9) Let us turn back to the initial question of the case to frame the major issue. A lecturette from time to time on some aspect of the case is the only "tell them" method permitted in the case method.

It is rewarding to develop a style of teaching which will be one's own rather than to propound dicta which students are expected to accept with little or with no question. Of course, it is the main objective of all good teaching to achieve student growth, but the teacher, too, must grow in order to bring about student growth. Therefore, there is no better means of stimulating a teacher's mental growth than to analyze case or situation data for presentation in the classroom with the aim of bringing about student and teacher growth in the solution of a case problem.

Then, too, another basic problem of education at the higher levels of high school and college is to develop the student capacity to deal with specific problems in this infinitely complex and continually changing society. No matter what method or technique the teachers use to accomplish this purpose, the personal conviction of the method or technique value must be in evidence to the student. In a word, the teacher, skillful in the art of teaching, must adapt a method or technique in teaching a capacity to see specific problems clearly and to seek solutions with reasonable conclusions.

There is really no stereotyped approach to each case problem in the teaching process. In the main, the student must learn to apply principles, rules, and theories by the test of relevance and the limits to attain "developed" generalizations in a succinct summary for future thinking. It will be helpful to attach social implications to such case solution generalization. This attitude of social reference should be inherent in the case method of teaching at all times. It will give zest to pursue with insight solutions for action instead of merely considering subject matter in its "vacuum" of intrinsic reasonability without social and civic reference.

Classroom activity under the case method of teaching is primarily the student's responsibility. The student's attitude is most important in the case method. In fact, it is the essence of the whole approach in this method to note and, if possible, to correct the withdrawal of the student into silence or over-aggressiveness lest the case method itself becomes one of "casing" the instructor rather than the problem at hand. Any such student attitude of dependence would block any real learning according to the sights of the case method of teaching.

It is essential, therefore, to establish the proper classroom atmosphere with student rapport in the case method of teaching so as not to give the impression that the case method is merely a device to give a "frame of attack" to the student for solving a problem buried in the facts as presented. Such approach would defeat the real purpose of the case method in developing the student's ability to think. Hence, the teacher must keep up his guard not to give a mere counting of the negative and positive points in a problem with the clever word interplay of cause-and-effect relation. Such procedure would create an either-or attitude for the student, and this would be ruinous to the "grays" in the spectrum of the black and white extremes of thinking, because there are facts also in the "grays."

There is an infinite variety of material that can be adapted to the case method of teaching. However, the teacher may find it helpful to confine his thinking of subject matter by simply noting the interactions among his students as well as by appraising the behavior and verbalized expressions among the students as indicative of their attitudes, emotions, values, and opinions. Besides, the teacher, at the early stage of case method presentation, should be careful not to reveal his own viewpoints so as not to condition the student's thinking with his advice or argumentation. Teacher interests too frequently are pressed by his questions to set the mode of class thinking in the beginning of the case method. A good rule for the teacher would be to listen so as to get the student's world of thought in accurate focus in order to use a terminal corrective summary as the solution of the case evolves according to the reactions of the class.

Psychologists have pointed out that learning consists in making modifications in the way the individual perceives the world. It is the function, therefore, of the teacher to seek out any conflict of point of view in the student's mind; look for the pattern block of the student's thinking; focus on what preparatory knowledge the student has; and, finally, create an atmosphere of confidence that the problem can be solved.

In the matter of semantics, in the case method of teaching a blackboard listing of the pivotal case words in order to focus attention on the facts of the case, these blackboard words can be used to initiate the discussion of the case. The whole class should be considered as a social unit in this work. Man is by nature a social animal as Aristotle pointed out over 2,000 years ago. This social emphasis may be considered the mental hygiene aspect of the case method of teaching which is a realistic down-to-earth method for encouraging student social participation in group work. Certainly no person is free to choose intelligently until he is sufficiently disciplined to see the implications of his choice. Does the case method of teaching not do this in a very superior way by reason of the social appraisal of the case in the class discussion?

By way of illustration of the case method of teaching, in conjunction with a situation in the area of method in education, the following case for analysis could be presented:

In a second-grade class in elementary school, the teacher spoke of the circus which came to town. A large picture of a clown was placed in the classroom. The children used this picture as a basis for drawing. Different clothes were colored on the clown in the children's drawing. At the conclusion of the children's drawing, each child was asked to comment on his own picture. Then a class critic was selected to choose the five better pictures from the group. The pupil critic was asked by the teacher to give the reasons for selecting the five better drawings. The pupil critic mentioned that color, size, and evenness (this is really symmetry). . . .

The questions may be: (1) Is this class procedure correct? (2) Is this procedure democratic? (3) Should appraisal criteria be given to the pupil critic? (4) Should the class teacher further evaluate the pictures rejected by the pupil critic?

The following principles from this procedure are: The selection of the class product should be made by the pupil critic rather than by the class teacher in order to set a standard by the class through a democratic procedure of one of the class group. The representative pupil-critic analysis could be used through a democratic selection as a basis of data for further teaching and evaluation by the teacher in a subsequent lesson.

The case method of teaching may be introduced by posing a case or a fact situation, a problem or a difficulty in which there is an opportunity for a teaching analysis; the tuning of questions to solve the problem proposed by the case; the training of students to "see" the implication of the problem;

there should be a class atmosphere for give-and-take discussion with the final compilation of the principle or rule of behavior in a reported solution from the deliberations of the whole class.

Since many viewpoints in the case method of teaching are given and rejected with reasons, the residue from this procedure may be that "truth will out" inevitably. In this, the whole method of the case study is an honest and charitable attempt to appraise all sides of a problem in a pointed pursuit with a designed purpose of seeking a reasonable solution for the "case" of facts at hand.

88

Defining "Discussion"

HARRY RUJA

Professor of philosophy, San Diego State College. At the time his article originally appeared in *School and Society* (July 11, 1953), he was assistant professor of philosophy and psychology.

The renewed interest—especially in the context of nondirective therapy[1]—in discussion as a college teaching method makes it desirable to have a common meaning for the term. There is, however, no such common meaning. "The teacher who reports to his wife, 'We had a good discussion today,'" writes Dean Ward of the University of Chicago, "may mean anything from 'Following my opening remarks (which occupied forty minutes), there were several good and pertinent questions from the floor, all of which I handled rather well,' to 'I hardly needed to say a word, once Smith and Thompson began to argue about immortality.'"[2] No attempt to evaluate the effectiveness of "discussion" procedures can be made, of course, in the face of such ambiguity.

Axelrod has recently distinguished four discussion methods as follows:[3]

1. *The lecturette.*—Here the instructor sets the problem, explains its significance, relates it to other problems, and asks for a solution. If a student proposes a solution, the instructor evaluates it. If the proposed solution, in the instructor's judgment, is not satisfactory, the instructor meets such student criticisms to his solution as are presented. In such a situation, students expect the instructor to "know the answers," and the instructor serves as a source of information (to the best of his ability).

[1] *See* C. R. Rogers, "Client-centered Therapy" (Houghton Mifflin, 1951), especially pp. 384–428; and M. J. Asch, "Nondirective Teaching in Psychology: An Experimental Study," *Psychological Monographs* (1951), LXV.
[2] F. Champion Ward, in J. Axelrod, B. S. Bloom, B. E. Ginsburg, W. O'Meara, and J. C. Williams, Jr., "Teaching by Discussion in the College Program," p. v. (University of Chicago Press, 1949).
[3] J. Axelrod, "The Technique of 'Group Discussion' in the College Class," *Journal of General Education,* II (April, 1948), 227–237.

2. *Recitation.*—Students respond to questions put to them by the instructor. The instructor chooses those questions which will lead to the "correct" answers. Here again the authority of the instructor is assumed, and the major responsibility for directing the "discussion" rests with him.

3. *Group conversation.*—Any topic is discussed which any student broaches and in any manner as he may desire and for as long as he wishes to continue doing so. The instructor may suggest topics or may limit discussion of a topic, if in his judgment it is too extraneous to the central concern of the group. Mostly, however, his role is passive: he serves as chairman of (or participant in) a "bull session," but does little more.

4. *Group discussion.*—At the beginning of each discussion period, some student summarizes progress to date. If a new topic is to be considered, the instructor presents it to the group asking the students to consider its significance. With his help they list subtopics relevant to the main topic. Then discussion of the subtopics gets under way. A student is asked (or volunteers) to formulate a hypothesis. To ensure understanding, the instructor rephrases it or asks another student to do so. The instructor asks a second student whether he agrees—if so, why, and if not, why not and what he has to offer in its place. If the second student offers an alternative, the instructor may seek to distinguish it from the original proposal or may ask a student to do so.

The role of the instructor is to enlist student participation in the analytic process. He seeks to minimize diffuseness; he participates in the identification of the problem and subproblems; and he contributes evaluations.

Helpful in many ways as this classification is, some overlapping and omission are present. For example, does not an instructor frequently speak haphazardly? Do not, then, methods 1 (the "lecturette") and 3 ("group conversation") sometimes have greater affinities than 2 and 4? What, indeed, is haphazard? May the instructor in 4 really have misanalyzed the problem so that the points his class (under his direction) have listed as germane to the topic may not be so and others which are germane may have been omitted? Who shall judge whether a "bull session" (method 3) is so haphazard? It may deal directly (and not always subtly) with matters of deep concern to the participants (*e.g.*, sex), while a carefully structured discussion (method 4) may deal with superficialities and trivialities.

Method 3 is uncontrolled group discussion and Method 4, instructor-controlled discussion. A third possibility is neglected: group-controlled group discussion. Here, the instructor does not pose the problem; the students do. He asks only: "What shall we consider today?" Students propose solutions on their own initiative and evaluate them if evaluation is felt by them to be called for. The instructor's role is to reflect the content and feelings of student comments so that students may be able to see more clearly what they are saying and how they feel.

The omission and overlapping occur in Axelrod's classification because he has used a double basis for classification. He began by classifying methods in terms of who does the talking. (In Method 1, the instructor does most of the talking; in Methods 3 and 4, the students do most of the talking; in Method 2 there is approximately equal division of the talking opportunities.) But at the end, he is distinguishing methods in terms of the structure of the discussion. Thus Methods 3 and 4 are highly similar to one another except that the former has virtually no structure while the latter has one imposed by the instructor.

In another place, Axelrod (with colleagues) expounds a scheme which uses degree of student participation as its *fundamentum divisionis*.[4] This expresses itself in a six-point continuum:

1. The student listens to the instructor expound a point.

2. The student asks questions in order to clarify in his own mind what the instructor has said.

3. The student challenges the instructor's statements.

4. The student propounds his own solution to a problem and has it approved or corrected by the instructor; if corrected, he listens to the instructor's reasons for modifying or rejecting.

5. The student propounds his own solution to a problem and is led by the instructor to elaborate and to defend it against attack, to relate it to other ideas, and to modify it, if necessary, in the light of the attacks.

6. The student participates in a group effort in which the tasks in step 5 are performed by other students as well as by himself.

A somewhat simpler approach is to classify in terms of who does the talking: who asks the questions, and who answers them? (To be sure, many classroom sessions deal with questions no one has asked nor wishes to ask nor is likely to ask. These we may perhaps dare to ignore.)

1. If the instructor asks the questions and answers them, we have the typical lecture situation.

2. If the instructor asks the questions and the students answer them, we have Axelrod's "recitation" method.

3. If the students ask and the instructor answers, we have what might be called a "reverse recitation" method. Often the time following a lecture labelled "discussion period" is spent in this way.

4. If the student asks and answers his own questions, we have the epitome of "discussion." The classroom is "student-centered," and learning is non-directive or self-directive. The method implies a maximum involvement of the participants both emotionally and intellectually.

Whether such involvement actually occurs is a proper subject for experimental investigation. But no experimentation is likely to be fruitful which employs unclear concepts. This paper has sought to perform this propaedeutic function of clarification.

[4] J. Axelrod, *et al., op. cit.,* p. 24.

89

Should Colleges Encourage Research and Writing?

CLYDE V. MARTIN

The late Clyde V. Martin was assistant professor of education, Long Beach State College, at the time his article originally appeared in *School and Society* (Oct. 25, 1958).

College administrators often seek to impress faculty members with the view that research and writing "interfere" with effective teaching. Time consumed by these activities is pictured as time that should have been used in classroom preparation. It is frequently asserted, in substantiation, that research experts and writers are more often than not poor teachers, presumably because their interests do not center upon the classroom. Moreover, it is said, there are large numbers of competent college teachers who never have published anything. We all recognize the assertion, too, that it is in the higher learning where the art of teaching reaches its lowest ebb.

The writer contends that research and writing serve to *reinforce* the college faculty member's teaching efforts rather than to compete with them. This contention is based on several points.

Students consider an instructor's knowledge to be relatively authoritative when the latter has published a substantial amount. They respond with a conscientious, reflective attitude toward their studies. High-calibre graduate programs, especially, demand the presence of faculty members who are recognized scholars.

One does not set down his views for publication lightly. A strong case can be made for the dictum, "Writing maketh an exacting man." The writer would urge, despite various popular psychological contentions to the contrary, that convictions and attitudes, habits and judgment, facts and concepts developed in one area of study are reflected broadly in a person's behavior.

A professor's *written* formulations influence his *spoken* formulations. The research and writing a professor does thus serve as effective modes of preparation for his classroom presentation. They are his natural allies, intellectually and psychologically, adding at once to the depth and breadth of his subject-matter grasp and to the dynamics of his instruction.

College teachers tend to allow their knowledge of subject matter to fall behind. It is a function of research to vitalize teaching by rendering it up to date. Wide-awake students react to few things more readily than being apprised of the "latest findings" in a field. They like instructors who are current.

It seems singularly appropriate in the case of instructors who are teaching "research" courses that they themselves be active investigators. Should we not be dubious as to the wisdom of instructors teaching the intricacies of research and writing if they themselves are relatively inexperienced (and seemingly disinterested) in these pursuits?

For run-of-the-mill students a dog-eared educational offering is sufficiently mystifying. The dull are lost to the cause in any case. But what of the gifted? We ought not to be satisfied to educate by and for mediocrity. The time is overdue for giving the bright student a break, for justly honoring America's natural intellectual gifts. If our colleges are adequately to challenge the brilliant student, instructors must exemplify the inquiring mind.

The learned men and women who comprise our college faculties should be speaking out in today's troubled world. Where faculty members possess knowledge which stands to benefit a wide audience, it is their duty to set forth their views in the public print. The responsibility of college instructors does not end with the classroom.

The college teacher tends, quite understandably, to specialize. Research and writing which deliberately seek concatenations and applications in diverse fields aid markedly in vitalizing his instruction.

Finally, the college faculty member is often interested in obtaining a research grant or foreign teaching assignment. His success in such quests often depends upon the quantity and quality of his writings.

90

Of Students, Professors, and Computers

CAMERON FINCHER

Associate director, Institute of Higher Education, University of Georgia. His article originally appeared in *School and Society* on March 4, 1967.

The much-publicized student protest at the University of California at Berkeley has become the most discussed event in American higher education. It has produced an inordinate amount of chittering, but there is still at the present time no indication of any outcome other than noise. The seemingly incessant references to the Berkeley crisis, student revolts, and campus demonstrations have spawned little in the way of intelligent criticism and virtually nothing in the way of adequate interpretations.

If we listen to the innumerable critics and analysts of the Berkeley problem, we receive a series of vignettes, half comic opera and half melodrama. An endless parade of explanations is apparently circling the block, so what comes after is merely what went before. We are told that students are in revolt because education has been dehumanized, depersonalized, automated; the students are in protest because they have no personal contact with the better teachers on campus, that they are excluded from the corridors of scholarship, that Mark Hopkins has deserted his end of the log; the students have risen because their individuality is being stifled by punchcards fed into a computer; they are no longer taught—they are processed.

That the Berkeley crisis has been much ado about nothing is not the contention made here. Rather, the contention is that the plethora of analyses and interpretations of the event has given rise to more myths than they have dispelled. The rash of explanations and interpretations are further tragic in that they have obfuscated rather than clarified a number of issues which existed prior to the student protest movement and which still need clarification.

Perhaps the issue that has been most obfuscated by the clamor over student protests is the changing role of the college faculty member. Vehement criticism of college teaching comes at a time when the role of the college instructor is undergoing extensive reorganization. In reacting to the criticism, it is imperative that college administrators do not permit the critics to impose upon the college an outmoded concept of the faculty member's role and functions.

The traditional conception of the successful college teacher is one in which the teacher is articulate and inspiring. Facility in expression, felicity of style, and an ability to raise the sights of students evidently weigh heavily in this conception. The primary function of the teacher is to convey to the student something of the love and mastery of subject matter that the teacher has gained from years of scholarship and broad-ranging experience.

Implicit in the notion of an inspiring teacher is the concept of leisure and intimate contact. The teacher has the time to become acquainted with the student, and the friendships born in class are continued throughout life. In brief, this conception of the good teacher is charming and wholesome, but it is mythical. In a day when higher education was "for gentlemen only," this conception of the teacher may have been a possibility, even if a rare one. In a day when education must serve highly diverse and pragmatic objectives, it is, at best, possible only at the graduate level in certain fields of inquiry.

There are numerous reasons why the traditional model for teaching will no longer suffice. One of these is the increasing distance between the scientist-scholar and the entering college freshman. The implications of the explosion of human knowledge in the past quarter-century are only vaguely understood by the majority of people and even less so by some of education's critics. The modern scientist or scholar, if he deserves the title at all, is at least eight years of higher education removed from the entering freshman. If the scientist or scholar continues to expand his own horizons and to grow and to develop professionally, as he is expected to do, he is receding rapidly from the entering freshman. To suggest that the scientist or scholar slow down while the freshman catches up is to suggest stagnation.

Just why the student is so desperate for dialogue with his professor has not been made clear by any of the critics. The student may often feel that his personal, social, or academic problems could be easily solved if he could but sit down and discuss them at length with an understanding faculty member. This may well be true, but it does not lessen the confusion between catharsis —the reduction of anxiety through talk— and the actual solution of problems.

Discussion of the student protest movement obfuscates matters further in that it has been so frequently cast in terms of a conflict between teaching and research. The issue is posed as if research and teaching were irreconcilable, and we are led to believe that professors can conduct research only at the expense of the student's education. To contend this is to assume that the student is incapable of learning without the continuous attention and assistance of the teacher. It smacks of a theory of education in which knowledge is finite and the student's faculties are developed through catechistic dialogue with his mentor.

Should the issue of research versus teaching be recast as a question of who should learn in the college, the faculty or the students, the answer is, of course, obvious—both should learn. One may seriously ask, then, if the anti-research attitude of so many vociferous critics is not, in fact, another upsurge of anti-intellectualism. To blame research for the Berkeley situation is to press hard, indeed, for a scapegoat.

To contend also that instruction at the undergraduate level suffers from an overemphasis on research is to assume that teachers are born, not made, and that for every faculty member conducting research one good teacher is lost. That many faculty members are neither good teachers nor good researchers appears not to have been mentioned. That good researchers are good teachers is definitely implied, however, and time spent in the laboratory or library by the faculty member is believed to be stolen from the student. One suspects that most critics have not taken graduate work and are unaware that poor teaching is as evident at the graduate level as the undergraduate.

The issue of research versus teaching is not a suitable leg on which to stand as a critic of higher education. There is no issue if one concedes that it would be to the advantage of society for each teacher to teach the students who can best learn from him. This implies that the research scientist or scholar who is laboring in a particular vineyard can teach best those students who are not too far behind, those who can see the relation between the faculty member's current research and the field of knowledge in which both teacher and student are interested. If this means that the best scientists and scholars will teach only graduate students, then so be it. To ask that the creative scientist conduct research at one level but teach at another is to induce further schism in higher education—not reduce it.

Just why computers should become the villain of the plot is not at all clear. Yet, for some inexplicable reason, there is a prevalent belief that the computer serves to depersonalize the individual through some strange process of transubstantiation and that the student becomes a mere card with holes punched in it. Criticisms of the use of computers appear to rest on the unquestioned tenets that oral communication is better than non-oral communication, that decisions are actually made by machines rather than people, and that an individual can convey information better if present in person. Each of these beliefs ignores the simple truth that most data processing methods actually are efforts to preserve the individual in a mass society and, at the present time, appear to be the only way in which the same kinds of information traditionally gathered about the individual can still be gathered and processed. A cogent argument can easily be devised to contend that the computer permits more of an individualized consideration of the student than the so-called personal interview. An interviewer can gather massive data about the individual, but there is no necessity that the information be applied in any way to the solution of the student's problems, and there certainly is no guarantee that the interviewee will be treated in a more humanistic or personal manner. Where human relations or interview rapport are concerned, an aloof, impassive interviewer can be as mechanistic as any computer. In all seriousness, one could argue that the computer is more "democratic" because its processing of information is not subject to the caprice so evident in humans. Having told the college administrator or faculty member all about his personal situation, the student can never know what information is stored in the central nervous system of the interviewer and which facts will be retrieved for making decisions affecting the student. That interviewers, regardless of well-meaning intent, are subject to quirks of memory, faulty recall, and even simple mistaken identity should be evident to all students of introductory psychology.

There are good reasons to question the use of computers in education, but they are not the reasons given by critics. The major shortcoming of computers and other data processing equipment may be that they actually perpetuate the errors of judgment so pervasive in traditional methods of student assessment and evaluation. By using a model of the traditional decision maker, data processing techniques merely may permit on a grandiose scale what has been occurring to a lesser degree all the time. There is a definite possibility that computers will be used merely to incorporate more and more information about the individual without seeking means of testing either the relevance or the interaction of the information gathered. A faulty decision based on a hundred facts rather than three or four is still a faulty decision and just as consequential for the individual concerned.

The question, therefore, is not whether to use computers—but whether to continue outmoded treatments of the individual. The limitations of the computer are the limitations of the human mind. Computers and other data processing equipment can do only what the human mind can do. The rapidity with which data are processed does not alter the fact that the same information is still being gathered and still being treated in the same old manner. The significance of the computer for education is the challenge it presents in devising new methods of administrative, instructional, and advisement uses.

Administrative uses of computers and data processing equipment are perhaps more easily visualized than instructional or evaluative applications. Basic to administrative decisions and actions are a great number of routine clerical tasks which the computer can readily handle. The innumerable man-hours consumed by scheduling classes, organizing courses, registering students, and recording course grades can be greatly reduced by proper use of data processing methods. These, however, are tasks of obvious burden, and, while students may bemoan the fact that they must fill out various forms in computer language—that is to say, in some form that has been precoded so as to permit conversion to punchcard or tape—most can understand the convenience or necessity of doing so. Indeed, there is good reason to believe that most students will quickly welcome the use of data processing methods if their use means faster registration, better scheduling of classes and course-work, and quicker reporting of final grades.

It is in the area of computer use for hitherto "personal" tasks and functions, such as instruction and evaluation, that students may balk at the intrusion of mechanized methods. Yet, the fields of instruction and evaluation are exactly the fields in which the use of computers may offer the best service to students and to the over-all purposes of education. These are areas in which the surface hardly has been scratched insofar as creative or constructive uses of the computer are concerned. They are also the areas in which resistance will necessitate that suitable groundwork be laid or that time be taken to prepare students, faculty members, and the general public for the applications of computer technology. In brief, it will be all the more important that the public understand that computers are of use in these areas because they can perform faster and more efficiently the same tasks that are now being performed by the human instructor.

Methods of programmed instruction have demonstrated quite clearly that students can learn without oral explication or lectures delivered in person by the teacher. They capitalize on the long-established psychological principle that students vary in the rate with which they assimilate information, and that students can learn in a situation where they set their own individual paces. They especially demonstrate that students need not be coerced or driven in order to learn. One rightly may suspect that programmed instruction is merely the introduction of technology into the formal learning situation and involves nothing in the way of learning principles that psychologists have not known for 30 to 50 years. The so-called technological revolution that is taking place in education is merely the application of certain principles derived and clearly established by another generation of psychologists.

No one rightly can claim that programmed instruction is the "best" way for students to learn. Indeed, if 60 years of research into the psychological principles of learning have established any final conclusion, it should be that there is no single best way to instruct or to teach. To the contrary, we must conclude that students can learn under almost any condition imposed upon them—a matter so much the better for civilization. The point, therefore, is not whether students can learn under this condition or that type of instruction but, rather, under which conditions and under which methods of instruction can which students learn which subject matters or skills more effectively? This, in a nutshell, is the question for all concerned with education to tackle.

If the majority of those involved in "the nation's largest business" can agree that the search for more effective means of instruction and more meaningful ways of evaluating student performance is a worthy project for our generation, an invitation to the computer would definitely seem in order. We would be foolish, indeed, to look to computer technology for all the answers or anything remotely resembling a final answer. What we can do is to use the methods of computer technology for the assistance they can provide, keep our systems of inquiry open, and stand ready to recognize failure when we stumble over it. If our educational system has survived the errors of past generations, the least that we can expect of our own is a willingness to try new methods that promise so much in the way of accomplishing the seemingly impossible task to which we are committed—the education of a nation's people according to their abilities and their interests.

The advent of computer technology will neither solve all the problems of education nor eliminate the need for education. What computer methods can accomplish is the provision of more effective methods of performing some of the tasks of drudgery that are inevitably involved in the process of education. If properly utilized, computer technology may literally free college instructors and teachers for the tasks they have so long professed to be their proper function. In other words, the teacher may actually establish a learning relationship with the student and achieve a learning situation in which the student can learn to think critically, to define meaningful problems, to analyze and interpret, to comprehend and apply principles and methods that he derives through his own forms of investigation, and to evaluate not only his own performance in a course of instruction, but the values and standards of his society.

Computer technology may permit us to accomplish what we have long professed to do in the area of student advisement. It may permit us to consider the student's individual objectives and expectations, to select a suitable combination of courses, to devise a workable schedule, and to provide a differential program of educational experience. In short, it may actually permit us to treat the student as the individual he would become.

If the computer can relieve the instructor or teacher of the tasks of scoring, grading, recording, and reporting, classroom instruction will not be depersonalized. To the contrary, most instructors would readily welcome relief from such clerical tasks and seek to use the time for promoting further learning on the student's part rather than less.

If, on the other hand, the student can acquire from other sources the information he has sought from the teacher, he will welcome the opportunity—provided his contact with the teacher can be spent to a better advantage by developing higher-level skills of analysis, synthesis, interpretation, and evaluation. Then, and only then, can the student enter into an intellectual dialogue with the teacher. If the student perceives the teacher's role as one of facilitating learning rather than transmitting information, both the teacher and the student will enjoy their respective tasks more. In short, the teacher can actually teach and the student can actually learn. A great deal of pretense on the part of both can be dropped and the educational level of the nation raised immeasurably.

PART **V**

The Student

From the New Youth to the "Forgotten Man"

91

The New Student in the Old College

EDWARD D. EDDY

President, Chatham College. His article originally appeared in *School and Society* on March 24, 1962, and was based on an address to the Ohio Association of Women Deans, Administrators, and Counselors, Akron, Oct. 27, 1961.

The advertising campaign in behalf of American colleges has posed the question: "When he's ready for college, will college be ready for him?" The question is directed to an enrollment crisis five to 10 years from now. A rephrased query is more important today: "When he has entered college, is college ready for him?" Unfortunately, there is only one realistic answer. It is a flat, honest, and perhaps cruel "No." The great majority of American colleges and universities are not ready for the kind and quality of student who is now knocking at the campus gate.

In the past two to three years, the students have changed faster than the colleges. During the '50's we could accuse the students of being lethargic and apathetic. The accusation then was a just one. Today it is a far more telling accusation of the colleges themselves.

Most colleges are not prepared for the new student. Far too many faculty members and administrators cling to tradition and ignore the rapidly rising level and the substantially changed attitude of American youth. Our colleges are in grave danger of short-changing both the students and the society they serve.

Vested interests on every campus prevent recognition of the obvious. Established customs, long-standing departmental and administrative structure, and sentimentalized traditions protected by alumni keep the colleges from responding with vigor and enthusiasm to the vigor and enthusiasm of the new students. The interest of the youngster who is ready for something new in the way of learning is quickly dampened by the self-oriented faculty member who sees a threat in change and resists it out of apprehension.

The so-called college admissions crisis has done a beautiful job of scaring American youth. In our readiness to prepare for a flood of youngsters beginning in 1964, we have succeeded in changing the attitude of the youngster of today. These students have a far greater appreciation of and regard for higher learning. The changed attitude has resulted in their readiness to be challenged deeply and consistently.

Many colleges have found that they must write ahead to ask visiting lecturers not to popularize their presentations, not to talk down and thus to underestimate their audiences. These are students who are willing to reach for the stars, even though they cannot yet understand the universe.

The failure of the colleges to respond to the new student has an amusing as well as disturbing aspect. For generations, college faculties have said that this is what they want. They have pleaded for vital, alive, and ardent young people to populate the campuses. Now they are here—but apparently the colleges do not know what to do with them. The time of fulfillment of faculty dreams has arrived, but faculty members are not ready to wake up. The alleged apathy seems to have boomeranged.

What is reported here is not true of every student, of course, just as it is not fair to label all college students as either liberal or conservative. But even if it be true of a minority, that minority is so fast growing as to become soon the dominant and vociferously dissatisfied group. Tomorrow's student is here today, but he is enrolled in yesterday's college.

What are the possible courses of action and reaction? How should the American college or university respond to the new student?

First, there are obvious courses of action which should not be taken. When faced with a sudden shift in the middle of the game, the temptation is great to recall the cards and reshuffle. In other words, the temptation is great just to shift the present program into higher gear and to make standards more rigid.

The new student already has been caught by some of these excesses. Witness the heavy reliance on—and thus preoccupation with—College Board scores. On one campus recently, until the situation could be rescued, freshman week almost turned into a hysterical comparison among the freshman students of individual scores which now are made known to each student by the College Board.

But students are not just score-happy before college. The near hysteria continues through the undergraduate years as each marking period looms and passes. An increasing number of students look forward to applying to "a good graduate school" and are conscious of their record as never before. More and more, undergraduate education is viewed as a necessary, almost evil stepping-stone toward the "real" process of education at the graduate level.

The typical response of the colleges is exactly what it should not be. Few faculty members make a sincere effort to change the content and method of the course to meet the new level. Few take a hard look at the total curricular offerings. Instead, longer assignments are handed out and the same curve in the grade scale is maintained. When the president announces at the opening faculty meeting that "this is the best class ever to enter our college," 500 pages of required reading are added almost automatically to each week's assignments.

Many college officials respond, too, by becoming more and more intolerant of individual deviation. We seem to have swallowed our own propaganda aimed at the mid-'60's. Some deans, for instance, honestly believe that they can hold students to a trouble-less conformity by mentioning the growing lines in front of the admissions office and cautioning the noncon-formist that 10 others are out there prepared to take his place. In the process, of course, the dean probably has killed whatever spark of creativity led the student away from the mass and to the dean's attention.

This growing internal crisis in higher education makes obvious one long-needed course of action. Institution by institution, colleges must buckle down to a realistic examination of the essential nature of the academic community as it could and should be in the setting of each campus. Both faculty members and administrators must be brave enough and selfless enough to discover again the true academic community in which group endeavor is balanced by individual creativity.

The conclusion is also obvious: It is high time to get rid of the trappings and trivia of traditional college life. It is time to strip the college down to what it exists for in the first place. Then—and only then—will higher education be worthy of the new student in the '60's.

This means taking a sharp look at what the college actually is, in comparison to what it pretends to be. For instance, colleges can stop the nonsense about pretending to act *in loco parentis*. They can stop telling students that "we will regard you as adults" and then build little walls to keep the children confined. They can stop telling parents that every little need will be satisfied and every comfort earnestly provided.

Today's student is sufficiently adult to merit the freedom which ought to come with life at the college level. The great majority of students will meet every expectation if given the chance, free from the prenatal cord which now strangles rather than nurtures.

Indeed, on many campuses the students are taking the intelligent lead without waiting for the college. They are the ones who have given the ax to the junior proms, the useless little clubs, and the meaningless meanderings and social gatherings. They have allowed to expire the organizations which meet to elect officers to revise the constitution in time to elect new officers, and so forth *ad nauseam*.

Now is the time for the colleges to step in and help the students. The initial introduction to campus life is a good place to start. If college faculties honestly believe that the business of college is the business of learning, then let them demonstrate this belief in the publications furnished freshmen before they enter college (which are read so avidly and frequently swallowed at face value) and in the activities scheduled for entering students during their first week on the campus.

This may mean cutting out the picnics and the rallies and the chummy little get-togethers, and, instead, sending the freshmen off promptly to the business of learning in the classroom. It is no longer defensible to keep the eager student from attending class while exhausting him with the trappings of campus life.

After orientation, the next step is to attack with vigor the entire experience of the freshman year. For a great many students today the freshman year is nothing but repetition and disappointment. College faculties know this to be true. It is time to stop talking about it and begin planning for something quite different and entirely challenging. A start can be made, for instance, by listening to what the freshmen themselves say about their first encounter with higher education. How a student receives his education, and the attitude he takes toward that "how," conditions substantially what he receives in the form of education.

The student is ready for a lot more than he is given credit for, partly because of a change in thinking about the necessity of higher learning and partly because of substantial improvement in the quality of his preparation. In many ways, the high schools have left the colleges far behind. The concept of the freshman year is based on a high school education which, for the most part, no longer exists. At Chatham College, for example, when the present seniors were freshmen, 29% passed a language exemption examination on the basis of their high school language work. This past fall, three years later, 49% of the entering class passed the same examination.

In the freshman year, as well as throughout the entire curriculum, colleges cannot afford to do anything less than to rip out without mercy the repetitious, the unnecessary, and the lock-step. If college officials are honest, they will realize that all of campus life needs a thorough overhauling. The American high school is now offering—in all its gory messiness—what used to be encountered in collegiate living. The over-emphasis on football, the marching bands, the drinking parties, the steady dating, and the endless line of prom queens are all flourishing at the junior and senior high school level. Let those who are in the colleges go to work on something different for the present-day student. This means beginning all over again and finding a new rationale, a new justification beyond custom and tradition, for the various extra-class activities on a college campus.

The present and potential growth of the live-at-home community college presents a special challenge to the residential institutions. If a student can receive just as good an intellectual experience by stripping college life almost to the bare essential of attending class, then residential colleges have some thorough soul-searching to do. They must make college living a genuinely important experience in all its phases or stop making false claims.

The courage to undertake the kind of reassessment proposed here demands college officers who are willing to lead and not merely to preserve. Unfortunately, the trend is not in the right direction due to an over-professionalization in college administration. And over-professionalization means protectionism rather than co-operative progress.

In the first half of the 20th century, college administration dropped from the hands of scholars who were specialists in academic disciplines into the hands of administrators who are specialists in methodology. The rapidly growing number and range of professional organizations in education confirm the process of specialization.

First, the personnel deans spent time trying to find their place in the academic sun. Then the directors of public relations began to cluster and worry about their status. This was followed by the directors of student unions. And right now there is a similar and potentially more dangerous movement among the professional fund-raisers. This is a highly disturbing trend for unified academic administration. Too often the members of these groups fail to realize that true prestige comes from essential contributions to the basic work of higher education and not from posture, place in the hierarchy, or size of budgets and offices.

To be worthy of the new student, the entire college must share a sense of purpose in the academic community which provides unity in means as well as ends. The whole experience of college life will not be a totality for the student if those who set the course are not unified. In the light of the hopes and aims of the new student, the only justifiable rallying ground is found in an honest answer to the question of why the college exists in the first place. By no means does all of this imply a kind of sweat-shop intellectualism. Nor does it imply abandonment of the total education of the individual, but only finding new ways to meet new demands of the new student.

The colleges must return, in Woodrow Wilson's terms, to a mode of association, to a "home for the spirit of learning" which makes them more than a scattered collection of prestige-seeking, status-aspiring individuals. And that mode begins with unity in purpose and process; that home begins with those who are the permanent inhabitants.

Failure to respond in unity to the new student will cripple not only him, but every high purpose which a college or university serves. Success will bring about the realization of the great potential for human good which now lies hidden within the youngster who earnestly seeks higher learning, within the college, and, hopefully and humbly we add, within each who seeks to serve both the scholar and scholarship.

92

Student Protest and Commitment

NATHAN M. PUSEY

President, Harvard University. His article originally appeared in *School and Society* on Dec. 11, 1965, and was based on a baccalaureate address, Harvard College, June 15, 1965.

A number of commentators already have pointed out that, viewed in perspective, the student demonstrations and disturbances which broke out on so many campuses in 1964–65 were less novel than at first appeared. For example, Harvard has been involved in student protests from her very beginning. Cotton Mather spoke of the "ungoverned youths in their ungovernableness" who made a travesty of everything President Hoar said or did in the 1670's. There have been "young plants turned to cudweeds" (to use Mather's phrase) throughout Harvard history. And in addition to mere disturbances, there have been very serious student "rebellions," as Prof. Samuel E. Morison calls them without equivocation in his *Three Centuries of Harvard*. These occurred in the 1760's and again in the early 19th century. Prof. Morison did not pursue the theme thereafter, but many still alive can continue the story and testify from personal experience that disturbances and riots have had a longer life among us than our Tercentenary historian's necessarily brief treatment might suggest.

One example will illustrate the kind: Speaking of methods used before non-violence had been heard of, Prof. Morison says of the Class of 1823 that it was "uncommonly rowdy." He says it indulged in "battles in commons, bonfires and explosions in the Yard, cannonballs dropped from upper windows, choruses of 'scraping' that drowned tutors' voices in classrooms and chapel, and plots that resulted in drenching their persons with buckets of ink and water." This particular disturbance began as a mere "demonstration," but it quickly turned into a "rebellion" when one of the original demonstrators, who had been apprehended through the perfidy of a student informer, was expelled. Upon this provocation, a considerable number of students swore an oath that they would leave the College until the expelled prankster had been reinstated and the hated informer had been deprived of his Commencement part. It is clear that a matter of high principle was involved, but the faculty (which at Harvard has had responsibility for student discipline from as far back as anyone can remember) was not impressed. Not only did they not concede the demand, but, completely unintimidated by this particular show of undergraduate intransigence, went on to expel 43 members of a class of 70 almost on the eve of commencement; and among those expelled was a son of John Quincy Adams, sixth President of the United States and first president of the Harvard Alumni Association.

An even more bitter family conflict occurred during Pres. Quincy's administration in 1834. In this episode, students were brought to their breaking point by what they considered the excessively harsh—it would appear now, the almost senseless—teaching methods of a particular member of the faculty. So they protested. But the other members of the faculty sided with their beleaguered colleague, and, facing up to the student attack, quickly voted to expel a number of the most vociferous protesters. This action of theirs, not surprisingly, was followed by more protest, at first merely by petition, but soon by increasingly severe acts of violence. In the end, the matter got completely out of hand and culminated at long last in the expulsion of the entire sophomore class. Repercussions from this rebellion echoed long in Harvard history. I myself have discovered, in talking to grandchildren of some of those expelled at that time, that the episode is not forgotten. Nor have Pres. Quincy or his faculty even yet been forgiven.

I should like to believe that we at Harvard have learned from these and other such harrowing episodes in our past; and that were new conflicts now to break out among us (as they almost certainly will), that because of past experience we could be relied on, from all sides, to confront new troubles with at least a modicum of understanding, charity, tolerance, and restraint. Surely manners contribute much toward the constructive settlement of disputes, and since community life in colleges is at best fraught with difficulty, it would be pleasant to believe that manners grow with experience. I do not know that this is so, but I hope it is.

It is almost certainly unwise, at this late date, to try to draw any generalized conclusion about the disturbances which upset so many campuses this past year. Pres. Clark Kerr, who was painfully involved in the most serious and widely publicized of them, has warned us in writing that the only simple observation which can be made about the events in Berkeley which is true is that no simple observation is true. I suspect he is right.

But most of the demonstrations this year did seem to many of us who occupy vulnerable positions to display a new and rather disturbing seriousness of tone. Certainly, they were no mere spring larks. If one is to believe the extravagant declamations of the fiercest of the student participants, the crudest displays of force were clearly intended to be no less than revolutionary struggles for power. But the great majority of the incidents were just as clearly earnest protests about very serious and important matters—such subjects of present national concern, for example, as civil rights and poverty, unfair employment practices, our government's policy in Viet Nam and in Santo Domingo, the involvement of American business in South Africa (and in Alabama and Mississippi); such weighty and pressing problems as these from outside the immediate sphere of reference of colleges and universities, and from within: institutional policies in regard to investment, an alleged growing indifference on the part of faculty toward students, especially undergraduate students, the rights of students to be heard and to participate in the formulation of policy, especially educational policy, and again an alleged excessive concern on the part of administrative officers for problems outside the institution at the expense of more important ones within—these and others. Together such real or fancied grievances led to widespread remonstrance and to a great deal of turmoil and soul-searching on campus after campus during the year. It may very well be that the end of these difficulties is not yet

What can one say about these episodes, which clearly raise difficult questions for us all? What specifically should a person's attitude be when such a storm blows up? Should he join a demonstration or should he not? Should he try to provoke one? I do not know how many have been tormented by such questions, but it seems to me many are, and that, in such circumstances, it is not easy to find a completely satisfactory answer.

Unqualified approbation of the activist role comes hard for one of my generation. In our time in college, not all of us, but (unless I am grievously mistaken) a very considerable majority of us, prided ourselves on standing aloof from causes and demonstrations. We left matters of these kinds for people we thought unimaginative and excessively earnest. If we were betrayed into any group activity of remonstrance, it was only when a beguiling element of farce could be introduced and when we therefore saw in a demonstration a possibility for hilarious good fun. I remember particularly, for example, the time H. L. Mencken came to the Boston Common to sell his *American Mercury* (which had been banned by the Watch and Ward Society) and to get himself arrested. What fun it was that day to join the throng which rallied about to escort him to jail! But it was really for him, and for us, essentially a lark. In our view, demonstrations were, as a rule, instigated and conducted by the humorless and self-righteous—and at their worst, the exhibitionist—among us, and we preferred to have no part in them.

Considering the events of this past year, how far away those days now seem! And how dated—if not benighted—our attitude! Or was it? Is there anything that can be said now in our defense? I believe something—for despite what even then surely must have appeared to many as an insufferable, supercilious attitude on our part, underneath we, too, in our way, were serious. Our most basic, conscious motivation was a determination not to be ensnared by cheap conventions, which Mencken and others had taught us to believe were all about us. It was rather our—I am willing to concede now—slightly pretentious determination to serve a deeper and worthier range of values than those which seemed to us to be held popularly in honor in our culture at that time. Starting with such a view, we came quickly to serve the very ancient, traditional Harvard idol of "indifference." But—and here I speak most seriously in our defense—we did not consider that this necessarily implied aloofness or unconcern. Rather, it seemed to us to bespeak a higher allegiance to judgment and discrimination. In our view, a chief function—perhaps *the* chief function—of education was criticism. Such present concerns as non-violence meant nothing to us. But we were nothing if not critical. Surely we must have appeared a disdainful lot; and I suspect, in large measure, we were.

Today—I take it—what we honored as indifference is held up by many to scorn. Involvement seems now to be everything; and I am prepared to concede if this is the student's view that it represents advance. At any rate, Harvard College is different from the one which my generation knew as undergraduates. And, on the whole, I believe it is a better one. I have endeavored on numerous occasions to indicate how this might be so. I do not mean to imply that I think the students are fundamentally better. I suspect if one could see deep within them, it would appear that their generation has as long a way to go to salvation—if I may use a manner of speaking appropriate in this place—as any of us have had, and have. By nature, they are no less basically selfish than we were and are, and just as prone to error. But it does seem to me that in comparison with those of their predecessors who affected to see in "indifference" a pre-eminent virtue (even if we did not quite believe it), the students do have a livelier under-standing than we did that ethics are not merely personal, but also and inescapably corporate and social. And beyond this, with a more intense realism than we could muster, the students have come to see that to be personally satisfying and life-giving, any ethics which are to command their assent have to be *their* ethics; they cannot be ethics devised and held by someone else or ethics acquired through words without personal involvement. And students want—at least a considerable number of them want—(and here they go way beyond us) to be associated with their fellow men, including the most humble and least educated among them, in a way we clearly did not. Surely, this is gain long overdue.

But, granting all this, a troublesome question remains: How do we participate in the dramatic upheavals of our time—in the weakness and sufferings of our world, and not rather simply seek refuge from them? What is there in all the confusion and conflicting claims in the busy world about us worthy of our devotion and best effort? And how, if we find it, do we engage with it and seek constructively to serve it, rather than under the cloak of pretentious words to continue to pursue our own interests? Here, surely, is a serious question—perhaps rather a series of serious questions.

Last year, a distinguished lady speaking to the graduating class of another college said on this point, "Our whole lives are spent in an attempt to discover when our refusal to bow to limitations is irresponsible escape from actualities, and when it is courage and rational faith, a valid expression of our deepest values."

I am sure all of us would like to take our stand with "courage and rational faith." The question is, how do we do this? How can we be sure we stand, with courage and with faith, on reason's side? It is hard to say—if we are thoughtful. No courses can be given in Harvard College in causes one should join or not join or in stands one should take or not take. Were such to be attempted, surely they would be full of special pleading, for such matters are rarely susceptible of exact assessment. And yet, we all could use such courses.

Against the background of the disturbances and demonstrations that rocked so many college communities this year, what I have wanted to say is that, if the fruits of college education are apathy, indifference, and self-justifying lack of concern, surely something has gone wrong. (This was an especial danger for my generation.) But something more is wrong if the alternative which presents itself is self-righteous, destructive action motivated by personal aggrandizement or hostility or even only by sullen discontent. There must be something better than these alternatives. And, of course, there is. I should like to say with all humility, as the University's spokesman, that this is a way toward which, in my judgment, Harvard throughout her history has been attempting to direct our gaze.

There is much evidence to prove my point. The University reveres the memory of men like John Harvard, whose convictions brought him to the new world to help establish a college in the wilderness; like Henry Dunster, who resigned his presidency rather than compromise his opinion that only adult believers should be baptized; like Charles W. Eliot, who defied entrenched interests to create a viable university; and James B. Conant, who as World War II drew on, mobilized Harvard to the defense of freedom. These were intelligent protesters who acted from conviction.

There is a certain irony in the origin of the new technique of civil disobedience which can be said to derive from the example of that graduate of the Class of 1837, Henry David Thoreau, whose example and whose writings are supposed to have influenced Gandhi and played a part in many contemporary uprisings, including the Negro Revolution of our time. Thoreau was not a remarkable undergraduate. He himself admitted in his classbook "that though bodily I have been a member of Harvard University,

heart and soul I have been far away among the scenes of my boyhood."
His college rebellion was escape to Concord, or to the College Library
where he read insatiably. In later life, he was wont to disparage his college
experiences, complaining in *Walden,* for example, that one year in his college
room cost more ($30) than the construction of his cabin. Yet, his college
life was happy and fruitful and relatively calm. The author of "Civil
Disobedience" played no part in the famous Rebellion of 1834, which took
place in the spring of his freshman year, although he is said to have come to
the defense of one of his Classmates unjustly charged with disorder. But
despite his later disparagement of his College, what he saw and did and
learned in Cambridge helped energize his creative will and develop his
fundamental slant on life.

One might say the same of some others who have affected our modes of
thought—Henry Adams, whose mournfully introspective and deprecatory
account of his education is not entirely borne out by the facts of his distinguished career; the champion of the vigorous life, Theodore Roosevelt,
whose self-discipline and Spartan self-reliance found popular acceptance in
a world given to large horizons; Franklin D. Roosevelt, socially successful
president of the Crimson, pushing good and polite causes, but not yet the
organizer of political and social reform; Walter Lippmann, symbol of the
flowering of undergraduate concern with the fundamental problems of
society, a founder of the Socialist Club, in an earlier Harvard era when
radicalism was in favor; John F. Kennedy, athletic, fond of a good time,
yet maturing to the point where he could produce a perceptive work in
international affairs. These are perhaps special examples, but there have
been many quite like them in other lines of public service, as well as scholars,
poets, teachers, musicians, lawyers, and all the rest.

What I have wanted to suggest is that undergraduate protestation, of
itself, is not necessarily a sign of virtue nor a requirement for significant
achievement. But certainly awareness is—awareness of shortcomings in
ourselves and others, awareness of abuses and chicanery, and also of human
need. And with awareness, knowledge, understanding, and concern. These
are qualities which Harvard would like to have helped to strengthen in
undergraduates. The examples of Harvard men I have cited were of patient
people who could bide their time, not people who would spend their power
to protest in a single youthful effort, justified or misguided, but individuals
who throughout their lives would keep on working constructively to strike
what blows they could for advance. And it is to the latter tribe we hope
students have elected to belong.

Looking about us for a path in the circumstances of our lives, again
and again we see on the one hand sloth, timidity, and escape from responsibility through rationalization; on the other, too frequently, assertiveness,
uninformed aggressiveness, and self-will. But where, between such unattrac-
tive opposites, lies the path of courage and rational faith; and how can we

develop the willingness to listen and learn and the unshakable determination to be of help? Where and how, indeed?

It always has seemed to me to be an excessively simple-minded person who believes this path is easy to be perceived, and an inexperienced or self-righteous person who believes it is easy to follow. But may I say that Harvard's deepest hope is that she may have contributed to help students to want to find, and move forward on, such a way.

93

The Great Revolt in Higher Education

WM. CLARK TROW

Emeritus professor of education, University of Michigan. His satirical article originally appeared in *School and Society* on Oct. 26, 1968.

The war on conformity had been won. Beginning with the conquest of Madison Avenue, the gray flannel suit disappeared and, somewhat later, all uniforms. Skirts and trousers on both sexes, after a period of rapid shrinkage, if worn at all, assumed any length or girth their wearers wished. For the insufficiently hirsute, wigs or false whiskers could be used to decorate either sex, as could jewelry and cosmetics.

Youth leaders had recognized early that nonconformity in dress and bathing was merely an outward symbol, and that the positive aspect of their revolt was freedom. Emancipation from all rules except those they made themselves gradually came to be achieved. Freedom of speech, including freedom from the restraints of grammatical rules and from what formerly had been matters of taste, not only in language, but also in behavior, was theirs. One could say and do what he wanted, whenever and wherever he wished. Such words as propriety, taste, good breeding, and the like, were the only filthy words left.

Such freedom was not attained without a struggle. Mass meetings, marches, placards, sit-downs, lie-downs, sit-ins, teach-ins, lie-ins, riots, and arrests continued for some time. On college campuses, black power fought white power, and white power fought black power until the Black-and-Whites took over, and continued the struggle, with the help of the Young Action Peoples' Society (YAPS) and the Social Nationalist Activists for Revolutionary Labor Schools (SNARLS). Gradually all arrived at enough of a consensus (which they usually spelled "concensus") to do business. When freedom from financial obligations came up as the next step in the reform of higher education, the opposition (all persons over 30) began to bestir itself. To meet the growing opposition, the students in one of the smaller state universities, one that earlier had been a teachers' college, achieved a breakthrough by smashing all precedent and promulgating the rule that students should constitute a majority on the Board of Regents. This went a long way toward clarifying the meaning of the earlier contention that students should have a voice in the determination of policy in matters in which they were concerned.

As would be expected, the constitutionality of the measure was questioned, and the state attorney general was asked to render an opinion. Surprisingly enough, he found that, by some oversight, the law stated that the control of the university should be vested in a duly elected board of regents. But it failed to state how many should serve on the board or by whom they should be elected. Great was the jubilation on the campus when the opinion was announced. The students forthwith duly elected 15 student members to counterbalance the 10 old members.

It was some time before the results of this momentous action began to make themselves felt. But gradually, a number of regental rulings were passed, all by a majority of 15–10. Among the first rulings was one under which rent paid by a student permitted him to live anywhere on the campus. Several readjustments were made under this ruling. Then one student who had a room to himself refused to permit another to occupy his room. The intruder claimed, under the regents' ruling, that he had a right to it, since he had paid his rent where he had been living. Angry words were followed by blows, and the intruder, after a struggle, threw the other out the window. The intruder was taken into custody, and the next day it was reported that he had no recollection of the incident. It was ascertained that he had purchased drugs at the student-operated book store. At the trial he was charged with murder, but he won his freedom on the defense lawyer's plea of temporary insanity.

Other minor incidents occurred, but the faculty raised no great objection since a later ruling released them from all teaching responsibilities because the movement required that all students should be free from rules about class attendance. A meeting of the liberal arts faculty was called to oppose the ruling, but it failed to bring out a quorum, and so no action was taken. The reason for the lack of interest was said to be the fact that the new plan gave faculty members practically full time for their research.

Things began to change, however, when, with the leadership of a few staff members from the sociology and mathematics departments, the regents were pressured to break all contracts with professors who were doing research on anything having to do with national defense, or which might be of possible use to the armed services or the war effort, and to spend at least six hours a day in personal contacts with students either in dormitories, other college buildings, or in their homes.

These rulings tended to increase the general opposition which, until now, had been only in the form of mutterings and complaints. At a secret rump session of the regents, to which the members of the student majority were not invited, the various actions that might be taken were discussed. Those that were voted gradually became evident in the days which followed.

The first event occurred at a student meeting at which a number of motions, amendments, and amendments to amendments, coupled with points of order and motions to adjourn so confused the student chairman and his cohorts that nothing was accomplished. The next occurrence was at an open meeting at which the speaker was a representative of the Cuban government. Questions came from the floor so rapidly that the speaker was unable to reply to them; and, though the chairman tried to channel them, he was unable to handle the situation and the speaker finally gave up. At a similar meeting, the applause began simultaneously with the speaker. The chairman tried to quiet the clapping and the shouts of "Bravo," pleading as he did so for the rights of free speech, when an unidentified voice yelled, "That's what *we* used to ask for."

These and similar happenings attracted little attention, however, as compared with the sit-in at the regents' meeting. The room was so crowded that neither the adult nor student regents could get in, and all moved to a larger room. The gathering soon became unruly and the police were called in. They arrested a dozen or so persons, supposedly faculty members; but they turned out, on further inquiry, to be non-professors.

What finally put an end to the nightmare was a motion made by a non-professor impersonating a non-student at a later meeting of the board of regents. (Since, for some time, the public had been invited to attend these meetings, it was felt that it also should be free to take part.)

The motion stated the fact that three-fifths of the cost of educating each university student was paid by the state. Hence, students were actually kept men (and women), their keepers being the despised over-30 age group. The motion called for the elimination of the unbearable situation. In the violent discussion that followed, someone yelled: "Can a kept man be a free man?" and the answer was a loud and vigorous "NO!" A number of the student regents realized what was going on, but were unable to keep their followers in line, and the motion passed.

After the students had voted themselves virtually out of college, other actions were reported by off-campus forces. The legislature voted to withhold all funds until the situation was stabilized. The AAUP issued a 56-page report on the situation and removed the university from its approved list. The State Department of Education withdrew accreditation, which meant that no teachers graduating from it legally would be certified to teach. A number of industrial firms sued for breach of contract. The university had failed to pay for some $500,000 worth of building equipment, and the firms were unable to get any reply to their inquiries. In one such case, the student advisor to the university treasurer had taken the statement home and lost it; he since had left college and his successor had not been appointed.

Meanwhile, the soap and clothing manufacturers had put on a vigorous advertising drive to increase their sales. As a result, conformity with former nonconformity in styles no longer was acceptable. Lacking the outward symbols of freedom, the movement began to fade out, hastened by the recognition on the part of the leaders that graduation time was approaching, and they soon would need to get a job from an employer who was over 30.

94

The University and the Unstudent

JOHN F. OHLES

Associate professor of secondary education, Kent State University. His article originally appeared in *School and Society* on Oct. 26, 1968.

It started, perhaps, at Berkeley, then moved through Chicago, Ohio State, Howard, Columbia, and eventually may spread to the most remote and least notable Podunk State and Private University. It is misnamed the Battle for Student Power; it should be called more correctly the War of the Unstudent.

This War of the Unstudent is distinguished by forceable occupations of college buildings in the name of free speech and by demands in the name of academic freedom to dictate university policy, from course content to the hiring and firing of professors, to where and whether buildings shall be erected, and to the rules or absence of them in dormitories. The struggle for power is not to assert student power as much as it is to demolish the power of the establishment; the resolve is not to replace one program with another, but to destroy the existing program. The deficiencies of the old order are detailed simply for they surround one, but the new order is explained only in the broadest terms: love, equality, justice, and flower power.

The roots of conflict in the university are ancient and honorable; they are centered in the struggle between the have-nots (students) and the haves (faculty), between those who have made it and those who are seeking to make it, between those who control destiny and those in search of it. The teacher has the knowledge which the student must wrest from him. The institution selects the student, exerts control over him, establishes the means by which he progresses through the ritual, and elects finally whether he should receive the symbol of success, the academic degree. Within this context is the arena where complaints about academic requirements, course content, and quality of instruction are relevant.

A second area of relevant contention between students and the academic establishment is in the *in loco parentis* role of the institution. The enforcement of extended adolescence upon maturing and resisting adults has been expressed traditionally in escape out of (and entry back through) windows, in smuggled bottles, in panty raids, water fights, and the rest. If the students are amateurs in academic affairs, they are experts in their own needs for maturity and self-realization, in resistance to strictures against their adult independence.

But the War of the Unstudent is not represented in the traditional conflicts in institutions of higher education. A new development, mass education, is bringing into the college classroom greater numbers of those who had been excluded from the past academic scene. Increasing technology and extended requirements for admission into many vocations have brought new hordes onto college campuses; many of these new collegians have substituted vocational aims for academic curiosity, but most of them readily or hesitantly accede to the demands of institutional conformity.

Burgeoning enrollments also have increased the numbers of faculty, with an extended range of purpose and competence. Many of the new breed of professors are as unsure as the students of their relation to the establishment, the reason for their being, the means to their own self-realization. Some college instructors are allied more commonly with rebellious students than with their own colleagues. Occasionally, the students are made use of by faculty in the pursuit of power and status in the academic world. There are times, too, when students become pawns of administrators who are in conflict with the faculty. And there are times when the student becomes the tool of the non-student, who finds the campus an ideal place to further his particular crusade.

There is, finally, a larger proportion among today's students who are unstudents, those who enter the university without a commitment and who continue to wander through the academic halls only because of parental expectations, or social pressures, or as means of avoiding the draft or work or the responsibility of meeting the demands of the independent adult. Most questions about the motivation or dreams or expectations or behavior of the unstudent are unanswered; the only question that has a ready answer is whether he will accept the institution, its program, classrooms, professors, and administrators. The answer is no. The size of his roar must not obscure the fact that he numbers far fewer than five per cent of the student body. Even his hundreds in the multiversity are but a pittance among the tens of thousands.

The unstudent is the lost soul, once along skid row, but now with a place to sleep and an assured eating schedule; he is the hobo who wanders between those classes he does attend; he is the stowaway sailor who journeys on student junkets or drug-elicited "trips." But of all the kicks he seeks, none is more inviting, more rewarding, or more convenient than to shake the institution that shelters him. Society may be his enemy, but the institution at hand is his target.

The charming thing about many unstudents is that they are intelligent, frequently among the more intelligent of the student body. But intelligence is part of the problem, for the unstudent may ignore the books and cut classes and still compete academically. And the time that others consume in fighting to stay in the academic community he spends in bemoaning his existence, plotting his revenge, organizing his few supporters, and warring against the establishment.

In times past, the unstudent was likely to leave the campus for skid row, the lumber camp or migrant farm trail, or the life of the hobo or seagoing wanderer, or in the non-warring armed forces; and he often came back to the campus as a more mature student. But, today, the unstudent has fewer outlets; he may join the hippie colony, but here he still is subject to the draft and under public censure. He knows that there are few real means of escape; his options are limited. Having once left the campus, he may have difficulty in returning. His surest shelter is the university, where he may gain status and even extend his tenure if the institution surrenders to his demands and agrees to operate with the rules that he first extracts and is then free to amend. If he can bend the university to his will, he may find at least a partial solution to his problems. At any rate, he may enjoy that temporary satisfaction that comes from even a minor victory against society.

The role of higher education in reacting to the unstudent is not a simple one. It is, however, the task of the university to reject the non-student and to seek to sort out the legitimate complaints of the students from the irrelevant gripes of the unstudent. An unpleasant and difficult task, the job of sorting requires that complaints shall be specific, supported by evidence, and relevant. Above all, the university must establish reasonable and responsible avenues through which the screening of criticism takes place. The institution should exercise patience and require of itself and its students the acceptance of deliberate processes uninhibited by emotional excess. The university should identify the demands of the unstudent and, in large part, choose to ignore them. It reluctantly should meet his crude force with its judicious use of power. It cannot permit him to run or to ruin the university.

That universities have problems in curriculum, teaching, and administration should be obvious to any serious onlooker. But it should be equally clear that to pursue the non-problems of the unstudents can only interfere with the resolution of the real problems of the students.

Universities exist solely for their students. They seek to protect the student from non-students, unstudents, and, sometimes, himself. The academic freedom that is bandied about so lightly and conveniently is, after all, freedom to learn rather than to teach or to administer. So that the student may freely learn, the professor is free to teach. And this freedom to learn requires that colleges and universities come swiftly to terms with the newest by-product of mass higher education, the confused and confusing unstudent. He is a new problem that must be solved swiftly, readily, sympathetically, humanely, and efficiently.

95

Dissent and the College Student in Revolt

CLYDE E. BLOCKER

President, Harrisburg (Pa.) Area Community College. His article originally appeared in *School and Society*, January, 1970.

The current student unrest on the American college campus has been discussed in such detail, using every method from reasoned logic to harsh invective, that it is difficult to think of a fresh way to begin a meaningful discussion of the problem. The quality of the discussion has varied from sheer rubbish to well-conceived suggestions for remediation. I would like to mention briefly some causes of our current problems and to suggest a number of institutional responses designed to cope with unrest and dissention on the campus.

There are two major contexts in which the causes of campus unrest must be discussed. One is the society-at-large with its multitudinous social problems; the second is the college itself. First, let us mention some of the dilemmas in our social order. Most authors ascribe the frustrations of students to the war in Vietnam, continuing racial discrimination, corruption in politics, unethical commercial exploitation of consumers, a breakdown in the American family structure, a continually weakening position of organized religion, and a massive shift in the values of individual citizens. In addition, there is the development of an economy and society based upon the exploitation of scientific knowledge, with virtually no commensurate progress made in the application of the social sciences to our political institutions and processes.[1]

Within this larger context, many colleges have drifted along serenely in the same old ways on the implicit assumption that theirs was the best of all possible systems and that the changes taking place on the larger scene

[1] Henry Mayer, "No Peace in Our Time," *Change in Higher Education*, 1:22–24, January–February, 1969.

would require minor institutional adjustments, if any were required at all. Some changes which have taken place on the campus during the last decade have aggravated the incipient frustrations of students to an even greater degree. The flight of professors from the classroom into research and service activities, combined with the massive influx of undergraduates, has made the dehumanization of the college experience inevitable. These changes have caused the colleges to field their second team, for the most part young and inexperienced graduate assistants, teaching fellows, and instructors. The freshmen and sophomores taught by these inexperienced young teachers recognize that they are being short-changed.[2]

Although it is difficult to generalize about American college students, there are some discernible changes in them which have had their effect upon interactions between student and institution. For instance, colleges and universities now have students from all socioeconomic strata—from the ghetto, the farm, the suburbs, and the factories. Most of these students come to the campus with the best of intentions. Many of them recognize the inevitable necessity of completing some post-secondary study if they are to achieve an acceptable level of occupational competence. Too often, however, they find courses that have questionable relevance to present-day problems and concerns, and they find many artificial hurdles which seem designed to eliminate, rather than include, as many as possible.[3]

After being bombarded for years with the necessity of higher education for personal and occupational fulfillment, a significant number of students become victims of what almost can be characterized as an anxiety neurosis resulting from continued exhortations to continue in higher education in spite of a rising tide of barriers, such as higher admissions standards and limited enrollments, and tortuous bureaucratic hurdles that exist within the college itself.

On a number of university campuses, protesting students have been joined by junior faculty members who are disenchanted with a system in which they are accorded inferior professional status and little-or-no power in the governance of the institution. A small, but significant, minority of young faculty not only are frustrated by institutional forms and procedures, but also find in student demonstrations fertile fields for the acting out of their own neurotic needs. When faculty and students join in protest, whatever their motivations, a college can be paralyzed completely.[4]

Any college may find itself attempting to cope with student disruption at any time. Although not as well-publicized, there have been a number of serious confrontations on the campuses of two-year colleges, and it is

[2] *Education at Berkeley: Report of the Select Committee on Education* (Berkeley: University of California, 1966), pp. 3–7.
[3] S. L. Halleck, "Hypotheses About Student Unrest," *Today's Education,* 57:22–24, September, 1968.
[4] *Education at Berkeley, op. cit.,* pp. 40–44.

probable that there will be many more before some reasonable social and political equilibrium is restored. The question to which constructive thinking should be addressed is: What conditions and relationships should be developed on the campus to diminish or eliminate the causes of student unrest?

The first institutional response, which, of necessity, will be interwoven with a number of following recommendations, is the need for a thorough and critical examination of the educational philosophy of the college, of its educational missions, and of the extent to which the community, trustees, administrators, faculty, and students understand these central concepts. Some of the questions which must be answered are the following: What is the philosophical stance of this college? Traditional? Liberal? A mix of these two?; Is the college truly student-oriented, or is there actually an emphasis upon the welfare of the professional staff and upon the *status quo* in the curriculum and instructional methods?; Are the educational missions of the college clearly defined and communicated to students and faculty?; Are the stated functions of the college appropriate for the population being served?; To what extent, and in what ways, can and should the college be involved in questions of social, political, and economic reform in the larger community?; and, finally, Is there general consensus in all segments of the community relative to these questions?

The answers to these questions are not easy, and the processes necessary to find answers are even more complex. Unprecedented changes in personal values and attitudes are taking place in the U.S., and a consensus for any point of view is very difficult to achieve. Regardless of the difficulties involved, such critical analysis of basic issues is absolutely essential. In the absence of such thinking and reappraisal by responsible elements in the college and community, there is every likelihood that extremists of both the right and left will fill the vacuum.

The seemingly bland questions posed above, and the process of critical analysis, hide in them more than meets the eye. If these questions are explored in more than a superficial way, those who participate in the discussions must face the pain resulting from a change in their own tightly held opinions and prejudices. Each of us is, simultaneously, the beneficiary and victim of our limited insights and life experiences. It is, therefore, difficult for us to internalize the needs of others effectively in an emotional way. Essential changes in colleges can come only after such deep introspection and objective analysis of the interrelationships among the college as an organization and the people being served by it.

Some community colleges have set forth their educational aims and how they are to be accomplished in succinct terms. They are the development of intellectual competence, a mature life style appropriate to the present and the future, occupational competence, and responsible behavior as a citizen in the academic community and the larger society. These objectives define the educational services for which such colleges originally were organized, and, properly interpreted, it is clear that community colleges are not arenas in which our current social ills will be solved. No doubt, community colleges can contribute to the solutions of social and economic inequities, but they are not instruments for immediate social change.

The tribe-like banding together of students into loose and shifting coalitions on the basis of "issues" has raised questions as to the efficacy of traditional student personnel services as they now exist in community colleges. Originally conceived as providing nonacademic services to students outside the classroom, it is entirely possible that, as presently organized, student personnel services and counseling are not relevant to the times. There is ample evidence that the staffs responsible for guidance and counseling, student activities, and related functions have not been effective in dealing with student unrest. The students, in many instances, simply ignore these staffs and occupy the president's office. That is where the action is. That is where the decisions are made. Do not bother us with deans or counselors.

The shifting sands of permissiveness on campus have isolated student personnel people rather effectively from meaningful interaction with students. These professionals suffer from outmoded education, training, and behavior patterns which have only limited significance on the campus today. Who is interested in counseling and facing one's personal psychological problems when there is a peer group which can provide exciting "action," and which makes it unnecessary for one to try to find solutions to one's own personality problems. It is a lot less painful to attack the administration or "the system" for real or imagined defects than to face the painful analysis essential to the development of an acceptable self-concept.

Heresy though it is, I am suggesting that colleges must reconsider carefully the organization and application of the guidance services as they are not related to this generation of students, and to succeeding waves of students who will be even more sophisticated and aggressive than those now in college. The old forms, attitudes, and domination of students by adults are ended. New approaches based upon adult relationships between college staff and students is the principle of the future. The dean of men and dean of women are dead. Long live the deans!

What can be done now? Professional personnel can hand the routine clerical work and paper shuffling to competent clerical workers and the computer. They can get out of their offices and mingle with students. They must be concerned effectively with students, their feelings, frustrations, and legitimate complaints. Given this, their recommendations must be heard and responded to by the college administration and trustees.

These days, students must be accepted and treated as adults. This does not imply that the generally accepted rules of adult behavior should be abandoned, but rather that students should be encouraged by every possible means to take responsibility for their own acts, both individually and in groups. Students can be responsible for budgeting activity funds, social activities, dress, campus discipline, and many other important aspects of campus life.

Another weak link in the structure of colleges is the business-oriented, educationally naive board of trustees. Traditionally, American colleges have been governed by lay boards of trustees, representing business, industrial, and professional groups. The contributions of these individuals to the growth and vitality of colleges must not be denigrated, for their influence and foresight have been a significant factor in the development of the most comprehensive and effective system of higher education in the world. But students today are asking that trustees take on an additional dimension of responsibility: a greater understanding of educational processes and a sharing of decision-making with faculty and students.[5]

The first step in this process of changing the roles of the board of trustees is the expansion of their knowledge about the characteristics of the students being served, the expansion of their understanding of curricula, and the revitalization of their concern with teaching methods. For too long, trustees have been concerned with buildings and budgets, and have been generally unmindful of the essence of education—the teaching-learning process. Admittedly, trustees can not, and should not, be professional educators, but they should spend time and effort evaluating the educational outcomes of the colleges for which they are responsible.

The second responsibility, which probably will be more difficult for trustees to accept, is the need for revision of college governance to include faculty and students. Grassroots democracy has been an American ideal for 250 years, but it has been achieved in only a few extraordinary instances. Student rebellion in the U.S. and other countries has been sparked time-after-time because students reject the outmoded concept that the conditions of their servitude are dictated by others. And it has been convenient and advantageous for some faculty to unite with students in order to bring their particular grievances to the attention of college governing bodies.

On this point, of course, one must be careful to delineate the areas of responsibility with which students and faculty legitimately can be concerned. There are some legal limitations and practical considerations which must be taken into account, e.g., ownership of property, control of college funds, and the execution of other legally mandated responsibilities. However, the sharing of power, or at least trustee responsiveness to the recommendations of students and faculty, is a reality that trustees must face, and quickly.

Last, it is essential that students, faculty, administrators, and trustees collectively develop policies and procedures for the governance of academic affairs, conditions of employment for faculty, and college-student relation-

[5] *Crisis at Columbia: Report of the Fact-Finding Commission Appointed to Investigate the Disturbances at Columbia University April and May 1968* (New York: Vintage Books, 1968), pp. 33–41.

ships. Cooperative development of policies and procedures by these four groups gives all of them a "piece of the action"; and with self-interest comes concern for the welfare of the college. "That which I have helped build, I will not destroy." The process of developing these essential policies is in itself a learning experience for all who are involved.[6]

Policies and procedures governing the college should be developed carefully before a crisis takes place. Rational thinking is difficult or impossible when the house is on fire. Properly developed, this aspect of the college will reflect the consent of the governed, and will provide for due process for individuals who have violated the rules of the academic community. Due process has been made a requirement of college governance by general usage on campus and by the Federal courts. In the absence of due process, state or Federal courts can, and will, intervene.

Every college should have a strong student government and a faculty organized into appropriate committees. The governance of today's college should be based on four groups, freely interacting with one another— trustees, administration, faculty, and students. It is important to define the areas in which students will be consulted and invited to advise in institutional policy-making. Equally important is the necessity of a clear definition of the faculty's role. The processes made possible by such an organization give all participants a feeling of meaningful interaction. Most importantly, the institution will cease to be segmented into adversary groups.

Although I am reluctant to end on a pessimistic note, it seems apparent that, if dissenting students wish to interrupt the legitimate activities of a college, they will do so despite any machinery designed to promote rational decision-making. A very small minority of students and ex-students have as their goal the destruction of institutions of higher education, or they are bent on converting our colleges into bases of political power on the South American model. Unreasonable demands by students or faculty cannot be negotiated. As a last resort, colleges cannot hesitate to use civil and criminal law enforcement agencies to protect the civil rights of the majority.[7]

There are profound changes taking place in society today. Colleges have no choice but to respond to these changes with immediacy, but not panic; with imagination, but not fear; and with flexibility, but not rigidity. It is clear, at least to me, that a small minority, made up of students and militant groups in the community, are attacking society through one of its most vulnerable points—schools and colleges. This phase will pass, for the majority will insist shortly that its members also have rights which must not be destroyed by the minority.

Thoughtful students and faculty have pointed out some of the weaknesses of colleges. They have laid bare some of the absurdities and contradictions

[6] Otis A. Singletary, *Freedom and Order on Campus* (Washington: American Council on Education, 1968).
[7] *A Declaration on Campus Unrest* (Washington: American Council on Education, 1969).

which we have assumed were educationally sound. Now is the time for change, rational reasoned change, which will make it possible for all to experience an individually fulfilling educational experience.

96

Facing the Issues of Student Unrest

FRANK J. SPARZO

Assistant Professor of Psychology, Ball State University. His article originally
appeared in *School and Society* on Oct. 26, 1968.

During the past few years, evidences of student unrest and effective protest
have become increasingly common on college campuses. Although this
student unrest has been exaggerated and misinterpreted by some journalists
and educators, it does seem to be developing into a significant factor on
college campuses throughout the nation.

A major fact has emerged since the Berkeley protests of 1964: the college
student today is exerting more and more power and influence on administrative decisions.[1] This new power can be labeled conveniently the "fourth
estate," and may take its place beside the three traditional estates of trustees,
administration, and faculty.

We see evidence of this new student power all around us. For example,
in some colleges and universities organized teacher evaluation by students
now is occurring. Students always have evaluated their professors, of
course, but recently they have systematized their evaluations and now are
sharing the written results with college administrators and the teachers
themselves. Obviously, some professors do not accept the new way in which
their students are evaluating them, nor do the faculty, administrators, and
students agree on just what should be done with the results.

Michigan State and a few other universities now have an Ombudsman,
a full-time position similar to that found on a national level in Denmark,
Sweden, Norway, and Finland. Protecting students from excesses of

---

[1] Influence will be taken, as synonymous with power, to be "the capacity of one actor to do
something affecting another actor, which changes the probable pattern of specified future
events." See Nelson W. Polsby, *Community Power and Political Theory* (New Haven: Yale
University Press, 1963), p. 3.

bureaucracy and helping them solve their problems informally and quickly are the major tasks of this official.

Reform also is taking place in student-faculty committee assignments. Many colleges are promoting student-faculty cooperation by instituting new student-faculty committees and increasing or adding student representation on faculty and administrative committees.

These are but three examples of many which indicate that a new concern for students and the power they can exert is developing on campuses across the country.

It is now clear that educators will make a grave error if they expect this current student bid for greater power and influence to wane. The trend is irreversible, and for good reason. Students are more conscious of their influence; they know that their efforts to gain power have paid off in many instances. They have learned that reforms are possible. Moreover, today's college student not only is more sophisticated in general, but also more sophisticated about the running of a college campus. He even may organize and plan courses on his own and, on a few campuses, for university-approved credit. He is making progress in solving what previously has been a major obstacle to student power—namely, his relatively short stay on the campus. As students develop more permanent structures, in much the same way as college fratrenal organizations have developed, they will make their influence felt continuously, regardless of the changing membership of the student body.

The use of the word "power," student power in particular, is undoubtedly unsettling to some educators. One can get the distinct impression of the students on one side opposing the faculty and the administration on the other. And this impression is quite correct. Often, both faculty and students act as if they belonged to peer groups destined to oppose one another. This attitude is a major obstacle in coping with student unrest.

We see one result of this opposition when students bring legal action against a college *and win*.[2] Such action tends to reaffirm the attitude of opposition. And, unfortunately, it also tends to define college-student relations in legalistic terms. Some educators like Cornell University's Pres. James A. Perkins are rightly concerned about the danger of substituting judicial processes for academic processes. The point is that college officials must anticipate and recognize student rights before a situation ends up in court or before students resort to irresponsible acts. Clearly, the fact that students are turning to the courts to win their rights implies something significant about the dialogue, or lack of dialogue, between college or school officials and students. It implies that something is wrong on the campus.

[2] For one example, a state college in Alabama was instructed to reinstate a student editor who had been expelled for failure to follow a directive from the president of the college regarding an editorial in the college newspaper. The judge ruled that the student's right to free speech has been violated.

With each new freshman class, more and more high schools and colleges will have to reconsider the question, "What rights, influences, and privileges should our students have?" And we shall have to consider this question in much the same spirit as we ask, "What influences and responsibilities do our faculty and administrators have?"

If there are to be continued student demands for greater power or influence, educators will have to face at least five issues which are related distinctly to student unrest. First, educators must learn more about the student's academic and non-academic life. Too many faculty and administrators have no idea of or completely ignore the fact that when students are living in overcrowded residence halls, and many are, there is a lack of privacy which can lead to significant problems for some. Too many ignore, decry, or minimize student sexual tensions. Too many openly verbalize their lack of interest in student problems and tend to regard themselves as academicians who necessarily have no responsibility to their students beyond the classroom lecture.

College educators must follow the lead of those who teach at the elementary and secondary level and become more sensitive to both academic and non-academic student problems. Facing this issue need not make higher education paternalistic or like high school, as some may say; it well may make higher education more like it ought to be.

Second, a related issue is one which has been recognized for many years by educators, as well as non-educators like Aldous Huxley, who remind us that we have neglected almost completely the non-symbolic aspects of the process of knowing. Educators persist in their neglect of the noncognitive and nonverbal aspects of behavior. We seem frightened, insecure, and confused when we deal with student emotionality or interpersonal relationships. Instead, we try to avoid facing these nonrational aspects of behavior, for example, by hiring such "professionals" as guidance counselors and staff psychologists or by limiting education to the higher mental processes, "thinking," reasoning and problem-solving or "cognitive" activities. Other dimensions of human-ness, such as emotion, feeling, interpersonal response—the so-called irrational—are neglected.

A distinct implication, then, is that we must see students as people first, not as organisms into which we put a "liberal education." Most educators surely know this; nevertheless, the issue is yet to be faced squarely, as it will have to be, if we are to break down this very significant barrier to education and to better student-faculty relationships.

Third, we must come to grips with the fact that the principle of *in loco parentis* has been withering for some time. Students are less willing to have their behavior controlled by colleges. Educators and psychiatrists also are calling for changes; *e.g.,* a recent study concluded that the private heterosexual and homosexual behavior of college students need not concern college administrators directly, although such behavior traditionally has been a concern of the college.[3] Students are saying more and more, "We have a right to be wrong, to make mistakes, and, if necessary, to suffer the consequences of our mistakes." The basic issue to be faced is one which has been mentioned already—namely, in what areas do students have a right to make decisions even though some of their decisions may be wrong?

Fourth, students are more aware than ever that college officials are concerned greatly with restricting the deviant student, a concern not difficult to understand. Unfortunately though, the majority of students, quite capable of acting responsibly, feel they are restricted unduly by rules and regulations developed for other students, but which essentially are hampering for them. Today's students are asking educators to treat them with more trust than they have in the past and not attempt to over-regulate their lives solely because of the actions of a few.

Fifth, the student relationship to the bureaucratic college structure must be re-examined. Students have become increasingly concerned with the difficulties involved in solving many of their legitimate problems. For example, college officials often seem completely helpless to react to a simple student request. On some issues, college officials would side with their students, but refrain from doing so because of pressures from parents and the public. When confronted with such situations or with a legitimate student problem, educators too often respond by informing students that they have no appreciation for the "complexity" of the situation or that they are immature and inexperienced. Students are finding it very difficult to accept this kind of treatment. They are demanding that educators face issues more honestly. The result is that college officials are increasingly likely to be charged with hypocrisy, particularly when the students have been told again and again that college exists for them.

If educators are to make the necessary realignments to meet the challenge of student unrest on the college campus, they must concern themselves fully with these five issues. Probably, the reader has noted that the question of whether students should have more to say about the running of a college was not raised. This is because the writer does not believe the basic issue is whether students should or should not have a greater part in decision-making. Rather, the real task is to discover and accept those areas of college life which students can and ought to handle either for themselves or handle conjointly with the faculty and administration, areas which, if students were allowed such participation, would contribute significantly to their educational and personal growth. Lest we commit an error known as the "fallacy of limited decisions," the writer should be quick to add that college officials need not necessarily abdicate their current rights, responsibilities,

[3] Group for the Advancement of Psychiatry, *Sex and the College Student* (New York: Atheneum, 1966).

and influences.[4] Nevertheless, realignments seem necessary. The problem is that neither the college nor the students really know or agree upon whether the college or the students, or both, should make the decisions in many controversial areas. Solving this basic and very complex problem well may depend upon facing the above issues honestly and creatively.[5]

[4] Some economists use the phrase "fallacy of limited decisions" to refer to the notion that during any particular period of time there is a fixed or limited number of decisions to be made in connection with operating the economy. If the government makes more decisions, the private sector necessarily will have fewer to make. Political scientists often refer to this kind of reasoning as the "fallacy of the zero sum game." We must guard against making a similar error when analyzing college-student relationships; e.g., if students are allowed more choices and more decision-making power, it does not follow automatically that the faculty and administration thereby will have less power and influence.

[5] For some similar views of student unrest expressed in terms of proposed realignments, see Joseph Katz and Nevitt Sanford, "The New Student and Needed Educational Reforms," Phi Delta Kappan, 47: 397-401, April, 1966.

97

Students and the 1970's: Calm After the Storm

JOSEPH P. GIUSTI

Director, Beaver Campus, The Pennsylvania State University, Monaca. His article originally appeared in the October, 1969, issue of *School and Society*.

Today, the academic community is quaking with internal problems, the tremor of which shall be felt for years to come. For, instead of imaginatively and ingeniously moving ahead, we find our progress has been interrupted. We are stymied, our human resources are smothering in an atmosphere thick with problems and tensions.

Whereas the 1950's spawned the uncommitted dropout—the "beatnik"; the 1960's have created the critical, defiant, nonconformist—the "peacenik." From "draft-card-burners" to "sit-in or lie-in" demonstrators, this form of student protest only could have been germinated in the climate of the 1960's. For the 1960's have ushered in a climate of "caring" which was conceived in an era of questioning, and achieves its fruition through the vehicle of protesting. It is a climate which invades every facet of today's living, since protesting has not been limited to student protest. As if the problems of increasing teachers' salaries and integrating black and white do not loom darkly enough, educational administrators are faced with handling, negotiating with, and appeasing student protesters.

There are many sociological reasons for the climate of caring (from prosperity to permissiveness). Instead of the disinterested student bent only upon fulfilling requirements for the prided parchment, today he is the well-read, well-spoken, well-versed, young adult. He is disenchanted with his world, he hates the war in Vietnam, he abhors social and radical inequities, he will not tolerate expediency or accommodation, and, in a nutshell, he wants his turn at trying to "right it all." The hippie, or passive segment of the young generation, simply ignores, at least temporarily, the structures of society; the activist is bent on restructuring his world with all its profound ills.

Generally, students are examining their own immediate surroundings and finding them wanting in many ways. The whole nature of the university is being studied, analyzed, and questioned. Is it truly the home of freedom of speech, academic freedom, justice and equality for all? Is it a privately managed corporation which offers academic services to qualified students, or is it a community of scholars who together pursue the good, the true, and the beautiful? Realistically, a true academic community is impossible today with the many varied interests and services a university performs. The relationship of the university to society is changing, and today's student wants to stabilize and define it. He finds it difficult, even impossible, to reconcile the theoretical and ideal with the practicalities of life. How, he says, can an institution devoted to the proliferation of knowledge be engaged in classified research? Why should a research professor outrank a gifted teacher on the basis of the former's research? Perhaps an acceptable general guideline for the what, why, and how of the university can be found in the statement of a Columbia University trustee, William S. Paley, chairman of the board of the Columbia Broadcasting System: "Our universities are not custodians of the old order, perpetuators of the proven, or curators of the established. They are open-ended ventures, selective of the past, critical of the present, and oriented to the future."[1]

The most dynamic difference evinced in the students of the 1960's is their attitude toward change. Not only do they discuss and analyze, but they march and demonstrate, for they sincerely feel they can change society and permanently affect the course of events. But is this really so surprising? Their generation, more than any before, grew up with change.

Specifically, the most important change students desire concerns their demand for an increasing role in the management of their university. This includes having deciding votes on basic policy decisions, on hiring faculty, on designing curricula, and in the disciplining of their own peers. Anthropologist Margaret Mead recently remarked that the events of the past five years have marked "an end of an epoch" in the way universities are governed. According to Paley, [. . . that] "a board of trustees should commit a university community to policies and actions without the components of that community participating in discussions leading to such commitments has become obsolete and unworkable. . . ."[2] Mutual cooperation and assistance is necessary in any viable organization.

As with all social movements of this nature, each episode gives rise to new ones. From the beginnings at Berkeley and on through Columbia, San Francisco State, and Chicago, from the Sorbonne to Frankfurt, student

[1] Commencement address, University of Pennsylvania, May 20, 1968. *University of Pennsylvania Two Hundred and Twelfth Commencement* (Philadelphia: University of Pennsylvania, [1968]), p. 20.
[2] *Ibid.*, p. 16.

demonstrations, protests, and seizures have risen to thunderous proportions. Students are appalled at certain aspects of their societies; they recognize the threats of human violence in the world, and are well-aware of the threats of technological violence.

Student protesters are asking just where university authority really lies; their rebellion thus is directed against administrators, for they symbolize the authority. Administrators, more than ever before, are catapulted into precarious positions of lone decision-making.

Inherently, an academic institution will, and always should, be troubled with unrest or intellectual disagreement; it houses strongly opinionated individuals with varied viewpoints and, consequently, it can not, and would not wish to, control or channel all thought into one vein. Those individuals who dream about a community of scholars jointly controlling the educational endeavor must be reminded that, practically speaking, this can not be wholly without the assistance of administrators. "In a world in which professors demand salaries and fringe benefits, in which credits are deemed necessary, and in which education requires expensive libraries and laboratories, there is no way to run a university without a highly skilled administration."[3] Effective institutions of higher learning will have to be the natural result of a strong administrator with intellectual leadership, seriousness of purpose, and sense of direction.

There are definite lessons to be learned by educational administrators everywhere. From within Columbia itself, we glean that members of activist groups only number about 200 out of better than 17,000 students on campus. Similar proportions exist within San Francisco State and elsewhere. Perhaps, future protests, demonstrations, and seizures can be deterred and issues resolved by immediate and positive administrative action before the die is cast. Hesitation, possibly born of fear of overreaction, of reprisals, of unfavorable publicity, and a host of other fears, affords time for activist recruitment.

Anarchy and mob tyranny can not be permitted to germinate. At its inception, positive action should be taken. It should be made clear from the outset that all individuals' rights shall be upheld—not only the rights of those who are dissenting, but the rights of those who are not. Regardless of the virtue of the cause or of those participating in it, initiating force or violence to achieve one's objectives is both illegal and immoral. Allowing the use of force to obtain one's own objectives, worthy though they may be, only opens the door for complete breakdown of law and order. Support for this conviction was voiced by former Supreme Court Justice Abe Fortas: "Campus and university facilities are public facilities; but public use does not authorize the general public or the university faculty or students to use them in a way which subverts their purpose and prevents their intended

[3] Paul Woodring, "Who Makes University Policy?" in Christopher G. Katope and Paul G. Zolbrod, eds., *Beyond Berkeley* (Cleveland: World Publishing Co., 1966), p. 149.

use by others. . . . I know of no legal principle which protects students on campus from the consequences of activities which would be violations of the law if undertaken elsewhere."[4] Moreover, "Dissent and dissenters have no monopoly on freedom. They must tolerate opposition. They must accept dissent from their dissent. And they must give it the respect and the latitude which they claim for themselves. Neither youth nor virtue can justify the disregard of this principle, in the classroom, in the public hall or on the streets. Protest does not justify hooliganism."[5]

Meeting "hooliganism" with appeasement only can lead to more "hooliganism." No one's life or property will remain safe unless university and civil authorities meet aggression with unified, firm action.

It is the obligation of educational administrators to protect the freedom of students and faculty alike, to maintain the academic services of the university, and to continue to provide and extend municipal and civil courtesies. Whenever persons or groups disrupt order, incite the constituants, and employ violent tactics, administrators have the responsibility to act immediately.

At the same time, administrators must work to keep the channels of communication free and open In a word, they must balance firmness with understanding and temper judgment with sensitivity—all this without releasing or lessening their basic authority or responsibility.

At this point, someone may declare: "But what about the students' demands?" Indeed, they are not crying to the wind, for they have many outspoken allies. And it is not difficult to sympathize with their disillusionment, for we all have felt it too. As students so succinctly put it: "You set up the atomic bomb. You were complacent with Dachau. Your depression wasn't so great. You got trapped in Korea. Now you want to threaten my life in someplace like Vietnam. You assassinated Kennedy and gave me in his place a professional politician from Texas. Your generation has failed us and yourselves utterly. We are much better equipped to make decisions and to take control."[6]

Insight into the students' concept of society and the university is vital to understanding their position. The university is to be the place in which this "new" and "perfect" society will germinate. Rather than being used by society, today's students see the university as being in society, confronting and solving a multitude of problems in today's world.

These students, 10-years-old when the New Frontier began, "were the youngest witnesses to the high hopes for a more open society that came in the early Sixties with its battles for civil rights and against poverty. In their

[4] Abe Fortas, *Concerning Dissent and Civil Disobedience* (New York: New American Library, 1968), pp. 46–47.
[5] *Ibid.*, p. 64.
[6] Bill Ward, "Why the Student Revolt," in Katope and Zolbrod, *op. cit.*, p. 233.

short span of history, they have seen on television the assassinations and funerals of three national leaders who embodied these hopes. . . . Still vitally young themselves, they have watched the nation's shift from a youthful sense of unlimited expectations to the middle-aged habit of assessing and conserving old strengths and former gains. Fed by the mass media, urged by parents and teachers to inquire, the students are sensitive to the larger world—and their limited role in it—as no generation before."[7]

Today's youth have been made dependent by an affluent society. Their cars, their education, the gratification of their wants and needs were given to them. They were refused the means by which they could pay their own way through work or other meaningful contributions to society. Society merely asked them to be silent, passive, and appreciative. The affluence, which freed them from worrying and working, permitted them more time to study, to travel, to compare, to judge, and to criticize. As a result, sophistication and disillusionment came at an early age.

Most certainly, today's knowledgeable students should be granted more authority in governing certain areas of their environment. However, permitting major student participation in certain other areas only can lead to chaos. The administrator, then, must recognize those issues on which students have a right and responsibility to speak, and those issues which definitely are not in the students' realm. Likewise, students should be urged to develop a capacity for judgment while maintaining their independent search for truth. It is most important, therefore, to provide an atmosphere of freedom of thought and expression, but, at the same time, to instill also a strong sense of responsibility toward the results and direction of one's actions.

An area which demands mature thought and responsible action is that of student housing and social rules. Herein lies the area which most justifiably should have student concurrence. The protesting students feel they unjustly are made to follow rules which their non-college peers outgrew years ago. Experience has shown that student rules are just as stringent (and perhaps more so at times) as administration rules. Nevertheless, they should be made aware that they are members of a social unit and, as such, they must obey certain rules.

With regard to curriculum planning and establishing requirements for degrees, there is no doubt that imaginative students can contribute greatly, for their insight is close to the situation. However, once again, an academic apprentice never could control fully such a vital area; foresight and experience, mandatory to this facet of educational planning, must be, by definition, inadequate in the student.

Whimsy might rule if students controlled the hiring and firing of faculty. Though it is certainly true that the students may know more of the teaching

[7] Diane Divoky, "The Way It's Going to Be," Saturday Review, Feb. 15, 1969, p. 84.

ability of a professor than does the administrator, the fact remains that the administrator is prepared professionally to assess the total professional qualifications of the professor. A university simply could not function with students controlling faculty attrition; students choose the faculty when they choose the institution.

We are brought logically to only one conclusion—student assistance and cooperation is laudatory, student control is impractical. Edward J. Shoben, former director, Commission on Academic Affairs, American Council on Education, stated: "Governmentally, the community of scholars cannot, by definition, be a society of equals. It is necessarily too sharply structured according to differences in training, demonstrated knowledge, and attainment. The power of decision can rest only with those who have met the essential requirements for senior membership in the academy and who have committed themselves in their careers to the values it represents."[8]

Unfortunately, the breakdown of communications at various institutions of higher learning is foremost among the headlines; little or no attention is directed to campuses such as American University, Washington, D.C., where student protest resulted in a peaceful student-faculty-administration cooperative venture. Indeed, we admire all the virtuous goals of today's youth—honesty, justice, and social and legal rights for all; but unquestionably they should add several old-fashioned, but still-valuable, attributes— good taste, respect, and propriety.

In return, a suggestion is made for administrators. Manifest a sincere trust and confidence in students. Listen to what they really are saying, instead of hurrying to extinguish the fire of their passionate appeals. Instead of fearing activism, rejoice that interested, caring students inhabit campuses; recognize that protest points to the necessity for reform; and, most importantly, consider the initiation and acceptance of change.

For, if education is to progress, many brilliant minds must channel their efforts in constructive veins, instead of being thwarted by problems of protest. Likewise, if a democratic society is to survive and flourish, principled men of reason will have to rally when the foundations of democracy are attacked.

Let us, then, build our hopes on the restless, questioning generation. Let their caring move us to care, let their critiques cause us to re-examine, let their protests force us to reform. Whereas the climate of the 1960's has been a decade of caring, probing, and searching, let us commission the 1970's as a decade of dedication to solving the problems of the 1960's, answering its questions, and building on its foundations—the calm after the storm.

[8] Edward J. Shoben, "Academic Freedom For Students," *NASPA Journal,* 5:28, July, 1967.

98

Touching Base with Our Youth

EUGENE F. McKIBBIN

Dean of Instruction for Liberal Arts, Fullerton Junior College. His article originally appeared in *School and Society* on Nov. 11, 1967.

Books have been written, lectures have been given, and workshops have been held, but we still are puzzling about the nature of today's college youth. The revolt at Berkeley, the New Left, and the telephone-booth-packing all make news, and nobody seems to understand.

As educators, we have seen the folly of one-variable analyses, but, in my opinion, at the risk of being considered an iconoclast, our desire to be scientific causes us to over-analyze, over-study, and over-complicate the picture. Furthermore, we even may be over-frantic. Our present college youth simply have not been given a base to examine, accept, reject, or modify, and this, to me, is their major predicament.

Most of us in education who are fortyish can remember quite clearly the days of right and wrong, of black and white, of clear-cut priority listings of values that were easy for us to recite and more easy to follow because we accepted or rejected them in total, and, if we did not understand completely, we took the "leap of faith," many times without intellectual inquiry. This is neither praise nor condemnation; it is the picture of the world of our youth now past. There was, as a result, greater uniformity in the accepted operational code; the base was there.

We were taught to achieve, to strive for the top, to compete, but we also were taught that it was wrong to do so at the expense of others. A value structure, then, based on what we recited as the "higher values," was our security. Whether we say this structure was a result of the Christian ethic, the cultural pattern, or the blending of ideas in the public schools is not as important, for purposes of description, as the premise that most of us were in agreement as to which values had accepted priority.

Childhood in a depression, adulthood in World War II, and, for many, unexpected college life after the war produced a group of parents and educators who began to question absolute values and direct counseling. The progeny of this group now are in college.

It became the vogue to be non-directive in parental direction and school counseling. When the children asked, "What is right?" or "What do you believe, Dad?" the response was, "How do you see it, Son?" or, "How does society see it?" All of this was a serious, sophisticated attempt to help the growing child to "stand on his own feet" in intellectual and moral pursuit.

While the concept itself had a great deal of merit, the results were not as productive as we might have expected, perhaps because those of us who constituted that educating, transmitting generation were not skillful in our counseling techniques. In our own ambivalence, we presented an unstable image to be emulated. We refused to teach values we questioned, and we had mixed feelings about the direction we were going. Moreover, we were not even certain that non-directive counseling was the answer.

The children of that type of conditioning became the college students of today, left to search for their own values. The search has resulted in finding many of the values of previous generations, but, in the process, some are overlooked. One such value frequently overlooked today is loyalty. Modern man can read Hemingway's *The Old Man and the Sea* and revel in the heroic virtues of courage, perseverance, and conquest and still completely miss the theme of the boy returning to the old man simply out of love and loyalty, a loyalty with no thought of gain. One can not help but ask, "Where does the real power lie?" The tragedy is that too few do ask.

Much of the searching is being done in a very courageous, positive manner in the fiery inquiry of our present youth. Some are asking tough, incisive questions, and others, who find it too difficult, retreat to a facade of not caring.

If, in the search, not enough values are found to satisfy the need for stability, then a route that frequently is taken is to attempt to attach to the norms of society rather than to its values. Norms are a much more elusive base to which to attach than are values for several reasons. Norms are related more immediately to behavior than are values that change more slowly. Norms are much more difficult to identify for an individual who is searching for them. For, if trained sociologists have difficulty in agreeing on what the norms are, then it becomes an even more formidable task for our youth to accept, reject, or modify norms for self-use.

Searching for the norm is complicated even more for our present college youth by the great mobility of our society. In many housing areas where the young grow up, neighbors and friends come from many ethnic backgrounds with a variety of cultural patterns. How does one find the norm in this type of movement? Searching for the ever-elusive norm has to be a very frustrating experience, and, frankly, I believe many of our youth really are asking for help.

The question, then, is how do we help. Again, the answer we give is simple; putting it into practice is not. When a cry for help goes out, a response must be given, not because the rule book says so, but simply because someone needs help.

The response is that of a committed person—most frequently the teacher who has done his homework, who has asked the questions of himself, who has, himself, traveled on the journey of learning so that he has ideas to challenge, answers to give, positions and beliefs to present and defend, to be available and willing when the student wants counsel, and, above all, to have the courage and vision to walk with the student as he dreams.

This is the base we have to offer. Let us make certain that it is solid enough.

99

Peace Corps: Antidote for Provincialism

ROBERT H. SHAFFER

Dean of Students, Indiana University. His article originally appeared in *School and Society* on April 15, 1967.

Many college students complain that their college experience, especially the formal curriculum, is irrelevant to the concerns which are important to them. Many educators agree with them, but blame out-of-class life on the university, which to them seems unreal and irrelevant to the problems, issues, and tensions facing the college student.

Both students and professors have responded to the situation in a variety of ways. Students have responded with increasingly rebellious attitudes, overt protests and demonstrations, and silent withdrawal from the demands of the educational establishment. "Leave us alone" has been a response of some who, at the same time, complain of anonymity and lack of a personal relationship. Many students have adopted a pseudo-beatnik behavior by exhibiting the characteristics and trappings of the individualistic "beats." In fact, many of this group are as conformist to their self-perceived non-conformity as the rank and file students who continue in their traditional vocationally oriented educational paths, leading to well-defined certificates and labels.

Many professors have responded to the new student by abdicating their leadership role in education and denying the authority of knowledge and experience. Student disenchantment with the educational establishment has been reinforced further by the widely disseminated view that the house of intellect has no substance or form. A general solution, to part of the problem at least, has been to advocate extensive student involvement in university policy formulation and decision-making as a means of reducing alienation from the educational community and the consequent feeling of the irrelevance of the traditional educational experience.

The conflict troubling students and teachers alike stems from

conflicting views of the educational process. Educators traditionally have
defined the role of the university as teaching, research, and public service,
with emphasis upon teaching at the college level. They see the dominant
teaching task as contributing to the academic growth and intellectual
development of the individual.

Contrary to this view, students feel that their own personal maturation,
the establishment of an identity, and the development of a philosophy of life
vis-à-vis the chaotic world are their most important educational problems.
Thus, the characteristics of traditional higher education, such as grades,
courses, majors, and subject-centered study, not only are meaningless, but
actually detrimental to their primary purpose of an education. Further, they
feel that the university must become an agent for social change, rather
than a neutral, sterile channel of truth. Given the feelings of students, the
structured content of most courses and the traditionally objective views of
world events support the new student view of a hypocritical, contradictory
world. The split between the two views of the college and university has been
exaggerated further as the work of the universities becomes related more
closely to the ongoing affairs of the world, and becomes separated still
further from value judgments and social standards.

To achieve relevance and coherence for its work, the university no longer
can live effectively with two worlds—the world the student experiences
and the educationally oriented world which the university envisions as
comprising the collegiate environment.

The difference between the experimental world and the educational
ideal always has concerned educators. There is little evidence that the gap
is wider. However, there is much evidence that the modern student is more
vocal and overt in voicing his objections. Further, because of such social
changes as increased material security, easier communication, and greater
mobility in the academic world, students are challenging more aggressively
the traditional educational status quo. They are demanding new roles, not only
for themselves in the process of higher education, but for the higher educational institutions themselves as power centers to correct the evils of
society. In short, outspoken students are demanding a role for higher
education in the U.S. similar to that envisaged for developing countries by
American educational consultants.

Many of the best students on any college campus are frustrated by the
operative indifference of educational authorities to welcome and accept
suggestions for educational improvement. Most college officials, administrators and professors alike, verbalize an eagerness for innovative, creative
suggestions. Their resistance, buoyed by tradition, departmentalization, and
limiting professionalism, is a matter of historical record. Consequently,
student reaction has been characterized by cynicism, distrust, and challenge.
A reaction based on such feelings rapidly deteriorates to irrelevant protest and
immature name-calling.

Unfortunately, the institutional nature of American higher education probably will not change markedly in the near future. Thus, the response by higher education holding the greatest potential for effectively meeting problems caused by current development in the student world probably will be incorporation of off-campus experience into the student's educational program. If such experience is to make a significant impact on the lives of individuals, it must be more than enjoyable travel, profitable work experience, or even intensive study abroad.

Their off-campus educational experience must be a period of personal challenge, coupled with opportunities for independence and responsibility in a setting which shatters the actual and mentally imposed limitations of provincialism, tradition, and custom. An international experience would seem to meet these requirements most fully. Peace Corps or similar service for those who can qualify would seem to be one of the best avenues for such experience.

The failure of educators to recognize the importance of such an addition to the traditional college program has not been caused by tradition and institutional formalism alone. Parents, teachers, counselors, and other educators have failed to comprehend its importance primarily because of their formative experiences arising out of the Depression and military service. These resulted in an emphasis upon time as a precious commodity and upon speed in "completing" one's education. Thus, any experience which did not result in credits toward a degree almost automatically was discounted and rejected in favor of accreditable study projects. The older generation could not understand "waiting two years" or "taking two years out of one's life." Despite the rather trite counseling view that taking time to develop skills, abilities, and understanding is the equivalent of sharpening a tool before undertaking a different task, the educational world, in general, rejects non-accredited experience.

Much has been written about the increased life expectancy of young people today. One authority has estimated an expectancy of 90 years for our present teenage population. Further, authorities talk of the apparent solution to most problems of material well-being for U.S. citizens. Young people today have the promise of a life without hunger and time to enjoy living if they only can build a personality and a body of experience which gives them the capacity to live. It is precisely the fear that they can not build such a life with today's traditional institutions and customs that causes so much alienation, frustration, and apparent aimless protest activity.

The real challenge to the university currently is to provide career and educational planning which is related to the concerns which the student feels to be most important in the planning—how his life is to be spent and what significance he will have in a world characterized by chaos and confusion.

While educationally and personally valuable, the dominant criterion of a Peace Corps job—significant production—removes every hint of a make-believe or irrelevant setting. The educational experience of Peace Corps work does not take place within the protecting cover of ivy-covered walls. This fact alone may be the most important reason for encouraging the inclusion of international service experience in the educational plans of most students.

Relevance to the world is available to the younger generation if it will consent to leave the pseudo-barrenness of their contrived pads and seek their challenge in eliminating the genuine barrenness of some people's lives. Paul Goodman has been quoted widely because of his comment that to grow up in America is to grow up "absurd." Bureaucracy and establishments may rob some individuals of their meaning and reduce them to absurdity, but many individuals rob themselves by refusing to consider the very experiences and opportunities which will give them meaning. The nonconformist establishment in most graduate schools is more deadly to creative response than the grey-flannel suit crowd because of its self-deceiving righteousness and nihilistic view of society.

The trite slogan, "I am a person. Do not fold, spindle, or mutilate," is a sad response to the challenge to combat conformity and anonymity in a complex world by action. Instead of burnishing the self-awarded halos of the so-called alienated youth, authors, educators, and journalists could interpret more effectively the creative, energetic response of young people by stressing service in tutorial programs, work camps, VISTA, hospital aid, the Peace Corps, and the many international projects sponsored by various religious organizations.

If the traditional idealism of the American college student is turning sour, the response by higher education must be creative, student-centered, and positively directed. It must be a renewing challenge to students to do more than express scorn and contempt through energetic protests, irritating sit-ins, or boorish walk-outs. It must challenge them to positive action directed at correcting some of the evils they verbalize so skillfully. Above all, it must challenge them to extend their range of interest and scope of concern beyond the confines of their campus and to base their actions on sounder motives than hate, cynicism, and mistrust.

Many activists defend their campus-centered programs concerned with women's visiting hours, liquor restrictions, and car bans as being "relevant" to the lives of students and, therefore, of meaning to them. Such a narrow view of student outreach is in sharp contrast to the idealistic conception of the modern student. Beer, women, and cars are titillating topics and effective political issues on any campus. In building a personal identity, however, they are a poor substitute for significant involvement on an international scale, such as Peace Corps experience.

Encouraging some type of service in an international setting, whereby the individual gets out of his rut and gives of himself, is an essential aspect of assisting college students to avoid "growing up absurd," to use Goodman's term. Through such experience, the young adult best can overcome many of the obstacles which he says prevent him from becoming a real person in his own eyes. It helps him to achieve a sense of relevance in his day-to-day work. It encourages a new image of himself as a significant individual in the world. He gains a new identity, freed from the limiting confines of various peer groups influencing him. It gives him a broader view of his problems and tensions in relation to those facing people in different cultures and countries. It will do what nearly every returning Peace Corps volunteer reports—"It made me a different person!"

In short, inclusion of an international service experience in an individual's educational and life plan will inject new spirit and confidence into the men and women who will lead our nation in responding creatively to the demands of the world.

100

The Rights of Students in the Classroom

RAYMOND E. WHITE

Assistant professor of history, Southeast Missouri State College. His article originally appeared in *School and Society* on April 15, 1967.

The principles of free thought and free speech are basic to American society. These concepts particularly are important to the college community, where the search for knowledge must be unencumbered and the spirit of free inquiry must prevail. The vitality of a democratic society demands that both professors and students be allowed to follow unfettered any avenue of knowledge and to discuss any idea or concept they think important. Indeed, teachers should encourage students to think deeply, broadly, and critically and to be persistent in the search for truth. Only in an atmosphere of intellectual freedom can students prepare themselves for the enormous responsibilities of national and world citizenship. Supreme Court Justice William O. Douglas expressed these ideas well when he wrote: "Every generation, if it is to grow to maturity and have understanding of man and the universe, must have no limits to its horizons. . . . Teachers [and one would also have to say students] must be allowed to pursue ideas into any domain. There must be no terminal points on discourse." *

The student's freedom to think, inquire, learn, and express himself in the academic community is dependent upon conditions and opportunities in the classroom. The responsibility to promote and maintain an atmosphere of academic freedom in the classroom mainly lies with the professor, but students ever must be vigilant that their freedom is secure.

In the classroom and in private conferences, the professor should stimulate free inquiry and discussion. Unless the student is permitted to think for himself, to question, to discuss, and to differ, his learning experience will lag. The intellectual environment of the classroom is invigorated most when the

---

* William O. Douglas, *The Right of the People* (Garden City, N.Y.: Doubleday, 1958), p.26.

student has the opportunity to express freely his ideas and his doubts. Certainly, the student has a responsibility to learn the subject matter of any course of study and to maintain the academic standards set by the professor, but he completely should be free to question the information and the opinions the professor offers. Such freedom in the classroom advances the knowledge of both student and professor. If the student is free to question, he is in the best environment for the acquisition of knowledge. On the other hand, nothing challenges the professor more than the keen questions of his students. Penetrating queries on the part of the student prompt the professor to maintain a firm comprehension of the subject matter and to present that material with clarity. Students and teachers have a common goal—to learn as much as they possibly can. In an atmosphere of free inquiry, they best can accomplish this goal.

Too many college professors, hidebound by tradition, limit the capabilities of their students by operating their classrooms on the pattern of an autocratic state—with the professor as the dictator. If free expression is discouraged in the classroom and the student merely is expected to accept without question the ideas and opinions of the professor, the professor is forcing upon the student a learning environment that the professor never would accept himself. This mode of teaching not only makes the professor autocratic and intolerant, but it also affects adversely the student by preventing the fullest development of his intellectual capacities. It is easy to be authoritarian and often difficult to accept the audacious questions and opinions of the probing student—but the mere exercise of authority and the mere assertion of the professor's superior knowledge benefits neither student nor instructor. The freedom to discuss, differ, and challenge without fear of repression and without fear of losing grade points is the type of learning environment the student needs.

The good teacher does not sermonize or expect the student to accept his ideas at face value on any subject, controversial or otherwise. Rather, the teacher states his thoughtful opinions on matters in his area of academic study. He appeals to the student to use his own reasoning powers and to challenge any of the information presented in the course. In following this avenue, the professor reveals his understanding of the enthusiastic and curious student who will not be fitted into the intellectual mold of his seniors. The student needs to think for himself, even if it means that his thinking becomes heretical and unorthodox.

Free expression in the classroom does not release the student from the obligation of learning thoroughly the subject matter of the course and performing academically in a manner the professor demands. At the same time, the student should be evaluated only on his knowledge of the subject matter, and not at all on his views or opinions. If a student has the feeling that his opinions might affect his grade adversely, he will hesitate to express them. Certainly, good, honest dialogue between student and professor creates excitement in learning and promotes the acquisition of knowledge. In any event, the professor never should allow opinions expressed in such dialogues to affect his evaluation of the student. In appraising academic ability, the professor should follow a systematic and intelligible procedure which protects the student from discriminatory and erratic evaluations. Moreover, a student has a right to know his academic standing at any time during the period of the course.

If the professor exercises care in evaluating student academic ability, he also must act with responsibility when called upon by prospective employers to furnish information about his students. Teachers, most certainly, can answer questions about a student's academic record and his qualifications for a particular job. But questions which relate to the student's opinions about politics, religion, and social and moral concepts might endanger the student-teacher relationship. If this relationship is damaged, the opportunities for learning are limited. The knowledge of student views and opinions, which the professor learns through his professional association with the student, should be considered confidential.

Fair and just evaluation of student abilities and freedom in the classroom are necessities in the 20th-century system of higher education. Professors must remember that colleges were created primarily for students and that students have rights, especially in the classroom. Too many professors cling to the idea that education ought to be carried on without the interference of students. Those encrusted professors who hold this view should shed it of their own volition; if the professors do not, students should demand it.

101

Cutting—Permissive or Controlled?

J. PAUL WILLIAMS

Professor emeritus of religion, Mount Holyoke College. At the time his article originally appeared in *School and Society* (Oct. 19, 1963), he was professor of religion.

"I never take the roll," said a colleague. "If a student has the ability to do the work without coming to class, why should I force him to attend?"

This proposition often is stated by college and university teachers as evidence of their educational emancipation, of the distance between their methods and those of the traditional schoolmaster. After experimenting with this "broad-minded" policy for a couple of decades, I have concluded that it hinders rather than aids the educational process in a large percentage of classes. Accordingly, at the beginning of most of my courses, I now make this statement: "Your presence here is essential to the adequate completion of the work of this course. Many of its objectives are very difficult if not impossible to achieve by independent study. Accordingly, I will expect you to appear here with the same regularity that you would appear at an office where you were employed."

The beneficial results of this policy seem clear. For one thing, under this regimen, the emphasis of the course need not be placed so squarely on subject matter. Every able college teacher includes more than subject matter among his offerings. He may seek to increase such qualities as independence, creativity, logicality, and appreciation; and he may have a high degree of success in helping some students to develop these qualities. Yet, devising methods of evaluating the extent to which a student acquires them is very difficult. On the other hand, devising methods of evaluating a student's knowledge of "the facts" is comparatively easy. Consequently, the teacher in courses where the attendance is spotty will emphasize subject matter by the type of examination he is forced to give, since he will wish to differentiate as fairly as he can among his students in his course grades.

Moreover, placing a near-to-exclusive emphasis on subject matter in the evaluation of achievement stimulates in students an unfortunate view of education: that mastery of factual content is the all-important end. Some students come to the class with a more mature view: they feel that, though the factual content is an essential foundation, it is not the end of their work. Such students in a class where the instructor examines subject matter closely are forced to stress memorization of the minutiae of their class notes and of a textbook. They take a risk if they pursue such tangential aspects of the course as may intrigue their interest.

Unlimited cutting also results in another problem. College and university teachers must face students who have a large variety of abilities, backgrounds, preparations, interests, etc. This built-in heterogeneity is increased by adding still another differentiating factor: uncertainty whether some students have covered outside the classroom what most students have covered inside the classroom. This additional heterogeneity should be tolerated only under exceptional circumstances.

These observations assume the present American arrangements in higher education. Some readers no doubt would wish to attack the problem by proposing a new set of arrangements: the Oxford plan, the tutorial system, no examinations until the end of a student's experience in a given institution and then examination in depth. Until such changes are made, the active teacher is confronted by the necessity of making plans for classes in which he must assign work, conduct examinations, and report course grades.

The courses where little harm is done by permissive attendance policies are, oddly enough, not those aimed at increasing such intangible qualities as independence and creativity, but, rather, courses whose aim is to transmit what scholars have agreed on as the essential factual material. Some students can master the basic material without listening to their instructor's lecture; why should these students be required to go to class? But there are other courses where the values must be obtained chiefly through prolonged give-and-take experiences.

The most important consideration in requiring attendance is that a student is most apt to acquire some of the essential values of education while he is in direct contact with the teacher. The courses where numerous class sessions and high standards of attendance seem mandatory are those where the emphasis goes beyond subject matter: seminars, laboratories, classes where intragroup reactions dominate, and classes where such things as attitudes, assumptions, skills, and thinking processes are under examination. The values of such courses usually cannot be obtained by independent study; if the student is absent, the work cannot be made up except by special tutoring by the teacher—and often not even then. The chief function of the teacher in conducting such courses is not to act as a transmission belt for facts, but to act as a coach in the development of special objectives. Every student misses his educational birthright unless he has continuing contact with teachers who look over his intellectual shoulder and ask, "Have you considered viewing it (doing it) this way?" To fail to require attendance in classes designed to provide direct student-teacher contact is to express our own uncertainty concerning the value of this important teaching function.

102

Conflict and Tension Areas on the Campus

WALTER I. MURRAY

The author was a member of the faculty of Southern University at the time his article originally appeared in *School and Society* (Nov. 27, 1954). Information about his current position is unavailable.

The persistence of conflict situations and tensions on the modern college campus, despite the tremendous advances in psychology and psychiatry, is a phenomenon of central importance in any analysis of the behavior of college students. One of the significant steps in this direction is the organization and operation of college psychological clinics. The clients of these clinics, in general, are individuals with so-called personality problems, financial difficulties, and poor interpersonal relationships.

The purpose of this survey is to discover areas on the campus where individual students have difficulties and conflicts which make for poor interpersonal relationships. Such a study aims to supply data to the college administrators which would indicate where improvement is needed and to furnish a basis upon which a technique might be developed to understand the individual pattern of poor interpersonal reationships.

Thirty students in an introductory course in sociology were asked to submit a list of areas in which they had personally encountered difficulties because of conflicts and tensions or where they have witnessed the experiences of others in this regard. This assignment was made because it enabled the students to use research methods in solving familiar problems, thus engendering self-confidence, and to apply sociological principles. The responses of these students were summarized and discussed by them. These summaries were submitted to another class of 28 students enrolled in sociology. Their reactions were noted with regard to the generality of the experiences and their evaluations. On the basis of these judgments, a check list was submitted to 265 students enrolled in Southern University.

This survey revealed that there are a number of areas in which tension and conflict arise on our campus. Those of us whose responsibility is that of assisting students to make satisfactory interpersonal adjustments should endeavor to find the causes which make for poor adjustment and should do something to improve the situation.

Table I

TENSION AREAS ON THE COLLEGE CAMPUS
AS REPORTED BY 265 STUDENTS

AREA	NUMBER OF STUDENTS	PER-CENT
1. Sorority-Fraternity Affiliation	105	39
2. Lines for Service		
a. Dining hall	138	52
b. Post Office	114	43
c. Movie	54	23
d. Registration	184	69
3. Clothing	70	26
4. Popularity Polls (such as Miss ROTC)	106	40
5. Student-Teacher Relationship	122	46
6. Skin Color Differences	105	39
7. Loafing Centers (benches, rails, halls)	99	37
8. Scholarship (grades and grade points)	110	45
9. Election of School Officers	96	36
10. Athletic Competition	49	19
11. Boyfriend-Girlfriend Relationship	107	43
12. Club or Church Membership	33	12
13. Car Parking	103	38
14. Dormitory Regulations	117	44
15. Classroom Neighbors	1	·4
16. Library	2	·8
17. Dances	1	·4
18. Crossing the Street	1	·4
19. School Employees	1	·4
20. Lavatory Problem	2	·8
21. Transportation	1	·4

103

Contributions of Counselors to Academic Standards

MARGUERITE HALL ALBJERG

The author was a counselor in the office of the Dean of Women, Purdue University, at the time her article originally appeared in *School and Society* (Nov. 5, 1960). Mrs. Albjerg is now retired.

An alert counselor no less than an able professor is aware that some students want to ride piggy-back from registration to commencement. If they, together with administrators and parents, should ever unite their efforts to elevate academic standards, this country might see its citizens reject the popular premise that "a standard of living is more important than a standard of thinking."

Both counselors and professors realize that improving the intellectual climate at a university requires the developing of campus mores which truly respect scholarly achievement. The admirable labors of professors in this field are recognized, but that counselors also make a worthy contribution in this area is less often known. Advisers make a contribution, first of all, by comprehending readily and valuing highly genuine scholarship and intellectual discipline. One cannot abet what one does not understand. A counselor need not be a Phi Beta Kappa nor have a doctor's degree nor have published a book, but she must appreciate what scholarship is and have the desire to see learning thrive. She may be incapable of doing this if she herself has not continued to grow intellectually since her own college experience. She should take care that the trivia of her job—selecting beauty queens, judging homecoming floats, chaperoning dances—do not so sap her energy and dull her intellectual curiosity so that she loses her penchant for poetry, or international affairs, or Greek philosophy.

A discerning counselor quickly recognizes that a university may have a number of worthy objectives but its primary goal is that of creating an atmosphere of learning and facilitating the student's mental growth. Such an adviser may try to communicate to her counselees that "the average is something to be risen above, not something to cling to."

Undergraduates are sometimes more inclined to listen to the counselor who can comprehend a quadratic equation or grasp a Supreme Court decision as long as she can, at the same time, understand *them*. They feel that such an adviser can help them bridge the gap between the classroom and campus. Almost any counselor will do a better job if she knows the library and how to use it, if she is interested in books and reads them, if she is aware of world problems and concerned about them.

Advisers are frequently charged with being indifferent to the academic program or with stressing students' personal adjustment as the paramount goal in college. A few may be so motivated just as the teaching faculty has a few who have no real regard for superior scholarship, yet neither group seems to comprise a sizable number in either profession. The interest of counselors in bettering the scholastic conditions on a campus is often in evidence. For example, in their participation in orientation and freshman interview programs, they emphasize consistently that the two imperative techniques for scholastic success in college are the development of good study habits, if one does not already have them, and handling effectively one's time.

Counselors also point out to the uncertain freshman that the academic program comes first, that if it cannot be managed competently along with the extracurricular functions, the latter should be by-passed. Then, too, they remind counselees who complain about too exacting assignments that the university is not "a glorified high school," that its basic purpose is to promote intellectual growth which is achieved primarily by the student's personal efforts. Teachers may indicate the way and stimulate the desire, but the student herself must travel the road to learning.

An observant counselor also may reassure a serious but able student that her undue concern about her courses is part of the price one usually pays for genuine learning and that the achievement of excellence is often preceded by personal anxiety. But the wise adviser often encourages such a disheartened student with the assurance that there is a special self-confidence and a unique exhilaration that comes to one who has developed a well-trained mind which operates effectively.

In working groups, counselors often are influential in persuading residence units to require less activity hours of their members whose extra-curricular duties are hindering their scholastic progress. Also, they discourage or deny the requests of student organizations for late hours or for permission to give more elaborate social affairs because these unduly exploit students' energy and interfere with their study time. Then, too, advisers actively have encouraged students to invite faculty to their residence units so that their participation in the group's conversation can stimulate provocative discussions.

However, any counselor worth her salt "does not mistake activity for achievement" any more than an able professor confuses "busy work" with learning. She well knows that if counselors or students "so run that we never rest, if we so talk that we never think, if we so exist that we never live," true learning is not possible, and anti-intellectualism is given another boost.

Counselors also can contribute to improving the campus climate by respecting the nonconformist. Those who prefer "to fit in" rather than "to stand out" usually support the standards of mediocrity and do little to elevate the intellectual tone of the campus. "If mediocrity is made welcome," it has been observed, "excellence will look elsewhere for its opportunity." Unquestionably, getting along with people is commendable, while intentionally cultivating the dissenter's role lacks merit. But doing what seems important and right and not being diverted by group disapproval or by improper rewards are the marks of an independent person or, perhaps, a nonconformist.

Often counselors are confronted with students who feel they should oppose a belief currently in vogue or the prevailing sentiment of a group. Here a sagacious adviser who is not overawed by the "togetherness" and "groupism" on the campus can help the student clarify her thinking, often encourage her, and yet indicate certain displeasing aspects of her position. The counselor can even point out that group approval is no substitute for personal integrity. Any adviser knows it is much easier to suggest that the student conform, but an enlightened counselor may recognize in the student's conduct a significant milestone in her intellectual maturing and, therefore, give her needed support.

Again, there is the coed who always wanted to take engineering but yielded to parental pleas to enter the more ladylike field of English. Still dissatisfied with her choice and facing the protests of her roommates and her boyfriend over her contemplated change, she drops in to talk to a counselor. After their candid but inspiriting discussion of her decision, the coed musters the courage to persevere with her plan.

Occasionally, students stop in ostensibly for one thing but actually to "test" their own iconoclastic views on some matter against the judgment of the adviser. Whether the student's ideas are untenable or feasible, she needs to be urged to think critically, honestly, and responsibly. And this is frequently just what a prudent counselor helps her to do. For there is no academic risk involved in consulting a counselor, whereas a student in conferring with a professor on some controversial topic may fear that he will take a disparaging view of her intellectual potential. When students believe an adviser is intelligent enough to grasp their concepts and is sufficiently flexible to give these impartial consideration, that individual is likely to be sought by college youth as a kind of academic confessor. Any time a student is spurred on to challenging mental activity and accountable action, the cause of intellectual excellence has been served.

A counselor, however, needs to be on her guard in dealing with one type of nonconformist. James R. Killian, Jr., has warned of this when he said that we are in danger of creating an institutional environment which is preoccupied not with learning but with "the self-conscious aspects of one's personality problems." Although a university undoubtedly hopes to improve the spirits and physiques of its students while it cultivates their minds, its primary commitment is not to the solution of serious personality difficulties. A gravely maladjusted student is often a nonconformist, too, and she and her family sometimes put great pressure on a counselor to endorse a special campus arrangement designed to help her solve her particular problems. To yield to such requests frequently is to impede the academic atmosphere of a housing unit or perhaps to overtax a busy counselor whose time should be given to matters more pertinent to the main purpose of college life.

Counselors who bring to their task an inquiring mind, a humane and intelligent concern for students, and fidelity to the chief purpose of the university can benefit youth, the institution, and society. If the adviser remembers to practice herself what she tries to suggest to her counselees— namely, never "become so overwhelmed with the urgent as to lose sight of the important"—then she may feel reasonably sure that she, too, has made a contribution to the intellectual climate of the campus.

104

New College Students Lack Study Techniques

L. S. HADLEY

The author was Director of Student Advising, Kent State University, at the time his article originally appeared in *School and Society* (Nov. 23, 1957). Dr. Hadley is now retired.

Few students entering college experience academic success which is commensurate with their measurable potentialities. This judgment is based on the following experiences by the writer: many years of teaching and supervision in secondary schools; observation of results from Mooney's Problem Check-List (and similar forms) completed by numerous sample groups composed of potential college students; direction of the program of orientation for new students at a good-sized state university for eight years; counseling with thousands of college students, as well as with their faculty advisers, during service as director of student advising.

I estimate conservatively that about 95% of those entering college lack adequate study skills, and this includes many high-school valedictorians. The typical high-school student studies very little outside of his school's organized study halls and seldom spends more than two hours outside of school on all of his subjects put together. His skills are geared to meet this demand. Suddenly he is confronted with college assignments, each of which may consume two hours, and there is no supervised study hall. Even though his school record may have been sufficiently high to rate him top honors, he finds himself greatly disillusioned when he must meet both the increased competition which college brings and the immediate demands for the more effective use of his time. A relatively small percentage of the beginning college students have reading speeds and comprehension skills adequate to handle all college assignments. Many never have experimented with reading for meaning but have continued verbalizing as if they were reading aloud. The shorter assignments never have required more. College classes are taught predominantly by the lecture method and one seldom meets a new college student who is able to take good and usable notes. A counselor has only to recall the numerous complaints of students about tests ("That wasn't a fair question; it isn't in the text book.") to realize that their previous school experiences have required no note-taking on class work.

Since secondary teachers have used more generally the so-called objective-type tests, it is not unusual to find numerous college beginners who experience great difficulty to organize in writing the answer to a test question. Other kinds of tests also disturb some students because "they just seldom show to good advantage on tests," yet most college professors judge course grades on the basis of test performance.

A few students adjust their study techniques without apparent interruption, while others appear utterly frustrated. Some acquire study skills in a hit-or-miss fashion and feel lucky when they get by, not thinking what they might have been able to achieve had they tried appropriate techniques. Others fail to meet the minimum requirements and are dropped.

Aside from foundations in written expression and computation skills, probably the most important assets a student has when he enters college are his academic work habits and study skills. But if he has not acquired the necessary techniques to become an effective college student with ordinary adjustments, then the problem is largely one of initiating his own programs of self-improvement. Many colleges offer organized courses in how to study in which the student may enroll, even for college credit. These are only as effective as each individual student makes them. Again, many excellent references are available and a student may conscientiously read all of the suggestions made to him, but nothing happens to his own reading or other study skills until he is motivated to try out some of the programs of improvement. Counseling may include a careful diagnosis of the student's individual difficulties, but, unless he becomes experimental to the point of developing some new approaches to his problems of being an adequate college student, his problem remains unsolved. All of these efforts on the part of college— courses, counseling, clinics, laboratories, suggested references—are needed and must be made available to students, but in the final analysis there are no short-cuts to success in improved reading or other study skills and each student must realize that only through practice can he change his own habits.

Living up to one's potentialities most of the time is the goal held by the mature student, and he does it without "outside" prodding.

105

Training in Ideas

SYLVIA ANGUS

Assistant professor of English, State University of New York, Canton. Her article originally appeared in *School and Society* on March 10, 1962.

Like most teachers of college English I have been plagued for years by the masses of freshmen who, told to write a paper discussing some idea in their reading, have thrown out two or three undeveloped thoughts or, even more pitifully, have asked in dismay how one could write 500 words about *that* kind of a subject. Only this year, after teaching a class of senior high-school students on an advanced standing program, has it become clear to me why college freshmen are so frequently incapable of dealing with ideas. Even those rarely favored high-school students who have written regular themes as part of their English course almost never have been required to discuss an idea. A list of typical high-school theme subjects and, I regret to add, often college theme subjects reads like this: "My Grandmother," "The First Time I Fell in Love," "My Summer Vacation," "My Favorite Relative," "How to Make Pizza," "The Salk Vaccine," "The Day I Kept House."

There is not an idea in the lot; the subjects are all descriptive or anecdotal. If a high-school student has a fair command of grammar, it is extremely simple for him to be wafted up to college with a straight A average in English. It is a rude shock to him as a college freshman to discover that he has no training whatever in writing the kind of analytical essay or examination which suddenly is demanded of him not only in English, but in History, Philosophy, Economics—practically all of his arts subjects.

It is not, as it sometimes seems to the frustrated college instructor, a matter of basic intelligence. I have had students of high intelligence and considerable literary imagination who have not known how to develop an idea. Asked to discuss, for instance, the difference between the Greek Gods and the Christian God, they will make a careful list of the most obvious differences. It does not occur to them that a list is not a discussion. They do not discuss, therefore, the *reasons* for the differences, the connection between the stage of civilization and the conception of God, the social utility of different ideas of God, or the economic or social implications of religious differences. Almost invariably, having made their lists, these students will conclude with a resounding peroration on the superiority of Christianity. They are accustomed to making strong statements of opinion, but since they have not been trained in unemotional, reasoned analysis, their judgments are too superficial to have any value. They are like the people who say, "I don't know anything about art, but I know what I like."

Unfortunately, this battered cliché is, in essence, the exact reverse of what should be the student's role. The job of the student is to suspend judgment. Ultimately, we hope, he will learn to make his choices, but before that time he needs to learn how to analyze, how to collect and weigh evidence, how to erect the sub-structure upon which sound judgments may be made. It is this technique, so lightly tossed off as "learning how to think," which is still the basic function of education and which is ignored or misunderstood in many high schools. If, in the high school, students were taught to examine ideas and to read other people's speculations about them, they would enter college with the most useful tool they could get for their continuing education.

Which brings us to the further point that not only are students not being taught to discuss ideas, they are not being taught to read for ideas either. Obviously, ideas neither can be discussed nor analyzed soundly without considerable reading background. The most brilliant mind in the world will produce only philosophic clichés if it is illiterate and can make no use of already explored ideas. It is necessary, therefore, that the student be taught not only to analyze, but to recognize the areas of his ignorance and to fill them in by reading widely.

Where, then, to make a start? Does one read everything first and then start to analyze, or does one first learn to analyze and then read as seems required? Clearly we have here the dilemma of the educational circle. Does one think to read or read to think? Just as clearly, we have here an educational universe, like the physical one, which cannot be said to begin, suddenly, anywhere. It is essential to consider the process of education a spiral rather than a circular one if we are to make any progress. We must tackle both reading and thinking at once. Since they will not remain with each other, even for a moment, they will push each other up the spiral. As thinking deepens, the need for more information will become evident. As reading broadens, we will see the necessity for comparing, for analyzing—in short, for thinking more deeply.

When our college freshman arrives on campus, we must begin at once the sadly delayed process of starting him on his educational spiral. How to do this? First, I believe, by shifting his attack on all questions from "what" to "why." Most college teachers do this automatically, of course, if they are any good at all. But it seems to me that it must be done more self-consciously.

We need to recognize that our students have been taught conscientiously to look *at* things rather than into or around them. This is not, of course, an evil. They must be trained to look at things. Unfortunately, they have not been taught that there is anything more to be done, that the most important questions are "why" and "how."

It seems evident that the process of teaching students the "what" of their reading should begin in grade school and junior high. By the time high school is reached, the shift to asking "why" should be taking place. By the time a student of college caliber matriculates, it should be possible to assume that he knows how to read for precise information and that the emphasis should be wholly on reading for ideas and for pleasure.

Obviously, this halcyon situation does not begin to exist. The thinking process must start somewhere, however, and the college English class is a logical place to begin. Assigned themes should be closely tied in with reading materials and the shift to "why" should be made. This means that instead of assigning themes on "Autumn" or "My Roommate," instructors will have to devote considerable thought to the creation of a list of pertinent subjects for discussion. It is important at first to find questions which can be handled analytically with a minimum of extra information. To begin by asking for an analysis of Greek religion would demand a great deal from a student whose first knowledge of the ancients is coming to him from a current class reading of "The Odyssey." It would be less demanding of background, while still making a start on analysis, to ask the student to write a paper discussing possible reasons why men should create Gods in their own image. There are, obviously, vast continents of sociological, psychological, and anthropological reasons for this which the student will not know. Nevertheless, it is a question which is possible for the student to speculate upon.

He probably will start with a simple statement such as the one that human-type gods are cosier than abstract ones. It then becomes the teacher's job to show how such a remark might be amplified and explored. He might ask why this should be so and, if it is true, why abstract conceptions of God should ever have been created at all. That question, of course, will bring up such additional questions as "What do people want in their God images anyway?" and "How may human-type gods be inadequate?"

At first these and similar questions will seem like a sneak attack to many students. You did not ask those questions in the theme topic, you may be told aggrievedly. Of course you did not. The thing they are learning from this is that discussion is not static, that it involves motion between ideas. Points bring up other points; statements resolve themselves into new and further questions. They begin at this stage to get a glimmering of what you mean when you ask them to expand an idea. They begin to realize that a few neatly turned comments are the merest beginning, just the visible top of an iceberg of thought. They begin also to perceive how much they do not know, a convenient moment to direct them to outside reading materials.

When the student has begun to see the relevance of reading to his ability to discuss in greater depth, it will become useful to involve the entire class in the thinking process as an exercise in cross-fertilization of thought. An effective method is for the instructor to read aloud one or more papers in each set and to ask that the class discuss a student's analysis. At first the instructor will have to lead the way by indicating weakly supported thoughts and by suggesting points which should have been made. In a remarkably short time, the other students join in with suggestions of how the ideas might be expanded, what more might be said.

There are, clearly, any number of techniques which the instructor might use successfully to train students to think more deeply. The urgent necessity is that teachers recognize that student ineptness in the handling of ideas is not congenital and that almost any student who makes it to college at all can be trained to improve in this area. If college English instructors can train their freshman students to be more analytical, more knowledgeable, and less prone to dogmatic statements, members of every other department will rise up and call them blessed.

106

A Program for the Talented College Student

PETER S. MOUSOLITE

Acting Regional Assistant Commissioner, U.S. Office of Education, Chicago. At the time his article originally appeared in *School and Society* (March 5, 1966), he was Acting Regional Representative.

It is reasonable to expect talented students to become leaders on the campus, and later in their communities. If they learn in college to apply all of their abilities to the solution of certain problems, they should carry considerable practical experience in solving difficulties into the community organization in which they will function.

If, on the other hand, they are allowed to fall far below their potential, they are likely to carry into the world habits of laziness and just getting by. This loss of sheer brain power, the power of the persons potentially most effective in society, is serious to a world facing seemingly insoluble problems.

As a technique for assisting the student in individual development, every college should have an adequate counseling and guidance system. The principal purpose of this system is to help the student make the best possible adjustment to his cultural and social environment, and to fit him for making those same adjustments later in the outside world. The guidance and counseling system often is only partially effective. It generally functions for students whose problems have become so acute that they have either come in for a voluntary interview, or have been sent by a faculty member who has noticed some scholastic difficulty. The talented student is in danger of seldom being touched by the guidance services. This will be due, probably, to the fact that instructors and administrators see achievement too much in the light of a competitive grade system rather than include achievement also in terms of a student's potential.

The problem has been and will be one of stimulation and motivation, of releasing power which is held in check by some personal or institutional control. With these students, as with others, the institution should think of adjusting to the needs of individuals somewhere along the four years of study. Instead of making students conform for four years to a rigid curriculum, the curriculum should be flexible so as to consider the needs of the students, both individually and as a group.

The fundamentals underlying all effective work with persons, whether it be in the field of politics, education, business, or religion, seem to be the same. The basic premise must be the value of the individual as a person and not as a cog in the social machine. Our most effective social organizations are based on the voluntary and personal contributions of individuals. If these social contributions are to be made by individuals, then certainly we must recognize the peculiar qualities and values which differentiate every human being from every other human being.

All students who desire to do so should be encouraged to enroll in an experimental program. As stated previously, if it can be demonstrated that counseling techniques applied to individualized education are effective in producing the fullest effectiveness of talented individuals, it should have significant effects. First of all, it would train a group of leaders to give all of their effort and ability to the solution of a given problem. Secondly, it would indicate that the techniques used for this group might be profitably extended to a wider range of students, perhaps to include all students.

As to the actual program of this experimental group, students should be enrolled, at the appropriate time, for a year of college rather than for courses. In conference with one of a number of faculty members who have demonstrated marked ability to adapt their courses to individual requirements, the student would begin work on some project which interested him. In the conference, student and advisor would work out any kind of program which seemed advisable, but the course of study would consist principally of projects, reports, and papers to be worked out by using all the necessary resources of the college and civic community.

In such a program, the faculty advisor should lead the student skillfully from one area of interest into another in such a way that he eventually would cover considerable ground in all the main fields of knowledge but always would be following his interests.

An example of such leading of the interests might be of value. Suppose the student is interested in such a question as "What were the causes of or the reasons for the failure of the League of Nations?" He would be led into the study of previous attempts at world government culminating with the present organization of the United Nations. He would find that to understand them he needed to inquire into history, politics, economics, psychology, religion, literature, and, certainly, problems of ethics and moral values would arise. Coming to the uses of atomic and nuclear energy, he would be compelled to go into the areas of the physical and biological sciences. In a contemporary study of the United Nations, he would have to use his knowledge of a foreign language to do further research in certain lines. In all of these fields, the knowledge acquired would be retained much better than in ordinary courses, because it would have some immediate application to the student's interests.

What is really important is that the student would acquire, early in his academic career, the tools for independent investigation and research and the incentive and motivation to want to do it. Once completed, the project would provide for the student the real reward—that of a deep, inner, personal satisfaction that comes from work well done.

A word of caution: There are certain reservations that must be stated with regard to those individuals who may exceed all bounds of common sense in attempting to accommodate the talented student so eagerly sought today. Lest we forget, one of the necessary requisites of any student is that he should accept a large measure of responsibility for his own development and for his own education. A student of unusual ability should be able to recognize unusual aspects of course assignments and classroom discussions in such a manner that he will explore on his own initiative those areas not limited by a three-credit course in any subject matter.

A student possessed of high ability is fortunate but not always successful in the attainment of his life's goals. The same student accepting considerable responsibility for his own education has better training for his career and is more likely to attain success.

107

Students Insist upon Examinations

VICTOR L. ALBJERG

Professor emeritus of history, Purdue University. At the time his article originally appeared in *School and Society* (May 23, 1953), he was professor of history.

When an examination is announced students invariably groan. They regard these periodic tests as inventions of the devil. But a kind word may be in order for Beelzebub himself. Did not Giosuè Carducci, eminent Italian, receive the Nobel Prize for his *Ode to Satan*? As a matter of fact students would grumble if examinations were eliminated. They want them for the same reason that for decades the public fought for the merit system. Citizens insisted upon the civil service because they favored appointments on the basis of merit rather than on that of favoritism. They demanded equality of opportunity in quest of office. To secure justice for himself each individual recognizes the necessity of extending the same fairness to others.

Students are as eager for justice as are their elders. The system of examinations is for students what the merit system is for adults. Some form of student evaluation is inescapable, and fundamentally students prefer to be rated on the basis of achievement rather than upon wealth, social position, or their appearance. Nothing could be more fair than to measure students on the basis of their performance; nothing so destructive of morale as to grade them by some capricious standard.

Winston Churchill admitted that, while he was First Lord of the Admiralty, he took meticulous care in drafting his reports to Mr. Asquith, the Prime Minister, who, he knew, scrutinized them with a discerning eye. When students realize that their labors are similarly observed, then they, too, will appreciate the utility of their efforts. If they are convinced that inadequate preparation inevitably yields low grades and that diligent application produces high grades, they, too, will recognize the value of serious study. Morale to a large extent depends upon the fairness of examinations.

Someone has said that nothing helps a man to concentrate so much as the realization that he is about to die. Examinations have much the same effect upon students, for failure in a test can impose academic execution.

Moreover, examinations should be given to exploit the competitive instinct in a free and competitive society. Almost everyone works harder when he knows that his efforts are being measured against those of others. Even a horse runs faster when it is running against other horses than when it lopes along alone. The Russian Communists also recognized this truism. Soon after their accession to power they acted upon the maxim, "To each according to his needs," and this produced a needy society. The Communists then changed the rule, "To each according to his deeds," with the result that they produced mighty deeds. By exploiting the competitive instinct the Reds changed Russia from a dive of drones to a hive of hustlers. By means of examinations students often can be reimbursed for intelligent activity that will spur them on to greater achievement. Academic equalitarianism is contrary to the American spirit.

Examinations should also be given in order to train students to meet the crises of normal existence. An examination is a crisis. Since daily living is full of such occurrences, students should be prepared to meet these climacterics by facing them in school. They should not be unfitted for practical living by being sheltered in an environment of unreality. A doctor, called to a critical case, must be able to discover the relevant facts and then to draw the proper conclusions. If he fails, the patient dies. Each difficult case is for him an examination. A lawyer who argues a case in court takes an examination each time he appears before the jury. If he cannot produce the evidence, the client loses. A banker with his vault bulging with capital takes an examination each time he faces an investment opportunity. If he flunks he may bankrupt his institution. The best training for any army is actual fighting. The best combat preparation for a student is to take examinations.

108

Imaginary Advice to Students on Taking Examinations

WM. CLARK TROW

Emeritus professor of education, University of Michigan. At the time his article originally appeared in *School and Society* (March 9, 1963), he was professor of education and of psychology.

It looks as if examinations are here to stay, so you might as well get used to the idea of taking at least one in each course—unless it is a seminar, in which case you might be able to talk your way through it. Some say it is important to know how to study, and there are even books on the subject, but this is an indirect approach. Whether you study or not, it is the examination that counts. So it is much better to know how to take examinations and meet the crucial issue head-on instead of going around Robin Hood's barn.

I am not talking about the true-false and multiple-choice type examination, because there is nothing to do about them except to go down the list marking the items more or less at random. If you are the conscientious type and feel that you ought to read the questions, mark according to your whims, for studies have shown that when you know something about a course, you will get more than 50% right and this will put you above most of the students who try to figure out what the instructor meant by each question. Never mark alternate items right and wrong. Though this is likely to pass you, it suggests a careless disinterest in the whole experience that instructors do not appreciate. It is better to mark the longer statements true and the shorter ones false, because it seems to take fewer words to write what is not so than what is.

But to get back to the regular examinations, the so-called essay type. I have taken a good many of these—more than most students because I usually take a make-up or repeat a course—so I think my experience should be valuable.

In the first place, there are many more important things in life than the niceties of the English language, so don't be too squeamish about spelling. Two "'s's" in "occasion," one "g" in "aggression," and an easy-going tolerance in the use of criteria or criterion allow one to devote his attention to more fundamental issues. The same is true about the antecedents to pronouns. If you get a little mixed up in one paragraph, start the next with: "This is of outstanding importance because . . . " and let the reader figure out to what "this" refers. And, incidentally, refer to yourself from time to time as "the author", "the writer," and "we." This keeps the reader guessing as to whether you are referring to a cited authority (which gives the impression of erudition) or to yourself (which builds you up into the same category).

Use as many nouns as possible. For example, don't write: "If the child prefers to do something else. . . ." It is much better to write: "If the child has a school need preference for some other value activity. . . ." Such expressions give a kind of scholarly stench to your writing.

Use whatever words come to mind when you are thinking of something to write. Words mean what you want them to mean. And in a sentence like "There are reasons and consequences of every event," never mind that "reason of" is not standard dialect; it is yours, and the reader should be able to get the drift. After all, what is he paid for?

Some think it is better to start writing as soon as you get to your seat, while your mind is still fresh and clear from the cramming you may have done the night before. My advice, however, is to wait until you receive the questions (to read them carefully is confusing) and then immediately write down the answers to the questions you thought would be on the examination, whether it is or not. Such immediate action gets you started so that you can proceed without fear of clutch (blanking out).

Sometimes it is helpful to read a question, since it may suggest something to write. However, do not be bound by it. If it asks for the causes of something or other, you might as well write on the results, especially if you know them better, and if you don't know either, write something that you do know about—if anything.

Readers differ in their attitudes toward organized misinformation. In general, it is better to present it in a disorganized form, since the numbers (1), (2), and (3) in the margin may create a tension in the reader that cannot be released until he learns what are these numbered points you are making. For him to obtain this knowledge might be disastrous; so it is better not to arouse the tension.

If three or four points—that is, causes, results, considerations, etc.—are important in discussing a topic, whether or not they are mentioned in the statement of the question, it is better to concentrate on one of them and not to think about the other possibilities, for this is distracting. Even if you could think of the others, you might not know anything about them; that would cause you anxiety and you might not be able to remember what you knew about the one you could think of. If you know nothing about that either, follow the directions above and write about something. Whatever you write on might be related to the question, whether you realize it or not.

Some readers prefer generalizations; others like specific facts. Usually you can tell from a course which the professor prefers; but he may not read the papers. Therefore, it is usually a good idea to learn three or four facts to be used, whatever the question is. And, by all means, never meet the point of the question directly, even if you can figure out what it is, for this, too, might cause the reader to suspect that you had prior knowledge. If you talk all around it, you get it encircled so that it cannot get away from you, and you can demolish it at your leisure, perhaps on the make-up, if you are still in college.

109

Changing Mores Concerning Cheating on Examinations

MARVIN L. HENRICKS

Professor of sociology, Indiana Central College. At the time his article originally appeared in *School and Society* (Nov. 22, 1958), he was associate professor of sociology.

On the basis of data obtained from a questionnaire given to students in a single college, one realizes that the student who sometimes cheats is a very ordinary person: 57% of all those questioned and nearly 75% of the seniors had cheated at some time during their college careers. The volume of the offenders will not surprise those who communicate with students, for they believe that cheating is common.

It is interesting to note the views of college people about the practice of cheating. Only 13% of the students think that the person who cheats is "basically dishonest," 33% are uncertain about this, but over 53% are quite sure that one who cheats is not to be thought of as possessing such a trait. In fact, only 34% are sure that they would not vote for such a person for the office of class treasurer, 22% say that this fact would not keep them from trusting the offender with class money, while the remaining 40% are uncertain.

Students say there is no reason to believe that, because a person cheats, he also would steal a five-dollar bill if given the opportunity. Only seven percent would say that stealing and cheating would necessarily go together. There is a great increase, however, in the belief that people who cheat on tests might also cheat on income tax, or on time cards, or vending machines.

Most students believe that, in the competitive system, their own grades suffer when other students cheat. A large 73% of them believe this, 20% are uncertain, but only seven percent think this is not so. Still, less than 20% feel a great deal of resentment against the cheaters, and only 13% say they feel none at all. In spite of the feeling that the practice worked against them, only

12% would co-operate with an honor system which asked them to inform on a fellow student, 33% were unsure, and 55% said they would not inform.

The suggested punishments were interesting because they reveal more than direct responses the feeling about the seriousness of the offense. Only one percent thought that cheating justifies expulsion from school. Only a few more, between two and three percent, thought an "F" in the course would be fair. Most suggested that the professor speak to the offending student, and some that an "F" on the test would be deserved.

The accumulated data suggest that cheating is widespread and not harshly condemned.[1] Is the increase in cheating a part of the general relaxation of an old code? The questions which dealt with such marginal decisions as income-tax evasion and fraudulent time-card punching are questions which concern individual responses to impersonal situations. It seems to be more acceptable to violate these demands. Much of our present-day living is characterized by this kind of impersonal relationship, and there is reason to wonder if the so-called breakdown of the moral code does not represent instead the dysfunction of a code built for rural people who dealt individually with one another.

The practice of cheating may be another one of these evidences. Students are parts of a system in which the attainment of knowledge has become secondary to the completion of a prescribed course which our culture demands. Examinations are a part of the process. One passes or one does not depending on his ability to beat the testing system. The system becomes a kind of game in which the professor has certain techniques and devices and the student has countermoves. Cheating has been used as one of these. If this is the case, one might ask what devices are available to replace the old personal code of ethics. Actually there seems to be no offered substitute as yet, and this may explain some of the social problems which plague modern society. The practice of cheating on school examinations seems to be a reflection of the dysfunctioning of the established moral code.

[1] The amount may vary from place to place. This study was made in a small college in a large urban community in the Midwest.

110

Student Ethics and the Honor System

CHARLES I. GLICKSBERG

Professor of English, Brooklyn College. At the time his article originally appeared in *School and Society* (May 25, 1957), he was associate professor of English.

If the confessions, written or oral, frankly made by thousands of students at Brooklyn College are representative of student thinking and student behavior in the U.S., then it is rare, indeed, to find a student who, at some time in his academic career, has not engaged in the practice of cheating. The practice (some students facetiously call it an art) is sufficiently widespread to warrant serious attention on the part of college teachers and administrators. If actions are a reliable index of moral values, then the vast majority of college students today would seem to have little regard for the ethical standards that should guide and control their behavior. If the young will "cheat" (an ugly word with ugly implications) while in college, what reason is there to assume that their code of behavior will be any higher when they enter the business or professional world?

Obviously, the practice of cheating has not reached epidemic proportions; the authorities take too many practical precautions and set up too many stringent safeguards. But many students are tempted at some time or other to cheat and many succumb weakly to temptation. The reasons they give to justify their actions are both curious and revealing.

The irony of the situation, on the face of it, is too strong to be missed. Here is a faculty composed of scholars, men and women dedicated to the single-minded pursuit of knowledge and truth, who must cope with this obnoxious practice of cheating. Students will copy term papers they have inherited from some other students who took the same course in the past; some will devise highly ingenious means of cheating on examinations; others will hand in themes, signed with their name, which are copied, practically verbatim, from some other source.

Fundamentally, when we are dealing with the problem of cheating in college, we are forced to take into account the mores and functioning morality of the business world. It is when the students venture to discuss this problem openly that we perceive why, according to them, they resort to such unethical practices. The reasons assigned vary, but a recurrent complaint, really a justification, is that the world puts too high a premium on "success." Later on no one stops to ask how, in what fair-minded manner, this was achieved. In our society, success is its own excuse for being, the alpha and omega of life, the crown and consummation of all striving. What is an accepted technique in the business world must be, *ipso facto,* equally "good" in the academic jungle. Why not? So long as one is not caught, it would be quixotic folly not to take advantage of each opportunity.

An equally important reason given for cheating is the competitive pressure that prevails in college, the undue emphasis placed on marks. Since that is the only way he knows how to survive, the student (and he believes he is thoroughly "realistic" in doing so) falls back upon "the art" of cheating. Those who are struggling hard to enter the dental or medical profession, for example, must keep their academic standing high. If their grades are low, their career is automatically brought to an end. Not that every student condones this practice, for cheating fails to solve the fundamental problem, the fact of competition. It is this problem itself, the students argue, that has to be corrected. The cause of student insecurity must be eliminated; the exaggerated value attached to high grades must be replaced by more worthy incentives.

Others maintain that the impersonal atmosphere to be found in college, with a huge enrollment and overcrowded classes, intensifies the impulse to cheat. No personal, friendly relationships exist between students and their teachers. Students are generally fearful of betraying their ignorance and seeking the help and guidance of their instructors. Indeed, teachers themselves are held in part responsible for this flourishing practice. Instead of getting to know their students individually and judging them in the light of a full term's work, these teachers base their final mark entirely on one or two examinations. Under these "adverse" circumstances, the students contend, they have no other alternative, when they are at a loss for an answer, but to cheat: one must learn how to survive in this academic rat race; one must master the difficult and complex art of getting ahead. The end, in short, justifies the means. As for moral values, the student who cheated felt unhappy and his self-respect thereby was impaired, but the temptation, unfortunately, was too strong to resist. When entrance to a professional school was at stake, who would hesitate to adopt these extreme measures?

Only a few students professed to believe that the end did not justify the means. What counted in the end, one girl maintained, was not the grade received but the positive benefits she derived from her education. If she felt compelled to cheat, then there was something radically wrong with her or the educational system. Besides, the cheating was not worth the damage done to her self-esteem, since she had to live with herself. But the majority, a group of cheerful conformists, insisted that one must do as others do. Such practices, they pointed out, went on all the time, undetected and unpunished and, in fact, often rewarded. As long as one is clever and resourceful and is never caught red-handed, what harm is done? As for the possibility of being apprehended, they are perfectly willing to run this calculated risk. What most of them strangely leave out of account is the cumulative burden of guilt, the operation of the inner check, the judgment of conscience. If the harassment of conscience becomes too painful, they dissipate the shadow of guilt by falling back upon the process of rationalization, hitting upon socially acceptable "reasons" for actions which cannot be thus defended. Since society is notoriously corrupt, why should college students remain inflexibly moral? Anyone who disagrees with this point of view is a naive, starry-eyed idealist, sadly unacquainted with the real facts of life.

That, in general, is the theme students sound in their compositions and in their offhand remarks during the discussion period. One student confesses that he has cheated, but so has every student in college. Were they taught a code of honesty by their parents and teachers? How can the honor system be made to work if the competitive pressure, even in the schools, is so great? Each one is urged to excel, to beat his competitor, to get a gold star, to make the Dean's List, to graduate *summa cum laude*. Yet, he is also exhorted to be honest and honorable in all his dealings. Thus, he is exposed to a double standard of morality. "It is wrong to cheat, but it is right to get good marks. How right is it to get good marks? Right enough to cheat?"

The honor system appeals to many of the students, despite their spirited defense of the necessity for cheating. One student, who pointed with pride to the way the "system" is used at West Point, realized that some students might take advantage of their new freedom, but, if the student body as a whole loyally co-operated, these delinquents soon would be weeded out. Hence, he urged that the honor system should be given a fair trial.

One student, writing on "The Honor System and Cheating," made it abundantly clear why he believed the honor system could not be made to work. But what, he asks, are the motives behind the practice of cheating? Man is born pure, but he is conditioned throughout life "to cheat with friends, to cheat in business, and to cheat even in love." Here, surprisingly enough, the moralist emerges. College youth cheat out of necessity, in order not to be left behind in the race of life, but they are not happy about this indulgence in "sin." The main desire of the young, in college as in high school, is to "get ahead, to get good marks, and, most of all, to please their parents." This young man's proposed solution is to eliminate the competitive system in college or lessen it to a point where it will not lead to cheating.

Even the imposition of strict standards of vigilance during examination periods—assigning many proctors, separating students so that they sit at a safe distance from each other, demanding that all books and papers be put aside—does not help to solve the situation. Such a policy simply recognizes that the situation exists and adopts a number of preventive measures. These students, if their confessions are to be trusted, are sincere in their conviction that cheating exists. Only the more mature students possess sufficient insight to realize that cheating never can be successful, for the cheater in the end cheats himself. A few are aware that cheating does not pay.

What conclusions are warranted from these voluntary confessions? In many cases, they are not to be taken at face value. Though cheating does go on, it is not so widespread as the students make it out to be. There is no doubt, too, that they feel uneasy about the practice of cheating, despite their brave attempts to justify it. If they had their way, they would put an end to cheating and institute the honor system on an experimental basis. Nevertheless, they seriously question whether, under the present academic regime, the honor system could be made to work.

The bravado with which these students expose their moral delinquencies (it is significant that they regard them as such) is not to be taken too literally. The urgency with which they cast about for convincing alibis for their misdeeds indicates that they are not unregenerate sinners. Their desire to change conditions, to eliminate the necessity for cheating, is not to be mistaken. If the movement for a higher standard of ethical behavior in college is to make any appreciable headway, it must find its dedicated leaders not only among teachers, but also among the student body. It is the more mature-minded student, we have noted, who most eloquently decries the practice of cheating and who is most eager to alter the conditions that tend to make cheating in college seem either necessary or desirable, or both. Were such student leaders to appear and set a proper example, then the honor system could be successfully put into practice. Before it is instituted, the young should be led to understand what the alternatives are. It is for them to realize that the success or failure of such a system, essentially co-operative in structure, depends entirely on them. It is time for them to grow up and accept responsibility for their actions. A new tradition, one based on honesty and honor and self-respect, can be established that each generation of college students will be proud to perpetuate.

111

"Reasons Why My Mark Should Be Raised"—By a Pre-Med

RAYMOND M. SELLE

The late Raymond M. Selle was professor of biology and director of the Moore Laboratory of Zoology, Occidental College, at the time his article originally appeared in *School and Society* (May 15, 1954).

Teachers are frequently amazed at the resourcefulness of students to put their fellow schoolmates in their proper places. Whenever a member of a group oversteps the bounds of good taste or propriety, more often than not a fellow member of the group will sense the situation and produce an effective antidote.

The academic competition among college premedical students for many years has been very keen. The great surplus of applicants for the first-year classes in the 80 medical schools in the United States has placed an emphasis upon the "getting of grades" that readily can become unwholesome. A number of years ago, in 1934 to be exact, in my class in human embryology, a course given primarily for premedical students, there was a young fellow who developed the "chronic gripes." He never was satisfied with the grading of his test papers and examinations; moreover, he became vociferous about it. Several of the other students in the class were annoyed by his grumbling.

One morning there appeared on my desk a neatly typed, unsigned paper, "Reasons Why My Mark Should Be Raised"—By a Pre-Med. I have kept the paper posted in the classroom since that day in 1934. Its fabric has yellowed and become brittle with age. Several hundred students have spied it, stopped, and tarried to read it, glanced furtively around and smiled. Many are they who have remarked about the paper. It is as effective today as it was 20 years ago.

With the permission of the original author, now T. T. Suzuki, M.D., we list the reasons:

1. There must be a mistake somewhere.

2. Neither the midterm nor at any time have I received an official warning; therefore, relying upon the college, I merely maintained my grade. Surely, this must be a satisfactory grade.

3. I know many members of the class who did not do such good work as I did and who got better marks. I was recognized among my classmates as a good student—you just ask any one of them.

4. I was not well at the time of the examination.

5. I was unwell on the night before the examination and couldn't study at all.

6. This mark ruined my prospect of entering medical school.

7. This mark ruined my prospect of getting a scholarship.

8. This mark grieved my mother (or father who is an M.D.) whose pride I am.

9. This is the only course in Biology where I received a poor grade.

10. It is not a higher mark that I seek; I care nothing for marks; I think marks are wicked and disapprove of them. However, this pernicious system of which I am the victim requires marks for achieving success and, therefore, I seek a higher mark.

11. Several people around me copied from my paper during the examination, yet they received higher marks than I did. Surely, this is not fair.

12. I live far away from the college and therefore should be given a bonus.

13. I have studied this subject from the broad philosophical viewpoint and, therefore, I was unable to answer your technical catch questions.

14. The questions were ambiguous and, therefore, my answers should be graded according to the reasonable interpretations that I made of your questions.

15. I misread your question because you were still writing the question on the board and you were standing in front of it.

16. The examination was unfair and unfairly distributed over the subject.

17. I have to work after school and at nights; therefore, I should be given a break.

18. The reason I did not do better is because I am very honest, whereas I do not wish to say anything against many of the other members of the class.

AMEN!

112

Students Estimate Their Own Grades

WENDELL S. DYSINGER and PHOEBE E. WILKINS

The authors are, respectively, vice-president and dean of the college emeritus and counselling coordinator and associate professor of education, MacMurray College. At the time their article originally appeared in *School and Society* (Dec. 25, 1954), they were, respectively, dean of the college and assistant professor of psychology.

The ability of students to estimate their own grades at the close of an academic term is a significant phase of the problem of grading of students. The correspondence of student grade estimates with grades assigned by teachers represents both the insight of the student as to the quality of his work and the communication of the teacher concerning his judgment about the quality of the work of the student.

At the close of the first semester of 1953–54, all students of MacMurray College were requested to offer grade estimates. Each student was asked to make such an estimate in each course taken. These grade estimates were made after final examinations had been taken, but they were reported before teachers' grades were assigned. Comparisons were made, then, between the grade which the student assigned to herself and the grade which the teacher assigned. Grades were assigned as A, B, C, D, E (condition), and F. Plus and minus signs were disregarded both as teacher grades and in student estimates.

These student grade estimates represented the voluntary co-operation of the student body. Only one general announcement of the project was made. Dormitory hostesses later co-operated in reminding students of this request. Grade estimates were offered for 82.6% of the possible number of grades. Out of 2,115 grades assigned at the close of the semester, there were 1,747 grade estimates. In some cases, students did not give grade estimates for all their courses. Grades in a few classes were eliminated from the study in advance, each for special reasons. The percentage of return was high enough that the returns doubtless represent the total satisfactorily.

The college teachers were told of this project at a faculty meeting early in December, 1953. Nothing more was said to the faculty about the matter. The grades were assigned early in February. It was hoped that the faculty would not discuss grades with individual students in more detail than was their usual practice. We believe that this purpose was achieved.

Students had varying backgrounds on which to judge their grades. Freshmen had had mid-semester grades in November. Upperclassmen had had this information only in courses in which the work was below a "C." The upperclassmen had obviously a longer experience in college work. Graded tests and papers had been available to students during the semester as a background for judgment following regular class practice. The number of such grade-guides varied in different classes. No consistent pattern could be found either in the number of tests or papers submitted or the number of faculty conferences which substantially influenced the accuracy of grade estimates.

Almost two thirds of the grade estimates of students (64.5%) were the same as the grade assigned by the teacher. The percentage of identical estimates was best for the seniors, and the other classes ranked in direct order with the freshmen showing the lowest percentage of accurate grade estimates. Some 33.5% of the students missed the grade assigned by the teacher by one grade level. Approximately half of these estimates were one grade level too low and another half, one grade level too high.

In one and a half percent of the cases (27 grade estimates), the student missed the grade assigned by the teacher by two full grade levels. Eleven of these were two grade levels low and 16 were two grade levels high. This seems to represent the number of cases on the campus in which the insight of students into the grade of a particular course was radically deficient.

The best students (2.5 and above where 3.0 is A) made better grade estimates than did the poorer students (.5 and under where 1.0 is C). The poorer students were quite optimistic about their grades, while the best students were somewhat pessimistic. Some 6% of the grade estimates of poor students were two grade points high, indicating unrealistic optimism, while no superior student estimated so optimistically (often there was no ceiling so high).

An analysis was made in terms of individual teachers, and we found no differences which seemed significant. The results were also analyzed in terms of the individual student and the number of correct and incorrect grade estimates which each student made. Slightly more than one third of the grade estimates did not correspond to the grades, and we studied the distribution of these inaccurate grade estimates among the students.

Only 16% of the students had all of their grade estimates correct. Some 31% had one wrong estimate; 30% had two wrong; 13% had three wrong; 5% had four wrong; 3% had all estimates wrong.

Some 78.1% of the students made two or fewer wrong estimates. These percentages vary among the different classes, with the junior and senior class having a better record than the freshman and sophomore classes. The weaker students again had the poorer record on grade estimates.

Several conclusions seem to be justified by this study. Students of MacMurray College have a fairly accurate understanding of the quality of work which they are doing or of the quality of work which the teachers think they are doing. The insight of students seems to improve somewhat as they progress in their academic work. Poor students tended to be optimistic about their grades, while the better students tended to be pessimistic. Students seldom missed in their grade estimates by more than one grade level, and a very small number of students missed all of their grade estimates.

In these discussions, the teacher's grade has been taken as the criterion, but the accuracy of the teacher's grade is not assumed. Student grade estimates may not be subject to much more error than the teacher's grade. Students seem to understand the quality of work which they are doing and are able to predict two thirds of their grades accurately and miss the other third by only one grade point level.

Other interpretations are suggested in terms of the communication of teachers concerning the quality of work done. Communication seems better from teacher to the strong students and to more advanced students.

Criticisms of the grading system are often offered in terms of the injury which may be suffered by weak students on one side and among strong students on the other. Students make comparisons with others who are inferior or superior to them. The competition for grades is thus interpreted as injurious from the point of view of mental hygiene. The results from the study suggest, on the other hand, that any effect is largely a function of the class situation rather than of the practice of grading. Students are able to compare their work with the work of other students and estimate with fair accuracy their achievement in comparsion with the standard set by the instructor. Some of this insight may come from other grades on the quiz, the test, the paper, but much of it must come from class recitation and from other obvious evidences of differences in achievement. The assignment of the grade by the teacher formalizes such differences, but this may well be a relatively unimportant factor when the student is able to sense his own progress.

113

Can Student Rating of Instructors Be Painless and Foolproof?

PRISCILLA R. MEYER and ROLLIN M. PATTON

The authors are, respectively, counseling and clinical psychologist, Veterans Administration Hospital, Waco, Tex., and chief of the Human Performance Branch, NASA Ames Research Center, Moffett Field, Calif. At the time their article originally appeared in *School and Society* (Dec. 25, 1954), they were, respectively, assistant professor of psychology and instructor in psychology, University of Akron.

More and more college students are rating their instructors and the instructors do not always like it. It is not easy to step from the role of king of the classroom to that of an intellectual entertainer, dependent for success on the latest poll of popularity.

"Just the same," cry proponents of rating, "students learn more awake than asleep, and they are better judges of their wakefulness than the droning professor with eyes glued to faded notes." That students are the best judges of what interests, informs, and enlightens them is hard to refute. Certainly much of the resistance to student ratings is coming from instructors who haven't gotten a point across in decades, and would prefer not to be told about it with means and percentages.

Not all faculty foot-dragging on the rating issue can be laid to the "I'd rather not know" attitude. Investigators agree that present evaluation methods have several things wrong with them. There is the problem of careless rating. Even after a semester of flawless instruction, if the student takes two minutes on his way out the door to put X's on the lines of a graphic rating scale, he may not weigh his responses very seriously.

If he does give the rating thought and care, the questions asked may not be revealing or helpful to his teacher. Of what value is it to know that one is "occasionally inspiring," to cite an item on a scale now in use. Lack of specificity and precision is apparent.

Then there is the eternal question, "Did the student tell me the truth?" This question is worth asking. There are many reasons for him to pick out the very best items and circle them. It's quicker, easier, and, if the rater can be identified, it's safer.

Finally, there is the teacher to consider. How will he react to being told the truth, assuming that it isn't all rosy? Psychologists reiterate that humans learn more with praise than punishment. The low-rated teacher is only human if he shrinks before denunciation and fails to profit from it.

In short, student ratings are likely to be careless, too general, biased, or unpalatable. These deficiencies are not necessarily the fault of the students. They have been the fault of rating scales, particularly graphic scales and checklists, since such scales came into use.

The armed forces and private industry have been using a radically different type of rating scale which attacks these objections. It is the forced-choice scale. Typically the forced-choice method presents the rater with a group of descriptive statements and asks him which are most true of the person he is rating. He must choose a required number (usually two out of four).

The statements are grouped to appear equally favorable to the rater. Each statement discriminates between effective and ineffective workers to some extent, and the amount of this discrimination is determined before the scale is made. A typical forced-choice tetrad is:

> *Select the two statements which best describe your teacher.*
> Has class members form committees (DI 18, FI 4.2)
> Omits chapters in textbook from lectures (DI 3, FI 4.2)
> Uses extensive vocabulary (DI 5, FI 4.2)
> Tells students to have a good time in college (DI 20, FI 4.2)

DI is discrimination index—the degree to which the statement distinguishes between good and poor teachers. It is established by having known good and poor teachers rated on these statements before they are put into blocks. FI is favorability index—the degree to which the statement looks favorable to the rater. It is established by having raters indicate how good each statement looks, considered independently. In the sample tetrad all statements appear equally favorable, but two discriminate and two do not. These sample DI's and FI's are fictitious and for illustration only.

To test this method in a university setting, we devised a 25-block, 100-item forced-choice form for college teachers, the *Instructor's Information Form,* and tried it out at two universities. University A was a large, private, urban institution; University B was a medium-sized rural state institution.

All statements on the Form were favorable in appearance and specific in content. They covered the following areas: method of teaching, examination and grading procedures, method of handling students' questions, student-teacher relations, textbooks and assignments, speech habits, and personal traits.

Using the method of high and low groups, we asked half the 208 students in the sample to rate the best college teacher they had ever had. The other half rated their worst teacher. Raters were limited to a teacher they had known in the last four years, from any college they had attended.

Table 1
SUMMARY OF RESULTS

		BEST TEACHERS		WORST TEACHERS		
	N	Mean	S. D.	Mean	S. D.	t (M)
University A	98	66.76	4.28	43.76	7.04	19.00*
University B	110	65.02	4.77	46.26	6.48	17.53*
Combined groups	208	65.92	4.62	44.22	6.99	26.20*

* Significant at .01 level.

The student sample, obtained during summer sessions, was unusually cosmopolitan. Over 57% were students from other colleges; they reported attendance at 73 colleges well scattered across the country. All were above the freshman level.

As Table 1 shows, the forced-choice scale discriminated between good and poor teachers very effectively. The Best and Worst groups constituted distinct distributions with little overlap. The split-half reliability of the scale, calculated on odd-even items, was .88.

The Form got a good reception from students and instructors. Not a single teacher who saw the scale considered it threatening in any way, and many students wrote spontaneous comments indicating approval of such ratings.

To discover if the scale could be faked by "apple-polishers," we asked 39 students to fill out the Form, trying to give the highest possible rating. If the scale could be perfectly falsified, the average faked ratings should be 84 (the highest possible score). Actually the mean faked rating was 63.90, 2.02 points below the mean of the Best teachers. The highest actual rating of a Best teacher was 80; the highest faked rating was 72. We concluded that the forced-choice scale was more foolproof than any of the graphic or checklist types.

In addition to differentiating good and poor teachers, the scale discriminates between good-sounding teaching practices which students find helpful, and equally favorable sounding practices which they consider of little importance. It would appear that the forced-choice method can take the curse off student rating of instructors and still permit the teacher to learn much that is valuable about the efficacy of his teaching practices.

114

Unpromising College Students Who Graduate

PAUL F. MUNGER

Professor of education, Indiana University. At the time his article originally appeared in *School and Society* (Feb. 28, 1959), he was professor of psychology, University of North Dakota.

Some colleges are confronted with entering students who, because of poor high-school records, are considered to have little scholastic promise. College teachers will agree that efforts beyond the average are necessary for such students to graduate. It should be of interest to those who are concerned about such students to know the number of semesters required to graduate and the number of semesters attempted by those who had enrolled for eight or more semesters and did not graduate.

The subjects of this investigation are 81 graduating, unpromising college students and 45 near-graduating, unpromising college students who completed eight or more semesters. These are a part of a group of 891 students who had graduated in the lower third of their high-school classes and who were admitted on a trial basis to the University of Toledo. As was previously reported,* a definite relationship between grade-point average in the first semester and length of residence was found. This relationship also was found between grades in various first courses and length of residence. The students in the present study were enrolled in five colleges: arts and sciences, business administration, education, engineering, and pharmacy.

This is a report of the varying lengths of residence and number of course failures of those who graduated and those who persisted for eight or more semesters and did not graduate.

The similarity between the two groups on gross scores of the Ohio State Psychological Examination, Form 20, is indicated in Table 1. Only six raw score points separate the graduates from the near-graduates. The

---

* P. F. Munger, SCHOOL AND SOCIETY, 81: 120–122, April 16, 1955.

Table 1
MEANS AND STANDARD DEVIATIONS OF GROSS SCORES ON
THE OHIO STATE PSYCHOLOGICAL EXAMINATION FOR
GRADUATING AND NEAR-GRADUATING, UNPROMISING
COLLEGE STUDENTS

	GRADUATES	NEAR-GRADUATES
M	64.7	59.1
SD	21.0	16.9
N	78	44

large standard deviations indicate a considerable spread of scores in both groups. The F value of the difference between the means of the two groups was not significant at the five percent level of confidence.

Table 2 shows that 35% of the 81 unpromising students who graduated

Table 2
NUMBER OF SEMESTERS ENROLLED OF GRADUATING AND
NEAR-GRADUATING UNPROMISING COLLEGE STUDENTS

NUMBER OF SEMESTERS	GRADUATES	NEAR-GRADUATES
8	29	23
9	33	9
10	10	9
11	8	3
12	2	1

did so in the usual eight semesters, 41% in nine semesters, and the others in as many as 12 semesters. The average number of semesters required by these students to graduate was slightly over nine. Of the 45 near-graduating students, 53% ceased to persist at the end of eight semesters, the others persisting up to 12 semesters. This indicates that graduation and number of semesters in residence are not synonymous.

In such an unpromising group it would be expected that many would fail several courses before graduating or dropping out. Table 3 gives a distribution of the number of course failures of graduating and near-graduating students. It is perhaps surprising that 30% of the graduates had no course failures and 27% had only one course failure. However, two graduates had eight course failures.

These figures suggest that slightly more than half of the unpromising graduating students were really rather typical students in spite of having graduated in the lower third of their high-school classes. Conversely, 43% overcame the difficulties of two or more course failures and graduated from college.

Table 3
NUMBER OF COURSE FAILURES OF GRADUATING AND
NEAR-GRADUATING UNPROMISING COLLEGE STUDENTS

NUMBER OF COURSE FAILURES	GRADUATES	NEAR-GRADUATES
0	24	2
1	22	2
2	17	5
3	9	7
4	4	5
5 or more	5	22

It is interesting to note that two near-graduates dropped out with no failing grades and two with only one failing grade. While the over-all grade-point average is not available for the two groups, the first semester mean grade-point average of the graduates was 1.22, or slightly better than a "C" average, the mean g.p.a. of the near-graduates was .82, or slightly less than a "C" average. The F value of the difference between these two means was significant at the one percent level of confidence.

Students who enter college from the lower third of their high-school graduating classes will continue to be doubtful risks and those who graduate will require an additional semester. The observing personnel worker may be able to recognize potential graduates by noting first-semester course grades and grade-point averages. Third-ranking appears to be too broad a category for use in predicting who will be successful in college.

115

The Meaning of a Bachelor's Degree

C. ARTHUR SANDEEN

Associate Dean of Students, Iowa State University. His article originally appeared in *School and Society* on Feb. 17, 1968.

Over 530,000 persons received bachelors' degrees in 1966 from a great variety of American institutions of higher education.[1] Apart from the varying quality of these colleges, their faculty, students, and facilities, what besides the successful accumulation of 120 semester credits do these degrees mean? Most of these colleges make idealistic statements concerning the purposes of their institutions, but to what extent are these purposes actually reflected in their student programs?

These questions, which have been discussed rather widely, have not been dealt with successfully by more than a few of our colleges. The writer believes that the bachelor's degree in its present form in most of our colleges means little more than the completion of minimum course requirements which may qualify a student for a job or graduate school (rarely for effective citizenship), and that this is one of the primary shortcomings of American higher education today.

Despite the fact that a student may have four years on a campus, at graduation it is hazardous, if not impossible, to answer any of the following questions about him: What does he stand for? What has meaning and relevance for him? What in his college experience really has made a difference? What experiences did the college consciously provide him which helped him confront the vital questions of his existence? Who knows him as a human being?

[1] U.S. Office of Education, *Digest of Educational Statistics* (Washington, D.C.: U.S. Government Printing Office, 1966), p. 80.

Because of the admitted difficulties in dealing with such questions, and the external pressures to graduate increasing numbers of students, colleges have concentrated on the easily visible and the quantitative aspects of educational programs. The educational aspects of the extracurriculum have been neglected by the faculty and left almost entirely to the personal whims of the undergraduates.

Some of the traditional sources of meaning on the campus have lost much of their significance. The quest for popularity and social success is declining in importance, and the activities oriented "college chap" of previous years is admired only by a handful of students. Purely academic efforts seem, to increasing numbers of students, largely unrelated to the really important questions of life. Many students evidently have decided that, if any meaning is to be found, it must be done apart from the actual structure of the college. The existence of the "free university movement" and the widely publicized student use of hallucinogenic drugs may be viewed, in part, as symptomatic of this situation.

The decision of the college not to concern itself actively with the existential concerns of students seriously hinders the quality of the educational program, and a possible consequence is to deliver over to students, in the form of neglect, the kind of freedom that breeds license. Keniston has studied students who feel alienated, and aptly has labled them the "disaffiliates." [2]

Perhaps the academically integrated and well-planned programs at colleges such as Cowell and Stevenson at Santa Cruz, Raymond and Covell at the University of the Pacific, or Justin Morrill and James Madison at Michigan State University may provide the stimulus for much of the needed change in American higher education. But, hopefully, a really exciting and intellectually meaningful education does not depend so much on external organization as it does on a changed attitude. Why could not more undergraduate schools experiment with a program similar to one used among graduate students at George Peabody College, which Hobbs describes as a "quarter at Woolsthorpe"? [3] It consists of a period free of all classes and assignments, where there are no reading lists, no required papers, no grades. The student simply is given what always will be, in our frenzied world, a most precious commodity—uninterrupted time. The origin of the name is significant. In 1665, a great plague swept England, and the universities were closed. An undistinguished Cambridge student went home to his mother's cottage at Woolsthorpe and there, with no one to bother him, invented the calculus.

[2] Kenneth Keniston, "Faces in the Lecture Room," in R. S. Morison, ed., *The Contemporary University* (Boston: Houghton Mifflin, 1966), p. 323.
[3] Nicholas Hobbs, "The Art of Getting Students into Trouble," in L. E. Dennis and J. K. Kauffman, *The College and the Student* (Washington: American Council on Education, 1966), p. 204.

Or, why cannot the curriculum itself be made sufficiently exciting and relevant so as to confront students with intellectually respectable and meaningful experiences? Out-of-class programs initiated by the college should be logical extensions of what goes on in the classroom, and deemed equally essential by the college in the fulfillment of its objectives.

If disturbing numbers of students have chosen to seek relevant experiences apart from the college itself, they have not so much rejected an actual program with which they did not agree as much as they have retreated from no program at all. Perhaps students are not reacting so much against the faculty acting *in loco parentis* as they are reacting against them *in absentia*.

Students need to be given a clear indication of what the college stands for, what it expects, and, in fact, what it demands of them. Students today see distressingly few significant differences among the great majority of colleges. Taking a degree at Midwest U. is not much different than taking one at Tech, because the colleges themselves have not defined or clearly publicized their own goals or distinctive qualities.

What is being advocated here is not a retreat to an earlier period when intellectual values and purposes in our college were secondary to the salvation of souls. Diversity long has been recognized as a strength of American higher education, but there is a danger today that the bachelor's degree may become so diluted and homogeneous that it may have no meaning at all. If we remain content to allow the bachelors' degree to become largely irrelevant to the undergraduate ("It's just a piece of paper," some students say), society itself will be the loser, as higher education will be viewed merely as a mechanical and burdensome task to be performed, rather than an exciting, intrinsically valuable, and indispensable enterprise of the human mind.

116

Is the College Student Becoming a "Forgotten Man"?

LOGAN WILSON

President, American Council on Education. His article originally appeared in *School and Society* on Feb. 6, 1965, and was based on a Founders Day address, Franklin and Marshall College, Oct. 22, 1964.

We are living in an age in which our institutions are valued to an unprecedented extent. We hear daily—on spot radio and television announcements urging financial support for the "college of your choice"—that "college is America's best friend." The advertisements of insurance companies and banks enticingly describe the increased lifetime earnings for those who attend college. Such an expenditure of time, effort, and money, we are assured, is nothing less than a hard-headed "investment" with "practical dividends."

Local, state, and Federal governments place the hope of the nation on institutions of higher education, both in creating the knowledge to maintain our economic and defense superiority in the world and in ameliorating the social disorganization induced by rapid technological change.

From the goals of "expanding and expounding knowledge" we have moved to the goals encompassed by the term "knowledge industry." Not only from our major metropolitan areas, but also from hundreds of communities across the land come the pressures to make colleges and universities mean all things to all people. The rest of the nation looks with envy at the economic growth of the California Bay region surrounding Stanford and the University of California, or at the burgeoning electronics industry on Route 128 in Boston which leans on Harvard and M.I.T., and it is presumed that this is to be emulated everywhere, by everyone, for the good of all.

In short, the pendulum has swung from expecting too little of our colleges and universities to perhaps expecting too much—of straining the essential foundation of higher education on the assumption that it can support a structure which will give solutions to all our problems.

The spate of new demands and new expectations, without carefully selected priorities, contributes to an increasing danger that the individual student may be crowded out of the picture. For some of us, there is a recurrent need to recall that colleges were created primarily for students. The many pressures and diversions that beset us could create a deplorable condition where the student is the "forgotten man."

The need to make higher education available to all qualified youth is being met by our unique American system of mass education, and in the process the notion is discarded that college is for only a small, elite group. Individual responses to the challenge by the 2,000 or so junior colleges and other colleges and universities in our country have been laudable. Physical plant expansion, the growth of graduate education to provide the necessary faculty members, and creative fund-raising for the support of all types of institutions have marked the past decade and will keep pace in the future.

One danger inherent in higher education's new-found success, however, is that created by a seller's market. With 40%, or more, of our youth seeking admission to college, it is all too easy for those of us engaged in teaching or administration to avoid confronting some of the issues involving students that should be at the heart of our concern. Because others are standing in line to take the places of the dropouts, there is a danger of our becoming indifferent, if not callous, to the sources of discontent and the causes of failure.

We know that the rate of expansion of enrollments in the next decade inevitably will have a heavy impact on student life. Increasingly, students may have less personal contact with professors and staff members of their institutions except when they find themselves in serious trouble and have to be dealt with in some official way. With the advent of programmed instruction may come the faceless anonymity that IBM cards, drop cards, seat numbers, and I.D. numbers represent. The depersonalization of the student, if allowed to go unchecked or unchallenged, represents a grave threat to the very purposes of higher education. We must not only sympathize with the student's desire to make a human or personal connection with his college; we also must assist him vigorously in making such a connection.

Let us take a brief look at three critical issues we must confront and resolve:

First, what factors obstruct or reinforce the learning goals of our colleges and universities?

Obviously, the first order of business in a college is learning. Yet, we know that this cannot be truly fruitful if it takes place only—and grudgingly —in the classroom and laboratory. A student spends most of his time outside the periods of formal instruction. Therefore, what happens during this time may well be crucial in the outcome of whether the goals of the college are obstructed or reinforced. The desire to learn, the cultivation of the mind and of individuality, the acquisition of literary judgment, aesthetic taste, and spiritual identity are goals for students that should pervade the atmosphere of the entire campus, not just the classroom.

We should consider several factors which affect this issue—extracurricular activities, faculty and administration values, and the climate and environment of the campus.

We need to re-examine the extracurricular life of our colleges in light of present conditions. It may well be that certain of the adolescent preoccupations of 19th-century college life are no longer fitting. I do not mean that any moment spent away from a book is a wasted or frivolous moment. Nor do I argue that entertainment has no place in institutions whose primary mission is edification. Everyone knows that leisure and diversion are necessary to keep our campuses from being grim, unsmiling, joyless places. But with the rising expectations and standards demanded of students and, I hope, the increasing level of student maturity, we can afford to drop the enervating and time-consuming activities that (on some campuses) preoccupy the energies of students and obstruct realization of the real goals of education.

Extracurricular life can be both enjoyable and constructive, and we should assist students in restructuring traditional student activities so that they have a more positive role in the campus environment. The pervading out-of-class values and climate of a campus are major factors in obstructing or reinforcing a student's acceptance of the intellectual mission of the college. In this sphere, too, the concepts of right and wrong, justice and injustice, truth or sham are learned and reinforced.

Much has been said, but little done, about the publish-or-perish syndrome and the low value attributed by faculty and administration to the effective and committed teaching of students. Consultantships, outside research grants and contracts, and publications seem to score more points for faculty members. For this, faculty and administrators must accept responsibility.

Dr. Clark Kerr, in his recent book, "The Uses of the University," summarizes it well in stating,

The undergraduate students are restless. Recent changes in the American university have done them little good—lower teaching loads for the faculty, larger classes, the use of substitute teachers for the regular faculty, the choice of faculty members based on research accomplishments rather than instructional capacity, the fragmentation of knowledge into endless subdivisions. There is an incipient revolt of undergraduate students against the faculty; the revolt that used to be against the faculty *in loco parentis* is now against the faculty *in absentia*.

If the college does not reward faculty members for their devotion to teaching and relating to students, the student body can infer only that such activity is not considered terribly important. If the faculty itself regards *relief from teaching* as the chief reward for accomplishment, or as the highest status symbol, and relegates undergraduate teaching to inexperienced graduate assistants, we may be sure that the students perceive this situation, too. Obviously, such matters can obstruct or reinforce whatever values a college seeks to attain.

In recent years, behavioral scientists have become interested in studying campus environments and climates as they affect student perceptions of college goals and values. This is a fascinating area of study, incidentally, which I urge colleges and universities to examine.

Many are familiar with the work of Nevitt Sanford and the other contributors to the book, "The American College." There is evidence enough to demonstrate that the environment in which learning takes place— or is supposed to take place—is of sufficient consequence to merit our efforts to do everything we can to improve it.

The work of Robert Pace of U.C.L.A. and George Stern of Syracuse University has a particular relevancy here. Using the earlier research studies, Dr. Pace and the Educational Testing Service have developed College and University Environment Scales (CUES) wherein some 150 statements about college life are rated by students as generally True or False with reference to their college. A wide variety of aspects of the institutional environment are rated in this manner, and the results yield a highly interesting description of the college from the students themselves. Because they are a part of the institution—live in it—they presumably are able to judge or describe best what that environment is.

Colleges are scored on five scales. They include a scale of *practicality, community, awareness, propriety,* and *scholarship.* I commend the significance of such research activities and hope that they will be helpful in re-examining the images we create, knowingly or unknowingly.

A second issue that demands our attention is student personal conduct and behavior. Our newspapers and magazines are featuring, with increasing frequency, popular articles on the subject of student morals, rebellion, drinking, and general strife.

Many self-styled experts are just discovering these problems, although those of us with long experience on campuses know that they are not of recent origin. Aristotle made a relevant comment when he said long ago,

... they [youth] have exalted notions, because they have not yet been humbled by life or learnt its necessary limitations; moreover their hopeful disposition makes them think themselves equal to great things—and that means having exalted notions. They would always rather do noble deeds than useful ones: their lives are regulated more by moral feeling than by reasoning—all their mistakes are in the direction of doing things excessively and vehemently. They overdo everything—they love too much, hate too much, and the same with everything else. ...

A problem *does* exist in the area of student behavior. Colleges and universities cannot be indifferent to questions of honesty, integrity, and morality, but it is not easy to reach a consensus on expected standards of behavior and the means of enforcing them.

In some of our "multiversities" the faculty apparently has disavowed any interest in student behavior outside the classroom or off the campus. Although individual faculty members privately may feel concern, the problems are so involved that they may adopt a "hands off" policy and leave the worries to the dean.

At the other extreme, there are colleges where the faculty take most seriously the *in loco parentis* concept. Student life, both on and off campus, is regulated by a system of elaborate rules and regulations. Students need permission to leave campus, they must be in dormitories at specified hours, the use of automobiles is denied, and freedom of behavior is severely circumscribed.

For most of our colleges and universities, however, the situation lies between these two extremes. Many of them are groping for answers to cope with the changing values and mores of our society and particularly those of our youth.

We must acknowledge that the home milieu in which many of today's students were reared is different from that of their teachers and deans. The postwar period of general prosperity, mobility, and redefinition of values has witnessed a reduction in community and family restraints. Some parents do not support the restrictions which colleges traditionally have placed on students in matters of personal conduct. Other parents, however, expect colleges to police their sons and daughters in ways which they themselves did not or could not do. Our colleges, of course, cannot reasonably be expected to accept responsibilities which really belong to mothers and fathers. Given all of this, it is no wonder that the present tension exists between students and institutions regarding rules, discipline, morals, rights, freedoms, and responsibilities.

The overburdened college president, possessing the ultimate responsibility, more often than not delegates matters affecting student life to other administrative officers, such as the dean of students, and the function of dealing with students in this crucial area becomes a segregated and negative one. The dean readily may become a scapegoat, for, without full faculty cooperation, he may be forced to promulgate proscriptions which he alone cannot enforce. This state of affairs is an open invitation to some students to protest, of course, but legitimate modes of protest and ground rules for settling grievances, both alleged and real, are unclear on many campuses.

The student newspaper is often a symbol of the tension that exists between undergraduates and local authority. Editors frequently want to be considered immune from responsibility or accountability—as though the campus or the principle of academic freedom provided a sanctuary from community standards of good taste, propriety, or responsibility. College officials may counter this situation, however, with a plea to the alumni and the community to recognize that the student newspaper is not an official spokesman for the institution and that one learns by doing and having to defend one's actions and words.

What are the answers to these and numerous other problems? Shall we do away with all rules and regulations? Do students really want to be left completely alone in non-academic areas, as they are in some European countries? Do they want enough control over operations to be able to shut them down, as is the case in some Latin-American countries?

There are no pat answers to these questions, and so we come back to the difficult job that each college or university must define for itself—the eternal question posed by freedom and responsibility. And the confrontation of this issue begins anew with each generation of students.

Every college or university has a responsibility for what happens to a student outside the classroom, and this is especially true for the residential college. That obligation cannot be sidestepped, no matter how much we may wish to avoid it. Qualities of character, conscience, and citizenship are part of the educational development of our students. All of us, faculty as well as students, make a tragic mistake if we proclaim that this is not the proper business of the college.

Let me turn briefly to the third and final issue, which is of interest to me because it represents a waste of human potential. It is the continuing high rate of student attrition in higher education.

Nationally, as shown by various studies, only about four out of every 10 entering freshmen are graduated from college four years later. While one or two more may finish sometime later, or somewhere else, the total picture is one of waste, inefficiency, and probably considerable personal unhappiness.

Some of these students are outright academic failures, but we have made real progress recently in our selection and prediction instruments that soon should reflect itself in a rapidly decreasing attrition rate for academic reasons. Still other students find themselves out of step with institutional requirements, schedules, and unrealistic faculty expectations. The fact that they do not "fit" a preconceived mold or are repelled by the pressures and irrelevancies put upon them should give us pause for reflection.

There is a ring of truth in Paul Goodman's statement that

. . . for most students, the abstractness of the curriculum, especially if the teaching is pedantic, can be utterly barren. The lessons are *only* exercises, with no relation to the real world: they are never "for keeps." And many of the teachers are not practicing professionals, but merely academics, interested in the words, not the thing.

In the race for "excellence," too many students who would have been successes a decade ago are found in the tally of casualties. A great many colleges and universities have tended to denigrate academic adequacy in student capability and performance and overemphasize a stringent definition of academic excellence.

A substantial portion of youth seek and can profit from higher education. We can demand adequacy for all students but excellence can be expected only from a few. The danger is that we will eliminate those whose motivation and capabilities are only average or slightly above. We do so at the peril of the nation, for by definition such young people make up the foundation on which our society rests.

I hope there will be no dichotomy between unrealistically high expectations and no standards at all. We should demand the best from each student. Despite that best effort, however, there still will be a bottom quarter in each class. In many cases, that category should not be regarded arbitrarily as failures. We can be flexible without being lax, and we can treat students as individuals without having academic chaos. Each of us should be challenged by this problem.

In sum, these three critical issues should engage the attention of faculties and students in our institutions of higher education: the factors which obstruct or reinforce the learning goals of our colleges; the problems of student personal conduct and behavior out of class; and the continuing high rates of student attrition that cause waste of human resources.

BIBLIOGRAPHY

Academic Freedom and Civil Liberties of Students. New York: American Civil Liberties Union, 1956.

Aitken, Jonathan, and Michael Beloff. *A Short Walk on the Campus.* New York: Atheneum, 1966.

Allen, Herman R. *Open Door to Learning: The Land-Grant System Enters Its Second Century.* Urbana: University of Illinois Press, 1963.

Anderson, Kenneth E., ed. *The Coming Crisis in the Selection of Students for College Entrance.* Washington, D.C.: American Educational Research Association, 1960.

Arbuckle, Dugald. *Student Personnel Services in Higher Education.* New York: McGraw-Hill, 1953.

Armour, Richard W. *Going Around in Circles: A Low View of Higher Education.* New York: McGraw-Hill, 1965.

Atkinson, Brooks, ed. *College in a Yard: Minutes by Thirty-nine Harvard Men.* Cambridge, Mass.: Harvard University Press, 1957.

Avorn, Jerry L., Robert Friedman, *et al. Up Against the Ivy Wall: A History of the Columbia Crisis.* New York: Atheneum, 1969.

Axt, Richard G. *The Federal Government and Financing Higher Education.* New York: Columbia University Press, 1952.

Babbidge, Homer D., Jr. *Student Financial Aid: Manual for Colleges and Universities.* Washington, D.C.: American College Personnel Association, 1960.

————, and Robert M. Rosenzweig. *The Federal Interest in Education.* New York: McGraw-Hill, 1962.

Bartky, John A. *Administration as Educational Leadership.* Stanford, Calif.: Stanford University Press, 1956.

Barzun, Jacques. *The American University.* New York: Harper, 1968.

————. *The House of Intellect.* New York: Harper, 1959.

Baskin, Samuel, ed. *Higher Education: Some Newer Developments.* New York: McGraw-Hill, 1965.

Bauer, Ronald C. *Cases in College Administration.* New York: Bureau of Publications, Teachers College, Columbia University, 1955.

Beach, Waldo. *Conscience on Campus: An Interpretation of Christian Ethics for College Life.* New York: Association Press, 1958.

Becker, Howard S., Blanche Greer, and Everett S. Hughes. *Making the Grade: The Academic Side of College Life.* New York: Wiley, 1968.

Bell, Daniel. *The Reforming of General Education: The Columbia College Experience in Its National Setting.* New York: Columbia University Press, 1965.

————, and Irving Kristol, eds. *Confrontation: The Student Rebellion and the Universities.* New York: Basic Books, 1969.

Bell, Norman T., Richard W. Burkhardt, and Victor B. Lawhead, eds. *Introduction to College Life: Meanings, Values, and Commitment.* Boston: Houghton Mifflin, 1966.

Benjamin, Harold. *Democracy in the Administration of Higher Education.* New York: Harper, 1950.

Bennett, Margaret E. *Getting the Most Out of College.* New York: McGraw-Hill, 1966.

Bernard, Jessie S. *Academic Women.* University Park, Pa.: Pennsylvania State University Press, 1964.

Bigelow, Karl W. *Selected Books for the College and University Administrator.* New York: Bureau of Publications, Teachers College, Columbia University, 1958.

Birmingham, Frederick A. *The Ivy League Today.* New York: Thomas Y. Crowell, 1961.

Blackwell, Thomas E. *College and University Administration.* New York: Center for Applied Research in Education, 1966.

—————. *College Law: A Guide for Administrators.* Washington, D.C.: American Council on Education, 1961.

Blegen, Theodore C., and Russell M. Cooper, eds. *The Preparation of College Teachers.* Washington, D.C.: American Council on Education, 1950.

Blocker, Clyde E., Robert H. Plummer, and Richard C. Richardson, Jr. *The Two-Year College: A Social Synthesis.* Englewood Cliffs, N.J.: Prentice-Hall, 1965.

Bogue, Jesse Parker. *The Community College.* New York: McGraw-Hill, 1950.

Bolman, Frederick deW. *How College Presidents Are Chosen.* Washington, D.C.: American Council on Education, 1965.

Boroff, David. *Campus U.S.A.: Portraits of American Colleges in Action.* New York: Harper, 1961.

Bowen, Robert O., ed. *The New Professors.* New York: Holt, Rinehart and Winston, 1960.

Bowers, William J. *Student Dishonesty and Its Control in College.* New York: Bureau of Applied Social Research, Columbia University, 1965.

Bowles, Frank H. *Admission to College: A Perspective for the 1960's.* Princeton, N.J.: College Entrance Examination Board, 1960.

Brembeck, Cole S. *The Discovery of Teaching.* Englewood Cliffs, N.J.: Prentice-Hall, 1962.

Brickman, William W., and Stanley Lehrer, eds. *Automation, Education, and Human Values.* New York: School & Society Books, 1966.

—————, and Stanley Lehrer, eds. *A Century of Higher Education: Classical Citadel to Collegiate Colossus.* New York: Society for the Advancement of Education, 1962.

Bronowski, Jacob, *et al. Imagination and the University.* Toronto, Canada: University of Toronto Press, 1964.

Brookover, Wilbur B., *et al. The College Student.* New York: Center for Applied Research in Education, 1965.

Brown, David G. *The Market for College Teachers: An Economic Analysis of Career Patterns Among Southeastern Social Scientists.* Chapel Hill: University of North Carolina Press, 1965.

—————. *The Mobile Professors.* Washington, D.C.: American Council on Education, 1967.

—————, ed. *Social Changes and the College Student.* Washington, D.C.: American Council on Education, 1960.

Brown, Nicholas C. *Higher Education: Incentives and Obstacles.* Washington, D.C.: American Council on Education, 1960.

—————. *Orientation to College Learning—A Reappraisal.* Washington, D.C.: American Council on Education, 1961.

Brubacher, John S. *Bases for Policy in Higher Education.* New York: McGraw-Hill, 1965

————, and Willis Rudy. *Higher Education in Transition: A History of American Colleges and Universities, 1636–1968.* New York: Harper, 1968.

Brumbaugh, A. J. *Establishing New Senior Colleges.* Atlanta, Ga.: Southern Regional Education Board, 1966.

————. *Problems in College Administration.* Nashville, Tenn.: Board of Education, The Methodist Church, 1959.

Burns, Gerald P. *Administrators in Higher Education: Their Functions and Coordination.* New York: Harper, 1962.

————. *Trustees in Higher Education: Their Functions and Coordination.* New York: Independent College Funds of America, 1966.

Bushnell, Don D., and Dwight W. Allen. *The Computer in American Education.* New York: Wiley, 1967.

Byse, Clark. *Tenure in American Higher Education: Plans, Practices, and the Law.* Ithaca, N.Y.: Cornell University Press, 1959.

Capen, Samuel P. *The Management of Universities.* Buffalo, N.Y.: Foster & Stewart Publishing Corp., 1953.

Caplow, Theodore, and Reece J. McGee. *The Academic Marketplace.* New York: Basic Books, 1958.

Carey, James T. *The College Drug Scene.* Englewood Cliffs, N.J.: Prentice-Hall, 1968.

Carpenter, Marjorie, ed. *The Larger Learning: Teaching Values to College Students.* Dubuque, Iowa: Wm. C. Brown, 1960.

Chambers, M. M. *The Campus and the People.* Danville, Ill.. Interstate Printers and Publishers, 1960.

————. *The Colleges and the Courts, 1962–1966.* Danville, Ill.: Interstate Printers and Publishers, 1967.

————. *Financing Higher Education.* Washington, D.C.: Center for Applied Research in Education, 1963.

————. *Freedom and Repression in Higher Education.* Bloomington, Ind.: Bloomcraft Press, 1965.

Chandler, B. J. *Education and the Teacher.* New York: Dodd, Mead, 1961.

Clark, Burton R. *The Open Door College: A Case Study.* New York: McGraw-Hill, 1960.

Cohen, Joseph W. *The Superior Student in American Higher Education.* New York: McGraw-Hill, 1966.

Cohen, Mitchell, and Dennis Hale. *The New Student Left: An Anthology.* Boston: Beacon Press, 1966.

Cohn-Bendit, Daniel and Gabriel. *Obsolete Communism: The Left-Wing Alternative.* New York: McGraw-Hill, 1969.

Coleman, James C., et al. *Success in College: A Guide to Freshman Orientation.* Chicago: Scott, Foresman, 1960.

Collier, K. G. *New Dimensions in Higher Education.* New York: Humanities Press,1968.

Colman, John E. *The Master Teachers and the Art of Teaching.* New York: Pitman, 1967.

Conant, James B. *The Citadel of Learning.* New Haven, Conn.: Yale University Press, 1956.

————. *The Education of American Teachers.* New York: McGraw-Hill, 1963.

Connelly, Thomas R. *The Registrar.* Newark, N.J.: Washington Irving Publishing Co., 1951.

Cooper, Russell, ed. *The College.* New York: Wiley, 1964.

————, ed. *The Two Ends of the Log: Learning and Teaching in Today's College.* Minneapolis: University of Minnesota Press, 1958.

Corson, John J. *Governance of Colleges and Universities.* New York: McGraw-Hill, 1960.

Crabs, Richard F., and Frank W. Holmquist. *United States Higher Education and World Affairs*. New York: Praeger, 1967.

Craig, Hardin. *Woodrow Wilson at Princeton*. Norman: University of Oklahoma Press, 1960.

Crisis at Columbia. New York: Vintage Books, 1968.

Curti, Merle E., and Roderick Nash. *Philanthropy in the Shaping of American Higher Education*. New Brunswick, N.J.: Rutgers University Press, 1965.

Daigneault, George H., ed. *The Changing University*. Chicago: Center for the Study of Liberal Education for Adults, 1959.

Danière, André. *Higher Education in the American Economy*. New York: Random House, 1964.

Darley, John Gordon. *Promise and Performance: A Study of Ability and Achievement in Higher Education*. Berkeley: Center of Higher Education, University of California, 1962.

Davis, James A. *Great Aspirations*. Chicago: Aldine, 1963.

————. *Undergraduate Career Decisions*. Chicago: Aldine, 1964.

Deane, Calvin J., *et al. Introduction to College*. Boston: Allyn and Bacon, 1958.

Deferrari, Roy J. *Workshop on Problems of Administration in the American College*. Washington, D.C.: Catholic University of America Press, 1955.

Demerath, Nicholas J., Richard W. Stephens, and R. Robb Taylor. *Power, Presidents, and Professors*. New York: Basic Books, 1967.

Dennis, Lawrence E., and Joseph F. Kauffman, eds. *The College and the Student: An Assessment of Relationships and Responsibilities in Undergraduate Education By Administrators, Faculty Members, and Public Officials*. Washington, D.C.: American Council on Education, 1966.

Deutsch, Monroe E. *The College from Within*. Berkeley: University of California Press, 1952.

DeVane, William C. *Higher Education in Twentieth-Century America*. Cambridge, Mass.: Harvard University Press, 1965.

Dibden, Arthur J. *The Academic Deanship in American Colleges and Universities*. Carbondale: Southern Illinois University Press, 1968.

————. *A Bibliography of College and University Life*. Galesburg, Ill.: Knox College, 1959.

Diekhoff, John S. *The Domain of the Faculty in Our Expanding Colleges*. New York: Harper, 1956.

Division of Student Mental Hygiene, Yale University. *Psychological Problems of College Men*. New Haven, Conn.: Yale University Press, 1958.

Dobbins, Charles G., and Calvin B. T. Lee, eds. *Whose Goals for American Higher Education*. Washington, D.C.: American Council on Education, 1968.

Dober, Richard P. *Campus Planning*. New York: Reinhold Publishing Corp., 1964.

Dodds, Harold W. *The Academic President—Educator or Caretaker?* New York: McGraw-Hill, 1962.

Donovan, John D. *The Academic Man in the Catholic College*. New York: Sheed & Ward, 1964.

Draper, Hal. *Berkeley: The New Student Revolt*. New York: Grove Press, 1965.

Dressel, Paul L., and Associates. *Evaluation in Higher Education*. Boston: Houghton Mifflin, 1961.

Dusenberry, Robert, ed. *Toward the 21st Century in Higher Education*. Corvallis: Oregon State University Press, 1968.

Earnest, Ernest. *Academic Procession: An Informal History of the American College, 1636–1953*. Indianapolis, Ind.: Bobbs-Merrill, 1953.

Eble, Kenneth E. *The Profane Comedy: American Higher Education in the Sixties*. New York: Macmillan, 1962.

Eddy, Edward D., Jr. *The College Influence on Student Character*. Washington, D.C.: American Council on Education, 1959.
————. *Colleges for Our Land and Time*. New York: Harper, 1957.
Education at Berkeley: Report of the Select Committee on Education. Berkeley: University of California Press, 1965.
Eells, Walter C. *College Teachers and College Teaching*. Atlanta, Ga.: Southern Regional Education Board, 1957.
————, and Ernest V. Hollis. *The College Presidency, 1900–1960: An Annotated Bibliography*. U.S. Office of Education. Washington, D.C.: Government Printing Office, 1961.
Estrin, Herman A., and Delmer M. Goode. *College and University Teaching*. Dubuque, Iowa: Wm. C. Brown, 1964.
Eurich, Alvin C., ed. *Campus 1980: The Shape of the Future in American Higher Education*. New York: Delta Books, 1968.
Evans, M. Stanton. *Revolt on the Campus*. Chicago: Regency Press, 1961.
Fairchild, Hoxie N., *et al. Religious Perspectives in College Teaching*. New York: Ronald Press, 1952.
Falvey, Frances E. *Student Participation in College Administration*. New York: Bureau of Publications, Teachers College, Columbia University, 1952.
Farnsworth, Dana L. *Mental Health in College and University*. Cambridge, Mass.: Harvard University Press, 1957.
Feuer, Lewis S. *The Conflict of Generations: The Character and Significance of Student Movements*. New York: Basic Books, 1969.
Ficken, Clarence E. *Building a Faculty in a Church-Related College of Liberal Arts*. Nashville, Tenn.: Board of Education, The Methodist Church, 1959.
Fields, Ralph R. *The Community College Movement*. New York: McGraw-Hill, 1962.
Flaugher, Ronald L., Margaret H. Mahoney, and Rita B. Messing. *Credit by Examination for College-Level Studies: An Annotated Bibliography*. New York: College Entrance Examination Board, 1967.
Frankel, Charles. *Current Issues in Higher Education*. Washington, D.C.: Association for Higher Education, National Education Association, 1961.
————. *Education and the Barricades*. New York: W. W. Norton, 1968.
————, ed. *Issues in University Education*. New York: Harper, 1959.
Frederiksen, Norman, and W. B. Schrader. *Adjustment to College: A Study of 10,000 Veteran and Nonveteran Students in Sixteen American Colleges*. Princeton, N.J.: Educational Testing Service, 1951.
Freedman, Mervin B. *The College Experience*. San Francisco: Jossey-Bass, 1967.
Freeman, Roger A. *Crisis in College Finance? Time for New Solutions*. Washington, D.C.: Institute for Social Science Research, 1965.
Freidson, Eliot, ed. *Student Leaders and the American College*. Philadelphia: United States Student Association, 1955.
French, John R. P., *et al. Work Load of University Professors*. Ann Arbor, Mich.: Institute for Social Research, University of Michigan, 1965.
Friedenberg, Edgar Z. *The Dignity of Youth and Other Atavisms*. Boston: Beacon Press, 1965.
Galanter, E. H. *Automatic Teaching: The State of the Art*. New York, Wiley: 1959.
Gardner, David P. *The California Oath Controversy*. Berkeley: University of California Press, 1967.
Gardner, John W. *Excellence*. New York: Harper, 1961.
Garrison, Roger H. *The Adventure of Learning in College*. New York: Harper, 1959.
————. *Junior College Faculty: Issues and Problems*. Washington, D.C.: American Association of Junior Colleges, 1967.

————. *Teaching in a Junior College*. Washington, D.C.: American Association of Junior Colleges and American Education Publishers Institute, 1968.

Gauss, Christian F., ed. *The Teaching of Religion in American Higher Education*. New York: Ronald Press, 1951.

Geier, Woodrow A., ed. *Today's Student and His University*. Nashville, Tenn.: Division of Higher Education, Board of Education, The Methodist Church, 1966.

Geiger, Louis G. *Higher Education in a Maturing Democracy*. Lincoln: University of Nebraska Press, 1963.

Getzels, Jacob, James M. Lipham, and Roald F. Campbell. *Educational Administration as a Social Process: Theory, Research, Practice*. New York: Harper, 1968.

Gezi, Kalil I., and James E. Myers. *Teaching in American Culture*. New York: Holt, Rinehart and Winston, 1968.

Glaze, Thomas E. *Business Administration for Colleges and Universities*. Baton Rouge: Louisiana State University Press, 1962.

Gleazer, Edmund J., Jr. *This Is the Community College*. Boston: Houghton Mifflin, 1968.

Glennon, Vincent J. *The Road Ahead in Teacher Education*. Syracuse, N.Y.: Syracuse University Press, 1957.

Glenny, Lyman A. *Autonomy of Public Colleges: The Challenge of Coordination*. New York: McGraw-Hill, 1959.

Goldsen, Rose K., et al. *What College Students Think*. Princeton, N.J.: Van Nostrand, 1960.

Goldstein, Richard. *1 in 7: Drugs on Campus*. New York: Walker, 1966.

Goodman, Paul. *The Community of Scholars*. New York: Random House, 1962.

Gordon, Richard E., and Katherine Gordon. *The Blight on the Ivy*. Englewood Cliffs, N.J.: Prentice-Hall, 1963.

Gordon, Robert A., and James E. Howell. *Higher Education for Business*. New York: Columbia University Press, 1959.

Gorovitz, Samuel, ed. *Freedom and Order in the University*. Cleveland, Ohio: Press of Western Reserve University, 1967.

Gould, Samuel B. *Knowledge Is Not Enough: Views on Higher Education*. Yellow Springs, Ohio: Antioch Press, 1959.

Greeley, Andrew M. *The Changing Catholic College*. Chicago: Aldine, 1967.

Greene, Gael. *Sex and the College Girl*. New York: Dial Press, 1964.

Griswold, A. Whitney. *In the University Tradition*. New Haven, Conn.: Yale University Press, 1957.

————. *Liberal Education and the Democratic Ideal*. New Haven, Conn.: Yale University Press, 1959.

————, et al. *The Fine Arts and the University*. New York: St. Martin's Press, 1965.

Gross, John D., ed. *Methodist Beginnings in Higher Education*. Nashville, Tenn.: Board of Education, The Methodist Church, 1959.

Group for the Advancement of Psychiatry. *Sex and the College Student*. New York: Atheneum, 1966.

Gustad, John W. *The Career Decisions of College Teachers*. Atlanta, Ga.: Southern Regional Education Board, 1960.

Habein, Margaret L. *Spotlight on the College Student*. Washington, D.C.: American Council on Education, 1959.

Harbert, Sylvia D. *College Registrar as a Career*. Cambridge, Mass.: Bellman, 1959.

Harris, Seymour E. *Higher Education: Resources and Finance*. New York: McGraw-Hill, 1962.

————, ed. *Higher Education in the United States: The Economic Problems*. Cambridge, Mass.: Harvard University Press, 1960.

Haskew, Laurence D., and Jonathon C. McLendon. *This Is Teaching*. Glenview, Ill.: Scott, Foresman, 1968.

Hassenger, Robert. *The Shape of Catholic Higher Education.* Chicago: University of Chicago Press, 1967.

Havemann, Ernest, and Patricia Salter West. *They Went to College: The College Graduate of Today.* New York: Harcourt, Brace, 1952.

Havighurst, Robert J. *American Higher Education in the 1960's.* Columbus: Ohio State University Press, 1960.

Heath, Douglas H. *Explorations of Maturity: Studies of Mature and Immature College Men.* New York: Appleton-Century-Crofts, 1965.

Henderson, Algo D. *Policies and Practices in Higher Education.* New York: Harper, 1960.

Henry, Nelson B., ed. *The Public Junior College.* Chicago: University of Chicago Press, 1956.

Hettlinger, Richard. *Living with Sex: The Students' Dilemma.* New York: Seabury Press, 1965.

Highet, Gilbert. *The Art of Teaching.* New York: Knopf, 1950.

Hill, Alfred T. *The Small College Meets the Challenge: The Story of CASC.* New York: McGraw-Hill, 1959.

Hillway, Tyrus. *The American Two-Year College.* New York: Harper, 1958.

Hodenfield, G. K., and T. M. Stinnett. *The Education of Teachers.* Englewood Cliffs, N.J.: Prentice-Hall, 1961.

Hofstadter, Richard, and C. DeWitt Hardy. *The Development and Scope of Higher Education in the United States.* New York: Columbia University Press, 1952.

————, and Walter P. Metzger. *The Development of Academic Freedom in the United States.* New York: Columbia University Press, 1955.

————, and Wilson Smith. *American Higher Education: A Documentary History.* 2 vols. Chicago: University of Chicago Press, 1961.

Hollinshead, Byron S. *Who Should Go to College.* New York: Columbia University Press, 1952.

Howes, Raymond F., ed. *Vision and Purpose in Higher Education.* Washington, D.C.: American Council on Education, 1962.

Huffman, Harry, and Syrell Rogovin. *Programmed College English.* New York: McGraw-Hill, 1968.

Hungate, Thad L. *Management in Higher Education.* New York: Bureau of Publications, Teachers College, Columbia University, 1964.

Hunt, Everett L. *Revolt of the College Intellectual.* Chicago: Aldine, 1964.

Hutchins, Robert M. *The University of Utopia.* Chicago: University of Chicago Press, 1953.

Hyman, Ronald T. *Teaching: Vantage Points for Study.* Philadelphia: Lippincott, 1968.

Jackson, Philip W. *The Teacher and the Machine.* Pittsburgh, Pa.: University of Pittsburgh Press, 1968.

Jacob, Philip E. *Changing Values in College: An Exploratory Study of the Impact of College Teaching.* New York: Harper, 1957.

Jacobs, Paul, and Saul Landau. *The New Radicals: A Report with Documents.* New York: Random House, 1966.

Jaffe, A. J., Walter Adams, and Sandra G. Meyers. *Negro Higher Education in the 1960's.* New York: Praeger, 1968.

Jencks, Christopher, and David Riesman. *The Academic Revolution.* Garden City, N.Y.: Doubleday, 1968.

Johnson, B. Lamar. *Starting a Community Junior College.* Washington, D.C.: American Association of Junior Colleges, 1964.

Joughin, Louis, ed. *Academic Freedom and Tenure.* Madison: University of Wisconsin Press, 1967.

Joyce, Bruce R., and Berj Harootunian. *The Structure of Teaching.* Chicago: Science Research Associates, 1967.

Justman, Joseph, and Walter H. Mais. *College Teaching: Its Practice and Its Potential.* New York: Harper, 1956.

Katope, Christopher G., and Paul G. Zobrod, eds. *Beyond Berkeley: A Sourcebook of Student Values.* Cleveland, Ohio: World, 1965.

Keats, John. *The Sheepskin Psychosis.* Philadelphia: Lippincott, 1965.

Keenan, Boyd R., ed. *Science and the University.* New York: Columbia University Press, 1965.

Keezer, Dexter M. *Financing Higher Education: 1960–70.* New York: McGraw-Hill, 1959.

Keniston, Kenneth. *The Uncommitted.* New York: Harcourt, Brace and World, 1965.

Kennan, George F. *Democracy and the Student Left.* Boston: Little, Brown, 1968.

Kerr, Clark. *The Uses of the University.* Cambridge, Mass.: Harvard University Press, 1963.

Kidd, Charles V. *American Universities and Federal Research.* Cambridge, Mass.: Harvard University Press, 1959.

King, Francis P. *Financing the College Education of Faculty Children.* New York: Holt, 1954.

Kirk, Russell. *Academic Freedom: An Essay in Definition.* Chicago: Regnery, 1955.

Klopf, Gordon. *College Student Government.* New York: Harper, 1960.

Klotsche, Martin J. *The Urban University and the Future of Our Cities.* New York: Harper, 1965.

Knapp, Robert H., and Joseph J. Greenbaum. *The Younger American Scholar: His Collegiate Origins.* Chicago: University of Chicago Press, 1953.

Knauth, Ernest F. *The College Business Manager.* New York: New York University Press, 1955.

Knight, Douglas M., ed. *The Federal Government and Higher Education.* Englewood Cliffs, N.J.: Prentice-Hall, 1960.

Knoell, Dorothy M., and Leland L. Medsker. *From Junior to Senior College: A National Study of the Transfer Student.* Washington, D.C.: American Council on Education, 1965.

Knorr, Owen A. *Order and Freedom on the Campus.* Boulder: Western Interstate Commission for Higher Education, University of Colorado, 1966.

Kronhausen, Phyllis, and Eberhard Kronhausen. *Sex Histories of American College Men.* New York: Ballantine Books, 1960.

Kunen, James S. *The Strawberry Statement: Notes of a College Revolutionary.* New York: Random House, 1969.

Landis, Paul H. *So This Is College.* New York: McGraw-Hill, 1954.

Lass, Abraham H., and Eugene S. Wilson. *The College Student's Handbook.* New York: David White, 1965.

Law, Glen C. *The Urgency of New Leadership in Higher Education.* Stamford, Conn.: Press-Tige Publishing Co., 1962.

Lawler, Justus G. *The Catholic Dimension in Higher Education.* Westminster, Md.: Newman, 1959.

Lazarsfeld, Paul F., and Wagner Thielens, Jr. *The Academic Mind: Social Scientists in an Age of Crisis.* Glencoe, Ill.: Free Press, 1956.

Leach, MacEdward, and Orval Filbeck. *College Campus Classroom and You.* Dubuque, Iowa: Wm. C. Brown, 1954.

Lee, Calvin B. T., ed. *Improving College Teaching.* Washington, D.C.: American Council on Education, 1967.

Libaw, Frieda B., and William D. Martinson. *Success in College.* Glenview, Ill.: Scott, Foresman, 1967.

Lineberry, William P., ed. *Colleges at the Crossroads.* New York: Wilson, 1966.

Lipset, Seymour M., and Sheldon S. Wolin, eds. *The Berkeley Student Revolt: Facts and Interpretations*. Garden City, N.Y.: Anchor Books, 1965.

Livingstone, Sir Richard Winn. *Education and the Spirit of the Age*. Oxford, England: Clarendon Press, 1952.

Lloyd-Jones, Esther M., and Herman A. Estrin, eds. *The American Student and His College*. Boston: Houghton Mifflin, 1967.

————, and Margaret Ruth Smith, eds. *Student Personnel Work as Deeper Teaching*. New York: Harper, 1954.

Longenecker, Herbert E. *University Faculty Compensation Policies and Practices in the United States*. Urbana: University of Illinois Press, 1956.

Luce, Phillip Abbott. *The New Left*. New York: McKay, 1966.

Ludden, A. *Plain Talk About College*. New York: Dodd, Mead, 1961.

Lunn, Harry Hyatt. *The Student's Role in College Policy-Making*. Washington, D.C.: American Council on Education, 1957.

Lyons, Gene M., and John W. Masland. *Education and Military Leadership: A Study of the R.O.T.C.* Princeton, N.J.: Princeton University Press, 1959.

MacIver, Robert M. *Academic Freedom in Our Time*. New York: Columbia University Press, 1955.

Madsen, David. *The National University, Enduring Dream of the USA*. Detroit, Mich.: Wayne State University Press, 1966.

Mallery, David. *Ferment on the Campus: An Encounter with the New College Generation*. New York: Harper, 1965.

Manier, Edward, and John W. Houck, eds. *Academic Freedom and the Catholic University*. Notre Dame, Ind.: Fides Publishers, 1967.

Margolis, John D., ed. *The Campus in the Modern World: Twenty-five Essays*. New York: Macmillan, 1969.

Marshall, Howard Drake. *The Mobility of College Faculties*. New York: Pageant Press, 1966.

Martin, Boyd A., ed. *Responsibilities of Colleges and Universities*. Corvallis: Oregon State University Press, 1966.

Martorana, S. V. *College Boards of Trustees*. Washington, D.C.: Center for Applied Research in Education, 1963.

Mayhew, Lewis B. *General Education: An Account and Appraisal*. New York: Harper, 1960.

————, ed. *Higher Education in the Revolutionary Decades*. Berkeley, Calif.: McCutchan Publishing Corp., 1967.

McCarthy, Mary. *The Groves of Academe*. New York: Harcourt, Brace, 1952.

McConnell, T. R. *A General Pattern for American Public Higher Education*. New York: McGraw-Hill, 1962.

McGrath, Earl J. *The Predominantly Negro Colleges and Universities in Transition*. New York: Bureau of Publications, Teachers College, Columbia University, 1965.

————, ed. *Universal Higher Education*. New York: McGraw-Hill, 1967.

Medsker, Leland L., and James W. Trent. *The Influence of Different Types of Public Higher Institutions on College Attendance from Varying Socioeconomic and Ability Levels*. Berkeley: Center for Study of Higher Education, University of California, 1965.

————. *The Junior College: Progress and Prospect*. New York: McGraw-Hill, 1960.

Meeth, L. Richards, ed. *Selected Issues in Higher Education: An Annotated Bibliography*. New York: Teachers College Press, Columbia University, 1965.

Menhase, Louis, and Ronald Radosh, eds. *Teach-ins: U.S.A.* New York: Praeger, 1967.

Meredith, James H. *Three Years in Mississippi*. Bloomington: Indiana University Press, 1966.

Michaelis, John U. *The Prediction of Success in Student Teaching from Personality and Attitude Inventories.* Berkeley: University of California Press, 1954.

Miel, Alice, ed. *Creativity in Teaching.* Belmont, Calif.: Wadsworth, 1961.

Miller, Michael V., and Susan Gilmore, eds. *Revolution at Berkeley: The Crisis in American Education.* New York: Dial Press, 1965.

Millett, John D. *The Academic Community: An Essay on Organization.* New York: McGraw-Hill, 1962.

————. *Financing Higher Education in the United States.* New York: Columbia University Press, 1952.

Milton, Ohmer, and E. J. Shoben, Jr. *Learning and the Professors.* Athens: Ohio University Press, 1968.

Mitchell, Joyce Slayton. *The Guide to College Life.* Englewood Cliffs, N.J.: Prentice-Hall, 1968.

Mobberley, David G., and Myron F. Wicke. *The Deanship of the Liberal Arts College.* Nashville, Tenn.: Division of Higher Education, Methodist Board of Education, 1962.

Montagu, Ashley. *Up the Ivy: Being Microcosmographia Academica Revisited, A True Blue Guide on How to Climb in the Academic World Without Appearing to Try.* New York: Hawthorne Books, 1966.

Moos, Malcolm, and Frances E. Rourke. *The Campus and the State.* Baltimore, Md.: Johns Hopkins Press, 1959.

Morison, Robert S., ed. *The Contemporary University: U.S.A.* Boston: Beacon Press, 1967.

Morrill, James L. *The Ongoing State University.* Minneapolis: University of Minnesota Press, 1960.

Mueller, Kate Hevner. *Student Personnel Work in Higher Education.* Boston: Houghton Mifflin, 1961.

Muller, Leo, ed. *New Horizons for College Women.* Washington, D.C.: Public Affairs Press, 1960.

————. *Selected Bibliography on the Advancement and Support of Higher Education.* Washington, D.C.: American College Public Relations Association, 1962.

Murphy, Lois B., and Esther Rauschenbush, eds. *Achievement in the College Years: A Record of Intellectual and Personal Growth.* New York: Harper, 1960.

Mushkin, Selma J., ed. *Economics of Higher Education.* Washington, D.C.: Government Printing Office, 1962.

Nevins, Allan. *The State Universities and Democracy.* Urbana: University of Illinois Press, 1962.

Newcomb, Theodore M. *College Peer Groups: Problems and Prospects for Research.* Chicago: Aldine, 1966.

————, et al. *Persistence and Change.* New York: Wiley, 1967.

Newcomer, Mabel. *A Century of Higher Education for American Women.* New York: Harper, 1959.

Newman, Jack. *A Prophetic Minority.* New York: New American Library, 1966.

Newsom, Carroll V. *A University President Speaks Out: On Current Education.* New York: Harper, 1961.

O'Connell, Thomas E. *Community Colleges: A President's View.* Urbana: University of Illinois Press, 1968.

Orlans, Harold. *The Effects of Federal Programs on Higher Education: A Study of Thirty-six Universities and Colleges.* Washington, D.C.: The Brookings Institution, 1962.

Parthemos, George S., ed. *Higher Education in a World of Conflict.* Athens: University of Georgia Press, 1962.

Pattillo, Manning M., Jr., and Donald M. Mackenzie. *Church-Sponsored Higher Education in the United States*. Washington, D.C.: American Council on Education, 1966.

Paulsen, F. Robert. *Selected Bibliographies for Administration in Higher Education*. Ann Arbor: Center for the Study of Higher Education, University of Michigan, 1960.

Perkins, James A. *The University in Transition*. Princeton, N.J.: Princeton University Press, 1965.

Perkins, John A. *Plain Talk from a Campus*. Newark, Del.: University of Delaware Press, 1959.

Pervin, Lawrence A., Louis E. Reik, and Willard Dalrymple. *The College Dropout and the Utilization of Talent*. Princeton, N.J.: Princeton University Press, 1966.

Peterson, George E. *The New England College in the Age of the University*. Amherst, Mass.: Amherst College Press, 1964.

Peterson, Richard E. *The Scope of Organized Student Protest in 1964–1965*. Princeton, N.J.: Educational Testing Service, 1966.

Pollard, John A. *Fund-Raising for Higher Education*. New York: Harper, 1958.

Power, Edward J. *A History of Catholic Higher Education in the United States*. Milwaukee, Wis.: Bruce, 1958.

Price, Jacob M., ed. *Reading for Life: Developing the College Student's Lifetime Reading Interest*. Ann Arbor: University of Michigan Press, 1959.

Psychedelics and the College Student. Princeton, N.J.: Princeton University Press, 1967.

Pullias, Earl V. *A Search for Understanding: Thoughts on Education and Personality in a Time of Transition*. Dubuque, Iowa: Wm. C. Brown, 1965.

Pusey, Nathan M. *The Age of the Scholar: Observations on Education in a Troubled Decade*. Cambridge, Mass.: Belknap Press, 1963.

Rader, Dotson. *I Ain't Marchin' Anymore*. New York: McKay, 1969.

Rarig, Emory W. *The Community Junior College*. New York: Teachers College Press, 1967.

Rauh, Morton A. *College and University Trusteeship*. Yellow Springs, Ohio: Antioch Press, 1959.

Rauschenbush, Esther. *The Student and His Studies*. Middletown, Conn.: Wesleyan University Press, 1964.

Reeves, Marjorie, ed. *Eighteen Plus: Unity and Diversity in Higher Education*. New York: Humanities Press, 1966.

Reid, Robert H. *American Degree Mills*. Washington, D.C.: American Council on Education, 1959.

Ridgeway, James. *The Closed Corporation: American Universities in Crisis*. New York: Random House, 1968.

Riesman, David. *Constraint and Variety in American Education*. Lincoln: University of Nebraska Press, 1956.

Riley, John W., Jr., Bryce F. Ryan, and Marcia Lipshitz. *The Student Looks at His Teacher: An Inquiry Into the Implications of Student Ratings at the College Level*. New Brunswick, N.J.: Rutgers University Press, 1950.

Rivlin, Alice M. *Research in the Economics of Higher Education: Progress and Problems*. Washington, D.C.: The Brookings Institution, 1962.

Rivlin, Harry N., Dorothy M. Fraser, and Milton R. Stern, eds. *The First Years in College: Preparing Students for a Successful College Career*. Boston: Little, Brown, 1965.

Rogers, Francis M. *Higher Education in the United States: A Summary View*. Cambridge, Mass.: Harvard University Press, 1960.

Root, E. Merrill. *Collectivism on the Campus: A Battle for the Mind in American Colleges*. New York: Devin-Adair, 1955.

Rosecrance, Francis C. *The American College and Its Teachers.* New York: Macmillan, 1963.

Rosentreter, Frederick M. *The Boundaries of the Campus.* Madison: University of Wisconsin Press, 1957.

Rourke, Francis E., and Glenn E. Brooks. *The Managerial Revolution in Higher Education.* Baltimore, Md.: Johns Hopkins Press, 1966.

Rudolph, Frederick. *The American College and University: A History.* New York: Knopf, 1962.

Ruml, Beardsley, and Donald H. Morrison. *Memo to a College Trustee: A Report on Financial and Structural Problems of the Liberal Arts College.* New York: McGraw-Hill, 1959.

Sammartino, Peter. *The President of a Small College.* Rutherford, N.J.: Fairleigh Dickinson University Press, 1954.

Sanford, Nevitt, ed. *The American College: A Psychological and Social Interpretation of the Higher Learning.* New York: Wiley, 1962.

————, ed. *College and Character.* New York: Wiley, 1965.

Schmidt, George P. *The Liberal Arts College: A Chapter in American Cultural History.* New Brunswick, N.J.: Rutgers University Press, 1957.

Schoenfeld, Clarence A., and Donald N. Zillman. *The American University in Summer.* Madison: University of Wisconsin Press, 1967.

Schwab, Joseph. *College Curriculum and Student Protest.* Chicago: University of Chicago Press, 1969.

Scimecca, Joseph, and Roland Damiano. *Crisis at St. John's: Strike and Revolution on the Catholic Campus.* New York: Random House, 1967.

Selden, William K. *Accreditation: A Struggle Over Standards in Higher Education.* New York: Harper, 1960.

Selznick, Philip. *Leadership in Administration.* Evanston, Ill.: Row, Peterson, 1957.

Sex and the College Student. New York: Atheneum, 1965.

Sexton, Patricia Cayo. *The American School: A Sociological Analysis.* Englewood Cliffs, N.J.: Prentice-Hall, 1967.

Seymour, Harold J. *Designs for Fund-Raising: Principles, Patterns, Techniques.* New York: McGraw-Hill, 1966.

Shaffer, Robert H. *Student Personnel Services in Higher Education.* New York: Center for Applied Research in Education, 1966.

Shiver, Elizabeth N., ed. *Higher Education and Public International Service.* Washington, D.C.: American Council on Education, 1967.

Shuster, George N. *Education and Moral Wisdom.* New York: Harper, 1960.

————. *The Ground I Walked on: Reflections of a College President.* New York: Farrar, Straus and Cudahy, 1961.

Siegel, Max, ed. *The Counseling of College Students: Function, Practice, and Technique.* New York: Free Press, 1968.

Smith, Elmer R., ed. *Teacher Education: A Reappraisal.* New York: Harper, 1962.

Smith, Huston. *The Purposes of Higher Education.* New York: Harper, 1955.

Snavely, Guy E. *The Church and the Four-Year College.* New York: Harper, 1955.

Sparrow, John. *Mark Pattison and the Idea of a University.* New York: Cambridge University Press, 1967.

Spectorsky, Auguste C., ed. *The College Years.* New York: Hawthorne Books, 1958.

Spender, Stephen. *The Year of the Young Rebels.* New York: Random House, 1969.

Sprague, Hall T., ed. *Research on College Students.* Boulder, Colo.: Western Interstate Commission for Higher Education, 1960.

Stephens, Richard W. *The Academic Administrator: The Role of the University President.* Ph.D. dissertation. Chapel Hill: University of North Carolina, 1956.

Stewart, George R. *The Year of the Oath: The Fight for Academic Freedom at the University of California.* Garden City, N.Y.: Doubleday, 1950.

Stickler, W. Hugh, ed. *Experimental Colleges: Their Role in American Higher Education.* Tallahassee: Florida State University Press, 1964.

Stigler, George J. *The Intellectual and the Market Place, and Other Essays.* New York: Free Press, 1963.

Stiles, Lindley J., *et al. Teacher Education in the United States.* New York: Ronald Press, 1960.

Stoke, Harold W. *The American College President.* New York: Harper, 1959.

Straus, Robert, and Selden D. Bacon. *Drinking in College.* New Haven, Conn.: Yale University Press, 1953.

Stroup, Herbert. *Toward a Philosophy of Organized Student Activities.* Minneapolis: University of Minnesota Press, 1964.

————. *Bureaucracy in Higher Education.* New York: Free Press, 1966.

Stroup, Thomas B., ed. *The University in the American Future.* Lexington: University of Kentucky Press, 1965.

Sugg, Redding S., Jr., and George H. Jones. *The Southern Regional Education Board: Ten Years of Regional Cooperation in Higher Education.* Baton Rouge: Louisiana State University Press, 1960.

Summers, Robert E. *Freedom and Loyalty in Our Colleges.* New York: Wilson, 1954.

Sutherland, Robert L., *et al.,* eds. *Personality Factors on the College Campus.* Austin: The Hogg Foundation for Mental Health, University of Texas, 1962.

Swanson, John E., Wesley Arden, and Homer E. Still, Jr. *Financial Analysis of Current Operations of Colleges and Universities.* Ann Arbor: Institute of Public Administration, University of Michigan, 1966.

Swift, Richard N. *World Affairs and the College Curriculum.* Washington, D.C.: American Council on Education, 1959.

Tannenbaum, F., ed. *A Community of Scholars.* New York: Praeger, 1965.

Taylor, Harold, ed. *Essays in Teaching.* New York: Harper, 1950.

————. *Students Without Teachers: The Crisis in the University.* New York: McGraw-Hill, 1969.

Taylor, Herbert G., Jr., ed. *New Knowledge: Its Impact on Higher Education.* Corvallis: Oregon State University Press, 1965.

Taylor, R. Robb. *The American University as a Behavioral System: Power Hierarchies in Selected Academic Departments.* Ph.D. dissertation. Chapel Hill: University of North Carolina, 1958.

Tead, Ordway. *The Climate of Learning: A Constructive Attack on Complacency in Higher Education.* New York: Harper, 1958.

Thornton, James W. *The Community Junior College.* New York: Wiley, 1960.

Totaro, Joseph V., ed. *Women in College and University Teaching.* Madison: School of Education, University of Wisconsin, 1963.

Townsend, Agatha. *College Freshmen Speak Out.* New York: Harper, 1958.

Trent, James W., with Jenette Golds. *Catholics in College: Religious Commitment and the Intellectual Life.* Chicago: University of Chicago Press, 1967.

The Troubled Campus. Boston: Atlantic-Little, Brown, 1966.

Trueblood, Elton. *The Idea of a College.* New York: Harper, 1959.

Tussman, Joseph. *Experiment at Berkeley.* New York: Oxford University Press, 1969.

United States Commission on Civil Rights. *Equal Protection of the Laws in Public Higher Education: 1960.* Washington, D.C.: Government Printing Office, 1961.

Veblen, Thorstein. *The Higher Learning in America.* New York: Sagamore Press, 1957.

Veysey, Laurence R. *The Emergence of the American University.* Chicago: University of Chicago Press, 1965.

von Hoffman, Nicholas. *The Multiversity: A Personal Report on What Happens to Today's Students at American Universities.* New York: Holt, Rinehart and Winston, 1966.

Wakin, Edward. *The Catholic Campus.* New York: Macmillan, 1963.

Wallace, Walter L. *Student Culture: Social Structure and Continuity in a Liberal Arts College.* Chicago: Aldine, 1966.

Walters, Raymond. *Four Decades of U.S. Collegiate Enrollments.* New York: Society for the Advancement of Education, 1960.

Warshaw, Steven. *The Trouble in Berkeley.* Berkeley, Calif.: Diablo Press, 1966.

Weatherford, Willis D., Jr., ed. *The Goals of Higher Education.* Cambridge, Mass.: Harvard University Press, 1960.

Wells, Harry L. *Higher Education Is Serious Business: A Study of University Business Management in Relation to Higher Education.* New York: Harper, 1953.

West, Elmer D. *Financial Aid to the Undergraduate: Issues and Implications.* Washington, D.C.: American Council on Education, 1963.

White, Goodrich C. *The Education of the Administrator.* Nashville, Tenn.: Division of Higher Education, Methodist Board of Education, 1959.

Wicke, Myron F. *Handbook for Trustees.* Nashville, Tenn.: Division of Higher Education, Methodist Board of Education, 1959.

—————. *On Teaching in a Christian College.* Nashville, Tenn.: Division of Higher Education, Methodist Board of Education, 1959.

Wiggins, Samuel P. *The Desegregation Era in Higher Education.* Berkeley, Calif.: McCutchan, 1966.

—————. *Higher Education in the South.* Berkeley, Calif.: McCutchan, 1966.

Williams, G. *Some of My Best Friends Are Professors: A Critical Commentary on Higher Education.* New York: Abelard-Schuman, 1958.

Williams, Robert L. *The Administration of Academic Affairs in Higher Education.* Ann Arbor: University of Michigan Press, 1965.

Williamson, E. G. *Student Personnel Services in Colleges and Universities.* New York: McGraw-Hill, 1961.

—————, and John L. Cowan. *The American Student's Freedom of Expression.* Minneapolis: University of Minnesota Press, 1966.

Wilson, Kenneth M., ed. *Institutional Research on College Students.* Atlanta, Ga.: Southern Regional Education Board, 1962.

Wilson, Logan. *The Academic Man: A Study in the Sociology of a Profession.* New York: Octagon Books, 1964.

—————. *Emerging Patterns in American Higher Education.* Washington, D.C.: American Council on Education, 1965.

Wise, W. Max. *They Come for the Best of Reasons: College Students Today.* Washington, D.C.: American Council on Education, 1958.

Woodburne, Lloyd S. *Faculty Personnel Policies in Higher Education.* New York: Harper, 1950.

—————. *Principles of College and University Administration.* Stanford, Calif.: Stanford University Press, 1958.

Woodring, Paul. *The Higher Learning in America: A Reassessment.* New York: McGraw-Hill, 1968.

Wriston, Henry M. *Academic Procession: Reflections of a College President.* New York: Columbia University Press, 1959.

Yamamoto, Kaoru, ed. *The College Student and His Culture: An Analysis.* Boston: Houghton Mifflin, 1968.

Zinn, Howard. *SNCC: The New Abolitionists.* Boston: Beacon Press, 1964.

INDEX

564

INDEX

in total, community, 275; role of, in
United States, 28–30, 38; role of ideas
in, 146–147; roots of conflict in, 438–
439; school of education as real link
between, and high school, 137;
"service station" programs of, 81–82;
society's mounting concern over what
goes on in, 23–24; -society relationship,
changing, 455; sports as function of,
81; stake in problems of high school
administrators, 138–142; students' concept of, 457–458; students increasingly examining whole nature of, 455;
student responsibility to, 29; system,
junior faculty members disenchanted
with, 443; teaching, improving, 359–
364; teaching loads in, trend toward
sharply reduced, 396–397; traditional
departmental barriers breaking down
within, 35; transformation of American colleges and, 1; trend toward
combined public-private interest in,
30; World War II as turning point in
evolution of, in America, 31–32; *see*
Multiversity *and* State colleges and
universities
University College, Leicester, England,
229
U.S. Department of Health, Education,
and Welfare, 109
U.S. Office of Education, 55, 109, 395
U.S.S.R.: *see* Communism; Moscow
University; Russia(n); *and* Soviet
U.S. Steel Corporation, 92–93

Value, conflicts, at schools of education,
289
Van Doren, Mark, 260
Vassar College, 365
Veblen, Thorstein, 328
Venezuela, 40–41
Veterans, World War II, attitudes
toward higher education, 15
Vietnam, 127, 146; war in, as cause of
student unrest, 14, 429, 442, 454
Virginia Military Institute, 70

Virginia, University Center in, coopera-
tive education programs of, 70–71
Virginia, University of, 70
Vision, theory of stature of man's, 49–50
Volunteers in Service to America, 466

Wabash College, 69, 94, 335–336
Walden, 432
Ward, F. Champion, 409
Warnath, Charles F., 2–3
Warner Construction Co., 194–195
Warner, Roy, 194
Washington, D.C., 32, 98, 346, 459;
inherent danger of Federal control
through central office in, as reason for
opposition to Federal aid, 85
Washington and Lee University, 70
Washington Post, 104
Watch and Ward Society, 429
Weekly Reader, 322
Wells, Herman B., 179
Wescoe, W. Clarke, 3
Wesleyan University, 55
West Chester State College, trustee-
president conflict at, 196–202
West Coast Conference on Trustee
Orientation, 96
Western, non-, providing insight into,
culture, 266; non-, studies, program of
seminars in, in cooperative colleges,
72; society, Christian doctrine and
development of church in, 78; thought,
providing understanding of major
contributions of, 266
West Point, honor system at, 498
Whitehead, Alfred North, 367
White House Conference on Education,
368
Why Johnny Can't Read, 276
Williams College, 114
Wilson, Charles, 44
Wilson, Logan, 144, 354
Wilson, Woodrow, 159–160, 393, 397,
426
Winter Park, Fla., 391
Wisconsin, 121–122
Wisconsin, University of, 98, 145
Witherspoon, John, 393